Twentieth-Century War and Conflict

Twentieth-Century War and Conflict

A Concise Encyclopedia

Edited by

Gordon Martel

WILEY Blackwell

Registered Office
John Wiley & Sons, Ltd, The Atrium, Southern Gate, Chichester, West Sussex, PO19 8SQ, UK

Editorial Offices
350 Main Street, Malden, MA 02148–5020, USA
9600 Garsington Road, Oxford, OX4 2DQ, UK
The Atrium, Southern Gate, Chichester, West Sussex, PO19 8SQ, UK

For details of our global editorial offices, for customer services, and for information about how to apply for permission to reuse the copyright material in this book please see our website at www.wiley.com/wiley-blackwell.

Library of Congress Cataloging-in-Publication Data applied for

Paperback ISBN: 978-1-118-88463-8

A catalogue record for this book is available from the British Library.

Cover image: © Jack Sullivan / Alamy.

Set in 9.5/11.5pt Minion by SPi Publisher Services, Pondicherry, India
Printed in Singapore by C.O.S. Printers Pte Ltd

1   2015

Contents

List of Entries

List of Maps

Chronological Guide to Entries

About the Editors

Editor-in-Chief:

Gordon Martel is Emeritus Professor of History at the University of Northern British Columbia and Adjunct Professor at the University of Victoria. He has written widely on the history of modern war. Among his best-known books are *Imperial Diplomacy* (1985) and *The Origins of the First World War* (revised 3rd edition, 2008). He was one of the founding editors of the leading scholarly journal, *The International History Review*, and is editor of "Seminar Studies in History." He has edited numerous scholarly publications, including *The World War Two Reader* (2004), *A Companion to Europe, 1900–1945* (Blackwell, 2006), and *A Companion to International History, 1900–2001* (Blackwell, 2007). His *The Month That Changed the World: July 1914* was published in June 2014.

Board of Advisory Editors:

Richard Bonney is Emeritus Professor at the University of Leicester and Professorial Research Fellow in South Asian Security at the Royal United Services Institute for Defence and Security Studies (RUSI), Whitehall.

Brian Campbell is Professor of Roman History in the School of History and Anthropology at Queen's University of Belfast.

Karl Friday is Professor of History at the University of Georgia.

Susan R. Grayzel is Professor of History at the University of Mississippi.

John Lamphear was Professor of History at the University of Texas until his retirement.

S. P. Mackenzie is Caroline McKissick Dial Professor of History at the University of South Carolina.

Stephen C. Neff is Reader in Public International Law at the University of Edinburgh.

Helen J. Nicholson is a Reader in History at Cardiff University, Wales, and publishes on the military orders, crusades, and related subjects.

Mark A. Stoler is Professor Emeritus of History at the University of Vermont where he taught US diplomatic and military history from 1970 to 2007.

David R. Stone is Pickett Professor of Military History at Kansas State University.

Bruce Vandervort is Professor of Modern European and African History at the Virginia Military Institute and is also the editor of the *Journal of Military History*.

Geoffrey Wawro is the General Olinto Mark Barsanti Professor of Military History and Director of the Military History Center at the University of North Texas.

Contributing Editors:

Virginia H. Aksan is Professor of History at McMaster University.

Stephen Badsey, MA (Cantab.), FRHistS, is Professor in Conflict Studies in the School of Law, Social Sciences, and Communications at the University of Wolverhampton, UK.

Stephen Conway is Professor of History at University College, London.

Kelly DeVries is Professor of History at Loyola University Maryland and Honorary Historical Consultant at the Royal Armouries, United Kingdom.

Alan Forrest is Professor of Modern History at the University of York.

J. Michael Francis is Professor of History at the University of North Florida.

Michael D. Gambone is Professor of History at Kutztown University of Pennsylvania.

Gian P. Gentile is a serving Army colonel and currently runs the Military History Program at West Point.

Kate Gilliver is Senior Lecturer in Ancient History at Cardiff University.

David M. Glantz is chief editor of the *Journal of Slavic Military Studies*.

John Haldon is Professor of History at Princeton University.

Matthew Hughes is Reader in History at Brunel University.

Norrie MacQueen is Honorary Research Fellow in the School of International Relations at the University of St Andrews.

K. A. J. McLay is Head of the Department of History and Archaeology at the University of Chester.

Alexander Mikaberidze is Assistant Professor of History at Louisiana State University (Shreveport).

Stephen Morillo is the Jane and Frederic M. Hadley Chair in History at Wabash College.

Douglas M. Peers is Dean of Graduate Studies at York University.

Heather R. Perry is Assistant Professor of German and Medical History at the University of North Carolina at Charlotte.

Brian Holden Reid is Professor of American History and Military Institutions, King's College, London.

Richard Reid is Reader in the History of Africa at the School of Oriental and African Studies, University of London.

Clifford J. Rogers is a Professor of History at the United States Military Academy.

Michael Sage is Professor in the Department of Classics at the University of Cincinnati.

Pedro Santoni is Professor of History and Department Chair at California State University, San Bernardino.

Matthew S. Seligmann is Reader in History at the University of Northampton.

Dennis Showalter is Professor of History at Colorado College.

Louis Sicking is Lecturer in History at the University of Leiden.

Jennifer Siegel is Associate Professor at the Ohio State University.

Armstrong Starkey is a Professor of History at Adelphi University.

Carol B. Stevens, PhD (University of Michigan, 1985), is Professor in the History Department at Colgate University, Hamilton, New York.

Frank Tallett is Head of the School of Humanities at the University of Reading.

Blair Turner holds appointments as Professor in the Departments of History and of International Studies and Political Science at the Virginia Military Institute and is an editor of the *Journal of Military History*.

Anne Sharp Wells is assistant editor of the *Journal of Military History* and assistant editor of *The Papers of George Catlett Marshall* (volume 6) for the George C. Marshall Foundation.

Peter H. Wilson is G. F. Grant Professor of History at the University of Hull.

David Zimmerman is Professor at the University of Victoria, Canada.

Notes on Contributors

Mary Elizabeth Ailes is a Professor of History at the University of Nebraska at Kearney. Her publications include *Military Migration and State Formation: The British Military Community in Seventeenth-Century Sweden* (2002) and "Wars, Widows, and State Formation in 17th-Century Sweden," *Scandinavian Journal of History* (March 2006).

John E. Ashbrook is an Associate Professor of History at Sweet Briar College. He teaches Modern European History and researches political and military history of eastern and central Europe and the Balkans.

Donald Avery is Professor Emeritus and Adjunct Research Professor in the Department of History, University of Western Ontario. His publications on biological and chemical warfare include *The Science of War: Canadian Scientists and Allied Military Technology During the Second World War* (1998).

Stephen Badsey, MA (Cantab.), FRHistS, is Professor in Conflict Studies in the School of Law, Social Sciences, and Communications at the University of Wolverhampton, UK. His personal website is www.stephenbadsey.com

Pradeep P. Barua is Professor of History at the University of Nebraska at Kearney. He is the author of *Gentlemen of the Raj: The Indian Army Officer Corps 1817–1949* (2003) and *The State at War in South Asia* (2005). He has published several articles on the military history of South Asia and the developing world.

Colin F. Baxter received his MA and PhD degrees from the University of Georgia. He is Emeritus Professor of History at East Tennessee State University where he served as chair of the department until 2008. His books include *The Normandy Campaign, 1944: A Selected Bibliography* (1992), *The War in North Africa, 1940–1943: A Selected Bibliography* (1996), and *Field Marshal Bernard Law Montgomery, 1887–1976: A Selected Bibliography* (1999).

Gary J. Bjorge is an Associate Professor in the Military History Department of the US Army Command and General Staff College, Fort Leavenworth, Kansas. His degrees include an MA in political science and a PhD in Chinese language and literature from the University of Wisconsin. His publications include English translations of Chinese fiction and articles and books on Chinese military history topics.

Laura Brandon is Historian, Art and War, at the Canadian War Museum and an Adjunct Professor in the School for Studies in Art and Culture at Carleton University, Ottawa. She is the author of *Art or Memorial? The Forgotten History of Canada's War Art* (2006) and *Art and War* (2007).

Ahron (Ronnie) Bregman was born in Israel in 1958. After six years of army service, during which he took part in the 1982 Lebanon war and reached the rank of captain, he left the army to work at the Knesset as a parliamentary assistant. He studied in Jerusalem and London, completing a doctorate in War Studies at King's College, London, in 1994. He is the author of *The Fifty Years War* (1998), *Israel's Wars: A History since 1947* (2000), *A History of Israel* (2002), and *Elusive Peace* (2005). He teaches at the Department of War Studies, King's College, London.

James Chapman is Professor of Film Studies at the University of Leicester. He has wide-ranging research interests in the history of film and television and in the representation of war and history in the media. His books include *The British at War: Cinema, State and Propaganda, 1939–1945* (1998), *Past and Present: National Identity and the British Historical Film* (2005), *War and Film* (2008), and *The New Film History: Sources, Methods, Approaches* (co-edited with Mark Glancy and Sue Harper, 2007).

Richard L. DiNardo is Professor For National Security Affairs at the United States Marine Corps Command and Staff College, Quantico, Virginia. He is the author of numerous books and articles on a wide variety of topics in military history. His most recent work, *Breakthrough: The Gorlice–Tarnow Campaign 1915*, was published in 2010.

Kenneth W. Estes, a US Marine Corps officer 1969–1993, earned a doctorate in European history (1984) and taught Military, European, and US History at Duke University, the US Naval Academy, and in adjunct positions in Seattle and Europe. He has written or edited over a dozen books, and published numerous articles.

Brian P. Farrell has been teaching military history at the National University of Singapore since 1993. His research focuses on the military history of the British empire and on problems of coalition warfare.

Giuseppe Finaldi teaches history at the University of Western Australia. He is the author of *Mussolini and Italian Fascism* (2008) and *Italian National Identity and the Scramble for Africa* (2009).

Michael D. Gambone received his doctorate from the University of Chicago in 1993. He is the author of *Capturing the Revolution: The United States, Central America, and Nicaragua, 1961–1972* (2001) and *The Greatest Generation Comes Home: The Veteran in American Society* (2005). Dr Gambone is currently a Professor of History at Kutztown University of Pennsylvania. He is a veteran of the 82nd Airborne Division. In 2006, Dr Gambone deployed to Iraq and served in the city of Mosul.

David M. Glantz is chief editor of the *Journal of Slavic Military Studies* and one of the first US members of the Soviet (now Russian) Academy of Natural Sciences.

Christopher E. Goscha is an Associate Professor in the History Department at the Université du Québec à Montréal. He has published widely on the Indochina War and colonial and postcolonial Indochina.

Susan R. Grayzel is Professor of History at the University of Mississippi. She is the author of *Women's Identities At War: Gender, Motherhood, and Politics in Britain and France during the First World War* (1999), *Women and the First World War* (2002), a global history, *At Home and Under Fire: Air Raids and Culture in Britain from the Great War to the Blitz* (2011), and *The First World War: A Brief History with Documents* (2013).

Richard C. Hall is a Professor of History at Georgia Southwestern State University. He has served in the US Army and also taught at Ohio State University, University of Nebraska, Minnesota State University, and the Air War College. He is the author of *Bulgaria's Road to the First World War* (1996), *The Balkan Wars 1912–1913* (2000), *Consumed by War : European Conflict in the 20th Century* (2009), and *Balkan Breakthrough: The Battle of Dobro Pole 1918* (2010).

José María Herrera earned his PhD in history from Purdue University in 2008. He is currently Assistant Professor at the University of Houston-Downtown in the Department of Urban Education. He specializes in United States foreign relations with Latin America, early national Mexican history, and twentieth-century guerrilla movements in the Southern Cone.

Chalmers Hood received his PhD from the University of Maryland. His *Royal Republicans: The French Naval Dynasties between the World Wars* (1985) examined the French naval officer corps later involved at Vichy. Currently, he is writing a biography of Admiral François Darlan, based on recently released papers. He teaches at the University of Mary Washington.

Matthew Hughes is Reader in History at Brunel University and from 2008 to 2010 he held the Major-General Matthew C. Horner Chair in Military Theory at the US Marine Corps University. His recent publications include co-editing *Palgrave Advances in Modern Military History* (2006).

Michael P. Infranco teaches in the Department of Political Science at Washington State University. Dr Infranco also instructs graduate courses in international relations and international law at Troy University's Western Region sites.

Douglas V. Johnson, II is a retired US Army officer with a PhD from Temple University. He was with the US Army Strategic Studies Institute from 1985 until 2009, first as Strategic Research Analyst and then as Research Professor of National Security Affairs.

Artemy Kalinovsky is an Assistant Professor of East European Studies at the University of Amsterdam and holds a PhD from the London School of Economics. He writes and teaches on Russia and the Soviet Union, the Cold War, and other aspects of international history.

W. H. Kautt received his PhD in modern history from the University of Ulster at Jordanstown and is the author of *The Anglo-Irish War* (1999) and *Ambushes and Armour* (2010). He is an Associate Professor of Military History at the US Army Command and General Staff College and is a Fellow of the Royal Historical Society.

John T. Kuehn is a retired naval aviator and serves on the faculty of the US Army Command and General Staff College. He is the author of the well-received *Agents of Innovation* (2008) and, with Dennis Giangreco, *Eyewitness Pacific Theater* (2008).

Steven Hugh Lee is Associate Professor of History at the University of British Columbia. He is author of *Outposts of Empire: Korea, Vietnam, and the Origins of the Cold War in Asia, 1949–1954* (1996) and *The Korean War* (2001), and co-editor, with Chang Yun-Shik, of *Transformations in Twentieth-Century Korea* (2006).

Norrie MacQueen is Honorary Research Fellow in the School of International Relations at the University of St Andrews. His most recent books include: *The United Nations: a Beginner's Guide* (Oneworld, 2010); *The United Nations, Peace Operations and the Cold War* (Pearson, 2011); and *Humanitarian Intervention and the United Nations* (Edinburgh University Press, 2011). He was an electoral adviser in the UN peacekeeping mission in Timor-Leste.

Randal Marlin has taught in the Philosophy Department at Carleton University, Ottawa, since 1966, specializing in philosophy of law, existentialism, and, more recently, in propaganda studies. He is the author of *Propaganda and the Ethics of Persuasion* (2002) and many newspaper articles. In 1979–1980 he held a Department of National Defense Fellowship enabling him to study with Jacques Ellul in Bordeaux, France.

Jennifer Gayle Mathers is a Senior Lecturer in the Department of International Politics at Aberystwyth University. Her published work includes "Women, Society and the Military: Women Soldiers in Post-Soviet Russia," in *Military and Society in Post-Soviet Russia*, edited by Stephen L. Webber and Jennifer G. Mathers (2006), and "Women and State Militaries," in *Women and Wars: Contested Histories, Uncertain Futures*, edited by Carol Cohn (2011).

Sean McGlynn is History Lecturer for the University of Plymouth at Strode College and the Open University. He is the author of *By Sword and Fire: Cruelty and Atrocity in Medieval Warfare* (2008) and *Blood Cries Afar: The Forgotten Invasion of England 1216* (2011). He is currently working on commissioned studies of medieval generals and the Albigensian Crusade.

John C. McManus is Associate Professor of US Military History at Missouri University of Science and Technology. He has authored nine books on the United States in World War II and the modern combat experience.

Seumas Miller is Professor of Philosophy at the Australian National University, Foundation Professor of Philosophy at Charles Sturt University (1994), and Foundation Director of the Centre for Applied Philosophy and Public Ethics, an Australian Research Council Special Research Centre (2000–2007). He is also a Senior Research Fellow at the 3TU Centre for Ethics and Technology at Delft University of Technology. His extensive publications include writings on social action and institutions, terrorism, business ethics, and police ethics.

Edwin Moïse (PhD University of Michigan, 1977), a historian of the Vietnam War and of modern China and Vietnam, is a Professor of History at Clemson University. He is the author of *Land Reform in China and North Vietnam* (1983), *Tonkin Gulf and the Escalation of the Vietnam War* (1996), and other books.

Dražen Petrović is the Principal Legal Officer of the International Labor Office (ILO) in Geneva. He received his LLB from the University in Sarajevo, MA from the University of Belgrade, LLM from the European University Institute in Florence, and PhD from the University of Geneva. He has been associated with both international organizations and universities.

Gervase Phillips is Principal Lecturer in History at the Manchester Metropolitan University. He is the author of *The Anglo-Scots Wars, 1513–1550* (1999) and has contributed to the *Journal of Military History*, *War in History*, *War and Society*, *Technology and Culture*, and the *Scottish Historical Review*.

David Pizzo is a Professor of History at Murray State University in Murray, Kentucky. He teaches courses on European, African, and imperial history as well as courses focusing on war and genocide. He has published a monograph on colonial warfare in German East Africa.

Fiona Reid lectures in history at the University of Glamorgan. She has published *Mending Mentally Broken Men: Shell Shock, Treatment and Recovery in Britain, 1914–1930* (2010). She has recently written on the French *Exode* (1940), and her interests include the broader medical and social history of modern warfare.

Stuart Robson is a graduate of the University of British Columbia and Oxford. He taught at Trent University for 34 years and now teaches at the University of Victoria. He specializes in German history and the two world wars.

David Schimmelpenninck van der Oye is Professor of Russian History at Brock University. His research interests focus on eighteenth-and nineteenth-century cultural, intellectual, diplomatic, and military history. He is the author of, among other works, *Toward the Rising Sun* and *Russian Orientalism*.

Timothy J. Stapleton is a Professor of African History at Trent University in Canada. He has taught history at Rhodes University and the University of Fort Hare in South Africa and was a Research Associate at the University of Zimbabwe. His books include *Maqoma: Xhosa Resistance to Colonial Advance 1798–1873* (1994), *Faku: Rulership and Colonialism in the Mpondo Kingdom 1780–1867* (2001), and *No Insignificant Part: The Rhodesia Native Regiment and the East African Campaign of the First World War* (2006).

David R. Stone received his PhD in history in 1997 from Yale University and is currently Pickett Professor of Military History at Kansas State University. He is the author of numerous books and articles on Russian/Soviet military and diplomatic history.

Michael Sturma is Chair of the History Program at Murdoch University in Perth, Australia. His books include *Death at a Distance: The Loss of the Legendary USS Harder* (2006) and *The USS Flier: Death and Survival on a World War II Submarine* (2008).

Blair Turner holds appointments as Professor in the Departments of History and of International Studies and Political Science at the Virginia Military Institute and is an editor of the *Journal of Military History*.

Ian van der Waag, MA (Pretoria), PhD (Cape Town), is Associate Professor of Military History at Stellenbosch University, South Africa. Recent publications include "Wyndhams, Parktown, 1901–1923: Domesticity and Servitude in an Early Twentieth-Century South African Household," *Journal of Family History* (2007); and "Rural Struggles and the Politics of a Colonial Command: The Southern Mounted Rifles of the Transvaal Volunteers, 1905–1912," in *Soldiers and Settlers in Africa, 1850–1918*, edited by S. Miller (2009). He is working on the first single-volume military history of South Africa.

Bruce Vandervort received a PhD in modern European history from the University of Virginia in 1989. He is a Professor of Modern European and African History at the Virginia Military Institute and is also the editor of the *Journal of Military History*.

James A. Winn is William Fairfield Warren Professor at Boston University, Director of the Boston University Humanities Foundation. His eight books include a prizewinning biography of Dryden. *The Poetry of War* (2008), Winn's book for general readers, is available from Cambridge University Press.

David R. Woodward is Professor Emeritus at Marshall University. His publications include *David Lloyd George and the Generals* (1983); *Military Correspondence of Field Marshal Sir William Robertson* (1989); *Field Marshal Sir William Robertson* (1998); *Trial by Friendship: Anglo-American Relations, 1917–1918* (2003); *Hell in the Holy Land* (2006); *America and World War I: A Selected Annotated Bibliography of English-Language Sources* (2007), and *World War I Almanac* (2009).

Eyal Zisser is Director of the Moshe Dayan Center for Middle Eastern and African Studies and the former Head of the Department of Middle Eastern and African History, both at Tel Aviv University. Professor Zisser has written extensively on the history and modern politics of Syria and Lebanon and the Arab–Israeli conflict.

Editor's Preface

The articles in this collection are drawn from the five-volume *Encyclopedia of War* (2012). It is the hope of the general editor, and the advisory and contributing editors, that this concise one-volume paperback version devoted to the twentieth century (and beyond) will make it accessible to students and general readers. We believe that the selection here will provide a useful introduction to the subject of war since 1900. Unfortunately, given the limitations of space and the wish to keep the price within reach of students, many of the entries in the full encyclopedia could not be included. In particular, the numerous biographical entries devoted to people like Churchill, Stalin, and Hitler (and less well-known figures such as generals Brusilov,

Liman von Sanders, and Nogi Maresuke) have been omitted here. Neither was there space for separate entries devoted to specific battles, such as the battles of Khalkin Gol and Stalingrad, the Gallipoli Campaign, and Operation Barbarossa. Many students will have access to the complete list of entries via their university library's subscription to the online version of the full encyclopedia, however.

I would like to thank the contributors to this concise version for their willingness to revise their articles and to bring up to date their suggestions for further reading.

Gordon Martel
Victoria
November 2013

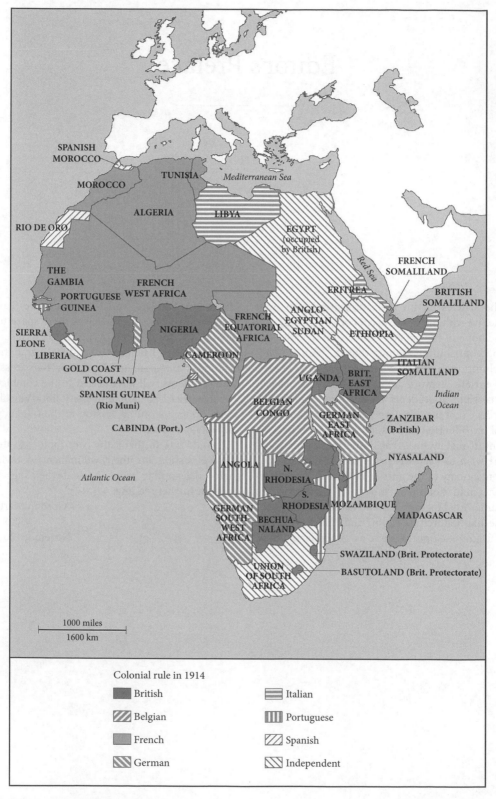

Map 1   Colonial Africa, 1914.

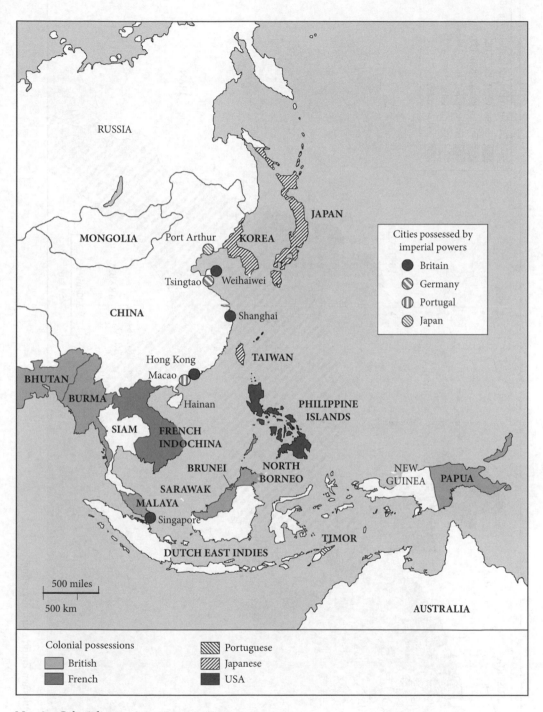

Map 2 Colonialism in Asia, 1914.

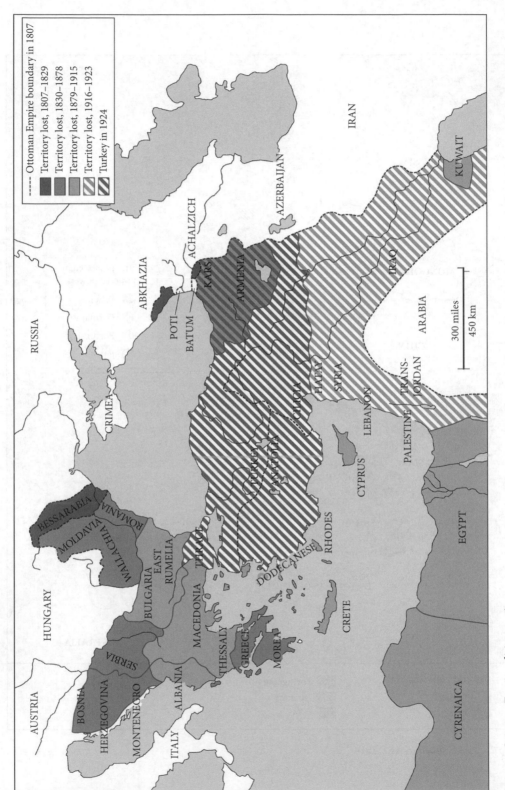

Map 3 Ottoman Empire: disintegration.

Legend:

- – – – Ottoman Empire boundary in 1807
- Territory lost, 1807–1829
- Territory lost, 1830–1878
- Territory lost, 1879–1915
- Territory lost, 1916–1923
- Turkey in 1924

Map labels:

AUSTRIA, HUNGARY, RUSSIA, IRAN, ITALY, ALBANIA, BOSNIA, HERZEGOVINA, MONTENEGRO, SERBIA, MOLDAVIA, WALLACHIA, ROMANIA, BESSARABIA, CRIMEA, ABKHAZIA, ACHALZICH, POTI, BATUM, KARS, ARMENIA, AZERBAIJAN, BULGARIA, EAST RUMELIA, MACEDONIA, THESSALY, GREECE, MOREA, THRACE, TURKEY ANATOLIA, CILICIA, HATAY, SYRIA, LEBANON, IRAQ, ARABIA, KUWAIT, TRANS-JORDAN, PALESTINE, CYPRUS, RHODES, DODECANESE, CRETE, EGYPT, CYRENAICA

300 miles
450 km

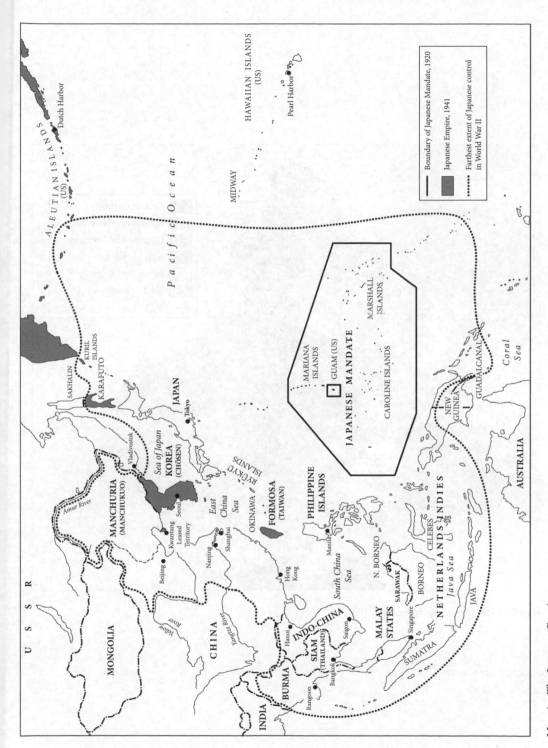

Map 4 The Japanese Empire.

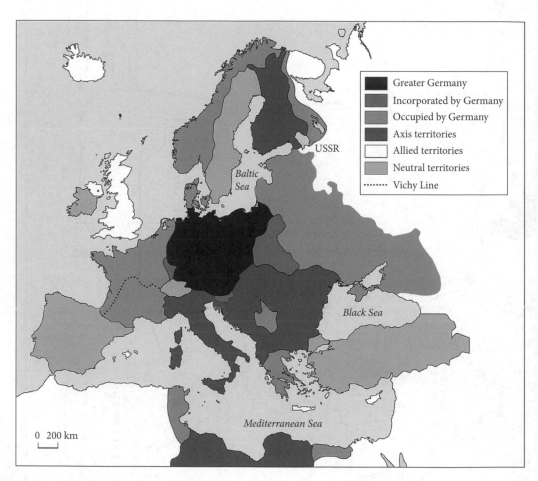

Map 5 German-occupied Europe, 1942.

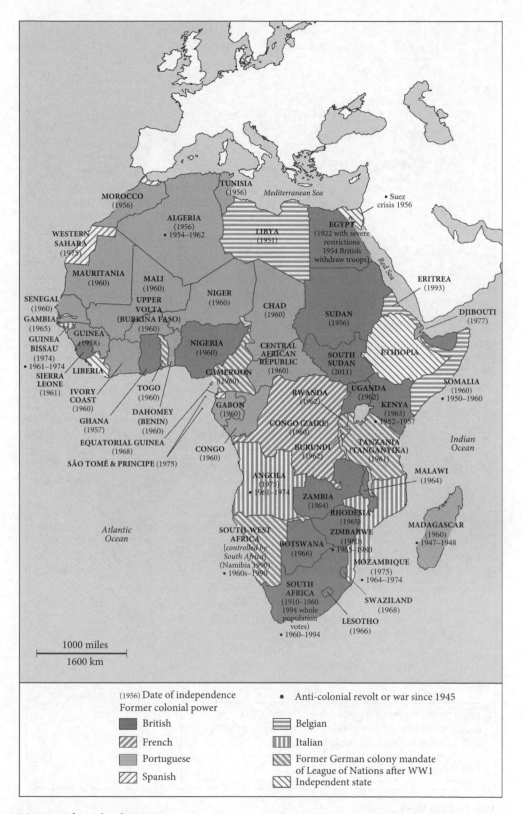

Map 6   Africa: decolonization.

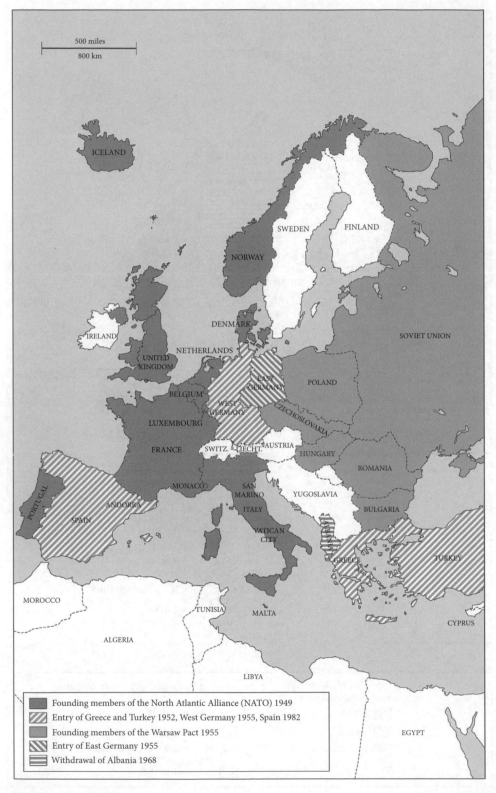

Map 7 Cold War Europe.

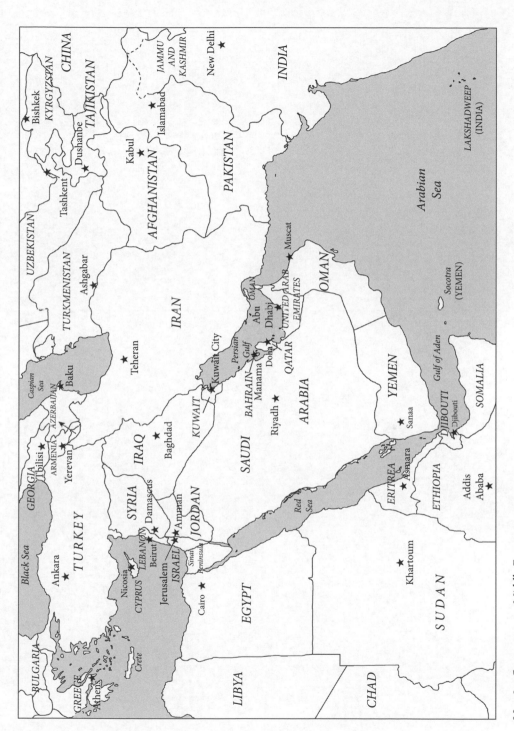

Map 8 Contemporary Middle East.

Algerian War of Independence (1954–1962)

BRIAN P. FARRELL

The Algerian War of Independence was one of the most controversial military conflicts associated with "decolonization," the dismantling of European overseas empires after World War II. The great majority of Algeria's population live in a long coastal plain along the southwestern shore of the Mediterranean Sea, and in mixed forest and mountain country intermingled with that coastal plain. Its location made Algeria coveted by ambitious empires throughout its history. Conflict between France and the Ottoman Turkish Empire prompted a French invasion in 1830, which framed the twentieth-century war of independence.

French hegemony in Algeria produced three developments that made the ultimate war of independence unique, complicated, and controversial. First, France declared its Algerian territories to be part of metropolitan France itself, not overseas colonial territories. Second, a large population of European settlers put down roots in Algeria. Third, successive French governments treated Algeria as part of France, but denied full political and civil rights and equality to residents of Algeria other than the European settler communities.

The Algerian population was diverse before France annexed the country. Berber peoples tended to live in the mountainous and desert areas, Arabs and Turks along the coastal plain. United to an extent by a shared religion, Islam, they were also frequently divided by disputes over land and customs. French rule was imposed by force in bitter campaigns stretching to the end of the 1840s. "Resistance" to French rule tended to be driven by local, ethnic, and religious factors, but did lay the foundation for an Algerian "national myth" of unified struggle against alien rule. The dispossession of non-Europeans from political and economic power reinforced that perception of suppressed national identity. But French efforts to integrate Algeria into French civilization also affected perceptions of identity. By the 1930s Algerians tended to divide into three broad groups. Many, led by Messali Hadj, wanted to oust French rule from Northwest Africa and restore independent states in Morocco, Tunisia, and Algeria. Many Muslim religious leaders saw the problem as a cultural struggle against French efforts to Europeanize a Muslim community. Their slogan was "Arabic is my language, Algeria is my country, Islam is my religion" (Horne 1977: 38). A smaller group of mainly urban professionals, led by Ferhat Abbas, distinguished between an ideal France of liberty, equality, and fraternity,

Twentieth-Century War and Conflict: A Concise Encyclopedia, First Edition. Edited by Gordon Martel.
© 2015 John Wiley & Sons, Ltd. Published 2015 by John Wiley & Sons, Ltd.

and the inequality imposed by European settlers in Algeria. They argued there was no reason Algerians could not be Muslim and French at the same time, providing liberal France lived up to its progressive ideals.

World War II was the decisive event that changed the course of modern Algerian history. The German conquest of France in June 1940 divided it politically and brought the war directly to Algeria. General Charles de Gaulle, a junior minister in the last government of the Third Republic, escaped to England to continue the war, and called on the French armed forces and people to rally to his call. But the constitutional government, taken in hand by Marshal Henri Philippe Pétain, accepted an armistice yet retained control of most French overseas territories – including Algeria. Pétain's Vichy France collaborated militarily with the Axis Powers. The French Empire became a military and political battleground between Vichy and Free France over the "French future." In Algeria, Vichy policies favored the political and economic dominance of the European community and widened the gulf between them and the non-Europeans. The Free French countered by declaring they would grant French overseas territories self-determination after the war. When Allied forces invaded Algeria and Morocco in November 1942 to drive Axis forces out of Africa, they ignited a confusing struggle for control of French territory and the armed forces. When France itself was liberated in autumn 1944 de Gaulle and his Free French established themselves as the Provisional Government of France. After the war ended with Allied victory in 1945, a Fourth Republic emerged. It faced daunting challenges. France was devastated physically, humiliated and divided politically. French leaders were determined to rebuild French prosperity, power, and prestige. To do this they needed to draw on the resources of the overseas territories. This clashed with rising expectations for political change in those territories.

Such expectations were spelled out in Algeria in June 1943 in a manifesto agreed by Messali Hadj and Ferhat Abbas, demanding post-war political independence. Algerian nationalism began to focus more on evolution outside any framework defined by France. This movement, combined with serious economic problems, triggered protests in May 1945 in the town of Sétif, during celebrations to mark the end of the war.

Police efforts to disperse the protests triggered violent reaction by Algerian farmers. The clashes escalated into an anti-European rampage, to which European settlers and the security forces responded massively. More than 100 Europeans and thousands of Algerians were killed. Sétif was a shocking wake-up call that exposed stark divisions pushing Algeria toward open conflict. Three agendas clashed. First, growing numbers of Algerians were no longer prepared to tolerate being second-class citizens in their own country. Common ground still existed, with many channels of intercourse. But dividing lines were very real: Muslim and non-European on the one hand, Christian and European on the other. Second, the French government needed first to rebuild France and simply could not drive radical changes overseas. Third, and most vexing, the European community was determined to prevent political change that would jeopardize its dominance of Algeria. This explosive combination of French weakness at home, European settler intransigence, and changing Algerian expectations produced the war of independence.

The clash at Sétif changed the political atmosphere in Algeria. The moment was met by a younger generation of Algerians, many of them veterans of the French armed forces. Frustration drove them forward, as did a larger international groundswell for political change and the dismantling of European overseas empires. Some of these younger leaders organized a political–military coalition to unite Algerian aspirations in a common front, to end the divisions that weakened Algerian nationalism. The formation of the *Front de Libération Nationale* (FLN) shaped what became the war of independence.

The FLN wanted to establish an independent modern Algerian state organized on socialist principles. It emerged from three things: French failure to satisfy Algerian demands for change, violent faction feuding between Algerian nationalist movements, and events elsewhere. French refusal in 1947 to grant real equality of status between Europeans and Algerians accelerated a shift towards armed struggle against French power. The principal nationalist party, the *Mouvement pour le Triomphe des Libertés Démocratiques* (MTLD), organized a paramilitary underground wing: the *Organization Spéciale* (OS). Most OS leaders wound up being arrested by French police. But this experience forged bonds between younger men from different regions and groups, bonds reinforced by growing impatience with pre-war leaders. They were also encouraged by nationalist challenges to European dominance elsewhere. French defeat in Indochina, culminating in the debacle at Dien Bien Phu in spring 1954, inspired a breakthrough in Algeria – it demonstrated that French power could be beaten.

Younger militants formed the *Comité Révolutionnaire pour l'Unité et l'Action* (CRUA), expressly to unite Algerian nationalists in armed struggle to end French rule in Algeria. CRUA leaders organized the FLN, and its military wing: the *Armée de Libération Nationale* (ALN). On November 1, 1954, the FLN staged more than 30 coordinated attacks, all over Algeria, against police stations, army barracks, factories, French civil servants, and Algerians working as state officials. The FLN announced itself to the world by claiming responsibility for the attacks, which killed seven people and provoked the French government to send paramilitary police and troops from the mainland to crush the outbreak. This launched a conflict that dragged on until July 1962, cost possibly half a million lives from a total population of 10 million, destroyed the Fourth Republic in France, sparked three rebellions against the Fifth Republic, provoked nearly the whole one-million-strong European community in Algeria to flee into permanent exile, and shaped both modern France and Algeria.

The FLN defined this conflict. They did so by waging a revolutionary war that ultimately forced France to abandon physical control of Algeria. This French–Algerian War combined three conflicts: civil war between the FLN and rival Algerian nationalist groups; guerrilla war between the FLN and the French army and police; *de facto* civil war among the French, in France and Algeria. The FLN identified three tasks: to convince the "Algerian people" to truly be the Algerian people; to establish the FLN as the undisputed leader of that people; to force the French government to leave Algeria to them. French war aims were more confused. The French government tried to bring about a stable Algeria still associated politically with France. The French army tried to preserve French power in Algeria by defeating what they wrongly identified as a "communist" military challenge to that power. And European settlers tried to prevent any change that would end their dominance of a French Algeria. Two other protagonists played vital roles by facing essential questions, pushed onto the agenda by the FLN. The Algerian people had to decide whether they were a united people, who wanted an independent nation, and if so what kind of nation, governed by whom. The people of France had to decide whether France should remain associated with Algeria, and if so how. The FLN's revolutionary war, designed to change Algeria as well as win independence, revolved around a central political question. This question became the preoccupation of French governments: could they find a "third voice" of moderation, lying between Algerian nationalism and European settler intransigence, with whom France could redefine its relationship with Algeria?

The central theme of FLN strategy was to force all Algerians into definitive conflict with the French. The "nine historic leaders" organized the movement into an external wing that would concentrate on winning international sympathy and support, led by Ahmed Ben Bella, and an internal wing that would wage revolutionary guerrilla war inside Algeria, whose major leaders included Belkacem Krim, Larbi Ben M'Hidi, and Rabah Bitat. From the first wave of attacks crucial targets were the so-called *béni oui ouis*, Algerians working for the French state, and MTLD supporters of Messali Hadj. The FLN insisted on forging one unified Algerian movement, through violence. But the structure of the organization reflected the country's internal divisions. The FLN divided Algeria into six districts, called *wilayas*, plus a special zone for the city of Algiers. Early operations in the *bled*, or countryside, did not gain much active support from Algerians. But they did provoke an uncompromising French government response. It could not negotiate independence with any Algerian groups because "ici, c'est la France." This position was at first popular in France, not least with an army smarting from defeat in Vietnam and determined to draw a line in Algeria. FLN external efforts enjoyed more success, sparking sympathy from the new Non-Aligned Movement and more tangible support from Arab nationalism, led by Gamal Abdel Nasser of Egypt. The struggle to make any progress in Algeria provoked FLN leaders deliberately to escalate the war in August 1955 by directly attacking European settlers near Philippeville, killing 103 civilians. The severe French military and civilian retribution that followed further poisoned relations between European settlers and Algerians. FLN terrorism, answered by French *ratonnade* ("rat hunt") retributions, sparked an escalating spiral of violence against civilians that played into FLN hands.

Such escalation reflected the center of gravity of the war: the political struggle to determine how civilian populations would answer those questions about the relationship between France and Algeria. French belated efforts to play catch-up by more liberal integration and social/economic development were directly attacked by the FLN strategy to target the European population and provoke retaliation. In March 1956, the French government granted "special powers" to Algerian authorities to suppress the FLN. In April, Ferhat Abbas disbanded his moderate party and joined the FLN. French executions of FLN prisoners provoked FLN attacks on policemen in Algiers; European policemen retaliated by planting bombs in the Casbah, the Arab quarter of the city.

The spiral of escalation prompted the FLN to organize its only wartime congress, in August, in the remote rural village of Soummam. This congress was controversial; none of the external leaders could attend and several denounced it. Nevertheless, the congress made two crucial decisions. First, the internal political struggle would remain paramount. Second, war aims and strategy were confirmed: violence would be used to destroy all voices of moderation or compromise, to force Algerians and French to answer their questions through conflict. To provoke this rupture, the FLN launched an even more aggressive campaign of urban terrorism in the heart of French Algeria: the capital city, Algiers.

The Battle of Algiers proved to be the major turning point in the Algerian War of Independence. The French won a military victory, but suffered an irreversible political defeat. On September 30, FLN guerrillas in Algiers, led by Larbi Ben M'Hidi and Saadi Yacef, launched a campaign of bombing attacks on civilian targets in the city, such as cafés and offices, frequented by Europeans. The FLN unit operated from the Casbah, provoking French police and troops to cordon off the quarter and strictly control movement in and out.

Yacef responded by using female fighters to smuggle out explosives and carry out attacks. On December 27, the FLN assassinated the European mayor of Algiers. This enraged the European community; hardliners tried to assassinate General Raoul Salan, the army commander in chief in Algeria, denouncing him as too weak to prosecute the war. Such rage forced the French government to turn over the capital to the army; on January 7, 1957, the 10th Parachute Division, commanded by General Jacques Massu, took over the defense of Algiers. The paratroopers were hardened regular veterans, more formidable and aggressive than the conscript soldiers they replaced. The FLN found out just how aggressive when it called a General Strike for January 28, to unite the Casbah in passive resistance to the French. The paratroopers broke the strike by forcing residents back to work. But this was just the beginning.

Massu's division worked with the clandestine 11th Shock Battalion, a counterintelligence unit secretly authorized by the French government to do "whatever it takes" to smash the FLN guerrillas in Algiers (Aussaresses 2005: 124–126). The paratroopers and the clandestine unit devised a strategy to implode the FLN, by smothering the Casbah with intrusive search and interrogation operations, using *agents provocateurs* and Algerian auxiliaries, or *harkis*, to identify FLN sympathizers, then using physical torture to force detained suspects to reveal the names, ranks, and locations of FLN fighters. The plan was to identify the enemy, then dismantle his force from within. This "urban protection" plan soon paid dividends. Larbi Ben M'Hidi was arrested then secretly executed by 11th Shock Battalion, his death proclaimed a suicide. French forces methodically hunted down and rounded up Saadi Yacef's unit, arresting Yacef himself on September 24. When paratroopers trapped and killed Ali LaPointe on October 10, the Battle of Algiers came to an end. But its repercussions changed the war, dividing the French, putting them on the political defensive, allowing the FLN to compete for the moral high ground.

During 1957, both the garrison commander of Algiers and its secretary general of police resigned in protest over the use of torture on detainees. Two governments in Paris were toppled by Algerian controversies. And in January 1958, Henri Alleg, a communist journalist in Algiers, made the issue an international scandal by publishing *La Question*, claiming he was tortured by the French army and police as part of a systematic policy. This inflamed already bitter controversies in France and abroad over French conduct of the war. In October 1956, the French forced a Moroccan airplane carrying Ben Bella and other external FLN leaders to land in Algeria, and arrested them. This helped turn Arab opinion against France, as did the French–British attack on Egypt over the Suez Canal controversy in November. After the French air force bombed the Tunisian village of Sakiet in error in February 1958, Algeria's now independent neighbors became even more willing to allow the ALN to operate from their territory. The Fourth Republic could not survive, especially because it could not control the European settlers in Algeria. When a European mob occupied government offices in Algiers on May 13, Massu and other senior officers and officials formed a Committee of Public Safety; the next day Salan declared the army had assumed temporary control of "French Algeria." Massu called on de Gaulle to come out of retirement to "save France." De Gaulle proclaimed: "I shall hold myself at the disposition of my country" (Horne 1977: 286–293).

The French turn to de Gaulle underlined a cardinal fact: France was paralyzed. The French people could not accept the tactics used to suppress the FLN. But the army insisted on following through its victory in Algiers, the European settlers insisted on *Algérie Française*, and the Fourth Republic could not bring either to heel. By June 1, de Gaulle agreed to form a government in France, with a mandate to govern with emergency powers for six months and draft a new Constitution to form a new republic. De Gaulle visited Algeria, parading in Algiers on June 4 in front of huge and delirious crowds, telling them "I have understood you." But the crowds did not understand what he really meant; nor did they realize it was already too late to preserve "French Algeria."

French divisions gave the FLN a chance to regain the initiative, a chance it seized ruthlessly. French success in Algiers, plus the arrest of Ben Bella, shifted momentum to the hard men of the field army. In May 1957, an ALN unit massacred more than 300 supporters of Messali Hadj in the village of Melouza. Such brutality, combined with the ongoing violent campaign to eliminate "Messalists" in the large Algerian community in France, cemented FLN dominance of Algerian nationalism. In December, ALN commanders lured Ramdane Abane, architect of the Soummam congress, to a meeting in Tunisia and assassinated him. ALN hardliners became ascendant in the FLN. They reworked its strategy: keep the army in being, pressure the French from outside Algeria, and galvanize "the people" inside the country (Stora 2001: 65–67). De Gaulle had to find the way forward between an Algerian nationalism now rallying behind a hardline FLN and European settlers standing fast on *Algérie Française*.

De Gaulle tried to create a "middle voice" by offering a "peace of the brave," launching a strategy combining carrot and stick. France launched its Fifth Republic in December 1958 with a Constitution shifting much power to the executive branch, and elected de Gaulle as president. De Gaulle pulled together efforts to promote social and economic development in Algeria in a new systematic Constantine Plan, to persuade Algerians to grow in association with France. This was balanced by the Challe Plan, named for the new commander in chief in Algeria, General Maurice Challe. The Morice Line, a deep belt of electronic sensors and fixed defense obstacles, was extended to cover the entire border with Tunisia. This impeded ALN incursions long enough to allow mobile forces to catch and smash them. Inside Algeria, conscript army units plus police forces were concentrated in one district at a time, to isolate and saturate it. This flushed out the ALN *katiba* – the typical combat unit, ranging from 30 to 100 fighters, equipped with a variety of weapons. The exposed *katiba* were then pounced on by regular army mobile units sweeping the target area, who scattered or shattered them. The offensive peaked in Operation Jumelles in the rugged Kabylia district in August 1959. ALN forces were punished so severely that their units inside Algeria were reduced to "penny-packets of shaken guerrillas" (Horne 1977: 339). But it was all too little too late.

The FLN responded by forming a Provisional Government of Algeria, insisting it would only negotiate one issue: full independence. Algerian opinion now lined up strongly behind the FLN, while the ALN remained "in being," posing a continued threat. De Gaulle was determined to "win" the war, to negotiate from a favorable military position – but not necessarily in order to keep Algeria as a French territory. He had a very different vision: to revive and redesign France as a united, strong, and modern Great Power. To his confidantes he spelled out the agenda bluntly: "I shall have to tell everyone concerned that colonies are finished. Let us come together and create a Community, with a common defense, foreign, and economic policy. Those that don't agree can go their own way and we will build a new French community with the rest" (Malraux 1968: 101).

De Gaulle wanted a new France to lead the way in the European Economic Community, to modernize itself as an economy, state, and society. Those overseas territories that could still fit into that vision would be welcome; the others would be let go. French power would no longer rest on territorial empire.

This left open the possibility for a continued relationship with Algeria, something de Gaulle certainly hoped to achieve. French ambitions to develop an independent nuclear deterrent relied on using the vast Algerian Sahara desert for testing, while oil and gas deposits being developed there would do much to support de Gaulle's agenda. This all made the FLN's success at rallying the Algerian people so important. By the time France was ready to talk about change, there was no one else to talk with. De Gaulle's willingness to consider real change – telling his advisors "the old Algeria is dead" (Stora 2001: 76) – provoked another European civilian uprising in Algiers in January 1960. "Barricades Week," escalating to violent clashes with the police, put another French government to the test. This time de Gaulle stood firm, faced down the demonstrations, assumed "special powers" for a year, and demonstrated he could not be intimidated by mob politics. His turn away from Algérie Française destroyed his relationship with the Europeans in Algeria and provoked a growing backlash among regular army officers. That made him more determined to resolve the Algerian conflict and move on with his larger agenda for change.

In 1960, de Gaulle tried hard to forge some sort of compromise that would leave a French presence in Algeria. On November 4, he went so far as to refer to "an Algerian Republic which will one day exist" (Horne 1977: 422). But when he visited Algiers in December the FLN organized four days of massive demonstrations that this time brought the capital to a standstill. They followed this show of strength by persuading the United Nations (UN) to support independence for Algeria. This turned the corner. When de Gaulle asked the French people in a referendum in January 1961 to support his policy to negotiate in Algeria, they did so. That launched the final stage of the conflict: direct negotiations between the FLN and the French government over the future of Algeria. These talks provoked virtual civil war between the French, which did much to determine the final settlement.

This final war within the war escalated beyond the point where the European community could remain in Algeria. Disgruntled army officers and European settler *ultras* formed in February a secret army dedicated to preserving *Algérie Française*, the *Organisation de l'Armée Secrète* (OAS). Days after the announcement that talks between the French government and the FLN would be held in the French town of Evian, the OAS murdered its mayor. In April, de Gaulle publicly referred to "a sovereign Algerian state" (Stora 2001: 256). Days later, Generals Salan and Challe launched a *putsch* in Algiers, supported by alienated army units led by the 1st Foreign Legion Parachute Regiment. They took over the city, called on the army and police to depose de Gaulle, and insisted Algeria would remain part of France. De Gaulle assumed drastic powers in a state of emergency and broadcast directly to the nation, reaching conscript soldiers through their transistor radios, denouncing the coup as illegal, calling on France to stand behind him. Senior French officials seriously feared a paratrooper assault on Paris, but the great majority of the army rallied to de Gaulle. Challe surrendered, but most other *putsch* leaders went underground and joined the OAS. The OAS now launched a violent campaign to destroy the negotiations, including a failed attempt to assassinate de Gaulle.

European settlers lined up behind the OAS as violence spread to France itself. OAS terrorism provoked such a backlash in France that in February 1962 de Gaulle openly conceded the majority now favored independence for Algeria. The final stage of negotiations provoked the OAS to switch their target, launching terror attacks against Algerians. Such attacks failed to prevent the signing of the Evian Accords on March 18, calling for an immediate ceasefire and a referendum in

Algeria within three months, on the question of independence. The OAS declared French forces "occupation troops in *Algérie Française*," rallied settler hardliners, and occupied the European working-class district of Bab El Oued in Algiers (Horne 1977: 523). Pitched battles with police and army provoked the final insanity. European settlers began to leave Algeria, provoking the OAS to order them to stay and fight for *Algérie Française* on pain of death. Good as their word, OAS terror attacks in Algerian cities became so violent the FLN warned that a race war might erupt as soon as the French army departed, if the indiscriminate terror did not stop. The OAS "scorched earth" response lashed out at the infrastructure of the cities of Algiers, as if to deny anyone the fruits of any victory. By the time the OAS and FLN declared a ceasefire on June 18 the damage was done. Algerian cities emptied, as European settlers, also known as *colons* or *pieds noirs*, emigrated in a mass flight for survival. More than 95 percent departed in 1962, reducing the European community to a tiny remnant. On July 1, the Algerian people voted overwhelmingly to support "an independent Algerian state cooperating with France," as per the Evian Accords. France recognized the Republic of Algeria as an independent sovereign state.

The lasting importance of the Algerian War of Independence comes from how the war was fought, and how it ended. The settlement allowed de Gaulle to forge his modern France. But this France remained bitterly divided by the Algerian experience. The *pieds noir* exodus left Algeria impoverished and France embittered. Algerian dependence on French aid and investment only increased, as did Algerian emigration to France. Controversies over torture and tactics were hidden away; not until 1999 did the French National Assembly resolve, in total silence, to declare that the Algerian conflict had indeed been a "war." Amnesties were granted to protect French officers from investigation. Full disclosures about 11th Shock Battalion and government policy only emerged in the twenty-first century, renewing bitter controversy. Algerians also had to swallow "fruit of the poisoned tree." One of the most famous justifications for violent resistance to colonial rule was written by Frantz Fanon, a medical doctor from Martinique who served in Algeria and came wholeheartedly to support the FLN. In *The Wretched of the Earth*, Fanon argued

that the only way for a people suppressed by alien rule to regain self-confidence, self-respect, and the strength to win back true freedom was to use force to evict the imperial power. This fit the FLN consensus that a people so long divided, in so many ways, could only unite against an outsider, and only armed struggle could build a united Algeria. FLN leaders won the war by persuading Algerians to accept them as the leader of a common cause – then lost the peace by refusing to accept pluralism in a plural society. The new leaders encouraged wholesale massacres of Algerians deemed to have collaborated with the French, then fell out among themselves even before French forces left Algeria. Authoritarian government produced such economic and social stagnation that in the 1990s a violent civil war erupted between Islamic reform movements and the army–FLN alliance. Fanon did not live to see how a country made by violence became one defined through it.

The twenty-first century "War on Terror" sparked renewed interest in the Algerian conflict. It seemed an example of a successful revolutionary war waged against western forces in a Muslim-dominated country. American military planners rediscovered *The Battle of Algiers*, one of the most powerful *cinéma vérité* films ever made. Filmed on location in Algiers, supported by Saadi Yacef himself, the film documented the political–military struggle between the French army and the FLN for control of the city. It captured the central themes: the social complexity of both European and Arab populations; the use of torture and terrorism; failure by French governments to control European settlers; FLN political success in imposing leadership on Algerians. Released in 1966, the film was banned in France for many years. Perhaps its most lasting lesson is the central lesson of the war. Revolutionary war separated the French and Algerian states. But it could not reinvent a French–Algerian relationship ultimately defined by economic forces. Nor could it heal the divisions inside Algeria that the long period of French rule only concealed. Algeria still suffers from the victory that made it independent.

SEE ALSO: National Liberation, Wars of; Terrorism, War Against; Vietnam War (1959–1975); World War II: Mediterranean Campaign; World War II: The Defeat and Occupation of France.

References

Aussaresses, P. (2005) *The Battle of the Casbah: Counter-Terrorism and Torture*. New York: Enigma Books.

Horne, A. (1977) *A Savage War of Peace: Algeria 1954–1962*. New York: Viking.

Malraux, A. (1968) *Anti-Memoirs*. New York: Holt, Rinehart and Winston.

Stora, B. (2001) *Algeria 1830–2000: A Short History*. Ithaca: Cornell University Press.

Further Reading

Evans, M. (1997) *The Memory of Resistance: French Opposition to the Algerian War*. Oxford: Berg.

Fanon, F. (1967) *The Wretched of the Earth*. London: Penguin.

Feraoun, M. (2000) *Journal 1955–1962: Reflections on the French–Algerian War*. Lincoln: University of Nebraska Press.

Henissart, P. (1970) *Wolves in the City: The Death of French Algeria*. New York: Simon and Schuster.

Hutchinson, M. C. (1978) *Revolutionary Terrorism: The FLN in Algeria 1954–1962*. Stanford: Hoover Institution Press.

LeSueur, J. D. (2001) *Uncivil War: Intellectuals and Identity Politics during the Decolonization of Algeria*. Lincoln: University of Nebraska Press.

Naylor, P. C. (2000) *France and Algeria: A History of Decolonization and Transformation*. Gainesville: University Press of Florida.

O'Ballance, E. (1967) *The Algerian Insurrection*. London: Faber and Faber.

Stora, B. (1998) *La gangrène et l'oubli: La mémoire de la guerre d'Algérie*. Paris: La Découverte.

Talbott, J. (1981) *The War Without a Name: France in Algeria*. London: Faber and Faber.

Windrow, M. (1997) *The Algerian War 1954–1962*. Oxford: Osprey.

Angolan Civil Wars (1975–2002)

IAN VAN DER WAAG

The Angolan conflict is in many ways the foremost African insurgency case study. Not only did this conflict follow a national liberation war, but it was also cast against the backdrop of the Cold War. Moreover, it covers the full range of combat, from low-intensity, insurgent conflict through to conventional warfare. The insurgency was fought throughout most of southern, central, and northern Angola, while the larger, semi-conventional war, conducted in southern Angola, involved until 1989 South African and Soviet-bloc forces (Turner 1998). The first civil war, ended by a fragile ceasefire, was followed in 1992 by renewed conflict, without the foreign forces, that continued, despite ongoing negotiations, through to the assassination of the leader of *União Nacional para a Independência Total de Angola* (UNITA), Jonas Savimbi, in 2002. It had additionally become a personal war; UNITA finally became indistinguishable from Savimbi, whose termination had become the only precondition for the end of the war.

The civil war was a continuation of the liberation war (1961–1975). As the Portuguese colonial empire collapsed, the nationalist movements, fractured along ethnic and ideological lines, intensified their struggles with each other. The *Movimento Popular de Libertação de Angola* (MPLA), essentially a Marxist party founded by "mestiços" (people of mixed European, native born indigenous Angolan and/or other indigenous African lineages), proclaimed a government in Luanda. A rival government was proclaimed in Ambriz by the *Frente Nacional de Libertação de Angola* (FNLA) and UNITA, groups that enjoyed strong support among the Bakongo and Ovimbundu. The MPLA, occupying the colonial capital and the major ports, drew Soviet and Cuban support. Cuba, acting independently of Moscow, soon took the lead (Gleijeses 2002). The FNLA looked to the United States and Zaire, and UNITA to South Africa, a country that was soon drawn to more direct involvement as a result of a growing refugee crisis and the presence of Soviet-bloc troops.

The MPLA faced a two-front war when Angola received formal independence on November 11, 1975. UNITA, cooperating with elements of the South African Defence Force (SADF) that crossed the Cunene River (which formed the border between Angola and the then South African occupied Namibia) in August, mounted an offensive in the south. The MPLA was repulsed and the SADF and UNITA, in a series of operations over difficult territory, occupied the southern ports as far as Lobito. However, the SADF advance soon outstripped supply. Moreover, the MPLA forces had been stiffened with Cuban troops and Cuban and Soviet weaponry. South Africa, concerned for casualties and the failure of American promises, withdrew from Angola in February 1976. The MPLA now had the upper hand, as the FNLA had been annihilated in an impulsive attack on Luanda, so ending Luanda's two-front war. The separatist movements in Cabinda, the northern exclave, were also contained.

The MPLA could concentrate on UNITA for much of the remainder of the war. Yet, despite the arrival of increasing numbers of Cubans, East Germans, Russians, and Vietnamese, the MPLA failed to secure victory. Support at critical times from South Africa and Zaire, whose president, Mobutu, enjoyed the support of the Bakongo within Zaire, bolstered UNITA. A revised SADF strategy included the creation of a UNITA insurgent army, and periodic, powerful, cross-border raids. As a result, UNITA harassed government forces, at times closing the Benguela railroad, which linked the Angolan port of Lobito with Zaire, and attacking strategic targets. Growing Soviet-bloc support for the MPLA tipped the balance. By 1989, the SADF had lost air superiority due to arms sanctions and the presence of East German aircrews. A major MPLA–Cuban offensive, launched toward the southeast and the UNITA capital at Jamba, was halted at the Lomba River. Attritional battles were fought around Cuito Cuanavale, with neither side able to destroy the other. Multinational negotiations led to the withdrawal of foreign troops and independence for Namibia in 1990.

The southwestern zone of operations closed with the South African withdrawal. The MPLA now focused on UNITA, which, deserted by erstwhile allies, was mauled in early 1990. Negotiations continued and the Bicesse Accords, resulting from pressures exerted by Washington, Moscow, and Lisbon, were signed in Portugal in May 1991, but the transition to a multi-party democracy foundered when Savimbi refused to accept the results of an ostensibly fraudulent election. The MPLA, who attacked demobilizing UNITA soldiers and civilian supporters in Luanda, controlled the seaboard, while UNITA, rooted firmly in the central highlands, controlled the hinterland. The MPLA devised a strategy to drive UNITA from its central position in the country and push the rebels further east, away from the oilfields and the sea. UNITA converged in the southeast, around Jamba, to regroup. Fortified with supplies stolen from the United Nations (UN) Angola Verification Mission (UNAVEM) or acquired from Zaire, UNITA regained control over several provinces. The battles for Huambo and Cuito were particularly severe, exacerbating the refugee and food crisis.

Ongoing negotiations led to further agreements, but these too collapsed under the weight of mutual distrust, poor international oversight, and the continuing importation of arms. UN sanctions followed and restrictions were placed on the trade of Angolan diamonds, a major source of UNITA wealth. Despite offensives against UNITA in 1998 and 1999, the MPLA could not bring Savimbi to a decisive battle and faced renewed separatist challenges in Cabinda. The war increased in fury. Civilians were used increasingly as targets and shields. Large areas were devastated by insurgent and counterinsurgent forces, both of whom used food as a weapon and strategy. Thousands of land mines were laid, maiming, killing, and disrupting patterns of life. The MPLA emptied the countryside of farmers, destroying Savimbi's base areas. UNITA had in the meantime lost American support, sanctions against conflict diamonds were biting, affecting the purchase of weaponry, and with the fall of Mobutu in 1997, Savimbi lost his remaining ally. The final blow came on February 22, 2002, when Savimbi was assassinated.

A new agreement was signed in April 2002. UNITA demobilized in August and became a political party. The war impacted heavily upon Angolan society and virtually destroyed the economy. Some 4.5 million people were internally displaced. Thousands of child soldiers had been impressed into service on all sides. The UNAVEM-III mission ended in December and the civil war, which saw seemingly irreconcilable violence and embraced the widest variety of forms, was over.

References

Gleijeses, P. (2002) *Conflicting Missions: Havana, Washington and South Africa, 1959–1976*. Chapel Hill: University of North Carolina Press.

Turner, J. W. (1998) *Continent Ablaze*. London: Arms and Armour.

Further Reading

Bridgland, F. (1986) *Jonas Savimbi: A Key to Africa*. Johannesburg: Macmillan.

Bridgland, F. (1992) *The War for Africa: Twelve Months that Transformed a Continent*. Rivonia: Ashanti.

Crocker, C. (1992) *High Noon in Southern Africa: Making Peace in a Rough Neighborhood*. New York: Norton.

de Vries, R. (2013) *Eye of the Firestorm: Strength Lies in Mobility*. Tyger Valley: Naledi.

George, E. (2005) *The Cuban Intervention in Angola, 1965–1991: From Che Guevara to Cuito Cuanavale*. London: Frank Cass.

Guimarães, F. A. (2001) *The Origins of the Angolan Civil War: Foreign Intervention and Domestic Political Conflict*. London: Macmillan.

Matloff, J. (1997) *Fragment of a Forgotten War*. London: Penguin.

Pearce, J. (2005) *An Outbreak of Peace; Angola's Situation of Confusion*. Claremont: David Philip.

Scholtz, L. (2013) *The SADF in the Border War, 1966–1989*. Cape Town: Tafelberg.

Stockwell, J. (1978) *In Search of Enemies: A CIA Story*. New York: Norton.

Van der Waag, I. and Visser, D. (2009) "War, Popular Memory and the South African Literature of the Angolan Conflict," *Journal of Contemporary History*, 34 (1): 113–140.

Arab–Israeli Conflict

AHRON BREGMAN

The Arab–Israeli conflict is usually seen as seven main wars: the 1948 war that followed Israel's independence; the Suez War of 1956; the June 1967 Six-Day War; the Israeli–Egyptian War of Attrition from 1968 to 1970; the October 1973 Yom Kippur War; the 1982 Israeli invasion of Lebanon; and finally the 2006 Second Lebanon War. There were also two major Palestinian insurgencies directed against the Israeli occupation in the Gaza Strip and the West Bank: from 1987 to 1993, which came to be known as the first *intifada*, and from 2000 to 2005, which is called the second, or the *Al-Aqsa intifada*.

However, before all of these conflicts there was a bloody civil war between Arabs and Jews in Palestine, an area that was under British control from 1917 to 1948. What sparked it was the changing demography of Palestine brought about by the influx of Jewish immigrants who came to Palestine in search of shelter from pogroms and persecution in their native countries. While the number of Jewish immigrants to Palestine was quite limited until the 1930s, the rise of Nazism in Germany led to some 200,000 Jews immigrating to Palestine between 1932 and 1938. Jews, who comprised only 4 percent of the total Palestinian population in 1882, formed 13 percent in 1922, 28 percent in 1935, and about 30 percent in 1939. By 1947 there were 608,230 Jews in Palestine, compared with about 1,364,330 Arabs (Bregman 2000: 4–5). This demographic transformation was accompanied by a geographical change as the new arrivals purchased large tracts of Palestinian land. The demographic and geographical changes increased tensions between Jews and Arabs in Palestine and led to violent clashes.

To end the Jewish–Arab strife, on November 29, 1947, the United Nations (UN) proposed to partition Palestine between the two peoples, allowing each community to form its own independent state on some of the land; it offered the Jews 55 percent of Palestine and the Arabs (still the majority) 45 percent. The Jews accepted the offer, but the Arabs objected and threatened that any attempt to divide Palestine would lead to war. The UN proceeded anyway and passed the partition resolution (United Nations Resolution 181); on the next day a civil war broke out in Palestine and went on until May 14, 1948.

The 1948 War

Friday, May 14, 1948, was the day the British departed Palestine and the Jews declared independence. Thus, the State of Israel was born and the Jews of Palestine became "Israelis." In response to the Israeli declaration of independence, the

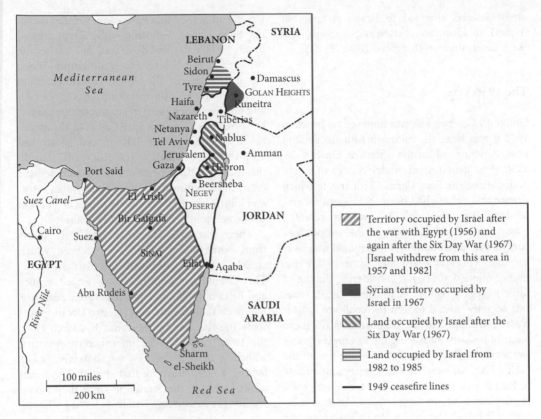

Map 9 Arab–Israeli conflict.

Arab armies of Egypt, Syria, Lebanon, Iraq, and Transjordan, supported by units from Saudi Arabia and Yemen, invaded. Their aim was to destroy Israel, help Arab Palestinians, or perhaps, as some scholars claim, to grab some land for themselves in the absence of the "British police-man." Thus, what started as a civil war between Jews and Arabs within Palestinian boundaries now became an all-out conventional war between the Israeli Defense Forces (IDF) and neighboring Arab armies. For the Israelis, this became their "War of Liberation," or "War of Independence," while for the Arab Palestinians, some 750,000 of whom became refugees as a result of the war, it became *al-Nakba*, "The Catastrophe."

The IDF managed to contain the Arab onslaught, counterattack, and seize some of the lands the UN had partitioned off to the Palestinians in 1947. Of the rest of this land allotted to the Palestinians, Egypt managed to capture the Gaza Strip and Transjordan took the West Bank. Thus, by the end of the first Arab–Israeli war, Palestine was indeed partitioned – not, however, between Jewish and Arab Palestinians as envisaged by the UN, but between Israelis, Jordanians, and Egyptians.

In terms of warfare, the 1948 war was quite a primitive encounter where the single soldier played a leading role while large formations – battalions, regiments, divisions, and so on – played little. Sophisticated weapons, tanks, and aircraft were hardly used at all. Contrary to popular belief, this war was not one between the "few" Israelis and "many" Arabs, or, as it is often put, a clash between David (Israel) and Goliath (the Arabs). In fact, careful analysis shows that the number of Israeli troops committed to the battle on the eve of the Arab invasion was roughly equal to that of the invaders. As the war progressed, the number of Arab troops increased only slightly, while the number of Israelis grew steadily, and, by the end of the war, Israel's fighting force was larger in absolute terms than that of the Arab armies put together. It was not a "miracle," as is often claimed, that led to Israeli victory, but numerical advantage, better organization, and sheer determination (Bregman 2000: 23–24).

The 1956 War

Unlike 1948, when war was imposed on Israel, in 1956 it was Israel, in collusion with Britain and France, who went on the offensive. On July 26, 1956, President Gamal Abdel Nasser of Egypt nationalized the Suez Canal Company, of which France and Britain had been the majority share-holders. The two colonial powers resented Nasser's unilateral decision, as they would lose control over an important international waterway through which vital supplies came to Europe. France and Britain began considering the use of force to regain control of the Suez Canal. Israel was secretly invited to join the coalition against Nasser, which provided an opportunity to achieve some of her own aims – mainly to gain control of the Straits of Tiran. The Straits, at the foot of the Gulf of Aqaba, were Israel's primary trade route to East Africa and Asia, but had for several years been blockaded by Egypt. Now, Israel conditioned that if she was to join the planned war she should be allowed to move her troops south to the Straits and remove the blockade.

A simple plan emerged: Israel would provide a pretext for French and British intervention by attacking Egypt from the east, approaching the Suez Canal. The British and French governments, as if taken by surprise, would appeal to the governments of Israel and Egypt to stop the fighting. They would stipulate that Egypt should: (i) halt all acts of war; (ii) withdraw all troops 10 miles from the canal; and (iii) accept temporary occupation by Britain and France of key positions on the canal. Israel (who of course would know the terms in advance) would be asked to: (i) halt all acts of war; and (ii) withdraw all troops 10 miles to the east of the canal. Israel would then accept the terms, and it was hoped that Egypt would follow suit, allowing French and British troops to regain effective control of the canal without bloodshed. However, if Nasser were to refuse the terms, France and Britain would intervene militarily and forcibly regain control of the canal.

The IDF struck on the afternoon of October 29, 1956, with aircraft parachuting troops at the Israeli end of the Mitla Pass, some 30 miles east of the Suez Canal. Following this, Egypt moved forces to face the invaders, and on October 30, Britain and France issued their ultimatum. When Egypt rejected it, the Anglo-French coalition struck from the air the following day, October 31, and on November 5 sent in ground troops to seize key positions along the Suez Canal. In the meantime, as planned, the IDF moved south and removed the blockade at the Straits of Tiran. In the course of this operation, Israel occupied the entire Sinai Peninsula, destroying Egyptian forces and killing hundreds of enemy troops at a cost of 172 Israeli soldiers killed and 700 wounded.

There was international outrage, particularly from America, at this blatant action, which smacked of old-fashioned colonial arrogance. The Eisenhower administration forced France and Britain to halt operations, accept a ceasefire, withdraw their troops, and agree to UN monitors replacing them along the canal. In March 1957, the Israelis, also under international pressure, withdrew from the Sinai – not, however, before issuing a stark warning that should Egypt ever again blockade the Straits of Tiran they would regard it as a *casus belli* and launch war on Egypt.

The 1967 War

Imposing a blockade on the Straits of Tiran to all Israel-bound ships was precisely what President Nasser did 10 years later on May 23, 1967. The debate continues as to why Nasser took this action, knowing full well that it amounted to a declaration of war. Perhaps Nasser – a self-declared leader of the Arab world – did it in response to growing pressure on him to stand up to Israel, or maybe he felt it was too good an opportunity to miss as Israel's aging premier and defense minister, Levi Eshkol, who lacked any military experience, might not respond to the challenge. Whatever the explanation, the blockade, along with other warlike actions such as removing UN observers from the Sinai, combined with bellicose rhetoric from Syria and Jordan, led to a significant escalation of tension in the Middle East. Feeling cornered, Israel decided to preempt any Arab attack and strike first.

Using almost all its aircraft, the Israeli Air Force (IAF), flying low to avoid Egyptian radar, came from behind Egyptian lines and in a massive three-hour attack destroyed almost the entire Egyptian air force (most of it still on the ground). It was a textbook strike, which can be compared to the Japanese attack on Pearl Harbor in 1941. But wars are rarely won from the air alone and Israeli ground forces then invaded the Sinai Peninsula and engaged the Egyptian army. Lacking any air support, the Egyptians stood little chance and retreated in a most unorganized fashion, chased by Israeli tanks and attacked intensely from the air. The Israelis again seized the Sinai Peninsula, reaching the Suez Canal; they also took the Gaza Strip, which had been under Egypt's control since 1948. The war quickly expanded to other fronts, where the IDF continued to inflict major defeats on Arab armies: from Jordan it occupied the West Bank and Arab East Jerusalem; and from Syria it captured the strategic Golan Heights. It was a short war that, as it is often put, changed the face of the Middle East.

The 1968–1970 War of Attrition

The Egyptian army, though badly beaten, had not been destroyed in the 1967 war, and reequipped by the Soviets with new arms, it attacked the IDF, which was now deployed along the eastern bank of the Suez Canal. The first major incident between Egypt and Israel after the June 1967 war took place on October 21, 1967, when an Egyptian destroyer torpedoed and sank the Israeli destroyer *Eilat* not far from Port Said. Israel retaliated by shelling Egyptian oil refineries close to the city of Suez and setting alight the adjoining oil storage tanks. Gradually, the situation along the Suez Canal escalated with more and more clashes. These, it is worth noting here, were not random incidents but rather part of a well-planned Egyptian military program which envisaged a total war against Israel in three main phases. The first of these was the "holding out" phase, or the steadfastness stage; the second was the "state of deterrence"; and the third was to be a total war of attrition against Israel. In a speech on January 21, 1969, President Nasser explained, "The first priority, the absolute priority in this battle, is the military front, for we must realize that the [Israeli] enemy will not withdraw [from land it occupied in 1967] unless we force him to withdraw through

fighting" (*Al-Ahram*, January 21, 1969). As the fighting dragged on and the number of casualties mounted, the Israeli general staff was obliged to seek ways of protecting the troops along the Suez Canal. This led to the construction of a defensive line of fortifications named after the chief of staff, Haim Bar-Lev. The line was a chain of 32 strong points stretching 180 km from Ras el-Aish in the north to Port Tawfik in the south. Each fort had firing positions, as well as a courtyard big enough to hold a few tanks and allow soldiers space to carry on with their daily lives and routines. A paved road linked the strongholds, and a sand ramp was built between it and the canal to prevent the Egyptians from observing the movements of troops inside the forts. The Bar-Lev line was completed in March 1969. That month, after a relatively calm period, Egypt resumed the war and carried out massive barrages of the Bar-Lev line, with 35,000 shells being fired between March 8 and 10. To this attack and those which followed, Israel's response was to send ground forces to carry out raids across the canal. But with Egyptian shelling of the Bar-Lev line continuing, the Israelis devised a new strategy of deep penetration by the air force, aimed at bombing positions deep within Egypt, thus relieving pressure on Israeli troops along the canal. The IAF began its bombardment on January 7, 1970, by attacking Egyptian military camps and other targets near the cities of Ismailia, Cairo, Insha, and Hilwan, and between January 1 and April 18, 1970, the period of the bombing campaign, the IAF flew 3,300 sorties and dropped 8,000 tons of ammunition on Egyptian positions. The pressure on the Egyptians was such that they were forced to reduce resources along the canal in order to protect the Egyptian interior, which in turn eased pressure on the Israelis along the Bar-Lev line and reduced casualties. But Israel also suffered heavily because the Egyptian anti-aircraft defense system, 30 times as powerful as it had been before the 1967 war, hit hard at the IAF. In August 1970, a ceasefire was agreed, and until the 1973 war the front was calm.

The 1973 War

After the 1967 war, Israel made it clear that she was reluctant to return the captured lands. She embarked on a creeping annexation, building settlements on the seized territories and exploiting resources such as oil in the Sinai and water in the Gaza Strip and West Bank. This deeply upset the Arabs. What is more, it seemed that the superpowers of the time – the United States and the Soviet Union – were enjoying an unusual period of détente and were reluctant to have their Middle Eastern clients ruining the improved atmosphere. Both, therefore, seemed to accept the new status quo and ignore Israel's gradual annexation of the seized lands. To break the deadlock and prevent the annexation becoming permanent, Egypt and Syria decided to launch a military attack on Israel, to liberate at least some of their lost land and perhaps force Israel into diplomatic negotiations over withdrawal from the rest.

Egypt and Syria decided to attack on October 6, 1973, which was Yom Kippur, the holiest day in the Jewish calendar, thus catching Israel by surprise and unprepared. The Arab offensive started with a massive Egyptian–Syrian air bombardment on Israeli targets in the Sinai and Golan Heights. In the Sinai, soon after the air strike, Egyptian guns opened a tremendous bombardment along the Suez Canal and, in the first minute of the attack, 10,500 shells landed on Israeli positions – a rate of 175 shells per second. In the Golan, Syrian guns opened a similar barrage on Israeli positions. Back at the Suez Canal, at 2:20 p.m., the 4,000 Egyptian troops of "Wave One" poured over the ramparts and slithered in disciplined lines down to the water's edge to begin crossing in small boats. Every 15 minutes a wave of troops crossed, and in 24 hours the Egyptians had managed to land 100,000 men, 1,000 tanks, and 13,500 vehicles on the Israeli side of the canal. Facing this invasion were a mere 505 Israeli troops, who could do little to stop the Egyptians. The Bar-Lev line of defense, which the Israelis had built along the canal after the 1967 war, quickly crumbled. On the Golan Heights, in the meantime, a first wave of 500 Syrian tanks, closely followed by a further 300, crashed through the Israeli lines along the entire front and penetrated deep into the Golan Heights.

It took the Israelis some time to mobilize their reserves – which form the main bulk of the IDF – and it was a number of hours before they began to get a grip on the situation. Their first priority was to contain the Syrian invasion of the Golan, where there was no strategic depth and Jewish settlements were close to the front line, unlike the Sinai where it would take Egyptian troops many hours before they came close to Jewish settlements or the Israeli border. They successfully halted the Syrian advance and began to push them back gradually, but it would take a week before it was the Syrians who were on the defensive as Israeli troops crossed east of the Golan toward Damascus.

Back in the Sinai, the IDF tried but failed to counterattack on October 8. Six days later, on October 14, they tried again and this time succeeded, inflicting heavy losses on the Egyptians, who made the mistake of moving away from their ground-to-air missile umbrella that so far had shielded them from the IAF. On the ground, General Ariel Sharon, a division commander, located a gap between the Egyptian 2nd and 3rd armies, through which he pushed his forces and approached the Suez Canal. He then crossed the canal to form a bridgehead on the Egyptian side of the water; by October 18, the IDF had a substantial force of three armored brigades and an infantry brigade on the western bank of the canal. Then, in a daring maneuver, Sharon completely cut off the 3rd Egyptian army from the rear, isolating about 45,000 Egyptian troops and 250 tanks from the rest of the Egyptian forces. By the end of the war, IDF forces were on proper Egyptian soil west of the canal and closer to Damascus than before the start of the war. It would not be wrong to say that, in military terms, the IDF's performance in the 1973 war – the way it recovered from the initial surprise, mobilized, and counterattacked – was even more impressive than its performance in the 1967 war. But in most people's minds at the time Egypt and Syria were the victors.

The 1982 War in Lebanon

Israel's military hero in 1973 was General Ariel Sharon. By 1982, he was no longer a soldier but defense minister. From the day of his appointment, Sharon's attention was firmly focused on Lebanon, where he identified two main problems. The first was the presence of Syrian troops and their ground-to-air missile system in the Beka'a Valley, which hindered the IAF's freedom to fly over Lebanon; the second was the presence of the Palestinian Liberation Organization (PLO), led by

Yasser Arafat, whom Sharon suspected of wanting to take over Lebanon and turn it into a base to attack Israel. Sharon wished to strike at both the PLO and the Syrians in Lebanon.

The opportunity came on June 3, 1982, when gunmen of a dissident Palestinian faction led by Abu Nidal shot the Israeli ambassador to London and seriously injured him. There was no reason intrinsically why such an incident should necessitate a substantial Israeli invasion to wipe out the PLO in Lebanon, especially given that Abu Nidal was a sworn enemy of the PLO. But such was the mood in Israel following the attempt on the life of the ambassador that hardly anyone seemed to care that the assassins were from Abu Nidal's group rather than Arafat's and most were willing to accept the view that Israel needed to attack the PLO.

At 3.15 p.m. on June 4, Israeli aircraft struck at nine PLO targets in Lebanon. The PLO hit back and for 24 hours shelled villages in northern Israel. On June 5, the Israeli cabinet convened and authorized an invasion of Lebanon, which it gave the name Operation Peace for Galilee; it would later come to be known as the War of Lebanon. It gave the IDF the mission of "freeing all the Galilee settlements from the range of fire of terrorists" and instructed that "the Syrian army [stationed in Lebanon] should not be attacked unless it attacks our forces." Defense Minister Sharon made it clear that the operation's objective was to remove the PLO from firing range of Israel's northern border, "approximately 45 kilometers" (Resolution 676 of the Israeli cabinet).

On June 6, 1982, the IDF invaded Lebanon. In the western sector along the Lebanese coast, forces moved northward, but, rather than stopping 45 km from the international border as instructed by the cabinet, Sharon ordered them to proceed up to Lebanon's capital Beirut in order to hunt down PLO leader Arafat. By July 1, Beirut was encircled and under siege.

In the eastern sector, after crossing the international border into Lebanon, troops advanced in the direction of the Syrians without firing at them. The Syrians, however, faced with Israeli tanks and troops moving in their direction, opened fire. With his forces "under attack," Sharon allowed them to return fire, sparking all-out war between Israeli and Syrian troops in Lebanon. Claiming that Syrian ground-to-air

missiles in the Beka'a Valley hindered IAF efforts to support the ground forces, Sharon persuaded the cabinet to allow him to destroy the Syrian missiles. The attack was delivered on June 8 by F-15 and F-16 aircraft that knocked out 17 of 19 Syrian batteries and severely damaged the remaining two (they were finally destroyed the next day). The Syrian air force intervened and lost 96 Migs without a single Israeli plane lost.

In the meantime, an immense artillery and air bombardment against Beirut also produced results (and many casualties among civilians), forcing the Lebanese government to demand that the PLO and its leader Arafat leave the city. On August 22, the first contingent of 379 PLO men departed and, over the course of the next 12 days, 14,398 Palestinian guerrillas were evacuated to other countries, including Arafat who went to Tunis; 5,200 Syrian troops also left Beirut for Syria. With Israeli permission, a Lebanese Christian militia entered the Palestinian refugee camps of Sabra and Shatila between September 16 and 18 in order to remove the 2,000 armed PLO fighters who, according to Israeli intelligence, remained in the camps after the Palestinian evacuation. The Christian militia found no armed Palestinians, only women, children, and the elderly – but they massacred hundreds of them anyway.

From a military point of view, the architect of the war, Defense Minister Sharon, did manage to achieve at least some of his aims: the IDF pushed the PLO and Syrian forces out of Beirut and the IAF destroyed the Syrian ground-to-air missiles in eastern Lebanon. But the price was high, as the war brought on Israel unprecedented international condemnation, particularly after the massacre in Sabra and Shatila. Israeli troops were to remain in Lebanon for 18 years, under constant harassment. Here was a lesson that the Israelis should have learned from the experience of others, notably from the Americans in Vietnam; that it is relatively easy to invade, but much more complicated to disengage. Armies can occupy territory in days, but getting out can take years.

The 1987 *Intifada*

Until 1987 the Arab–Israeli conflict had mainly been an encounter between conventional armies, but things were about to change when the IDF was confronted by an uprising in lands under its occupation. Like many other major events in history, notably World War I, the Palestinian uprising was sparked by a minor event – a car crash. On December 8, 1987, an Israeli vehicle collided with a Palestinian one, killing four Palestinians and wounding seven others. Rumors spread among the Palestinians that the car crash was somehow deliberate. At the victims' funerals in the Jabalya refugee camp in Gaza, angry Palestinians hurled stones at nearby Israeli army units. A soldier opened fire and killed a Palestinian, which led to riots. These quickly spread from Jabalya to refugee camps throughout the Gaza Strip, and then engulfed the more secular and affluent West Bank. These events were the beginnings of the *intifada*, "shaking off" in Arabic, which saw the highly trained and well-equipped Israeli army come into conflict with loose gangs of Palestinians, often no more than children, often armed only with rocks. This asymmetry was to prove a major problem for the Israelis. By avoiding a classic guerrilla war, the Palestinians effectively neutralized Israel's vast military superiority. Faced by civilians wielding stones, bottles, iron bars, and burning tires, the best military in the Middle East was simply too powerful to apply its might.

The IDF was caught off guard by the riots and was initially slow to react. It had neither the appropriate equipment nor the expertise to deal with what turned out to be an all-out civilian uprising, where women and children led demonstrations. The army was slow to send in reinforcements and was too selective in its use of the curfew – a standard means of restoring order by providing an opportunity to cool off. Thus, Palestinian demonstrations continued without respite and grew in size and vehemence. But the army soon got a grip on the situation and, by mid-January 1988, deployed two divisional commands to the West Bank and a third in the Gaza Strip, and started to use a variety of measures to put down the uprising. Unable to use its sophisticated arsenal against civilians with only primitive weapons, the IDF had to downgrade its weapons to suit, while retaining an advantage over the Palestinians. This would later lead to the invention of such "weapons" as a stone-hurling machine to counterattack youthful rock throwers, or vehicles equipped to fire canisters of hard rubber balls and small explosive propellants into crowds. The army made mass arrests which it conducted under curfews, deported activists, demolished houses of suspected terrorists, uprooted orchards to eliminate areas from which Palestinians could strike, and applied enormous pressure on the Palestinian population to submit.

By the end of 1988, the army was in fairly firm control of events in the occupied territories, but still they were just managing the situation rather than solving it. The uprising would continue for some six years, and it was to be a political deal between Israeli and Palestinian leaders in Oslo in September 1993 that ended it, rather than military might.

The Second *Intifada*

Seven years after the end of the first *intifada*, a new uprising erupted, which soon came to be known as the *Al-Aqsa intifada*, named after the mosque in Jerusalem's Old City where riots first began. The perspective of history will probably identify this insurgency in the occupied territories, from 2000 to 2005, as the continuation of the first *intifada*, though there are significant differences between the two events. While the stone and the bottle were the symbols and indeed the main weapons of the Palestinians during the first *intifada*, in the second uprising they were superseded by rifles, pistols, hand grenades, mortars, and suicide bombs. And while in the first *intifada* clashes between Palestinian insurgents and Israeli security forces took place in the center of Palestinian towns and cities, by the time of the second *intifada* these urban areas were no longer routinely patrolled by Israeli forces – the Israelis having withdrawn from them as part of the 1993 deal – and as a result, clashes now took place on the edges of towns and cities.

The second *intifada* was sparked by a visit of the right-wing opposition leader Ariel Sharon on September 28, 2000, to Temple Mount, the holiest site in Judaism, located in Jerusalem. On the ruins of the Jewish Temple stands a compound the Muslims call Haram Al-Sharif ("the Noble Sanctuary"), which Sharon planned to tour, and which contains a number of mosques, including Al-Aqsa, which is holy to Muslims. Palestinians therefore regarded Sharon's visit as a deliberately provocative move. There were only limited disturbances during the visit, but for the remainder of the day there were sporadic outbreaks of Palestinian stone throwing at Israeli police on Temple Mount and in its vicinity. These incidents, we know in hindsight, were the opening of the *Al-Aqsa intifada*. Violence intensified while international efforts to stop it failed, and, with suicide bombers blowing themselves up in Israeli towns and cities, the Israelis resorted to a variety of measures to stop the insurgency, including assassinations of Palestinian leaders.

The emergence of Sharon as Israel's prime minister in 2001 marked a new phase in the second *intifada*. Sharon ordered F-16s to fire rockets against Palestinian targets, intensified Israel's policy of assassinations and, following a suicide attack during Passover 2002, he ordered an all-out invasion of the West Bank – this was Operation Defensive Shield, which also included a siege on Arafat's headquarters in Ramallah.

In August 2005, Prime Minister Sharon withdrew Israeli forces and settlers from the Gaza Strip. Now, with no targets to attack in Gaza proper, Palestinians resorted to a new tactic: the firing of missiles and rockets from the Strip into Israeli territory.

The Second Lebanon War

On July 12, 2006, at 9:03 a.m., Hezbollah guerrillas attacked an IDF border patrol on the Israeli side of the border with Lebanon, killing three soldiers and capturing two others. Hezbollah planned to hold the two captives to ransom, wishing to exchange them for Lebanese held in Israeli prisons. Responding to an attack from across an internationally recognized border was perhaps justified; however, the sheer scale of the Israeli military reaction was such that it led to an all-out war with Hezbollah. Indeed, when attacked, Hezbollah responded by launching 22 rockets against towns and villages in Galilee, northern Israel. This was not the first time Israel's populated areas had come under rocket or missile attack – in the 1991 Gulf War Saddam Hussein fired 39 Scud missiles into Israel – but here, in July–August 2006, sustained and continuous rocket and missile strikes against the Israeli home front became the backbone of Hezbollah's tactics.

On July 13, the IAF carried out a lightning 34-minute strike and, in what came to be known as the Night of the Fajrs, it destroyed almost all of Hezbollah's arsenal of 240-mm Fajr-3 missiles, which were armed with a 45-kg warhead and had a range of 45 km. In the coming days the IAF would also wipe out most of Hezbollah's 320-mm Fajrs-5, which had a range of more than 75 km. Still, despite pulverizing air strikes, Hezbollah continued to carry out rocket attacks; on July 13 it fired 125 rockets, some of which hit Haifa, Israel's third-largest city.

Sustained air strikes were aimed at depleting Hezbollah's military ranks and arsenals (including, vitally, their stocks of rockets and launchers), but also at damaging their morale. Israel also targeted Lebanon proper: its roads, bridges, power stations, and, most notably, Beirut International Airport, a transfer point for weapons and supplies to Hezbollah. The IDF's chief of staff, Dan Halutz, a former pilot and chief of the IAF who had learned the lessons of the air campaigns in Bosnia and Kosovo, strongly believed that air strikes alone would be sufficient to bring Hezbollah to its knees. But, while successful in eliminating Hezbollah's long- and medium-range missiles, the IAF failed to destroy Hezbollah's short-range rockets, which continued to land on Israel.

The only way for Israel to tackle this latter problem was to embark on a full-scale ground assault into southern Lebanon. Transferring war into the enemy's territory has always been one of the main tenets of the IDF doctrine of warfare. Moving the battle into enemy territory ensured that the damage was done far from home, and it forced the enemy to protect itself, thus leaving it little time to strike at Israel. However, there was little appetite in the Israeli political–military establishment to embark on such an operation at a time when it was still believed that decisive attacks from the air, coupled with other measures, would gradually degrade Hezbollah's military capabilities and motivation to prevail.

However, as it became apparent that a major ground operation was needed, on August 7 the military reported that preparations for an all-out invasion of southern Lebanon were complete. Its plan called for an invasion by a force composed of three divisions, whose task would be to reach the Litani River and then, over a period of three to four weeks, clear the area between the Litani and the international border, searching for and destroying Hezbollah's short-range rockets. On August 11, at 9 p.m., 9,800 Israeli troops moved across the border into Lebanon. But their advance was slower than expected and the diplomatic clock was ticking fast: on August 12 the UN Security Council passed Resolution 1701, calling for a halt to hostilities in Lebanon. The Lebanese government accepted it and, on the next day, cracking under growing international pressure, the Israeli government accepted it too; the UN then announced that the ceasefire would come into effect on Monday, August 14, at 8 a.m. That day Hezbollah fired a barrage of 217 rockets into Israel to show that it was keeping up the bombardment right up until the end of the war and the Israelis, on the morning of August 14, just before the ceasefire came into effect, launched their last attack against Dahia, in southern Beirut.

In 34 days of battle, Israel lost 164 people of whom 109 were soldiers and 45 civilians; many more were wounded. Close to 4,000 rockets landed on Israel's home front causing much damage and disrupting day-to-day life. More than 1,000 Lebanese were killed during the war and scores more were wounded. Israel failed to achieve most of the goals it had set for itself at the onset of the war. The Winograd Commission, set up by the government to investigate both the political and military leadership of the war, concluded: "The IDF … failed to fulfil its missions … in most cases … the IDF demonstrated … powerlessness … in its contest with Hezbollah."

Reference

Bregman, A. (2000) *Israel's Wars: A History since 1947*. London: Routledge.

Further Reading

Bar-Joseph, U. (2005) *The Watchman Fell Asleep: The Surprise of Yom Kippur and Its Sources*. New York: SUNY Press.

Bar-Siman-Tov, Y. (1980) *The Israeli–Egyptian War of Attrition, 1969–1970*. New York: Columbia University Press.

Beverley Milton, E. (2009) *The Israeli–Palestinian Conflict*. London: Routledge.

Catignani, S. (2008) *Israeli Counter-Insurgency and the Intifadas: Dilemmas of a Conventional Army*. London: Routledge.

Dayan, M. (1976) *Story of My Life*. London: Weidenfeld and Nicolson.

Dayan, M. (1991) *Diary of the Sinai Campaign*. London: Weidenfeld and Nicolson.

Ginor, I. and Remez, G. (2007) *Foxbats over Dimona: The Soviets' Nuclear Gamble in the Six-Day War*. New Haven: Yale University Press.

Harel, A. and Issacharoff, A. (2008) *34 Days: Israel, Hezbollah and the War in Lebanon*. London: Macmillan.

Heikal, M. (1975) *The Road to Ramadan: The Inside Story of How the Arabs Prepared for and Almost Won the October War of 1973*. London: Collins.

Herzog, C. (1998) *The War of Atonement: The Inside Story of the Yom Kippur War, 1973*. London: Stackpole Books.

La Guardia, A. (2007) *Holy Land, Unholy War: Israelis and Palestinians*. London: Penguin.

Lesch, D. W. (2007) *The Arab-Israeli Conflict: A History*. New York: Oxford University Press.

Love, K. (1969) *Suez*. New York: McGraw-Hill.

Ovendale, R. (1984) *The Origins of the Arab–Israeli Wars*. London: Longman.

Pollack, K. M. (2004) *Arabs at War: Military Effectiveness, 1948–1991*. Lincoln: University of Nebraska Press.

Qassem, N. (2002) *Hizbullah: The Story from Within*. London: Saqi.

Rabinovich, A. (2005) *The Yom Kippur War: The Epic Encounter that Transformed the Middle East*. New York: Schocken.

Randal, J. (1990) *The Tragedy of Lebanon*. London: Chatto and Windus.

Rogan, E. and Shlaim, A. (Eds.) (2007) *The War for Palestine: Rewiring the History of 1948*. Cambridge: Cambridge University Press.

Schiff, Z. and Ya'ari, E. (1984) *Israel's Lebanon War*. New York: Simon and Schuster.

Schulze, K. E. (2008) *The Arab–Israeli Conflict*. London: Longman.

Sharon, A. (1989) *Warrior: The Autobiography of Ariel Sharon*. New York: Simon and Schuster.

el-Shazli, S. (1980) *The Crossing of Suez: The October War (1973)*. London: Third World Centre.

van Creveld, M. (1998) *The Sword and the Olive: A Critical History of the Israeli Defense Force*. New York: Public Affairs.

B

Balkan Wars (1912–1913)

RICHARD C. HALL

In the second half of the nineteenth century, the Balkan Peninsula increasingly became an area of nationalist restiveness, directed mainly against the waning power of the Ottoman Empire. During the mid-1870s, revolts erupted in Bosnia and Bulgaria to challenge Ottoman authority, and in 1876 war broke out between Serbia and the Ottomans. In an effort to maintain stability and to safeguard their interests, the Great Powers of Europe at the Congress of Berlin in 1878 intervened to impose an overall settlement on the region. This settlement failed to meet the national aspirations of the peoples living there. The Bulgarians, Greeks, Montenegrins, and Serbs all sought additional territories from the Ottoman Empire to realize their national unity. Until the early twentieth century, however, their mutual rivalries for Ottoman territories precluded the development of any Balkan alliance directed against the Ottoman Empire. For the Bulgarians, Greeks, and Serbs, these rivalries all overlapped in Macedonia. There, rival Bulgarian, Greek, and Serbian irregulars fought against the Ottoman authorities as well as against each other.

The Young Turk coup of 1908 aroused fears among these Balkan states that resulting reforms could strengthen the Ottoman Empire and thus deny the Bulgarians, Greeks, Montenegrins, and Serbs Ottoman territories containing their co-nationals. These concerns enabled the Balkan states to overcome their national rivalries and to cooperate against the Ottomans before the Young Turk reforms had a chance to succeed. By the summer of 1912, with Russian encouragement, these efforts resulted in the establishment of a loose Balkan League directed against the Ottoman Empire. It consisted of bilateral treaties among Bulgaria, Greece, Montenegro, and Serbia. The most important of these agreements was the Bulgarian–Serbian alliance of March 1912. It allotted northern Albania to Serbia and most of Macedonia to Bulgaria. The disposition of north-western Macedonia remained contentious. The Russian tsar assumed the responsibility to resolve any disagreement that might arise between the two Balkan allies over the so-called "disputed zone" there.

The Balkan League decided to act in the fall of 1912, before the anticipated end of the Italo-Turkish War could bring additional Ottoman forces to the Balkans. Montenegro began the war on October 8, 1912. The war became general 10

Twentieth-Century War and Conflict: A Concise Encyclopedia, First Edition. Edited by Gordon Martel.
© 2015 John Wiley & Sons, Ltd. Published 2015 by John Wiley & Sons, Ltd.

days later. Each of the Balkan allies fought separate campaigns against the common Ottoman enemy. Geography dictated that Thrace, located between the Bulgarian border and the Ottoman capital Constantinople, became the main theater of war. Three Bulgarian armies invaded eastern Thrace. One Bulgarian army screened the important Ottoman fortress town of Adrianople (Bulgarian: Odrin; Turkish: Edirne), while on October 29–31 the other two smashed the Ottoman forces in the Battle of Lyule Burgas-Buni Hisar (Turkish: Lüle Burgaz-Pinarhisar). This was the largest battle in Europe between the Franco-German War and World War I. The victorious Bulgarians pursued the Ottomans to their defensive positions at Chataldzha (Turkish: Çatalca), about 20 miles outside of Constantinople. There, on November 16–17, the Bulgarians attempted to force the lines and seize the ancient imperial city. Cholera and exhaustion, plus determined Ottoman resistance, prevented the Bulgarians from attaining their objective. They then settled into trench positions in front of Chataldzha.

Meanwhile, the Serbian army crushed the Ottoman forces in western Macedonia at Kumanovo on October 24. While Ottoman remnants retreated into central Albania, the Serbs occupied Kosovo and much of northern Albania. To the south, the Greek navy played an important role in bottling up the Ottoman fleet in the Dardanelles. This meant that the Ottomans were unable to transfer troops from Anatolia to the Balkans by sea. Their control of the sea also enabled the Greeks to occupy most of the Aegean islands. The Greek army advanced into Ottoman territory along two axes. One element hurried north to Salonika (Greek: Thessaloniki), which it entered on November 8, one day ahead of a Bulgarian force that had the same objective. The Bulgarians and Greeks then established an uneasy condominium in the city. The other Greek army moved in the northwest to bring the town of Janina (Greek: Ioannina) under siege. A small Montenegrin force entered the Sandjak of Novi Pazar. Most Montenegrin troops, however, brought the northern Albanian town of Scutari (Albanian: Shkodër) under siege. All their attempts to take the town by direct assault failed.

Having suffered defeat on every front, the Ottomans requested an armistice. This was finalized at Chataldzha on December 3, 1912. At this point, Ottoman Europe consisted of only the territory between the Chataldzha lines and Constantinople, the Gallipoli Peninsula, and the three besieged cities of Adrianople, Janina, and Scutari. The Greeks remained apart from the armistice, and continued fighting around Janina. After the conclusion of the armistice, negotiations between the Balkan allies and the Ottomans shifted to London. Two parallel conferences held there during December attempted to resolve the conflict. The first was a meeting of the representatives of the belligerent sides. Delegations from Bulgaria, Greece, Montenegro, Serbia, and the Ottoman Empire attended the London Peace Conference. At the same time the ambassadors of the Great Powers to Great Britain also met, presided over by the British foreign secretary, Edward Grey, in the London Ambassadors Conference to ensure that their own interests in the Balkans were preserved by any settlement. When the extent of the Ottoman defeat became clear, a group of Albanian notables in Vlorë proclaimed an independent Albanian state on November 28, 1912. Urged on by the representatives of Austria-Hungary and Italy, the Ambassadors Conference soon recognized the new state. This new Albania claimed much territory overrun by the Serbs. The Austrian and Italian protectors of the new state insisted that the Serbs evacuate northern Albania. Meanwhile, the London conference of belligerents foundered mainly on the issue of Adrianople, which the Ottomans insisted on retaining. When the Young Turks again seized power in Constantinople at the end of January 1913, they denounced the armistice.

The war resumed on February 3, 1913. The three besieged Ottoman cities soon fell. Janina surrendered to the Greeks on March 6. The Bulgarians, with some Serbian help, took Adrianople on March 26. Austrian pressure forced Serbian troops aiding the Montenegrins at Scutari to withdraw in April. Even though the Great Powers decided at London to include Scutari in the new Albanian state, Montenegrin forces continued the siege. The weary defenders of Scutari finally negotiated its surrender on April 22. This provoked an international crisis. On Austrian insistence, the Great Powers backed their demand that the Montenegrins withdraw with threats of armed intervention. Under these circumstances, the Montenegrins agreed to leave Scutari on May 5, 1913. After these further losses,

Map 10   Balkan wars, 1912–1913.

RUSSIA

AUSTRIA-HUNGARY

ROMANIA

BOSNIA · Belgrade · Bucharest

HERCEGOVINA
Sarajevo ·

SERBIA

BULGARIA

MONTENEGRO · Sofia

*Black
Sea*

Skopje ·

ALBANIA

Monastir
(Bitola) ·

THRACE

Constantinople ·

MACEDONIA

· Saloniki
(Thessaloniki)

ITALY

OTTOMAN
EMPIRE

CORFU

Aegean Sea

GREECE

· Athens

Ionian Sea

DODECANESE
(to Italy)

RHODES

CRETE

— Boundary of the Ottoman Empire in 1912 before the Balkan Wars

▓ Territory lost by the Ottoman Empire during the Balkan Wars, 1912–13

--- International boundaries in 1913 after the Balkan Wars

100 miles

200 km

the Ottomans agreed to terms. The Balkan War belligerents signed a preliminary peace treaty in London on May 30, 1913. This agreement limited the Ottoman presence in Europe to territory east of a straight line drawn from Enez on the Aegean Sea to Midye on the Black Sea.

Meanwhile, tensions were rising among the Balkan allies. The failure of the Serbs to retain northern Albania increased their determination to retain Macedonia in the face of growing Bulgarian opposition. The Bulgarians and Greeks failed to reach any agreement for the disposition of conquered Ottoman territories and soon fell to skirmishing over northern Macedonia. By May 5, 1913, the Greeks and Serbs had concluded an alliance directed against Bulgaria. To complicate the situation, the Romanians, who wanted compensation for any Bulgarian gains in the war, began to make demands on Bulgarian (southern) Dobrudzha. A Great Powers ambassadors' conference held in St Petersburg in April 1913 failed to resolve the issue to the satisfaction of either the Bulgarians or Romanians. The conclusion of the London treaty enabled the Bulgarians to transfer the bulk of their army from the Chataldzha lines to the southwestern part of their country in order to enforce their claims to Macedonia. Before the Russians could act upon their promise to mediate the dispute, an explosion occurred.

On the night of June 29, 1913, Bulgarian troops attacked Serbian positions in southeastern Macedonia. This began the Second Balkan War. Greek and Serbian counterattacks drove the Bulgarians back. The Greeks soon eliminated the Bulgarian presence in Salonika. By early July, however, the Bulgarian army had largely contained the Greek and Serbian advance along the line of the old Bulgarian frontier. At this point, the Ottomans and the Romanians intervened against Bulgaria. The Romanians wanted all of Bulgarian Dobrudzha. The Ottomans sought to regain Adrianople, which they had lost earlier that year. The Romanians invaded Bulgaria on July 10, the Ottomans two days later. The Bulgarian army, committed along the southwestern Bulgarian border against the Greeks and Serbs, could not oppose either action. With no help forthcoming from any quarter, the Bulgarians had to seek terms. Negotiations with the Greeks, Romanians, and Serbs resulted in the Treaty of Bucharest, signed August 10, 1913. Here Bulgaria acknowledged the loss of most of Macedonia as well as southern Dobrudzha. A separate treaty signed in Constantinople on September 30, 1913, confirmed the loss of Adrianople and northern Thrace to the Ottomans. Bulgaria, the main victor of the First Balkan War, became the victim of the Second Balkan War.

The two Balkan Wars resulted in significant changes on the map of southeastern Europe. A fragile Albania emerged, challenged by Greek and Serbian territorial claims and protected by Austria-Hungary and Italy. Bulgaria, despite its defeat in the Second Balkan War, gained territory all along its southern frontier, including an outlet to the Aegean with the port of Dedeagach (Greek: Alexandroúpolis). Greece obtained clear title to Crete, Epirus, much of southern Macedonia including the important city of Salonika, and most of the Aegean islands. Montenegro received half of the Sandjak of Novi Pazar, but was denied Scutari. Romania took southern Dobrudzha. Serbia got Kosovo, the largest portion of Macedonia, and half of the Sandjak of Novi Pazar.

The peace settlement satisfied no one. The Greeks sought additional Ottoman territories in Thrace and Anatolia. The Serbs wanted northern Albania, as well as the Habsburg territories of Bosnia-Hercegovina and parts of Dalmatia and Slavonia. The Bulgarians, bitter about their defeat and the failure of Russia to intervene to save Macedonia for them, turned to Austria-Hungary and Germany for redress. Serbia remained as Russia's only secure Balkan ally. Clearly, the ability of the Great Powers to determine events in the Balkan Peninsula was limited. A year after the end of the Balkan Wars, southeastern Europe was again at war.

The Balkan Wars were the first armed European conflicts of the twentieth century. In many ways they were the initial stage of World War I. Many aspects of World War I made their initial appearance during the Balkan Wars. These included massed infantry attacks against entrenched positions, concentrated artillery barrages, military use of airplanes, and huge casualties. The Balkan Wars resulted in at least 150,000 dead soldiers, with the Bulgarians and the Ottomans sustaining the heaviest losses. In addition, many civilians perished from deliberate atrocity, perpetrated from all sides, and from epidemic disease. Hundreds of thousands of civilians became refugees. The total cost of the Balkan Wars in terms of lives and material is difficult to ascertain, because of the short interval between the end of the Second Balkan War and the beginning of World War I. For much of the Balkan Peninsula, the war began in October 1912 and ended six years later. Many of the same battlefields, such as northern Albania, Doiran, Gallipoli, and Kosovo, again became the scenes of fighting. The issues over which the Balkan Wars were fought continued to plague southeastern Europe for the rest of the twentieth century.

SEE ALSO: World War I: Southern Front.

Further Reading

Erickson, E. J. (2003) *Defeat in Detail: The Ottoman Army in the Balkans, 1912–1913*. Westport: Praeger.

Hall, R. C. (2000) *The Balkan Wars 1912–1913: Prelude to the First World War*. London: Routledge.

Hellenic Army General Staff, Army History Directorate (1998) *A Concise History of the Balkan Wars 1912–1913*. Athens: Hellenic Army General Staff.

Helmreich, E. C. (1938) *The Diplomacy of the Balkan Wars 1912–1913*. Cambridge, MA: Harvard University Press.

International Commission to Inquire into the Causes and Conduct of the Balkan Wars (1993) *The Other Balkan Wars*. Washington, DC: Carnegie Endowment.

Király, B. K. and Djordevic, D. (Eds.) (1987) *East Central European Society and the Balkan Wars*. Boulder: Social Science Monographs.

Biological Warfare: Past, Present, and Future

DONALD AVERY

Definitions and Concepts

Biological warfare can be defined as a form of warfare that uses living organisms and natural poisons (toxins) to produce death and debilitation in humans, animals, or plants. While biological weapons (BWs) are often equated with nuclear and chemical weapons (CWs), in reality they are quite different since they are composed of, or derived from, living organisms, which can replicate themselves inside the host, thereby allowing an attacker "to use a small amount of a biological weapon to inflict mass casualties" (Koblentz 2009: 5). Another major difference is the diversity of pathogenic micro-organisms and toxins that can be used as biological weapons, particularly given the enormous advances in the biosciences during the past 40 years. As a result, there has been a major change in the concept of bioweapons, which traditionally meant "a warhead with massive quantities of refined agents that were specifically designed for instant and catastrophic release … [while] now a biological weapon might be merely a test tube of pathogens that are capable of wide replication or a tiny device that can carry a pathogen through the body" (Kellman 2007: 208).

Until the past decade, there has been a tendency for scholars and government officials to place biological warfare within the omnibus category of Weapons of Mass Destruction (WMDs), along with chemical and nuclear warfare. In part, this categorization has a historical dimension given the 1947 declaration by the United Nations (UN) that all three weapons systems represented different aspects of WMDs, and were quite distinct from conventional forms of warfare. During the next 50 years there was a common tendency to consider BWs and CWs as closely related weapon systems, along with the recognition that nuclear weapons, particularly after the 1950s development of thermonuclear devices, were in a class by themselves, given their capability of destroying the planet.

There are, of course, many ways that biological and chemical weapons are alike. Both use similar delivery systems, including bombs, shells, aircraft spray tanks, and other devices in the dissemination of pathogenic and toxic agents. Both are biospecific, eliminating living things rather than causing physical damage to the existing infrastructure. Both are effective over large areas, causing indiscriminate casualties. Both are likely to be devastating against unprotected troops and civilian communities. And both are cheap to produce, thereby providing an attractive alternative to conventional or nuclear weaponry. But, whereas poison gas was extensively used in World War I and the bloody Iran–Iraq conflict (1980–1988), germ warfare remains relatively untested. There are few operational examples of biological warfare, with the exception of sporadic Japanese

BW use against Chinese forces during World War II, and a few isolated cases of bioterrorism, such as the anthrax letter attacks of 2001. Another difference is that, historically, biological warfare researchers have been shadowy and self-conscious, in part because as medical doctors they were committed professionally to saving, not taking, lives.

Historical Background

While biological warfare was only institutionalized and made part of national military strategy during World War II, it has a long historical legacy. Indeed, hostilities between states have always been accompanied by an increase in infectious diseases, given problems of sanitation, poor nourishment, overcrowding, and the carnage of the battlefield. In fact, until the twentieth century, deaths from disease usually far exceeded the numbers killed in combat, a situation that encouraged rival armies to exploit disease outbreaks in order to gain a strategic advantage. This was evident during the famous 1346 siege of Caffa, when the Mongol army catapulted thousands of plague-infected cadavers into the Genoese city, causing a serious outbreak of bubonic plague. Another widely cited example of deliberate use was the 1763 decision of the British commander Sir Jeffrey Amherst to weaken those Native American tribes who had been involved with the Pontiac Rebellion in the Ohio Valley through the distribution of smallpox-infected blankets. The results were devastating (Fenn 2001: 88–89).

Overall, during the nineteenth century, biological warfare was not regarded as a serious military threat. Nor was it mentioned by the Hague Conventions of 1899 and 1907, which sought to establish civilized norms for the conduct of war. Germ warfare also did not occur on European battlefields during World War I, although many soldiers died of disease. Of particular importance was the devastating "Spanish influenza" of 1918–1919 that claimed millions of lives in Europe and the United Kingdom, among populations weakened by four years of sustained warfare. But in terms of the intentional use of disease, there were only crude attempts, by German agents, to use anthrax and glanders against American war horses destined for the Western Front. According to US microbiologist Mark Wheelis, Germany's attempts at veterinary BWs established a number of important precedents, since it was "(a) the first national programme of offensive biological warfare; and (b) the first biological warfare programme of any kind with a scientific foundation … [and] was directed against neutrals not belligerents, and targeted animals not humans" (Wheelis 1999: 59–60). On the other hand, other scholars have pointed out that neither the Versailles Treaty of 1919, nor the various post-war disarmament conferences, made any reference to biological weapons. All this would change during the June 1925 League of Nations meetings in Geneva, when the delegates decided that, in addition to outlawing "asphyxiating, poisonous and deleterious gases," they should "extend this prohibition to the use of bacteriological methods of warfare" (cited in Wright 1990: 368).

Despite this international taboo, global concern about germ warfare remained relatively low until 1934 when Wickham Steed, a British journalist, claimed that he had obtained secret German documents outlining plans to use anthrax and other biological agents against London's subway system. While the veracity of Steed's accusations was challenged by government experts, they did serve as a catalyst for even more sensationalist predictions about imminent biological warfare. In Canada, for example, the *Toronto Star* ran a series of revelations under the lurid title "Disease germs going to flood cities when next war comes." But all of these stories were wrong. In reality, no meaningful biological weapons research was being carried out in Nazi Germany, despite its large number of gifted microbiologists and its well-endowed life sciences research centers. The reason for this scientific inactivity was simple: "any offensive programme was barred by [Adolf] Hitler's interdict against BW development" (Geissler 1999: 99). Significantly, no such prohibitions existed for Germany's ally Japan, where biological warfare research became an important military priority during the 1930s, particularly after July 1937 with the outbreak of the Second Sino-Japanese War (1937–1945). Indeed, even before this date General Ishii Shiro, a highly regarded medical microbiologist, had established a research facility near Harbin, Manchuria, where his secret team of scientists (Unit 731) carried out a variety of military trials with anthrax, plague, cholera, dysentery, and other pathogens, using thousands of human subjects in these gruesome experiments.

Yet despite Japan's evolving BW program, the attention of most western military leaders remained focused on Germany and Italy. This was evident when, in September 1937, Nobel laureate Sir Frederick Banting warned the Canadian government that the country was vulnerable to a German germ warfare attack that would have a paralyzing effect on both the military and civilian population. In his brief, Banting prepared a detailed analysis of the various air-, water-, and insect-borne BW agents that German scientists had probably weaponized, including anthrax, botulinum toxin, and typhoid. With the support of General A. G. L. McNaughton, president of the Canadian Research Council, Banting carried out an intense campaign to convince both Canadian and British military officials about the importance of adopting effective defensive and offensive measures in order to meet the German BW threat. But to no avail (Avery 1998: 151–157).

World War II

Given their individual and collective aversion toward biological weapons, most high-ranking British military officers did not believe that the German army would use germ warfare. This confidence in the rules of war changed abruptly in June 1940 after the German *Blitzkrieg* violated numerous taboos, notably the massive bombing of civilian targets. Now they were faced with the prospect of invasion by a ruthless and resourceful enemy, who, it appeared, would use germ and gas weapons to achieve military victory.

As a result, throughout the next year the British government gradually moved toward an institutionalized and sustained response to the threat of germ warfare that included steady funding from the Ministry of Supply, the cooperation of the British Medical Research Council, and the September 1940 appointment of Dr Paul Fildes as director of BW research at Porton Down. Another asset was the 1941 establishment of the Anglo-Canadian joint chemical warfare facility at Experimental Station Suffield, in southern Alberta, which was subsequently expanded to include the testing of a number of

biological and toxin weapons. The British BW program also benefited from the fact that Prime Minister Winston Churchill had no reservations about developing an offensive biological warfare capability for retaliatory purposes if it would deter a German attack or advance the Allied military cause.

Although the United States did not become a belligerent until after Pearl Harbor, President Roosevelt authorized a number of military aid programs to help the United Kingdom and Canada resist the Axis powers. But, on the biological weapons front, the US military initially had little to offer, since its program was underdeveloped until after December 1941. Residual isolationist sentiments, limited defense budgets, and the US Army's general distrust of chemical and biological weapons (CBWs) hampered any sustained weapons development. And even when war was declared, the American BW program was divided between the Chemical Warfare Service for the offensive dimensions and the Surgeon General's Office for the defensive side. But most of the original ideas for biological agent development came from civilian bacteriologists and virologists, who operated out of the so-called War Bureau of Consultants Committee, under the chairmanship of Professor Edwin B. Fred of the University of Wisconsin. The important role of this organization was evident in February 1942 when the WBC submitted its first report to Secretary of War Henry Stimson, which called for a comprehensive study of biological warfare, with a special warning that the Japanese might deploy these weapons operationally in the Pacific theater, and possibly against the American mainland. Nor were these fears misplaced, since there was growing evidence that Japanese forces were using plague, cholera, and other biological agents against Chinese civilian and military targets.

During 1942, there was increased cooperation between American, British, and Canadian scientists as all three countries attempted to deal with the imminent biological warfare crisis. Part of this response focused on the development of improved defensive measures, such as vaccines, prophylactic drugs, and improved gas masks. Of particular importance was the July 1942 creation of a combined Canadian–American project at the small Canadian island of Grosse Île, near Quebec City, to research, develop, and produce a vaccine against rinderpest, a deadly animal virus. Shortly afterwards, Grosse Île became the home of a combined Anglo-Canadian undertaking to produce weaponized anthrax spores, an essential aspect of Britain's attempt to develop a retaliatory biological weapon. Despite hazardous working conditions, by 1944 the Grosse Île scientific team managed to produce over 500 liters of anthrax spores, the largest stock of this deadly BW agent in the world. The next stage was the proposed testing of anthrax cluster bombs at the vast Experimental Station Suffield, Alberta, prior to their going into mass production in the United States. This project was, however, canceled, in part because of health and environmental concerns about the site, and in part because the US Chemical Corps now wanted firm control over how the Allies' major offensive weapon would be developed (Avery 1998: 159–172).

Despite its slow start, the scale of the US biological warfare operation soon eclipsed its two partners because of its high level of funding, its large pool of qualified scientists, its extensive organizational structures, and its political support at the highest levels of government, including President Roosevelt. The development of BW munitions was a complex process. At the initial research stage many projects were farmed out to scientific experts at various universities, but the actual weapons developmental work was focused at Camp Detrick, Maryland, where thousands of scientists worked on a wide range of possible BW agents. While many different bacteria, fungi, viruses, and toxins were considered, most of the weaponization work concentrated on the bacteria that caused anthrax, plague, tularemia, and brucellosis, along with botulinum toxin, the world's deadliest poison. Once the Detrick pilot plant had produced sufficient quantities of these BW agents, or related simulants, they were tested at Horn Island (Mississippi) and Granite Peaks (Colorado) using aerial bombs and sprays, artillery shells, and even insect vectors. In early 1945, American and British military leaders also decided to produce over a million 4-lb anthrax bombs, which would be produced at the special plant at Vigo, Indiana, tested at Granite Peaks, and then shipped overseas for possible use against Germany, as the ultimate known weapon of mass destruction (Moon 2006: 215–227).

Pressure for the rapid development of anthrax anti-personnel bombs had been a British priority since the early stages of the war. As Porton Down scientists pointed out, most defensive measures would be futile against undetectable pathogens whose destructive work could take several days to detect, since they were usually indistinguishable from naturally occurring infectious diseases. Nor did they believe that the initial deterrent, crude anthrax cakes that targeted Germany's livestock industry, would be that effective. The situation became more critical in December 1943 when the United States Office of Strategic Services (OSS) reported that the German military had weaponized botulinum toxin and were prepared to use this deadly poison against Allied troops massed on the beaches of Normandy during the D-Day invasion. During the next four months there was an intense debate between American, British, and Canadian defense scientists about the most appropriate response to this serious threat, with the Canadian team pushing hard for large-scale immunization of assault troops with the newly developed "Bot Tox" toxoid. In the end, this did not occur because of the enormous logistical challenge in carrying out immunization on this scale, and concerns that such measures would alert German intelligence about the forthcoming invasion.

This incident provided another example of the weakness of Allied intelligence in obtaining accurate information about the biological warfare activities of the Axis powers. Fortunately, in the case of Germany, there was virtually no germ warfare program, despite strong interest on the part of the leadership of the SchutzStaffel, and the fact that the German occupying forces had gained access to France's early BW work. Nor were American and British intelligence aware of how Soviet dictator Joseph Stalin and his military advisors regarded biological weapons, despite their suspicions that the Kremlin was interested in the BW option. But the most serious intelligence breakdown occurred in November 1944 with the unanticipated appearance of hundreds of Japanese balloons, potentially carrying human and animal BW agents, carried by prevailing winds over the North American west coast. During this long civil defense crisis there was considerable consternation in Washington and

Ottawa that their countries might be facing a full-scale biological weapons attack. On the positive side, however, the incident generated an impressive civil defense response in both Canada and the United States that combined the talents of their respective military, law enforcement, public health, and medical communities. It also resulted in an unparalleled level of cooperation between civil defense planners of the two countries.

The biological warfare capabilities of the United States and its two allies continued to develop during the latter stages of the war. In the United States, all offensive biological weapons work was directed by the Chemical Warfare Service through its operational headquarters at Camp Detrick. Of particular importance was the task of coordinating the Anglo-American project to develop over a million anthrax cluster bombs, which continued after the defeat of Germany, leaving the clear impression that these anti-personnel weapons were being considered as part of the US arsenal during the proposed 1946 invasion of Japan. While this question never reached the strategic planning stage in Washington, the use of biological plant inhibitors such as rice blast (fungus) against Japanese agricultural targets was under review, as were chemical defoliants and toxic poison gas. All of these deliberations ended with the US atomic bomb attacks on Hiroshima and Nagasaki in August 1945.

Biological Weapons and the Cold War

The US military also took the lead in encouraging Canada and the United Kingdom to resume their wartime cooperation with the United States through the 1947 Tripartite Biological and Chemical Weapons Agreement. Yet despite many shared interests, namely the importance of deterring Soviet use of biological weapons, the three countries had quite different perspectives. For British military planners, lacking a nuclear deterrent until 1954, developing a biological and chemical weapons deterrent became a necessary priority during the immediate post-war years, particularly since the country lived in a dangerous neighborhood. Most of the research and development work was carried out at the Microbiological Research Department at Porton Down, with strong financial and administrative support from both the Labour and Conservative governments, and under a pervasive cloak of secrecy.

For Canada, there were less obvious advantages for remaining involved with offensive biological warfare research and testing, particularly since the country did not face the same strategic threats as the United Kingdom. Nor did Canada intend to develop atomic weapons, despite the important wartime contributions made by the Montreal-based Anglo-Canadian nuclear laboratory. But, within the context of the early Cold War, there were compelling arguments for being a member of the Tripartite Agreement: Canadian scientists were highly regarded for their BW expertise; the country had unique testing and research facilities at Suffield and Grosse Île; and, most important of all, this BW commitment provided an opportunity for reimbursing the US military for its ongoing protection of North America.

American post-war biological warfare planning had a number of important characteristics. One of these was that the United States, with its vast scientific and industrial resources, was the dominant force in determining what biological weapons would be developed, whether they would be mass produced, and what delivery systems would be used. On the other hand, during the immediate post-war years, the United States largely depended on its overwhelming nuclear weapons superiority to deter possible Soviet aggression, with its BW program being relegated to a minor back-up position. This situation changed during the Korean War (1949–1953) when the Pentagon became increasingly concerned that the Soviet Union might gain a strategic advantage over the United States because of its more advanced biological warfare capabilities. As a result, during the next two decades there was a major expansion of BW research and development at Fort Detrick, along with the initiation of production activities at Pine Bluff, Arkansas, focusing on the familiar bacterial agents and toxins of World War II. Throughout this period there was, however, considerable innovation in the selection of new anti-personnel agents, with viruses such as variola (smallpox), Venezuelan equine encephalitis, and Rift Valley fever, along with toxins such as ricin, saxitoxin (shellfish), and staphylococcal enterotoxin being considered as BW candidates.

While the army's Chemical Warfare Corps maintained its administrative control over the US biowarfare program, there was often significant input from the White House and Congress concerning the broader strategic dimensions of the country's BW policies. In October 1950, for example, the Stevenson Committee advised the secretary of defense that not only should the United States greatly expand its BW preparation, it should also abandon its traditional no-first-use policy, a recommendation that was eventually accepted in 1956, and incorporated into national defense priorities of the second Eisenhower administration (1956–1960). This major change of BW policy was, however, not made public. On the other hand, because of congressional oversight, the American BW program was more transparent than the British, Canadian, and French counterparts, although the dictates of national security prevented informed debate about specific goals and programs. For instance, no information was provided about the questionable 1945 US decision to grant Japanese bioscientists such as General Ishii immunity from prosecution as war criminals in exchange for information about their BW experiments on humans (Guillemin 2005: 92–111).

This "cover-up" would come back to haunt the US military during the Korean War, when the American biological warfare program came under attack by the Soviet Union and its communist-bloc allies. In particular, there were allegations that US military units had used germ warfare in North Korea and northeastern China – part of a sustained propaganda campaign, which sought to portray the United States as a barbarous, war-mongering nation. For over a year there were a series of investigations by pro-communist peace groups and scientific experts, whose findings were rigorously challenged and rejected by the United States. In 1953, the germ warfare controversy abruptly ended, following the death of Stalin and the Korean armistice.

After World War II, the Soviet Union devoted considerable resources to the development of its own biological warfare capabilities. During the first phase, BWs were viewed as a temporary substitute for the Russian atomic bomb, which

was successfully tested in September 1949. The second phase of the Kremlin's policy had a somewhat different perspective that viewed biological and chemical warfare as part of an alternative weapons system, which could be used against NATO forces in Europe when the inevitable conflict occurred. Most of the emphasis was, however, placed on poison gas rather than germs. Nevertheless, during this period the Soviet Union established an impressive biological warfare infrastructure. BW research was carried out in secret laboratories, many of which were attached to universities and technical institutes, with considerable assistance from the Soviet Academy of Sciences, the Ministry of Health, and the Anti-Plague Department institutes. In addition, there were a number of development and production facilities, such as the Military-Technical Science Research Institute of the Ministry of Defense at Sverdlovsk (Ukraine). At this secret plant, special attention was devoted to modeling the behavior of BW agents, determining persistency of different pathogenic aerosols, and the development of ever more lethal anthrax, plague, and smallpox agents. Once these munitions were deemed operational, they were tested at the BW field facilities on Vorzrozdeniye Island located in the Aral Sea, which became one of the most contaminated places on earth (Hart 2006: 132–146).

Attempts by the UN and its agencies to establish international control over biological weapons developed very slowly. That is not so say that the international community was not concerned about germ warfare. This was evident in September 1949 when Dr Brock Chisholm, the Canadian-born director general of the World Health Organization, gave the following warning in an address to the World Union of Peace Organizations: "Biological warfare is not a new kind of war, it is just the latest step …. Some seven ounces of a certain biological agent, if it could be effectively distributed, would be sufficient to kill all the people of the world" (cited in Avery 2006: 91). Yet, despite this appeal, few of the UN-sponsored disarmament negotiations during the next two decades included biological warfare on their agenda, largely because neither of the two superpowers was prepared to admit that they had an offensive BW program.

This situation changed dramatically during the Vietnam War when the US military's use of non-lethal chemical weapons (tear gas) and herbicides attracted sustained international criticism, reinforced by the fact that the United States had not ratified the 1925 Geneva Protocol. In addition, there were growing concerns about the possibilities of BW proliferation among non-aligned nations that would substantially increase the possibilities that biological weapons would be used in future conflicts. As a result, there was a flurry of disarmament activity at the UN, including the 1968 debate of the British proposal that separate disarmament conventions be established for biological and chemical weapons. This option was reinforced by the report of the UN secretary general's panel of CBW experts, which explored the scientific dimensions of the subject. The essential question was whether the two superpowers would play the game.

Fortunately for the arms control advocates, there were several reasons why the US government of Richard Nixon was prepared to reconsider the military viability and political acceptability of its offensive BW program. One of these was the growing public criticism about the militarization of American science, which was particularly pronounced among younger microbiologists, who campaigned against the linkages between their professional organization and the BW research facility at Fort Detrick. Another factor was the negative publicity associated with a series of incidents involving nerve gas accidents at Dugway, Utah, and other facilities, particularly since the two weapon systems were so closely linked. There was also a spate of sensationalist media reports, newspaper articles, and books about the "dark secrets" of the US biological warfare program, with the most powerful indictment coming from Seymour Hersch's bestselling book *Chemical and Biological Warfare* (1968). But most important of all was the decline of support for offensive biological warfare on the part of the US Department of Defense, notably Secretary of Defense William Laird, who saw these weapons as dangerous to produce, with minimal strategic advantages. Nor did the Joint Chiefs of Staff, despite their previous endorsement of the offensive BW option, disagree, reasoning that it was better to sacrifice biological weapons if they could retain the use of chemical non-lethals and their new CW lethal binary munitions. The final step was the November 25, 1969, statement by President Nixon: "Biological weapons have massive, unpredictable and potentially uncontrollable consequences. They may produce global epidemics and impair the health of future generations. I have therefore decided that the United States shall renounce the use of lethal biological agents and weapons, and all other methods of biological warfare. The United States will confine its biological research to defensive measures such as immunization and safety measures" (cited in Moon 2006: 35).

Was the American BW program hopelessly flawed, or could it be argued that scientific and technological developments during the previous 10 years had transformed US bioweapons into a viable offensive alternative to the nuclear option? The historical evidence suggests that the latter position is more convincing for a number of reasons. First, the United States and its Canadian and British allies had advanced into the second and third generation of BW agents, through improvements in the quality of the major agents (anthrax, plague, tularemia, brucellosis), along with their work on the weaponization of viral agents such as variola (smallpox), Venezuelan equine encephalitis, Rift Valley fever, and even Influenza A. Second, with major advances in DNA research since the landmark discoveries by Crick and Watson in 1954, there was now the possibility of altering the genetic structure of existing BW pathogens, making them resistant to antibiotics, and expanding the host range. Third, there were important innovations in the strategic aspects of BW delivery systems through the Large Area Coverage (LAC) system. This meant that through extensive spraying by high-performance aircraft, large aerosol clouds of pathogens could be created that would be carried by prevailing winds over designated targets. Nor were these mere speculative war games. Under the 1960s' Project 112 the American armed forces carried out a number of secret LAC trials in Alaska and several tropical locations, as well as several joint ventures with their Canadian ally. And finally, in 1969, plans for the use of medium-range and intercontinental missiles, carrying BW warheads, were also on the drawing board. Taking all these factors together, it is not surprising that the 15,000 defense scientists and technicians at Fort Detrick and other BW facilities were outraged by Nixon's November 1969 declaration. From their perspective, not only had they lost interesting and well-paid jobs, but the United States had forfeited the strategic advantages of an exciting program that was on the verge of realizing its potential. Moreover, as Bill Patrick, a veteran Detrick scientist put it, the "stuff is too damn good to go away" (Goldman 2009).

Between 1969 and 1975 the international community moved inexorably toward the establishment of the Biological Weapons Convention (BWC). It was officially proclaimed on March 26, 1975, once the required number of countries (22) had ratified the previous April 1972 Agreement. A relatively short document, the BWC contains 15 articles, the most important being the statement of principles in Article I:

Each State Party to this Convention undertakes never in any circumstances to develop, produce, stockpile or otherwise acquire or retain: 1. Microbial or other biological agents or toxins whatever their origin or method of production, of types and in quantities that have no justification for prophylactic, protective or other peaceful purposes; 2. Weapons, equipment or means of delivery designed to use such agents or toxins for hostile purposes or in armed conflict. (Cited in Wright 1990: 371)

In many ways the BWC was an amazing achievement since it outlawed an entire weapon system, based on a powerful international taboo. Unfortunately, moral strictures proved to be a poor substitute for an effective verification system, as would become evident during the next two decades.

Throughout the late 1970s, American intelligence reports cited growing evidence that Soviet scientists were still working on offensive biological weapons, in violation of the BWC's "gentleman's agreement." These suspicions were confirmed in April 1979 when an accidental release of weaponized anthrax spores at the Soviet military facility in Sverdlovsk killed 66 people, all of whom were in the path of the deadly plume. This image of Soviet CBW aggression was reinforced by a July 1980 report about a series of incidents involving "Yellow Rain" in Kampuchea and Laos, which American bioweapons experts claimed involved trichothecene mycotoxins, a possible third generation of biological/toxin weapons. Between 1980 and 1984, the United States submitted all of these allegations to the UN. In turn, the UN secretary general authorized a number of scientific investigations, including a Canadian team, that examined suspected mycotoxin casualties in several of these southeastern Asian countries. Overall, these UN-sponsored enquiries proved inconclusive, largely because of long delays in the collection of samples, questionable scientific analysis and, above all, the refusal of the many governments in this region to admit UN inspectors.

There were a number of useful lessons associated with these BW controversies. For a start, the BWC system of dealing with violations of its principles was obviously inadequate, given the lack of an effective verification and investigation system. Nor were there any serious consequences for the perpetrators. Although the Sverdlovsk incident was obviously embarrassing for the Soviet leadership, they were able to prevent international censure because of their claims that the anthrax outbreaks were caused by tainted meat, and by their vigorous counterattack against the Reagan administration, which they branded as militaristic imperialists who threatened world peace. Moreover, because Soviet "cheating" went unpunished, many other countries were encouraged to develop their own BW system as an effective way of advancing their national security goals.

Why did the Soviets accelerate their biological warfare program after signing the BWC? This is a difficult question to answer, given problems of access to Soviet-era archives. Fortunately, there are a number of first-hand accounts from a number of prominent Soviet-era defense scientists, including Kanatjan Alibekov (Ken Alibek), who was chief scientist and deputy director of the massive state-owned pharmaceutical company Biopreparat, prior to his 1995 defection to the United States. Several important trends emerge from these testimonials. One of these was the vast scale of the civilian-based BW program, with Biopreparat having over 60,000 people working in some 50 different laboratories, including the massive Vector facility at Koltsova (Siberia) that specialized in weaponized viruses such as variola (smallpox), ebola, Marburg, and Lassa. Soviet defense scientists also experimented with a number of genetically manipulated agents, notably anthrax and plague, along with certain "BW cocktails" that combined "smallpox with a hemor-rhagic disease virus to make it more lethal and an encephalitis virus to make it more transmissible from person to person" (Henderson 2009: 273). There were also four major military laboratories where many of the actual munitions were pre-pared. These were directly linked with the vast testing grounds at Vorzrozdeniye Island, where trials with different biological weapons delivery systems took place. In turn, a range of biological warheads were assembled for battlefield use on Scud short-range rockets, and on intercontinental missiles for the purpose of attacking North American cities if World War III should break out. All these developments were shrouded in secrecy, given the Soviets' pervasive security system with its strict "right to know" principles. Weapons sci-entists were also repeatedly told that their work was essential for the safety and well-being of the USSR, since the United States was well ahead in the BW arms race. As Ken Alibek explained, "We didn't believe a word of Nixon's announcement. Even though the massive US biological munitions stockpile was ordered to be destroyed, and some twenty-two hundred researchers and technicians lost their jobs, we thought the Americans were only wrapping a thicker coat around their activi-ties" (Alibek 1999: 234).

New Threats, New Players

While a number of countries considered acquir-ing biological weapons during the 1980s, only South Africa and Iraq actually achieved that goal. There are some interesting comparisons associ-ated with these two illegal programs, in terms of goals and scale of operation. In both cases the governments were non-democratic and fearful that they might be replaced by an internal civil war. Both also felt vulnerable to external attack, either by their neighbors or by UN-sanctioned intervention. Both were able to mobilize suffi-cient scientific talent and industrial resources to undertake the modest production and weaponi-zation of a select number of second generation BW agents. And, despite the BWC and western attempts at export control, both countries were able to acquire the necessary bacterial and viral seed stocks for their defense laboratories, and vital equipment for their production facilities.

On the other hand, there were substantial dif-ferences between these two clandestine biological warfare operations. In the case of South Africa's Project Coast, based at the Roodeplaat Research Laboratory, it was primarily interested in devel-oping specific weapons to control the country's black population. As a result, germ warfare was not integrated into South Africa's military and strategic planning. In contrast, Iraq's dictator Saddam Hussein regarded biological weapons as an essential part of his offensive and defensive priorities, which, along with poison gas, would allow him to confront his two major nuclear-armed rivals – Israel and the United States. This resolve was tested during the first Gulf War (1990–1991), when the American-led UN forces anticipated that they would encounter Iraqi anthrax or botulinum toxin munitions delivered by Scud missiles, aerial bombs, or artillery shells. While this did not occur, the United Nations Special Commission (UNSCOM) eventually dis-covered that Iraq had surreptitiously developed the second most potent BW offensive capability in the world, revelations that were obtained through diligent site inspections by hundreds of UNSCOM inspectors, and by the "confessions" of key members of Saddam Hussein's government.

At the international level, the legacy of the Iraqi, South African, and Soviet biological weapons pro-grams provided considerable ammunition for arms control advocates, who claimed that the BWC required drastic improvement. This reform process was enhanced by the end of the Cold War, the 1991 dissolution of the Soviet Union, and the 1992 decree by the Russian president that all BW work in his country should be terminated. Moreover, there was clear evidence that the overall membership of the BWC, despite its ideological blocs, was anxious to establish an effective verifica-tion system. This was evident during the 1991 Review Conference, and at subsequent meetings of scientific experts leading up to the crucial 2001 Review Conference. Unfortunately, despite the consensus for change, a number of countries demanded major concessions in the proposed ver-ification protocol, including China, Russia, and the United States. As the world's dominant super-power, American support of the reform process was critical, but in Washington there was consider-able concern about changing the BWC, summa-rized by three major questions. Would the amendments to the BWC jeopardize the proprietary and patent rights of American pharmaceutical and biotechnology companies, and weaken their global competitiveness? How would the protocol deal with recent progress in biological technology such as the ability to transfer certain genetic traits into non-select agents, thereby creating new biological agents? And what measures could be adopted so that legitimate US defensive research would not be obstructed or ostracized, particularly given the growing threat of bioterrorism? Despite desperate attempts by Canada, the United Kingdom, and other NATO countries, American officials ultimately decided that the response to its concerns was inadequate. In December 2001, the recently elected administration of George W. Bush rejected the entire reform process, and instead submitted its own list of incremental improvements.

Bioterrorism and New Biological Weapons

The threat of the covert use of biological weapons by agents of foreign powers or non-state terrorist groups is not a new phenomenon. As previously mentioned, during World War I, German agents attempted to attack American veterinarian targets. But the challenge assumed much greater proportions in World War II when there were numerous reports of German or Japanese saboteurs poisoning water reservoirs or releasing dangerous pathogens in North American cities. American and Canadian security agencies also remained vigilant throughout the Cold War years, carrying out a number of preventive exercises in anticipation of enemy attacks on urban subway systems or government buildings. By the 1970s, however, attention shifted to international and domestic terrorist groups, whom it was feared might use CBWs against the Montreal Olympics (1976) or other high-profile global events.

These concerns were intensified during the 1980s as different groups of terrorists appeared. In 1984, for example, US law enforcement agencies were forced to deal with the religious cult Rajneesh, which was responsible for the outbreak of restaurant-acquired salmonellosis in a small community near Portland, Oregon. In addition, there was evidence that certain white supremacist groups were trying to make crude anthrax and

plague bombs, as a possible sequel to their bombings in Oklahoma City. But the bioterrorism event that had the greatest impact was the 1995 revelation that the Japanese cult Aum Shinrikyo attempted to develop anthrax and ebola agents for use against Tokyo and other Japanese cities, although their eventual weapon of choice was sarin nerve gas. As a result of these events, the threat of bioterrorism was transformed from a remote theoretical possibility to the level of an imminent threat, particularly in Washington where both the Clinton (1992–2000) and Bush (2000–2008) administrations became convinced that there was a powerful linkage between terrorist groups and weapons of mass destruction. And bioterrorism now became the primary threat to the American homeland.

Although the al-Qaeda bombings of 9/11 did not involve biological weapons, these traumatic events were immediately followed by a series of attacks by means of anthrax-tainted letters that infected 22 Americans, killing five and forcing 7,000 more to receive medical treatment. Above all, this three-month bioterrorism siege caused widespread panic not only in the United States, but throughout the western world, particularly given the large number of copy-cat bogus incidents.

Since 2001, the US government has spent over 60 billion dollars on various civilian-related biodefense programs, the most important being Project BioShield, for the urgent development of vaccines against smallpox, anthrax, tularemia, ebola, and plague. Project BioWatch, on the other hand, is geared to the development of expensive new technology to overcome traditional problems of surveillance, detection, and diagnosis of deadly pathogens. Washington also provided extensive funds for the expansion of high containment (BSL-4) laboratories, despite criticism that these facilities might create additional biosecurity and biosafety problems. Another federal initiative was the creation of stringent new guidelines for American scientific researchers, under the 2002 Select Agent legislation, and through mandatory reviews of their projects by federal agencies, including the FBI. Yet despite these intrusive measures, there have been growing demands from private groups and government agencies for even more stringent biodefense measures. This sense of hysteria was evident in the January 2010 report of the US Senate Commission on the Prevention of Weapons of Mass Destruction Proliferation and Terrorism, which predicted "that a weapon of mass destruction (WMD) will be used in a terrorist attack somewhere in the world by the end of 2013 … [and] that weapon is more likely to be biological than nuclear" (Report Card 2010).

The future threat of biological warfare is a hotly debated topic. For critics of the massive funding of the US biodefense program, the threat is exaggerated, and there is little likelihood that international terrorist organizations such as al-Qaeda, or even "rogue" states such as North Korea, would be able to advance beyond the traditional BW agents. In contrast, the BW preparedness experts claim that in the near future terrorists will be able to acquire fourth generation BW agents, based on biologically engineered pathogens that can evade existing vaccines and antibiotics/ antivirals. There is also the possibility, these experts claim, that rapid advances in biotechnology will produce even more formidable germ weapons such as synthetic "chimera" viruses, host-swapping agents, and designer diseases. As one author grimly predicted, "the First World War was chemical; the Second World War was nuclear, and that the Third World War – God forbid – will be biological" (Ainscough 2004: 186).

SEE ALSO: Chemical Warfare; Gulf Wars (1990–1991, 2003–Present); Iraq–Iran War (1980–1988); Korean War (1949–1953); Vietnam War (1959–1975).

References

Ainscough, M. (2004) "Next Generation Bioweapons: Genetic Engineering and Biological Warfare." In J. Davis and B. Schneider (Eds.), *The Gathering Biological Warfare Storm*. Westport: Praeger.

Alibek, K. (1999) *Biohazard: The Chilling True Story of the Largest Covert Biological Weapons Program in the World – Told from Inside by the Man Who Ran It*. New York: Random House.

Avery, D. (1998) *The Science of War: Canadian Scientists and Allied Military Technology During the Second World War*. Toronto: University of Toronto Press.

Avery, D. (2006) "The Canadian Biological Weapons Program and the Tripartite Alliance." In M. Wheelis,

L. Rozsa, and M. Dando (Eds.), *Deadly Cultures: Biological Weapons Since 1945*. Cambridge, MA: Harvard University Press.

Fenn, E. (2001) *Pox Americana: The Great Smallpox Epidemic of 1775–8*. New York: Hill and Wang.

Geissler, E. (1999) "Biological Warfare Activities in Germany, 1923–45." In E. Geissler and J. E. van Courtland Moon (Eds.), *Biological and Toxin Weapons: Research, Development and Use from the Middle Ages to 1945*. Oxford: Oxford University Press.

Goldman, D. (2009) "The Generals and the Germs: The Army Leadership's Response to Nixon's Review of Chemical and Biological Warfare Policies in 1969," *War and Society*, 73 (2): 531–569.

Guillemin, J. (2005) *Biological Weapons: From the Invention of State-Sponsored Programs to Contemporary Bioterrorism*. New York: Columbia University Press.

Hart, J. (2006) "The Soviet Biological Weapons Program." In M. Wheelis, L. Rozsa, and M. Dando (Eds.), *Deadly Cultures: Biological Weapons Since 1945*. Cambridge, MA: Harvard University Press.

Henderson, D. A. (2009) *Smallpox, The Death of a Disease: The Inside Story of Eradicating a Worldwide Killer*. New York: Prometheus.

Kellman, B. (2007) *Bioviolence: Preventing Biological Terror and Crime*. Cambridge: Cambridge University Press.

Koblentz, G. (2009) *Living Weapons: Biological Warfare and International Security*. Ithaca: Cornell University Press.

Moon, J. (2006) "The US Biological Weapons Program." In M. Wheelis, L. Rozsa, and M. Dando (Eds.), *Deadly Cultures: Biological Weapons Since 1945*. Cambridge, MA: Harvard University Press.

Report Card (2010) "Government Filing to Protect America from Grave Threats of WMD Proliferation and Terrorism, January 26, 2010." US Senate, Joint Commission on the Prevention of Weapons of Mass Destruction, Proliferation and Terrorism.

Wheelis, M. (1999) "Biological Sabotage in World War I." In E. Geissler and J. E. van Courtland Moon (Eds.), *Biological and Toxin Weapons: Research, Development and Use from the Middle Ages to 1945*. Oxford: Oxford University Press.

Wright, S. (Ed.) (1990) *Preventing a Biological Arms Race*. Cambridge, MA: MIT Press.

Further Reading

Balmer, B. (2001) *Britain and Biological Warfare: Expert Advice and Science Policy, 1930–65*. London: Palgrave.

Chari, P. R. and Chandran, S. (2005) *Bio-Terrorism and Bio-Defence*. New Dehli: Monohar Publishers.

Clunan, A., Lovoy, P., and Martin, S. (Eds.) (2008) *Terrorism, War, or Disease: Unraveling the Use of Biological Weapons*. Stanford: Stanford University Press.

Cole, L. (1997) *The Eleventh Plague: The Politics of Biological and Chemical Warfare*. New York: W. H. Freeman.

Dando, M. (1994) *Biological Warfare in the 21st Century: Biotechnology and the Proliferation of Biological Weapons*. London: Brassey's.

Davis, J. and Schneider, B. (Eds.) (2004) *The Gathering Biological Warfare Storm*. Westport: Praeger.

Fidler, D. and Gostin, L. (2008) *Biosecurity in the Global Age: Biological Weapons, Public Health and the Rule of Law*. Stanford: Stanford University Press.

Gould, C. and Folb, P. (2002) *Project Coast: Apartheid's Chemical and Biological Warfare Programme*. Geneva: United Nations Institute for Disarmament Research.

Harris, S. (1994) *Factories of Death: Japanese Biological Warfare 1932–45 and the American Cover-Up*. New York: Routledge.

Lederberg, J. (1999) *Biological Weapons: Limit the Threat*. Cambridge, MA: MIT Press.

Leitenberg, M. (2005) *Assessing the Biological Weapon and Bioterrorism Threat*. Carlisle, PA: Strategic Studies Institute, US Army War College.

Miller, J., Engleberg, S., and Broad, W. (2001) *Germs: Biological Weapons and America's Secret War*. New York: Simon and Schuster.

National Academies Press (2004) *Biotechnology Research in an Age of Terrorism*. Washington, DC: National Academies Press.

National Academies Press (2006) *Globalization, Biosecurity, and the Future of the Life Sciences*. Washington, DC: National Academies Press.

Piller, C. and Yamamoto, K. (1988) *Gene Wars: Military Control over the New Genetic Technologies*. New York: William Morrow.

Regis, E. (1999) *The Biology of Doom: The History of America's Secret Germ Warfare Project*. New York: Holt.

C

Chechnya Wars (1990s–Present)

DAVID R. STONE

A bitter and bloody insurgency pitting separatist Chechens and Islamic allies against the Russian state.

The Chechens, a Muslim people living on the north slopes of the Caucasus mountains, had been brought under control of the Russian Empire over the course of the nineteenth century in long and vicious guerrilla wars. Only partly pacified, the Chechens retained their ethnic cohesion and resentment of outside domination through the final years of the Russian Empire and into the early period of Soviet rule. During World War II, Chechen territory came under brief German occupation and Soviet dictator Joseph Stalin became convinced that the Chechens had collaborated with the Germans. He then imposed a collective punishment on the entire Chechen people, deporting them en masse to Central Asia in 1944. Though after Stalin's death in 1953 the Chechens gradually returned to the Caucasus, the enormous suffering and death imposed by the Soviet regime left deep scars.

As the Soviet Union began to disintegrate in the late 1980s, Chechen nationalism took advantage of new freedoms to reassert Chechen identity and demands for autonomy. Chechnya itself lay within the boundaries of the Russian Republic, the largest of the 15 Soviet republics. After the December 1991 Soviet break-up, the question of Chechen independence was now a matter for Russian president Boris Yeltsin. Yeltsin and other key figures in his government regarded secession as utterly unacceptable, since any such concession could result in the flight of other sections of the sprawling and ethnically diverse Russian Federation, particularly among Chechnya's turbulent neighboring territories of the North Caucasus. Most ethnic separatist movements in Russia reached some accommodation with Moscow providing for limited autonomy; those efforts failed in Chechnya.

A number of factors prevented a settlement. The presence of oil in Chechnya raised the stakes of control, while the particular historical experience of the Chechens bred special resentment of Russian rule. Chechen president Dzhokhar Dudaev, a former Soviet air force general, proved capable of rallying Chechen nationalism but not of imposing order and effective government on Chechnya, where loyalty to family and clan far outweighed allegiance to a Chechen state. Chechnya degenerated into anarchy, becoming a haven for smuggling and organized crime which

Twentieth-Century War and Conflict: A Concise Encyclopedia, First Edition. Edited by Gordon Martel.
© 2015 John Wiley & Sons, Ltd. Published 2015 by John Wiley & Sons, Ltd.

spilled over into Russia proper, notably the regions of Ingushetia and Dagestan. When Russian sponsorship of Chechen opposition to Dudaev failed to bring down his regime, Yeltsin's team moved closer to armed intervention, fueled by overconfidence. Yeltsin's defense minister Pavel Grachev boasted that two hours and a regiment of paratroops would be enough to restore order.

The result of the political deadlock was Russian armed intervention on December 11, 1994, beginning the First Chechen War (1994–1996). Russian public opinion was decidedly lukewarm, and the Russian military as well as its paramilitary internal troops were made up largely of demoralized and unprepared conscripts. Chechen nationalism was galvanized by the Russian invasion, and the disparate clans united around the common struggle. The low point was the First Battle of Groznyi, capital of Chechnya, at the end of December 1994 and beginning of January 1995. Multiple Russian armored columns converged on the center of Groznyi, but were uncoordinated and fought badly in the narrow confines of the city. Small groups of Chechen fighters ambushed the columns with rocket-propelled grenades, isolating small detachments and wiping them out, killing hundreds, perhaps thousands, of Russian soldiers. Denied a quick victory, the Russian military turned to the massive application of overwhelming force, involving the intense shelling and bombing of Groznyi itself as well as other Chechen towns and cities. This not only produced massive casualties among Chechen civilians, who were after all Russian citizens, but further embittered the Chechen population against the imposition of Russian rule.

The war degenerated into a protracted insurgency, where Chechens employed infiltration and ambush against Russian efforts to extend and maintain their authority. Russian forces could exert some control over flatter ground in northern Chechnya, but in the south, made up of the foothills of the Caucasus mountains, Chechen guerrillas found a natural stronghold. The war altered Chechen society, as the Chechens' loose and tolerant practice of Islam was radicalized by Russian repression and the increasing presence of Muslim volunteers from around the world. The Russian military responded to this dirty war with indiscriminate use of force as well as the brutal filtration of the Chechen population to imprison or execute suspected militants. The clan-based nature of Chechen society which had made it so difficult for Dudaev to build an orderly state now served to make the Russian task harder, as the decentralized Chechen resistance proved impervious to the elimination of its leaders. Dudaev himself, for example, was killed in April 1996 by a missile strike tracking his mobile phone, but the insurgency continued. Chechens also resorted to terrorist tactics. In June 1995, Chechen militants managed to travel in force well outside Chechnya, passing through seemingly secure Russian territory, to capture a hospital and other buildings in the town of Budennovsk, and over 100 people were killed in the ensuing battle.

The war dragged on through the summer of 1996, when Yeltsin's reelection campaign required some progress on the issue. To boost his own popularity before the final round of voting against communist candidate Gennadii Ziuganov, Yeltsin commissioned popular retired general and moderate Russian nationalist Aleksandr Lebed to attempt to reach a peace settlement. In an effort to humiliate Yeltsin, Chechen forces managed a stunning surprise recapture of Groznyi from Russian forces. This final blow provided the impetus for Lebed to negotiate a peace settlement with Chechen leader Aslan Maskhadov. Yeltsin had no choice but to approve a peace settlement which gave Chechnya everything short of full legal independence from Russia, and major hostilities ceased.

But this end to the First Chechen War did not bring peace to Chechnya. The smuggling and organized crime, including kidnapping for ransom on an enormous scale, returned and worsened in Chechnya's devastated society. The Chechen nationalism which had sparked the first war became overshadowed by Islamic radicalism. Maskhadov was unable or unwilling to establish order, and the spillover of Chechen anarchy and growing Islamic fundamentalism destabilized surrounding Russian territory. Radical Islamists among the Chechen population, such as Shamil Basayev, saw the *de facto* independence of the republic as an opportunity for *jihad* (Holy War) among all the Islamic peoples of the North Caucasus. Low levels of violence, including attacks on Russian policemen and soldiers, continued despite the peace accord.

By 1999, the situation was explosive. The precise origins of the Second Chechen War remain deeply controversial. In August 1999, almost simultaneously, Russian president Boris Yeltsin appointed Vladimir Putin as prime minister, and Shamil Basayev launched an invasion from Chechen territory into the neighboring region of Dagestan. Putin's hardline response to the invasion, and Basayev's clear violation of the tenuous peace, pushed Russian public opinion toward support for a second Chechen war. The next month, a series of bombings of apartment buildings in Russia, blamed by the Russian government on Chechen terrorists, killed hundreds of people and further solidified Russian support for renewed war. Political opponents of Vladimir Putin have argued that the bombings were engineered by the Russian government itself to provide further justification for war.

Appalling levels of criminality and violence in Chechnya had exhausted any remaining Russian public sympathy for the Chechen cause. This, combined with Russia's far better performance in the Second Chechen War, produced mass popularity for Putin. The ailing Yeltsin resigned the presidency unexpectedly on December 31, 1999. This left Putin as acting president and put him in an ideal position to win the resulting presidential election in early 2000.

The Russian army had clearly learned a great deal from its experience in the First Chechen War. Since the end of the first war, tactical reforms and contingency plans were in preparation for the possibility of a second. Command and control, particularly coordination between the Russian army and troops belonging to the Ministry of Internal Affairs, was much better. The Russians also cut down on the earlier practice of throwing ill-trained conscripts into close combat with dedicated and experienced Chechen fighters. Instead, the Russians relied heavily on firepower – artillery, air bombardment, minefields, and even fuel–air (thermobaric) munitions – to reduce the expenditure of manpower. In particular, rather than risk troops in a man-to-man fight for Groznyi, Russian forces leveled the city with shells and bombs. Slow and systematic advance provided areas of relative safety north of the Terek River dividing Chechnya where Chechens, exhausted from unceasing violence, could achieve relative security. All this was combined with effective management of the Russian media, which displayed in the Second Chechen War none of the sympathy for the rebels that it had in the first. Putin skillfully employed the terrorist attacks of September 11, 2001, to portray the Second Chechen War as part of the global war on terror, quieting western criticism of Russian methods. Combined with effective use of Chechen allies and paramilitary formations, the result was a far more successful campaign than the first, though it took years to achieve an end to serious resistance.

The final major event of the Second Chechen War was the horrific September 2004 takeover of a school in the Ossetian town of Beslan by a few dozen Chechen sympathizers, who killed over 300 people, nearly 200 of them children, before being killed or captured. While Putin used this crisis to further centralize power in Moscow's hands, major terrorist acts associated with the Chechen insurgency dwindled, perhaps in response to worldwide revulsion at the deaths of so many children.

Though not evident at the time, Beslan marked the beginning of the end of large-scale Chechen resistance. Guerrilla resistance dwindled as Chechen fighters were lost through attrition and an increasing number of Chechens grew exhausted with the struggle. Key leaders of the insurrection were either killed or came to terms with continued membership in the Russian Federation. Maskhadov was killed in a fight with Russian special forces in 2005, and Basayev, who had claimed responsibility for organizing the Beslan attack, died in an explosion in 2006. Other Chechen leaders accepted Russian rule. Akhmad Kadyrov, who had joined Putin's team as administrative head of Chechnya in 2000, presided over the gradual pacification of the region until his assassination by a bomb while in a stadium for a parade in 2004. After a brief interval, his son Ramzan Kadyrov became Chechen prime minister in 2005 and then president in his own right in 2007. Kadyrov and Putin established a working arrangement whereby Russian backing and substantial funds for reconstruction of the devastated region flowed to Kadyrov. Kadyrov in return accepted Russian suzerainty and maintained order in Chechnya. Putin turned a blind eye to Kadyrov's authoritarian rule, and to the string of Kadyrov's political rivals and investigative journalists who ended up dead. Though small groups of guerrillas remained active in Chechnya's mountains, Putin's successor as Russian president Dmitrii Medvedev declared the counterinsurgency ended in March 2009. Ethnic and religious tensions remain strong throughout the North Caucasus.. Chechnya itself is relatively pacified, but bombings, assassinations, and low-level clashes between nationalist and Islamist militants and local security forces remain endemic.

SEE ALSO: Terrorism, War Against.

Further Reading

Gall, C. and de Waal, T. (1998) *Chechnya: Calamity in the Caucasus*. New York: New York University Press.

Gammer, M. (2005) *The Lone Wolf and the Bear: Three Centuries of Chechen Defiance of Russian Rule*. London: Hurst.

Hughes, J. (2007) *Chechnya: From Nationalism to Jihad*. Philadelphia: University of Pennsylvania Press.

Lieven, A. (1998) *Chechnya: Tombstone of Russian Power*. New Haven: Yale University Press.

Russell, J. (2007) *Chechnya – Russia's "War on Terror."* New York: Routledge.

Smith, S. (2005) *Allah's Mountains: The Battle for Chechnya*. London: Tauris.

Chemical Warfare

DONALD AVERY

Definitions and Categories of Weapons

Chemical warfare involves the use of chemical agents to kill or incapacitate, either on the battlefield, or within a civilian context. Because of their diversity, chemical weapons (CW) are usually described by their physical properties or how they affect humans. During World War I, for example, the warring nations developed and used different categories of choking gases (chlorine, phosgene), blood gases (hydrogen cyanide), persistent blister agents (HS mustard gas and lewisite), and non-lethal irritating gases such as CS tear gas. These remained the standard CW

munitions until World War II when the Germans secretly developed three deadly, non-persistent nerve agents (tabun, sarin, soman), which greatly expanded the strategic importance of chemical warfare. During the 1950s, another generation of nerve gases emerged with the British discovery of VX, which was both more toxic than the G-agents and relatively persistent, meaning that it could contaminate the battlefield for an extended period of time. Another category of gas weapon of this era was non-lethal "psychochemicals" such as BZ and LSD, which could cause serious psychological disorientation among enemy troops, although these agents proved difficult to use within a battlefield context. Toxin weapons, defined as toxic substances derived from living organisms, were another promising field, with most of the attention being devoted to the weaponization of ricin (plant), staphylococcal enterotoxin (bacterium), botulinum toxin (bacterium), and trichothecene mycotoxins (fungi).

Another generation of chemical weapons emerged from the extended CW arms race that took place after 1960, as both the United States and the Soviet Union attempted to utilize non-conventional weapons that would give them a strategic advantage, while avoiding a nuclear confrontation. These innovations included more effective nerve gases along with the binary munition that combined two CW precursors during the flight of the shell or bomb. Fortunately, the 1997 Chemical Weapons Convention (CWC), now supported by 190 countries, has curtailed the research, development, testing, and use of poison gas for military purposes. It has not, however, prevented work on new non-lethal CW agents, such as anesthetic fentanyl and bio-regulators/peptides, since they are not covered by the CWC because of their exclusive use in law enforcement and peacekeeping purposes.

It should be noted that this chapter does not deal with the development and use of flamethrowers, incendiary bombs, and napalm devices, since these are normally categorized as conventional weapons and were not subject to the dictates of the 1925 Geneva Protocol or the 1997 CWC. Also excluded from discussion are smoke weapons, used in battlefield situations during

World War II. Instead, the focus of this chapter is on "asphyxiating, poisonous or other gases," as defined by the Protocol.

Poison and Early Chemical Weapons

Chemical warfare is closely associated with the age-old phenomenon of intentional poisoning. Indeed, history abounds with examples of individual or large-scale incidents of death by poison, with the Renaissance-era Borgia family having a special place in this pantheon of infamous assassinators. Another dimension of this nefarious activity was the availability of certain toxic substances such as hemlock, opium, lead, arsenic, snake venom, and a wide range of industrial chemicals such as chlorine, the first battlefield poison gas. On the other hand, a number of scholars have stressed the importance of long-standing taboos against the use of poison weapons that "may have had its origin in the linkage of medicine, poisons, and mysticism common to societies everywhere" (Cole 1998: 119).

Unfortunately, there are many historical examples where primitive gas weapons were used. One of the more famous occurred in 673 CE when the Byzantine Greeks used sulfur dioxide mixtures (Greek Fire) to defend Constantinople from the attacking Saracens. Chemical weapons were also in evidence during the military campaigns of Genghis Khan (1162–1227), who often shot huge missiles of burning pitch and sulfur into cities he was besieging. During the nineteenth century, deployment of poison gas was proposed in a number of major conflicts, notably the Crimean War and the American Civil War, when both Confederate and Northern military strategists explored this military option. It did not occur; in fact, later in the century there was a movement to outlaw any form of chemical warfare. This was evident during the 1899 Hague Peace Conference, where the national representatives, as part of their general attempts to reduce the inhumanity of warfare, proposed a permanent ban on the use of asphyxiating or deleterious gases, a taboo that remained in effect until World War I. For some scholars, this was a noble initiative to ban a weapon system before it became militarily important, particularly since these weapons did not discriminate between combatants and innocent civilians, and therefore violated "the just war doctrine" (Price 1997: 34). In contrast, other experts claim that this ban was a futile effort, partly because the major industrialized nations had copious amounts of toxic chemicals, and partly because of the dictates of modern technological warfare, which emphasized killing capacity over military chivalry.

World War I and Poison Gas

Between 1914 and 1918 scientists of the warring states became aware, either as members of the armed forces or as wartime researchers, of the ways that science could transform military conflict. This was particularly true for approximately 5,400 Allied and enemy chemists, who were involved in creating a number of lethal chemical weapons. Between 1915 and 1918, over 124,200 tons of poison gas were used, causing over a million casualties, including 91,000 deaths. Overall, this represented an average of about 6 percent of total battlefield deaths, but soldiers in the poorly equipped Russian army had a much higher level of fatalities.

Chemical warfare began in April 1915 after the brilliant chemist Fritz Haber managed to convince the German High Command that the surprise use of poison gas would bring about a major victory on the Western Front. And in some ways he was right. The massive chlorine gas attack of April 22, at the second Battle of Ypres, did achieve impressive tactical results, creating an 8-km hole in the Allied defensive position and causing about 15,000 casualties among the French and Canadian troops. Gas did not, however, become the "winning weapon" that Haber had promised. This was in part because the crude delivery system of gas cylinders was often offset by sudden changes in wind direction, and in part because of the difficulty of integrating the use of chemical weapons into German strategic planning and military culture. In addition, the British and French quickly adopted various defensive measures, notably the use of charcoal respirators, and developed their own offensive capabilities. But the initiative in creating new chemical weapons remained with the German military. This was evident on July 12, 1917, when a series of attacks was launched at the Western Front using mustard gas, a persistent vesicant agent that disabled more soldiers than it killed. In turn, the British, French, and Americans expanded their use of poison gas weapons in the form of shells, bombs, and aerial sprays. During the last year of the war, over 65,000 tons of chemical weapons were used on the Western Front, including the seven major non-persistent gases (chlorine, phosgene, diphosgene, chloropicrin, hydrogen cyanide, cyanogen chloride), along with two persistent agents (HS mustard gas and lewisite).

By 1918, chemical warfare had developed a number of institutional characteristics. For battlefield use, it was employed in a tactical doctrine that sought to paralyze enemy soldiers in their trenches, disrupt artillery batteries, and sever communication linkages. On the defensive side, use of mustard was useful in covering withdrawals and retreats, and denying frontal areas for troop concentrations. Increasingly, execution of these functions was carried out by specialized chemical warfare units, who were also responsible for training troops in the appropriate offensive and defensive techniques. This systematic approach to CW preparations also occurred at the home front, where the large-scale production of war gases required considerable industrial planning, along with the challenge of establishing safe but efficient facilities. In addition, it was necessary to select isolated and restricted areas for the testing of new agents and munitions, with Porton Down becoming the focus of British CW activity, and Edgewood Arsenal, Maryland, performing a similar function for the US Chemical Warfare Service.

Above all, poison gas was a weapon of fear. First, since it blanketed everyone in a large area, there was no place to run, and little chance of changing the outcome of the attack through heroic action. Second, even when defensive measures were adopted, troops had to rely on their respirators and protective clothing to protect themselves from approaching clouds of toxic gases, uncertain whether they would experience horrible death by asphyxiation or multiple mustard gas burns. Third, given problems of detection, soldiers in the trenches never felt really safe from these deadly stealth weapons. As a result, they were more likely to experience the

psychoneuroses "gas fright," a unique form of battle exhaustion (Utgoff 1990: 10). Nor was the civilian population of France and the United Kingdom spared from fear of poison gas, particularly given concerns that Germany might resort to aero-chemical warfare as part of its late-war bombing campaigns.

Interwar Years

After World War I, there were various international attempts to ban the use and possession of chemical weapons. One of these was the drafting of Article 171 of the Versailles Treaty, which specifically prohibited Germany from possessing chemical weapons as a penalty for having initiated this uncivilized form of warfare. In 1922, the Washington Conference on Disarmament attempted to establish an international ban on gas warfare. While the prospect of renouncing a functioning weapon system was generally contentious, the most spirited debate about chemical warfare took place in the United States where there was a formidable partnership of pro-gas spokesmen, including representatives of the US chemical industry, the leadership of the Chemical Warfare Service, veterans groups, and even prominent scientists such as the chemist James Conant, who questioned "why tearing a man's guts out by a high-explosive shell is to be preferred to maiming him by attacking his lungs or skin" (cited in Russell 2001: 43). On the other side of the issue were American religious organizations, peace groups, prominent politicians, and even leading military officials such as General John Pershing, former commander of US forces in Europe, who branded the use of chemical weapons as barbarous and vengeful. In the court of public opinion, however, the anti-gas groups carried the day, as revealed by a prominent survey that showed only 19 Americans favored the US Army having gas weapons, while 367,000 opposed this concept.

Two years later another important study of chemical warfare was carried out by technical specialists of the 1924 Temporary Mixed Commission of the League of Nations, who warned "that all nations should realise the full and terrible danger which threatens them" (Spiers 1986: 44). This latter initiative would eventually result in the June 1925 Geneva Protocol, which banned "the use in war of asphyxiating, poison-ous or other gases ... materials or devices ... [which] has been justly condemned by the gen-eral opinion of the civilised world" (Price 1997: 91). The Protocol was initially signed by 38 coun-tries, including the United Kingdom, Germany, France, Italy, Canada, Japan, and the United States, although for a variety of reasons the latter two countries did not ratify the Convention until many years later. Moreover, even those states' parties who supported the international ban insisted on major reservations, including the right to retaliate as part of their national security strategies.

Despite the Geneva Protocol, during the 1930s there was considerable discussion about the mili-tary potential and public morality of chemical warfare. One aspect of this ongoing debate com-prised publications by former experts, such as Major-General C. H. Foulkes, who had been in charge of Britain's CW operation during World War I, and British chemist J. B. S. Haldane, whose popular book *Callinicus: A Defence of Chemical Warfare* argued that gas was ultimately a more humane form of warfare than high explosives or other conventional weapons since it primarily incapacitated, rather than killed, enemy soldiers. On the other hand, there was a growing body of literature that warned about the future threat of aero-chemical attacks on European and North American urban centers, reinforced by growing evidence that Italy and Germany were developing powerful air forces and the prevailing view that the attacking bombers would always reach their target.

In 1935, the debate over chemical warfare changed abruptly after the Italian air force used mustard gas bombs and spray against poorly equipped Ethiopian troops and vulnerable civil-ian targets. The Fascist government of Benito Mussolini was not punished by the international community for its extensive use of poison gas, even though the official investigation by the League of Nations forced Italian authorities to justify why they had violated the Geneva Convention. But this exercise in sophistry and rationalization only served to further disillusion world leaders. As British Prime Minister Stanley Baldwin lamented, "if a great European nation, in spite of its having given its signature to the Geneva Protocol against the use of such gases, employs them in Africa, what guarantee have we

that they not be used in Europe?" (Spiers 1986: 53). The lessons of the Abyssinian War also had a powerful influence on British, French, and American military planners, who became increas-ingly concerned that their CW preparations lagged far behind those of Fascist Italy, Nazi Germany, and Imperial Japan.

World War II

Remarkably, poison gas was not deployed strate-gically during World War II. That it not to say, however, that either the Axis Powers or the Allies believed that their adversaries would desist from using chemical weapons if an advantageous situa-tion emerged or a deadly new gas munition was available. Indeed, there were at least seven situa-tions when chemical warfare appeared imminent, but each of these crises passed, and gas was not used. Historians have marshaled three major arguments to explain this phenomenon. The first emphasizes ethical issues, arguing that interna-tional prohibitions and massive public revulsion toward poison gas prevented both the Axis Powers and the Western Allies, along with their Russian partner, from initiating use of this weapon system. A second viewpoint stresses the strategic dimensions, namely, that political and military leaders of the warring states realized that no decisive advantage would be gained by deploy-ing chemical weapons, since the other side could effectively retaliate and inflict high casualties. The third argument points out that chemical weapons did not fit into the military culture of any of the belligerents, being inconsistent with the prevailing "way of war" that the British, German, and American military hierarchies embraced (Legro 1995: 144).

In September 1939, British, Canadian, and American military planners were forced to antici-pate a German chemical warfare attack that would deploy not only the "popular" chemical weapons of World War I, but possibly deadly new gases derived from industrial poisons as well. These discussions were temporarily stilled by the realization that the dazzling victories of the Wehrmacht in western Europe had been achieved without poison gas. But it was a short hiatus. By June 1940, the central issue was not German CW aggression but whether the desperate and depleted British military forces should use poison gas to repel an imminent Nazi invasion. In the end, despite arguments that Britain would be violating international moral standards, Prime Minister Winston Churchill authorized the operational use of CW weapons since, in his opinion, German troops on the landing beaches would be an ideal target for British mustard gas and phosgene weapons.

Allied chemical warfare planning was also affected by the deliberations of the August 1940 British defense mission to North America, led by the eminent scientist Henry Tizard. During this high-level tour, arrangements were made for British and Canadian chemical weapons specialists to tour US facilities at Edgewood Arsenal, and to meet with key members of the US Chemical Warfare Service. As a result of these deliberations, an extensive exchange system between the three countries was instituted that lasted until the end of the war. Another dimension of this CW Alliance was the bilateral arrangement between Ottawa and London in March 1941 for the formation of the Anglo-Canadian Experimental Establishment Station, a 1,000-acre site in southern Alberta for the development and testing of CW munitions. During the next four years, numerous trials were conducted with virtually the entire poison gas arsenal of the Canadian, British, and American armed forces.

The possibility that Germany might develop a powerful new poison gas was another subject of mutual interest for Allied defense officials. For the most part, however, British and American intelligence dismissed rumors about secret "nerve gas" weapons as baseless, assuming that they, not the Germans, had the most effective CW research and development capabilities. What they did not realize was that in 1936, the IG Farben chemist Dr Gerhard Schrader, while searching for new insecticides, had discovered the organophosphate compound tabun, the world's first nerve gas. It was a frightening weapon: a colorless, odorless gas that brought rapid death through convulsions and asphyxiation. In September 1939, the German High Command authorized the production of tabun at a newly constructed plant in the Silesian village of Dyhernfurth, despite its problems of rapid vaporization in battlefield use and its tendency to decompose during storage. Two years later, IG Farben scientists discovered sarin,

an even more effective nerve agent because of its high toxicity and stability. By 1943, both tabun and sarin were scheduled for military use once Germany either initiated chemical warfare or used these weapons in retaliation. In reality, neither of these prospects would materialize.

The official position of the Western Allies on the use of chemical weapons was set forth in two dramatic statements during the spring of 1942. On May 10, Prime Minister Churchill warned that German use of poison gas against the Soviet Union, Britain's wartime ally, would be regarded "as if it were used on ourselves … and we will use our great and growing air superiority in the west to carry gas warfare on the largest possible scale far and wide upon the towns and cities of Germany." On June 5, President Roosevelt sent a similar message to Japanese authorities: "if Japan persists in this inhuman form of warfare against China or against any of the United Nations, such action will be regarded by this government as though taken against the United States, and retaliation in kind and in full measure will be meted out" (cited in Avery 1998: 136). Despite this impressive rhetoric, the reality was that in 1942 neither the British nor the US military had the capability of "retaliation in kind." Indeed, despite strenuous attempts to stimulate the production of various war gases in the United Kingdom, United States, and Canada, there was no possibility that there would be sufficient CW munitions for even the European theater of war until 1944. Fortunately for the Allies, throughout this critical period Germany showed little interest in using chemical weapons on the battlefield, despite having its newly developed nerve gases.

By the spring of 1944, the situation had dramatically changed. Now, there were at least three major reasons why German military authorities might consider launching a series of CW attacks. First, the moral taboo had been violated since the Nazi regime had already used chemical weapons in the form of Zyklon B against millions of concentration camp victims. Second, German security officials had managed to maintain a cloak of secrecy around their nerve gas projects, with strict "right to know" guidelines. As a result, British, American, and Soviet intelligence appear to have been unaware of the serious threat they were facing. Third, and most important, there were two major targets where tabun and sarin munitions might make a major difference to Germany's war effort. One of these was on the Eastern Front, where nerve gas could have stalled the relentless advance of the Red Army; the other ideal target was the Normandy landing grounds, where thousands of Allied soldiers would have been vulnerable to these novel weapons. And, even though its nerve gas munitions were limited, Germany did have large supplies of mustard gas, which, as a persistent vesicant agent, would have contaminated the battlefields in France and eastern Europe, providing additional defensive assets to the beleaguered Third Reich.

On the other side of the equation, there were major reasons why Nazi Germany was deterred from a first-use CW policy. By the spring of 1944, the Luftwaffe had lost its air superiority, at least on the Western Front, which meant that German cities were vulnerable to massive CW retaliatory action. On the Eastern Front, there was also the awareness that the Red Army had a reputation for integrating chemical warfare into its military doctrine, and was therefore capable of inflicting heavy casualties on German troops, who were not well trained or equipped for gas warfare. And finally, since German dictator Adolf Hitler rejected all proposals for a proactive chemical warfare position, the Wehrmacht was unable to develop the necessary infrastructure, logistical measures, and command structures for an effective poison gas attack before the war was lost.

German planners were not alone in considering the offensive CW option. During the latter stages of World War II there were several situations where the United Kingdom and the United States considered a first-use gas attack. In July 1944, for example, Prime Minister Churchill, shocked and enraged by ever-increasing German V-1 rocket attacks on London, demanded that the British Chiefs of Staff consider the possibilities of using chemical weapons to "drench the cities of the Ruhr and many other cities in Germany in such a way that most of the population would be requiring constant medical attention ... I do not see why we should always have all the disadvantages of being the gentlemen, while they have all the advantages of being the cad" (Avery 1998: 146–147). The British Chiefs of Staff strenuously objected, despite the fact that they had sufficient chemical weapons on hand for a major offensive, given previous concerns that Germany might use poison gas at Normandy. But, in their opinion, the outbreak of chemical warfare at this stage of the global conflict should be avoided at all costs, since it would seriously impede the progress of Allied armies as they sought to topple the Third Reich.

A more likely prospect was that the United States would use chemical weapons against Japan, in part because of the remote possibility that Japan would eventually use its limited CW resources against US troops, and in part because this "war without mercy" was producing enormous American casualties. After the carnage of Iwo Jima and Okinawa, even Army Chief of Staff George Marshall was convinced that poison gas should be added to the US arsenal. As he explained to Secretary of War H. L. Stimson, "drench them and sicken them so that the fight would be taken out of them ... The character of the weapon was no less humane than phosphorous and flame throwers and need not be used against dense populations of civilians – merely against these last pockets of resistance" (van Courtland Moon 1989: 304). This first-use policy gained further momentum during the summer of 1945 when the US Joint Chiefs of Staff considered a feasibility study that recommended that gas be used during the projected November 1945 invasion of Kyushu (Operation Olympia), and the March 1946 landing on the main island of Honshu (Operation Coronet), on the grounds that it would save the lives of American soldiers and shorten the war. These plans were, however, shelved after the August atomic bomb attacks on Hiroshima and Nagasaki.

Post-War Developments

It was quite remarkable that a major weapon system, extensively used in a previous war, remained on the shelf during a subsequent conflict. This did not mean, however, that there was no interest in chemical weapons after World War II. On the contrary, once the Western Allies and the Soviets took control of their respective occupation zones in Germany, both sides made enormous efforts to develop production techniques for the German nerve gases (tabun, sarin, and soman) by using captured technology and munitions, along with the assistance of "seconded" German scientists.

For Russian and British military authorities there were special incentives to transform CW into an operational weapon of mass destruction, since it would offset their temporary lack of nuclear weapons.

While the United States, with its stock of atomic bombs, was in a more fortunate strategic situation, there was strong lobbying by political and military groups for the development of viable chemical warfare capability. There were a number of reasons for this policy. From a strategic perspective, it would provide the United States with a flexible response in dealing with a possible Soviet CW attack, which appeared more likely after the 1956 statements from the Kremlin that it was prepared to use all of its weapons of mass destruction (nuclear, chemical, biological) against the United States if World War III should occur. As a result, in March 1956, President Eisenhower amended the national security policy against first use, with the provision that, "to the extent that the military effectiveness of the armed forces will be enhanced by their use, the United States will be prepared to use chemical and bacteriological weapons in general war" (Tucker 2006: 155). Significantly, this first-use policy was at variance with the policies of Canada and the United Kingdom, although neither country voiced any complaints.

Technological developments that improved the efficiency of chemical warfare provided another reason why Washington moved away from the Roosevelt retaliation-only tradition. Many of these innovations occurred within the tripartite chemical and biological research agreement between the United States, the United Kingdom, and Canada, whereby each side focused on certain CW problems and shared its information with the other two partners. Given its vast scientific and industrial resources, the United States assumed a leading role within this system, with most of the research, production, and testing being coordinated by the Chemical Warfare Corps (after 1947), including its vast research and development facilities at Edgewood, the sarin production plant at Mussel Shoals, Alabama, and the Dugway Proving Grounds in Utah.

Among the CW innovations developed under the tripartite system were the lethal VX family of organo-phosphorous gases, which not only exceeded sarin in lethality, but also were much more effective in penetrating protective masks and clothing. In addition, there were new forms of non-lethal gases such as BZ and LSD, which caused psychoneuroses and were lauded as a humane weapon because of their ability to incapacitate large numbers of enemy combatants. In addition, there were marked technical improvements in CW delivery systems such as the M-24 cluster aerial bomb, the 155-mm artillery shell, the Honest John rocket, and, above all, binary CW munitions. This latter device was based on the principle that the two chemical components of the nerve gas were combined during flight, and did not become lethal until impact. As a result, binaries overcame many of the formidable problems associated with transporting, storing, and using chemical weapons.

During these years, the tripartite allies also concentrated on other strategies in their ongoing preparations for chemical warfare. One of these was the attempt to prepare American, British, and Canadian troops for combat in a toxic battlefield, which included testing nerve gases on human volunteers, sometimes with unfortunate results. For example, in May 1953 British airman Ronald Maddison died of sarin poisoning during a "controlled" experiment at Porton Down, an accident that was cloaked in secrecy until the 1990s. Another defensive initiative, adopted by all three countries, was the establishment of various civil defense programs for protecting the civilian population from a chemical and biological weapons attack, as was evident during the 1962 Cuban Missile Crisis. On this occasion, there was widespread concern that while the Soviets' first strike would be nuclear, chemical weapons would be used in the next stage, after the infrastructure of the United States and its allies had been destroyed.

During the late 1960s a number of incidents undermined the ability of the United States to wage gas warfare. High on the list was international condemnation of its use of incapacitating gases (tear gas) and herbicides, along with the fact that the United States had not yet ratified the 1925 Geneva Protocol. Another factor was the November 1969 decision by the government of Richard Nixon to unilaterally terminate its offensive biological weapons program and work toward an international ban on this frightening form of warfare. There was also a series of embarrassing domestic accidents involving chemical weapons. The most controversial of these were the February

1969 VX aerial trials (part of 1,200 tests since 1951) at the Dugway Proving Grounds, which produced a poisonous cloud that drifted outside the facility, killing at least 3,800 sheep in neighboring Skull Valley. The Pentagon's clumsy attempts to deny responsibility and claim that its extensive open-air testing program was completely safe did not enhance its reputation for either competence or honesty. As a result, there was a public outcry that all offensive CW work should be canceled in the United States and internationally.

Why did the CWC not materialize until April 1997? How does one explain the 22-year difference between the enactment of the Biological Weapons Convention and the CWC, particularly since the two weapons were invariably linked together as non-conventional forms of warfare? There are a number of plausible explanations, all associated with the Cold War. First, the United States and its allies suspected that the Soviet Union was trying to improve its chemical warfare capabilities, notably in the development of fourth-generation weapons such as fungus-based trichothecene mycotoxins and new nerve gases such as Foliant, with enhanced "toxicity, stability, persistence and ease of production" (Tucker 2006: 231). These concerns were intensified by reports of Soviet troops using sarin and mustard gas against the mujahideen in Afghanistan after their 1979 invasion of that country, along with the possible deployment of mycotoxins (yellow rain) in southeastern Asia. Because of American allegations, the United Nations carried out a series of investigations that were hampered by poor science and the refusal of many pro-communist countries in the region to grant access. A second factor was that, unlike biological weapons, the US Joint Chiefs of Staff regarded gas warfare as a viable military option. They had, for example, strenuously defended the use of non-lethal tear gas and Agent Orange defoliants during the Vietnam War, and they also felt that the United States should have the ability to retaliate in kind if the Soviets launched a CW attack on North Atlantic Treaty Organization forces in western Europe. As US Secretary of Defense Melvin Laird put it, "if we want to make sure this weapon is never used, we must have the capability to use it" (Mauroni 2000: 49). Third, there was growing concern that user-friendly binary CW weapons represented a destabilizing threat to the international arms control regime, since they would not only accelerate the arms race between the United States and the USSR, but also encourage many smaller countries to develop their own chemical warfare potential, as the poor nations' atomic bomb.

In reality, the 1980s witnessed the proliferation of gas warfare technology, with the number of countries suspected of having CW capabilities increasing from 13 in 1980 to 25 in 1990. In the case of South Africa, for instance, its primary interest in having chemical weapons was for domestic use against insurgent groups such as the African National Congress, who threatened to overthrow the white supremacist government. But the most substantial CW activity took place in the Middle East, where many Arab countries justified their gas programs as a counterweight to Israel's nuclear capabilities. Nor was the use of poison gas in the region a new phenomenon. Two decades earlier there had been evidence of Egyptian military chemical weapons during their intervention in Yemen, although Cairo strenuously denied the allegations. But the 1980s pattern of state interest in chemical warfare was more widespread, and more successful. This was evident when Libya's strongman, Col Muammar Gaddafi, managed to develop CW technology through a range of secret deals with unscrupulous western-based companies, despite attempts by the United States to block his goals. Meanwhile, Iraqi dictator Saddam Hussein had embarked upon an even more ambitious chemical and biological warfare program, which was greatly accelerated during the long and bloody war with neighboring Iran (1980–1988).

There are a number of important questions associated with this incident. Why did the international community not punish Iraq, through sweeping sanctions, for its flagrant violation of the Geneva Protocol, despite attempts by Iranian authorities to obtain support from the United Nations and its member nations? Why did the United States refuse to officially condemn Saddam Hussein's government until the late 1980s, even though there was ample evidence that Iraq had gradually integrated poison gas into its military strategy? This included the devastating use of mustard and nerve gas munitions on the battlefield against massive frontal attacks by poorly equipped Iranian infantry, and by gas attacks against Iranian and Kurdish civilian communities. Why was Iraq able to produce large quantities of sarin, VX, and mustard gas in its own secret industrial plants, despite international export controls? And finally, why did Saddam Hussein and his henchmen continue to view poison gas as a "winning weapon," not only on the battlefield, but also as an instrument of terror in suppressing political dissent by Kurdish and Shi'ite rebels?

Iraq's sustained use of chemical weapons created an unfortunate legacy. First, there was the prospect that Saddam Hussein would resort to gas in future conflicts, even against the nuclear-armed United States. Second, Iraq's successful operational use of CW weapons greatly increased their popularity with other "rogue" nations, such as Syria, Libya, and North Korea. Third, there was increased concern that non-state parties might use poison gas to attract international attention, particularly after the radical Islamist group al-Qaeda emerged as a serious international threat. Significantly, the only terrorist gas attack has come from an obscure Japanese religious cult, Aum Shinrikyo, which in March 1995 used crude sarin weapons against the Tokyo subway system. Although only 12 people died in the assault, it had a devastating impact on the city, with thousands of people seeking medical attention. For many western security experts, the Aum Shinrikyo phenomenon represented a new era, where terrorist groups sought to maximize fatalities through the targeted use of chemical, biological, and radiological weapons against urban populations. It also demonstrated that a well-funded non-state group could acquire some of the world's most frightening instruments of death, particularly since Aum had attempted to develop anthrax and ebola devices.

Ironically, the 1995 Tokyo incident coincided with the last stages of debate in the United States Senate on whether that country would ratify the CWC. Although it was a long, hard struggle, the pro-CWC advocates took advantage of the rapprochement between Washington and Moscow and of the new international consensus that poison gas was a terrible instrument of war. This resolve had been strengthened by the Gulf War chemical warfare scare (1990–1991). Even though Saddam Hussein did not authorize the use of poison gas, the US military and its allies were forced to assume the worst-case scenario:

the possibilities of a toxic battlefield. For the soldiers involved, this was often a traumatic experience, given the physical fatigue and discomfort of wearing CW-resistant equipment and the fear that their nerve gas antidotes might not be effective. There were also claims that frontline troops were exposed to accidental nerve gas explosions that subsequently produced a form of chronic illness labeled "the Gulf War Syndrome." A more positive legacy of the 1990–1991 Gulf War was the appointment, and work, of the United Nations Special Commission, consisting of specialized weapons of mass destruction inspection teams. In the case of chemical weapons, it was demonstrated that on-site inspections could be effective, even when a country such as Iraq attempts to conceal its CW agents, munitions, and delivery systems.

The CWC is a unique international agreement. Not only does it outlaw an entire weapon system, including research and development, but it also provides for an invasive form of inspection and verification, which is carried out by a permanent and independent secretariat known as the Organization for the Prohibition of Chemical Weapons (OPCW). Moreover, while the chemical industries in the member nations, notably the United States, requested specific measures to protect proprietary information, these demands were quite limited, and dual-use problems do not impede the effectiveness of the OPCW. Equally important is that membership in the CWC has continued to grow; by October 2013, 190 out of 195 countries recognized by the United Nations had ratified the Convention.

Future Concerns

Chemical warfare remains a global threat for a number of reasons. First, despite the fact that most countries are members of the CWC, a number of countries with possible CW aspirations still refuse to join. Second, there are concerns that terrorist groups might gain access to Russia's vast stockpile of chemical weapons, despite efforts on the part of the G7 Partnership for Peace Program (2003) to ensure that destruction of these munitions occurs in a timely and safe fashion. In addition, there have been troubling reports from US intelligence agencies that the Russian military may be concealing its most advanced binary chemical programs. Third, there is the contentious issue of so-called non-lethals, which remain outside the scope of the CWC on the grounds that they are essential for law enforcement, peacekeeping, or counterterrorist activities. Questions about the legitimacy of these devices were reinforced after the October 23, 2002, siege of the Dubrovka theater in Moscow, when Russian security forces used a narcotic gas (anesthetic fentanyl) that accidentally killed 129 of the 800 hostages. Fourth, because of advances in biotechnology, differences between chemical and biological weapons have become even more blurred, with the prospect that there will be "an immense range of new technologies for novel toxins and chemical weapons." (Wheelis and Dando 2003: 36). And finally, there is the continuous threat that rogue states will not only use poison gas against rival state parties, but also against their own citizens. Such was the case on August 21, 2013, when the Syrian government launched a deadly sarin attack against dissident groups in Damascus, killing thousands of men, women, and children. Yet despite widespread condemnation from most countries of the world, it remains unclear whether this blatant violation of the CWC and international human rights will go unpunished. Indeed, even with the possibility that the UN Security Council will monitor Syria's pledge to destroy its CW arsenal, suspicions remain that the government of Bashar al-Assad will sabotage the disarmament process and "will do even worse things than he already has" (Smithson 2013: 4).

SEE ALSO: Biological Warfare: Past, Present, And Future; Gulf Wars (1990–1991, 2003–Present); Terrorism, War Against.

References

Avery, D. (1998) *The Science of War: Canadian Scientists and Allied Military Technology during the Second World War*. Toronto: University of Toronto Press.

Cole, L. (1998) "The Poison Weapons Taboo: Biology, Culture, and Policy," *Politics and the Life Sciences*, 17 (2): 119–132.

Legro, J. (1995) *Cooperation under Fire: Anglo-German Restraint during World War II*. Ithaca: Cornell University Press.

Mauroni, A. J. (2000) *America's Struggle with Chemical-Biological Warfare*. Westport: Praeger.

Price, R. (1997) *The Chemical Weapons Taboo*. Ithaca: Cornell University Press.

Russell, E. (2001) *War and Nature: Fighting Humans and Insects with Chemicals from World War I to Silent Spring*. New York: Cambridge University Press.

Smithson, A. (2013) "How to Dismantle a Chemical Bomb: Lessons for the United Nations in Syria," *Foreign Affairs* (Council on Foreign Relations), http://www.foreignaffairs.com/print/137103 (accessed January 17, 2014).

Spiers, E. (1986) *Chemical Warfare*. London: Macmillan.

Tucker, J. (2006) *War of Nerves: Chemical Warfare from World War to al-Qaeda*. New York: Pantheon.

Utgoff, V. (1990) *The Challenge of Chemical Weapons: An American Perspective*. New York: Macmillan.

van Courtland Moon, J. E. (1989) "Project SPHINX: The Question of the Use of Gas in the Planned Invasion of Japan," *Journal of Strategic Studies*, 12 (3): 303–323.

Wheelis, M. and Dando, M. (2003) "New Technology and Future Developments in Biological Warfare," *Military Technology*, 5: 52–56.

Further Reading

Bard, M. (2008) *A Strange and Formidable Weapon: British Response to World War I Poison Gas*. Lincoln: University of Nebraska Press.

Brown, F. (1968) *Chemical Warfare: A Study in Restraints*. Princeton: Princeton University Press.

Cole, L. (1997) *The Politics of Biological and Chemical Warfare*. New York: W. H. Freeman.

Cook, T. (1999) *No Place to Run: The Canadian Corps and Gas Warfare in the First World War*. Vancouver: University of British Columbia Press.

Goodwin, B. (1998) *Keen as Mustard: Britain's Horrific Chemical Warfare Experiments in Australia*. St. Lucia, Queensland: University of Queensland Press.

Gould, C. and Folb, P. (2002) *Project Coast: Apartheid's Chemical and Biological Warfare Programme*. Geneva: United Nations Institute for Disarmament Research.

Haber, L. F. (1986) *The Poisonous Cloud: Chemical Warfare in the First World War*. Oxford: Clarendon Press.

Johnston, H. (2003) *A Bridge Not Attacked: Chemical Warfare Civilian Research During World War II*. Singapore: World Publishing.

Krause, J. and Mallory, C. (1992) *Chemical Weapons in Soviet Military Doctrine: Military and Historical Experience, 1915–1991*. Boulder, CO: Westview Press.

Palazzo, A. (2000) *Seeking Victory on the Western Front: The British Army and Chemical Warfare in World War I.* Lincoln: University of Nebraska Press.

Sidel, F., Takafuji, E., and Franz, D. (Eds.) (1997) *Medical Aspects of Chemical and Biological Warfare.* Washington, DC: Borden Institute, Walter Reed Army Medical Center.

Tucker, J. (Ed.) (2000) *Toxic Terror: Assessing Terrorist Use of Chemical and Biological Weapons.* Cambridge, MA: MIT Press.

van Courtland Moon, J. E. (1984) "Chemical Weapons and Deterrence: The World War II Experience," *International Security*, 8 (4): 3–35.

China, Invasion of (1931, 1937–1945)

GARY J. BJORGE

Japan's invasions of China during the 1930s initiated and then expanded the largest war fought between two countries during the twentieth century. For Japan, this was a war fought for resources and geopolitical position. For China, it was a war for national survival. Japan possessed a powerful modern army and pursued a strategy of quick decisive victory. China responded with masses of soldiers and traded space for time in an attrition strategy. In the initial invasion of 1931, Japan rapidly gained control over the three northeastern provinces of China known as Manchuria. In the subsequent major thrust of 1937–1938, the Japanese overran most of northern and central China. Yet the Chinese refused to surrender and Japan found herself stuck in an unforeseen quagmire. Unable to extricate herself from this strategic predicament, Japan compounded her problems by responding to the outbreak of war in Europe in ways that eventually led to her decision to attack the United States. By this action, Japan made her war with China part of World War II, a war in which she met total defeat and was forced to surrender all she had gained in China since 1931 and more.

These invasions were an extension of Japan's long-standing national security goal of establishing control over adjacent areas on the Asian continent. Such control was considered necessary in order to counter possible military threats and ensure access to the natural resources needed to guarantee Japan's economic independence. By

defeating Russia in the Russo-Japanese War of 1904–1905, Japan acquired possession of Russia's Liaodong Peninsula Leasehold, which she renamed the Kwantung Leased Territory, and the South Manchurian Railroad. In 1910, she annexed Korea. Manchuria then became the focal point of Japanese expansionist aspirations because of its mineral wealth, rich farmland, and potential value as a buffer shielding Korea from both China and Russia, later the Soviet Union. Relying on their relationship with Zhang Zuolin, a former bandit whom they had helped become the independent warlord in control of Manchuria after China's Manchu Dynasty collapsed in 1911, the Japanese moved to deepen their influence in the area. During the 1920s, many officers in the Kwantung army, the army that Japan had established to maintain order in the Kwantung Leased Territory and the South Manchurian Railroad Zone, came to believe that Japan should seize Manchuria and annex it, as had been done with Korea. Increasingly impatient with what they considered to be Japanese government timidity, some began plotting to take Manchuria by direct military action. In 1931, such a plot brought about the first invasion of China in the 1930s.

The plot of 1931 was not the first attempt by Kwantung army officers to seize control of Manchuria. In 1928, the Kwantung army chief of staff, upset with Zhang Zuolin because he had ignored Japanese advice to stay out of Chinese political affairs, arranged to blow up his train and kill him while he was returning to Manchuria from Beijing on June 4, 1928. His hope was that Zhang's death would provoke anti-Japanese riots and give the Kwantung army a pretext to seize control of major cities across Manchuria. However, there was no eruption of violence, Zhang Zuolin's son, Zhang Xueliang, wisely did not take an anti-Japanese position, and the Japanese consulate in Mukden called for calm. Kwantung army units did not move and the plan failed.

The lesson expansionist zealots learned from this failure was to be more patient and more thorough in preparation. By the summer of 1931 another group of plotters felt that conditions were ripe for action. The plan was simple. A bomb was to be exploded along the railroad south of Mukden to provide an excuse for Kwantung army units to seize the nearby Manchurian army

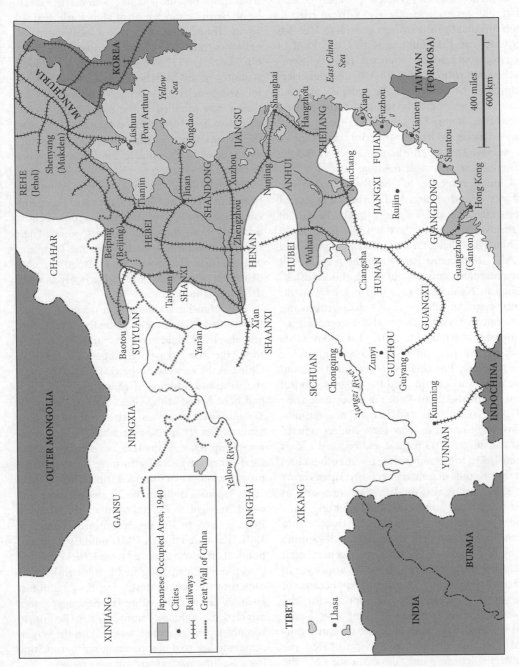

Map 11 Invasion of China.

Japanese Occupied Area, 1940
Cities
Railways
Great Wall of China

OUTER MONGOLIA

XINJIANG

GANSU

NINGXIA

QINGHAI

XIKANG

TIBET
Lhasa

INDIA

BURMA

INDOCHINA

YUNNAN
Kunming

SICHUAN
Chongqing

GUIZHOU
Guiyang
Zunyi

GUANGXI

Yangzi River

Changsha
HUNAN

GUANGDONG
Guangzhou (Canton)
Hong Kong

JIANGXI
Ruijin

Nanchang

FUJIAN
Fuzhou
Xiamen
Shantou
Xiapu

TAIWAN (FORMOSA)

East China Sea

ZHEJIANG
Hangzhou
Shanghai

JIANGSU
Nanjing

ANHUI

HUBEI
Wuhan

HENAN
Zhengzhou

SHAANXI
Xian
Yanan

SHANXI
Taiyuan

SUIYUAN
Baotou

CHAHAR

Beijing (Beiping)
HEBEI
Tianjin

SHANDONG
Jinan
Qingdao
Xuzhou

Yellow Sea

Lüshun (Port Arthur)
Shenyang (Mukden)

REHE (Jehol)

MANCHURIA

KOREA

Yellow River

400 miles
600 km

barracks and the arsenal in the city. Once those objectives were taken, the area under Kwantung army control was to be gradually expanded until all of Manchuria was occupied. The army general staff and government officials in Tokyo tried to stop this plot by dispatching a general to Mukden to warn the Kwantung army that this kind of activity would not be supported. However, sympathizers within the Tokyo headquarters informed the plotters of the general's mission. Instead of waiting to be restrained, the plotters acted first. Before the general had the opportunity to issue his warning, during the night of September 18, 1931, the bomb was set off and the Kwantung army went into action.

China's response to the Kwantung army's attacks in and around Mukden was a policy of non-resistance and an appeal to the League of Nations for support. At this time, Jiang Jieshi (Chiang Kai-shek), the leader of the Guomindang (GMD/ Nationalist Party) and the president of the nationalist government that had been established in Nanjing in 1928, did not want a war with Japan. In 1927, civil war had broken out between the nationalists and the communists. Jiang was determined to destroy the communists and achieve internal unity before confronting the Japanese. The Japanese government also did not want war and directed the Japanese consul general in Mukden to ask the Kwantung army to cease operations and join in negotiations. However, Kwantung army commanders refused the consul general's request and rejected orders from Tokyo to stop advancing toward other cities on the grounds of military necessity. Japan's army in Korea army also used military necessity as justification for supporting the Kwantung army and, contrary to orders, sent troops into Manchuria. Powerless to bring the Kwantung army under control, first the army general staff and then the government began to acquiesce in what was happening. In part this was because of the great wave of popular support for the Kwantung army that was sweeping over Japan. But it was also because, although the army general staff and the government considered the military actions and disobedience of the Kwantung army to be completely unacceptable, they shared with its officers the belief that, ultimately, separating Manchuria from China was in Japan's national interest.

In December 1931, a cabinet more sympathetic to the actions of the Kwantung army was organized in Tokyo and the separation of Manchuria from China became Japanese policy. There was to be no Japanese annexation of Manchuria. Instead, Japan created the fiction that a local independence movement had gained freedom from China. On March 1, 1932, the founding of Manchukuo (country of the Manchus) was declared and the following week Pu Yi, the last Manchu emperor of China, was installed as the new country's chief executive. Two years later, on March 1, 1934, after the Kwantung army had occupied Jehol province and added it to Manchukuo, Pu Yi was enthroned as the country's emperor.

By establishing Manchukuo, Japan committed herself to a policy of self-reliance and independent action. The basis of strategy was to be security achieved through national military power. There would be no turning back. After the League of Nations Assembly voted 42–1 (Japan) to condemn her occupation of Manchuria, Japan withdrew from the League.

With Manchuria's status as a Japanese puppet state settled in Japanese eyes, the Kwantung army, and also the Tianjin garrison, continued to push for an increase in Japanese influence in northern China at the expense of the GMD. In May 1933, the westward advance of Kwantung army units had been halted at the Great Wall passes by the Tanggu Truce negotiated between the Kwantung army and local Chinese authorities. But this truce agreement left the Japanese in a strong position for further advances by turning Eastern Hebei province into a demilitarized zone. Then, in May 1935, Japan's Tianjin garrison, a small force that owed its right to be stationed in the Tianjin–Beiping area to the Boxer Protocol signed in 1901, demanded that all GMD military units and political offices be removed from Hebei province. Two months later, Jiang Jieshi, still firmly committed to the goal of destroying his communist enemies before confronting Japanese aggression, directed his military commander in Beijing to comply. Japan, it seemed, was well on the way to achieving her goal of separating northern China from Nanjing government administration.

In a bid to confirm these gains, in October 1935, the Japanese prime minister proposed that China recognize Manchukuo, join with Manchukuo and Japan to develop northern

China's economy, and cooperate with Japan to combat communism. Given the intensity of anti-Japanese anger in China, acceptance of such a proposal by Jiang's government was impossible. This anger eventually also forced Jiang to end his anti-communist crusade. When he went to Xi'an in December 1936 to energize another extermination campaign, two generals took him into custody and demanded that he fight the Japanese instead of other Chinese. As a condition for his release, Jiang had to agree to end anti-communist operations and form a united front with them to resist Japan.

The formation of the united front to resist Japanese aggression put Chinese nationalism on a collision course with Japanese nationalism and expansionism. The collision finally came as the result of an incident that occurred on the night of July 7, 1937, near the Marco Polo Bridge (Lugouqiao) southwest of Beiping. A Tianjin garrison unit that was conducting maneuvers in a sensitive area containing the railroads linking Beiping to central China and the sea encountered unanticipated Chinese interference and shots were fired. For several days it appeared that the crisis would pass, as a ceasefire agreement was reached by the local commanders. The Japanese government and army general staff did not want a war with China. Just a few months earlier Japan had signed an anti-Comintern pact with Germany in order to strengthen her position relative to the Soviet Union. A war with China would weaken her ability to meet the perceived Soviet threat. However, the Kwantung army, out of concern that the badly outnumbered Tianjin garrison could be defeated in battle, immediately started moving troops into Hebei province. On July 17, Jiang Jieshi ordered more Chinese troops to move toward Beiping and announced a policy of no retreat. Unwilling to appear hesitant or weak in the face of strong Chinese pronouncements and troop movements, the Japanese government began to deploy forces from the home islands to Hebei. With emotions running high on both sides, negotiations faltered. At that point, with several divisions in position, the Japanese decided to teach the Chinese a lesson and reorder the political situation in northern China through military action. On July 27, they launched a major offensive that quickly took Tianjin and Beiping and continued to advance toward the west and south against ineffective Chinese resistance.

The Japanese hoped that their offensive would force the Chinese to concede defeat without expanding the war beyond northern China. Jiang Jieshi, on the other hand, thought opening a front in the Shanghai area offered China a chance to inflict heavy losses on the Japanese and possibly bring the United States and other western powers into the conflict on his side. In late July, he laid down a challenge to Japan by ordering his best German-trained divisions into the demilitarized zone that had been established west of Shanghai as part of the agreement to end heavy fighting between Japanese and Chinese forces in early 1932. The Japanese responded by sending more forces to Shanghai, and, after the Chinese air force tried to bomb Japanese naval vessels, on August 14 they launched a major attack. The Chinese fought fiercely and held their positions for nearly three months, but on November 5 the Japanese outflanked the Chinese defense line by conducting an amphibious landing on the north shore of Hangzhou Bay. Moving rapidly to the west in pursuit of the retreating Chinese, the Japanese captured Nanjing on December 13, and then began a shocking campaign of violence against the city's inhabitants.

During the autumn, the Japanese offered surrender terms to the Chinese government, but meeting their demands would have compromised Chinese sovereignty to such an extent that Jiang Jieshi had no alternative but to reject them. Before Nanjing fell he ordered the evacuation of the government to Chongqing, a city several hundred miles to the west of Nanjing. On December 17, he vowed to fight to the end. The Japanese thus faced a difficult situation. This unplanned war in China was tying down several hundred thousand soldiers and other military resources, and victory was not in sight.

For most of 1938 the Japanese continued trying to force a Chinese surrender through direct military action. Major operations that inflicted heavy losses on Chinese armies and greatly expanded the area under Japanese control were carried out. This strategy culminated in October after they seized Guangzhou (Canton), the major port in southern China, and Wuhan, the large city in central China that had become a symbol of resistance after the fall of Nanjing. In an attempt to limit the conflict in China and keep it from further undermining their grand strategy of preparing to win a war with the Soviet Union, the Japanese ended large-scale offensives. They instituted a blockade of the nationalist-controlled territory and turned their attention to governing the large part of China they now occupied.

Japan was never able to effectively implement this new strategy. Regarding the blockade of the nationalist-controlled area, in the summer of 1940 Japan was able to deepen the isolation of the nationalist government by getting France's Vichy government to shut down the railroad from Vietnam into China, and Great Britain to close the highway from Burma into China. However, after Japan signed the Tripartite Pact with Germany and Italy in September 1940, Britain decided to reopen the Burma Road and, after Japan cut this route by occupying Burma in early 1942, United States aid was still able to reach China by air from India. As far as governance was concerned, the Japanese achieved a political coup in March 1940 when they established a new National Government of China in Nanjing with the former second-ranking leader of the GMD, Wang Jingwei, as president. However, they never created an effective puppet-government political system because they could not bring themselves to give the Wang government or other puppet governments the authority and independence they needed to become, in the eyes of the Chinese people, legitimate representatives of Chinese interests in dealings with the Japanese. In addition, insufficient troop strength forced the Japanese to adopt a strategy of protecting cities and lines of communication and basically ignoring large areas of the countryside. Bereft of nationalist soldiers and local government officials because the Japanese invasion had driven them away, these areas became fertile ground for communist expansion and growth.

In large measure, from 1939 to the time of Japan's surrender to the Allied Powers in August 1945, the war between Japan and China took the form of a military stalemate. The only major offensive by the Japanese during those six years was Operation Ichi-Go, a campaign launched in the spring of 1944 with the aim of destroying American air bases in southern and southwestern China. As for Chinese military operations, the nationalists and communists never took their eyes off each other, even as they faced the

Japanese. Fighting between them during the war and preparations for the resumption of their conflict after Japan's defeat worked to reduce the military pressure they put on the Japanese.

Ironically, Japan's war with China facilitated communist preparation to face the nationalists in the coming Chinese civil war even as it weakened the nationalist government. Japan had invaded China, in part, to destroy communism. Yet, by driving the nationalist army out of large areas of China and creating widespread anger and a spirit of resistance among the rural population with its brutal behavior, the Japanese army created a situation that facilitated the mobilization of millions of Chinese by the communists. By the time the Japanese surrendered, communist strength vis-à-vis the nationalists was much greater than it had been in 1937. This war is significant in military history because of its scale, length, number of military and civilian casualties, and its brutality. It marked the end of a long period of Japanese expansion. But what is arguably the most consequential aspect of the war is how Japan inadvertently helped the communists establish the foundation for victory in the Chinese civil war of 1946–1949.

SEE ALSO: Chinese Civil War (Modern); World War II: War in Asia.

Further Reading

Boyle, J. (1972) *China and Japan at War, 1937–45: The Politics of Collaboration.* Stanford: Stanford University Press.

Ch'i, H. S. (1982) *Nationalist China at War: Military Defeats and Political Collapse, 1937–45.* Ann Arbor: University of Michigan Press.

Crowley, J. (1974) "Japan's Military Foreign Policies." In J. Morley (Ed.), *Japan's Foreign Policy, 1868–1941: A Research Guide.* New York: Columbia University Press.

Dorn, F. (1974) *The Sino-Japanese War, 1937–41: From Marco Polo Bridge to Pearl Harbor.* New York: Macmillan.

Harries, M. and Harries, S. (1991) *Soldiers of the Sun: The Rise and Fall of the Imperial Japanese Army.* New York: Random House.

Hsiung, J. and Levine, S. (1992) *China's Bitter Victory: The War with Japan, 1937–1945.* Armonk, NY: M. E. Sharpe.

Ienaga, S. (1978) *The Pacific War: World War II and the Japanese, 1931–1945.* New York: Pantheon Books.

Johnson, C. (1962) *Peasant Nationalism and Communist Power: The Emergence of Revolutionary China, 1937–1945.* Stanford: Stanford University Press.

Li, L. (1975) *The Japanese Army in North China 1937–1941: Problems of Political and Economic Control.* Tokyo: Oxford University Press.

MacKinnon, S. (2008) *Wuhan, 1938: War, Refugees, and the Making of Modern China.* Berkeley: University of California Press.

MacKinnon, S., Lary, D., and Vogel, E. (Eds.) (2007) *China at War: Regions of China 1937–1945.* Stanford: Stanford University Press.

Mao, Z. D. (1963) *Selected Military Writings of Mao Tse-tung.* Peking: Foreign Language Press.

Wilson, D. (1982) *When Tigers Fight: The Story of the Sino-Japanese War, 1937–1945.* New York: Viking.

Chinese Civil War (Modern)

GARY J. BJORGE

The war between the Guomindang (GMD/Nationalist Party) and the Gongchandang (CP/Communist Party) for control of China was a lengthy struggle that, during the years 1946–1949, became one of the major wars of the twentieth century, ranking just behind the two world wars in terms of scale, number of casualties, and political impact. The war also became significant as the original example of Mao Zedong's (Mao Tse-tung) approach to waging revolutionary war and overthrowing governmental power. By leading the CP to victory, Mao became the preeminent revolutionary war theorist of his time. His ideas inspired revolutionaries in many countries and the path he took to win the war became a model for them to follow.

The war began in 1927. The communists and the nationalists had been collaborating since January 1923 when the Comintern directed CP members to join the GMD. This collaboration, however, was fraught with tension from the beginning. GMD leaders quickly sensed that the communist goal was to subvert the GMD from within, but the need for Soviet aid kept them from breaking their relationship. In 1927, however, simmering disputes and suspicions reached boiling point and violent conflict

between the two parties broke out across large areas of China. In April, Jiang Jieshi (Chiang Kai-shek), at the time the commander in chief of the GMD's National Revolutionary Army, decided that before the communists moved against him, he would strike against them. He issued orders to purge all communists in Shanghai, Nanjing, and adjacent areas controlled by his force. This action eventually led to the revolt of communist-led army units and fighting between communist and nationalist units. Mao joined in this anti-Jiang movement by leading an unsuccessful peasant uprising against the GMD in Hunan province. In December he participated in the communists' seizure of Guangzhou. After three days, GMD forces retook the city and executed many communists, but Mao escaped. While Jiang was consolidating his power, Mao was fleeing to the remote Jinggang mountains along the Hunan–Jiangxi border.

In the Jinggang mountains, Mao began to implement his concept of revolutionary war. Contrary to orthodox Marxism, he envisioned the peasantry, not the urban proletariat, to be the best source of revolutionary energy. He believed that if the CP could mobilize and lead the peasants, it would become strong enough to eventually prevail over the GMD. His strategy and tactics owed much to the ancient military strategist Sun Zi (Sun Tzu): avoid strength; attack weakness; achieve information superiority; maneuver; prepare; acquire supplies, weapons, and manpower from the enemy; only fight battles you can win; and gain popular support through policies that benefit the masses. These were some of the ideas from Sun Zi's *The Art of War* that Mao used successfully. He emphasized study, analysis, and the need to understand the war situation as a whole. He was confident that if the CP moved forward carefully step by step it could organize the peasantry into a powerful revolutionary force.

Mao had little to start with in early 1928. Taking the desperate peasants, disillusioned intellectuals, and defeated soldiers who straggled into the mountains to avoid GMD retribution, he and Zhu De, an officer with a long record of military service in various armies, joined together to organize what they called the 4th Red Corps. Zhu was the commander and Mao was the political commissar. In total, the force numbered around 10,000, with about 2,000 men armed. With this small force, Mao started to mobilize and organize the peasantry and set up a rural base. To win over the peasants, he used his military to create some kind of economic benefit for the great majority of peasants and then pushed ideological education. This education process was facilitated by the establishment of organizations that involved most people in a village. In order to avoid placing a large economic burden on the peasants, while increasing the size and capability of his military, he implemented a three-tier organizational structure. In addition to the regular Red Army, two irregular military organizations, the Red Guards and "insurrectionary detachments," were established. They provided military capability while allowing their members to continue normal productive labor. In this way Mao gradually created the ability to defend his base area and expand it.

As Mao and Zhu increased the size of their military force, the CP leadership operating underground in the French Concession in Shanghai and their mentors in Moscow became fascinated by the possibilities it seemed to represent. In 1930, they decided to use this force in a campaign aimed at awakening the revolutionary consciousness of the urban proletariat by capturing cities. They ordered Mao and Zhu to lead their peasant force out of the mountains to attack Changsha, the capital of Hunan, and Wuhan. Changsha was taken and held for three days, but there was no proletarian uprising and the operation ended disastrously with heavy losses.

The attack on Changsha alerted the government in Nanjing to the dangers posed by the base area that Mao had established in Jiangxi. This GMD-dominated government had been established on October 10, 1928, with Jiang Jieshi as president. Nominally, it was a government that had ultimate authority across all of China. In reality, local warlords wielded power in many areas, foreign concessions were beyond its reach, and the Japanese were exerting immense pressure against it in Manchuria. Weak and struggling to become stronger, the government had limited resources to deal with the communist threat posed by Mao, but after the attacks in central China Jiang felt that he had no choice but to act. In December, he launched a bandit-suppression campaign to wipe out the communist menace once and for all.

Communist forces outmaneuvered the nationalist forces and this campaign quickly ended in failure. Three more campaigns launched during the next two years also failed because they had to be cut short to address threats posed by Japanese aggression. Finally, the fifth suppression campaign, which began in October 1933, did meet with success. Jiang massed around 700,000 troops and, in accordance with the advice of his German advisors, completely encircled the communist area and then progressively compressed it. This operational concept proved effective. To save themselves, on October 15, 1934, some 85,000 soldiers and 15,000 CP and government officials broke through nationalist lines and fled to the west.

During the period of the fifth bandit-suppression campaign, Mao Zedong's status as a leading CP figure was in eclipse. In mid-January 1935, however, at a Political Bureau meeting held at Zunyi in eastern Guizhou province, Mao and his supporters regained control of the CP. For the remainder of the civil war and beyond, Mao would be the dominant figure within the CP.

In October 1935, the remnants of the communist force that had departed southern Jiangxi a year earlier reached northern Shaanxi province. Only a small percentage of those who had started what eventually became the 6,000-mile Long March completed the harsh journey, and in their new base area they continued to face attempts by government forces to eradicate them. Then Japanese aggression against China again provided them with a respite. In December 1936, Jiang Jieshi was kidnapped in Xi'an by two generals who wanted to fight the Japanese instead of their fellow Chinese. As part of the terms for his release, Jiang agreed to work with the communists to resist Japan. His anti-communist campaign ended, and in February 1937 a communist delegation arrived in the Chinese capital, Nanjing, for the start of formal negotiations aimed at establishing a nationalist–communist united front against Japan.

After full-scale war between China and Japan began in July 1937, the nationalists and the communists reached a number of agreements on military collaboration. The main communist military force in Shaanxi province was reorganized and became the Eighth Route Army of the national army. Communist regular army units and guerrillas in the eight provinces of Henan, Hubei, Hunan, Guangdong, Jiangxi, Fujian, Zhejiang, and Anhui were reorganized as the New Fourth

Army of the national army. The government agreed to provide a monetary subsidy to the communist forces and supply them with a small quantity of ammunition. However, due to ideological differences and deep mistrust, cooperation had its limits. The communists refused to place their forces in the field under the operational command of national army officers and rebuffed national army requests to direct the training of their soldiers. In 1939, the government resumed the suppression of communist organizations and initiated a blockade of the communist areas. Fighting between nationalist and communist units began to occur. In 1940, the nationalists were so concerned about communist mobilization of peasants in the lower Yangzi River valley that they ordered the New Fourth Army to shift northward and operate in the Yellow River area. In January 1941, government forces attacked the New Fourth Army headquarters and attached units as they were preparing to cross the Yangzi and killed several thousand soldiers. This incident drew international attention and all but ended the united front.

The reality was that no matter how hard it tried, the government could not successfully counter the growth in communist activity and influence that the Japanese invasion made possible. Japanese offensives in northern and central China during 1937 and 1938 captured most major cities and the railroads between them. They also created vast areas that were open to communist infiltration because nationalist forces and governmental officials had withdrawn. Mao saw the opportunities that lay before him and ordered his army into these areas to conduct political mobilization and establish base areas. This work was greatly facilitated by the brutality of the Japanese army. Japanese behavior forced the peasants into a spirit of resistance and made it easy for the communists to organize them into military organizations and establish CP-dominated political structures. During the war, the communists did not attempt to initiate class struggle in rural villages. There was no need to stir up a mass movement to build support for them when Japanese army depredations were producing this effect. Not wanting to weaken their position as leaders of all Chinese people in the fight against Japan, the communists implemented a modest rent-reduction/interest-reduction program that did

not drastically threaten anyone's economic livelihood. They emphasized political indoctrination, developed mass organizations, and greatly increased the size of their military forces. What they achieved was amazing. In 1937, the communists had about 80,000 soldiers and controlled an area with approximately 1.5 million inhabitants. In 1945, they governed nearly 100 million people and had around one million regulars and two million militiamen.

This was a great increase in strength vis-à-vis the nationalists. Furthermore, it had been achieved through the principles of self-reliance, self-sufficiency, and acquiring material from the enemy. The communists, in other words, had built their formidable war machine on a relatively simple and stable economic foundation. They also had a strong political system in place. On both counts, the nationalists became weaker as the war progressed. Ineffective political and military leadership, weak government administration, and deepening economic problems hampered the war effort against Japan and made it harder to compete against the communists. An egregious example of GMD incompetence occurred during the Henan famine of 1943–1944. Many thousands starved to death because officials failed to meet their responsibilities. Resentment toward the government among the peasantry was so great that when the Japanese launched an offensive in Henan in the spring of 1944, the peasants rose up and disarmed 50,000 nationalist soldiers rather than let them requisition livestock and food for the war effort.

After the Japanese attacked Pearl Harbor on December 7, 1941, the United States became involved in the civil war by providing military aid to the Chinese government. Also, after Japan's surrender on August 14, 1945, the United States helped the nationalists regain the major cities of eastern China by landing marines to occupy the Tianjin–Beiping area and transporting hundreds of thousands of nationalist soldiers from southwestern China into the areas still occupied by the Japanese. At the same time, the US tried to promote a political resolution of GMD–CP differences. In August 1945, the US ambassador to China flew to Yenan, the communist capital, and escorted Mao Zedong back to Chongqing for negotiations with Jiang Jieshi. In late 1945, President Truman sent General George C.

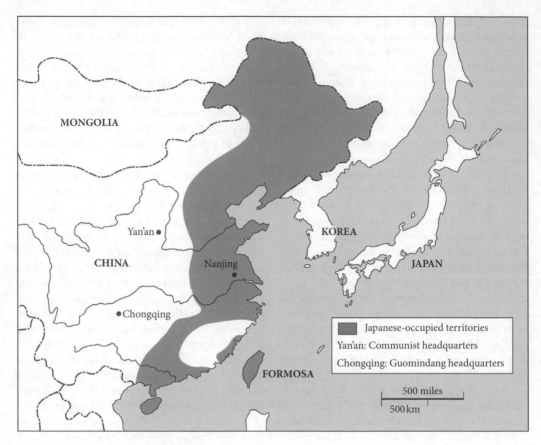

Map 12   Guomindang and the Japanese occupation.

Marshall to China to act as a mediator. Nothing the United States did, however, could stop the slide toward full-scale civil war.

Fighting between nationalist and communist forces had broken out after the Japanese surrender as both sides rushed to seize as much territory from the Japanese as possible. The situation was especially acute in the race for Manchuria and, despite Marshall's efforts to establish an effective ceasefire, the fighting there intensified in the spring of 1946. Both sides were confident that they would prevail on the battlefield and in July 1946 all-out war began.

Initially, because of their 3:1 advantage in regular troop strength and the combat power of divisions trained and equipped by the United States during World War II, the nationalists achieved a series of victories. However, they failed to destroy any sizable communist force or achieve any decisive results. After one year

their offensive was reaching a culmination point. They had been unable to fully replace battlefield losses and were stretched to the limit with few reserves.

During 1947 the communists seized the strategic initiative. They delivered their first strategic counterblow in the spring in Manchuria when Lin Biao sent the large army he had created using Japanese weapons and tens of thousands of former Manchukuo troops into the field. In a series of battles, he isolated the major nationalist troop concentrations from each other. In late summer 1947, Liu Bocheng and Deng Xiaoping broke through the nationalist defense line along the Yellow River, dropped their logistics line of communication to their Shandong base area, and marched to the Dabie mountains, 300 miles away in southwestern Anhui. There they started mobilizing the masses and building new rural bases in a strategic area close to the Yangzi River and the major cities of

Wuhan and Nanjing. This maneuver forced the nationalists to redeploy their forces, weakened their offensive capability, and created more areas of vulnerability. In addition, governmental misman- agement and corruption was sapping support for the government. Very high inflation was weaken- ing the economy. Looking at the war situation as a whole, the outlook was in the communists' favor.

The year of decision in the war was 1948. After conducting successful large-scale mobile operations during the summer, the communists launched three large campaigns during the fall. These were the Liao-Shen campaign in Manchuria, the Huai-Hai campaign in eastern central China, and the Ping-Jin campaign in the Beiping–Tianjin area. All three produced great communist victo- ries. In the space of about four months the nation- alists lost over a million troops and virtually all of their positions north of the Yangzi River.

On April 21, 1949, communist forces attacked across the Yangzi on a 500-km front centered about 100 km west of Nanjing. Nanjing was taken on 23 April, Hangzhou on 3 May, and Shanghai on 27 May. In early May, troops transferred from Manchuria opened a new front in the Wuhan area. During the next several months the com- munist armies continued to advance against little opposition, and on October 1, 1949, with most of China under communist control, Mao Zedong proclaimed the establishment of the People's Republic of China (PRC). Roughly 22 years after Jiang Jieshi's forces had sent Mao and other com- munists fleeing to the Jinggang mountains, Mao Zedong had forced Jiang and others to seek safety across the sea on Taiwan.

After 1949 the civil war became a form of stale- mate. During the 1950s, the PRC launched attacks against various nationalist-held offshore islands and captured several of them. However, Taiwan could not be reached. Over the years, Taiwan became a multi-party democracy and, for the first eight years of the twenty-first century, the presi- dent of Taiwan belonged to a party other than the CP's former civil war foe, the GMD. What the future holds is unclear. Taiwan is a *de facto* independent country, but the CP regime in Beijing remains unwilling to accept a *de jure* independent Taiwan. It also refuses to rule out a military attack against the island. Sixty years after the founding of the PRC, the last chapter of this civil war remains to be written.

SEE ALSO: China, Invasion of (1931, 1937–1945); World War II: War in Asia.

Further Reading

Benton, G. (1992) *Mountain Fires: The Red Army's Three-Year War in South China, 1934–1938*. Berkeley: University of California Press.

Bjorge, G. (2005) *Moving the Enemy: Operational Art in the Chinese PLA's Huai Hai Campaign*. Ft. Leavenworth, KS: Combat Studies Institute Press.

Donovan, P. (1976) *The Red Army in Kiangsi, 1931–1934*. Ithaca: China–Japan Program, Cornell University.

Johnson, C. (1962) *Peasant Nationalism and Communist Power: The Emergence of Revolutionary China, 1937–1945*. Stanford: Stanford University Press.

Klein, D. and Clark, A. (1971) *Biographic Dictionary of Chinese Communism, 1921–1965*. Cambridge, MA: Harvard University Press.

Mao, Z. D. (1967) *Selected Works of Mao Tse-tung*. Peking: Foreign Language Press.

Pepper, S. (1980) *Civil War in China: The Political Struggle, 1945–1949*. Berkeley: University of California Press.

Salisbury, H. (1985) *The Long March: The Untold Story*. New York: Harper and Row.

Smedley, A. (1956) *The Great Road: The Life and Times of Chu Teh*. New York: Monthly Review Press.

Van de Ven, H. (2003) *War and Nationalism in China, 1925–1945*. New York: Routledge Curzon.

Wei, W. (1985) *Counterrevolution in China: The Nationalists in Jiangxi during the Soviet Period*. Ann Arbor: University of Michigan Press.

Whitson, W. with Huang, C. H. (1973) *The Chinese High Command: A History of Communist Military Politics, 1927–71*. New York: Praeger.

Combat Film

JAMES CHAPMAN

What is a "war film"? In the film industry the term was first used to describe films set during the American Civil War, such as *The Birth of a Nation* (dir. D. W. Griffith, 1915), and reflects the fact that this was the first major war to be the sub- ject of dramatic representation in film. (For a critical taxonomy of "war films," see Neale 2000: 125–133.) The term also came to be applied to actuality films of World War I, such as *The Battle of the Somme* (dir. Geoffrey Malins and J. B.

McDowell, 1916), and later to fiction films, such as *All Quiet on the Western Front* (dir. Lewis Milestone, 1930), that presented a harrowing account of the experience of the trenches. In fact, the war film – like other genres such as *film noir* or melodrama – is one that has no fixed boundaries. Film critics and historians disagree on the parameters of the genre. R. E. Shain, for example, avers that war films "do not have to be situated in combat zones" and that they may deal "with the roles of civilians, espionage agents, and soldiers in any of the aspects of war (i.e. preparation, cause, prevention, conduct, daily life, and consequences or aftermath)" (Shain 1976: 20). Under this definition we would include films about the experiences of prisoners of war, such as *La Grande Illusion* (dir. Jean Renoir, 1937), and home-front dramas, such as *Mrs. Miniver* (dir. William Wyler, 1942) and *Millions Like Us* (dir. Frank Launder and Sidney Gilliat, 1943).

Other commentators, however, have suggested that such inclusive definitions are rather too vague and propose a more specific category that focuses directly on the military conduct of war. Jeanine Basinger, in her study of American films of World War II, prefers the term "combat film" to describe films that concern groups of servicemen engaged in fighting and that excludes films not involving combat. She also argues for a historically based understanding of genre that sees the emergence of certain narrative conventions and visual motifs as being culturally and historically specific. To this end she suggests that the combat film was a product of the industrial and ideological conditions of World War II: "World War II gave birth to the isolation of a story pattern which came to be known and recognized as the combat genre, whether it is ultimately set in World War II, in the Korean War, or in Vietnam, or inside some other genre such as the Western" (Basinger 2003: 13). This chapter examines the history of the combat film, focusing specifically on the American film industry where the genre took shape.

World War II and the Emergence of the Combat Film

The emergence of the combat film needs to be understood in the context of the propaganda imperatives of the US government following its entry into World War II. The Office of War Information (OWI) was set up in June 1942 under the direction of Elmer Davies. The OWI in turn had a Bureau of Motion Pictures, run by ex-newspapermen Lowell Mallett and Nelson Poynter, whose role was to act as liaison between the War Department and the film industry. The relationship between the OWI and the Hollywood studios was not without some friction. When the OWI threatened to become interventionist by demanding approval of scripts – this was motivated by its dissatisfaction with the film industry's early attempts at war propaganda – there was an outcry in Hollywood and the OWI was forced to back down. By 1943 the OWI had established a good working relationship with the studios that proved mutually beneficial. The OWI was able to see the sort of films it wanted made, while the studios, for their part, realized that working with the OWI rather than against it could work to their advantage as audiences were hungry for war-themed entertainment and war films tended to be profitable.

While war propaganda found its way into most genres, including spy films, detective films, comedies, and even musicals, the combat film was a new genre mandated by the OWI. It was the ideal form for articulating messages such as "why we fight" (an essential theme of US propaganda given the strong isolationist sentiment that had prevailed right up to Pearl Harbor) and for instilling faith in the strength of America's armed forces. The combat film also stressed unity of purpose (a recurring narrative convention is the heterogeneous social group – army platoon, submarine crew, jungle patrol, air crew – who overcome their personal differences for the common cause) and showed that war would not be a painless experience (usually at least one sympathetic member of the group will die in battle). However, it took some time for these conventions to take shape. Hollywood's early efforts at war propaganda had been films like *A Yank in the RAF* (dir. Henry King, 1941) – actually in production before the United States entered the war – and *Eagle Squadron* (dir. Arthur Lubin, 1942) that mixed romantic melodrama with sensational heroics. They were successful at the box office, largely because they were among the first war subjects, no matter how heavily fictionalized, but it soon became apparent that audiences (and the OWI) preferred a more realistic treatment.

Basinger argues that the conventions of the combat film began to emerge in a number of films released in 1942 – including *Desperate Journey* (dir. Raoul Walsh), *Flying Tigers* (dir. David Miller), and *Wake Island* (dir. John Farrow) – and had become firmly established by 1943 in films such as *Air Force* (dir. Howard Hawks), *Action in the North Atlantic* (dir. Lloyd Bacon), *Guadalcanal Diary* (dir. Lewis Seiler), *Bataan* (dir. Tay Garnett), and *Sahara* (dir. Zoltan Korda). In these films we see the emergence of the main conventions: the focus on a small combat unit tasked with a specific military objective, the preparation for combat, tensions within the group that are overcome by shared experiences, the death of one or more members of the group, and the climax in which the objective is secured. The recurring motifs include the presence of an observer or commentator (often a war correspondent or someone keeping a diary), the prominence of rituals of service life (receiving mail, cleaning weapons), and patriotic music (typically "Halls of Montezuma" sung by a male chorus). Several films were based on actual battles (*Wake Island*, *Guadalcanal Diary*, *Bataan*), while others were representative of particular theaters of war (*Action in the North Atlantic*, *Air Force*, *Sahara*). All these films were strongly patriotic in tone and, while they acknowledged the fact of death, it was invariably presented as a heroic sacrifice in a just and righteous cause.

Another cycle of combat films in 1944–1945 – including *They Were Expendable* (dir. John Ford, 1944), *Objective: Burma!* (dir. Raoul Walsh, 1945), *The Story of G.I. Joe* (dir. William Wellman, 1945), and *A Walk in the Sun* (dir. Lewis Milestone, 1945) – represent what Basinger describes as the "mature" combat film in that they "reflect a realism that is still based on the war itself but that has taken on an increasingly distanced presentation" (Basinger 2003: 136). These films are less assertively patriotic than some of the earlier films and suggest a greater level of psychological realism in their characterization of men in battle. Combat is a grim business and the mood is somber rather than upbeat. *Objective: Burma!* is a good example. The content of this film has been entirely overshadowed by the controversy it provoked when it was released in Britain: the British press objected loudly to a film which, in their eyes, had Errol Flynn and a platoon of Yanks winning the war in Burma without any reference to the role of the British Fourteenth Army (Jarvie 1981). However, this was a grossly unfair reaction to a film that is far from the fictitious farrago that its detractors claimed. *Objective: Burma!* was based on the activities of American special operations units in Burma such as Brigadier General Frank Merrill's 5307th Provisional Regiment, and far from suggesting that the Yanks won the war in Burma, it focuses on a single patrol with limited tactical objectives. Moreover, *Objective: Burma!* offers a realistic representation of the physical hardships of jungle warfare – the platoon is decimated by a combination of Japanese attacks and disease – and acknowledges the human cost of war in that many of the men die. The film ends with Flynn's Captain Nelson holding the dog tags of his men killed during the mission and saying: "Here's what it cost." By 1945 the need for pro-war propaganda had passed, and the combat film could afford a more somber tone.

The contemporary response to these films suggests that they were understood to be highly realistic in their representation of the combat experience. We may take the reviews of Bosley Crowther, senior film critic of the *New York Times*, as a barometer of critical taste. He admired *Wake Island* for its "harsh and bitter detail" and found it "a realistic picture about heroes who do not pose as such." *Bataan* was "a picture about war in true and ugly detail." *They Were Expendable* demonstrated "complete authenticity" in its representation of the war in the Pacific. *Objective: Burma!* "achieved a startling degree of realism … the whole picture has a strong documentary quality." And *The Story of G.I. Joe* "has all the integrity and the uncompromising reality of those other great pictorial documents of the Second World War, *The True Glory*, *Desert Victory* and *The Battle of San Pietro*" (*New York Times*, September 2, 1942, p. 9; June 4, 1943, p. 17; January 27, 1945, p. 15; December 21, 1945, p. 24; October 6, 1945, p. 9). For Crowther, then, by the end of the war the fictional combat film had achieved a level of realism that put it alongside combat documentaries compiled from actuality footage.

The Development of the Combat Film after World War II

The World War II combat film remained a major genre of American cinema for two decades after the end of the war itself. On one level its persistence demonstrates the success of the formula that had emerged during the war. Some post-war combat films, such as *Sands of Iwo Jima* (dir. Allan Dwan, 1949) and *Merrill's Marauders* (dir. Samuel Fuller, 1962), are virtually indistinguishable (except, in the latter case, for its color cinematography) from the films being produced at the end of the war. Realism continued to be the yardstick for critics. Crowther felt that *Sands of Iwo Jima* was a film of "savage realism." *Battleground* (dir. William Wellman, 1949) was "witheringly authentic" and *Attack!* (dir. Robert Aldrich, 1956) was "a ruthlessly realistic drama." *Halls of Montezuma* (dir. Lewis Milestone, 1951) was "a remarkably real and agonizing demonstration of the horribleness of war" (*New York Times*, December 31, 1949, p. 9; November 12, 1949, p. 8; September 20, 1956, p. 29; January 6, 1951, p. 9). As the combat film no longer needed to fulfill a propagandist role, filmmakers were able to go to greater lengths of realism in their representation of war.

The Korean War (1950–1953) prompted a cycle of combat films that simply transposed the conventions of the World War II films to Korea. These included *The Steel Helmet* (dir. Samuel Fuller, 1951), *Battle Zone* (dir. Lesley Selander, 1952), *Retreat, Hell!* (dir. Joseph H. Lewis, 1952), *The Glory Brigade* (dir. Robert D. Webb, 1953), and *Pork Chop Hill* (dir. Lewis Milestone, 1959). Stylistically these films were similar to the mature World War II combat film in that they allowed space for discussing the ethics of war and suggested a degree of detachment and even cynicism about the conduct of war. There is an ideological imperative at work of course – communism is now the faceless enemy rather than National Socialism or Japanese militarism – but Basinger contends that the Korean War variant was also responding to other issues prevailing in American society. She suggests that "the Korean films present a grab bag of current ideological and social problems that might be on the minds of people in the 1950s audience:

communism, race relations, the morality of killing, juvenile delinquency, divorce, and family conflict" (Basinger 2003: 161). The platoon in *The Steel Helmet*, for example, includes both an African American and a Japanese American, whose presence is used to explore racial prejudice, while *The Bridges at Toko-Ri* (dir. Mark Robson, 1955) is a combination of the combat film and the family melodrama that examines how absence on combat tours affects the domestic lives of pilots and their wives.

From the mid-1950s the combat film began to fracture into several different lineages. While most wartime films had featured archetypal characters rather than "real" people – the imperative of wartime propaganda had been to project the common experience of combatants rather than tales of individual heroics – the war "biopic" based on true stories reemerged in the 1950s in films such as *To Hell and Back* (dir. Jesse Hibbs, 1956) and *Battle Hymn* (dir. Douglas Sirk, 1957). *Battle Hymn* was a biopic of United States Army Air Forces Colonel Dean Hess, the "flying parson" who accidentally bombed a school during World War II and atones by setting up an orphanage in Korea. *To Hell and Back* was a biopic of Audie Murphy, America's most decorated soldier, who won 28 combat honors including the Congressional Medal of Honor and was credited with killing or capturing 240 German soldiers in North Africa and Europe. In a bizarre merging of fact and fiction, Murphy, who after the war became a movie actor starring mainly in low-budget westerns, plays himself. The war biopic reached its apotheosis in *Patton* (dir. Franklin J. Schaffner, 1970), for which George C. Scott won an Academy Award for his performance as the controversial, vainglorious general.

Patton can also be placed in a lineage of big-budget films based on the events of World War II that flourished in the 1960s and 1970s. The prototype for these films was Darryl F. Zanuck's *The Longest Day* (dir. Andrew Marton, Ken Annakin, and Bernhard Wicki, 1962), a reconstruction of the D-Day landings that told the story from the perspective of each of the combatant nations (America, Britain, Germany, France). Zanuck assembled an all-star cast (including John Wayne, Robert Mitchum, Henry Fonda, Robert Ryan, Richard Burton, Richard Todd, Peter Lawford,

Kenneth More, Robert Wagner, Jeffrey Hunter, and Curt Jurgens) and shot on location in Normandy (Ambrose 1996). *The Longest Day* was shot in black and white (at a time when color had become the standard) in order to approximate the documentary-realist style of wartime films. It was an enormous box-office success and prompted several other epic reconstructions of key battles of World War II, including *Battle of the Bulge* (dir. Ken Annakin, 1965), *Anzio* (dir. Edward Dmytryk, 1968), *Battle of Britain* (dir. Guy Hamilton, 1969), *Tora! Tora! Tora!* (dir. Richard Fleischer, 1970), *Midway* (dir. Jack Smight, 1976), and *A Bridge Too Far* (dir. Richard Attenborough, 1977). These films shared similar conventions: they attempted to present a balanced account of historical events that included the perspectives of all sides involved and they cast big stars as major characters in order to help audiences understand the complex narratives.

The big-budget international reconstruction emerged in parallel with another type of combat film: what I have termed elsewhere the "men on a mission" movie (Chapman 2008: 204–227). These were a cycle of noisy war-adventure films with an emphasis on visual spectacle and violent action. Unlike the historical war epics they made no pretense to realism, though occasionally, as in *The Guns of Navarone* (dir. J. Lee Thompson, 1961), there was space for a discussion of the ethical conduct of war. Perhaps the key film in this cycle was *The Dirty Dozen* (dir. Robert Aldrich, 1967). In this film a group of US servicemen facing execution or long prison terms for a range of serious crimes including murder and rape are offered pardons if they volunteer for a suicide mission. The "dirty dozen" are recruited and trained by the tough Maj. Reisman (Lee Marvin), who transforms a group of ill-adjusted misfits into a crack commando unit. The actual mission – to assassinate a group of high-ranking German staff officers the night before D-Day – is a coda to the film. *The Dirty Dozen* was a major box-office hit, but it prompted controversy for a sequence in which Reisman orders his men to pour petrol through the air vents of an underground bunker where the wives and aides of the German officers have taken shelter and then to throw in hand grenades. It is an entirely gratuitous act: the prisoners have been confined and represent no threat to the success of the mission. Film critic Stephen Farber concluded his review with the suggestion that "the war being fought in the movie, though it is called World War II, is really the Vietnam War" (Farber 1967–1968).

The success of *The Dirty Dozen* prompted a cycle of violent, cynical combat films in which the nominal heroes were characterized as much as criminals as they were soldiers. *Play Dirty* (dir. André de Toth, 1969) even made this parallel explicit when the colonel in charge of an irregular unit declares: "War is a criminal enterprise and I fight it with criminals." Other variations on this formula were *The Devil's Brigade* (dir. Andrew V. McLaglen, 1968) and *Too Late the Hero* (dir. Robert Aldrich, 1970). *Kelly's Heroes* (dir. Brian G. Hutton, 1970) – a follow-up to the same director's *Where Eagles Dare* (1969) with the same star (Clint Eastwood) – combined the war film with the crime caper as Private Kelly leads a motley group to rob gold bullion from a bank behind enemy lines. With its references to the spaghetti western (as Eastwood and his co-stars Telly Savalas and Donald Sutherland face off against a German Tiger tank) and to the hippy counterculture, *Kelly's Heroes* demonstrates that by this time the content and style of the World War II combat film had been transformed out of all recognition from the genre that emerged 25 years earlier.

The Vietnam War Film

The combat film was radically transformed by the Vietnam War. There was, in fact, only one major film about Vietnam during the war itself. *The Green Berets* (dir. John Wayne, 1968) was a patriotic epic endorsing the role of the US military in the campaign against the Vietcong. Based on Robin Moore's 1965 bestseller about the activities of US Special Forces in Vietnam, *The Green Berets* was produced by Wayne's own company, Batjac Productions, with the cooperation of the US Department of Defense, which provided military hardware and some 250 army personnel for the film. Wayne saw it as a vehicle for inspiring "a patriotic spirit" among Americans and to explain to the world "why it is necessary for us to be there" (quoted in Shaw 2007: 211). *The Green Berets* represents nothing if not a throwback to the propaganda films of 1942–1943, directly transposing the conventions of the World War II combat film to Vietnam. Its politics are highly simplistic (Americans are unequivocally good, the Vietcong unequivocally bad), and, rather like Wayne's other major directorial effort, *The Alamo* (1960), it features several scenes where characters deliver long propagandizing speeches. It was derided by the critics, who focused on its ponderous narrative, lethargic direction, and clichéd script, not to mention the improbable casting of the 61-year-old Wayne as a Special Forces colonel, but it was a major box-office success that grossed $11 million in America and $9 million overseas. When it was shown to servicemen in Vietnam, however, it was reportedly met with derision for its unrealistic representation of war and its unintentionally funny moments (Shaw 2007: 220–224).

Apart from this one aberration (albeit, it must be stressed, one that was popular at the time), Hollywood's response to the Vietnam War was tardy. The war was absent from screens until the late 1970s. That said, westerns such as *Soldier Blue* (dir. Ralph Nelson, 1970) and *Little Big Man* (dir. Arthur Penn, 1970) have been understood as Vietnam allegories, while the moral confusion of the war was reflected in the satirical comedies *M*A*S*H* (dir. Robert Altman, 1970) and *Catch 22* (dir. Mike Nichols, 1970), set, respectively, in Korea and World War II. It was only after the last US troops had been withdrawn in 1975 that Hollywood felt able to address the Vietnam War directly. *Go Tell the Spartans* (dir. Ted Post, 1978) and *Apocalypse Now* (dir. Francis Ford Coppola, 1979) were the first Vietnam combat films. The latter, which adopted the basic narrative of Joseph Conrad's novella *Heart of Darkness*, was intended by Coppola as "a film experience that would give its audience a sense of the horror, the madness, the sensuousness, and the moral dilemma of the Vietnam War" (quoted in Hagen 1983: 231). Critics admired *Apocalypse Now* for its cinematography and its brilliant set pieces, particularly the helicopter attack on a Vietcong village overlaid with Wagner's "Ride of the Valkyries," though they felt that its narrative – as Captain Willard (Martin Sheen) is sent to "terminate with extreme prejudice" the rogue Colonel

Kurtz (Marlon Brando) – was too disjointed and its conclusion incoherent.

The Vietnam films that followed *Apocalypse Now* fall into two distinct groups. The first group – exemplified by *Missing in Action* (dir. Joseph Zito, 1984) and its sequels and the hugely successful *Rambo: First Blood Part II* (dir. George Pan Cosmatos, 1985) – exemplify what have been called "the politics of Reaganite entertainment" (Maltby 1985: 385). These films can be seen as part of an ideological project to erase the memory of America's defeat in Vietnam through narratives in which elite Special Forces return to rescue "MIAs": servicemen reported "missing in action" whom sections of the American media claimed were still being held in prison camps in Vietnam. Thus cartoonish characters such as Braddock (Chuck Norris) and Rambo (Sylvester Stallone) are dispatched to Vietnam where they reassert American pride and military might. As Rambo remarks when offered the chance to return to Vietnam: "Do we get to win this time?" These films can also be seen as an attempt to rehabilitate the reputation of the Vietnam veteran that had suffered in the wake of My Lai and other incidents. *Rambo*, in particular, was attacked in some quarters for its ideologically reactionary politics, though as a film it is a rather more satisfying experience than *Apocalypse Now*. *Rambo* adheres closely to the conventions of the action adventure – *The Last of the Mohicans* in particular is a point of reference – and lacks the pretentiousness of Coppola's overblown epic.

A second group of films in the later 1980s – *Platoon* (dir. Oliver Stone, 1986), *Full Metal Jacket* (dir. Stanley Kubrick, 1987), *Hamburger Hill* (dir. John Irvin, 1987), and *Casualties of War* (dir. Brian de Palma, 1989) – collectively represent a more realistic version of the Vietnam War. Indeed, the critical reception of these films recalls the vocabulary used to describe the combat films of the 1940s and 1950s. Thus *Platoon* was described as "brutal, vicious, surpassingly ugly – in a word realistic," while *Hamburger Hill* was "the most realistic portrayal of the Vietnam War ever filmed" (Gates 2005: 299). The realism of these films to some extent reflected actual experiences of Vietnam. Oliver Stone had served in Vietnam, as had James Carabatsos, screenwriter of *Hamburger Hill*. *Full Metal Jacket* also aspired to a level of authenticity through the casting of a former drill instructor, R. Lee Ermey, as the sadistic and foul-mouthed Gunnery Sergeant Hartman.

These films entirely subvert the conventions of the World War II combat film. While the World War II films demonstrate unity among Americans to face a common enemy, the Vietnam films focus on conflict within the unit. The most schematic example is *Platoon*, where the Americans are literally fighting among themselves: the "good" sergeant Elias (Willem Dafoe) is shot and killed by the "bad" sergeant Barnes (Tom Berenger). Unlike the World War II films, which usually have a distinct sense of time and place, the Vietnam films seem to detach the war from its historical context. One reviewer wrote that *Platoon* "seems hermetically sealed off from history, taking place in a self-contained dramatic world" (*Monthly Film Bulletin*, 639 [April 1987]: 123). The sense of being outside history is accentuated by the loose and fragmentary narratives in contrast to the usually tightly structured World War II combat films: *Hamburger Hill* consists of a series of "contacts" that seem random and unconnected. The most significant feature of these films, however, is that they show American servicemen committing what amount to war crimes. *Platoon* features a sequence in which US soldiers, angered by the death of one of their comrades, terrorize a village, shooting and beating the inhabitants, while *Casualties of War* revolves around the rape and murder of a Vietnamese girl by an American platoon.

Full Metal Jacket represents the apotheosis of the cycle. Stanley Kubrick had already made one of the outstanding anti-war films, *Paths of Glory* (1957): *Full Metal Jacket* takes up the earlier film's condemnation of the futility of war and the inhumanity of militarism. What particularly distinguishes *Full Metal Jacket* is that it considers not only the war itself but also the process of training and indoctrination that turns men into killers. The first part of the film is set at the US Marine boot camp at Parris Island, South Carolina, where a group of new recruits are subjected to the brutal training regime of Sergeant Hartman, whose methods include both verbal and physical abuse. A parallel is drawn between military training and ideological indoctrination: the men are taught to love their rifles and to hate the enemy. One recruit, the overweight "Private Pyle" (Hartman renames the recruits according to his whim), is victimized for his failure to meet the physical demands of training and is bullied by the others when they are punished for his shortcomings. The film suggests that the training process is even more brutalizing and dehumanizing than the experience of war itself. When the action shifts to Vietnam, Kubrick offers a commentary not only on war but also on the war film: a documentary crew interviews men on camera for "Vietnam – The Movie" and "Private Joker" (Matthew Modine) impersonates John Wayne. These and other sequences have led film historian Thomas Doherty to argue that *Full Metal Jacket* represents Vietnam as a "cinematic, not historical, experience … a cinematic usurpation of the historical record that reaffirms the vital cultural function of genre" (Doherty 1988–1989: 24). In other words, we have come to understand the Vietnam War through the conventions of the Vietnam film rather than in its own right.

Saving Private Ryan and the Revival of the Combat Film

The idea that the combat film has reached a stage in its history where its points of reference are not war itself but rather other combat films is illustrated by the film that revived the genre in the late 1990s: *Saving Private Ryan* (dir. Steven Spielberg, 1998). Following the end of the Vietnam cycle in 1989, the combat film had been moribund for the best part of a decade. The conventions of the combat film were transferred into other genres, particularly science fiction films such as *Aliens* (dir. James Cameron, 1986), *Independence Day* (dir. Roland Emmerich, 1996), and *Starship Troopers* (dir. Paul Verhoeven, 1997). However, the success of *Saving Private Ryan*, which grossed over $480 million worldwide, signaled a new wave of combat films including *The Thin Red Line* (dir. Terrence Malick, 1998), *Three Kings* (dir. David O. Russell, 1999), *Enemy at the Gates* (dir. Jean-Jacques Annaud, 2001), *Black Hawk Down* (dir. Ridley Scott, 2001), *We Were Soldiers* (dir. Wallace Randall, 2002), *Windtalkers* (dir. John Woo, 2002), and *Flags of Our Fathers* (dir. Clint Eastwood,

2006). The cycle includes films about Vietnam (*We Were Soldiers*), the First Gulf War (*Three Kings*), and the US intervention in Somalia (*Black Hawk Down*) as well as World War II. It was Spielberg's film, however, that had the greatest popular and critical success.

Critical commentary on *Saving Private Ryan* has focused almost exclusively on its representation of the Omaha beach landings – a sequence that is held to have set new standards of realism for the combat film. The film has been described as "Hollywood's most grimly realistic and historically accurate depiction of a World II battlefield" (Landon 1998: 58). Spielberg and his production team went to extraordinary lengths to ensure visual and aural realism. Thus, to simulate the noise of bullets ripping apart flesh, the sound editor recorded live rounds being fired into meat carcasses wrapped in cloth (using the same caliber ammunition as used in 1944), and cinematographer Janusz Kaminski used desaturated colors to replicate the "look" of color combat footage. Yet *Saving Private Ryan* is significant for other reasons too. On one level it can be seen as part of an ideological project to reclaim the memory of World War II as "the good war" in response to the cycle of critical Vietnam movies (Auster 2002). The framing device of *Saving Private Ryan* is a Normandy veteran (later revealed to be James Ryan) returning to pay his respects to fallen comrades. In using this device, *Saving Private Ryan* can be located in the culture of remembrance and commemoration: its aim is to honor the memory of a generation of young Americans who died "on the altar of freedom."

The sheer visceral impact of the Omaha beach sequence – comprising some 24 minutes of a film with a total running time of 163 minutes – entirely overshadows the rest of the film. Following the Omaha sequence, *Saving Private Ryan* adopts the conventions of the patrol movie as Captain Miller (Tom Hanks) and his socially diverse platoon are sent on an extraction mission to find Private Ryan (Matt Damon) – believed to be the only survivor of four brothers – and bring him home. The patrol movie has been a staple of the genre since *A Walk in the Sun*, to which *Saving Private Ryan* includes several narrative and visual references. So many of the conventions of the combat film are employed in *Saving Private Ryan*, indeed, that it becomes a virtual compendium of the genre. The allusions to other films are too many to list in their entirety: a few examples will suffice. The screen-filling image of the Stars and Stripes that opens and closes the film brings to mind *Patton*. The beach assault and the burning of enemy pillboxes with flamethrowers recalls *Sands of Iwo Jima*. The soldier who loses his rifle on the beach and the breaching of the German defenses with bangalore torpedoes (long tubes packed with explosives) are both borrowed from *The Longest Day*. The characterization of Captain Miller is modeled on Captain Wilson (Robert Mitchum) in *The Story of G.I. Joe*, who similarly dies at the end of the film, while Southern sharpshooter Private Jackson bears affinities with the protagonist of *Sergeant York* (dir. Howard Hawks, 1941) and with a similar character in *Kelly's Heroes*. While the story of *Saving Private Ryan* is fictional, there were several instances during World War II of brothers killed in action: the most famous were the Sullivan brothers, who all perished when the USS *Juneau* was sunk in the Pacific. Their story was dramatized in *The Sullivans* (dir. Lloyd Bacon, 1944), from which *Saving Private Ryan* borrows the scene of the men's mother receiving the telegram informing her of their deaths.

What this suggests is that the frame of reference for *Saving Private Ryan* was not so much World War II itself but rather the history of the World War II combat film. This is not, perhaps, difficult to understand. The vast majority of cinemagoers in the late 1990s would have no personal memory of the war and in most cases no experience of combat. Their frame of reference would, instead, be other films they had seen on television. *The Longest Day*, for example, has become a television staple, usually screened to coincide with the anniversary of the Normandy landings. In a broader sense this illustrates how the experience of combat has come to be mediated through cinema. What the success of *Saving Private Ryan* demonstrates is how the popular memory of World War II has been kept alive for a generation who did not experience it through the medium of the combat film.

SEE ALSO: War and Cinema; War Photography; War Poetry; War Propaganda.

References

Ambrose, S. E. (1996) "*The Longest Day*: 'Blockbuster' History." In John Whiteclay Chambers II and David Culbert (Eds.), *World War II, Film and History*. New York: Oxford University Press, pp. 97–106.

Auster, A. (2002) "*Saving Private Ryan* and American Triumphalism," *Journal of Popular Film and Television*, 30 (2): 98–104.

Basinger, J. (2003) *The World War II Combat Movie: Anatomy of a Genre*, rev. ed. Middletown, CT: Wesleyan University Press.

Chapman, J. (2008) *War and Film*. London: Reaktion.

Doherty, T. (1988–1989) "Full Metal Genre: Stanley Kubrick's Vietnam Combat Movie," *Film Quarterly*, 42 (2): 24–30.

Farber, S. (1967–1968) "Shooting the Wars," *Film Quarterly*, 21 (2): 39.

Gates, P. (2005) "'Fighting the Good Fight': The Real and the Moral in the Contemporary Hollywood Combat Film," *Quarterly Review of Film and Video*, 22 (4): 297–310.

Hagen, W. H. (1983) "*Apocalypse Now* (1979): Joseph Conrad and the Television War." In Peter C. Rollins (Ed.), *Hollywood As Historian: American Film in a Cultural Context*. Lexington: University of Kentucky Press.

Jarvie, I. C. (1981) "Fanning the Flames: Anti-American Reaction to *Operation Burma* [*sic*] (1945)," *Historical Journal of Film, Radio and Television*, 1 (2): 17–137.

Landon, P. (1998) "Realism, Genre and *Saving Private Ryan*," *Film and History*, 28 (3–4): 58–63.

Maltby, R. (1985) *Hollywood Cinema: An Introduction*. Oxford: Blackwell.

Neale, S. (2000) *Genre and Hollywood*. London: Routledge.

Shain, R. E. (1976) *An Analysis of Motion Pictures About War Released by the American Film Industry, 1930–1970*. New York: Arno Press.

Shaw, T. (2007) *Hollywood's Cold War*. Edinburgh: Edinburgh University Press.

Further Reading

Adair, G. (1989) *Hollywood's Vietnam: From "The Green Berets" to "Full Metal Jacket,"* 2nd ed. London: Heinemann.

Chambers, J. W. and Culbert, D. (Eds.) (1996) *World War II, Film and History*. New York: Oxford University Press.

Doherty, T. (1993) *Projections of War: Hollywood, American Culture and World War II*. New York: Columbia University Press.

Koppes, C. R. and Black, G. D. (1987) *Hollywood Goes to War: How Politics, Profits and Propaganda Shaped World War II Movies*. Berkeley: University of California Press.

Manvell, R. (1974) *Films and the Second World War*. London: J. M. Dent and Sons.

McCrisken, T. and Pepper, A. (2005) *American History and Contemporary Hollywood Film*. Edinburgh: Edinburgh University Press.

Suid, L. H. (2002) *Guts and Glory: The Making of the American Military Image in Film*. Lexington: University of Kentucky Press.

Taylor, M. (2003) *The Vietnam War in History, Literature and Film*. Edinburgh: Edinburgh University Press.

Congo Wars (1960s–2000s)

TIMOTHY J. STAPLETON

During the 1950s, Belgian colonial rulers failed to prepare Congo for independence. The many Belgians in the civil service meant that few black Congolese gained administrative experience or western education. With much of the rest of Africa moving toward independence, Congolese political movements emerged along regional and ethnic lines. When the Belgians finally decided to decolonize, they did so with only six months preparation, intending that a weak Congo would be dependent upon their assistance. In 1960, the first independent government was led by Prime Minister Patrice Lumumba, a Pan-Africanist from the northeast, and President Joseph Kasavubu, a Bakongo irredentist from the west. Continued Belgian control of the army quickly led to mutiny, attacks on Belgian civilians, and Belgian withdrawal from the capital. Albert Kalongi declared the diamond mining area of Kasai independent, though this was suppressed by Lumumba's new army, transported in Soviet-supplied trucks and aircraft. In the mineral-rich southern province of Katanga, Moise Tshombe declared secession, supported by western mining interests and the Belgians. Belgian soldiers disarmed Congolese army units in the area and organized a Katanga military with Belgian, French, South African, and Rhodesian mercenaries.

While Lumumba called for United Nations (UN) assistance, international peacekeepers undermined his authority by seizing the country's airports, disarming soldiers loyal to him, and refusing to crush Katanga separation. Lumumba and Kasavubu dismissed each other, and the former was placed under house arrest by army commander Joseph Mobutu. Lumumba attempted escape but was recaptured and flown to Katanga where, in February 1961, he was killed on Tshombe's orders.

Throughout 1962, UN forces, mostly Swedish and Indian, and Mobutu's Congolese army invaded Katanga, and in January 1963 Tshombe capitulated. In 1964, Congolese army brutality caused an uprising in the east in which Simba (Lion) fighters were armed by the Soviet Union. Tshombe, the former separatist who was now prime minister, planned to suppress the rebellion by hiring western mercenaries, and Americans paid for combat aircraft flown by Cuban exiles. In November 1964, 1,800 western hostages held by the Simbas in Stanleyville were rescued by Belgian paratroopers dropped by American aircraft and a motorized column of mercenaries. From April to November 1965, Che Guevara led a Cuban contingent into eastern Congo to support the rebels, but withdrew when he realized there was little revolutionary potential. In November 1965, Mobutu overthrew President Kasavubu, established an American-backed anti-communist dictatorship, and eventually renamed the country Zaire. In 1966 and 1967, based on rumors that the exiled Tshombe would return, western mercenaries and former Katangese soldiers staged unsuccessful mutinies in Kisangani (Stanleyville).

Mobutu's involvement in failed American and South African intervention in Angola in 1975 backfired as the new government in Luanda, along with Cuban troops, began to assist exiled Katangese separatists. In March 1977, 2,000 armed insurgents of the *Front National pour la Libération du Congo* crossed from Angola to the Zairean province of Shaba (Katanga), advanced on Kolwezi, and were repelled by Zairean and Moroccan troops, the latter flown in by French aircraft. In May 1978, another insurgent force reached Kolwezi and Zairean paratroopers could only hold the town's airstrip. Responding to Mobutu's call, French Foreign Legion paratroopers recaptured the town and evacuated western civilians.

Although Mobutu lost his American support when the Cold War ended in the early 1990s, he delayed demands for democratization. After the 1994 Rwanda genocide, Hutu extremists moved into eastern Zaire, victimized local Tutsi, and raided their home country. In late 1996, Rwanda and its ally Uganda organized an uprising in eastern Zaire led by 1960s pro-Lumumba rebel Laurent Kabila under the banner of the Alliance of Democratic Forces for the Liberation of Congo-Zaire (ADFL). Angola also supported the ADFL because of Mobutu's assistance to National Union for the Total Independence of Angola insurgents. The rebels, along with Rwandese and Ugandan soldiers, advanced west and by May 1997 arrived at Kinshasa and Lubumbashi. Mobutu fled the country and Kabila took over, renaming it the Democratic Republic of Congo (DRC). Fast becoming authoritarian, Kabila fell out with his Rwandese and Ugandan allies, who he expelled in July 1998. In early August, another rebellion began in the east, supported by troops from Rwanda, Uganda, and Burundi. With rebels and foreign troops on the outskirts of the capital, Kabila's situation looked bleak. Forces from Zimbabwe, Namibia, and Angola arrived in September, under the auspices of the Southern African Development Community (SADC), and pushed the rebels and their allies eastward. Not all SADC members supported this intervention, with South Africa, Botswana, and Zambia remaining neutral. By the end of 1998, the rebels had split into two groups: the Rally for Congolese Democracy, backed by Rwanda, and the Movement for the Liberation of Congo, supported by Uganda. In August 1999, Rwandese and Ugandan units fought over control of Kisangani. Despite a January 1999 ceasefire, fighting continued and the DRC became divided into government- and various rebel-held zones. With soldiers from at least six neighboring countries involved, the Second DRC War was dubbed "Africa's World War." Involving few large battles, it was characterized by widespread looting of natural resources such as diamonds and coltan. Between two and three million people, mostly civilians, died from disease and hunger. The assassination of Laurent Kabila by his bodyguards in January 2001 resulted in the rise of his son Joseph Kabila, who quickly engaged in negotiations that resulted in foreign forces withdrawing in 2002. Major rebel groups were eventually incorporated into a new army. However, various insurgent forces, including Rwandese Hutu extremists of the Democratic Liberation Forces of Rwanda, control mines in the east, which is still plagued by violence despite the presence of a large UN peacekeeping force.

SEE ALSO: Angolan Civil Wars (1975–2002); Peacekeeping.

Further Reading

Nzongola-Ntalaja, G. (2002) *The Congo: From Leopold to Kabila*. London: Zed Books.

Prunier, G. (2008) *Africa's World War: Congo, the Rwandan Genocide and the Making of a Continental Catastrophe*. Oxford: Oxford University Press.

Turner, T. (2007) *Congo Wars: Conflict, Myth and Reality*. London: Zed Books.

E

Ethnic Cleansing

DRAŽEN PETROVIĆ

Definition

Although this term is widely used, its exact
meaning is difficult to determine. It still appears to
be a political rather than legal term. Many official
documents and witnesses describe ethnic cleansing in different ways.

Ethnic cleansing is a well-defined policy toward
the systematic elimination of one or several groups
of persons from a given territory by another
group, on distinctions based on ethnic or national
origins. The policy of ethnic cleansing is directly
or indirectly connected with the systematic use of
violence and very often with military operations.
The goal of ethnic cleansing is the establishment
of ethnically homogeneous regions and it is
therefore not a consequence but rather the purpose of a war. Such elimination is achieved by any
means possible, ranging from discrimination,
through expulsion, forced migration and population change, to extermination. Consequently,
these means include violations of human rights
and international humanitarian law. As the aim
and methods of this policy are contrary to

international law, the policy itself amounts to a
violation of international law, albeit not well
defined.

Ethnic cleansing is a literal translation of the
expression *etničko čišćenje* in the Bosnian,
Croatian, or Serbian languages. In general terms,
the idiom *čist* (clean) means "without any dirt" or
"contamination." It therefore tends to convey a
positive connotation that hides the destructive
character of "cleansing." The use of the term
"cleansing" in the criminal context involving ethnicities can be traced back to the 1912 Balkan
War and World War II. The term "clean" should
not be understood to mean that an ethnic group
is "unclean" in any vision of racial hygiene that
should justify its elimination, but rather as a
reference to an "ethnically pure" land.

Origin

The origin of this term – even in its original
languages – is difficult to ascertain. In the 1980s
some local media in Yugoslavia claimed that
Kosovo Albanians wanted to create "ethnically
clean territories" by intimidating the Serbian
minority in what was then an autonomous province within Serbia and Yugoslavia and forcing
them to leave. At the time, the term was basically

Twentieth-Century War and Conflict: A Concise Encyclopedia, First Edition. Edited by Gordon Martel.
© 2015 John Wiley & Sons, Ltd. Published 2015 by John Wiley & Sons, Ltd.

associated with administrative and non-openly violent methods.

The term acquired its present meaning during the war in Bosnia and Herzegovina (1992–1996). It was widely used by all warring and other parties concerned in wars in Croatia, Bosnia and Herzegovina, and later in Kosovo. It appears impossible to establish who was first to employ it and in which context it was applied. One may surmise that the term originated in military vocabulary, as military officers of the former Yugoslav People's Army had a preponderant role in all these wars. The expression "to clean the territory" refers to military operations aimed at eliminating enemy forces and is used mainly in the final phase of combat in order to totally control the conquered territory, which may also be known as "mopping up." In the case of ethnic cleansing, it is assumed that the enemy to be eliminated encompasses individuals of different ethnic origin.

The term has been widely used by journalists and politicians to describe events in the former Yugoslavia. It has also been established as a part of the official vocabulary of the United Nations (UN) Security Council and other UN institutions, as well as other governmental and non-governmental international organizations. Lawyers are more prudent in using it.

It has subsequently been used outside the scope of the former Yugoslavia, such as in the context of the Middle East, Abkhazia (Georgia), Cyprus, and Burundi. It has also been used to describe some events from the past, long before it appeared in the context of the former Yugoslavia.

Although the term is recent, situations to which it could apply have been recognized throughout history. Some of its patterns can be clearly identified in the deportation of Armenians and Greeks in Turkey, in the forced deportation of entire ethnic groups in the Soviet Union in the 1940s (Crimean Tatars, Ingush Meskhetian Turks, and so on), in the Nazi campaign against Jews in the 1930s, in the treatment of Serbs in the occupied territories of Yugoslavia during World War II, in the forced deportation of German minorities from eastern European countries after the end of World War II, and so on. Some aspects of genocides, such as the one in Rwanda, can also be defined as ethnic cleansing.

What Is Ethnic Cleansing?

The very nature of ethnic cleansing is still controversial. On various occasions it has been described as a systematic process, campaign, pattern, strategy, policy, and practice, or a combination of these.

Although it may seem insignificant, the difference in terms indicates a substantial variation in approach to ethnic cleansing. Some consider it as a crime, possibly even synonymous with genocide.

Ethnic cleansing takes different forms – from simple administrative and economic discrimination to the extermination of a targeted group or groups. What determines the various forms, methods, and targets of ethnic cleansing depends on the means at the disposal of those who practice it and its ultimate aim.

Ethnic Cleansing as a Practice

As a practice, ethnic cleansing encompasses a set of actions, directly or indirectly related to military operations, committed by one group against the members of another (or other) ethnic groups living in the same territory. In this context, ethnic cleansing may be defined by its elements and methods, which may vary from administrative measures to military actions, although this cannot be understood as a rigid distinction because some may overlap.

Administrative measures are not directly connected with military operations. The former may be applied before or after military operations, and may include, for example, forced removal of the legally elected authorities; dismissals from work, in particular from public service; restrictions in the distribution of food; discrimination; constant identity checks of members of a particular ethnic group; evictions from premises using property rights as a pretext; public warnings that the personal security of the targeted ethnic group cannot be guaranteed; forced labor, including that on the front lines; changing of name and religion; settlement of "appropriate" population (very often refugees or internally displaced persons) in the region controlled by one nation; lack of effective protection by the authorities or any rule of law; discriminatory and repressive legislation; refusal of hospital treatment, including childbirth; "voluntary" transfer of property following the departure and forced signature of a document stating that the departee would never return or conditioning departure with that of the entire family; expropriation of property; telephone disconnection; restriction of freedom of movement.

Non-violent measures other than administrative could include local media inciting fear and hatred, physical and verbal abuse in the street, harassing telephone calls (including death threats), and publishing lists of individuals indicating their ethnic origin. Food may not be sold to members of the target group and its members may not have access to adequate medical care. They are marginalized in all aspects of social life.

Terror-inspiring measures may be undertaken by regular soldiers or paramilitary forces, but are not directly connected with military operations. They are usually illegal and may involve: robbery, terrorization, and intimidation in the street; massive deportation, detention, and ill- treatment of the civilian population and their transfer to prisons and camps; forced labor; harassment and eviction of the civilian population; shooting at selected civilian targets or blowing-up by explosives and setting fire to homes, shops, and places of business; destruction of cultural and religious monuments and sites; instigation of massive displacement of population; mass forced transfer or relocation of population; discrimination, humiliation, and harassment of refugees belonging to a group of different ethnic origin. During forced deportation, many may have to go through transit camps or are forced to go on death marches. Consequently, many people die of hunger, deprivation, disease, or exhaustion.

A very specific element of ethnic cleansing is rape and other forms of sexual abuse, including castration. Such things may be connected with military operations, but often occur after their cessation. Rape includes that of women of all ages, often very young girls and virgins. It may be performed in front of a victim's parents, children, or other family members in order to reinforce its terror effect. It is done in a systematic manner. The intention of rape is very often pregnancy, and such intention may be expressed either verbally or by keeping the raped woman in detention until a late stage of pregnancy when it is too late for an abortion. It can be defined as forced impregnation. This is supposed not only to affect the honor and morals of the target group and limit its reproduction and future demographic growth, but even more to create the next generation of the nation to which the perpetrators belong.

Military measures are considered as patterns formed during military operations and directly connected with them. Some of the acts that may be considered in this category are summary executions and the deliberate killing and on-the-spot torture of certain categories of civilians, mainly prominent members of the local community (such as religious leaders, teachers, judges, educated individuals, police officers, political leaders, or local business people). Other methods comprise the siege of towns and villages – including cutting off of food, water, and gas supplies, as well as other essentials, to the civilian population; deliberate shelling of civilian targets (especially food-production and transport facilities, means of communication, post offices), cultural and architectural monuments, religious buildings, and medical institutions; reprisals against civilian targets and populations; the taking of hostages and detention of civilians for exchange; use of civilians as human shields; and attacking refugee camps.

The dilemma here is that because all of these acts may be analyzed as isolated violations of human rights and international humanitarian law, one risks neglecting the root system behind them. As the practice of ethnic cleansing does not always include all of these elements, the problem is to determine which specific elements could be considered as characterizing ethnic cleansing, and which could not. The main criterion is that violations of human rights and international humanitarian law are not just isolated acts, but are part of a wider system. Authorities often support this process, either by participation or instigation, or at least by non-opposition (prevention or punishment).

Ethnic Cleansing as a Policy

The aim of the policy of ethnic cleansing may be defined on the local and global level, as well as in the short and long term. Some goals could be regarded merely as elements of the ultimate goal.

On the local level, the aim may be to create fear, humiliation, and terror of the "other" population, an effective control over a given territory, reprisals, stealing of property, or provocation of flight of the other group. On the global level, the aim may be defined as an irreversible change in the demographic structure of a region with the establishment of ethnically homogeneous areas, so achieving a stronger position in future political negotiation that owes its logic to division based on ethnic criteria. The ultimate goal may also be elimination by means of the extermination of certain groups of people from a given territory, including elimination of the physical traces of their presence.

The goals of this policy could be of a short- or long-term nature. The short-term goal may be effective control over territory for military or strategic reasons, facilitated by the flight of the other population. The long-term goal may be to create such living conditions that would make the return of a displaced population impossible, thus endorsing a definitive gain of territory and a definitive change in demographic structure, to foster a territorial and national unity and create a firm basis for territorial aspirations.

These are several important characteristics of the policy of ethnic cleansing, but one key element is its systematic character. Ethnic cleansing is used against a particular group of people according to their ethnic, national, religious, or other specificity. It means that it is directed against all members of a given population, including women, children, and non-combatants. The targeted group is defined by its personal characteristics, such as ethnic origin, and not by its activity as combatants.

Ethnic Cleansing as a Crime

Those advocating the policy of ethnic cleansing cannot respect international humanitarian law because it implies losing the means, methods, and objectives that are essential for achieving the goals of this policy. The relation between the policy of ethnic cleansing and international criminal law can be analyzed at three levels, which may overlap.

Most measures used in an ethnic cleansing policy represent grave breaches of the 1949 Geneva Conventions and the 1977 Additional Protocols. A simple reading of the list presented above confirms this view. The UN Security Council, when it employed the term "ethnic cleansing" for the first time in its Resolution 771

(1992) of August 13, 1992, strongly condemned any violations of international humanitarian law "including those involved in the practice of 'ethnic cleansing.'"

The policy of ethnic cleansing can be considered through the prism of crimes against humanity as described in the Charter of the International Military Tribunal ("Nuremberg Tribunal"), the Statute of the International Criminal Tribunal for the former Yugoslavia, or the Rome Statute of the International Criminal Court. It is obvious that this policy, aimed at the elimination of a particular population from a given territory, without precise designation of target group and without any clear intention of their destruction as a group, easily fits the definition of crimes against humanity. If one can make a relationship between violations of human rights and crimes against humanity, it may be useful to note that on April 27, 1999, the UN Commission on Human Rights adopted Resolution 1999/47 "deploring practices of forced displacement, in particular 'ethnic cleansing' and the negative impact they constitute for the enjoyment of fundamental human rights by large groups of populations."

The elimination of a given ethnic group from a territory can also be done with an intention to destroy it, in whole or in part. If this is the case, ethnic cleansing may be considered as synonymous with genocide. This is a source of division among scholars, as many do not share this view, perhaps because they fail to see that in its extreme form ethnic cleansing may well be genocide. The UN General Assembly, in its Resolution 47/121 of December 18, 1992, referred to "the abhorrent policy of 'ethnic cleansing' (which) is a form of genocide." This enlargement of the definition of genocide given by the 1948 Convention on the Prevention and Punishment of the Crime of Genocide was not followed by judicial bodies. For example, the case of *Prosecutor v. Krstic* (IT-98–33–T, judgment of August 2, 2001, Sections 577–580) expressly disagreed with such an approach. The same view was expressed by the International Court of Justice in its judgment of February 26, 2007, in the case of *Bosnia and Herzegovina v. Serbia and Montenegro* (concerning the application of the Convention on the Prevention and Punishment of the Crime of Genocide), which found in Section 190 that "neither the intent, as a matter of policy, to render an area 'ethnically homogeneous,' nor the operations that may be carried out to implement such policy, can *as such* be designated as genocide."

Does ethnic cleansing have any legal meaning as such? The term is absent from both the Statute of the International Criminal Tribunal for the former Yugoslavia and the Rome Statute of the International Criminal Court. Ethnic cleansing has to be considered under war crimes, crimes against humanity, and genocide, as it does not exist as a separate category. The Trial Chamber in Case No. IT-00–39–A (*Prosecutor v. Momčilo Krajišnik*) before the International Criminal Tribunal for the former Yugoslavia stated that "it has not treated the term as legally significant," although it has been used by witnesses and reports. In other cases, however, both the Trial and Appeal chambers used an established instance of ethnic cleansing in the Lašva Valley and Krajina as a basis for their judgments. Nevertheless, although the description of ethnic cleansing by the media largely justified the creation of the International Criminal Tribunal for the former Yugoslavia, this term seems to be used more often by prosecutors than by judges. Although they refer to it, they sometimes try to fit it into already existing categories. For example, in the Separate and Partly Dissenting Opinion in the Appeal Chamber judgment in Case No. IT-98–34–A (*Prosecutor v. Mladen Naletilic, a.k.a. "Tuta" and Vinko Martinovic, a.k.a. "Stela"*), Judge Shomburg stated that "the crime of ethnic cleansing by uprooting specific parts of a population needs to be called by the name it deserves: Deportation."

One can regret this cautious approach. Ethnic cleansing could well be a separate crime on its own. The phenomenon of ethnic cleansing surpasses the specific case of the former Yugoslavia. It can easily occur in situations such as the redefining of frontiers or rights over a given territory in areas with a mixed population. Such a logic of conflict implies violent acts against an "enemy" civilian population on a large scale, and not war *per se* in its traditional meaning as a conflict between defined armies. Examples in world history are numerous, although the situations in question have not been defined as ethnic cleansing.

SEE ALSO: Yugoslav Succession, Wars of (1990–1999).

Further Reading

Bell-Fialkoff, A. (1993) "A Brief History of Ethnic Cleansing," *Foreign Affairs*, 72 (3): 110–121.

Calic, M.-J. (2009) "Ethnic Cleansing and War Crimes, 1991–1995." In C. Ingrao and T. Emmert (Eds.), *Confronting the Yugoslav Controversies: A Scholars' Initiative*. West Lafayette: Purdue University Press.

De Zayas, A. (2003) "Ethnic Cleansing: Applicable Norms, Emerging Jurisprudence, Implementable Remedies," *International Humanitarian Law*, 1: 283–313.

Fisher, S. (2006) "Occupation of the Womb: Forced Impregnation as Genocide," *Duke Law Journal*, 91: 97–133.

Naimark, N. (2001) *Fires of Hatred: Ethnic Cleansing in Twentieth-Century Europe*. Cambridge, MA: Harvard University Press.

Naimark, N. (2007) "Ethnic Cleansing." *Online Encyclopedia of Mass Violence*. http://www.massviolence.org/Ethnic-Cleansing, ISSN 1961–9898.

Pajic, Z. (1993) *Violation of Fundamental Rights in Former Yugoslavia. Vol. 1: The Conflict in Bosnia and Herzegovina*. London: David Davies Memorial Institute of International Studies.

Petrovic, D. (1994) "Ethnic Cleansing – An Attempt at Methodology," *European Journal of International Law*, 5 (3): 342–359.

Petrovic, D. (1995) "Beyond Xenophobia: Ethnic Cleansing." In B. Baumgartl and A. Favell (Eds.), *New Xenophobia in Europe*. Boston: Kluwer.

Schabas, W. (2009) "Genocide Law in the Time of Transition," *Rutgers Law Review*, 61 (1): 161–192.

Shaw, M. (2010) "The Minimal Euphemism: The Substitution of Ethnic Cleansing for Genocide." In *Genocide: Critical Concepts in Historical Studies*, vol. 1. London: Routledge.

F

Falklands War (1982)

BLAIR TURNER

The world awoke on April 3, 1982, to the shocking news that an Argentine invasion force had landed on the desolate Falkland Islands in the far South Atlantic, subdued the small force of Royal Marines stationed at the capital, Port Stanley, and proclaimed the islands *nuestras* – "our" – Malvinas (Argentina would follow up with the capture of a tiny garrison on South Georgia Island that same day). No one except the invasion force and a few planners in the Argentine military staffs knew of the expedition until it was over. There had been long and drawn-out discussions in the United Nations (UN) and other venues for decades about the contentious issue of sovereign control of the islands. Multiple conflicting claims dating back to the Seven Years' War of the eighteenth century ensured that both sides had established rather rigid positions: Britain in favor of "self-determination" for the few settlers on the islands (Scots and Welsh) and the Argentines in favor of exclusive sovereignty over islands on the Argentine continental shelf, with guarantees of civil rights for the settlers as Argentine citizens. Even so, the notion of actual hostilities over the islands seemed remote. The Argentine plan was based on forcing a *fait accompli*. That the British would undertake the costly and huge operation necessary to recover the islands some 8,500 miles distant in the coming South Atlantic winter was deemed too unlikely; a negotiated settlement would be reached. Argentine planners understood, however, that defeat was a distinct probability if the British did fight.

And fight they did. The British navy, not having sailed forth in anger since the frustrating Suez Crisis, mobilized immediately. The nuclear submarine HMS *Conqueror* – just one example of British military superiority – departed for the South Atlantic on April 4. Surface forces, including Britain's two aircraft carriers, deployed from Portsmouth on April 5. On April 9, troop transports, loaded with British paratroop and marine units, deployed, and on April 12, Britain announced a 200-mile exclusion zone around the islands. Even though not yet in theater, British forces were on the offensive; the Argentines sat pat.

The UN condemned the invasion and called for withdrawal of Argentine forces, cessation of hostilities, and a negotiated settlement. The United States embarked on shuttle diplomacy between Washington, Buenos Aires, and London in an attempt to effect some kind of settlement. But American efforts came to naught. The

Twentieth-Century War and Conflict: A Concise Encyclopedia, First Edition. Edited by Gordon Martel.
© 2015 John Wiley & Sons, Ltd. Published 2015 by John Wiley & Sons, Ltd.

Argentines were suspicious – correctly – of the neutrality of America's good offices and the British were determined to press forward. Eventually, the United States offered logistical and intelligence support to the UK and helped pressure the Organization of American States and virtually every American republic to stand aside. Only two Latin American nations involved themselves directly in the conflict and in very limited roles: Peru flew some sorties in support of Argentina; Chile rendered support to Britain.

By May 1, British operations had reached the point that an active offensive could be launched. Royal Marines had recaptured the small base on remote South Georgia Island in late April. With that flank secured, a direct approach to the Falklands was open and the war was on. On May 1, Vulcan bombers from the UK reached and bombed the airstrip at Fort Stanley, the British task force entered the exclusion zone, and Harrier "jump-jets" from the carriers bombed targets on the Falklands. In opposition, the Argentine navy was not an inconsiderable force: it had the *Veinticinco de Mayo*, one of only two carriers in Latin American maritime forces. It also boasted the heavy cruiser *Belgrano*, some reasonably modern frigates, and somewhat older diesel submarines. And the navy operated a significant number of attack aircraft. However, once HMS *Conqueror* torpedoed and sank the *Belgrano* on May 2 (the heaviest loss of life of any incident in the war) the navy did not sortie to offer battle to the British forces: arguably a missed opportunity. In response, Argentine naval aircraft, French-made Super Étendards carrying Exocet missiles, successfully attacked HMS *Sheffield* on May 4. The pattern of the largest naval conflict since Okinawa was set: the British controlled the sea, but Argentine aircraft sent six British ships to the bottom and damaged 10 others.

On land, the issue was more one-sided. Once the British landing was completed in the inland sea of San Carlos Water (Falkland Sound) between the large East and West Falklands on May 21, the outcome was not in doubt. Not that the fighting was easy: the Argentines put up stiff resistance at Goose Green and Darwin on the southern flank of the British landing zone, but were overcome on May 28. Argentine air forces continued to pound landing ships and escort vessels in San Carlos Water and on the southern coast of the East Island, as the British attempted to leap-frog by water towards Port Stanley. Eventually, the British land forces had to march cross-country and attack the capital from the west. This required subduing dug-in Argentine infantry on several mountain ridges, but this was done in good order and all Argentine forces on the islands surrendered on June 14.

The costs of the war were not light: the British lost 255 personnel killed and some 777 wounded; Argentine losses were 652 dead and missing, and an unspecified but larger number of wounded. Most Argentine losses were at sea. Materially, Britain could absorb the number of ships lost, but Argentina could not; in addition to the *Belgrano*, she lost a submarine and virtually all of her troop carrier capability. The Argentine air arm, both navy and air force, was cut off; perhaps as many as 109 aircraft were lost. But the real costs to Argentina were political. The military government – now demonstrably incapable of performing even its most basic function of national defense – was entirely discredited and stepped down, ending an era of military dominance of political power begun in 1930. The military has not returned to power since. And the British commitment to hold the islands is more solid today than it was before the war.

SEE ALSO: Submarine Warfare.

Further Reading

Freedman, L. *et al.* (2007) *The Official History of the Falklands Campaign*, 2 vols. London: Routledge.

Moro, R. O. (1986) *La guerra inaudita: historia del conflicto del Atlántico Sur*. Buenos Aires: Editorial Pleamar.

First Indochina War (1945–1954)

CHRISTOPHER E. GOSCHA

The Indochina War was a colonial and civil conflict, a violent hotspot in the Cold War, as well as a social, cultural, and ideological battle. The conflict divided the French and the Vietnamese, opposed Vietnamese, engulfed the Lao and the Cambodians, and involved the Chinese, British, Soviets, and Americans, among others.

At the outset, the conflict was above all a clash between opposing French and Vietnamese nationalists over who would control Indochina. During most of World War II the French remained in their Asian colony thanks to a condominium worked out with the Japanese. Given that Vichy aligned France with the Axis powers following the fall of France in 1940, Tokyo kept the French on to run Indochina, while the Japanese focused on fighting the war. The Allied invasion of France in 1944 and the emergence of a new French order under Charles de Gaulle changed all that. Worried that the French in Indochina would now support the Allies as the Americans focused their full attention on Japan, on March 9, 1945, the Japanese engineered a *coup d'état*, ending some 80 years of French rule.

For de Gaulle, the empire had been essential to the survival of his resistance government. Recovering it, including the missing Indochinese piece, would be equally important to the restoration of France's national and international prestige lost in the humiliating defeat of 1940 and Vichy's collaboration. In Brazzaville in early 1944, Gaullist colonial officials hammered out a package of seemingly liberal colonial reforms designed to provide increased autonomy to restless colonial nationalists. Federalism was the linchpin. Indeed, the French saw Indochina as the litmus test for a federal conception of colonial rule. Gaullists announced this idea in their March 23, 1945, Declaration on Indochina. However, a wide range of Vietnamese nationalists rejected it, calling on the French to acknowledge their independence. Coming weeks after the Japanese coup and the end of colonial rule, how could it be otherwise? they asked. De Gaulle and a wide range of French politicians saw it differently. Although the term "French Union," enshrined in the 1946 Constitution, may have replaced the outdated word "Empire," the French had no intention of creating the equivalent of a British Commonwealth within which independent nation-states would emerge. In September 1945, de Gaulle selected Admiral Georges Thierry d'Argenlieu to serve as the new high commissioner for Indochina. General Philippe Leclerc took command of the Expeditionary Corps. De Gaulle's instructions

were clear: reestablish French national sovereignty over all of Indochina in the form of an Indochinese Federation. Backed by de Gaulle, the admiral followed those instructions to the letter, with dangerous consequences.

Like de Gaulle, Ho Chi Minh had also created a nationalist front during World War II, designed to recover Vietnamese national sovereignty once the Allies had defeated the Axis powers. In 1941, Ho presided over the formation of the Vietminh Doc Lap Dong Minh or the Vietnamese Independence League (Vietminh for short). Led by the Indochinese Communist Party, this broad-based nationalist organization was designed to attract support from all segments of Vietnamese society in favor of national independence. Ho put talk of radical social revolution on hold. On August 19, 1945, a few days after the Japanese capitulation to the Allies, but before the Allies or Gaullists could land their troops, the communist-led Vietminh rode a famine-driven wave of popular discontent to power (starvation killed around a million Vietnamese between 1944 and 1945). On September 2, 1945, in Hanoi, Ho Chi Minh declared the birth of the Democratic Republic of Vietnam (DRV). Two new nationalist leaders had emerged from World War II – one French, one Vietnamese – each of whom was determined to impose sovereignty over the Vietnamese space vacated by the Japanese. It was an explosive mix.

Foreign countries also profoundly influenced the nature of the conflict between French and Vietnamese nationalists. Having been knocked out of World War II early on, de Gaulle was not always privy to major global decisions made by the British, Americans, Soviets, and the Chinese as the war drew to an unexpectedly early end in the Pacific. The Allies did not consult de Gaulle about the agreement reached at Potsdam in July 1945 dividing Indochina into two operational zones at the 16th parallel, confiding the southern part to the British South East Asia Command and the northern half to the China Theater. Following the Japanese surrender, President Harry Truman approved Order No. 1 allowing the British and the Chinese to occupy and accept the Japanese surrender in their respective zones. This international division of Indochina had important repercussions locally. For one, the British under General Douglas Gracey allowed French forces disarmed by the Japanese in March to execute a *coup de force* in Saigon on September 23, 1945, pushing the DRV's southern forces into the countryside as the arriving Expeditionary Corps under Leclerc took control of the cities, roads, and bridges in southern Indochina from October.

Although the Indochina War began in the south in September 1945, it was not yet a full-scale war. Determined to avoid the instability the British had unleashed in the south, local Chinese officers blocked any French return to northern Indochina until the Franco-Chinese accord of February 28, 1946, could be signed, authorizing the French to replace Chinese troops in an orderly fashion. Even the signing of the preliminary March 6 Accords in 1946 recognizing the DRV as a "free state" within the Indochinese Federation and the French Union was due less to a liberal moment in French colonial thinking than to the intense pressure local Chinese commanders placed upon French and Vietnamese negotiators to sign an agreement before French troops disembarked. A military annex authorized the French to station in all 15,000 troops in the north. Thanks to the Republic of China, DRV leaders thus continued to operate their state and negotiate with the French in the north, while simultaneously fighting the latter's forces below the 16th parallel.

Could decolonization be achieved peacefully? While the violence in the south did not make the Indochina War inevitable, the French determination to apply the federal project at the expense of Vietnamese independence aspirations set the two states on a dangerous collision course. The main dividing issue was the unification of the French colony of Cochinchina, or southern Vietnam, with the rest of the DRV/Vietnam based out of Hanoi. According to the March Accords, the French recognized the DRV as one "free state" (*Etat libre*) among three other "free states" that would constitute, together, the Indochinese Federation – the DRV (Vietnam above the 16th parallel), Cochinchina (Vietnam below the 16th parallel), Laos, and Cambodia. The organization of a referendum in the south would determine the future status of Cochinchina.

While Ho Chi Minh sought to avoid war, he could only compromise on this issue so far without discrediting himself and his cause. Anti-communist and anti-French nationalist parties like the Vietnamese National Party and the Greater Vietnam parties were highly critical of any negotiations with the French. They too believed in an independent and unified Vietnam, but without the French colonialists and the Vietnamese communists. Indeed, Ho gambled when he agreed in the Accords to place the DRV within the Indochinese Federation, allowed the French to station troops in the north, and counted on Paris to hold a referendum on the unification of Cochinchina with the rest of the DRV.

Ho lost his bet when follow-up conferences designed to take up the unresolved issues of the March 6 Accords failed, first in Dalat and then in France in mid-1946. The failure of the French and the Vietnamese at Fontainebleau to resolve the question of Cochinchina allowed hardliners on both sides of the divide to take matters into their own hands. And this made reaching an overall compromise solution increasingly difficult to achieve. In a desperate move, Ho Chi Minh obtained a *modus vivendi* in September 1946 prescribing, among other things, a ceasefire in the south. However, the lack of political will in France, exacerbated by ever changing governments in Paris, allowed local authorities in Indochina led by Thierry d'Argenlieu to roll back the DRV's sovereignty in favor of that of the colonial Federation. Such brinkmanship led to serious clashes in Lang Son and Haiphong in November 1946 before the Vietnamese, their backs up against the wall, lashed out in Hanoi on December 19, 1946. Long spoiling for a fight, local French authorities replied with force. Full-scale war had now broken out in all of Indochina and would rage for almost 10 more years across Vietnam, Laos, and Cambodia, killing 112,000 men in the French Union forces and an estimated 500,000 Vietnamese, civilians and soldiers alike.

Wars of decolonization almost always spawn civil violence as different groups vie for control over the postcolonial state and its nature. The civil war was most prominent in eastern Indochina, where communism had divided Vietnamese nationalists since the 1920s. If the French army had initially supported Vo Nguyen Giap's destruction of the anti-Vietminh and anti-French opposition parties in July 1946, French political leaders regretted that they suddenly found themselves face to face with the DRV. As early as January 1947, Léon Pignon, a longtime Indochina hand and one of France's best colonial minds, advised his superiors that the French colonial conflict with the DRV had to be transposed to a Vietnamese playing field, using the Vietminh's adversaries to do the fighting. It was in this context that the French rallied the southern Hoa Hao and Cao Dai religious sects to the French cause in 1947, setting off a violent civil war with the DRV in the Mekong Delta. The French also turned to the former emperor Bao Dai, now living in exile in China and unhappy with the DRV, to build a counter-revolutionary state, around which non-communist nationalists would rally and through which the French would maintain their presence in Vietnam. Vietnamese non-communists hoped that their anti-communism and the Cold War would force Paris to accord them the independence denied to Ho Chi Minh's government. True, the French convinced Bao Dai to return to Vietnam and abandoned the Federation in favor of the Associated State of Vietnam incorporating Cochinchina by 1949. However, the French only slowly granted non-communist nationalists real sovereignty. And by trying to "Vietnamize" the war against the DRV, the French only exacerbated the violence among Vietnamese. In 1950, the French created a Vietnamese army for the Associated State. When the guns went silent in 1954, the Vietnamese accounted for the majority of battlefield deaths in the French Union forces.

On top of this, the Indochina War was also one of the hottest battlegrounds in the Cold War. While the onset of the Cold War in Europe may have made itself felt in Indochina shortly after World War II, the Chinese communist victory of October 1949 and the outbreak of the Korean War in June 1950 firmly shifted the Cold War eastwards along a Eurasian axis, creating a communist bloc stretching from the Elbe River to the South China Sea. If Stalin handed over the Asian side of world revolution to Mao Zedong, who supported his long-time communist allies in Korea and Vietnam, the Americans were determined to hold the line in Indochina against the spread of Sino-Soviet communism. Washington was ready to do this even if it meant prolonging the French colonial presence in Indochina to the national detriment of the Associated State of Vietnam. By the end of the war, the Americans were financing two-thirds of the French war in Indochina, while the Chinese communists were heavily backing the DRV.

As in Korea, internationalization rapidly made Indochina the theater of an increasingly lethal conflagration. Sino-American military assistance and training provided to the belligerents augmented battlefield violence, bombing raids, and increased the number of casualties among civilians and soldiers, as the DRV's general staff took the battle to the French, often using wave tactics, instead of relying uniquely on less intensive guerrilla warfare. This was particularly true in northern Vietnam, where Chinese assistance helped the DRV to outfit and train six combat divisions by the end of the conflict. Set-piece battles at Vinh Yen, Dong Trieu, Na San, and Dien Bien Phu cost tens of thousands of lives. Vietnamese statistics confirm that from 1950 artillery and machine gun fire mowed down young soldiers attacking in waves against fortified positions. The French air force used napalm supplied by the Americans with devastating effect, whereas the People's Army of Vietnam fired artillery cannons and, in the closing days of the battle of Dien Bien Phu, opened up on French Union troops with Soviet-supplied, truck-mounted multiple rocket launchers ("Katyusha" or Stalin's Organs) (Goscha 2010). The Algerian War of Independence (1954–1962) never registered this level of battlefield violence.

However, no one knew in 1950 that the French would lose the battle of Dien Bien Phu in 1954. Although General Vo Nguyen Giap scored an important victory at Cao Bang in late 1950, securing much of the northern border from the French, his attempts to march on Hanoi in the open Red River delta were overly optimistic, as the stinging defeat he suffered at Vinh Yen in January 1951 demonstrated. Indeed, the newly arrived commander in chief, General Jean de Lattre de Tassigny, welcomed his adversary's determination to fight in the delta, convinced that French firepower and Union forces, including the expanding army of the Associated State of Vietnam, could inflict defeat on the Vietminh in such circumstances. While the DRV's shift to large-scale battles forced the French to transfer troops from other areas in Indochina, thereby allowing the DRV to increase its influence territorially via guerrilla tactics, the People's Army was not going to take the delta from the French any time soon. Vietnamese strategists, seconded by Chinese advisors, shifted their attention to the northwest highlands. In September 1951, the DRV used wave tactics and attacked by night in order to overrun the French camp in Nghia Lo. General Raoul Salan responded by ordering his men to regroup and reinforce the French camp at Na San in order to stop the Vietnamese march on

Tai territories in the highlands and into Laos. When the Vietnamese moved on Na San in late 1952, Salan confronted them with a full-blown entrenched camp, supplied by air, and outfitted with heavy artillery. The Vietnamese victory at Nghia Lo turned into a severe defeat for Vo Nguyen Giap at Na San.

Nevertheless, one of the results of this shift to the uplands and western Indochina was that violence spilled into Laos, upland non-Vietnamese territories, and eventually into eastern Cambodia as Chinese aid allowed the DRV's armed forces to move battalions and even entire divisions across long distances. In 1953–1954, during two Vietnamese thrusts westwards across the Annamese Chain, Cambodians, Lao, and upland minorities began to die in greater numbers as the war entered its most intensive phase. On another front, the expansion of the DRV's forces into western Indochina also allowed Vietnamese communists to install their own "resistance governments" in Laos and Cambodia, led by the Pathet Lao and the Khmer Issarak. In so doing, the Vietnamese, thanks to the new international conjuncture and Chinese aid, created a counter set of "Associated States" and armies and thus ensured, with the French and Americans, that civil war would come to Laos and Cambodia.

The internationalization of the Indochina War also linked France, Vietnam, Laos, and Cambodia to events taking place around the world. This was particularly the case for the French, who found it increasingly hard to balance the growing costs of the intensifying war in Indochina with their global commitments in manpower and money to the defense of western Europe, their role in the North Atlantic Treaty Organization, and need to match the rearmament of West Germany. How could France contribute to the European Defense Community when much of its army and officers were bogged down in Indochina? Things were also heating up in French North Africa. As Tertrais (2002: 23) has shown, the final blow to the French did not necessarily occur on the battlefield at Dien Bien Phu in 1954, but rather on the economic front in Europe: "While all problems may not be financial [at the outset]," Pierre Mendès France had already warned at the time of the Cao Bang defeat, "they become so one day."

With this in mind, the Joseph Laniel government named General Henri Navarre commander in chief of the armed forces in Indochina on May 8, 1953, instructing him to create the necessary military conditions for an acceptable political solution to the war, *une sortie honorable*. Navarre devised a plan for 1953–1954 designed to avoid large-scale battles with the enemy in order to rebuild French Union forces. In 1954–1955, the army would deliver decisive military blows to Vo Nguyen Giap's army in order to force the enemy to the negotiating table on terms favorable to the French. The Americans were involved in the making of the plan and paid most of its bill, hoping to keep the French in the war and containment alive without having to commit troops themselves. In July 1953, the French government approved the Navarre Plan. Upon arriving in Indochina, Navarre focused his attention on the delta and launching his main offensive, Operation Atlante, against DRV positions in central Vietnam. In September 1953, thanks in part to the Chinese intelligence services, the DRV acquired a good understanding of the basic elements of the Navarre Plan and used it in preparing the 1953–1954 Winter–Spring campaign. Rather than trying to attack the delta, where the French could concentrate their artillery and airpower easily on the attacking forces, the Politburo decided to try to disperse the French as much as possible by attacking toward the northwest at Lai Chau and Phongsaly in Laos, then toward central and southern Laos, and even as far as northeast Cambodia if need be. The Politburo never had the intention to "take" Laos; the strategic goal was rather to disperse the French Union forces across Indochina.

It was in this context that Navarre surprised his adversaries when he decided to commit to a battle in the remote northwestern valley at Dien Bien Phu in order to block the DRV from taking Laos. Not only did Navarre dig in at Dien Bien Phu, providing the Vietnamese with a battle in the highlands, but he also went ahead with Operation Atlante in central Vietnam, thereby dispersing his forces across Indochina just as the DRV high command had hoped. Vo Nguyen Giap could not believe his luck when his intelligence services guaranteed him that Navarre would not pull out of Dien Bien Phu. Backed by the Politburo, Giap received full authorization to knock out the French camp at Dien Bien Phu in order to inflict a major battle defeat on the French before opening negotiations in Geneva on terms favorable to the DRV.

This was a battle the Vietnamese side simply could not lose. So much so that Vo Nguyen Giap, in agreement with his Chinese advisor, postponed the first attack set to begin in mid-January 1954. The artillery had not yet been moved into position, Giap explained, and the Vietnamese had never attacked in waves in broad daylight. Artillery was essential to knocking out the French airbase, something the Vietnamese had failed to do at Na San. Thanks to his military intelligence services, Navarre reported to his superiors in early January 1954 that Giap was moving his artillery into positions around Dien Bien Phu, adding that if his adversary succeeded in doing so, he could no longer guarantee a French victory at Dien Bien Phu. However, rather than increasing his troops in Dien Bien Phu, Navarre went ahead simultaneously with Operation Atlante. Giap obliged the French general by sending troops into the central highlands, Laos, and even as far as eastern Cambodia in order to disperse the French so that he could concentrate on winning *the* decisive battle at Dien Bien Phu. On March 13, confident that its artillery was in place and that French forces were sufficiently dispersed, the Vietnamese high command opened artillery fire on the French airstrip, took it out, and, following a two-month battle that resembled the trench warfare of Verdun more than the wave tactics of Korea, overwhelmed the French Union forces. On May 7, 1954, the French camp at Dien Bien Phu fell, as did Navarre's attempt to recover central Vietnam. The colonized had scored a historic victory over the western colonizer in a set-piece, modern battle; one that resounded across the third world, above all in Algeria.

However, the internationalization of the war posed formidable obstacles to the DRV. The shift toward peaceful coexistence in Moscow and Beijing after Stalin's death in 1953 and the armistice in Korea a few months later put Vietnamese communists in a difficult position. In early 1954, the big powers, even the United States, agreed to meet in Geneva to discuss the two hot wars in Asia, the Korean and Indochinese ones. Zhou Enlai led a Chinese delegation determined to find a diplomatic solution to prevent the Americans from replacing the French on his southern flank. While the Vietnamese may have handed the French an astonishing military defeat at Dien Bien Phu, securing all of Vietnam at the negotiating table turned out to be impossible. Vietnamese communists would have to let go of southern Vietnam on the diplomatic front. Like the Chinese, Vietnamese communists feared that if a solution were not reached at the negotiating table, the Americans would intervene militarily. The Vietnamese, Chinese, and Soviets concurred. After arduous negotiations, in the early hours of July 21, 1954, it was agreed that Vietnam would be temporarily divided at the 17th parallel until elections could be held in 1956 to unify the entire country under one national leadership. As in the March Accords of 1946, the Vietnamese communist leadership gambled on the organization of a referendum in order to achieve unification via political instead of military means. In the meantime, the DRV withdrew its armed forces and personnel to areas above the 17th parallel, while those of the French Union moved to the south. An armistice was signed and an international commission designated to oversee the implementation of the accords.

Significantly, neither the Americans nor the State of Vietnam ever signed on. Nor was there a mechanism for enforcing compliance by any side. When Ngo Dinh Diem transformed the State of Vietnam into the fully independent Republic of Vietnam in 1955, he made it clear that he wanted nothing to do with the accords signed in Geneva. In 1956, the French withdrew their armed forces from southern Vietnam. The Indochina War was over, but the possibility for renewed civil and Cold War most certainly was not.

SEE ALSO: Algerian War of Independence (1954–1962); Korean War (1949–1953); Vietnam War (1959–1975); World War II: The Defeat and Occupation of France; World War II: War in Asia.

References

Goscha, C. (2010) "'Hell in a Very Small Place': Cold War and Decolonization in the Assault on the Vietnamese Body at Dien Bien Phu," *European Journal of East Asian Studies*, 9 (2).

Tertrais, H. (2002) *La piastre et le fusil: le coût de la guerre d'Indochine, 1945–1954*. Paris: Comité pour l'histoire économique et financière de la France.

Further Reading

Devillers, P. (1952) *Histoire du Vietnam de 1940 à 1952*. Paris: Le Seuil.

Dommen, A. (2001) *The Indochinese Experience of the French and the Americans: Nationalism and Communism in Cambodia, Laos and Vietnam*. Bloomington: Indiana University Press.

Fall, B. (1960) *Le Viet Minh: La république démocratique du Viet Nam, 1945–1960*. Paris: Librairie FNSP/Armand Colin.

Goscha, C. (2011) *Vietnam: Un Etat né de la guerre*. Paris: Armand Colin.

Joyaux, F. (1979) *La Chine et le règlement du premier conflit d'Indochine, Genève 1954*. Paris: Publications de la Sorbonne.

Lawrence, M. (2005) *Assuming the Burden: Europe and the American Commitment to War in Vietnam*. Berkeley: University of California Press.

Lawrence, M. A. and Logevall, F. (Eds.) (2007) *The First Vietnam War: Colonial Conflict and Cold War Crisis*. Cambridge, MA: Harvard University Press.

Logevall, F. (2012) *Embers of War*. New York: Random House.

Marr, D. (1995) *Vietnam 1945: The Quest for Power*. Berkeley: University of California Press.

Morgan, T. (2010) *Valley of Death: The Tragedy at Dien Bien Phu that Led America into the Vietnam War*. New York: Random House.

Shipway, M. (1996) *The Road to War: France and Vietnam, 1944–1947*. Oxford: Berghahn Books.

Tonnesson, S. (2009) *Vietnam 1946: How the War Began*. Berkeley: University of California Press.

Turpin, F. (2005) *De Gaulle, les gaullistes et l'Indochine, 1940–1956*. Paris: Les Indes Savantes.

G

Greco-Turkish War (1919–1922)

DAVID PIZZO

The Greco-Turkish War was a conflict fought in Anatolia between the Kingdom of Greece and the new Turkish Republic in the wake of World War I. The war represented both the final stage of disintegration of the Ottoman Empire and the culmination of the Greek "Megali [Great] Idea" of uniting all Greeks in the eastern Mediterranean under a single Greek state. Early Greek successes seemed to offer the prospect of a pan-Hellenic Greek state on both sides of the Aegean, but the Turkish revolutionaries' military successes of 1921–1922 turned victory into catastrophe, resulting in the collapse of Greek irredentist dreams, large refugee flows, and the destruction of both the Greek communities in Anatolia and Turkish communities in Greece. For the Turkish national movement, on the other hand, the war represented a crucial phase of their war of independence. The negotiations that ended the war also mandated state-organized population exchanges which profoundly changed the cultural and ethnic composition of the region.

Greek politics had been incredibly divided about entering World War I, and Greece only officially joined the Entente near the war's conclusion. It had been party to discussions among the Allies about the division of the post-war Ottoman Empire, as the Entente powers sought to balance their various and competing claims to Ottoman territory. Prime Minister Eleftherios Venizelos, the Megali Idea's best-known advocate and the primary architect of Greece's joining the Entente, pushed very hard at the Paris Peace Conference for a Greek military occupation of western Anatolia, particularly of the city of Smyrna. The British soon came to view this as a preferable outcome to the region falling under Italian control, as Lloyd George and other British officials feared that the Italians, who had originally been promised Smyrna, were more likely to reach an agreement with the Turks. The British and French both hoped to contain or defeat the Turkish nationalists, and they hoped to impose some version of the zonal agreements reached between themselves, Italy, and Greece. Britain in particular hoped to impose a harsh settlement on the Ottomans and prevent the victory of the nationalists without directly committing its own forces (Bloxham 2005: 154–155). The Entente's "Anglo-Greek policy" aimed to use the Greeks as a proxy army to enforce their will in Anatolia. Entente interest in maintaining a presence in Asia Minor therefore dovetailed with irredentist Greek

Twentieth-Century War and Conflict: A Concise Encyclopedia, First Edition. Edited by Gordon Martel.
© 2015 John Wiley & Sons, Ltd. Published 2015 by John Wiley & Sons, Ltd.

demands to "liberate" the areas of Anatolia with large Greek minorities, and a Greek expeditionary force landed at Smyrna on May 15, 1919.

Commanded by High Commissioner Aristidis Stergiadis, the Greek force quickly secured Smyrna and the surrounding areas. While the Greek population, a substantial minority (and by Greek reckonings a majority) in Smyrna welcomed the expeditionary force as liberators, much of the Muslim population reacted with fear and revulsion. The deaths of almost 400 Turkish citizens of Smyrna in the initial landings did not bode well for the campaign to come. Indeed, the Greek landings served as one of the primary catalysts of the emerging Turkish

nationalist movement under Mustafa Kemal, and many Turks believed that the Greeks intended to exterminate or drive them out of western Anatolia altogether. Nonetheless, the Turkish response was initially weak (with other Allied armies simultaneously occupying Constantinople and other areas of Anatolia), and Greek forces soon pushed outwards from Smyrna in an offensive that had seized Ushak, Panderma, Bursa, and Adrianople by the end of July 1919. Irregular warfare between Turks and the Greek army and between Turks and Anatolian Greeks continued throughout 1919 and 1920, the harshness of Greek occupation doing much to bolster the nationalists' cause. At the Conference of

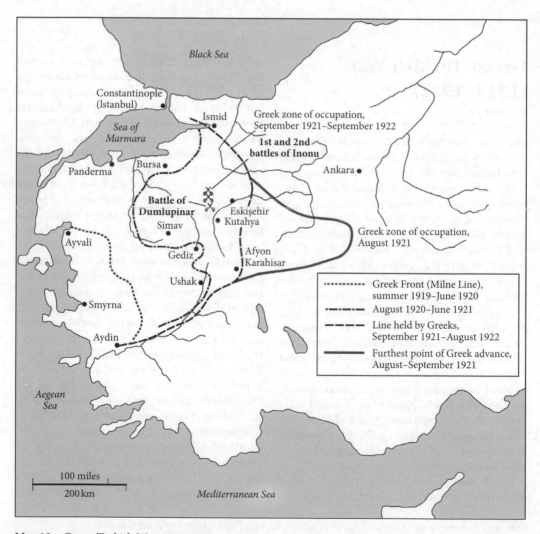

Map 13   Greco-Turkish War, 1919–1922.

London of February–March 1921 – an Allied attempt to mediate the conflict in Anatolia – neither the Greeks nor the Turks were willing to compromise, as the former had committed too much to the cause already, and the latter saw the conflict with the Greeks as a struggle for their very existence.

Over a year after the initial Greek landings, the weak government of Sultan Mehmed VI felt compelled on August 10, 1920, to sign the Treaty of Sèvres with the Entente. The dreams of Venizelos and other proponents of the Megali Idea seemed to be on the verge of being realized. The supporters of Venizelos "talked excitedly of his having created a Greece of the two continents and of the five seas," the two continents being Europe and Asia and the five seas being the Mediterranean, the Aegean, the Ionian, the Sea of Marmara, and the Black Sea (Clogg 2002: 95). The aspiration to create Greater Greece, which had led to a military disaster in the previous Greco-Turkish War of 1897, seemed as if it were about to be fulfilled. Two months later, however, King Alexander died, and the election that followed in November turned into an ugly battle between Venizelos's supporters and those royalists who supported the return of exiled King Constantine (who had been expelled during the National Schism of 1914–1917). To the astonishment of Venizelos as well as many foreign observers, "Greater Greece's" main architect was soundly defeated, unable to hold even his own seat in parliament. This result was a clear a sign of the hostility of much of the Greek population toward continued warfare after nearly eight years of constant mobilization. The Anti-Venizelists now formed a majority government, but despite their earlier criticism of the war effort in Asia Minor, it soon became clear that they had no intention of withdrawing from Anatolia. Indeed, they felt strong enough to launch a renewed offensive in January 1921, and both the scale and the violence of the Greco-Turkish War would escalate dramatically in 1921 and 1922.

Greek forces pushed toward Eskişehir, but Turkish nationalist revolutionaries halted their advance at the First Battle of İnönü (January 9–11, 1921). The Turkish army's defense of İnönü was one of the nationalists' first military victories, and it did much to bolster the revolutionaries' legitimacy and in part led to negotiations with the Soviets, resulting in the Treaty of Moscow on March 16, 1921. This agreement secured Turkey's eastern frontier and allowed the nationalists to concentrate their forces on the invading Greeks. Turkish forces halted the Greeks again at the Second Battle of İnönü (March 26–31, 1921). The Greeks launched yet another offensive that summer, this time seizing Eskişehir on July 17 and reaching the Sakarya River. This push put the Greeks within 80 km of the nationalists' headquarters at Ankara, but they were unable to advance any further. Both Kemal's effective leadership and the extreme difficulties of supplying an army spread over such a broad front deep in the interior of Anatolia meant a victory for the Turks at the Battle of the Sakarya River (August 23–September 13, 1921). After holding the line at the Sakarya River through September, the Greeks felt compelled to withdraw to a defensive line just east of Eskişehir and Afyonkarahisar before the onset of winter.

Kemal's armies consolidated their control over much of Anatolia throughout 1922. Kemal had already secured a French withdrawal from Cilicia on October 20, 1921, and Italy had also renounced its territorial ambitions. Even the British became ever more lukewarm toward continued commitment to the Greek occupation, and by the end of 1921 they were sending neither arms nor financial support to their erstwhile Greek allies. The growing strength of the Turkish nationalists combined with the crumbling commitment of the Great Powers left the Greeks in a highly vulnerable position. By August 26, Kemal felt strong enough to launch a major offensive against the Greek lines, quickly seizing Afyonkarahisar and Bursa. The nationalist army then drove the Greeks back along the rail line to Smyrna. At this point, the Greek army engaged in a scorched-earth policy as it retreated, destroying entire villages and engaging in frequent massacres. Their retreat soon turned into a desperate drive to escape encirclement and annihilation. The advancing Turkish nationalists likewise killed large numbers of Anatolian Christians, creating a massive refugee flow toward Smyrna. Greek forces began their evacuation on September 8, and the Turks finally launched their attack on Smyrna on September 9, 1922. During and after the assault, the Turks killed large numbers of Armenian and Greek civilians, seen as a fifth column that had brought the Greeks into Anatolia.

Clogg (2002: 97) states that about 30,000 Greek and Armenian Christians were massacred as the Turkish army and Turkish civilians rampaged through the city. While there is a debate as to who set the fires, the Greek sector of Smyrna was burned to the ground, and Greek soldiers and Anatolian Christian civilians massed on the coast in an attempt to escape the burning wreckage of the city. The frantic evacuation from Smyrna, henceforth known as Izmir, and the events that followed effectively ended both the pan-Hellenic Megali Idea and the more than two-millennia presence of Greek peoples in Asia Minor.

The military debacle in Anatolia was followed by treaty negotiations at Lausanne, Switzerland. There the Allies abandoned the zonal divisions of Asia Minor envisioned by the now defunct Treaty of Sèvres. The Treaty of Lausanne (July 24, 1923) recognized Turkey's current borders (indeed, as Bloxham (2005: 166) points out, it is the only post-war settlement to have survived to the present day) and sought to settle the "demographic" issues that resulted from the Turkish victory. The chaotic and murderous grassroots ethnic cleansing of 1921 and 1922 was to be replaced by a state-sponsored exchange of populations. By Naimark's (2001: 54) estimate, the treaty aimed to relocate about 350,000 "Turks" and between 1.2 and 1.5 million "Greeks," both groups defined by their religion rather than their linguistic or cultural identity, in an attempt to create ethnically homogeneous nation-states. As Hirschon (2003: 9) points out, this compulsory population exchange marked a watershed in the history of the eastern Mediterranean. It caused great suffering to those dislocated, but it did seem to create the conditions for more stable relations between Greece and Turkey in the interwar period. The war was nothing short of a catastrophe for the Greeks, and their defeat poisoned post-war politics for decades. For the creators of the new Turkish Republic, on the other hand, the war served as the foundational struggle of their War of Independence. The Treaty of Lausanne may have helped secure better relations between Greece and Turkey, but as Mazower (1999: 41–75) argues, it also served as an ominous precedent for subsequent regimes that sought to solve "ethnic problems" through forced population transfers.

SEE ALSO: Balkan Wars (1912–1913); Ethnic Cleansing.

References

Bloxham, D. (2005) *The Great Game of Genocide: Imperialism, Nationalism, and the Destruction of the Ottoman Armenians*. Oxford: Oxford University Press.

Clogg, R. (2002) *A Concise History of Modern Greece*, 2nd ed. Cambridge: Cambridge University Press.

Hirschon, R. (Ed.) (2003) *Crossing the Aegean: An Appraisal of the 1923 Compulsory Population Exchange between Greece and Turkey*. New York: Berghan Books.

Mazower, M. (1999) *Dark Continent: Europe's Twentieth Century*. New York: Knopf.

Naimark, N. M. (2001) *Fires of Hatred: Ethnic Cleansing in Twentieth-Century Europe*. Cambridge, MA: Harvard University Press.

Further Reading

Clark, B. (2009) *Twice a Stranger: The Mass Expulsions that Forged Modern Greece and Turkey*. Cambridge, MA: Harvard University Press.

Fortna, B. C., Katsikas, S., Kamouzis, D., and Konortas, P. (Eds.) (2012) *State-Nationalisms in the Ottoman Empire, Greece and Turkey: Orthodox and Muslims, 1830–1945*. New York: Routledge.

Gingeras, R. (2009) *Sorrowful Shores: Violence, Ethnicity, and the End of the Ottoman Empire 1912–1923*. New York: Oxford University Press.

Mazower, M. (2002) *The Balkans: A Short History*. New York: Modern Library.

Milton, G. (2008) *Paradise Lost: Smyrna 1922: The Destruction of a Christian City in the Islamic World*. New York: Basic Books.

Panayi, P. and Virdee, P. (Eds.) (2011) *Refugees and the End of Empire: Imperial Collapse and Forced Migration in the Twentieth Century*. New York: Palgrave Macmillan.

Smith, M. L. (1998) *Ionian Vision: Greece in Asia Minor, 1919–1922*. Ann Arbor: University of Michigan Press.

Gulf Wars (1990–1991, 2003–Present)

KENNETH W. ESTES

Known in the region as the Second and Third Gulf Wars, with the Iraq–Iran War (1980–1988) as the first of the series, these conflicts marked the apogee and nadir of the regime of the Iraqi dictator Saddam Hussein. In the case of the subject wars, each consisted of a coalition war organized by the United States to first limit and then overthrow the Iraqi regime, with the aim of improving peace and stability in the petroleum-rich region so vital to the economies of most of the rest of the world.

Gulf War (1990–1991)

Curiously enshrouded today with doubts because of its successor campaign of 2003, the Gulf War of 1990–1991 between Iraq and a US-led international coalition organized under United Nations (UN) auspices decisively reversed the issue of Iraq's seizure of Kuwait on August 2, 1991. It inaugurated the permanent introduction of US ground and air forces into a region previously frequented only by its naval forces on a regular basis. In the process, US foreign policy became entangled with the relations and problems of the Islamic states of this region more than ever before.

The 1990–1991 Gulf War drew some origins from the Iraq–Iran War of 1980–1988, which began similarly with a surprise attack by Iraqi forces. In July 1988, both sides ceased hostilities. Less than two years later, Iraq then seized Kuwait, partly out of the need to recover financially from the ravages of the First Gulf War. Kuwait had loaned Saddam Hussein's government 14 billion dollars in the interval and was loathe to remit any of it, despite Iraqi requests. Given incipient quarrels with Kuwait over borders and slant drilling into the Rumelia oil fields, Hussein determined to settle the issue by outright conquest.

Iraqi forces, in the strength of three divisions, crossed into Kuwait on August 2, 1990. Within a few days, US President George H. W. Bush ordered forces to reinforce and defend Saudi Arabia and the Persian Gulf emirates, at the same time fomenting a growing coalition determined to resist and ultimately expel the Iraqi forces. In doing so, President Bush responded to the urging of British Prime Minister Margaret Thatcher, who had taken a similar tough stance against the Argentine seizure of the Falklands (Malvinas) Islands in 1982.

With international support growing in the UN, and with it the material and military contributions to a coalition effort, the United States fashioned and led a defensive effort to safeguard the remaining Arab states of the Gulf region from Iraq. The United States, despite an announced defense cutback at the end of the Cold War, benefited immensely from previous war plans and major military infrastructure built in the region (particularly in Saudi Arabia) to defend it against Soviet invasion. Air and naval bases, storage facilities, barracks, and operations centers had all been built by Gulf states and US contractors. The US Central Command had been formed in the wake of the Soviet invasion of Afghanistan (1979) and since had received the lion's share of planned reinforcements, equipment, and exercises in the US defense establishment. The US modified its deployment plans made for the defense of the Gulf against the Soviet Union. Thus, with little warning, massive forces and support echelons moved to the Gulf for this new occasion.

US aircraft reached Saudi Arabia beginning on August 8, 1990, followed by US Army Airborne and Marine Corps ground units, backed up by naval aviation from offshore aircraft carriers and supporting land bases. Within a month, enough forces had been established in Saudi Arabia to block any further Iraqi moves. The US forces dubbed the defensive build-up "Operation Desert Shield," an operation aimed at confining Iraqi moves to the Kuwaiti territory already seized. From Riyadh, the Saudi capital city, the commander in chief of US Central Command, army General Norman H. Schwarzkopf, and the largely titular Arab coalition commander, Saudi Lieutenant General Prince Khalid bin Sultan bin Abdul Aziz Al-Saud, began planning offensive moves in order to expel the Iraqis from Kuwait, supported by parallel diplomatic deliberations in the UN. On October 31, President Bush authorized a doubling of US forces in preparation for the offensive.

US diplomacy ran into complex problems on various levels. Arab states sending forces to the coalition would fight only under Arab major commanders, and some, such as Syria, disliked the new offensive mission. The Iraqi threat to fire missiles into Israel if attacked by the coalition introduced further anomalies into the Arab–western coalition. The Russians, long military patrons and suppliers to Iraqi forces, saw their considerable investments at stake and urged a diplomatic solution, even offering their good offices apart from the UN for a last-minute settlement short of war.

The Iraqis had little hope for resisting the coalition of US, British, French, Saudi, Egyptian, and Gulf contingents on the ground, let alone the overwhelming air and naval armadas that included even more national contingents. But Israel warned that it would not ignore Iraqi attacks, and Iraq clearly hoped to unhinge the Arab–western alliance by bringing Israel into any outbreak of fighting. US forces deployed defensive missile batteries to protect Israel, while directing more missions of coalition aviation and special forces into the western Iraqi desert, from which any missiles would be launched to bombard Israel.

The US deployment to the Gulf region exceeded any similar undertaking since World War II. More than 500,000 troops, including a major mobilization of national guardsmen and reservists, deployed to the Gulf in a six-month period, and other major deployments from the United States replaced units detailed to the Gulf region. Bases in all the Gulf states from Bahrain to Oman received US naval and air forces and the growing logistic structure necessary to support them.

After Iraq resisted UN and US calls for abandoning Kuwait, the UN authorized the use of force "by all means necessary" on November 29, 1990, and the US Congress authorized the president to use force against Iraq on January 9, 1991. The offensive operation, dubbed "Operation Desert Storm" by the US and "Operation Granby" by the UK, began with an air campaign on January 17. Coalition aircraft and US cruise missiles struck strategic and tactical targets in Kuwait and Iraq on a continuous basis through the beginning of the ground combat phase.

On February 24, 1991, the Marine Corps ground combat contingents attacked into Kuwait, opening the coalition ground offensive by forcing their way through the Iraqi barriers and brushing aside the frontline resistance. Flanked by two joint corps of Arab contingents, the attacking US forces destroyed or captured whole brigades of Iraqi troops and swept through the burning oil fields toward the capital of Kuwait City.

Within the following 24 hours, a vast field army of mechanized, armored, and air assault divisions of the US, British, and French armies rolled across the Saudi–Iraqi border. Overwhelming weak defenses, these forces, organized under the US Army XVIII Airborne Corps and VII Corps, wheeled north and east to outmaneuver and destroy the main fighting forces of the Iraqi army and to move along the Euphrates River, completing a massive encirclement of Kuwait and southern Iraq. They maneuvered by day and night through sandstorms and other problems, despite the challenge of distinguishing friend from foe. A few Iraqi counterattacks were beaten off with hardly any casualties. After 100 hours of combat, the coalition forces dominated Kuwait and the Arab coalition units cleared its capital of remaining Iraqis.

The Iraqi units in this war lacked the skills or stamina necessary to inflict damage. The Iraqi air force scattered, making only a few efforts to engage, with most aircraft voluntarily interned in Iran, and the small Iraqi naval forces withered under overwhelming air attacks. The elite Iraqi Republican Guard ground corps, held in reserve from the immediate battle area, suffered catastrophic losses fighting the US Army-led encirclement, and the slight Iraqi resistance in Kuwait melted within the first 48 hours of the ground offensive.

Iraq launched missile strikes against Israel as the air campaign began, with the first ballistic missiles fired on January 18. US anti-aircraft missile batteries seemed to counter most incoming missiles, but later analysis demonstrated that most Iraqi missiles broke up in flight. In any case, the missiles contained no chemical warheads, and the much-feared Iraqi arsenal of chemical weapons played no part in this war. Moreover, coalition air and special forces strikes against Iraqi launch sites made unnecessary any Israeli participation that might have threatened coalition political cohesion.

As the nature of the Iraqi collapse became apparent, President Bush accepted the advice of his staff to cease fire and halt what was emerging as a slaughter of now ineffective Iraqi forces. A hurriedly assembled armistice meeting on the Kuwaiti frontier allowed two Iraqi generals meeting with Prince Khalid and General Schwarzkopf on March 3 to pledge Iraqi adherence to the various UN demands, as well as to arrange for prisoner exchanges and other military requirements.

The decision to end the fighting spawned endless second-guessing to the present day over possible outcomes had the coalition continued military operations to occupy Baghdad and depose the regime of Saddam Hussein. The unexpected resistance of Iraqis to occupation in the 2003 campaign has apparently not quelled speculation that Iraq might have fallen easily into foreign domination in 1991.

As a result of the Second Gulf War, Kuwait was restored to its emir, Iraqi military power was crippled, UN inspection teams certified the destruction of newly prohibited munitions and weapons, and allied (later Anglo-American) air patrols were established over the northern and southern sectors of Iraq. A continuing US military presence settled in the Gulf region after the war.

US forces and equipment had performed well and the expenses of the 1990–1991 Gulf War were touted as "covered" by the $75 billion in contributions promised by coalition partners. However, only some $49 billion was actually donated, some of it in the form of goods and services, and none of the contributions covered the immense wear placed on US and coalition matériel. Despite this factor, this conflict suggested that future wars could be fought economically by the United States to advance its national aims.

Gulf War (2003–Present)

As extraordinary as it would have seemed years ago, nobody could have predicted that the drama of the 2001 terrorist attack on New York and Washington would have been upstaged by any other event in the presidential administration of George W. Bush. However, this became the case with the unilaterally initiated US invasion of Iraq, which produced vigorous debate in an already polarized diplomatic and US political landscape. The Iraq campaign of 2003 (inaugurating the Third Gulf War) nevertheless met the needs of the US political leadership to settle its issues with Iraq.

During 2002, indicators continued to build signaling impending US military action against Iraq. The US government had already demonstrated its desire to settle direct and latent threats to security in the aftermath of the September 11, 2001, attacks on US soil. Thus, even before the campaign against Afghanistan reached its culminating point in the establishment of a friendly interim government there, planning

continued for removing the onerous government of Iraq and removing any future threat it presented to the region and US interests.

The incoming administration of Mr Bush had already indicated its wish to take new initiatives against Iraq in 2000. Maintaining the US-led aerial over-watch of "no-fly" zones in Iraq from Turkish and Saudi bases cost too much in funds, equipment, and increasingly scarce military manpower. Moreover, the former coalition arrayed against Iraq had tired of the UN sanctions and embargos that followed the conclusion of that conflict. Several of these nations openly anticipated the resumption of trade relations. Moreover, Iraqi dictator–president Saddam Hussein had defiantly resisted and obstructed the efforts of UN weapons inspection organizations monitoring the disarmament clauses of the 1991 armistice agreed to by the Iraqis. In a manner still unexplained to this day, Iraq withheld the remaining details of the creation and scrapping of its ballistic missile, chemical, and biological weapons programs, and its research in nuclear weapons. Iraqi military forces had approached the Kuwaiti border several times in the 1990s, and expensive military deployments by the US had been ordered to demonstrate resolve and to continue to demonstrate military superiority in the Gulf region.

Any doubts in the Bush administration on how best to put an end to the seemingly endless defense drain posed by the Saddam Hussein regime quickly evaporated with the destruction of the World Trade Center and the resulting need to provide a strong response to reassert US power in the region and destroy the amorphous band that could be held responsible for the attacks. Even as the quick reprisal campaign against Afghanistan to destroy terrorist bases of operations took shape, US deployments and war planning efforts against Iraq could be discerned. The US Army V Corps headquarters, in Heidelberg, Germany, received its assignment to begin planning operations in "Southwest Asia" during the first week of November 2001.

If the United States intended to wage a "global war on terrorism," then states sponsoring terrorism or known to sympathize with terrorist acts could be added to the list of likely targets. This facet scarcely implicated Iraq and Saddam Hussein's regime, but Paul Wolfowitz, the US deputy secretary of defense, revealed publicly that the emphasis on Iraq's rumored possession of weapons of mass destruction was brandished most vigorously because the US public would grasp it as a threat, making war justification more easily than the other possibilities.

While the US Army planned, war gamed, and revised concepts of operations against Iraq, President Bush announced the key phrase "Axis of Evil" in the 2002 State of the Union address, identifying Iraq as a nation of interest and setting the tone for a year of build-up of both policy and military readiness for a campaign against Iraq. The immediate objective aimed at overthrowing Saddam Hussein and installing a more friendly government that would ease tensions, isolate other opponents (such as Iran, also included in the Axis of Evil), and permit greater US influence in the region, including military basing rights.

As laudable as these objectives remained with the public, the concept of unilateral military action, even with British and Australian forces participating, did not prove endearing in the United States or among her usual allies. But the United States carried out extensive deployments of forces and supplies through the summer of 2002, and it appears that Bush both overestimated war fervor and deployed the forces to the region far faster than allies or the UN Security Council were willing to act. Arab allies that had supported the 1990–1991 Gulf War also proved less motivated toward a showdown with Iraq. Although allies from the 1990–1991 conflict viewed Hussein as at least a latent threat to their nations, the notions of a US-sponsored invasion to accomplish regime change found little favor in the traditional autocracies of the Arab world.

By late summer 2002, therefore, the United States had stationed several brigades of ground troops in Kuwait, moved at least five sets of prepositioned equipment (each sufficient to outfit a mechanized or armored brigade) from other sites to Kuwait, and had more ships entering the Persian Gulf each week with cargos of general supplies and equipment.

By this time, Army V Corps planning considered using both the 3rd Infantry Division and the 1st Armored Division as the leading elements of the attack, supported by the 101st Airborne Division. Other major units, such as the 4th Infantry Division, 1st Cavalry Division, and 82nd Airborne Division would reinforce or perform supporting missions for V Corps. However, by February 2003, the V Corps's force lists had been stripped of many units and revised plans called for a starkly reduced attack force, with reinforcements to be "rolled" into the theater after combat began.

Convinced of a cheap and rapid victory, the Bush administration approved an air attack against an alleged hideaway of Hussein late on March 19 and launched the ground offensive on March 20, 2003. The evident weakness of Iraq – defeated in 1991 and embargoed since then – suggested that no long air campaign or overwhelming build-up of forces would be needed. Fewer than 50,000 US and UK troops initially crossed into Iraq from staging bases in Kuwait, with another 100,000 en route to the assembly areas in Kuwait. Dubbed "Operation Iraqi Freedom" by US forces, the campaign was called "Operation Telic" by British forces and "Operation Falconer" by the Australian units involved. While British and US Marine Corps troops isolated the major southern Iraqi city of Basra and the nearby Faw Peninsula, the remainder of the US forces thrust along the Euphrates River as far as Al Nasiriya, before splitting into two axes of advance.

The Army V Corps and the companion I Marine Expeditionary Force thus began the fastest offensive in US military history, covering the distance from the Kuwaiti border to their penetration of downtown Baghdad – a straight-line distance of 540 km – in a mere 16 days. Combat involved not only the leading assault elements of the two corps but many combat support and service support units, as they followed along the lengthening lines of communications. The soldiers and marines responded to changing situations and enemy tactics, adapting their own tactics, techniques, and procedures to defeat the enemy wherever found. For example, the appearance of irregular forces as the more dangerous tactical opponent required adjustment to engagement methods. In the end, however, the surprising speed with which they approached and penetrated into the capital city with armored forces brought a quick end to organized resistance.

As the Iraqi government fled the city, military resistance melted from all but die-hard factions, some of which required neutralization by additional US divisions arriving at Kuwaiti ports. Allied special forces, used in record numbers in this conflict, secured airfields at the Iraqi city of Kirkuk for the 173rd Airborne Brigade to land and occupy the Kurdish northern provinces of Iraq.

Between April 7 and April 20, a mopping-up of isolated pockets of Iraqi units continued to the south of Baghdad, while the occupation of the area to the north of the city and south of Kirkuk completed the combat phase of the campaign. After defeating the Iraqi armed forces and toppling the regime of Saddam Hussein, the focus of the effort now shifted to the Iraqi population and the need to provide a safe and secure environment for reconstruction, humanitarian assistance, and the inevitable nation building that now faced the United States and its coalition partners in Iraq.

Despite the attention given by the US forces to restrict the bombardment and fire support to minimize collateral damage, nearly all available services in Iraq collapsed as a result of the combat operations: civil servants and other public workers fled, and buildings and infrastructure were looted of matériel (even items of little apparent value were carried off by the mobs). There ensued no rapid restoration of services on the part of the Iraqis, and the US military forces had not prepared to provide them or to begin the reconstruction of the Iraqi infrastructure. The "rolling start" method of the 2003 campaign minimized the employment of forces of all kinds. An eventual build-up of forces was planned in the event that Iraqi resistance continued or setbacks to the offensive required new operations to be launched. But the rapid movement of the initial assault forces brought about the "decapitation" of the Saddam Hussein regime in a mere 16 days, leaving the same assault forces also in charge of a large and unplanned recovery and stabilization operation. In fact, a nation-building program far in excess of that conducted in the 1990s by the North Atlantic Treaty Organization in the Balkans now beckoned the United States and its coalition partners. But the assault forces stood alone, recovering from their own exertions, and the follow-on forces scheduled to conduct the remainder of the fighting expected in Iraq, such as the 1st Armored and 4th Infantry Divisions, were still arriving and assembling. Even if the United States had planned for an occupation

and nation-building effort, none of the requisite forces had been sent, nor would any arrive for the foreseeable future.

A great improvisation now took place, a "rolling occupation" plan was devised to match the "rolling start" campaign. But no time remained. The opportunities for an early restoration of order had already vanished. By all accounts, the US invasion of Iraq, undertaken in conjunction with British and Australian combat forces, had succeeded in its mission. Although the term "coalition of the willing" had been frequently cited by US spokespersons, only five of the 30 nations initially named had sent combat troops, and the small Polish and Romanian contingents took no part in the fighting.

President Bush proclaimed major combat operations at an end on May 1, 2003, but in the months that followed the war became a struggle of resistance and insurrection by varied groups against the US-led occupation of the country. Again, US military planners had not taken serious account of the possibility of a resistance movement and, even with the creation of a "sovereign" Iraqi provisional government in July 2004, there seemed no end in sight for the Anglo-American campaign to pacify Iraq. Two major risings in the Shi'ia-dominated southern provinces, led by the Iraqi cleric Muqtada al-Sadr, challenged the US establishment of the provisional government, and open combat flared during April–September 2004. Successive elections, constitutions, and governments later, the insurrection movements demonstrated no loss of energy. In contrast, the coalition partners showed real fatigue in continuing the security and economic reconstruction of Iraq. In the end, only the acquiescence of Iraqi tribal leaders and the fielding of a coalition-trained Iraqi army, constabulary, and police force allowed the Iraqi government to exercise sovereignty and the US and allied troops to begin a gradual withdrawal from the country.

Conclusions

The US invasion of Iraq in 2003 stemmed from an overly enthusiastic and ambitious concept that had been reinforced in unintended fashion by the ease of victory in the 1990–1991 Gulf War. The deployment then of overwhelming US and coalition forces in six months time had resulted in an aerial campaign of roughly 30 days and a 100-hour ground war that had eliminated the threat of Iraq to the region and settled the United States into a commanding presence in the Gulf region. The apparent ease of that victory influenced the more ambitious schemes of invading and occupying Iraq in 2003.

Unfortunately, the fortunes of war and the intrinsic play of chance against even the best-laid plans make the simplest things in war difficult. A typical example of such oversimplification came when US Secretary of Defense Donald Rumsfeld called upon Iraq to surrender on the first day of ground operations in 2003, as if the "game" were up and there would be no need for the armed forces of a sovereign nation to attempt to do its duty and defend itself, no matter how hopeless the odds.

As a result of such wishful thinking and harsh realities left unanticipated or miscalculated, the 2003 invasion and subsequent occupation of Iraq brought numerous problems for which few solutions remained at hand: national resistance, misconduct of troops, trials, prisons and prisoner handling, rules of engagement, trial procedures, collaboration, and use of torture among an endless list of concerns. The shortage in the United States of Arabic speakers and other knowledgeable experts formed a poor basis for establishing hegemony in a part of the world unfamiliar at best to American eyes. If nothing else, the US experience with the Iraq War of 2003 has served as a warning to those who consider war a facile tool to be exploited in the hands of designated craftsmen.

SEE ALSO: Chemical Warfare; Falklands War (1982); Iraq–Iran War (1980–1988).

Further Reading

Atkinson, R. (1999) *Crusade: The Unknown Story of the Persian Gulf War*. Boston: Houghton Mifflin.

Atkinson, R. (2004) *In the Company of Soldiers: A Chronicle of Combat in Iraq*. New York: Henry Holt.

Beck, S. and Downing, M. (2003) *The Battle for Iraq: BBC News Correspondents on the War Against Saddam*. Baltimore: Johns Hopkins University Press.

Fallows, J. (2006) *Blind Into Baghdad: America's War in Iraq*. New York: Vintage.

Fontenoy, G., Degen, E. J., and Tohn, D. (1991) *On Point: The United States Army in Operation Iraqi Freedom*. Fort Leavenworth: Combat Studies Institute Press.

Friedman, N. (1991) *Desert Victory: The War for Kuwait*. Annapolis: Naval Institute Press.

Gordon, M. R. and Trainor, B. E. (2006) *Cobra II: The Inside Story of the Invasion and Occupation of Iraq*. New York: Pantheon.

Putney, D. (2004) *Airpower Advantage: Planning the Gulf War Air Campaign 1989–1991*. Washington, DC: Air Force History and Museums Program.

Record, J. (1993) *Hollow Victory: A Contrary View of the Gulf War*. Potomac, MD: Potomac Books.

Record, J. (2004) *Dark Victory: America's Second War against Iraq*. Annapolis: Naval Institute Press.

Ricks, T. E. (2009) *The Gamble: General David Petraeus and the American Military Adventure in Iraq, 2006–2008*. New York: Penguin.

Schubert, F. N. and Kraus, T. L. (Eds.) (2000) *The Whirlwind War: The United States Army in Operations Desert Shield and Desert Storm*. Washington, DC: Center of Military History.

van Creveld, M. (1991) *The Transformation of War*. New York: Free Press.

I

Indo-Pakistani Wars (1947–1948, 1965, 1971)

PRADEEP P. BARUA

India and Pakistan became independent nations in 1947. Almost at their very inception the two nations went to war over the disputed territory of Kashmir. The Kashmir conflict would lead to war again in 1965, and in 1971 the creation of the new nation of Bangladesh was cause for yet another war. These three wars have been a defining factor in relations between the two countries and the region in general.

1947–1948

On August 15, 1947, the old British Raj gave way to the independent nations of India and Pakistan. Within months the two new nations were in dispute over the kingdom of Jammu and Kashmir. The Hindu ruler of Jammu and Kashmir, Maharaja Hari Singh, wanted his princely state to be independent. However, the Pakistani president, Mohammed Ali Jinnah, was determined that the Muslim majority state be a part of Pakistan. On October 22, Jinnah launched Operation Gulmarg, a full-scale guerrilla invasion of Kashmir by tribal raiders recruited and supported by the Pakistani army. On October 26, Hari Singh signed the instrument of accession handing over his kingdom to India. The next day India flew the 1st Sikhs (infantry battalion) into the capital, Srinagar.

The Indian army's first priority was to defend Srinagar. This came under the responsibility of the 161st Infantry Brigade. Despite intense pressure, the Indian forces were able to outflank and devastate the tribal raiders at the Battle of Shalateng on the Baramula to Srinagar highway. Within a few weeks, the brigade managed to clear the entire Sri Valley of thousands of marauding tribesmen. By November, the Indian forces in Kashmir had increased to division strength (Jammu & Kashmir Division). By the end of the month, the division had retaken several towns, including Naushera, Jhangar, Kotli, and Mirpur. The onset of winter brought an end to further offensive operations. When fighting resumed in late January, Pakistan committed its regular forces to aiding the raiders. Jhangar fell to Pakistani forces in January, but was retaken by an Indian counterattack in February. Indian forces were also able to retake Kot on January 31. In April, Indian advances secured more territory, including the town of Rajauri. Pakistan responded by committing more and more forces and in May they were able to stop a major Indian attack

Twentieth-Century War and Conflict: A Concise Encyclopedia, First Edition. Edited by Gordon Martel.
© 2015 John Wiley & Sons, Ltd. Published 2015 by John Wiley & Sons, Ltd.

toward Chakothi, thereby ending Indian operations west of Srinagar.

To the south, the Indian forces had been waging an intense campaign since November to maintain the besieged town of Punch, which sheltered 40,000 refugees. On September 14, the Indian army launched Operation Easy to relieve Punch. In a methodical campaign using infantry, artillery, and air support, the Indian forces advanced steadily through intense opposition and broke the siege on November 19. All operations in the southern sector ended when the ceasefire came into effect in December.

The biggest territorial gains for Pakistan came in the northern part of Kashmir. Here, at the start of the conflict, the Pakistani forces gained a major coup when the pro-Pakistani British commander of the Gilgit Scouts overthrew Hari Singh's control in the north. On August 14, Colonel Thapa, the Skardu garrison's commander, surrendered Skardu to the raiders. Kargil and Dras had already fallen in May and June. The end result was that Leh, the capital of Ladakh, was cut off from the rest of Indian-controlled Kashmir. The Indian army launched its counterattack in the north in June with Operation Erase. A two-battalion assault took the town of Gurias to the northwest of Dras and Kargil. In September, an attack was opened against Dras and Kargil. After a hurried and challenging engineering operation to build a road through the Zoji La Pass, Stuart light tanks were used in the attack. The tanks' appearance unnerved the defenders and Dras fell on November 15, with Kargil falling on November 24. The road to Leh was opened a few days later.

The 1947–1948 Kashmir War was the longest of the three wars fought between Pakistan and India. Coming on the heels of World War II and Independence, it enabled the two countries to showcase their military capabilities. Despite operating close to its supply bases and enjoying a huge numerical advantage, the Pakistani army was unable to press home its advantage. Its main weakness was the shortage of trained and experienced officers. The Indian army, on the other hand, had a large number of trained and battle-hardened officers who had just emerged from years of operational experience in World War II. This experience emerged during the Kashmir War. The Indian army displayed considerable operational flexibility to deal with raiders and the Pakistani army. It also made effective use of its positional warfare doctrines learned during World War II. Whenever possible, commanders made full use of artillery and air support to aid the infantry in its operations. The Indian army's officers and non-commissioned officers displayed skill, determination, and discipline in checking and even reversing many of Pakistan's initial gains.

1965

The 1965 or Second Kashmir War, as it is sometimes called, began with yet another ambitious Pakistani plan to use guerrillas to destabilize Indian Kashmir. Codenamed Operation Gibraltar, the plan envisaged the use of 7,000 guerrillas, who would infiltrate the Kashmir Valley and instigate an uprising by the local Kashmiris. The assault commenced on August 7, 1965. India's response was swift and decisive. Indian forces crossed the ceasefire line, seized a number of Pakistani posts, including the Haji Pir Pass, and crushed the guerrillas.

The Pakistani high command, surprised and incensed by the Indian willingness to cross the ceasefire line, escalated the conflict by initiating Operation Grand-Slam, an offensive into Southern Kashmir (Jammu), on September 1. This assault took the Indians by surprise and they lost much of the vulnerable Chammb-Akhnur salient to the Pakistani 12th Infantry Division. The Indians, who were restricted by treaty obligations to the number of troops they could send into Kashmir, now decided to take the Pakistani pressure off Jammu by launching a new offensive toward the Pakistani cities of Lahore and Sialkot. In the case of Lahore, the objective was not to take the city, but to threaten it and destroy most of Pakistan's armored forces in the process. The operation pitted three Indian infantry divisions – the 4th, 7th, and 15th – and one armored brigade – the 2nd – against two Pakistani infantry divisions – the 10th and 11th – and the Pakistani 1st Armored Division. The attack commenced on September 6. All three Indian infantry divisions were tasked with seizing bridges on the Ichogil Canal outside Lahore. After bitter fighting, the 7th Indian Division seized the crossing at Burki on September 11. The 15th Indian Division secured its canal crossing at Dograi on September 21 after bitter hand-to-hand fighting. However, when the

4th Indian Division advanced toward the Inchogil Canal on September 6, it ran headlong into a Pakistani counterattack by elements of the Pakistani 11th Infantry Division and the 1st Armored Division, which were moving towards Lahore. The 4th Indian Division was forced to fall back and establish a defensive position between Asal-Uttar and Chima. In the war's largest tank battle, Indian Centurion tanks from the 3rd Cavalry and Deccan Horse stopped the M-47 Patton tanks of the Pakistani 1st Armored Division. On September 8–10, the Pakistani 1st Armored Division made repeated and futile attempts to break through, but was repulsed with heavy losses. Aside from smaller probing actions, this sector remained stable until the ceasefire on September 23.

The Lahore offensive was followed by an offensive operation toward the Pakistani city of Sialkot. The 1st Indian Army Corps was tasked with cutting the northern Pakistani city's communication links with Lahore. The Indian 1st Army included the 6th and 26th Infantry Divisions and the powerful 1st Armored Division. Its objectives were the Pakistani towns of Phillora, Chawinda, and Pagowal on the road connecting Sialkot to Lahore. The attack commenced on September 8, but slow progress due to rain and mud and Pakistani resistance enabled the Pakistanis to rush in their 6th Armored Division to Chawinda. On September 12–13, the Indian forces seized Phillora and Pagowal in the face of heavy resistance from Pakistani armor. However, Chawinda continued to hold out against several Indian attacks until the ceasefire.

The 1965 war also saw the air forces of the two countries engage in a short but intense air campaign. The Indian Air Force (IAF) began the conflict with a concerted effort to provide ground support to Indian forces, but the lack of adequate air–ground coordination and planning meant that these operations were largely ineffective, and resulted in heavy losses to defending Pakistani fighters. The Pakistani Air Force (PAF) stayed largely on the defensive, with a few raids against Indian air bases and defense installations. The IAF, however, used its superior numbers to launch a sustained operation against Pakistani air bases, with special emphasis on the largest of them, Sargodha. Pakistan claimed to have repelled these attacks by inflicting heavy losses on the attacking IAF planes. The overall effectiveness of either side's efforts, however, proved to be sporadic at best. This was due largely to the limited offensive operational effectiveness of each side's aircraft. With the exception of a few squadrons of Canberra medium bombers (the PAF used the American version, the B-57), both sides relied on first-generation subsonic fighters. The IAF used a mix of British and French aircraft, including the Hunter, Gant, Vampire, Mystère, and Ouragon. The PAF used the American-built F-86 Sabre. All these fighters were lightly armed, primarily equipped with canons, rockets, and small iron bombs (a few Pakistani squadrons were equipped with Sidewinder air-to-air missiles), and with very limited range. At the end of the war, the PAF claimed 113 Indian aircraft downed to the IAF's claim of 73 Pakistani aircraft.

The 1965 War saw both India and Pakistan utilize substantially larger air and ground assets than during the First Kashmir War. Pakistan in particular was eager to show off its new mechanized formations utilizing their American-supplied M-47/48 battle tanks and M-113 armored personnel carriers. The Indians, by contrast, stuck to basic World War II-style infantry and artillery operations with tanks operating in a supporting and anti-tank role. On the whole, Pakistan's attempts to offset India's numerical advantage with mechanized warfare tactics failed, as their units were not capable of operating as effective combined arms units. With the exception of the Chaamb battle, the Pakistanis suffered heavy losses near Amritsar and Khem Karan.

1971

The Third Indo-Pakistan War was caused not by events in Kashmir, but by the outbreak of civil war in East Pakistan. In December 1970, Bengali Muslim nationalists won an overwhelming victory in the East Pakistan elections. General Yahya Khan, the military dictator, refused to accept this result and ordered the Pakistani military garrison in East Pakistan to seize control, triggering a violent civil war. Millions of refugees flooded into India, creating immense pressure on the Indian government. In April 1971, the prime minister of India ordered General Sam Manekshaw, the army chief and the chairman of the joint chiefs, to prepare for military intervention in East Pakistan in support of the Bengali Muslims who were fighting to create the independent state of Bangladesh.

As the Indian build-up on the border with East Pakistan gathered steam, Pakistan sought to launch a preemptive strike in the west. The Pakistani plan was to seize territory in the west to offset any Indian gains in East Pakistan. In accordance with this plan the Pakistani commander in East Pakistan, General Niazi, formulated a "fortress" concept of defense. Key towns along likely Indian routes of advance into East Pakistan were to be converted into fortresses. They were Jessore, Jhenida, Bogra, Rangpur, Jamalpur, Mymensigh, Sylhet, Bhairab Bazar, Comilla, and Chittagong. This defensive plan was based on the assumption that the Indians would have a narrow window of opportunity to seize chunks of territory in East Pakistan before international pressure brought an end to the conflict. However, in August 1971, India and the Soviet Union signed a treaty of friendship. This provided India with cover in the United Nations Security Council and alleviated any chance that China might intervene on Pakistan's behalf. Furthermore, war games conducted in October 1971 indicated that Indian troops could bypass the Pakistani fortresses and bring a quick end to the conflict. All these factors influenced the Indians to modify their objectives to plan for the complete seizure of East Pakistan. Pakistani planners were completely oblivious to this change of plan.

Pakistan initiated the attack with a preemptive airstrike against Indian airfields in the early hours of December 3. Within hours the Indians initiated their assault on East Pakistan. General Jagjit Singh Aurora's Eastern Command was responsible for the assault on East Pakistan. General Aurora used three army corps, the 2nd, 4th, and 33rd. The three Indian corps would attack from three different directions: the west (Jessore), north (Rangpur–Bogra), and east (Comilla–Sylhet). The Indian advances went according to plan. The "fortresses" were largely ignored, and by bypassing the main road networks, the Indians outflanked the Pakistani defenses. Indian light infantry formations proved adept at traversing East Pakistan's heavily forested and riverine terrain. Two significant -airborne operations, the heliborne lift of a battalion of soldiers to Sylhet and a parachute drop in Tangail, helped confuse the Pakistani defenders

and hastened the Pakistani forces' surrender in East Pakistan on December 16.

Pakistan had hoped to offset territorial losses in East Pakistan with offensive gains in the west. According to this plan, Pakistani forces would capture Poonch in Jammu and Ramgarh near Jaislamer. Pakistan's powerful 2nd Corps, its headquarter reserve, would also launch attacks in the Punjab. Indian plans were largely defensive, the only exception being the seizure of strategically important positions along the Kashmir ceasefire line. Major fighting took place in Chaamb, where the Pakistani 23rd Infantry Division seized territory west of the Tawi River. In response, the Indian 26th Division seized a small section of Pakistani territory known as the "chicken's neck," jutting into Akhnur. The major fighting in the west, however, took place in the Shakargarh Bulge, a large section of Pakistani territory jutting into India in the Punjab. Here the Indian 1st Corps struck at the defending Pakistani 1st Corps. After heavy fighting the Indians captured much of the bulge by December 15. On December 16, heavy tank battles erupted as Pakistani counterattacks sought to stem the Indian advance. Fighting ceased on December 17. Smaller ground actions took place in southern Punjab and Rajasthan, with Indian and Pakistani forces launching probing actions and raids across the international border.

The IAF and the PAF planned and mounted major air campaigns during the 1971 two-week war. The PAF initiated the air war with a preemptive airstrike against Indian airfields on December 3. However, this attack met with little success as all Indian fighters were dispersed and deployed in hardened shelters. The IAF struck back with a major counter air offensive. Unlike 1965, the IAF made ground support a major priority in 1971, and it showed. Of the total of 6,000 sorties launched, some 3,978 were dedicated ground support missions. In East Pakistan, the IAF quickly suppressed the single PAF Sabre squadron and then commenced to provide effective ground support to the Indian army. In the west, the IAF followed a mix of deep-strike and close-support tasks. The PAF tried to respond in kind, but found itself tied up in air defense missions. IAF strikes against Pakistani oil storage facilities were particularly effective and accounted for destruction of 40 percent of Pakistan's oil reserves. Heavy air battles occurred throughout the war's duration, with both sides making exaggerated kill claims.

The Indian navy played a substantial role in the 1971 War. Its greatly expanded fleet conducted a blockade of both East and West Pakistan. India's lone carrier, INS *Vikrant*, operating in the Bay of Bengal, conducted air strikes against the Pakistani port of Chittagong. In the west, the Indian navy's Osa missile boats attacked the Pakistani port of Karachi, sinking a Pakistani destroyer, PNS *Khaiber*, and the minesweeper *Muhafiz*. Other Indian ships shelled the Pakistani ports of Pasni, Gwadwer, and Jiwani. The Pakistani surface fleet remained in port, but its submarines were able to venture out. On December 8, the Pakistani Daphne-class submarine, the *Hangor*, sank the Indian corvette INS *Khukri* off the Rajasthan coast. Another Pakistani submarine, PNS *Ghazi*, attempted to enter the eastern Indian port of Cochin, but was sunk by the Indian destroyer INS *Rajput*.

The 1971 War culminated in a decisive victory for India. The war showcased India's growing military capabilities and the maturation of its defensive–offensive military doctrines. In sharp contrast, the war highlighted Pakistan's significant military weakness vis-à-vis its larger neighbor. It would define relations between the two countries for decades to come as they marched into the twenty-first century.

Further Reading

Brines, R. (1968) *The Indo-Pakistan Conflict*: London: Pall Mall Press.

Jagan Mohan, P.V.S. and Chopra, S. (2006) *The India–Pakistan Air War of 1965*. New Delhi: Manohar Books.

Kohli, S. N. (1989) *We Dared: Maritime Operations in the 1971 War*. New Delhi: Lancer International.

Musa, M. (1983) *My Version: India–Pakistan War, 1965*. Lahore: Wajidalis.

Musa, M. (1984) *Jawan to General: Reflections of a Pakistani Soldier*. Karachi: East and West Publishing.

Prasad, S. N. (1987) *History of the Operations in Jammu and Kashmir*. New Delhi: Government of India.

Saliq, S. (1977) *Witness to Surrender*. Karachi: Oxford University Press.

Shaheen Foundation (1988) *The Story of the Pakistan Air Force*. Islamabad: Shaheen Foundation.

Singh, J. (1993) *Behind the Scene: An Analysis of India's Military Operations, 1947–1971*. New Delhi: Lancer International.

Sisson, R. and Rose, L. E. (1990) *War and Secession: Pakistan, India and the Creation of Bangladesh*. Berkeley: University of California Press.

Iraq–Iran War (1980–1988)

DOUGLAS V. JOHNSON, II

This eight-year war began as a series of miscalculations and spiraled out of control as new tactics brought forth unexpected reactions, the way most wars develop. In the end, the Iraqis overcame their ideological prejudices to produce a professional military with which they achieved military victory. The Iranians could not overcome their revolution's ideological influences. Ultimately, the Ayatollah Khomeini's religious stature may have been the only factor preventing the Iranian government's collapse. The centrality of oil made the war a matter of serious interest to all industrialized nations and brought about some strange cooperative actions which are the subject for another study. By war's end, both sides were exhausted, but Iraq had access to reserves Iran did not possess and could have continued the war for a while longer; however, its debt settlement issues led to the invasion of Kuwait in 1989 and the coalition counterstroke, Operation Desert Storm. In the process, both societies were reordered, one by revolutionary zeal, the other by modernization – for a while.

Wars do not usually begin over long-standing animosities alone. In the case of Iran and Iraq those animosities go back at least 300 years and some would say even more. The rise of the secular Ba'ath Party in Iraq and, somewhat later, the emergence of the Persian Islamic revival under the Ayatollah Khomeini accentuated the long-standing animosities between the two nations. The secularist Ba'ath political program resembled the firm centralized control and strict internal security of the East Germans who served as advisors. Internal security matters most in dictatorships. One source claims that 20 percent of Iraqi government employees worked for the security services. Those animosities alone, however, did not precipitate combat. In this case even the deep disagreement over the status of the Shatt-al-Arab waterway was, while significant, a mere pretext. The real reason was that a window of opportunity opened for Iraq and it stepped through it. The calculus had to have been approximately as follows: the Ayatollah Khomeini came to power on the strength of Islamic renewal and had been seeking the overthrow of the Ba'ath Party and Saddam Hussein as apostates. Khomeini had been attempting to incite the large Iraqi Shi'a population in southern Iraq to join the revolution and overthrow the apostate Hussein. Saddam seems to have judged the verbal vitriol from Tehran to be dangerous enough possibly to upset the Shi'a and thus create a serious threat to his position, the issue that ultimately mattered most. The Iranian Revolution had destroyed the foundation of the country's military forces through purges of the officer corps and many of the technically trained personnel in the military because of their close association with Americans. The time for Iraq to act was at hand, as weakness and confusion were clearly evident in Iran. Not only should Iraq be able to seize control of the Shatt, but it might also be able to discredit and thus see the removal of Khomeini. Once Khomeini was gone, all the Gulf States could breathe a sigh of relief and would then be beholden to Saddam, the protector of "true" Islam and the Gulf community.

Early in the war Saddam Hussein turned his attention to securing the population from dissent. One of the mysteries of this war was the active participation by the non-Sunni portions of the Iraqi population. The Ayatollah Khomeini counted upon Iraqi Shi'ite gravitation to his brand of Islam, only to find little resonance and nominal participation among the Iraqi Shi'a population. Charles Tripp (in Karsh 1989) explains this as stemming from the unique structures of varied Shi'a communities in Iraq, including the secularization of urban Shi'a and their corresponding rejection of the previous domination by Iranian-linked clerics. Communism and Ba'ath philosophies of social justice and land reform resonated with this younger group. Ruthless government suppression of all pre-war Islamist activities helped minimize popular dissent. Iraqi society was closely watched and regulated. For the Iraqi Shi'a soldier the equation was simple: die in battle and the family would be rewarded; desert and the family might be destroyed. Saddam employed Iraqi nationalism with remarkable effect, strengthened his internal security forces, periodically discovered plots and acted swiftly and publically against them. His most difficult problem was managing the domestic financial problems

brought on by massive arms spending, sharply reduced oil revenues, and heavy mobilization demands. Women entered the workforce in unprecedented numbers, and strict consumption constraints became necessary. Mobilization demands made the import of foreign labor essential. These workers – some estimates run as high as two million – sent most of their wages home, eventually causing the Iraqi government to place strict caps on foreign worker remittances – which caused further labor shortages.

In Iran, the Khomeini revolution installed a strict Islamic administration resting increasingly on the "Have-Nots" of the population. The "Haves" were too closely associated with the former shah's regime, overthrown in significant measure because of its secularist orientation.

Social turmoil always accompanies a revolution, as it is frequently the tool to bring it about. Revolutionary governments benefit from an external, proximate enemy upon whom to focus the anxieties and uncertainties of the people naturally resulting from revolutionary upheaval. Khomeini used Saddam Hussein and the Ba'ath in Iraq. The rhetoric from Tehran became increasingly virulent as the Ayatollah attacked Saddam's legitimacy. While Saddam and the Ba'ath provided an easy external target, it was not enough to settle domestic factionalism. As it became clear that the Khomeini revolution would be dominated by a Persian, Islamic fundamentalist orientation, latent factionalism grew in intensity. Westernized, leftist intellectuals were split, with a large group forming an armed body, the Mujahideen-al-Khalq, who were eventually crushed in 1982, but reappeared in Iraq. The pro-Soviet Tudeh Party suffered as Moscow funneled an estimated 20 billion dollars in weapons to Iraq, while providing only 0.6 billion to Iran. The Soviets were very uncomfortable over the spread of Islamic fundamentalist ideology among its Muslim populations in the south. The Tudeh Party was eventually crushed too.

The Kurds were among the first to feel the effects of the revolution's heavy-handedness. The Kurds have never been a unified political entity and both Iraq and Iran used various levers to secure their support or submission, leaving many thousands dead in the process. Kurdish factions had been at war with one or the other combatants and the Turks as well, well before 1980. Iran moved first to quash Kurdish activity in the border regions in 1979, but only after 1986 did the Kurds organize significantly against Baghdad, for which they suffered serious retribution immediately following the 1988 ceasefire. Iran seemed to be in a state of continual chaos; perhaps the best time to attack it.

On September 22, 1980, the Iraqis committed seven of their 12 divisions in attacks on Kuzestan, attempting to seize the cities of Khoramanshahr, Abadan, Dezful, and Ahvaz, as well as the more northern cities of Penjwin, Qasr Sherin, and Mehran. The capture of the southern cities would effectively deliver control of the Shatt-al-Arab and important oil facilities into Iraqi hands. It appears to have been a limited-objective attack simply to signal to the Khomeini regime to stop interfering in Iraqi internal affairs, and to seize territory possibly in exchange for control of the Shatt.

The Iraqi attack included a substantial air strike against 10 major Iranian airfields. The Iraqis advanced without serious casualties on either side, but seemed to lack a clear strategic objective, reinforcing the supposition that Saddam sought merely to signal to the Iranian regime. What transpired next surprised observers. The Iranians fought back with unexpected effectiveness, capitalizing on the combination of their American-trained regulars and the revolutionary zeal of the masses partly motivated by a sense of nationalism. The first surprise was the response of the Iranian air force, which, on the day following the attack against its facilities, retaliated with a 100-plane strike. The Iraqis were driven back and the Iranians proceeded to press their counterattacks into Iraq proper. Neither side was ready to back down. The stage was set for eight years of blood-letting, the reintroduction of chemical weapons, economic warfare, the complete upset of the hitherto stable oil market system, and the progressive involvement of the United States in the region's affairs, not to mention the reordering of two societies.

While ultimate Iraqi ends remain somewhat clouded, the rate of advance of the Iraqi ground units suggested timidity borne of unpreparedness and ambivalent leadership. There is little to suggest that Iraq's army had ever undergone the kind of operational training required to successfully execute a multi-division, combined arms offensive. Khoramanshahr proved to be a more difficult objective than the Iraqis expected. It was a large city and the Iraqi army had never trained for urban warfare. At the United Nations' insistence, the Iraqis halted operations, but the Iranians refused to do so. Saddam Hussein was forced to send in his commandos, who cleared the city by October 24. Having been successful in these limited objective operations, the Iraqis stopped, apparently hoping that the Iranian defeats would suffice to bring down the Khomeini regime.

Iraq had a population base of approximately 16 million at the time, as opposed to some 45 million Iranians. As a consequence, the Iraqis, who suffered fairly substantial casualties in the fight for Khoramanshahr, adopted a casualty-averse strategy whenever possible. From then on, the Iraqis, who had spent lavishly on weaponry of fairly high technology, attempted to substitute technology and equipment for manpower wherever possible. The Iranian army, purged of many of its American-trained officers and non-commissioned officers, was engaged in border security missions and was neither positioned nor trained to repel an invasion. The Prussians discovered at the Battle of Valmy in 1792 that even an *ad hoc* military force, if motivated by revolutionary zeal and a stiffening of regular soldiers, can defeat an attack upon the nation's soil. The Prussians were halted by poor generalship and a mob. The Iraqis were likewise halted by poor generalship and a mob. In both cases, the "mob" was a mixture of revolutionary paramilitary forces and remains of the pre-revolutionary army.

Operations in 1981 opened with a major tank battle near the town of Susangerd, each side employing roughly 300 tanks. Iraqi tactics proved superior as they executed a classic double envelopment, destroying some 200 Iranian tanks. This signaled another major change in the Iranian military organization as it set the already confused and fractured command structure off on another revolutionary cleansing. Already suspect in the Islamists' eyes, much of the remaining regular officer corps was forced to flee the country.

The fractionalizing of Iranian society was present in the Iranian armed forces as well. By mid-1979 three forces other than the regular army had come into being, with the Pasdaran (Revolutionary Guards) under Khomeini's direct supervision. Pasdaran were roughly analogous to early western militia in that they had little formal training, elected their officers, and were politically powerful. The Hizbollah, as a force under the control of the Islamic Revolutionary Party, exerted control locally. The Pasdaran were augmented by the "Mobilization of the Oppressed," the Baseej – raw, marginally trained men from anywhere, expected to rush into battle whenever called upon. Their tactics were simple – charge the enemy regardless of cost. Death in battle was a guarantee of a passport to heaven. The Baseej provided manpower for the Pasdaran. All of these detracted from the potential strength of the regulars. Under the shah, the regular armed forces had been trained by Americans and were, therefore, suspect from the start. Rather than reconcile the roles and missions of these disparate forces, they were allowed to exist and to prosper or wither in tandem with the fortunes of their political supporters. Unified effort was never achieved and the war was lost before the regime could bring itself to resolve this problem.

On November 29, 1981, the Iraqi frontline militia, the marginally trained Iraqi Popular Army, witnessed the effectiveness of this new, highly motivated Pasdaran–Baseej force. Attacked at several locations by human waves of fanatics and finding themselves unable to kill the Iranians fast enough, the Popular Army broke and fled.

Winter brought operations to a halt, but the success of the new Iranian tactics was unnerving. The following spring, the Iranians recaptured Abadan and Khoramanshahr. Casualty counts vary enormously with sources, one saying the Iraqis lost 30,000 in the Khoramanshahr fight, another saying none – they abandoned the city. This fight may have been seminal in both camps. In one, the efficacy of the untrained but enthusiastic masses offered much promise; in the other, the need for means to exterminate such "vermin," as Iraqi media labeled them, led toward more technological remedies, including chemical weapons. The tactics and techniques involved in chemical warfare are relatively simple, but take time to master and produce more psychological effect than actual casualties. Death rates from chemical warfare were similar to those of World War I, around 2 percent. On the other hand, use of chemical weapons produces large numbers of wounded requiring extensive treatment and support. In June 1982, the Iraqis withdrew to their original border, ending the first phase of the war.

Having failed to harm the Iranian regime seriously, Saddam sought a negotiated settlement which the Ayatollah vigorously rejected, letting it be known that he was set on freeing southern, largely Shi'a, Iraq from Ba'athist control. Success here would destroy Iraq. It would gut Iraqi manpower and compromise its oil operations. The fight that followed should be named the Battle for Basrah. It became the critical point, akin to Verdun during World War I. Geography limited the maneuver room required by Iraqi armored forces, so Iraqi Engineers set to work creating an iron ring around the town, including an artificial lake. The Iranians tested the defenses on July 13, 1982. Sacrificial mine clearers led the way, followed by the Baseej, then the Pasdaran and the regulars. Once again the Iraqis led them into a double envelopment, inflicting severe casualties at the cost, however, of the 9th Iraqi Armored Division reportedly suffering over 30 percent losses.

Saddam initiated a review of what had gone wrong, a remarkable step for a dictator. Ba'athist Party hacks in the officer corps were found wanting and were purged. The Iraqi regular officer corps had performed well. Many were well educated and professionally trained and Saddam began to rely upon them within the normal parameters of a dictatorship. As the war progressed, the Iraqi regular army demonstrated remarkable competence, eventually demonstrating the ability to move corps (multi-division) units with ease throughout the operational theater, and to do so without detection. Iraqi Engineers proved capable in both offensive and defensive techniques, eventually developing "forts" whose reduction seriously worried US Army Engineers before the later Operation Desert Storm.

The year 1983 saw a resumption of Iranian offensives, this time around Fakkeh. It was a costly operation resulting in very limited gains. While this was disappointing to the Iranians, they were more seriously disturbed by the failure of the Iraqi Shi'a community to rally to their cause. Ideology began to give way to professional military operations and the Iranian regular army was placed in command. Instead of massive, single-point assaults, the Iranians began a series of attacks along the 730-mile border most likely intended to hone atrophied skills and to throw the Iraqis off balance. Attacking Haj Umran and Mehran in the Central region and later Penjwin in the north, the Iranian regulars succeeded with far lower casualty rates than the Pasdaran-led operations. While Iraqi territorial losses were small, these defeats set the Iraqi Engineers to work on a massive lateral road-building program that would provide their armored forces operational interior lines, the ability to move laterally faster than their opponent.

The Pasdaran, feeling shunted aside, launched a political campaign criticizing the limited territorial gains and the lack of effort against the critical point – Basrah. Winning the political battle, they took charge of military operations again, but showed they too had learned and began a series of indirect attacks against the Basrah stronghold. Operation Beida rested upon infiltration of the lightly protected Hawizah Marshes near Qurnah and north of the Majnoon Island oil fields. The Iraqi generals commanding the sector reacted effectively to each Iranian effort to gain a solid foothold, defeating each of three successive attempts. However, the Iranians captured and held the Majnoon oil complex.

Maintaining their focus on Basrah, the Iranians tried again in March 1985, further south nearer Qurnah. Here they succeeded in establishing a foothold on the Tigris River roadway. The Iraqis were prepared and once again crushed the effort in a pincer movement with the Republican Guards participating. The Republican Guards had not been employed outside of Baghdad as they were Saddam's personal protective force. These units had the best of everything in terms of equipment, but, of course, for these units political reliability trumped all other considerations. This operation marked the beginning of their regular participation in counteroffensive operations. It also ended phase two of the war. The Iranians had demonstrated commitment and callousness, while the Iraqis had demonstrated equal commitment, but increasing professionalism, including critical attention to casualty management.

On February 10, 1986, the Iranians stunned everyone by seizing the Al Faw Peninsula. Feinting toward the Hawizah Marshes, the Iranians conducted an assault crossing of the Shatt-al-Arab waterway, against the poorly trained Iraqi Popular Army units protecting the area. The Al Faw Peninsula is largely under water during periods of the year with only a few elevated roadways available for movement, thus channeling any vehicle attacks along them. Iraqi mechanized efforts to recapture Al Faw were thus seriously restricted and forced into frontal attacks along the narrow roadways. Republican Guard units dispatched to recover the ground became stuck in the mud and were then blasted by guns from across the waterway. Three weeks of counterattacks ensued without any substantial ground being retaken, but neither could the Iranians advance out of the peninsula.

Saddam now attempted another low-casualty gambit and directed the seizure of Mehran, which the Iraqi army accomplished. He then offered to trade Mehran for Al Faw, suggesting he would continue his seizures until Khomeini relinquished Al Faw, but the Iraqis failed to provide sufficient forces to hold the heights around Mehran and the Iranians quickly recaptured it.

Buoyed by their success, the regime in Tehran began announcing plans to conclude the war through a massive mobilization of 100,000 more Iranians into the "Mohammed Corps," and another 100,000 into the "Mahdi Corps," for the final campaign. These numbers never materialized, signaling war-weariness.

The fighting in 1986–1987 had been well photographed and publicized, allowing more and more pundits to offer evaluations of the contestant capabilities. The loss of Al Faw caused concern in the West as some began to speak of the imminent collapse of the Iraqi army. That was a mistake. The Iraqis mobilized to a level beyond that to which they had hitherto been willing to go and expanded the Republican Guard significantly. Women increasingly found employment replacing the men called up for army service.

The last battle of 1986 was probably the first phase of the 1987 Iranian campaign. The Iranian Karbala IV campaign began with an attempt to seize Umm Rassas Island in the Shatt. It failed at enormous cost. The Iranians attacked again – Operation Karbala V – on January 9, 1987, initiating a campaign that lasted until April that year. Karbala IV, V, and VIII were all fought in the vicinity of Basrah; Karbala VI and VII took place in the Central Front and in Kurdistan. None succeeded and the attacks may have cost Iran upwards of 70,000 casualties versus an estimated 10,000 Iraqi casualties.

The war had dragged on for seven years and casualties were certainly high. In addition, extraordinary amounts had been spent on arms. Adaptations from *Military Balance* show Iranian army manpower growing from 150,000 in 1980 to 550,000 in 1988, with 400,000 more-or-less reserve soldiers. During the same period, Iraqi strength grew from 200,000 to a million, with only 75,000 reservists. During similar periods, Iranian armor suffered declines from 1,735 tanks and 1,075 Other Armored Vehicles (OAVs) to 550 tanks and 750 OAVs. In contrast, Iraq increased its inventories from 2,750 tanks and 2,500 OAVs in 1980 to 5,500 and 4,750, respectively, in 1988. Artillery is mentioned separately here because it was the primary means of chemical weapons delivery and some differentiation must be made within these numbers. Iran's artillery establishment dropped from 1,000 weapons to 875, while Iraq's grew from 1,240 to over 3,000. Of these 3,000, however, one must include a sizable increase in proportion of battlefield rocket systems capable of delivering large quantities of chemical warfare agents. To be most effective, chemical agents need to be delivered in large quantities at the same time, something of which battlefield rocket systems are uniquely capable.

Chemical weapons were employed with increasing liberality by the Iraqis. They became adept at chemical weapon use, settling on mustard gas as their preferred agent. Mustard gas is a "blister" agent, literally blistering any skin it contacts, and is thus very dangerous to eyes and nasal areas. Mustard gas is dispensed in droplet form and even though it is eventually neutralized by heat and water, it has a nasty tendency to contaminate the area in which it is employed. The Iraqis found it particularly useful in wet areas like the Hawizah Marshes. Dispensed there, it would float on top of the water and injure any Iranian soldier attempting to move through the water, by any means. A more insidious form of mustard was dispensed in powdered form and had a longer dwell-time in arid operational areas.

Two "wars" emerged within this war – the War on the Cities and the Tanker War – perhaps better called the Oil War. Both sides early recognized the central importance of oil revenue and quickly attacked each other's facilities physically and diplomatically. Neither had a sound understanding of what serious economic warfare required. What

physical damage was done was quickly repaired or mitigated by both sides. Iran was able to close off Iraqi exports through Syria by diplomatic measures. The Iraqis responded by constructing additional pipelines through Turkey and Saudi Arabia and recovered some of the lost capacity. The Iraqis initiated military attacks on Iranian production facilities and on tankers carrying Iranian oil. In 1984, Iran began to attack Iraqi oil transports. Iraq modulated its attacks carefully, but Iranian threats, backed by a naval capability strong enough to make the threats credible, made tanker escort through the Gulf necessary. At Kuwait's request – and following the Russian offer to do so – western navies began escorting tankers through the Gulf into the Indian Ocean and back. One of the first escorted by the US Navy, the *Bridgeton*, hit a mine. This expanded the US Navy's actions and in due course an Iranian mine-laying vessel loaded with mines was caught by a US Navy patrol and the evidence filmed for all to see. The subsequent mining of the US Navy frigate *Samuel B. Roberts* set off a retaliatory strike that crippled the Iranian navy. The War on the Cities recalled the German bombing of London early in World War II. Both Iraqis and Iranians struck at the vulnerable populations of the enemy capital cities. The difference was that Iranians and Iraqis fired missiles. The effects were limited even though unnerving to the residents. The Iranians initiated the attacks in 1985; Iraq struck back. Iraq fired some 120 missiles at not only Tehran, but also Isfahan and the Shi'a holy city, Qom. This was three times the size of the Iranian attacks on Baghdad. While the War on the Cities was largely ineffectual, the Tanker War cost Iran revenues and her navy. A tragic sidelight of the naval hostilities occurred when, through a series of procedural errors on both sides, the US Navy shot down an Iranian civilian airliner (Cordesman and Wagner 1990: 392–394).

The Iraqi air force grew in numbers throughout the war and was always well equipped with sophisticated French aircraft. Saddam rarely committed his air force to ground support, preferring to employ attack helicopters. The Americans had trained the Iranians in the tactics of these weapons and early in the war they performed well. They remained a potent force as the United States traded helicopter-launched missiles in 1985–1986 for American hostages. The Iraqis quickly adopted what worked and gradually built up a sizable force that became progressively integrated into their operations.

Iran's economic problems, like Iraq's, initially revolved around a sharp drop in oil-generated income as world petroleum prices declined sharply. The upheaval of revolution severely disrupted the domestic economy, which was further disrupted by the imposition of Islamic economic principles that were at odds with what had been a burgeoning capitalist economy. Appeals to merchants to follow the Islamic path of dealing equitably with their brothers, coupled with strict applications of justice, had some effect, but the government was forced to adopt a rationing system while tacitly allowing the operation of a black market. Self-sufficiency was pursued in agriculture with some success, but industry suffered from lack of skills and resources. Ironically, Iran's inability to spend billions on armaments, and almost no-cost ability to recruit fighters through the Baseej, gave it some room to manage its finances and domestic economy. These measures notwithstanding, Iran's military expenditures tended toward 60 percent of the budget (Hiro 1991: 109–113).

Iraq entered the war with $35 billion in foreign reserves, but these dwindled quickly toward zero as the war wore on. Oil revenues dominated the economy, but Iraq was slow to recognize that the war would be long and only adopted domestic austerity measures after the third year. While these involved some decentralization of the domestic economy, which had previously been built on a Soviet-style centralized, collective model, the price of oil and the quantity exported dominated everything. There are numerous estimates of both Iraqi and Iranian oil production, but they vary considerably by source and by estimates of covert transactions.

Another ambiguous part of the economic picture is what may variously be labeled loans, subsidies, gifts, or protection money by Saudi Arabia, Kuwait, and the other Gulf states to Iraq. While the Gulf countries were wary of the increasing secularization and aggressiveness of Iraq, they feared the Islamic revolutionary appeal to their large Shi'a communities even more and provided substantial financial support to Iraq in the tens of billions of dollars, some estimates suggesting over $60 billion from Saudi Arabia alone (Kanovsky in Karsh 1989: 231–252). After the war, Iraq insisted

this support was a form of contribution to secure the Gulf from Iranian domination.

Foreign military aid was vital to both combatants as neither had significant domestic arms manufacturing capabilities. Both had alienated their principal suppliers before the war. Iraq had suppressed the Iraqi Communist Party, as did Iran – as noted above – a few years later. The United States had built up the shah of Iran's armed forces with weapons, supplies, and extensive training, and the United Kingdom supplied some material as well. With the overthrow of the shah and subsequent seizure of American embassy personnel, that pipeline shut down. Nevertheless, foreign military sales, overt and covert, seemed to involve every nation capable of supplying the combatant's needs. It was a Devil's playground, with the United States covertly supplying Iran while eventually providing satellite intelligence to Iraq. France, West Germany, the USSR, and Soviet satellite states supplied both sides. All figures on this subject are approximations.

As examples, France supplied Iraq with air and air defense material before and during the war. In 1983, as Iran strengthened forces on its islands athwart the Gulf shipping lanes, France delivered $500 million in military aid, including Exocet (anti-ship) and other missiles, to Iraq. Before the war Iraq had contracted for Italian manufacture of several naval vessels, including four frigates. These were embargoed for the duration of the war, but several ships built in Britain for Iran were released and allowed to proceed.

There was much to learn from this war at this point, but for the most part the world was aghast at the bloodshed and the utter lack of restraint by either side – if they could, they did.

While fending off the last serious Iranian Karbala attacks, the Iraqis had been developing their plans for 1988. *Tawakalna Ala Allah* – "In God We Trust" – was maturing as, again largely unnoticed, the Iraqi Engineers were constructing a full-scale mock-up of the Al Faw Peninsula and quietly training division after division in specific roles.

On April 17, 1988, the Iraqi army attacked Al Faw, in the kind of combined arms operation the Iraqis had gradually developed and for which they trained intensively. The Iraqis employed enough troops to make the outcome certain – reportedly some 200,000 in the battle and surrounding support area.

Estimated Iranian numbers were only about 15,000. Iraqi tactics had been honed and they executed a very complex, multi-pronged assault to perfection. Two corps assaulted the flanks of the peninsula, and executed two amphibious assaults as well, while Republican Guard forces attacked in the center. For the first time in years the Iraqis also committed major elements of their air forces and augmented these with their substantial attack helicopter forces. This was unusual enough that the Iranians charged the United States with assisting in the battle.

Possibly to prevent last-ditch measures of defense, the Iraqis left one of three bridges back across the Shatt intact and filmed masses of Iranians fleeing to the safety of the far shore. The numbers fleeing undermined the then-prominent idea that the Iraqis simply gassed everyone on the peninsula. Then, following an on-site press conference, the Iraqis turned in very businesslike fashion to the next task following directly in the wake of the seasonal drying of the ground.

At one-month intervals – when the ground had dried and the objective-specific training had been completed – the Iraqi army struck the next objective. The attack on Fish Lake began at 9:30 a.m., May 25, 1988, and was over by 6 p.m. that day. It was another application of brute force on chosen ground simply crushing those who chose to stand. As in the Faw attack, there was no attempt at pursuit. The Iraqis retook Majnoon in four hours, but showed some subtlety this time with one corps swinging around behind the island to protect the flank of the attacking force and cut off the Iranian retreat route. Thereafter the Iraqis concentrated on gutting Iranian force capabilities, capturing and destroying huge amounts of equipment and taking many prisoners. The attack at Dehloran/Zubiadat on July 12 began at 7:15 a.m. and resulted in a 45-km penetration by 11:00 a.m. It took four days to evacuate the material captured in this brief fight. The final battle took place after the ceasefire and carried all the hallmarks of an unmistakable message to the Iranian regime. This deep-penetration raid drove 40 miles into Iran against marginal opposition. Iran had ceased to exist as a military power.

Iraqi war aims were partially attained – Iran was militarily prostrate. The Iraqi Shi'a popula-tion had fought and bled for Saddam Hussein, utterly rejecting the Persian brand of Islamic revival. The Kurdish annoyance would be dealt with summarily in the months to come with the follow-on Anfal campaign of retribution. Saddam's hands were free from Persian distur-bances, but his debts were enormous and Iraqi society would have to adjust to a non-war foot-ing, which has never been an easy task. Iran, battered and ostracized by much of the world, had to ponder the future – which is the subject of another study.

SEE ALSO: Chemical Warfare.

References

Cordesman, A. H. and Wagner, A. R. (1990) *The Lessons of Modern War. Volume 2: The Iran–Iraq War*. Boulder: Westview Press.

Hiro, D. (1991) *The Longest War: The Iran–Iraq Military Conflict*. New York: Routledge.

Karsh, E. (Ed.) (1989) *The Iran–Iraq War: Impact and Implications*. New York: St. Martin's Press.

Further Reading

Axelgard, F. W. (1988) "*Iraq: Looking Beyond the War*," Middle East International, January 24.

Bergquist, R. (1988) *The Role of Airpower in the Iran–Iraq War*. Maxwell Air Force Base: Air University Press.

Cordesman, A. H. (1994) *Iran and Iraq: The Threat from the Northern Gulf*. Boulder: Westview Press.

Doran, C. F. and Buck, S. W. (Eds.) (1991) *The Gulf, Energy, and Global Security: Political and Economic Issues*. Boulder: Lynn Rienner.

Herzog, C. (1989) "A Military–Strategic Overview." In E. Karsh (Ed.), *The Iran–Iraq War: Impact and Implications*. New York: St. Martin's Press.

International Institute for Strategic Studies (n.d.) *IISS Military Balance*. (Annual edition for each successive year.) London: International Institute for Strategic Studies.

Islam al Khafaji (1988) "Iraq's Seventh Year: Saddam's Quart d'Heure?" *Middle East Report*, March–April.

Jansen, G. (1987) "The Battle for Basrah," *Middle East International*, January 23.

Laffin, J. (1989) *The World in Conflict, 1989. War Annual 3*. London: Brassey's.

Metz, H. C. (Ed.) (1990) *Iraq: A Country Study*. Washington, DC: US Government Printing Office.

Muir, J. (1988) "Rout of the Revolutionaries," *The Sunday Times*, April 24.

O'Balance, E. (1987) "Iran vs. Iraq: Quantity vs. Quality?" *Defense Attaché*, 1.

O'Balance, E. (1988) *The Gulf War*. London: Brassey's.

Palmer, M. A. (1992) *Guardians of the Gulf: A History of America's Expanding Role in the Persian Gulf, 1833–1992*. New York: Free Press.

Pelletiere, S. C. and Johnson, D. V., II (1991) *Lessons Learned: The Iran–Iraq War*. Carlisle Barracks, PA: Strategic Studies Institute.

Pelletiere, S. C., Johnson, D. V., II, and Rosenberger, L. R. (1990) *Iraqi Power and US Security in the Middle East*. Carlisle Barracks, PA: Strategic Studies Institute.

Segal, D. (1988) "The Iran–Iraq War: A Military Analysis," *Foreign Affairs*, Summer.

Sherrill, M. S. (1988) "Iran on the Defensive," *Time*, June 20.

Sick, G. (1989) "Trial by Fire: Reflections on the Iran–Iraq War," *Middle East Journal*, Spring.

Tucker, A. R. (1988) "Armored Warfare in the Gulf," *Armed Forces*, May.

Tyler, P. E. (1988) "Rout of Iran from Faw Still Puzzling to the West," *Washington Post*, May 3.

Wagner, J. S. (1983) "Iraq." In R. A. Gabriel (Ed.), *Fighting Armies: Antagonists in the Middle East – A Combat Assessment*. Westport: Greenwood Press.

Irish Revolution, Wars of the

W. H. KAUTT

The Irish revolution is a phrase and concept increasingly being used by historians to describe the events in Ireland from 1911 to 1923, although the starting date is by no means agreed. During this long decade, Ireland underwent a political transformation brought about by the convergence of resurgent Irish nationalism and the catastrophe of the Great War. While the effects of this revolution were not as violent as some, and it was not as overtly transformative socially, its longer effects, both within Ireland and elsewhere, were as important as any other revolution.

There were several stages to this war, consisting of the three constituent conflicts and events leading to or following them. It began with a considerable political fight over home rule, followed by organizing and arming by those for and against home rule. Then came World War I and the 1916 Easter Rebellion, the War of Independence (1919–1921), and the Civil War (1922–1923). The connection of this era to the later "Troubles" of the late twentieth century is problematic and made more difficult by both republican and loyalist groups trying to make such links to further their agendas.

Background to the Irish Revolution

Anglo-Normans invaded Ireland in the 1170s, but largely intermarried with Irish and were, like many invaders before them, absorbed into Gaelic Irish culture. By the late sixteenth and early seventeenth centuries, with the Protestant Reformation fully engaged in Great Britain, Elizabeth, and later James I, instituted what became known as the Plantation of Ulster whereby lowland Scots Protestant settlers were brought in to settle the Catholic country, mostly in the northern counties. This, combined with the after effects of the English Civil War (1642–1651) and the later Williamite War (1689–1691), created the Protestant Ascendancy. Thus, the majority of the land was controlled by a religious and, frequently ethnic, minority. As a result of these conflicts, sectarian strife continued in varying levels of intensity into the twenty-first century.

Prior to the 1790s, rebellions in Ireland were led by local elites. Thereafter, inspired by the French Revolution, republicanism was the revolutionaries' means to freedom. In 1798, the United Irishmen sought to join Protestant and Catholic working-class people to establish a republic in Ireland. Great Britain reacted politically by bringing Ireland into the United Kingdom with the Act of Union of 1800.

The only other significant rebellion from then on was the so-called "Young Ireland" rebellion of 1848. Its only lasting effect was the foundation of the Irish Republican Brotherhood (IRB). This was a secret organization dedicated to the creation of an Irish republic through infiltration of other nationalist groups and using their assets.

Home Rule and Unionism

Nationalism in Ireland was not limited to republicanism. Growing out of the political machinery that helped pass Catholic Emancipation in 1829, the Repeal Movement sought to revoke the Act of Union to establish a government and parliament in Dublin. Following the collapse of this movement around the time of the Young Ireland Rebellion, this constitutionalist approach was eventually taken up by the home rule movement beginning in the 1860s. Home rule meant to establish an Irish parliament in Dublin to govern Irish local affairs, but otherwise remain in the United Kingdom.

Beginning in the 1880s, successive Liberal governments introduced multiple home rule bills; while several passed the Commons, they were defeated in the Lords.

In 1912, after the defeat of the third home rule bill, Unionists in northern counties, many descendants of the Protestants who colonized in the seventeenth century, began to prepare to resist the implementation of a home rule bill if it should ever become law. In September, they formed the Ulster Volunteer Force (UVF) to resist with violence if necessary. The UVF then set about training and arming itself, while continuing to increase its numbers; at its height, the UVF claimed over 100,000 enrolled members.

Within months, the disparate nationalist community responded by forming their own Irish Volunteers to defend home rule and Ireland. Founded in Dublin in late 1913, they envisioned the UVF as their primary threat. They, likewise, claimed about 100,000 members.

The similarities between the two organizations were striking: similar size and organization; similar, although opposing, membership; both even bought weapons from arms dealers in Germany. Yet that is where the similarities ended, because the UVF, unlike the Irish Volunteer Force, had a large percentage of army veterans in its ranks. This included both officers and enlisted men and allowed them to develop more rapidly into a credible force. The Irish Volunteer Force was composed largely of amateurs.

The political situation in the United Kingdom, which had long favored the home rulers, changed dramatically with the outbreak of war in August 1914. The UVF, seizing an opportunity to demonstrate their loyalty to king and country, as well as their heartfelt patriotism, volunteered to fight as a unit in the British Army. Many UVF units helped constitute the 36th (Ulster) Division, where they gained a legendary reputation at the Battle of the Somme in July 1916. Home rulers and other nationalists also fought in the war, forming the bulk of the 10th and the 16th (Irish) Divisions, the former fighting valiantly, if not futilely, at Suvla Bay in 1915 at Gallipoli.

As the Unionists feared, the home rule bill eventually passed, but contained a provision for the exclusion of six of the Ulster counties. Further, its implementation was delayed for the duration of the war. John Redmond, the leading home rule MP, who had taken over the leadership of the group early in its infancy, assisted British recruiting efforts in Ireland. In September 1914, in a speech to the Irish Volunteers at Woodenbridge, Co. Wicklow, he said they should help defend Ireland's interests and fight wherever needed. Although innocuous, this went too far for a small republican minority of about 13,000, who separated and formed a new group called the Irish Volunteers. Redmond's remaining 100,000 moderates officially became the National Volunteers.

The separation was over more than just cooperation with the British. The republicans saw a fundamental flaw in the British cause in the war. If they were fighting for the "rights of small nations" (Belgium), what about Ireland? It was a small nation too. Further, the republicans felt the new home rule law was also flawed because it instituted partition. Moreover, there were considerable signs that the Cabinet never intended to implement home rule (Fanning 2012: 136). Of course, the republicans saw Britain's "danger was Ireland's opportunity." They wanted a republic totally separated from the British Empire. At this crucial juncture, the IRB came back into the picture after a generation in the background, starting a chain of events that led Ireland to war.

The Easter Rising, April 24–29, 1916

The Easter Rising has taken hold of popular imagination, especially with modern republicans in Ireland. This is partly due to the romanticism that has grown up around it, but also because it represents the commencement of the modern violent struggle for an independent Irish republic. At its core, this battle was a transition from the traditional Irish rebellion to the modern struggle for independence. This was the last time Irish rebels rose to fight in a conventional manner against militarily superior British forces.

Eoin MacNeill, leader of the Irish Volunteers after their separation from the National Volunteers, felt that an uprising would be suicidal.

In the background, the IRB, more of an *agent provocateur*, having already infiltrated most of the Volunteer leadership, prepared to bring about a general rebellion. They made contact with the Germans in an attempt to facilitate an invasion. When that failed they asked for arms, which eventually were sent.

The choice of Easter was both symbolic and practical. Easter represented to the primarily Catholic Irish a sacrifice to, and rebirth of, Éire, while in practical terms, preparations for the national holiday meant that the primarily working-class rank and file would get off work early on Saturday, while Easter Monday was also a holiday. This has led to the legends about the desire on the part of the IRB leaders of the Rising, particularly Patrick Pearse, to seek martyrdom through sacrifice that would propel the cause of the republic to the fore in the popular mind. This has been effectively dispelled by J. J. Lee, but persists in the popular imagination (Lee 1973).

MacNeill discovered the plot a few days prior and tried to prevent it by canceling the annual Volunteer Easter review and maneuvers. Pearse, MacNeill's deputy but also leader of the IRB plotters, countermanded the cancelation and delayed it all until the Monday after Easter (April 24) to allow the brigades to muster as much strength as possible. Yet, due to these orders and counter-orders, only a fraction the men showed, and primarily only in Dublin.

They originally intended to rise up all over the country at the same time. They would seize key points throughout the country, especially in Dublin and Cork, and sever communications with Britain. This was a plan that would have fit well on the Western Front, but had little chance of success without well-trained and well-armed troops; the rebels had neither. This did not stop them.

Eventually, the rebels occupied many of the important points in various parts of the city: the Irish Citizen Army (ICA) took the City Hall and St Stephen's Green, while the 1st Irish Volunteer (IV) Battalion held North King Street area, the Four Courts, and the Mendicity Institute; the 2nd IV Battalion was at Jacob's Biscuit Factory; the 3rd IV Battalion held the Beggar's Bush district and the approach to it at the Mount Street Bridge across the Grand Canal; the 4th IV Battalion took the South Dublin Union; and the headquarters elements of both the Irish

Volunteers and the ICA occupied the General Post Office on Sackville Street.

They tried but failed to occupy several other key sites around Dublin. One of these was Dublin Castle, the seat of the Irish government. Another was Trinity College, which was centrally located in the city, but also housed an armory for the Officer Training Corps (OTC). The officers and cadets of the OTC held the position, which was later used to launch counterattacks against strong rebel positions to the north. The other important sites they could not secure were railway stations at Amiens Street, Broadstone, Harcourt Street, and Kingsbridge. The rebels certainly understood the importance of these positions, but did not have sufficient men to take and hold them.

The General Post Office

Around noon, some 150 rebels marched up the street, halted in front of the General Post Office, faced left and charged, bayonets fixed, into that magnificent building. Shortly thereafter, having taken over the Hotel Metropole next door, they began storing supplies in it and fortifying their positions (McNally 2007: 46; Béaslaí 2009: 101; Sceilg 2009a: 134).

Around 12:30 p.m., Pearse, *de facto* commander of the rebels and president of the Provisional Republic, stepped in front of the building and read the "Proclamation of the Republic" to a small crowd of amused Dubliners who gathered outside to watch the goings-on. Just after he finished, a mounted reconnaissance patrol of at least two troops of the 6th Reserve Cavalry rounded the corner onto Sackville Street to the cheers of the Dubliners. Volunteers of the Rathfarnham Company fired on the troopers from concealed positions, killing three men and one horse and mortally wounding another man (McNally 2007: 46–47; Sceilg 2009a: 131–133). The survivors beat a hasty retreat back to barracks.

The South Dublin Union

The 4th IV Battalion was placed in the southwest of the city and the most intense fighting in that area took place at the compound known as the South Dublin Union. Eamon Ceannt and his vice commandant, Cathal Brugha, with only about 50 of their company, occupied and fortified several buildings in the Union compound (Sceilg 2009b:

62–63). The South Dublin Union stood in between the junction of forces and lines of communication and Dublin Castle, the location of the civil administration, the headquarters of the national police, as well as the Dublin Brigade headquarters.

St Stephen's Green

One of the major ICA strongpoints in the city during the Rising was at St Stephen's Green, the largest park in the city center. The ICA commander, Captain Michael Mallin, seized the Green and immediately pressed male passersby to dig trenches in the lawns. It served as a link between the 2nd and the 3rd IV Battalions, at Jacob's biscuit factory and Beggar's Bush district respectively. The rebels occupied several buildings around the Green to provide support, but not the Shelbourne Hotel, which commanded the entirety of the northeast of the Green. This failure cost them dearly (McNally 2007: 41; Fox 2009: 107–109).

North King Street

The 1st Dublin IV Battalion's mission was to secure and hold the North King Street area from the north bank of the Liffey to the north of the city. Being positioned between the military complex at Parkgate and the rebel general headquarters at the General Post Office, the 1st Battalion held the latter's western flank (Béaslaí 2009: 100–101).

Captain Séan Heuston, commander of D Company, 1st IV Battalion, took the Mendicity Institute just off Usher's Quay on the south bank of the Liffey. With the river between the 1st Battalion and the Four Courts, the nearest 1st Battalion strongpoint, this small detachment of about 25 men of D Company was cut off from support. James Connolly ordered Heuston to hold the position for three hours; in the end, he held it for three days against impossible odds (McNally 2007: 39; Béaslaí 2009: 101; Brennan 2009: 210–211).

Resistance to the Rebels

The three British infantry battalions of the Dublin Brigade deployed their standby forces to Dublin Castle. They had to fight their way in and suffered heavy casualties from the ill-armed and ill-trained rebels who were, nevertheless, in commanding and fortified positions. While the British contained the Rising in the City of Dublin by the end of the first day through the use of various *ad hoc* units consisting of garrison troops, the OTC at Trinity, Musketry School personnel, retired soldiers and men on leave, along with cavalry reinforcements from the Curragh (Co. Kildare), this was not a considerable feat since there was no attempt by the rebels to go any further. The rebels were holding their positions until the British "invaded."

Brigadier General W. H. M. Lowe arrived early Tuesday morning with two more infantry battalions and assumed command of British forces in the city. He concentrated on the area south of the Liffey. The importance of the rebel failure to secure the lines of communication into the city became apparent as more troops arrived from north Belfast by rail.

At 3:00 a.m. Tuesday, the Curragh Mobile Column, with 100 men, took over the Shelbourne Hotel commanding the ICA positions on St Stephen's Green. Shortly after coming under intense machine-gun fire, the ICA abandoned their trenches on the Green and took up in the Royal College of Surgeons. Mallin's men left most of their ammunition behind when they evacuated their positions. Around the same time, the army established machine-gun positions in the Kilmainham Hospital from which they raked the South Dublin Union along with sniper fire. While under this intense fire, the Volunteers regrouped and consolidated their positions within the Union (McNally 2007: 51–2, 48; Sceilg 2009b: 70–71).

As the gunboat *Helga II*, having steamed up the Liffey, pounded the area near Boland's Mill, elements of the 5th Reserve Artillery Brigade arrived from Athlone, Co. Westmeath, and set up two of their four worn-out 18-pounders on the grounds of the Grangegorman Lunatic Asylum. The other two were used on the south side of the Liffey. But they had only shrapnel rounds to attack the fortified positions and thus had limited effect (McNally 2007: 55).

As these forces pressed into the city, rebel positions were being systematically reduced and Lowe now had sufficient troops to conduct larger operations on both sides of the Liffey. At the Mendicity Institute, on the south side of the Liffey, the Royal Dublin Fusiliers stormed in after some 15 minutes of intense fighting. Using teams of hand-grenadiers, the infantrymen kept up continuous fire. Heuston's became the first rebel position actually to surrender, at noon (McNally 2007: 61).

The Advance of the Foresters

After being mobbed by cheering crowds of Dubliners, the 2/7th and 2/8th Sherwood Foresters marched north in tactical formation. Several members of the 3rd IV Battalion lay in ambush on the approach to the beaten zone of the rest of their battalion just across the Grand Canal ringing the southern part of the city. The Volunteers prepared their sites well, barricading themselves in with a layered defense. As the British troops moved up the street, other Forester elements assaulted the bridge at Mount Street. This withered away when they took heavy fire from other positions of the 3rd IV Battalion.

Friday, April 28, 1916

By around 2 a.m. on Friday, General Sir John Maxwell arrived to assume overall command of the situation. He ordered the 2/5 and 2/6th South Staffordshires to attack across the Liffey at the Four Courts and the rest of the 177th Brigade, reinforced by the 176th (Lincoln and Leicester) Brigade, to attack Éamon de Valera's 3rd IV Battalion (McNally 2007: 84).

Saturday, April 29, 1916

At around 9 a.m. Saturday morning, Ned Daly's 1st IV Battalion were holding the 2/6th South Staffordshires' advance in check. The 2/5th South Staffordshires broke in and resistance began to collapse. The situation rapidly became untenable for the rebels throughout the city. For Pearse, the final straw was when he supposedly witnessed a family fleeing "their burning home under cover of a white flag being cut down by British fire." He wrote orders, countersigned by Connolly, for the rebels to surrender. By Sunday morning, the last of the rebel positions, the ICA at the Royal College of Surgeons off St Stephen's Green, surrendered. The Rising was over; some 36 square miles of the city had been destroyed, causing £2.5 million (some £1,050,000,000 today) in damage (Officer 2008). British military casualties were 550; rebels

lost about 200; and 2,500 civilians were killed or wounded. But the aftermath was frequently as cruel as the fighting (McNally 2007: 87).

Courts-Martial

The rebel leaders were put on trial, and some 161 courts-martial occurred within just two weeks of the Rising. Historian McNally summed it up well saying that,

> The proceedings were pursued with an indecent haste that made a mockery of the court itself. When Eamon Ceannt was on trial, he was offered the opportunity to call a defence witness and named his senior officer Thomas MacDonagh, only to be told he was indisposed and could not testify. What was not admitted was that the prospective witness had been executed that morning. (McNally 2007: 90)

In the end, 15 of the 65 men and one woman sentenced to die were shot, including Pearse, the badly wounded James Connolly, and the young Heuston. The executions were especially hard to take for the Dublin populace (including even the majority who opposed the Rising) because the rebel forces did not behave like most modern revolutionaries; they maintained discipline and fought honorably (Sceilg 2009a: 134–135).

The same cannot be said of the British Army. Leaving aside the inevitable issues of the post-Rising executions, British forces made some grievous errors that cannot be excused as the result of being in combat and their leadership conspired to cover up these activities (House of Commons Debate, 20. vii. 1916, *Hansard*, vol. 84, Sections 1171–1172). There were three types of general mistreatment of civilians or rebels *hors de combat*: that which occurred during the fighting in general, that occurring during actual combat, and that occurring after the Rising ended (Donnelly 2001: 1). In this heavy-handed way, the British "lost the peace," acting as if the people of Dublin were an enemy population in an occupied city, rather than the liberated people of their own country.

Several thousand rebels were interned in Britain just after the Rising, the majority of whom were eventually congregated in Frongoch Camp in Wales. While historians debate the effects of bringing many like-minded leaders together in one camp, the result is telling: most of the leaders of the later War of Independence and Civil War were "graduates" of Frongoch "Rebel University." These men did not stay interned long; the first of them were freed by Christmas.

Although the obscure nationalist party Sinn Féin had nothing to do with the Rising, the press and government blamed them for it. As a result, the republican leadership, on release from internment by 1917, took over the small group. Deciding to contest the parliamentary elections in December 1918, the republicans took some 70 percent of the Irish seats in Westminster. Refusing to go to London, they met instead at the Mansion House in Dublin and declared the Irish republic of 1916 was valid and still working. This became the First Dáil Éireann (literally, "assembly of Ireland").

The Irish War of Independence, 1919–1921

The new war began on January 21, 1919, the same day as the first meeting of the Dáil, when a small group of Tipperary Volunteers ambushed an explosives shipment at Soloheadbeg, killing the two elderly policemen who escorted it. The Irish Volunteers spent 1919 raiding Royal Irish Constabulary (RIC) barracks and private homes for arms, while occasionally conducting ambushes. Thus, the war began slowly.

The early part of the war was typified by attacks against policemen, which served several purposes. First was the ever-present need for arms and munitions. The Irish Volunteers, who eventually became the Irish Republican Army (IRA), lost most of their weapons in the Rising. So, afterward, they stole them from those who had them: police, military, and private persons. Small-scale activities soon led to larger-scale raids on police barracks.

Raids on police barracks met several needs. They provided new arms and ammunition, if successful. At the same time, these attacks also provided training for the Volunteers, who usually learned through trial and error. They were also attacks against authority, a largely symbolic gesture, but an insult nonetheless. Finally, the police gathered intelligence for the government,

and attacking them meant potentially blinding the authorities in a given area. Over time, the experience from these attacks, combined with raids and other operations, led to the IRA ambush doctrine that came out more fully in 1920 and 1921 (Kautt 2010: 99).

These attacks also placed great strain on the policemen and their families, who were Irish too. The policemen caught in this situation in 1919 had two choices, quit or endure. What hurt the Constabulary more than resignations, retirements, deaths, or dismissals were the cumulative effects these had on recruitment. As more men left the RIC, drastically fewer joined the once-prestigious force. The government's reaction to this campaign in 1919 was to treat it as nothing but crime. When this failed to produce any discernible result, the government realized that it needed to shore up the RIC and strike at the rebels.

Politically unwilling to use military force, the government decided to recruit non-Irishmen into the RIC from among the three million demobilized servicemen from the war. These men, hired as "temporary constables," became known as the "Black and Tans" due to their combined police and army uniforms. With little or no police training, they were inserted directly into existing police barracks as individual replacements.

1920: The War Intensifies

By the beginning of the year, the police were weakening and the rebels growing stronger. The RIC, still some months from receiving reinforcements, was forced to consolidate its strength by abandoning smaller, indefensible barracks in the countryside. The leadership reasoned this would allow it to strike out in greater strength, but, while this was true, it did not change the reality that it looked to everyone like a retreat, while leaving a vacuum the rebels filled. Worse yet, police morale plummeted.

With the rebels gaining strength, the government decided that a more aggressive approach was necessary. Consequently, it made Sir Hamar Greenwood the new chief secretary for Ireland and brought in some effective civil servants to improve the administration there. It also made Major General Sir H. H. Tudor head of the RIC as police advisor to the viceroy and

General Sir Nevil Macready commander of the army in Ireland.

The new leadership brought a renewed intensity to the fight against the rebels that had hitherto been lacking. The influx of the Black and Tans brought much-needed manpower, while Tudor's rearming them as soldiers gave them the firepower. What they needed was to take the fight to the rebels. The army, with new motor vehicles and a new mandate to help the police, provided the transport, but the government needed a force to bridge between the army and the police.

There had long been talk of a "special gendarmerie" to act as a strike force capable of independent action. The Auxiliary Division, RIC (ADRIC) was created in the summer of 1920 from demobilized military officers. The "Auxies," frequently and mistakenly called Black and Tans, earned a reputation for fierceness and brutality.

In the late summer of 1920, the British forces struck back. Moving quickly, they conducted raids and searches on a scale not seen since the Rising. This quickly affected the rebels, forcing many to go on the run. In some cases, police reoccupied barracks they abandoned just months earlier.

While this caused disruption in rebel forces, it had unforeseen results. Many of those forced on the run hid in rebel strongholds in the south or in Dublin, thus providing these active areas with more men with nothing to do but fight. Violence and casualties increased on both sides. The other result was that, with mass arrests, much of the rebel leadership was behind bars, thus leaving the war effort to others. In this case, the new leaders were younger and more radical. This was the case with Michael Collins and IRA Chief of Staff Richard Mulcahy. With these multiple forces at work, the rebels fought back. There were many incidents in the autumn of 1920 that typify the rebel attempts to stem the tide of the British forces, but none that seized the imagination as much as Bloody Sunday and the Kilmichael Ambush.

Bloody Sunday

Collins, in his guise as IRA director of intelligence (he was also Dáil Éireann minister of finance, president of the IRB supreme council,

IRA adjutant general, and IRA director of organization), decided to strike at British intelligence capabilities by organizing the assassination of almost two dozen men whom he believed were enemy agents. The assassination teams moved out early in the morning on Sunday, November 21, 1920, catching many in bed, while missing others completely. Historians have long argued whether the victims were agents or not; some certainly were, some probably were not, and some were innocent bystanders, including the first two Auxies killed. The killings had a chilling effect throughout Dublin.

Later that same day, a group of ADRIC and regular RIC entered the crowded stadium at Croke Park, expecting to find some of the murderers in the crowd there. Although the evidence is unclear about why, they suddenly started shooting at the crowd, killing almost a dozen people. While there is no credible evidence that they came under fire as they claimed, there has been none to prove this was a deliberate reprisal either. This demonstrated the elusiveness of the rebel gunmen and the strain they put on British forces.

Kilmichael Ambush

Just a week later, with these events still fresh, the 3rd West Cork Brigade flying column, under Tom Barry, caught two ADRIC trucks on a lonely road, ambushing them and massacring the passengers almost to the last man. The savagery of the attack shocked and horrified the authorities. That the rebels had destroyed an elite unit of 19 men rocked them because it indicated the rebels were more capable than they thought, or wanted to admit. While this was not the end of the British offensive, it demonstrated that the IRA was by no means beaten and was capable of striking back.

The remainder of the year saw increasing levels of violence. The ADRIC reputation for violence was well earned when K Company, ADRIC, burned much of the center of Cork City on the night of December 11–12 in retaliation for IRA attacks every day since Kilmichael. British troops were not going to endure what they saw as murder without response. Their leadership sympathized, some collaborated, but there was little they could do to prevent retribution.

1921: Boiling Point

The New Year came with little hope for change for the better. The British Army used its new armored vehicles with greater efficacy and the IRA switched from direct attacks against British forces to attacking transportation infrastructure – bridges and roads. While British authorities derided these activities, by mid-spring they found they could not maneuver their forces, and that the IRA was slowly isolating the outlying districts. This situation had worsened to the point that by the spring, it was easier, faster, and safer to sail around Ireland than to try to cross it by the shorter overland route.

As the conflict continued, IRA capabilities slowly increased and it began conducting larger and more violent operations in late May, while the British Army began a massive build-up of forces. Their plan was for a general offensive in the late summer with combined arms techniques, using infantry (vehicle-mounted and dismounted), cavalry, artillery, and police in unison. They had already practiced these techniques in the spring. In early July, however, politicians on both sides agreed to a formal truce, which began on July 11, 1921. The negotiations for a settlement dragged on until December, and the Anglo-Irish Treaty was finally signed on December 6. It acknowledged the formal partition of Ireland into the Irish Free State in the south and Northern Ireland (since June 1921), but it did not grant total independence or a republic.

After the Treaty was signed, it had to be ratified by the Dáil Éireann to come into force. The Treaty debates continued for a week before the final vote barely passed the resolution, approving it on January 7, 1922. At issue between those for and against the Treaty were three simple facts: it did not give the long-sought republic; it established the partition of Ulster; and it required an oath of allegiance to the king. In the end, the pro-Treaty side won by a narrow margin; the anti-Treaty side, calling themselves "Republicans," walked out.

Civil War, 1922–1923

The anti-Treaty IRA set about preparing to fight, while the Provisional Government of the Irish Free State prepared to assume control of the country from the British. By March, friction between the pro- and anti-Treaty IRA men boiled over in the south. The National Army formed from the pro-Treaty minority of the IRA, with Collins as chief of staff and Mulcahy as minister for defence.

The anti-Treaty side, led by de Valera, postured, and even tried to provoke. Arthur Griffith, interim president, and Collins tried to get the anti-Treaty side to come to a settlement, but they refused to compromise. Both sides decided to wait until the results of the general elections in June 1922; Collins and de Valera agreed, in writing, to accept the results. The election decisively (by 73 percent) demonstrated that the will of the people of southern Ireland was pro-Treaty. The people were tired of IRA violence. De Valera renounced his agreement with Collins.

The Battle of Dublin (June 28–July 5, 1922)

In early April 1922, about 200 anti-Treaty IRA had seized the Four Courts in Dublin. They remained there until July. After the results of the election and de Valera's response, and after giving the anti-Treaty IRA a final chance to surrender the Four Courts, on June 28, the National Army of the Free State began a bombardment of the site with artillery borrowed from the British Army. The bombardment lasted three days before the rebels, under famed Dublin IRA man Rory O'Connor, surrendered on June 30.

Anti-Treaty IRA men had taken up arms elsewhere in the city, notably on O'Connell (formerly Sackville) Street. Commanded by Cathal Brugha, they fought until July 5. After ordering his men to lay down their arms, Brugha refused to surrender and was killed (English 2003: 35–37).

The fighting spread throughout the east and south of the Free State. In Drogheda (Co. Louth), rebels drove out the pro-Treaty factions. The National Army moved south into Limerick and, eventually, into the anti-Treaty stronghold of Cork. Both Limerick and Cork fell in August 1922.

The anti-Treaty men hoped that they could invalidate the Treaty by preventing the Free State from assuming actual control, while provoking the British Army to fight. Although they had a distinct advantage in both numbers and experience against the National Army, the anti-Treaty IRA were unable to take the offensive in any effective manner. After August, they had no chance of victory.

They continued with sporadic guerrilla warfare and assassination. They killed Collins toward the end of August in an ambush in Cork and assassinated several high-level Free State officials. In retaliation, the Free State government executed anti-Treaty IRA leaders it held. This was problematic, as the men had usually surrendered in good faith. Rory O'Connor and several other famous leaders met their deaths in this manner. In the end, however, the policy was effective. The Free State executed 77 anti-Treaty men, more, indeed, than the British had executed during the previous war (English 2003: 37).

The ambushes and killings continued into 1923. Although the anti-Treaty forces were large, they did not have the support of the people. The end came with a ceasefire order on May 24, 1923. Although the violence continued for another year, the war was effectively over.

The Irish revolutionary era lasted slightly longer than a decade, during which much of Ireland changed. The revolution occurred during a time of great political, economic, and social upheaval, brought about, in part, by the Great War, and marked the passing of an era. It was the end of the almost exclusive control of politics by the wealthy, which was the death, in part, of home rule. It was the last of the great Irish uprisings and the start of a new type of revolutionary violence against individuals on a wide scale. While revolutionaries targeted groups, the violence was usually singular, targeting a particular person or family in the wider context of their group. Finally, the revolution experienced abject failure in the north, in many ways condemning those six counties to varying levels of strife ever since.

References

Béaslaí, P. (2009) "The North King Street Area." In *Dublin's Fighting Story 1916–21: Told by the Men Who Made It.* Intro. D. Ferriter. Cork: Mercier Press.

Brennan, J. (2009) "The Executed Leaders." In *Dublin's Fighting Story 1916–21: Told by the Men Who Made It.* Intro. D. Ferriter. Cork: Mercier Press.

Donnelly, R. (2001) "Files Confirm Unarmed Civilians Shot in 1916," *The Irish Times,* January 11: 1.

English, R. (2003) *Armed Struggle: The History of the IRA.* Oxford: Oxford University Press.

Fanning, R. (2013) *Fatal Path: British Government and Irish Revolution, 1910–1922.* London: Faber and Faber Ltd.

Ferriter, D. (2009) *Dublin's Fighting Story 1916–21: Told by the Men Who Made It.* Intro. Cork: Mercier Press.

Fox, R. M. (2009) "Citizen Army Posts." In *Dublin's Fighting Story 1916–21: Told by the Men Who Made It.* Intro. D. Ferriter. Cork: Mercier Press.

Kautt, W. H. (2010) *Ambushes and Armour, 1919–1921: The Irish Rebellion.* Dublin: Irish Academic Press.

Lee, J. J. (1973) *The Modernisation of Irish Society, 1848–1918.* Dublin: Gill and Macmillan.

McNally, M. (2007) *The Easter Rising.* Wellingborough: Osprey.

Officer, L. H. (2008) "Five Ways to Compute the Relative Value of a UK Pound Amount, 1830 to Present," *MeasuringWorth.* http://www.measuringworth.com/ukcompare/ (accessed January 22, 2014).

Sceilg (O'Kelly, J. J.) (2009a) "The GPO." In *Dublin's Fighting Story 1916–21: Told by the Men Who Made It.* Intro. D. Ferriter. Cork: Mercier Press.

Sceilg (O'Kelly, J. J.) (2009b) "The South Dublin Union." In *Dublin's Fighting Story 1916–21: Told by the Men Who Made It.* Intro. D. Ferriter. Cork: Mercier Press.

Further Reading

Augusteijn, J. (Ed.) (2002) *The Irish Revolution, 1913–1923.* Basingstoke: Palgrave.

Barry, T. (1995) *Guerrilla Days in Ireland: A Personal Account of the Anglo-Irish War.* Boulder: Roberts Reinhart.

Bartlett, T. and Jeffery, K. (Eds.) (1996) *A Military History of Ireland.* Cambridge: Cambridge University Press.

Béaslaí, P. (2009) "How the Fight Began!" In *Dublin's Fighting Story 1916–21: Told by the Men Who Made It.* Intro. D. Ferriter. Cork: Mercier Press.

Breen, D. (1964) *My Fight for Irish Freedom.* New York: Anvil.

Briscoe, R. (1958) *For the Life of Me.* Boston: Little, Brown.

Caulfield, M. (1963) *The Easter Rebellion.* New York: Holt, Rinehart, and Winston.

Coates, T. (2001) *The Irish Uprising, 1914–1921: Papers from the British Parliamentary Archive.* London: The Stationery Office.

Coffey, T. M. (1969) *Agony at Easter: The 1916 Irish Uprising.* New York: Macmillan.

Crozier, Brigadier-General F. P. (1930) *Impressions and Recollections.* London: T. Werner Laurie.

Doerries, R. (1999) *Prelude to the Easter Rising: Sir Roger Casement in Imperial Germany.* New York: Frank Cass.

Duff, C. (1966) *Six Days to Shake an Empire*. New York: A. S. Barnes.

Duff, D. V. (1937) *Sword for Hire: The Saga of a Modern Free-Companion*. London: John Murray.

Edwards, O. D. and Pyle, F. (Eds.) (1968) *1916: The Easter Rising*. London: MacGibbon and Kee.

Fanning, R., Kennedy, M., Keogh, D., and O'Halpin, E. (Eds.) (1998) *Documents on Irish Foreign Policy. Volume 1: 1919–1921*. Dublin: Royal Irish Academy.

Foster, R. F. (1988) *Modern Ireland: 1600–1972*. London: Penguin.

Hart, P. (1998) *The IRA and Its Enemies: Violence and Community in Cork, 1916–1923*. New York: Oxford University Press.

Hart, P. (2004) *The IRA at War, 1916–1923*. Oxford: Oxford University Press.

Hopkinson, M. A. (2002) *The Irish War of Independence*. Montreal: McGill-Queen's University Press.

Jeffery, K. (1984) *The British Army and the Crisis of Empire, 1918–22*. Manchester: Manchester University Press.

Kautt, W. (1999) *The Anglo-Irish War, 1916–1921: A People's War*. Westport: Praeger.

Kiberd, D. (Ed.) (1998) *1916 Rebellion Handbook*. Dublin: Mourne River Press.

Lynch, D. (1957) *The IRB and the 1916 Insurrection: A Record of the Preparations for the Rising, with Comments on Published Works Relating Thereto, and A Report on Operations in the GPO Garrison Area During Easter Week, 1916*. Cork: Mercier Press.

Macready, General, The Rt. Hon. Sir Nevil, Bt., GCMG, KCB (1925) *Annals of an Active Life*, vol. 2. London: Hutchinson and Co.

McCarthy, Colonel J. M. (Ed.) (n.d.) *Limerick's Fighting Story: From 1916 to the Truce with Britain*. London: Anvil Books.

McGuinness, C. J. (1935) *Sailor of Fortune: Adventures of an Irish Sailor, Soldier, Pirate, Pearl-Fisher, Gun-Runner, Rebel, and Antarctic Explorer*. London: Macrae-Smith.

O'Malley, E. (1937) *Army without Banners: Adventures of an Irish Volunteer*. Cambridge, MA: Riverside Press.

O'Malley, E. (1978) *The Singing Flame*. Dublin: Anvil Books.

O'Malley, E. (1982) *Raids and Rallies*. Dublin: Anvil Books.

Pearse, P. H. (1922/1913) "The Coming Revolution." In *Collected Works of P. H. Pearse*. Dublin: Maunsel and Roberts, pp. 91–99.

Pinkman, J. A. (1998) *In the Legion of the Vanguard*. Cork: Mercier Press.

Redmond-Howard, L. G. (1916) *Six Days of the Irish Republic: A Narrative and Critical Account of the Latest Phase of Irish Politics*. Boston: John W. Luce.

Stephens, J. (1916) *The Insurrection in Dublin*. New York: Macmillan.

Stewart, A. T. Q. (1967) *The Ulster Crisis: Resistance to Home Rule, 1912–14*. London: Faber and Faber.

Townshend, C. (1975) *The British Campaign in Ireland, 1919–1921: The Development of Political and Military Policies*. Oxford: Oxford University Press.

Various authors (2009) *Kerry's Fighting Story, 1916–21: Told by the Men Who Made It*. Cork: Mercier Press.

Various authors (n.d.) *Rebel Cork's Fighting Story, from 1916 to the Truce with Britain*. Tralee, Co. Kerry: Kerryman Anvil Books.

Winter, Sir Ormonde l'Épée (1955) *Winter's Tale: An Autobiography*. London: Richards Press.

Italo-Abyssinian Wars

GIUSEPPE FINALDI

First Italo-Abyssinian War (1887–1896)

In February 1896, a force of around 15,000 Italians assembled in the Italian colony of Eritrea and prepared to invade Abyssinia. Fighting on unfamiliar terrain and armed with defective maps, the Italian column split into four and confronted more than 100,000 disorganized and heavily fatigued Abyssinians. What would become a disastrous defeat at Adowa commenced at dawn on March 1. By the afternoon, the Italians were retreating in disarray, leaving the field, thousands of rifles, and all artillery in the hands of the enemy. More than 5,000 Italians perished and a further 1,000 were taken prisoner. The remnants of the shattered Italian forces made it back to the Italian colony although King Menelik was unable or unwilling to definitively clear them from Eritrea. Adowa was the greatest defeat suffered by any European power during the Scramble for Africa. In Italy, Francesco Crispi was humiliatingly dismissed as prime minister and the costs of mounting yet another African campaign were deemed as excessive. The "protectorate" had been liquidated and the remarkable fact of Ethiopian independence in an Africa completely dominated by European powers emerged as the most important legacy of the Italo-Abyssinian conflict. A black African nation had forced Europe to recognize its right to exist and it had done so with its own resources; when next Ethiopia would be attacked by a European power (again by Italy in 1935) a sense that such an act was arbitrary and illegal had emerged at the international level, a vitally important factor underpinning the decolonization of Africa in the decades after World War II.

Second Italo-Abyssinian War (1935–1936)

Accepting the defeat of Adowa as final was a bitter pill for some Italians to swallow and an undercurrent of dissatisfaction with what was considered to be an abdicating and humiliatingly weak Italian state provided some of the impetus behind the forces that would converge in Fascism in the years after World War I. Mussolini's regime, established in 1922–1925, made much of its having renewed the Italian nation and transformed the country's international status, but it was only with the coming to power of Hitler in Germany in 1933 that the conjunction of the European balance of power gave Italy room to maneuver with regards to its old African enemy. Yet the conquest of Ethiopia had never been an overtly stated ambition of Italian Fascism. Mussolini's decision to return Italy to a forward policy in Abyssinia was related to the need to recast his regime at home after the difficulties brought on by the Great Depression and by the fact that with Hitler's dynamism in full view, the "Fascist Revolution" in Italy appeared to be tired and lacking in direction The prestige of the regime both at home and abroad is the key to understanding Mussolini's reignition of the Scramble for Africa in the mid-1930s.

Yet, at least on the surface, the Scramble was over; Ethiopia was a member of the League of Nations and its young emperor Haile Selassie was familiar with Europe and European diplomacy in a way that would have been unthinkable in the days of Menelik. Ethiopia's acceptance into the League in 1923 was seen in Addis Ababa as a cast-iron guarantee of Ethiopian independence, a major achievement for an empire which was attempting to modernize along European lines. Haile Selassie had begun to transform the old Ethiopian feudal system of governance, concentrating power in his own hands and providing the country with a fledgling administration. The Ethiopian army, which under Menelik had been recruited in the traditional manner (through feudal levies), had been radically reorganized, although as a modern fighting force it was in the mid-1930s very much a work in progress. Unlike Menelik, Haile Selassie trusted in Europe

but was perhaps unaware that with the rise to power of Hitler, the League (and indeed the Versailles settlement) had become a dead letter. This change was sensed in Rome and a pretext was found in 1934 on the Somali-Ethiopian border to ignite a crisis. Terrified of a rearming and boisterous Germany, Britain and France needed to morally condemn Italy for being belligerent with another League member but hoped that Germany's open arms would not entice Mussolini to join Hitler in a bellicose and revisionist alliance in Europe. Thus, when war did break out in October 1935, the League condemned Italy as the aggressor but Britain and France did not want to seriously cripple the Italian war effort by imposing oil sanctions, let alone by closing the Suez Canal to Italian shipping. Sacrificing Ethiopia may have angered a morally outraged British public, but to appeasing British politicians the disappearance of the last island of African independence was far less significant than the hope that Hitler's Germany would remain isolated in its revisionist aims. In the event, the verbal condemnation of Italy and the ineffectual sanctions imposed by the League (it should also be added that the United States, not a League member, was willing to supply Fascist Italy's oil needs) combined to bolster Mussolini's regime, which could pose as having been condemned by the hypocritical imperial powers but which had pluckily stood up for Italy's interests notwithstanding.

Mussolini's popularity at home reached its peak during the Ethiopian war. Free to pursue its ambitions in Ethiopia, Italy this time poured vast resources into taking on the African nation. It was paramount for Mussolini's regime to distinguish itself from the bungling of liberal Italy that had supposedly been the cause of the Adowa disaster, and no expense was spared to ensure success. Half a million men and enormous quantities of ordnance were shipped to East Africa. While in 1896 the discrepancy between the Italian and Ethiopian military had been slight in terms of technology, in 1935 Italy possessed an air force, up-to-date artillery, a wide variety of armored vehicles, and a motorized supply line that eventually ran from the Red Sea coast to Addis Ababa. When Ethiopian resistance to this enormous war machine (nothing like it had ever been seen in Africa) proved sterner than expected, the Italians felt no compulsion to abide by the rules of the Geneva Convention and used gas bombs and terroristic methods to ensure rapid success. The Ethiopian war effort collapsed in little more than six months (although partisan armed resistance was to continue throughout the Italian occupation) and it was left to Mussolini to announce to an enthusiastic Italian public that Italy had finally earned itself an empire. Flouting the authority of France and Britain had paid off and a closer relationship with the Third Reich and its ambition to transform the post-Versailles status quo was in the offing. Haile Selassie escaped to Europe and appealed in person to the League, in which his trust had been misplaced, but his condemnation of Fascism's unchecked brutality and his warning that the horror he had witnessed in Ethiopia would soon be visited upon the rest of the world proved to be prophetic.

SEE ALSO: War Crimes.

Further Reading

Bosworth, R. (2002) *Mussolini*. London: Arnold.

Finaldi, G. (2001) "Italy's Scramble for Africa: From Dogali to Adowa." In J. Dickie and J. Foot (Eds.), *Disastro! Disasters in Italy since 1860: Culture, Politics, Society*. New York: Palgrave.

Mockler, A. (1984) *Haile Selassie's War: The Italian–Ethiopian Campaign, 1935–1941*. London: Random House.

Rubenson, S. (1976) *The Survival of Ethiopian Independence*. London: Heinemann.

Zewde, B. (1991) *A History of Modern Ethiopia*. London: James Currey.

K

Korean War (1949–1953)

STEVEN HUGH LEE

Korea's Partition and the Emergence of Rival Korean Regimes, 1945–1948

The ideological and political foundations of the Korean War lie in the Japanese imperial era, in the evolution of diverse and divisive strands of Korean nationalism, efforts by Koreans to eliminate Japanese colonial rule from the Korean Peninsula, the impact of the Russian Revolution on Asia, and the influence of Christianity and ideas of constitutional governance on Koreans. It was in this period that Koreans first encountered each other as modern ideological enemies, for example, as Japanese collaborators in the imperial army and as guerrilla partisans. The conjunction of forces that led to the Korean conflict, however, were also rooted in the immediate post-World War II era, in Soviet and American objectives toward Korea, the global beginnings of the Cold War, and the creation and consolidation of two rival Korean regimes.

During World War II the Allied powers advocated a qualified Korean independence. The Cairo Declaration of 1943, signed by Britain, the United States, and China, stipulated Korea would achieve independence "in due course." For much of the war, American and Soviet policy was predicated on establishing Korean sovereignty through a multi-power trusteeship over the peninsula. The end of World War II in Asia, however, opened new political possibilities for Koreans. In the wake of the abrupt termination of Japanese colonial rule, a coalition of politically active Koreans established a network of People's Committees across the newly liberated country. On September 6, 1945, a representative assembly met in Seoul and proclaimed the establishment of the Korean People's Republic.

In the aftermath of the Soviet declaration of war on Japan on August 8, 1945, American officials worried about the rapid expansion of Soviet influence in Northeast Asia. To contain Soviet power in the region, the US government asked the Soviet Union to divide Korea between Soviet and American spheres of influence at the 38th parallel. The division of the peninsula was meant as a temporary policy, and in theory, subject to a big power trusteeship. Soviet Premier Joseph Stalin agreed to the partition on August 15, tragically, the day Koreans celebrated their independence from Japan. The early post-war cooperation between the Soviet Union and the United States soon yielded to Cold War frictions between the

Twentieth-Century War and Conflict: A Concise Encyclopedia, First Edition. Edited by Gordon Martel.
© 2015 John Wiley & Sons, Ltd. Published 2015 by John Wiley & Sons, Ltd.

superpowers. Discord also emerged between the superpowers and Koreans and among Koreans of different political ideologies. The division of the peninsula was a fundamental starting point for peninsula-wide political and social conflict.

In the southern zone, American occupation forces refused to accept the authority of the Korean People's Republic and imposed a military government on the population, one which initially retained, in positions of local and central power, Koreans who had collaborated with the Japanese colonial regime. This policy exacerbated tensions in the south, especially in regions where People's Committees had been strong. Peasant and worker discontentment over food shortages and working conditions led to major urban and rural uprisings in late 1946. The conservatives, led by Syngman Rhee, a Korean Christian nationalist who had spent many years in the United States, criticized big power efforts to set up a trusteeship for Korea. The venue for these discussions was the US–Soviet Joint Commission, established in December 1945 at Moscow, but by the spring of 1946 negotiations had become deadlocked over which Koreans should be consulted in a process supposed to lead to the creation of a provisional Korean government.

The Korean Communist Party in the colonial era was weak due to Japanese infiltration and repression, but party members built up a base in the south after 1945 under Pak Hon Yong. Korean communists who had worked with the Chinese Communist Party returned to Korea, as did Soviet Koreans and partisan guerrillas like Kim Il Sung. In the 1930s, Kim had been a member of the Chinese Communist Party and an active guerrilla soldier in Manchuria with the Chinese-led Northeast Anti-Japanese United Army. His partisan group fled the region in 1941 and took asylum in the Soviet Union. Kim returned to northern Korea with Soviet occupation forces in 1945. By 1947, he led a coalition of communists, which included Pak Hon Yong, who were determined to fight a revolutionary war for Korea's independence and to defeat southern "traitors" who had worked closely with Japanese or American "imperialists." In 1948, Kim became premier of the newly created Democratic People's Republic of Korea (DPRK). Koreans from the north went to Manchuria to fight with the Chinese communists in the Chinese civil war, thus gaining valuable battle experience

for the forthcoming revolutionary war on the Korean Peninsula. Korean communists viewed the Korean revolution as part of a long-term struggle against Japanese colonialism and international imperialism.

In southern Korea, after the repression of the left and revolutionary peasants in late 1946 and 1947, Syngman Rhee became a leading spokesman for the conservatives. Much of the moderate and leftist political opposition had been eliminated in the political violence of the era. American occupation authorities, especially commander General John Hodge, treated Rhee with suspicion, but the Korean National Assembly voted him president of the newly established Republic of Korea (ROK) in the summer of 1948.

Civil and International War, 1948–1950

Historians and political scientists have distinguished between "civil" and "international" dimensions of conflict on the Korean Peninsula. These two concepts were closely intertwined, however, as "international" developments such as the ostensibly temporary division of the peninsula at the 38th parallel in 1945 had significant implications for the character of the emerging "civil war" by 1948 and 1949. Civil conflict in Korea existed from the time of the initial Soviet and American occupations. In the aftermath of the establishment of the North and South Korean regimes, as Syngman Rhee and Kim Il Sung sought to extend their power over both Koreas, the violence became more intensely linked to the future of the peninsula. In the south, civil war on the island of Cheju led to a rebellion by South Korean army soldiers who disobeyed the government's orders to side with the rightists. After May 1949, significant border fighting also erupted between southern and northern forces along the 38th parallel. Both Rhee and Kim also sought military support from their big power allies.

Until 1950 neither the United States nor the Soviet Union was prepared to underwrite their respective allies in a war over the peninsula. In late January 1950, however, Stalin agreed to provide North Korea with assistance for a southern invasion. In April, Stalin told the North Koreans to consult with the Chinese communists in planning their attack. In a conversation with Kim Il Sung in

Beijing in May 1950, Chinese leader Mao Zedong agreed to the northern offensive. Even so, Mao had reservations about Kim's plans, and was concerned that an American military intervention might prevent the Chinese communists from defeating nationalist forces in Taiwan. Stalin's decision in January helped to internationalize the conflict on the peninsula, but it was Kim and not Stalin who ordered the attack against South Korea on June 25. The date of the northern offensive is often given as the start of the Korean War, but the conflict had effectively begun in 1949, with the onset of the border fighting between the two Koreas.

After June 1950 the Korean War was characterized by guerrilla warfare and large-scale military offensives. The Soviet Union provided strategic planning assistance and tanks for the initial North Korean assault, which involved seven Korean People's Army divisions, several hundred aircraft, and an armored brigade attacking simultaneously along three corridors leading to the Han River and Seoul. Their objective was rapidly to defeat the South Korean army and to capture the capital city, thus ensuring a quick victory against President Rhee.

Concerned about America's global prestige, wanting to preserve the United States' sphere of influence in Japan, believing erroneously that Stalin ordered the North Korean invasion, and searching for ways to gain domestic and international support for a global rearmament program against the Soviets, the US government of Harry Truman ordered its representative on the United Nations (UN) Security Council to mobilize a coalition of anti-communist states to confront the northern offensive. The Soviet representative on the Security Council had withdrawn from the body to protest the UN's decision to retain Chinese nationalist representation and to deny communist China a seat at the UN. Without a Soviet veto, the Security Council passed resolutions demanding that the North cease its offensive and withdraw its soldiers from South Korea. On June 25–26 President Truman ordered the US Air Force and navy to intervene in the conflict and sent the US Seventh Fleet to the Taiwanese Straits, thus preventing Mao from organizing an invasion of Taiwan while preserving the islands for American strategy in the Pacific. Several days later, in an effort to contain the northern offensive, he authorized the sending of two divisions of American

troops from Japan to Korea. On July 1, a battalion from the 24th Infantry Division of the US Eighth Army (nicknamed "Task Force Smith" after its commanding officer) arrived in Korea from Kyushu, though these soldiers were as unsuccessful as the South Korean troops in stemming the North Korean attacks. The US Air Force, however, did rapidly achieve air superiority. Six days later, the UN, under American leadership, established a United Nations Command (UNC), headed by General Douglas MacArthur, the supreme commander for the Allied powers in Japan. In mid-July Rhee authorized the Korean military to come under the direction of the UNC. The war was ostensibly led by UN forces, but the anti-communist war effort was largely a product of American policy and resources.

South Korea's eight divisions lacked the necessary military equipment, personnel, and experience to contain North Korea's mechanized offensive, and early battles heavily favored the communists. DPRK soldiers occupied Seoul within three days of their attack in late June, mobilized several more divisions of troops for another major offensive in August, and had almost defeated UNC armies by the late summer of 1950. Only a rectangular strip of land known as the Pusan Perimeter, in southeastern Korea, remained under the control of UNC forces. Operation Chromite, a bold amphibious offensive organized by MacArthur against the west coast port city of Incheon in September, was coordinated with naval attacks and air raids which dropped napalm, killing dozens of villagers. In planning the operation, the American military established "X Corps," composed of American and South Korean infantry and marine units. Led by General Edward M. Almond, the attacking force divided the North Korean army and cut its supply lines, forcing the communists into retreat. By the end of September 1950 the UNC faced a major strategic decision: whether or not to cross the 38th parallel and occupy North Korea. Government and public opinion in the United States, as well as the Rhee regime, favored an offensive across the political boundary between the two Koreas. On October 7, with the Soviet Union's representative back on the Security Council, the United States and its allies in the UN General Assembly led the way in passing a resolution recommending that UN forces in Korea take measures to establish "stability" across the peninsula. The political and strategic decision to cross the parallel and unify the peninsula, however, had already been made by American officials. Despite warnings from the People's Republic of China (PRC) that its soldiers would intervene should UNC armies cross the parallel, the UNC ordered South Korean and other UN forces across the parallel in late September and October 1950. The UNC occupation of North Korea was an ill-fated and ill-defined strategic gamble, one which led to Chinese intervention in the Korean War.

Occupations and Atrocities

The northern invasion initiated a series of occupations of the Korean Peninsula: a northern occupation of South Korea which lasted until the UN counteroffensive in September 1950, a brief but very bloody UN occupation of northern Korea until December 1950, another American military occupation in the south, and a Chinese military occupation of North Korea. The rapid transition of occupation regimes in the first year of the conflict created almost indescribable hardship and trauma for Koreans. Ubiquitous violence confronted refugee civilians as they sought succor from soldiers who attacked from land, air, and sea. Many massacres occurred in the first six months of the war. As northern armies moved into South Korea, ROK soldiers and police murdered political prisoners in large numbers. In July 1950, for example, ROK authorities killed between 4,000 and 7,000 inmates held in the city of Daejeon. Many of the prisoners were not linked to communism, but had been picked up in anti-communist raids prior to the invasion. Investigations by the South Korean Truth and Reconciliation Commission in the 2000s suggest that Korean police and soldiers killed 100,000 or more civilians, including women and children, in the summer of 1950. American soldiers also committed atrocities. In late July, at the village of No Gun Ri, for example, US troops killed several hundred Korean refugees.

As northern soldiers and officials occupied the south, they rebuilt People's Committees and began the process of integrating the region into the northern regime. Members of the communist South Korean Workers' Party cooperated with occupation officials, though northerners held the bulk of the high-level political positions. Northerners established youth, women's, peasants', and workers' organizations to help coordinate the occupation. Communists also enacted land reform, but the Rhee regime's land reforms prior to the invasion limited the impact of this initiative. In Seoul and other cities, northerners set up tribunals and arrested former pro-Japanese or pro-American collaborators, landowners, or others they considered enemies of the DPRK. During their occupation of the south, North Korean soldiers and officials were responsible for about 30,000 civilian deaths. The South Korean army also committed many atrocities during its occupation of North Korea in the fall of 1950. Southern troops killed tens of thousands of civilians who had collaborated with the northern regime. In the northern capital of Pyongyang, for example, South Korean courts sentenced to death several thousand North Koreans. South Korean atrocities attracted the ire of British diplomats, who complained to the American Department of State about the massacres. American soldiers, however, were also ordered to destroy the North Korean government and to liquidate the northern Workers' Party. In some cases, American military authorities abetted ROK executions by turning over their prisoners to ROK soldiers. Up to 90,000 North Korean prisoners of the southern military may have perished as a result of mistreatment during the South Korean army's retreat after Chinese troops intervened in the war in the late fall of 1950.

Chinese Intervention

In the aftermath of the UNC September counteroffensive, on September 29, 1950, Kim Il Sung asked Stalin for help in mobilizing soldiers from China and other people's democracies. The Soviet premier responded on October 1 by asking Mao Zedong to assist the beleaguered DRPK forces. Mao viewed the UN offensive against North Korea with grave concern, partly for national security reasons. Convinced of the need to stem American imperialism in Asia, he took the lead within the Chinese government in advocating the use of Chinese troops in Korea. The Chinese government had taken initial steps to defend its territory in July, when it established the Northeast

Defense Frontier Army in Manchuria. By the end of the month, the soldiers stationed along the Sino-Korean border included those of the 38th, 39th, and 40th Armies of the Fourth Field Army, some of the best units of the People's Liberation Army. In early October, the Frontier Army, numbering some 250,000 troops, became known as the Chinese People's Volunteers (CPV), commanded by General Peng Dehuai, who had led Chinese forces during World War II and the Chinese civil war. Mao gave the initial order to send the volunteers to Korea on October 8, a decision confirmed in subsequent weeks. In late October and early November, the CPV, under threat from the air attacks of the US Fifth Air Force, engaged UNC troops for the first time, organizing deadly night raids against American, South Korean, Commonwealth, and other UNC-led soldiers. The CPV then suddenly ended its attacks and drew UNC forces into a strategic trap in northern Korea. Reinforced with a dozen divisions (150,000 soldiers) from the Chinese Ninth Army Group, the CPV struck again in late November and December, forcing UN soldiers to retreat south of Seoul. The UNC military failure created panic in western capitals, made worse by President Harry Truman's and General MacArthur's willingness to consider using atomic bombs in Korea or against Chinese cities. Mao sought to expel the enemy completely from the peninsula, but UNC counteroffensives stemmed the communist advances, and by the spring of 1951 the battle line had stabilized around the 38th parallel. The Chinese offensive had taught the US military the perils of any additional major offensive into communist territory, but American officials had also achieved many of their rearmament objectives after 1950, and concentrated their attention on their Europe-first strategy. The costs of another "rollback" offensive also dissuaded them from using military power to defeat the combined Chinese and North Korean forces. After MacArthur had sabotaged an initial effort to establish armistice talks, President Truman dismissed the general, much to the relief of America's North Atlantic Treaty Organization allies. The Truman administration thus asserted the primacy of executive authority over a military commander and ended MacArthur's hopes for military glory and a post-war political career. In the spring and early summer of 1951, the Soviets took initiatives to begin discussions for an armistice, which began in July 1951 in the Korean town of Kaeseong.

Prisoners of War

Although the initial discussions toward an armistice seemed promising, the negotiations stalled over the issue of repatriation of prisoners of war (POWs). The Geneva Convention of 1949 required states at war to repatriate prisoners to their home states, but in 1951 President Truman decided that prisoners should decide where they wanted to go after the signing of an armistice. North Korea had not been a party to the Geneva Convention, and the United States had signed but not ratified the agreement. The decision by the United States to demand nonforcible repatriation not only broke its earlier support of the Convention, but also extended the war. North Koreans appeared to have wanted to negotiate an armistice, though Stalin and Mao were willing to delay an agreement until they got one that they felt was advantageous in strategic and political terms. By contrast, the Syngman Rhee administration adamantly opposed an armistice. Rhee wanted to continue the war, and his regime organized rallies demanding that North Korea be defeated and incorporated into the south's constitutional structure. The American government, however, refused to support South Korea's belligerency. The UNC even limited the amount of ammunition issued to South Korean soldiers so they would not be able to initiate a sustained offensive against northern positions.

During the armistice negotiations, many Koreans and other armies' soldiers perished or were wounded in the war, both along the entrenched battle lines around the 38th parallel and in North Korea, where US bombing raids devastated the northern economy and society. UNC bombing raids leveled towns and villages, knocked out power and production facilities, and even targeted irrigation dams in an effort to destroy food supplies. The Korean War thus set precedents for US negotiating behavior in other conflicts, particularly Vietnam. In South Korea partisans continued to conduct guerrilla operations until 1954.

Armistice

In November 1952, Americans elected Dwight D. Eisenhower president of the United States, partly on a promise to end the Korean conflict. His administration soon considered additional ways of increasing military pressure on the communist side as a means of accelerating an armistice agreement. In particular, Eisenhower and his secretary of state, John Foster Dulles, were prepared to threaten the use of nuclear weapons to gain an armistice. The president even told a group of senior advisors in March 1953 that he was willing to use such weapons if they resulted in military victory over the communists and movement of the battle lines northward to Korea's "waist." The administration's atomic diplomacy came to the fore in the aftermath of Stalin's death in March 1953. Through diplomatic and military signaling, the US government made it clear to Chinese communists that it was prepared to use nuclear weapons to achieve an armistice to its liking. The Chinese leaders, however, were more concerned with economic development than prolonging the conflict over Korea, and in early June the communist side agreed to the American terms transmitted on May 20, 1953, accepting the principle of non-forcible repatriation of POWs.

Before the formal signing of the armistice, the Rhee government attempted to undermine the agreement: ROK guards at a POW camp released all North Korean prisoners. This did not wreck the armistice, but did result in a sustained communist offensive aimed at South Korean positions along the front lines, designed to demonstrate that the southern regime could not win the war on its own terms. On July 27, 1953, the Chinese, the UNC, and North Koreans signed the armistice. The Rhee regime, opposed to ending the war, was not a formal part of the negotiations, and South Korea has never formally adhered to the agreement. In the absence of a peace treaty, a state of war continues to this day on the Korean Peninsula.

Legacies

The Korean War had a tremendous impact on international society. It resulted in a major rearmament drive, an acceleration of American military support to its anti-communist allies, tensions within the Sino-Soviet alliance, an extended isolation of the PRC and North Korea from the capitalist-world economies, the creation, on the Korean Peninsula, of two of the world's largest armies, and the continued division of Korea and the two Chinas. The conflict's human and psychological legacies continue to shape the policies and perspectives of Koreans across the north–south divide.

SEE ALSO: Chinese Civil War (Modern); Peacekeeping; Vietnam War (1959–1975); World War II: War in Asia.

Further Reading

Chen, J. (1994) *China's Road to the Korean War: The Making of the Sino-American Confrontation.* New York: Columbia University Press.

Cumings, B. (1981) *The Origins of the Korean War: Liberation and the Emergence of Separate Regimes.* Princeton: Princeton University Press.

Cumings, B. (1990) *The Origins of the Korean War: The Roaring of the Cataract 1947–1950.* Princeton: Princeton University Press.

Cumings, B. (2002) "War Crimes and Historical Memory: The United Nations Occupation of Korea in 1950." In D. Carter and R. Clifton (Eds.), *War and Cold War in American Foreign Policy, 1942–1967.* New York: Palgrave.

Cumings, B. (2010) *The Korean War: A History.* New York: Modern Library.

Foot, R. (1985) *The Wrong War: American Policy and the Dimensions of the Korean Conflict, 1950–1953.* Ithaca: Cornell University Press.

Foot, R. (1990) *A Substitute for Victory: The Politics of Peacemaking at the Korean Armistice Talks.* Ithaca: Cornell University Press.

Goncharov, S., Lewis, J., and Xue Litai (1993) *Uncertain Partners: Stalin, Mao and the Korean War.* Stanford: Stanford University Press.

Hanley, C. J., Mendoza, M., and Sang-hun Choe (2001) *The Bridge at No Gun Ri: A Hidden Chapter from the Korean War.* New York: Henry Holt.

Hunt, M. (1992) "Beijing and the Korean Crisis, June 1950–June 1951," *Political Science Quarterly,* 107 (3): 453–478.

Kaufman, B. (1997) *The Korean War: Challenges in Crisis, Credibility and Command.* Philadelphia: Temple University Press.

Kim, Dong-Choon (2009) *The Unending Korean War: A Social History.* Honolulu: University of Hawaii Press.

Korean Institute of Military History (2000) *The Korean War*, 3 vols. Lincoln: University of Nebraska Press.

Lee, S. H. (2001) *The Korean War*. New York: Longman.

Lowe, P. (1997) *The Origins of the Korean War*. New York: Longman.

Matray, J. (1985) *The Reluctant Crusade: American Foreign Policy in Korea, 1941–1950*. Honolulu: University of Hawaii Press.

Millett, A. R. (2005) *The War for Korea, 1945–1950: A House Burning*. Lawrence: University Press of Kansas.

Millett, A. R. (2010) *The War for Korea, 1950–1951: They Came from the North*. Lawrence: University Press of Kansas.

Stueck, W. (1996) *The Korean War: An International History*. Princeton: Princeton University Press.

L

Lebanese Civil War (1975–1990)

EYAL ZISSER

From April 1975 to October 1990, Lebanon suffered a bloody civil war. At its peak it threatened to bring about the complete collapse and disintegration of the Lebanese state. During the fighting nearly 150,000 people were killed and another 200,000 wounded. Six hundred thousand people were made homeless, and nearly 250,000 left Lebanon, most of whom never returned. All this took place among a population that numbered merely 3.1 million at the beginning of the war.

It was difficult from the very beginning of the civil war to distinguish the various camps fighting each other or to demarcate the various stages of the conflict. It can be seen, in fact, as a conglomeration of internal Lebanese conflicts, joined by regional confrontations that were being acted out on Lebanese soil, which all merged into a war of all against all. The several struggles inside the Lebanese arena included those between the various religious communities, those within these communities between the notable families, and sometimes even struggles within these families between different branches of the family, or between different generations or age groups. Thus, during the civil war we find Maronites fighting Sunnis, Druze fighting Maronites, Druze fighting Shi'ites, and Shi'ites fighting Sunnis, as well as Maronites, Druze, and Shi'ites fighting other members of their own community.

As far as the regional and international aspects of the warfare are concerned, Lebanon quickly turned into an arena where the Great Powers, the Arab states, and other regional powers took part in the struggle. Three foreign actors in particular played a role: Syria, Israel, and the Palestine Liberation Organization (PLO). Iran also intervened at a later stage. To complicate matters even more, the various factions involved in the Lebanese Civil War, both those from within the country and those from abroad, could be found changing sides more than once.

Roots of the Civil War

Lebanon was established in September 1920 by French Mandate on the basis of the "Mount Lebanon autonomous district" (the *Mutasarrifiyya*) established by the Ottoman Empire under pressure from the western powers in the mid-nineteenth century. The founding of the Lebanese state created a new entity whose demographic composition and numerical balance between Christians and

Twentieth-Century War and Conflict: A Concise Encyclopedia, First Edition. Edited by Gordon Martel.
© 2015 John Wiley & Sons, Ltd. Published 2015 by John Wiley & Sons, Ltd.

Muslims, as well as between the different communities within each religious group, was totally different from those that had prevailed in the Ottoman district of Mount Lebanon, upon which Lebanon was based. The ratio of Christians in the general population was reduced to about 54 percent in the new Lebanese state. Maronite Christians, the hard core of the Lebanese state, were the biggest community with 29 percent of the Lebanese population; the Sunni Muslim community amounted to about 22 percent; the Muslim Shi'ites amounted to about 18 percent. Even these figures were soon to be changed. However, from the very beginning of the new Lebanon, the Muslims, led by the Sunni community, were perceived as seeking to challenge the very existence of the Lebanese state, as well as seeking to challenge the Maronites' dominance and hegemony.

As early as 1958, Lebanon witnessed an outbreak of violence, which was called "the civil war of 1958." This violence erupted when the incumbent president, Camille Chamoun, was seeking to extend his term beyond the six years fixed by the Lebanese Constitution. Tensions over the question of what international and regional orientation Lebanon should take also contributed to the wave of violence. Most of the Christians favored supporting the moderate and pro-western bloc in the Arab world, while the Muslims were attracted to supporting the pan-Arab nationalist camp led by Egyptian president Gamal Abdel Nasser. The violence lasted for several months and ended in a compromise, which came about to a large degree thanks to the efforts of the United States, which dispatched several hundred Marines to Lebanon in July 1958 with the aim of helping to restore peace.

Apart from this short outbreak of violence in the summer of 1958, the Lebanese state experienced, until the outbreak of the civil war in April 1975, considerable political stability and even economic prosperity. This was due to the success of the various communities in formulating and maintaining over time the "national pact" of 1943, a formula for dividing up the positions of power and the resources of the state among the different communities, and of no less importance, among the notable families in each of the different communities. The national pact was an unwritten agreement between the Shi'ite, Sunni, and Maronite leaderships that laid the foundation of Lebanon as a multi-confessional state, and has shaped the country to this day. Among the key points of the agreement were that the Maronites would accept Lebanon as an Arab affiliated country; the Sunnis would abandon their aspirations to unite with Syria; and in addition, the president of the Republic would always be Maronite, the prime minister Sunni, and the president of the chamber of representatives Shi'a. Members of parliament were to be in a ratio of 6:5 Christians and Muslims.

However, the situation in Lebanon began to change at the beginning of the 1970s. The demographic balance between the religious communities was shifting, with the Muslims becoming a clear majority in the country. This led to Muslim demands to adjust the national pact to the new demographic realities in Lebanon. In addition, the Palestinians became a factor on the domestic scene. Almost 120,000 Palestinian refugees had come to Lebanon in the wake of the 1948 war. As a result of the signing of the Cairo Agreement (November 1969), followed by the events of Black September (1970) and the expulsion of the PLO from Jordan by King Hussein, the PLO became an armed presence on Lebanese soil. This quickly led to the border with Israel heating up and Israel intervening more and more in Lebanese affairs. This situation placed a burden on the Lebanese system that it found difficult to cope with.

Civil War in Lebanon: Main Stages

Civil war broke out on April 13, 1975, in the wake of an exchange of fire between Palestinian and Maronite Phalangist fighters near a church in 'Ayn al-Rumana, one of the Christian neighborhoods of East Beirut. The fighting quickly spread all over Lebanon. From this point on, four main stages can be distinguished in the development of the civil war:

• 1975–1976: During this period the war could be characterized as a limited, internal Lebanese confrontation. On one side were the Maronite Militia, the "Lebanese Forces," headed by the Phalange Party. On the other side were the Sunni and Druze militias, backed up by the PLO. The confrontation at this stage involved mostly exchanges of fire, as well as acts of murder and massacre, which took place mainly along the strips of territory separating Christian and Muslim residential neighborhoods, mostly in the city of Beirut.

- 1976–1977: On June 1, 1976, Syrian soldiers entered Lebanon at the invitation of the Lebanese government. Using a divide-and-rule policy, Syria aimed at securing a presence in the country in order to return quiet and stability, but also in order to have Lebanon under its own control. The Syrians, assisted initially by the Christian militias, came up against PLO forces and Sunni and Druze militias that intended to block their way. The Syrian forces managed to gain a foothold in certain parts of Lebanon, but they failed to gain mastery of the situation and bring the civil war to an end. The leaders of the Christian militias quickly changed their position and abandoned Syria and linked up with Israel in an effort to expel the PLO, and even the Syrians, from Lebanon.

- 1977–1982: The struggle between Israel and Syria for dominance in Lebanon developed finally into all-out warfare when Israel launched Operation Peace for the Galilee on June 6, 1982. In two weeks Israeli forces reached Beirut and on August 23, 1982, brought about the election of Israel's ally, Bashir Jumayyil, as president of Lebanon. However, two weeks after his election as president, on September 14, Bashir was killed by a bomb planted at his headquarters. In the wake of his assassination, the Maronite "Lebanese Forces" carried out a massacre in the Sabra and Shatila Palestinian refugee camps, which they were allowed to enter by the Israeli army. Under international pressure, Israel was compelled to withdraw its forces from Beirut. The Israeli forces were soon to be replaced by a multinational force led by the Americans.

- 1982–1989: This phase began with the withdrawal of foreign military forces. The PLO removed its forces from Lebanon in August 1982, and later in the year Israel also began withdrawing from most of the territory it had seized during its invasion in the summer of 1982. During 1984, the United States and other nations that took part in the multinational force, like France and Italy, also removed their soldiers from the country in the wake of terrorist attacks carried out by radical Shi'ites, possibly Hezbollah members,

against their forces stationed in Beirut. (On April 18, 1983, the American embassy in Beirut had been blown up by a suicide bomber: 61 people were killed and 120 wounded. On October 23, the headquarters of the US Marines and those of the French forces in Beirut were attacked in a similar manner: 241 Marines and 23 French soldiers were killed, with another 100 injured.)

Along with all this it became evident that the power of the Maronite and Sunni communities in Lebanon was on the decline. Their place was being taken by the Shi'ite community, which became the biggest community in Lebanon (estimated at around 30–35 percent of the entire population). At first the Shi'ites were led by the Amal movement, which was established by the Shi'ite cleric Musa al-Sadr in 1975, but weakened after his mysterious disappearance in 1978 during a visit to Libya. Later the Shi'ites were led by the Hezbollah organization, which was established with Iranian aid in 1982, but announced its existence in 1985.

The war of all against all in Lebanon raged continuously during most of the 1980s and included mini-wars within the larger war. The "Mountain War" (September–October 1983) saw Maronite Phalangist and Druze fighters battling for control of southern Lebanon's Shuf mountains. The struggle ended in a Druze victory and the flight of hundreds of thousands of Christian residents from the mountains. The "War of the Camps" (1985–1986) was a Shi'ite–Palestinian struggle for control over southern Lebanon and Shi'ite neighborhoods and the Palestinian refugee camps in the country's large towns. It ended with a Shi'ite victory and the Palestinians being forced back into the refugee camps. In the "War of Shi'ites versus Shi'ites" (1988–1989), Amal fought Hezbollah for hegemony over the Shi'ite community. The struggle ended in reconciliation, through Syrian and Iranian mediation, but with Hezbollah having the upper hand.

In September 1988, Lebanese president Amin Jumayyil's term of office came to an end. Since it proved impossible to elect anyone in his place, Jumayyil appointed the Maronite commander of the army, General Michel Aoun, as acting president. Once appointed, Aoun launched an all-out war, first of all against the "Lebanese Forces," his former allies, second, against the Druze and the Shi'ites who were besieging Beirut, and third, a "war of liberation" against the Syrians. Aoun hoped that his struggles would help him end the chaos plaguing the country, but in fact they brought about Lebanon's further decline into bloodshed.

Fatigue and exhaustion amid the prevailing chaos finally made it possible to bring the civil war to an end. Following inter-Arab efforts at mediation, to which Syria also contributed, on October 22, 1989, in Taif, Saudi Arabia, representatives of the various Lebanese communities signed a reconciliation agreement. It was an updated and expanded version of the national pact of 1943. Following the signing of the agreement, the Lebanese chamber of representatives elected a president, René Moawad, on November 5, 1989. When Moawad was assassinated on November 22, after serving for only 17 days, Elias Hirawi was elected the next day to replace him. Gradually, political and legislative life resumed and calm returned to the Lebanese state.

However, the way to the implementation of the Taif Agreement was still blocked by General Michel Aoun, who firmly rejected it. Then, when the Gulf crisis erupted in August 1990, following Iraq's invasion of Kuwait, the Syrians were given the opportunity they had been waiting for to get rid of Aoun. On October 13, the Syrian army attacked the enclave he held around the presidential palace in Ba'adba and took control. With this the Syrians completed the imposition of their control over all of Lebanon, and the civil war was terminated.

In the end, Lebanon remained a fractured and fragmented state among the religious communities. From this perspective, it is possible to view the civil war as just another link in the ongoing struggle between religious communities that has characterized the history of the Lebanon for hundreds of years. The Taif Agreement granted advantages to a coalition led by the Sunni community, in partnership with the Druze and parts of the Maronite community. At the same time, the agreement tended to ignore the Shi'ites, who had become the biggest community in the country. Thus the foundations were laid for the tensions that have plagued Lebanon since the end of the civil war.

SEE ALSO: Arab–Israeli Conflict.

Further Reading

Abraham, A. J. (1996) *The Lebanon War*. London: Praeger.

Hanf, T. (1993) *Coexistence in Wartime Lebanon: Decline of the State and Rise of a Nation*. London: I. B. Tauris.

Johnson, M. (2001) *All Honorable Men: The Social Origins of War in Lebanon*. London: I. B. Tauris.

el-Khazen, F. (2000) *The Breakdown of the State in Lebanon, 1967–1976*. London: I. B. Tauris.

Salibi, K. S. (1976) *Crossroads to Civil War: Lebanon 1958–1967*. Delmar, NY: Caravan.

M

Malayan Emergency (1948–1960)

BRIAN P. FARRELL

The Malayan Emergency is widely seen as the most successful counterinsurgency campaign in modern warfare. The Emergency was an armed struggle launched by the Malayan Communist Party (MCP) in June 1948 to drive British colonialism out of Malaya and ignite socialist revolution. It was officially terminated in July 1960, although intermittent violence broke out again in later years, and a definitive peace settlement was only concluded in 1989. British, Malayan, and Commonwealth security forces comprehensively defeated armed insurrection in a conflict that made the phrase "hearts and minds" an axiom of counterinsurgency.

From start to finish one demographic reality, and one question, drove the conflict. Malaya was made up of different ethnic communities which did not get along very well, but no one could impose on the others. The Malay community, nearly all Muslim, was 50 percent of the population but mainly rural. The Chinese community was 38 percent of the population and economically dominant. An Indian community combining rubber plantation workers and city-dwellers made up 8 percent. The central question was: what kind of Malaya could these communities be persuaded to accept?

The Emergency was produced by several factors: the spread of communism in Malaya and China, the impact of World War II, and running tensions between ethnic communities. The Japanese occupation of Malaya during World War II set the table. Japanese divide and rule policy exacerbated friction between the Malay community, which regarded itself as the native race, and the Chinese community, whom the Malays considered expatriate sojourners. The Chinese community dominated commerce, but many Chinese were forced by the occupation to squat on the fringes of the jungle as subsistence farmers, without secure land title. British political control of Malaya, part colony part protectorate, had made it possible to manage communal tensions. But defeat in Malaya in 1942 humiliated the British, forcing them to consider fundamental changes in order to modernize Malaya without losing their position there. Meanwhile, the MCP took the lead organizing resistance to the Japanese. It drew strength from the Chinese community but nevertheless could not dominate that community, nor attract more than a handful of Malay supporters. When the Japanese surrendered in September 1945 the MCP exploited a brief vacuum of power to exact

Twentieth-Century War and Conflict: A Concise Encyclopedia, First Edition. Edited by Gordon Martel.
© 2015 John Wiley & Sons, Ltd. Published 2015 by John Wiley & Sons, Ltd.

violent retribution against so-called collaborators. Because many victims were Malay, this provoked retaliation, only brought under control
when Allied forces restored order. And after
long years of occupation the Malayan economy
was near collapse. These problems framed a
volatile situation when in 1946 the British
launched their plans to modernize Malaya.

British efforts to make Malaya a unitary colonial
state provoked a Malay backlash that produced an
organized nationalist political party, the United
Malays National Organization (UMNO). This put
the British between a rock and a hard place.
Modernizing the state included granting citizenship and land title to the Chinese and terminating
the prerogatives of the sultans of the different
states, through whom the British had exercised
real but indirect control. This infuriated many
Malays. They saw the sultans as expressions of
sovereignty in their own land, and feared that having already lost the economy to the Chinese they
would now lose the state as well. But when UMNO
pressure forced the British to scrap their Malayan
Union and replace it with a Federation of Malaya,
restoring the sultans' prerogatives and restricting
citizenship to "sons of the soil," this angered many
Chinese. Meanwhile, the MCP ostensibly disarmed its Malayan People's Anti-Japanese Army,
and concentrated on stirring up discontent in the
cities. But when the general secretary of the party
disappeared in 1947, taking party funds with him,
this discredited his urban strategy. This shifted the
balance of power to younger leaders who wanted
to directly challenge British rule. That was reinforced by the progress of communism elsewhere in
Asia, especially in China where the strategy to rely
on revolution in the countryside seemed to be
vindicated. These developments persuaded MCP
leaders to launch an armed struggle.

While the revolution was pre-planned, the
attacks in the state of Perak in June 1948 that set it
off were not. Local leaders took matters into their
own hands by attacking European plantations
before the Central Committee was ready to trigger a coordinated national uprising. This underlined a crippling weakness that dogged the MCP
from start to finish: communications. The grand
strategy was to implement revolutionary warfare
as preached and practiced by Mao Zedong in
China. This involved combining military and
political operations to discredit the government,

provoke it into a heavy-handed backlash, and
persuade the population their future lay with
socialist revolution. Winning national independence by driving out the British was presented as
the primary objective, but it was to lead to
revolution and a different kind of modern Malaya.
The campaign would be conducted through three
stages: using terror and violence to destabilize the
countryside and undermine the government;
establishing liberated areas in which the MCP
could erect a *de facto* government and build
stronger forces to more aggressively engage the
enemy; building an army that could drive the
British out of Malaya. But with no more than
8,000 armed fighters at any given time, at first
barely half that number, the armed wing the party
revived to fight the war, the Malayan Races
Liberation Army (MRLA), had to disperse into
small units, and rely on terrorism and guerrilla
hit-and-run operations, to carry the war to a
much larger enemy. This made it difficult to
communicate orders and coordinate operations
across a large country dominated by jungle and
mountain ranges. Nevertheless, Party General
Secretary Chin Peng accepted the *fait accompli*
after the British high commissioner gave in to
pressure from alarmed Europeans and declared a
state of emergency.

Both combatants struggled at first to find a
strategy to address the central question. MRLA
attacks included assaults on rural police stations,
vandalism of rubber trees, intimidation and murder of plantation workers or villagers who refused
to support the cause, and sabotage of railroad
lines. The British coined the phrase "Communist
Terrorist" or CT to denigrate their enemy, and
MRLA tactics helped them do this. Not until
October 1951 did the Central Committee conclude that such tactics did more harm than good,
turning an already suspicious population against
them. They changed the name of the army to the
Malayan National Liberation Army (MNLA) and
changed its strategy to more direct assaults on
government installations and security forces. It
turned out to be too late.

British grand strategy was at first equally ineffective. Little effort was made to resolve political
tensions provoked by establishing the Federation,
and military strategy focused on heavy-handed,
large-scale sweep-and-clear operations by infantry units. Such operations rarely encountered any

CTs but angered the local populations they disrupted. The way forward was indicated by successful intelligence, infiltration, and ambush operations by the police Special Branch, which did some damage to the MRLA leadership. The tide began to turn in 1950 when Harold Briggs, a very experienced British army officer, was appointed director of operations. Briggs devised a strategy that focused not on military contact with the MRLA but rather on isolating it from the population, then winning that population over. It took time for the elements of the Briggs Plan to be put in place, but the plan provided the blueprint by which counterinsurgency destroyed the MCP.

The tactical focus of the Briggs Plan was to cut off the CTs from the community on which they most relied: the so called *Min Yuen*, or sympathizers, who consisted mostly of Chinese squatters on the jungle fringe and residents of small towns. They provided essential supplies of food, passed information, offered safe houses, and provided recruits. Numbering perhaps 40,000 active sympathizers, they hid inside the larger Chinese community, whose ultimate loyalty became the center of gravity of the conflict. Briggs singled them out as the target: cut them off from the communists physically, politically, and psychologically, and the war would be won. The physical core of the plan was the literally titled New Villages; villages built from scratch into which Chinese squatters and suspected sympathizers were resettled. They were then secured behind barbed wire and fixed defenses, manned by police and Home Guard units that controlled movement in and out. This was reinforced by measures such as communal cooking, to deny food supply to the CTs. This approach helped push the MCP to change its strategy in October 1951.

The most dramatic MCP success of the war came on October 6, 1951, when they assassinated High Commissioner Sir Henry Gurney in a roadside ambush. This provoked a newly elected Conservative government in the United Kingdom to appoint General Sir Gerald Templer as high commissioner and grant him full executive control of both government and the security forces. Along with this proconsular authority, Templer was authorized to pursue whatever measures were necessary in order to destroy the communist insurrection. The moment and the mandate were matched by the man.

Templer supplied the drive and leadership to pull together the ideas sketched out by Briggs and implement the strategy. Four elements dominated implementation: political change, leadership, organization, and intelligence. Templer pressured the political leaders of the different communities of Malaya to find the necessary compromises, to allow the British to midwife a new Malayan state that could fend off communism from within. It took time but they did so, forging an alliance of communal political parties, led by UMNO, that built a durable anti-communist consensus across communal lines. This persuaded the British to negotiate independence as part of the strategy to destroy the communists, rather than wait until after the Emergency was settled. This was a truly decisive breakthrough that made the Malayans partners in the Emergency, fighting to secure their own path to independence. Meanwhile, Templer brought together the civil government, police, and armed forces in a network of executive committees that coordinated operations at the national, state, and district levels. And he entrenched intelligence operations and the police Special Branch, relying on Chinese detectives, as the leading force through which the enemy would be infiltrated, identified, and destroyed. The whole coordinated effort rested on a framework provided by saturating the countryside with police and Home Guard units, backed up by regular infantry and special forces, which mounted long-range jungle patrols to flush out MNLA units. At peak strength the combined security forces numbered more than 80,000 men. Total air superiority provided the means to move forces rapidly, drop propaganda leaflets, and mount rapid attacks on ground targets. Command of the sea ensured that supplies from abroad were reduced to an intermittent trickle.

Templer's strategy, driven forward after his departure in 1954 by Robert Thompson as director of operations, focused on concentrating great force to "clear" one state at a time. Too often these operations have been described as a brilliant use of political measures such as economic and community development, and political inclusiveness, to win over a community without using much force. This is a distortion of the strategy by which counterinsurgency did prevail. That strategy rested on a very determined application of power and force, to "screw down the population" by strict control (Hack 2001: 128–131). The key was to combine carrot and stick. Such strict controls were placed on every aspect of everyday life that, when they were lifted, the population was keen to give the government no excuse to reimpose them. This worked because it was combined with carefully calibrated use of force aimed to avoid unnecessary casualties, visible change in national politics that promised a new and better future, intelligence operations that greatly disrupted the enemy from within, and physical security that made the population feel safe in rejecting MCP intimidation.

This comprehensive grand strategy made such good progress that in 1955 Chin Peng came out of the jungle to negotiate peace with the new Malayan Alliance, led by UMNO leader Tunku Abdul Rahman. Chin Peng failed to persuade the Tunku to allow the MCP to operate as a political party in a soon-to-be independent Malaya. He returned to the jungle, retreating along with many of his fighters across the border to southern Thailand, to fight on. But the government now had the initiative. The Tunku destroyed the strongest political argument the MCP had by negotiating independence with the British, consummated on August 31, 1957. As that door closed, intelligence and Special Branch operations unraveled the MNLA from within. Psychological warfare assumed first place in strategy. The MNLA was systematically imploded by cash bribes and promises of amnesty and relocation that induced fighters to turn on their commanders and abandon the struggle. By July 1960, the situation was calm enough for the Malayan government to declare the Emergency terminated, at a cost of 2,478 civilians, 1,865 security personnel, and 6,710 CTs killed.

British success in Malaya is still being compared to the American counterinsurgency campaign in Vietnam. The comparison is stretched. The MCP was far weaker in every respect than its counterpart in Vietnam. It did not enjoy a common border with China, and never had much chance to persuade the Malay Muslim community that a Chinese-dominated socialist system was the best future for Malaya. The British did not use massive firepower because they did not have to. But they did use severe pressure to grind down the insurgency. They also diagnosed the conflict effectively and found the will to make the political changes necessary

to win it. Most important, the British never lost sight of a concrete objective: to destroy the MCP. Their decision to grant Malaya independence in order to accomplish this made it impossible for the MCP to prevail.

SEE ALSO: Chinese Civil War (Modern); National Liberation, Wars of; Psychological Warfare; World War II: War in Asia.

Reference

Hack, K. (2001) *Defence and Decolonization in Southeast Asia: Britain, Malaya and Singapore 1941–68*. London: Curzon.

Further Reading

Barber, N. (1989) *The War of the Running Dogs: Malaya 1948–1960*. London: Arrow Books.

Chin, C. C. and Hack, K. (Eds.) (2004) *Dialogues with Chin Peng: New Light on the Malayan Communist Party*. Singapore: Singapore University Press.

Chin Peng (2003) *My Side of History*. Singapore: Media Masters.

Clutterbuck, R. (2003) *The Long Long War: The Emergency in Malaya 1948–1960*. Singapore: Cultured Lotus.

Comber, L. (2008) *Malaya's Secret Police 1945–60*. Singapore: ISEAS.

Ramakrishnan, K. (2002) *Emergency Propaganda: The Winning of Malayan Hearts and Minds 1948–1958*. London: Curzon.

Short, A. (2000) *In Pursuit of Mountain Rats: The Communist Insurrection in Malaya*. Singapore: Cultured Lotus.

Stewart, B. (2004) *Smashing Terrorism in the Malayan Emergency*. Subang Jaya: Pelanduk Publications.

Stubbs, R. (1989) *Hearts and Minds in Guerrilla Warfare: The Malayan Emergency 1948–1960*. Oxford: Oxford University Press.

Mau Mau Emergency (1952–1960)

TIMOTHY J. STAPLETON

During the 1930s and 1940s, white settlers in the central highlands of British colonial Kenya expelled most of the indigenous Kikuyu from their land. The Kikuyu became squatters working for low pay on white-owned commercial farms, lived in small, infertile, and overcrowded reserves, or moved to growing slums in Nairobi. A small number of Kikuyu gained land for farming and cultivated ties with the colonial administration. Protest began in the early 1940s with a series of labor strikes, livestock maiming, and burning of farm buildings and crops. By the late 1940s, loyalty and unity among rebels was enforced by secret oath ceremonies. Led by Jomo Kenyatta, the moderate Kenya African Union failed to win any political reforms from the colonial regime in the early 1950s. Violence escalated in late 1952 with attacks on Kikuyu loyalists and the killing of a Kikuyu chief. Soon after arriving in Kenya, the new governor, Sir Evelyn Baring, declared a state of emergency on October 20, 1952. Beginning on the same day, colonial security forces launched Operation Jock Scott in which 100 African political leaders, including Kenyatta, and 8,000 others were arrested to remove the leadership of what was now called Mau Mau. In reality, African political leaders had little to do with this grassroots rebellion by mostly illiterate people. Violence against Europeans and loyalist Kikuyu increased with the first killing of settlers in January 1953. Calling themselves the Land and Freedom Army, insurgents organized a "passive wing" of noncombatants who supplied food, sanctuary, and information to the "active wing," which amounted to around 12,000 at the beginning of the conflict. In late March 1953, the insurgents launched their two largest attacks; 80 rebels raided a police station at Naivasha killing two policemen and another group massacred 84 African civilians at Lari. The Land and Freedom Army had few firearms, fought mostly with spears and machetes, and its leaders lacked military experience.

Colonial security forces in Kenya initially consisted of two infantry battalions of the King's African Rifles (KAR), African soldiers under white officers, and a small police force. When the emergency was declared, three other KAR battalions were brought in from other East African territories. Between October 1952 and September 1953, five British infantry battalions and 700 police volunteers arrived in Kenya. The Royal Air Force used heavy bombers and dive bombers against Mau Mau forest hideouts, and the Police Reserve Air Wing flew light civilian aircraft on reconnaissance missions. The death penalty was imposed for administering oaths and possessing firearms and ammunition. British counterinsurgency in Kenya was modeled to some extent on the campaign already underway in Malaya. Around one million Kikuyu were concentrated and confined in "protected villages" defended by a loyalist armed Kikuyu Home Guard formed in March 1953 that would eventually number 25,000. Insurgents were pushed into "free-fire zones" where there was little food and hunted by "pseudo gangs" of former rebels working for the security forces. Eventually, British army and police patrols entered the more remote forests of the Aberdare mountains in search of the insurgents and set ambushes on their supply routes. An insurgent network also operated in the city and, in April 1954, security forces, in Operation Anvil, surrounded Nairobi and over 16,000 people were arrested and detained. Around 78,000 detainees were sent to rehabilitation camps where they were subject to hard labor, discipline, and indoctrination. The British government was greatly embarrassed when news came out that, in March 1959, at Hola camp, 11 prisoners had been beaten to death for refusing to work. By May 1955, only 3,000 insurgents remained active and, by early 1956, the number had shrunk to around 900. The capture of key Mau Mau leader Dedan Kimathi in October 1956 – later tried and hanged – signaled the end of the counterinsurgency campaign, though the emergency remained until 1960.

Official British reports claim that 11,500 insurgents and 590 security force members (including 63 Europeans) were killed, and that, among civilians, 1,800 loyalist Africans, 32 Europeans, and 26 Asians lost their lives. These figures have been criticized for ignoring the thousands of civilians who were shot trying to escape or murdered by the Home Guard. In recent years there has been an intense academic debate over the total number of Africans who died in the conflict. David Anderson (2005) maintains that the number is closer to 20,000, Caroline Elkins (2005) claimed that at least 70,000 and perhaps as many as 300,000 died, and John Blacker (2007) puts the figure at around 50,000, half of whom were children. Most of these deaths occurred because of hunger and disease in "protected villages" and camps.

As a result of Mau Mau, the British granted reforms that allowed the formation of African political parties, encouraged the growth of conservative African elites from among loyalists, accepted the principle of African majority rule, and rejected the political aspirations of white settlers. The cost and embarrassment of suppressing Mau Mau was an important factor in speeding up British decolonization not only in Kenya but the rest of Africa as well. From independence in 1963, Kenya became a pro-western state with entrenched private property rights that protected landowners. While the ruling elite celebrated the struggle for freedom, Land and Freedom Army veterans have had little influence in postcolonial Kenya.

SEE ALSO: Malayan Emergency (1948–1960).

References

Anderson, D. (2005) *Histories of the Hanged: The Dirty War in Kenya and the End of Empire*. New York: Norton.

Blacker, J. (2007) "The Demography of Mau Mau: Fertility and Mortality in Kenya in the 1950s: A Demographer's Viewpoint," *African Affairs*, 106 (423): 205–227.

Elkins, C. (2005) *Imperial Reckoning: The Untold Story of Britain's Gulag in Kenya*. New York: Henry Holt.

Further Reading

Clayton, A. (1976) *Counter-Insurgency in Kenya*. Nairobi: Transafrica.

Maloba, W. (1993) *Mau Mau and Kenya: An Analysis of a Peasant Revolt*. Oxford: James Currey.

N

National Liberation, Wars of

TIMOTHY J. STAPLETON

The term "war of national liberation" is problematic and biased. It is often adopted by armed groups seeking to mobilize supporters on the basis of an imagined sense of national identity, usually defined in terms of common language, ethnicity, origin, or culture. These groups struggle to expel foreign occupation and achieve self-determination or overthrow objectionable internal regimes. It could be argued that the rebellions of ancient Jews against the Roman Empire in the first and second centuries were some of the first wars of national liberation. However, the term is more generally understood to apply to conflicts fought in Europe and the Americas during the Enlightenment period of the late 1700s and early 1800s, and to wars of independence fought in Asia and Africa during the Cold War of the second half of the twentieth century. Wars of national liberation, particularly since 1945, could be described as asymmetrical conflicts in that they typically began as small insurgencies using hit-and-run tactics against large conventional occupation forces. These conflicts are almost always civil wars in that

nationalist fighters characterize local people working for the state as traitors to the nation and target them for violence. Wars of national liberation, especially during the Cold War, were often proxy wars, as rival superpowers not wanting to confront each other directly backed opposite sides in regional conflicts. They also usually required insurgents to maintain a sanctuary and staging area in a neighboring territory. Perspective is important, as members of national liberation movements often celebrate themselves as freedom fighters, while their enemies deride them as terrorists or separatists.

Modern nationalism began in eighteenth-century Europe with the rise of ideas about popular sovereignty that inspired revolution against monarchies on both sides of the Atlantic. During the American Revolution, settlers in 13 North American colonies rejected the authority of the British parliament in which they had no representation and formed separate independent states. Coming together to defend themselves from the British in the American Revolutionary War (1775–1783), they created the United States as a nation based on the sovereignty of the people and cast off their allegiance to the British monarchy. The French Revolution of 1789, which was caused by famine and disease as much as Enlightenment political philosophies, saw the

Twentieth-Century War and Conflict: A Concise Encyclopedia, First Edition. Edited by Gordon Martel.
© 2015 John Wiley & Sons, Ltd. Published 2015 by John Wiley & Sons, Ltd.

overthrow of an absolute monarchy and the beginning of a government based on citizenship. Inspired by events in France and poor living conditions at home, the black slave majority in the French colony of Saint Domingue rose up in 1791 and by 1804 had abolished slavery and established the Republic of Haiti. With Napoleon's invasion of Spain in 1808 and the cutting off of Spain from its American colonies by the Royal Navy, independence movements emerged in the Spanish colonies during the early nineteenth century and fought a series of wars to achieve autonomy for what became the states of Latin America. In the 1820s, Greeks, who had been ruled by the Ottoman Empire for centuries, took up arms and gained independence in 1832. While there is a long history of Irish resistance to British rule, the failed Easter Rising of 1916 and the guerrilla war fought by the Irish Republican Army against British and loyalist forces from 1919 to 1921 resulted in independence for most of Ireland.

The European colonization of Asia and Africa during the nineteenth century led to the development of local westernized elites who spread concepts of nationalism among their own subject peoples. Nationalist movements in Asia and Africa gained strength during World War II, which the Allied powers who were also the colonial powers saw as a struggle for democracy and national self-determination. In the 1950s and 1960s, nationalism in the colonies was encouraged by the officially anti-colonial stance of superpowers, the United States and Soviet Union, and the weakening of colonial rulers. Many nationalist leaders were inspired by communist ideals as a way to address the injustice and inequity of colonial rule. In 1961, Soviet leader Nikita Khrushchev declared support for wars of national liberation.

In parts of Asia, Japanese occupation during World War II had weakened European colonial states and encouraged nationalists who sometimes gained administrative experience as part of Japanese puppet regimes or military experience as part of resistance forces. After Chinese nationalists and communists fought to liberate their country from Japanese occupation during World War II, the 1949 victory of Mao's communists in the civil war meant that China became an active sponsor of liberation movements in Asia and sometimes Africa. In 1945, the Dutch tried to regain control of Indonesia, where nationalists had declared independence immediately after Japanese surrender. This led to a nationalist insurgency in which the Dutch lost control of the countryside and withdrew in 1949. When the French reasserted control over Indochina in 1946, a Vietnamese Nationalist Army (Vietminh) launched a low-level insurgency that gained strength and developed into a full-scale conventional war in the early 1950s. With support from the Soviet Union and China, the Vietminh defeated the French at the Battle of Dien Bien Phu in 1954. In turn, the French withdrew and Cold War rivalries led to the division of North and South Vietnam. Beginning in 1959, the American-backed regime in the South was challenged by the communist Vietcong or National Liberation Front, which launched a guerrilla war backed by North Vietnam and the Soviet Union. Despite the conventional and controversial military intervention of the United States from 1965 to 1973, North Vietnamese forces gained the upper hand and reunited the country in 1975.

In post-war Malaya, economic problems and lack of voting rights for ethnic Chinese led to the establishment of the communist Malayan National Liberation Army, which fought a guerrilla war against British colonial rule from 1948 to 1960. British counterinsurgency, which included large-scale resettlement, worked because the insurgents were mostly ethnic Chinese and not indigenous people, they had limited external sponsorship, the Chinese gained the vote, and the war only seemed to delay decolonization. After independence, another communist insurgency began in Malaysia in the late 1960s and lasted until 1989.

In most of Africa during the 1950s and 1960s, decolonization was a negotiated process between outgoing European colonial powers and local nationalist leaders who would inherit the state. However, stubborn resistance to change by white settlers in some areas led to nationalist movements embarking on armed liberation struggles. In 1945, when there were around two million French settlers in Algeria, the colonial police opened fire on peaceful nationalist protesters in the town of Sétif, killing more than 100 Europeans and 8,000 Algerian Muslims. In 1954, the *Front de Libération Nationale* was formed and fought a protracted insurgency against the French.

Although the French brought in half a million troops and adopted increasingly brutal methods, the insurgency gained momentum and France eventually agreed to abandon settler interests and grant independence in 1962. Some authors claim that the rebellion of the Land Freedom Army (Mau Mau) in British colonial Kenya during the 1950s represented a national liberation movement, but the lack of literate leadership and outside support meant that there was little evidence of typical nationalist rhetoric and goals. The Algerian and Kenyan conflicts would speed up decolonization in much of the rest of Africa, as European powers did not want the expense or embarrassment of putting down similar rebellions.

Southern Africa, dominated by settler colonial regimes, would be the scene of insurgent warfare from the early 1960s to early 1990s. The Sharpeville Massacre of March 1960 convinced African nationalist leaders that non-violent protest against South Africa's apartheid regime was futile. Consequently, the African National Congress formed Umkhonto we Sizwe (Spear of the Nation, or MK), which organized a bombing campaign that sought to avoid loss of life, while the Pan-Africanist Congress formed Poqo (Alone) which focused on killing whites. While both early armed campaigns were suppressed by security forces, these organizations went into exile and continued their armed struggle. By the 1980s, MK was embarking on more lethal operations in coordination with local mass protest. Poqo developed into the Azanian People's Liberation Army, but its attempts to launch a Maoist peasant insurgency failed because of violent internal conflict in exile. Mounting international sanctions, failed military intervention in Angola, and mass anti-apartheid protest at home ultimately led to a negotiated transition in the early 1990s.

The 1965 Unilateral Declaration of Independence by the white minority regime in the British colony of Southern Rhodesia prompted African nationalists to form armed wings that would wage liberation war from neighboring countries. During the 1970s, the Zimbabwe People's Revolutionary Army, based in Zambia, received Soviet assistance and adopted a Leninist revolutionary strategy of cultivating a small professional force that would seize power at a critical moment. At the same time, the Zimbabwe African National Liberation Army was supported by China and pursued Maoist-style guerrilla warfare and politicization of rural communities along the border with Mozambique. By the late 1970s, insurgents controlled most rural areas and a British-sponsored negotiation led to majority rule and the independence of Zimbabwe in 1980.

Frustrated by years of failed passive resistance against a South African occupation that dated back to World War I, the South West African People's Organization formed an armed wing called the People's Liberation Army of Namibia (PLAN) in 1965. PLAN infiltrated guerrillas into South West Africa from Zambia and Angola to attack local agents of the state and settlers, and plant landmines. The South African Defence Force created a long, depopulated strip along South West Africa's northern border, employed more indigenous troops, and pursued PLAN fighters into Angola in the late 1970s and 1980s. However, defeat by Cuban–Angolan conventional forces in the late 1980s resulted in Namibian independence in 1989 and political changes in South Africa.

Unlike other European powers, the authoritarian Portuguese government refused to decolonize, claiming that its African territories – including Guinea-Bissau, Angola, and Mozambique – were integral parts of the mother country. In the early 1960s, African nationalist insurgencies, supported by the Soviet Union and Cuba, began in all three colonies. Portuguese counterinsurgency was most successful in Angola because of South African support, the division of three rival liberation movements, and the long distance to staging areas in neighboring countries. By 1969, the Front for the Liberation of Mozambique, with Tanzania as a sanctuary, had gained control of one third of the country and established an embryonic administration in "liberated zones." Based in the neighboring Republic of Guinea, the African Party for the Independence of Guinea and Cape Verde controlled a significant portion of the small West African territory of Guinea-Bissau by 1967 and although the Portuguese began serious offensives in 1970, it was too late. With the 1974 coup in Lisbon, partly caused by the stress of fighting three wars in Africa, the Portuguese withdrew quickly from their colonies, which became independent states governed by former liberation movements. This represented a major turning point in the history of southern Africa as apartheid South Africa and settler Rhodesia lost a valuable ally and liberation movements gained support from the new governments in Angola and Mozambique, which also became friendly to the Soviet Union.

In Cold War-era Latin America, socialist revolutionary movements waged liberation wars against repressive and exploitive American-supported dictatorships. In 1959, Cuban revolutionaries led by Fidel Castro overthrew the American-sponsored regime of Fulgencio Batista. In 1961, at the Bay of Pigs, Castro's force repelled a seaborne invasion by Cuban exiles trained and supplied by the American Central Intelligence Agency. The Castro regime, with Soviet assistance, became a sponsor of liberation movements in Africa, Asia, and other parts of Latin America. After many years of guerrilla warfare, the Sandinista National Liberation Front of Nicaragua, aided by Cuba, ended several generations of dictatorial rule by the Samoza family in 1979. They then faced counter-revolutionary insurgency from the American-backed Contras based in neighboring Honduras. Similar communist-inspired insurgencies flared up in other parts of Latin America, such as El Salvador and Colombia, prompting brutal counterinsurgency campaigns. Latin American insurrections were not always successful. For example, Che Guevara, who had played an important role in the Cuban Revolution, launched the small National Liberation Army of Bolivia but lack of local support meant that he was hunted down and killed by American-trained security forces in 1967.

Postcolonial Africa continued to experience wars of national liberation, often waged by regional groups for self-determination or against oppressive dictatorships. From the early 1980s to 2005, the Sudanese People's Liberation Army (SPLA) fought for independence of the black and mainly Christian southern Sudanese from the dominance of Arab Muslim northerners. In a pattern that would become typical of African insurgencies, Uganda backed the SPLA while the Sudanese government supported the Lord's Resistance Army in northern Uganda. Initially fighting against Spanish rule in Western Sahara, the Polisario Front began a guerrilla war against Moroccan occupation in 1975 and was backed by

Algeria. Ethiopia faced many armed separatist movements. The Eritrean People's Liberation Front fought a 30-year guerrilla war against Ethiopian occupation that contributed to the fall of the regime of Mengistu Haile Mariam in 1991 and the independence of Eritrea in 1993. From northern Ethiopia, the Tigrayan People's Liberation Front also fought against the Mengistu administration from the mid-1970s and took over the Ethiopian state in 1991. The Western Somali Liberation Front (WSLF), backed by an irredentist regime in Somalia, fought an insurgency against the Ethiopian state in the 1970s and early 1980s to unite the Ogaden area with Somalia. After the failed Somali invasion of Ethiopia in 1977–1978, the WSLF was replaced by the Ogaden National Liberation Front, which continued guerrilla operations into the 2000s.

Some opportunistic leaders, mainly interested in acquiring power and wealth, have cynically exploited desires for national liberation to mobilize followers. This is well illustrated by the recent history of conflict in the Democratic Republic of Congo. In 1996 and 1997 the Alliance of Democratic Forces for the Liberation of Congo, led by Laurent Kabila, strongly backed by troops from Rwanda and Uganda, crossed Congo from east to west and overthrew the notoriously corrupt dictatorship of Mobutu Sese Seko. Once in power, Kabila quickly became as authoritarian as his predecessor, sparking another rebellion in the east by the Rally for Congolese Democracy and the Movement for the Liberation of Congo, supported by invasion forces from Rwanda and Uganda now concerned about Kabila's alliance with insurgents from their own countries. Kabila's regime was saved by the military intervention of Zimbabwe, Namibia, and Angola, which claimed to be fighting for Congo's liberation against western-backed neocolonial forces. From 1998 to 2002, in what has been called Africa's World War, the Congolese army, various rebel groups, and at least five different foreign armies looted Congo's natural resources, particularly valuable minerals. Central to the conflict was first Mobutu's and then Kabila's relationship with Hutu extremist perpetrators of the 1994 Tutsi genocide in Rwanda who were exiled in eastern Congo and plotting a return to their home country. These Hutu believed that they represented the indigenous nation of Rwanda, which had been unjustly usurped by

Tutsi who were imagined as foreigners from the Horn of Africa.

Wars of national liberation during the late twentieth century were not confined to Asia and Africa. Following the violent state repression of a civil rights movement in Northern Ireland in the late 1960s, the Provisional Irish Republican Army began a vigorous defense of Catholic communities and an urban guerrilla war against British and loyalist forces that was framed within the context of liberation. After British withdrawal from Palestine in 1948, Jewish settlers declared the State of Israel and defeated invasion by Egypt, Jordan, Syria, Iraq, and Lebanon in what they would call the War of Liberation. Conversely, expelled Palestinian Arabs formed the Palestinian Liberation Organization in 1964 and embarked on guerrilla war to regain land taken by Israel and achieve self-determination. Afghan resistance to Soviet invasion in the 1980s and the presence of North Atlantic Treaty Organization forces in the 2000s, Iraqi resistance to US and British occupation from 2003, and Chechen rebellion against Russian control from the 1990s onward, could all be considered wars of national liberation.

With many former colonies entering the United Nations in the 1950s and 1960s, the General Assembly became more sympathetic to armed national liberation movements. In 1973, it passed a resolution that declared that wars of national liberation against colonial, foreign, or racist regimes would be legally considered as international conflict and combatants would be eligible for rights under the 1949 Geneva Convention. The American-led "War on Terror" in the 2000s reopened debates about the legal status of captured insurgents, many of whom would consider themselves as liberationist fighters.

SEE ALSO: Chechnya Wars (1990s–Present); Chinese Civil War (Modern); Congo Wars (1960s–2000s); Irish Revolution, Wars of the; Mau Mau Emergency (1952–1960); Soviet War in Afghanistan (1979–1992); Terrorism, War Against; Vietnam War (1959–1975).

Further Reading

Bayly, C., and Harper, T. (2007) *Forgotten Wars: Freedom and Revolution in Southeast Asia*. Cambridge, MA: Harvard University Press.

Beckett, I. (2001) *Modern Insurgencies and Counter-Insurgencies*. London: Routledge.

Moran, D. (2006) *Wars of National Liberation*. New York: HarperCollins.

O'Neill, B. (2005) *From Revolution to Apocalypse: Insurgency and Terrorism*. Dulles: Potomac Books.

Schultz, R. H. (1988) *The Soviet Union and Revolutionary Warfare: Principles, Practices and Regional Comparisons*. Stanford: Hoover Institution.

Turner, J. W. (1998) *Continent Ablaze: The Insurgency Wars in Africa 1960 to the Present*. Johannesburg: Jonathan Ball.

Wilson, H. A. (1988) *International Law and the Use of Force by National Liberation Movements*. Oxford: Clarendon Press.

Nigerian Civil War (1967–1970)

TIMOTHY J. STAPLETON

During the colonial period, the British ruled the large and populous territory of Nigeria as three separate regions. Although Nigeria has a vast number of ethnicities, each region was associated with a major ethnic group: the Igbo in the east, the Yoruba in the west, and the Hausa-Fulani in the north. The two coastal southern regions, east and west, became relatively more prosperous and predominantly Christian, with a significant western-educated elite. Comparatively poor and marginalized, the predominantly Muslim north was controlled by conservative local elites.

In Nigeria the decolonization process of the 1950s was characterized by negotiation between the outgoing British and emerging political leaders from the three regions over what form the postcolonial state would take. Nigeria became independent in 1960 as a federation with three regions, and since northerners constituted a majority, they dominated the federal government. The development of an oil industry in the Niger Delta during the 1960s encouraged northern leaders to drop ideas of separating from Nigeria and created resentment among easterners that the wealth of their region was being stolen. In January 1966, a group of mostly Igbo army officers led by Major Kaduna Nzeugwu staged a coup that ousted civilian politicians from the north, who were accused of electoral fraud, and eventually brought General Johnson Aguiyi-Ironsi, another Igbo, to power. Yoruba and Hausa leaders were killed, including Prime Minister Abubakar Tafawa Balewa, who was from the North, and the Sardauna of Sokoto, who was a northern traditional leader, and it appeared that Igbo officers were being promoted within the army. This led to a counter-coup by northern officers led by Lieutenant Colonel Murtala Mohammed that installed Lieutenant Colonel Yakuba Gowon, a northern Christian, as military ruler. Many southern army officers, including Ironsi, were killed and in September the massacre of over 10,000 Igbo living in the north resulted in 1.5 million refugees flooding into the eastern region. Given the federal government's failure to stop the killings, the administration of the east, under military governor Lieutenant Colonel Emeka Ojukwu, refused to recognize Gowon as head of state. At the Aburi Conference in Ghana in January 1967, both sides agreed to a non-violent solution to the crisis. Regions would gain "confederal" status without a change to boundaries, all members of a supreme military council would have veto power, all regions would have to agree on major decisions, salaries would be paid to displaced people, and the federal head of state would be recognized as commander of the armed forces. However, by mid-March both Gowon and Ojukwu had reneged on aspects of the agreement.

On May 30, 1967, Ojukwu, authorized by the Eastern Region Consultative Assembly and Advisory Committee of Chiefs and Elders, declared the secession of the eastern region as the independent Republic of Biafra (named for the geographic Bight of Biafra) with its capital at Enugu. Around the same time, Gowon declared emergency powers including press censorship and a ban on political activity, and broke up large regions by reorganizing the country into 12 smaller states. Once Biafra declared independence, the federal government began mass military mobilization and acquisition of weapons. On July 6, 1967, the federal government launched a military campaign to suppress Biafra's secession. Conducting what was initially called a police action, federal units in the north formed the First Infantry Division and advanced south into Biafra in two columns. The left column (on the east side) captured Garkem-Ogoja on July 12 and the right column (on the west side) took Nsukka on July 14. Biafran forces had put up stiff resistance at Nsukka but were hampered by lack of ammunition. During July and August, Biafra responded by invading the mid-western region west of the Niger River with the aim of distracting Nigerian forces from the north by threatening the federal capital of Lagos. Three Biafran battalions advanced through Benin City and eventually

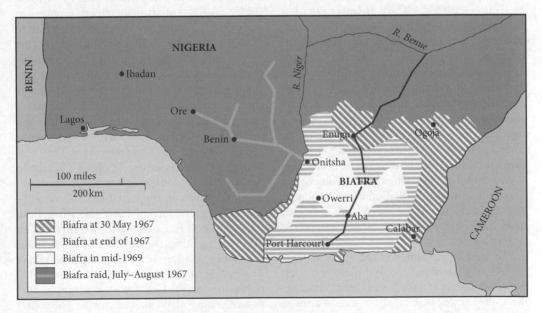

Map 14   Nigerian Civil War, 1967–1970.

halted at Ore, 100 miles east of Lagos, on August 21, with just one federal battalion of recruits in their way.

The Biafrans had believed that the mixed Yoruba and Igbo population of the mid-west would support them, but this backfired as the invasion and subsequent looting seemed to discredit Biafra's claim to be acting in self-defense. Brigadier Victor Banjo, commander of the invasion force, whose Yoruba ethnicity, it was hoped, would appeal to mid-westerners, was discovered to be plotting against Ojukwu and was executed. Under instructions from Gowon, General Murtala Mohammed assembled and took command of the new Second Infantry Division, advanced eastward through the mid-west, and on September 22 drove Biafran forces out of Benin City and ultimately to the east bank of the Niger River. Between October and December, the Second Infantry Division made three unsuccessful attempts to cross the river and capture the Biafran city of Onitsha, suffering heavy losses in personnel and equipment. Murtala launched these disastrous amphibious attacks against the advice of other senior officers and army headquarters. Each assault was announced by bugle calls, which he thought would inflict fear on the enemy, and he reputedly used a soothsayer to determine the timing of the operations. Around the same time, federal troops from the Lagos garrison – called the Third Infantry Division, but later renamed Third Marine Commando Division – were landed on the coast of the Niger Delta, capturing the cities of Bonny and Okrika on July 26 and Calabar on October 13. Bonny was an important oil industry terminal and its capture blocked supply ships from access to Biafran-occupied Port Harcourt. Since Biafra had no significant navy, the Nigerian navy controlled the coastal waters, which left Port Harcourt airport as Biafra's only link to the outside world. On October 4, the First Infantry Division, pushing down from the north, captured the Biafran capital of Enugu. Biafran forces were now surrounded and confined to the Igbo heartland, which was packed with refugees.

The need for oil trumped Cold War rivalries as the federal government received military support from both Britain and the Soviet Union. Although the United States prohibited the sale of arms to either side, pro-Biafran journalists, humanitarian organizations, and missionaries used television and print media to gain support from the American public. No country provided official military support to Biafra. French President Charles de Gaulle openly expressed sympathy for Biafra and France sought to take over British oil interests. In turn, France covertly sent military supplies to Biafra through its former colonies of Côte d'Ivoire and Gabon. The humanitarian services of French doctors in Biafra, including Bernard Kouchner, and their criticism of Nigerian army violence against Biafran civilians, led to the creation of *Médecins sans Frontières* (Doctors without Borders). Fighting African nationalist insurgents and desperate for friends on the continent, Portugal and Rhodesia also provided clandestine support to Biafra. Only four African countries – Côte d'Ivoire, Gabon, Zambia, and Tanzania – formally recognized Biafra. Apartheid South Africa also supported Biafra and late in the war sent a small special forces team to train Biafran partisans for operations behind federal lines.

From the beginning of 1968, the war became a stalemate, with the gradually shrinking and overcrowded Biafra under blockade by federal forces. The federal army was expanded to 70,000 men equipped with British small arms and armored vehicles. In addition, the federal air force received Ilyushin-28 bombers and MiG-17 fighters from the Soviet Union. The Biafrans built air strips on straight roads and tried to import supplies. In early 1968, Murtala finally abandoned his plan to cross the Niger River and took Onitsha by having his Second Division move around via the Enugu–Onitsha road. However, with Biafran forces harassing its supply lines and its demoralized soldiers abusing civilians and looting, the division never recovered as a fighting force and Murtala was replaced. A Nigerian offensive from April to June 1968 further reduced Biafran territory. The Third Marine Division under Colonel Benjamin Adekunle had considerable success. At the end of April, the division, supported by artillery, initiated a large crossing of the Cross River from Calabar to Port Harcourt, which was captured on May 19. Fighting through the area's swamps, Adekunle's division advanced northeast, taking Aba in August and Owerri in September. To the north, the federal First Division advanced cautiously, seizing Abakaliki and Afikpo. The arrival of French weapons enabled the Biafrans to regroup at the end of 1968 and they stubbornly held the Uli airfield, surrounded federal units at Owerri, and threatened Aba.

The federal military then concentrated on maintaining the blockade to starve Biafra into submission. Biafran leaders and western humanitarian organizations accused the Gowon regime of genocide against the Igbo by preventing delivery of food. Nigerian authorities responded that airlifts of food aid were also being used to deliver weapons and ammunition. Desperate Biafran forces began to employ foreign mercenaries like German Rolf Steiner and Swedish pilot Carl Gustav von Rosen. Although the Nigerian government criticized Biafra's use of mercenaries, many of its Soviet-supplied airplanes were flown by Egyptian and other foreign pilots. In April and May 1969, the First Division launched an offensive that captured the new Biafran capital of Umuahia. In June, Biafra launched a desperate offensive meant to knock federal forces off balance. Owerri was recaptured and civilian aircraft fitted with rockets for ground attack damaged oil and ammunition storage facilities and raided federal air fields, destroying Soviet-supplied warplanes. However, Biafra did not have the resources to exploit success and Nigerian forces quickly recovered. In December 1969, federal commanders initiated a final offensive that would end the war. In January 1970, the Third Marine Commando Division, now under Colonel Olusegun Obasanjo (future military ruler and civilian president of Nigeria), who has been described as the most capable officer to emerge from the conflict, pushed up from the coast with armored vehicles penetrating Biafran lines. On January 9, federal troops once again took Owerri and, on January 13, captured the last Biafran-held town, Amichi. Ojukwu flew to exile in Côte d'Ivoire leaving Phillip Effiong, Biafra's army commander, to effect the formal capitulation.

Biafra simply did not have enough resources or international support to challenge the large and well-supplied Nigerian forces. The federal military had expanded from around 8,000 personnel just before the war to 120,000 in 1968 and 250,000 in 1970. Biafra began the war with 3,000 troops and ended with 30,000. Biafra was easily besieged as it had extremely limited air combat, air defense, and naval capabilities.

Although estimates of civilian fatalities vary from half a million to three million, it is clear that the vast majority were from the eastern region and perished from starvation or disease. Estimates of total combat casualties vary from 90,000 to 120,000. By famously declaring that there was "no victor and no vanquished," Gowon embarked on a policy of national reconciliation, began a reconstruction program in the east, and banned ethnically based political parties. However, resentments lingered as during the war many Igbo had lost their property in other parts of the country, many did not get back previous government jobs, minimal compensation was offered for useless Biafran currency, and the easterners still maintained that they were not receiving their rightful share of oil revenues squandered by subsequent military regimes.

Further Reading

Akpan, N. U. (1976) *The Struggle for Secession 1966–70: A Personal Account of the Nigerian Civil War.* London: Frank Cass.

De St. Jorre, J. (1972) *The Nigerian Civil War.* London: Hodder and Stoughton.

Forsyth, F. (1969) *The Biafra Story.* London: Penguin.

Obasanjo, O. (1980) *My Command: An Account of the Nigerian Civil War 1967–70.* Ibadan: Heinemann.

Siollun, M. (2009) *Oil, Politics and Violence: Nigeria's Military Coup Culture, 1966–76.* New York: Algora Publishing.

P

Peacekeeping

NORRIE MACQUEEN

From the middle of the twentieth century and particularly since the end of the Cold War, peacekeeping has become increasingly important as a means of conflict management and resolution. It remains a very difficult activity to define precisely, however. Although peacekeeping has long been a key activity of the United Nations (UN) (more than 60 operations have been undertaken since the late 1940s), the term does not appear in the organization's charter. Its utilization as a response to conflict accelerated after it became clear that the UN's much more ambitious plan for a comprehensive system of collective security by enforcement was unachievable in the polarized world of the Cold War. Yet peacekeeping was not a UN innovation. The general technique had been employed by the League of Nations and other international actors in the interwar years, and multinational security operations had already been pursued in the nineteenth century. Peacekeeping has been undertaken by a number of regional organizations and other coalitions, although the role of the United Nations has remained dominant.

Problem of Definition

The difficulty in arriving at a clear definition of the term "peacekeeping" arises mainly because of the wide variety of activities undertaken under its name. Peacekeeping can embrace small military observation missions mandated to monitor ceasefires, large-scale exercises in neutral interposition between armies, and even the exercise of quasi-state powers in territories in transition. It may be interstate or intrastate in nature. It may be conducted by the UN, another international organization, or by so-called "coalitions of the willing" which may or may not be authorized by the UN. The problem of definition is further compounded, however, by the misuse of the term for political and propaganda purposes by those who wish to present other less benign behavior in a more respectable light. The ambiguity of the term has been exploited to disguise actions that have had only tenuous connections with impartial conflict resolution. At various times, Britain in Northern Ireland, India in Sri Lanka, and Russia in Transcaucasia have claimed to be involved in peacekeeping, though their adversaries would have rejected such a description.

Twentieth-Century War and Conflict: A Concise Encyclopedia, First Edition. Edited by Gordon Martel.
© 2015 John Wiley & Sons, Ltd. Published 2015 by John Wiley & Sons, Ltd.

The United Nations Department of Peacekeeping Operations offers the following definition:

> Peacekeeping is a way to help countries torn by conflict create conditions for sustainable peace. UN peacekeepers – soldiers and military officers, civilian police officers and civilian personnel from many countries – monitor and observe peace processes that emerge in post-conflict situations and assist ex-combatants to implement the peace agreements they have signed. Such assistance comes in many forms, including confidence-building measures, power-sharing arrangements, electoral support, strengthening the rule of law, and economic and social development.

This is a considerable advance on the original UN conception of peacekeeping that emerged from the experience of operations in the 1940s and 1950s. The classic peacekeeping mission of this early period was defined by three essential characteristics:

1. It could only be undertaken with the full consent of the parties to the conflict it was designed to help resolve.
2. The peacekeeping presence had to be entirely neutral in respect of the merits of the conflicting positions.
3. Peacekeepers could use force only in self-defense and in the last resort.

That rather austere and minimalist view of the peacekeeping project did not stand up to subsequent realities. It was based on a view of peacekeeping as a response to interstate disputes in which peace (defined merely as a cessation of violence) had already been agreed by the parties. Those parties would then seek an external agency to supervise the maintenance of the ceasefire and facilitate a longer-term process of peacemaking. Long before the complex and dangerous deployments of the 1990s, from the former Yugoslavia to sub-Saharan Africa, this traditional construction had already proved inadequate. It did not embrace peacekeeping in intrastate conflicts where "consent" might be fragile and variable and where violence was still underway or liable to re-erupt. The classic definition was also inapplicable to

situations such as those in Bosnia and Rwanda where the peacekeepers' neutrality and refusal to use force were tantamount to complicity in crimes against humanity.

Nevertheless, the central notions of consent, impartiality, and minimum use of force, while rarely applicable in full, offer a useful means of conceptualizing peacekeeping in relation to other forms of armed intervention.

Origins of Peacekeeping

The huge growth in peacekeeping by the UN and other agencies that followed the end of the Cold War tends to distort the longer historical narrative. Examples can be found of multilateral military action that at least approached the modern conception of peacekeeping even in the nineteenth century. These might include joint European naval action against the Atlantic slave trade and multinational "police" units in China. Closer to the classic ideal, perhaps, would be the Swedish intervention between Denmark and Prussia in Schleswig Holstein in the 1860s.

In the 1920s and 1930s, the Associated Powers (the allied victors of World War I) as well as the UN's direct predecessor, the League of Nations, had deployed international forces in various parts of Europe. Much of this activity involved the supervision and management of plebiscites in disputed border regions as a new map of Europe began to emerge. New national and ethnic frontiers – between Germany and Poland, between Austria and Yugoslavia, and in the new Baltic states – were created under the supervision of multinational military missions. Perhaps the most substantial of these undertakings was in the disputed Saar territory on the Franco-German border. The League of Nations provided a transitional administration there between 1920 and 1935 and then created a multinational force (composed of British, Italian, Dutch, and Swedish contingents) to oversee the tense referendum campaign which eventually resulted in the return of the Saar to Germany.

The UN had established something recognizable as a peacekeeping operation shortly after its foundation when, in 1948, it sent international military observers to the borders of the new state of Israel. This Truce Supervision Organization was responsible for monitoring and reporting on the ceasefire agreed between Israel and the Arab states after the war precipitated by the declaration of Israeli statehood. This was followed quickly by the Military Observer Group in India and Pakistan, which was created to carry out a similar role in the disputed region of Kashmir.

These early military observer missions were followed in 1956 with the first large-scale peace-keeping "force." Following Egypt's nationalization of the Suez Canal, Britain, France, and Israel con-spired to seize control of the waterway by force. This act of apparent neoimperialist aggression was almost universally condemned internation-ally and it fell to the UN to deal with the ensuing crisis. A plan was constructed jointly by the UN Secretary General Dag Hammarskjöld and Canadian foreign minister Lester Pearson to deploy a multinational force to the region: the United Nations Emergency Force (UNEF). This was composed of contingents volunteered by UN members and was interposed as a buffer between the sides and mandated to supervise military dis-engagement. Essentially, the operation was a larger-scale version of the earlier military obser-vation missions. In Suez, the UN presence would take the form of a large "force" rather than a small observer group, but the fundamental principles of neutral supervision legitimized by the moral authority of the UN were the same. The political impartiality of the UN force underpinned a par-ticularly valuable part of the peacekeeping for-mula: each side in the dispute could gloss the operation in their own way and construct their own preferred narratives. For Egypt, UNEF vin-dicated its claims of neocolonial bullying, having been deployed to end the aggression of Britain, France, and Israel. Britain and France, in contrast, could also claim that the Emergency Force justi-fied their behavior. Having acted quickly to uphold proper standards of international legality, the Anglo-French force could now hand over responsibility to the UN. However contradictory these competing narratives might be, there was no likelihood that the peacekeepers would meet violence or obstruction from either side. As state members of the UN, all the actors had fully con-sented to the intervention, and in the propaganda war that followed the actual hostilities they were all anxious to be seen as responsible members of the international community.

The supposed lessons of UNEF were drawn together by Secretary General Hammarskjöld two years later in his "Summary Study of the Experience Derived from the Establishment of the United Nations Emergency Force" (General Assembly Document A/3943, October 9, 1958). The classic trio of peacekeeping characteristics – consent, neutrality, and force only in self-defense – was first articulated in this. Peacekeeping contrasted with the enforcement model of UN collective security in every key respect. Enforcement required the identification and punishment of an "aggressor"; peacekeeping need only identify a crisis. Enforcement action was designed to secure a military outcome, while peacekeeping was about neutral interposition. Peacekeeping forces were formed by voluntary contributors, while participation in enforcement action was in principle an obligation of UN membership. The peacekeepers themselves, in Hammarskjöld's conceptualization, would ideally come from small and middle-range powers rather than from big states whose presence might further destabilize the situation.

Despite this attention to the lessons of the peacekeeping experience, its legal basis remained vague if not non-existent. Clearly, peacekeeping was not the type of military action envisaged by Chapter VII of the United Nations Charter in which the organization's military enforcement powers were set out. But it was difficult to locate it anywhere else. Chapter VI, which deals with "The Pacific Settlement of Disputes," was a pos-sible legal home for peacekeeping, but this made no reference to the use of military forces by the UN. From this situation there emerged an infor-mal notion of peacekeeping as a "chapter six-and-a-half" activity. But while this representation helped to convey a sense of what peacekeeping was about, it was obviously meaningless in formal legal terms.

Peacekeeping in the Cold War

One of the fundamental purposes of peacekeep-ing between the 1940s and the 1970s was to ease the interlinked pressures on the international system generated by the Cold War and decoloni-zation. Peacekeeping was used to immunize local conflicts, many of which were a consequence of the end of imperial rule, from the larger infection of the Cold War. Or, looked at another way, peacekeeping was designed to protect the stability of the central balance in the Cold War from the dangerous irritants of peripheral conflicts. Two years after the creation of UNEF for Suez, UN military observers helped divert a looming conflict on the Lebanon–Syria border which threatened superpower involvement. Another intervention in the Yemen–Saudi Arabia frontier area during 1963 and 1964 served a very similar purpose. Meanwhile, in 1962–1963, a UN operation had seen the transfer of the contested territory of West New Guinea from Dutch to Indonesian control. This undertaking involved the creation of what amounted to a transitional UN state in the territory.

The success of these missions in fencing off regional conflicts from larger Cold War tensions was, however, overshadowed by the problems that afflicted the world's most ambitious peacekeeping project of the period. This took place in the former Belgian Congo between 1960 and 1964. Instead of preventing a local crisis from seeping into the Cold War, UN involvement in the Congo itself became a cause of serious East–West confrontation. The Congo operation also challenged the classic view of peacekeeping as an interstate activity founded on the basic principles of consent, neutrality, and force only in self-defense. The UN intervention took place amid a disintegrating state where the idea of consent had no real meaning. Neutrality became an equally empty concept as there was no obvious political center ground that the peacekeepers could occupy. Amid this chaos, the UN was accused by the Soviet Union and many Afro-Asian states of protecting neocolonial interests seeking the break-up of the new Congo. The operation also led to the death of Dag Hammarskjöld in a plane crash in 1961 as he traveled to crisis negotiations in the region.

The possibilities for peacekeeping improved in the 1970s during the interlude of superpower détente. For a time at least, East and West – now aware of the implications of nuclear mutually assured destruction – sought actively to cooperate to defuse crises that might draw them in. This approach was evident in the peacekeeping operations established in the Middle East following the Arab–Israeli war of 1973 when, on the initiative of the superpowers themselves, UN forces were deployed on Israel's borders with both Egypt and Syria. This détente peacekeeping was relatively short-lived, however. It had its final expression in the Interim Force in Lebanon created in 1978 amid vicious civil war, Israeli invasion, and Syrian threat. The unraveling of the larger fabric of détente at this time meant that the superpower pressure on local clients, which was essential to any hope of success for the operation, was soon withdrawn. The ensuing "second" Cold War meant that the Security Council unanimity necessary for the formation of any new operation could not be achieved. The result was a decade of dormancy in UN peacekeeping.

Peacekeeping after the Cold War

The end of the Cold War not only brought UN military intervention back to the international stage, it did so at a massively expanded level. This was not altogether a marker of a new, positive multilateralism. Certainly, peacekeeping could now take place in a much wider space, both in the political sense and in the geographical sense. Regions and conflicts that had been off-limits because of superpower sensitivities to spheres of influence were opened up. Central America, Afghanistan, and Southeast Asia were now subject to multilateral intervention. But a major reason for this was that areas that had once been stabilized by superpower control had been abandoned by their former patrons, leaving the UN to deal with the consequences. For example, the regime in Somalia, which had been bolstered by American backing because of the strategic importance of the Horn of Africa, was now left to the mercy of its many internal enemies. The result was the effective collapse of the state and a humanitarian disaster. Peacekeeping, therefore, did not merely encounter new possibilities with the end of the Cold War, it faced new demands as well.

In response to these dramatically changed conditions, UN Secretary General Boutros Boutros-Ghali in 1992 produced *An Agenda for Peace*. This was the first major discussion document on peacekeeping since Hammarskjöld's "Summary Study" in 1958. Boutros-Ghali urged a root-and-branch reform of the way peacekeeping was organized and funded. Formal contributors' agreements were proposed as a way of easing the problems of supply of peacekeepers in the face of spiraling demand. The creation of a large reserve fund was suggested to remove the financial uncertainty of peacekeeping. The threatening crisis of resources also led Boutros-Ghali to urge a greater peacekeeping role for regional organizations. In the operational realm his proposed reforms were modest. He did though propose a more robust approach in one specific circumstance. In the 1990s, UN forces were increasingly involved in supervising peace settlements reached between local antagonists. In such circumstances the UN should be permitted to enforce compliance with prior agreements. To this end new "peace enforcement units" should be formed.

In the event, few of Boutros-Ghali's proposals were adopted. The relatively optimistic, if pressured, environment in which *An Agenda for Peace* was written did not last. Setbacks in Bosnia, the debacle of Somalia, and the genocide in Rwanda all damaged the image of peacekeeping as an effective means of conflict management. Perhaps aware of their own responsibility for these failures, the leading members of the UN generally preferred to avert their collective gaze.

Peacekeeping Beyond the UN

Although there is a close association of peacekeeping with the UN, it not only existed long before the organization was established, it also exists as an activity either wholly apart from the UN or in some form of partnership with it. The freezing of the possibilities for UN peacekeeping during the second Cold War in the 1980s led to the establishment of non-UN forces in critical areas of the Middle East by states acting among themselves. In 1979, the Soviet Union refused to renew the mandate of the UN's Egypt–Israel mission begun after the 1973 war. The main function of this force would now be to oversee the implementation of the 1978 Camp David agreement. This was unacceptable to Moscow, which was hostile to the western-brokered settlement. The Multinational Force and Observers was therefore created from among North Atlantic Treaty Organization (NATO) members to replace the UN presence. In Lebanon in 1982 and 1983, a

similar arrangement saw the establishment of two US-led Multinational Forces (MNF-I and MNF-II), which operated in the Beirut area to which the UN force's mandate did not extend. Inevitably, however, without Security Council authorization the legitimacy of these forces was open to question.

Since the end of the Cold War a number of organizations have sought to develop an autonomous peacekeeping identity. NATO claimed a peacekeeping role, though its operations in Bosnia, Kosovo, and Afghanistan were primarily enforcement operations. Both the European Union and the Organization for Security and Cooperation in Europe have attempted to develop a peacekeeping function, though the tangible outcomes have been limited.

The most commonly adopted approach by regional organizations has been one of partnership with the UN. This involves either parallel ventures by both organizations or the deployment of non-UN forces with the formal authorization of the UN. The American Unified Task Force in Somalia in 1992–1993 operated along with the UN operations in Somalia. Interventions by the Economic Community of West African States Military Observer Group (ECOMOG) in Liberia and Sierra Leone in the mid-1990s also worked in parallel with a UN mission. A UN observer group was responsible for monitoring the activities of Russian-led peacekeepers on the borders of Georgia. Perhaps the most ambitious of this type of operation was the "hybrid" force in Darfur where the UN and the African Union were engaged in a joint operation from 2007. The second model – where UN authorization is given to an otherwise independent peacekeeping operation – could be seen in East Timor in 1999 when an Australian-led "coalition of the willing" intervened in the violence following a referendum on the territory's future.

The benefits and weaknesses of non-UN peacekeeping are finely balanced. The resources of the UN are not infinite and peacekeeping by other agencies is an important means of burden-sharing. Conflict management may benefit from the involvement of regional organizations as they may be more sensitive and responsive to specific local conditions. Similarly, regional bodies may have a stronger self-interest in resolving conflicts in their own areas. But some of these supposed strengths may equally be weaknesses. Local agencies may pursue local political agendas that have little to do with impartial conflict resolution. Regional organizations often have a single dominant member whose national interests may be pursued at the expense of peacekeeping neutrality. In West Africa, for example, there was suspicion of Nigeria's dominant position in the region and in ECOMOG, which raised questions about the motives for sending its troops to Liberia and Sierra Leone. At a practical level too, regional bodies may not be as effective as the UN in the operational aspects of peacekeeping. Peacekeeping endeavors by the African Union, notably in Darfur before direct UN involvement, and later in Somalia, were limited by shortages of equipment and resources among the contributing contingents and by weaknesses in training.

A "New Peacekeeping?"

Since the end of the Cold War, and more particularly since the beginning of the twenty-first century, there have been claims that the practice of peacekeeping was undergoing fundamental changes both in its methods and in its objectives. The suggestion was that the peacekeeping project had broken decisively with the traditional model set out in the 1950s. Consent, neutrality, and force only in the last resort were no longer appropriate criteria as they did not reflect the horizons of a "new peacekeeping."

In terms of methods, the new peacekeeping had supposedly moved beyond the observation and interposition of the classic model. Peacekeeping was now multifunctional and would usually involve a number of tasks. These might stretch from humanitarian intervention dealing with the immediate needs of civilians to long-term peace-building involving political as much as military activity. This multifunctionality had been an inevitable result of the increasing tendency of peacekeeping interventions to take place within countries in response to civil conflicts rather than between hostile sovereign states. Yet, while it is undoubtedly true that interventions after the end of the Cold War became overwhelmingly intrastate in character, this was not a new phenomenon. The Congo and Cyprus

Table 1 United Nations peacekeeping operations (multiple operations have taken place in some locations)

Date	Location
1948–present	Palestine
1949–present	Kashmir
1956–1967	Suez
1958	Lebanon
1960–1964	Congo
1962–1963	West New Guinea
1965–1966	India–Pakistan
1963–1964	Yemen
1964–present	Cyprus
1965–1966	Dominican Republic
1973–1979	Sinai
1974–present	Golan Heights
1978–present	Lebanon
1988–1990	Afghanistan–Pakistan
1988–1991	Iran–Iraq
1988–1999	Angola
1989–1990	Namibia
1989–1992	Central America
1991 present	Western Sahara
1991–1993	Cambodia
1991–1995	El Salvador
1991–2003	Iraq–Kuwait
1992–1994	Mozambique
1992–1995	Somalia
1992–1999	Macedonia
1992–2002	Bosnia
1992–2002	Croatia
1993–present	Georgia; Haiti; Liberia
1993–1994	Uganda–Rwanda
1993–1996	Rwanda
1994	Chad–Libya
1994–2000	Tajikistan
1997	Guatemala
1998–2000	Central African Republic
1998–2005	Sierra Leone
1999–present	Democratic Republic of the Congo; Kosovo; East Timor
2000–2008	Ethiopia–Eritrea
2004–present	Côte d'Ivoire
2004–2006	Burundi
2005–present	Sudan
2007–present	Central African Republic–Chad; Darfur

operations in the 1960s were, after all, addressing civil conflicts and, in the former case at least, were widely multifunctional in method. The change, in other words, may be one of degree and intensity rather than one of kind.

The proposition that the objectives of peace-keeping changed fundamentally is more complex and was based on the assumption that there had been a basic alteration in the nature of the international system in recent times. This had been driven in part by the process of globalization. The traditional power and sovereignty of states had been reduced by a global economic transformation which national politicians could not control. This raised the prospect of a transition from a world politics based on a "system of states" to one built around something that could truly be described as an "international community." In this framework, peacekeeping did not (should not) serve the traditional state system but, instead, human needs. The implications of this for consent, neutrality, and the proper use of force are evident. Did (should) peacekeeping be dependent on the consent of increasingly irrelevant host states which may themselves be at the root of the problem in hand? Could (should) human needs be secured by a bogus neutrality between morally unequal interests? Did (should) peacekeepers have a responsibility to physically protect civilians and, if so, how could this be compatible with the non-use of force? The debate is inconclusive and is frequently complicated by confusions between description and prescription, as the syntax of the previous sentences suggests. It reflects, however, a continuing and vigorous intellectual engagement with an activity whose significance has grown steadily since the beginning of the twentieth century.

SEE ALSO: Angolan Civil Wars (1975–2002); Arab–Israeli Conflict; Congo Wars (1960s–2000s); Yugoslav Succession, Wars of (1990–1999).

Further Reading

Bellamy, A. *et al.* (2010) *Understanding Peacekeeping*. Cambridge: Polity Press.

Boutros-Ghali, B. (1992) *An Agenda for Peace: Preventive Diplomacy, Peacemaking and Peacekeeping*. New York: United Nations.

Durch, W. (Ed.) (1993) *The Evolution of UN Peacekeeping: Case Studies and Comparative Analysis*. New York: St. Martin's Press.

Higgins, R. (1969, 1970, 1980, 1981) *United Nations Peacekeeping 1946–67: Documents and Commentary: Vol. 1 The Middle East; Vol. 2 Asia; Vol. 3 Africa; Vol. 4 Europe*. Oxford: Oxford University Press.

James, A. (1990) *Peacekeeping in International Politics*. London: Macmillan.

MacQueen, N. (2006) *Peacekeeping and the International System*. London: Routledge.

Wheeler, N. (2003) *Saving Strangers: Humanitarian Intervention in International Society*. Oxford: Oxford University Press.

White, N. D. (1997) *Keeping the Peace: The United Nations and the Maintenance of International Peace and Security*. Manchester: Manchester University Press.

Post-Traumatic Stress Disorder

FIONA REID

Definitions

Post-traumatic stress disorder (PTSD) is a relatively new diagnosis. PTSD first appeared in the American Psychiatric Association's (APA) *Diagnostic and Statistical Manual of Mental Disorders* in 1980 (*DSM-III*). Commonly regarded as the bible of the APA, *DSM-III* is an inventory of about 200 named mental disorders. The initial diagnostic criteria stated that PTSD was promoted by "a recognizable stressor that would evoke significant symptoms of distress in almost anyone"; the 1987 revision (*DSM-III-R*) insisted that such an event should be "outside the range of usual human experience" and would "be markedly distressing to almost anyone." *DSM-IV* (1994) states that "By definition, PTSD always follows a traumatic event which causes intense fear and/or helplessness in an individual." The symptoms of PTSD include sleeping disorders, concentration difficulties, obsessive thoughts, and flashbacks. Sufferers are often extremely anxious, highly irritable, and easily startled; they tend to re-experience or re-live the original trauma and so have to avoid situations that might provoke traumatic memories. These may all seem like very general descriptors, but the diagnosis of PTSD was the direct result of research into the particular mental health problems of Vietnam War veterans in the United States, and of much political pressure by those veterans and their advocates.

Although PTSD is a recent diagnosis, men have long suffered troubling after-effects from the stress of combat. After World War I, Sir

John Fortescue, historian of the British Army, commented that "numbers of men went out of their minds in the old campaigns, as they still do ... even the bravest man cannot endure to be under fire for more than a certain number of consecutive days, even if the fire be not very heavy" (War Office Committee 1922: 8–9). His words were echoed by Charles Moran, a medical officer during World War I and Winston Churchill's physician during World War II: "men wear out in war like clothes" (Moran 1945: 70). The words of Fortescue and Moran imply that there is some universal quality to mental breakdown in combat: it has always happened and it is always likely to happen. Yet while men (and latterly women) may always have "gone out of their minds" in wars, models of psychological understanding have changed. The role of the military doctor has altered, as have soldiers' expectations about treatment, pension entitlement, long-term health prospects, and welfare policies. The multitude of ways we have conceptualized military mental breakdown can be seen in the number of words and terms that have been employed to describe it: nostalgia, melancholia, wind contusion, cerebro-spinal shock, palpitations, irritable heart, disorderly action of the heart (DAH), effort syndrome, neurasthenia, war shock, shell shock, war neurosis, anxiety neurosis, Not Yet Diagnosed Nervous (NYDN), exhaustion, combat stress, low moral fiber (LMF), old sergeant syndrome, post-traumatic stress disorder.

Some of these terms – melancholia, neurasthenia, PTSD – have been used to describe civilian as well as military anguish. Others existed only within the armed forces: DAH, an unexplained somatic disorder, was the scourge of the nineteenth-century British Army, and LMF was an expression used exclusively by the Royal Air Force during World War II. It is tempting to read all these previous diagnoses as undiagnosed PTSD or PTSD under another name. However, it is important to emphasize that PTSD was not a discovery, but simply a new way of describing a range of recognizable symptoms, and, like all other such labels, it tells us more about the society that awarded the label than about any intrinsic or universal response to warfare. The history of PTSD is no simple progress narrative, but its roots lie in previous approaches

to mental breakdown among troops. In addition, although a distinct medical–military culture has been evident since the early modern period, at all times, the history of trauma in wartime is inseparable from the history of peacetime or civilian trauma.

Nostalgia, Nervousness, and the Modern Man

The psychological disorders of war were implicitly recognized in the early modern welfare system. The Royal Hospital at Chelsea, London, began to award daily allowances to old or disabled soldiers from 1685, and those who were mentally incapacitated were as eligible as their physically wounded comrades. "Nostalgia" was widely recognized as a mental malady among early modern European armies, and Dominique Larrey, one of Napoleon's physicians, interpreted it as a specific form of insanity brought on by the stresses of long and arduous military campaigns, and the associated strain of years away from homes and families. The diagnosis of nostalgia was an enduring one, and it later featured in medical accounts of the American Civil War. Generally regarded as the first "modern" war, the American Civil War was characterized by unprecedented levels of firepower, high explosives, and intense fighting. For the first time, combatant breakdown was attributed to the particular strains of industrial warfare.

Yet, it was not just the nature of modern warfare that provoked nervousness, anxiety, and mental breakdown. Modern industrial life was perceived as intensely stressful, and "railway spine" was one symptom of this stress. The mid-Victorian railway may have been the symbol of great technological progress, but it was also the symbol of all that was violent, dangerous, and terrifying about the new industrial world. Passengers involved in railway accidents were often left in a disturbed state, displaying a range of symptoms such as backache, loss of memory, dizziness, local paralysis, insomnia, and lassitude. John Erich Erichsen argued that this was because the central nervous system had been disturbed by the violent physical shock of the original accident. The extent to which the symptoms of railway spine were in fact psychological was a matter for debate. In

1883, Dr Herbert Page, surgeon to the London and North Western Railway, argued that "fright alone" could account for them. Page clearly felt that his own work had been marginalized, and, in 1920, he wrote to the wartime psychologist Millais Culpin, declaring that "all the symptoms of shell shock" could be found in *Railway Injuries*, the book he had published in 1891 (Jones and Wessely 2005).

Railway accidents were thought to trigger a range of troubling disorders, including neurasthenia, a nervous complaint which proliferated throughout the late nineteenth century. In 1869, George Beard, an American physician and neurologist, described neurasthenia as a nervous disorder and a disease of advanced civilization. Patients suffered from headaches, impotence, anxiety, neuralgia (pain caused by damaged nerves), depression, and loss of memory. Sometimes they displayed physical symptoms ranging from general aches and pains to paralysis or blindness. Many doctors argued that neurasthenia was caused by the hectic demands of modern life: businessmen competing in the fierce and highly technological cities of the modern United States were quite simply being depleted of vital nerve force. The diagnosis was not universally accepted throughout the western world – some doubted its existence – but it did become popular in some circles, largely because it was a way of describing a mental illness without attributing shame to the sufferer or the sufferer's family. Patients were frequently treated in fashionable spas, and women in particular were often prescribed a "rest cure." Silas Weir Mitchell devised the rest cure as a result of his work with traumatized soldiers in the American Civil War, and his program demanded bed-rest, tranquility, and solitude: the lack of stimulation would allow frayed nerves to heal. Mitchell's methods were later modified and used to treat British officers during World War I.

Hysteria was a less respectable but equally prolific condition in the late nineteenth century. Jean-Martin Charcot, neurologist and director of Paris's Salpêtrière Hospital, became famous for his research into hysteria. Just as Mitchell's rest cure is commonly described as a way of managing hysterical Victorian ladies, Charcot is similarly remembered for his work with hysterical women. However, he also published extensive case studies on his hysterical male patients. Consequently, the concept of masculine hysteria became accepted within mainstream medical communities by the 1890s (Micale 1990). By the early twentieth century, Sigmund Freud was arguing that traumatic neurosis was not the result of physical shock, but was a consequence of the way in which the patient remembered the initial traumatic event. The history of trauma can thus be seen as having two branches. One – best exemplified by Erichsen – emphasizes the importance of neurological mechanisms. The other, best represented by Charcot and then Freud, argues for a recognition of the psychological origins of trauma.

In retrospect, railway spine, neurasthenia, and hysteria can all be seen as purely psychological conditions. Mainstream nineteenth and early twentieth-century commentators were not blind to the pain of mental illness but by and large they adhered to physical explanations. During 1915, commentators in the *Lancet* explained that shell shock was the result of the wind of the explosives or the wind of the bullet which had caused organic, but imperceptible, damage to the central nervous system. This was widely accepted within both French and British armies. Popular perceptions of nervous conditions similarly recognized no clear boundary between the mental and the physical, as advertisements for popular nerve tonics had long indicated. The Wincarnis Remedy – a tonic wine – was one of many "nerve products" sold to cure a range of debilitating conditions from colds and chills to sleeplessness and "brain-fag" (*The Times*, February 2, 1910; December 17, 1913). These concerns about the weak nerves of modern man were explicitly linked to the nation's readiness for war. In 1910, Kaiser Wilhelm II announced that victory in the next war would demand "healthy nerves" (Lerner 2003: 40). Similar sentiments were expressed in Britain where advertisements for "Mr. Sandow's fitness campaign" proclaimed that "health, fitness and endurance" were "the nation's vital assets," and that "weakness is a crime today" (*The Times*, November 4, 1914). By this stage, men in particular had a patriotic duty to overcome feeble nerves.

World War I and Shell Shock

The European armies that went to war in 1914 were not thoroughly prepared for the psychological casualties that would follow. Yet, military psychiatry had advanced throughout the early years of the twentieth century. During the Russo-Japanese War, the Russian army set up centers for the forward treatment of psychiatric casualties, and established a psychiatric hospital behind the battle lines in Harbin, Manchuria. The forward treatment of psychiatric casualties was unprecedented at the time, but is now accepted as one of the basic principles of modern military psychiatry. The Russian treatment of mentally wounded casualties was discussed in French and German medical journals during the war, and in US journals afterwards. However, the developments were not mentioned in the British War Office review of the treatment of the sick and wounded in the Russo-Japanese War, even though British observers had been present. Nor was there one unified understanding of the relationship between war and trauma. While there was some recognition that war could cause mental breakdown, there was also a belief that men who had previously suffered from weak nerves could benefit from the experience of war, in short, that war could be a nerve-corrective and could heal the damage caused by enervating, modern lifestyles.

World War I was a massive, highly industrial conflict which lasted for more than four years, and British, French, and German authorities all noted a worrying number of psychological casualties within the first few months of the war. The range of symptoms was bewildering, and included functional paralysis, speech disturbances, amnesia, nightmares, mutism, deafness, deaf-mutism, ambylopia (bent back), tremblings, tics, sleeplessness, nervous debility, indecision, loss of self-confidence, neurasthenia, confusion, anxiety, and depression. Dr Charles Myers, a Cambridge academic who became consultant psychologist to the British Expeditionary Force, first referred to "shell shock" in an article in the *Lancet* in February 1915. He did not invent the phrase but he did provide it with some credibility and so legitimized its widespread use. Yet Myers (1940: 13) quickly realized that shell shock was a medically imprecise term because a shell "may play no part whatever in the causation of 'shell shock': excessive emotion, e.g. sudden horror or fear indeed any 'psychical trauma' or 'inadjustable experience' is sufficient." It was clear that shell shock was a misleading term but it is also simple,

alliterative, and powerful. Despite official attempts to replace it, with, for example, Not Yet Diagnosed Nervous (NYDN), shell shock remained (Babington 1997: 62).

In many ways, shell shock seemed like a new problem during World War I. When appealing for funds for "Special Hospitals," Lord Knutsford explained that "These hospitals are a product of this war. No other wars have made them necessary" (*The Times*, January 31, 1916). Many medical staff agreed with him, and seemed frankly baffled by shell-shocked patients. In September 1915, Lieutenant Francesco Ummarino was admitted to an Italian hospital after being struck dumb by a violent explosion. He remained mute for several days until the official visit of King Victor Emmanuel. As soon as the king appeared on the ward, Lieutenant Ummarino leapt to his feet, cried "Il re, sua maestà!" (His Majesty the King!), then burst into tears and recovered, fit for duty. The king and the ward staff were all visibly moved. Clearly, the medical staff had no other plans for recovering his speech. Of course, not all medical professionals were so taken aback by shell shock. Grafton Elliot Smith, professor of anatomy at Manchester University Medical School, and his colleague Tom Pear, lecturer in experimental psychology, noted that a violent shock could often cure mutism – this was obviously Ummarino's experience – they also commented that "shell-shock involves no new symptoms or disorders. Every one was known beforehand in civil life" (Smith and Pear 1918: 24).

If the symptoms of shell shock had all been known beforehand, why was shell shock seen as such a significant crisis during World War I? The answer lies partly in the scale of the problem. Mental breakdown in war was not new, but the conscription of literally millions of men for a prolonged period of industrial warfare was new. Wastage was a serious issue and no army could afford to lose too many men to mental collapse. At the same time, the soldiers in these vast modern armies tended to see themselves as citizens with associated rights. None of the powers involved were democracies in the modern sense, but many of the key powers – France, Belgium, Britain, the USA, Italy – had governments that were representational in some way. Even in autocratic Imperial Germany, many workers had developed a sense of entitlement, largely as a result of the state welfare and compensation system. While some men could be accused of cowardice or pathological idleness, it was simply not possible for modern governments to conscript millions of men, treat them as cannon fodder, and expect charities to care for them afterwards. For this reason, the British government introduced statutory pensions in 1915, and the post-war German government – the new Weimar Republic – built on pre-war legislation to award special treatment rights to veterans and their families. This, of course, presented another problem: post-war governments could not abandon wounded ex-soldiers, but nor could they burden themselves with excessive pension bills. This was one of the reasons behind the US Army's program of psychiatric screening, introduced in 1917: by weeding out potentially vulnerable recruits, they were trying to protect the rights of weak citizens at the same time as minimizing future state expenditure. In December 1917, the Germans also introduced psychological testing, although the German tests focused more on measuring intelligence than identifying tendencies toward neurosis.

There was an increased sense of state responsibility toward ordinary soldiers during World War I, but this did not lead to high-level care for all mentally wounded men. On the contrary, the shell-shocked veterans of victorious and vanquished nations alike often received inadequate pensions and very little care. The key issues of World War I – the high number of overall casualties, the apparent inability to manage psychological casualties, and the rights of citizen soldiers – all later reappeared in debates about the soldiers of the Vietnam War. The issues may have been similar, but the main conclusion of the medical military experts after World War I differed significantly from those reached by the specialists involved with Vietnam veterans. Firstly, although some doctors perceived shell shock as a psychological problem, there was a widespread medical consensus after 1918 that a mental breakdown had a strong physiological element. According to this thinking, psychological symptoms were a product of physical damage. More significantly, although there was some acceptance that every man had his breaking point, military medical authorities also assumed that all healthy men would recover reasonably quickly. Those who broke down permanently were considered to

have some kind of a predisposition: the flaw lay in the man rather than the war.

Many mentally damaged veterans did not recover after World War I. In Britain 65,000 ex-servicemen were receiving pension awards for neurasthenia and shell shock in 1921. Similarly, in the United States, men continued to develop symptoms of war neurosis long after the Armistice. Consequently, medical and military elites were keen to ensure that psychological casualties would not cause such problems in any forthcoming conflicts. In Britain, Lord Southborough's post-war Committee of Enquiry argued that shell shock was "a grievous misnomer for the disorder or disorders grouped under that head" (War Office Committee 1922: 4); moreover, any medical label was unhelpful, and should be avoided in all future wars. In addition, most of the witnesses thought that psychological casualties could be minimized by effective training, good discipline, and the maintenance of high morale.

The resistance to medicalization was partially successful in that the term "shell shock" was not used in future wars. Yet, during the interwar years, those who had been characterized as shell shocked still required medical and financial help. While it was widely accepted that many good men had clearly broken down in battle, there were also concerns that shell shock had somehow made fear respectable or had even allowed men "an open sesame to the base" (Butler 1938: 72). In 1926, the German government decided to stop awarding pensions for traumatic neuroses, whether accident- or war-related. There were clear economic motives for this decision, but therapeutic reasons were presented too: pensions caused neurotics to become even more debilitated; the cure for neurosis was not idleness, but work. The Germans were not alone in privileging the therapeutic value of employment. British and US authorities similarly encouraged veterans to work, although, unlike their German counterparts, they tended to stress the particular suitability of rural occupations for neurotic pensioners.

World War II: No "Open Sesame" to the Base

By the outbreak of World War II, British policy had been framed in a conscious attempt to discourage neuroses. Dr Francis Prideaux, who had dealt with shell-shocked patients in World War I and had joined the Ministry of Pensions afterwards, drew up a memorandum to establish the lessons of the war and to outline effective approaches to future cases of war neuroses. Arguing that most neurotic pensioners had not been on the front line and that cases of "delayed shell shock" were bogus, Prideaux made the following recommendations: that no soldier should be discharged from service because of psychoneurosis; that pensions should not be awarded for neuroses; that no medical label should be attached to men with war neuroses. At the Horder Conference (1939) it was agreed that mentally damaged servicemen would be offered treatment rather than pensions (Shephard 2001: 166–168). Quite literally, there was to be no repeat of "shell shock" and its "open sesame" to the base.

Of course, British troops did suffer from mental breakdown in World War II, as did troops from all combatant nations, although neither Nazi Germany nor the Soviet Union formally recognized any kind of psychological or psychiatric breakdown. The British Army established the Directorate of Army Psychiatry in April 1942. Influenced by Myer's work in World War I, it advocated "forward psychiatry," based on the principles of PIE (proximity to combat, immediacy, and expectation of recovery). The American Army Medical Corps similarly aimed to treat most mentally wounded casualties close to the front line, although in all cases more severe breakdowns were sent to the base. Initially, men were diagnosed with "exhaustion," thus avoiding a medical label; "exhaustion" also implied easy, or at least straightforward, recovery. Nevertheless, the British government did recognize psychological breakdown as a war wound. The rate of psychological casualties varied throughout the war but, according to official figures, a total of about 10 percent of veterans' pensions were categorized as either psychological or neurological disorders (Jones and Wessely 2005: 8). The military experiences of World War II indicated that mental breakdown was linked to intensity of combat, and that, although issues of morale and leadership were pertinent, the basic conclusion of the Southborough report – that well-trained, highly disciplined units with good morale did not suffer from psychiatric casualties – was incorrect.

The Development of PTSD

One of the primary lessons of World War II, certainly in the British and the US armies, was that men had to be trained to manage their fears. If men did break down, the damage could be limited by forward psychiatry, and by a refusal either to hospitalize or to reward financially the patient. However, there was little interest in the study of war neurosis once the conflict was over, and the interest was not fully rekindled until the US involvement in Vietnam.

There had initially been optimism about low levels of psychological casualties in Vietnam. Men were allocated a Date of Expected Return from Overseas (DEROS) and so were scheduled to spend only a year in combat, a policy designed to minimize stress. However, by the early 1970s it was clear that this confidence had been misplaced. Throughout the United States, mental health professionals were noting high levels of drug addiction, alcoholism, mental instability, and even suicide among veterans. The "Vietnam vet" – seriously disturbed, asocial, deeply traumatized – had become the symbol of an unpopular and dirty war. One key difference between the traumatized Vietnam veteran and the mentally wounded soldiers of previous wars was that some of them attributed their trauma not just to the stresses and strains of the battlefield, but also to acute moral dilemmas, principally their role in atrocities. This was then exacerbated by the public's response to these atrocities. One example has become emblematic of the US presence in Vietnam. In 1968, American servicemen massacred over 500 civilians, mainly women and children, in the village of My Lai, and news of this filtered through to the American public the following year. As a result of this and other episodes, veterans returned home to a public that was often vocal about its shame. After the liberation of Europe, American servicemen could see themselves as heroic figures: they were large and handsome, and technological superiority had helped them to win the war. Soviet troops may have raped and plundered but the GIs were charming and they dispensed cigarettes and chewing gum with liberality. Recent accounts of post-war Europe have been more critical about the role of GIs, but, nevertheless, it was possible for World War II veterans to feel like – and to be treated like – heroes (Roberts 2013). This option was simply not available for the veterans of Vietnam.

Vietnam Veterans Against the War (VVAW) was founded in 1967 in direct response to the controversies of the conflict and to the lack of post-conflict support. Like previous veterans' organizations, the VVAW championed the rights of ex-military personnel, calling for increased health and welfare provision. Unlike previous veterans' organizations, it explicitly condemned the war its members had fought, and presented the combatants primarily as victims of the war. Given the anger at some of the atrocities associated with the Vietnam War, it is pertinent to ask how the men responsible for such brutal acts came to perceive themselves – and to be perceived as – war victims. This is largely because veterans were able to articulate and to share their emotions through the "rap groups" they had created. Given the lack of care from established health services, many men created their own centers for debriefing, mutual support, and therapy. One clear message came out of these groups: the bitter experiences in the jungles of Vietnam had brutalized American servicemen and damaged them psychologically. The flaw lay in the war rather than the man.

Another key difference between the conflict in Vietnam and previous conflicts was the role of the medical profession. In previous wars, mentally traumatized soldiers encountered doctors who, although they might well have been personally sympathetic, supported the ongoing war. During the Vietnam War, a significant number of mental health professionals became opposed to the war, and they were able to mobilize on behalf of the disturbed veterans. In 1972, Dr Chaim Shatan published an article in the *New York Times* identifying a condition he described as "post-Vietnam syndrome" (Shephard 2001: 357). Dr Robert Lifton, another psychiatrist, published *Home From the War* (1974), based on his conversations with veterans. Until this point, the received wisdom was that battlefield trauma could be managed, but Lifton argued that the psychological effects of serving in the Vietnam War were overwhelming, and that military psychia-

trists were culpable because they had served the interests of the military and not those of the patient (Young 1995: 109). This is an argument that would have made little sense in previous wars: individual doctors may have had qualms about their actions, but there was a consensus that the role of the military doctor was to preserve the strength of the fighting unit, not to care for individual patients.

By the mid-1970s, combatant trauma was a politically potent issue. At the same time, there were significant changes taking place within the psychiatric profession. Psychoanalytic approaches had dominated in the years immediately after World War II, but from the 1950s the development of psycho-active drugs began to change clinical practice. By the 1960s, doctors were prescribing specific drugs for discrete categories of mental illness, and this encouraged a move away from psychoanalytic approaches toward a more biological, evidence-based science. The key turning point came in 1975 when Dr Robert Spitzer began to draw up *DSM-III*. He jettisoned all those who had been involved in the creation of *DSM-II* and gathered together a team committed to diagnostic research, in his own words, a team with "its roots in St. Louis rather than Vienna" (Young 1995: 99). The main point of *DSM-III* was to provide practitioners of all persuasions with one clear and objective language. As a result, conversations between those from different theoretical backgrounds would be possible, as would direct communication between researchers and clinicians. Shatan and Lifton wanted their work to be reflected in the forthcoming *DSM*. They were both active in "rap groups" and wanted official recognition for the disturbed veterans they had encountered, and a secure pathway to ensure financial compensation for them. Shatan established a working group to collect evidence on post-combat trauma and to lobby for support, and in 1978 the group presented a report to Spitzer's Committee on Reactive Disorders. As a result, PTSD was included in *DSM-III* under the heading of anxiety disorders.

After *DSM-III*

The acceptance of the PTSD diagnosis was initially controversial. Opponents, such as the

Veterans' Administration, recognized that there would be large compensation claims from veterans, and that these would be hard to deny. Those who supported the diagnosis argued that it was clearly wrong to deny veterans access to a diagnosis that would enable them to claim much-needed medical care and financial compensation. This was an effective argument and the concept of PTSD was rapidly accepted throughout the world. *DSM-IV* provides a long list of traumatic events that can provoke PTSD. The list begins with military combat and goes on to include violent personal assault, incarceration, natural or man-made disasters, and automobile accidents or being diagnosed with a life-threatening illness. In addition, PTSD can be provoked by witnessing or learning about someone else's trauma. PTSD can therefore be applied in a wide range of cases, and symptoms can be found in, for example, the observers of violent accidents or those suffering as a result of the unexpected death of a relative or close friend. Whole populations who have lived through periods of violence and disorder – such as those living in Belfast during the "Troubles" in Northern Ireland – have been identified as suffering from PTSD. The condition is considered to be acute if the duration of symptoms is less than three months and chronic if the duration of symptoms is three months or more. PTSD is categorized as "Delayed onset" if the symptoms begin at least six months after the stressor. Throughout the western world it has now become common practice to provide counselors at disaster scenes, not just for the wounded, but also for the medical staff and bystanders. There has been an impact on the academic world too, as historians are now turning their attention to the trauma of medical staff in wartime, and to the way in which catastrophes have been retold and remembered.

Yet PTSD still provokes controversy. The newly-released *DSM-V* (2013) is more specific about describing what constitutes a traumatic event in its description of PTSD, but this has not ended all concerns. Some military leaders believe that the word "disorder" is unhelpful because it makes troops reluctant to ask for help and they would prefer a change to the term "posttraumatic stress injury." Despite these protests, *DSM-V* retains the term "Posttraumatic Stress Disorder." On a more general level, it is possible that the medicaliza-

tion of emotional trauma undermines other, less formal defense mechanisms: talking with family and friends; humor; group or community rituals such as commemoration services. As well as weakening other forms of support, reliance upon professional intervention may well turn into a dependency. More specifically, recent research indicates distortions in the PTSD database. Working from an admittedly small sample, taken from a Veterans' Affairs PTSD clinic, researchers conclude that some veterans have fabricated or exaggerated their wartime experiences. Men who have not been involved in combat have reported stress stemming from specific combat situations; men have reported stress as a result of committing atrocities when there is no evidence of them having committed atrocities (Frueh *et al.* 2005). One can understand why men exaggerate their combat experiences. Men have always done so in part to gain more status, and in the particular circumstances of Vietnam veterans it also allowed them access to financial compensation and medical care. But why should men deliberately implicate themselves in acts of cruelty and barbarism? These stories of fake atrocities are atypical, but they are important as they pinpoint changes in conceptions of combat trauma. In earlier wars breakdown had often been expressed in terms of weakness: shell-shocked men had allegedly run from the trenches; the combat-stressed soldiers of World War II were unable to support their comrades. These men were seen as either poorly trained or intrinsically weak. The traumatized veteran who attributed his nervous collapse to his part in an atrocity was in quite a different position. In confessing to an outrage – the rape of a woman, the destruction of a village, the murder of a child – the man was attributing his collapse to the fact that the war had forced him to take part in, or even initiate, a baseless act. These false claims may have been simple fabrications or they may have been false memories. In either case, by publicly recognizing the inhumanity of his actions, the man was reclaiming his own moral worth at the same time as castigating those responsible for such a dehumanizing war. Alongside the moral issues, these findings have clinical repercussions too. Research with Vietnam combat veterans has been used to create and refine the *DSM* criteria for PTSD, yet if the initial data is flawed, the criteria will be too (Frueh *et al.* 2005).

More recent wars have resulted in further research into the psychological consequences of modern warfare. Current findings gleaned from British troops in Iraq argue that support troops and reservists were the most vulnerable to psychological collapse during the recent war. Their problems must therefore be due to issues of deployment, acclimatization, and difficulties with homecoming rather than to the intensity of combat (Turner 2005; Browne *et al.* 2007). This particular research is focused once again on managing troops and managing trauma. It is a move away from the approaches adopted by the likes of Lifton and Shatan during the Vietnam War. Most crucially, this research emphasizes the importance of establishing exactly why the combatant has become traumatized. Although PTSD describes a common pathway to trauma, there are significant differences between combatant and non-combatant breakdowns and they require different treatments. There has also been a move away from the original universalizing model. Responses to traumatic and painful events vary from individual to individual and from culture to culture; some people are more resilient than others, and resilience can be developed. In short, a traumatic event alone is not responsible for mental breakdown because personal and collective reactions have their impact too.

We can recognize that key emotions are universal: in all societies at all times people recognize fear, terror, anxiety, rage, and so forth. Yet, while these emotions are universal, responses to traumatic events are historically and culturally contingent. PTSD has been a useful diagnostic tool, but it does not fully describe the myriad ways in which people respond to the stress of combat.

SEE ALSO: Vietnam War (1959–1975); World War I: Western Front.

References

Babington, A. (1997) *A History of the Changing Attitudes to War Neurosis*. London: Leo Cooper.

Browne, T., Hull, L., Horn, O., Jones, M., and Murphy, D. (2007) "Explanations for the Increase in Mental Health Problems in UK Reserve Forces Who Have Served in Iraq," *British Journal of Psychiatry*, 190: 484–489.

Butler, A. G. (Ed.) (1938) *The Australian Army Medical Services in the War of 1914–1918*. Melbourne: Australian War Memorial.

Frueh, B. C., Elhai J. D., Grubaugh, A. L., *et al.* (2005) "Documented Combat Exposure of US Veterans Seeking Treatment for Combat-Related Post-Traumatic Stress Disorder," *British Journal of Psychiatry*, 186: 467–472.

Jones, E. and Wessely, S. (2005) *Shell Shock to PTSD: Military Psychiatry from 1900 to the Gulf War*. New York: Psychology Press.

Lerner, P. (2003) *Hysterical Men: War, Psychiatry and the Politics of War in Germany 1890–1930*. Ithaca: Cornell University Press.

Lifton, R. J. (1974) *Home from the War: Vietnam Veterans, Neither Victims nor Executioners*. London: Wildwood House.

Micale, M. (1990) "Charcot and the Idea of Hysteria in the Male: Gender, Mental Science, and Medical Diagnosis in Late Nineteenth-Century France," *Medical History*, 34 (4): 363–411.

Moran, C. (1945) *The Anatomy of Courage*. London: Constable.

Myers, C. S. (1940) *Shell Shock in France, 1914–1918*. Cambridge: Cambridge University Press.

Page, H. (1891/2012) *Railway Injuries: With Special Reference to Those of the Back and Nervous System, in Their Medico-Legal and Clinical Aspects*. London: Forgotten Books.

Roberts, M-L. (2013) *What Soldiers Do: Sex and the American GI in World War Two France*. Chicago, University of Chicago Press.

Shephard, B. (2001) *A War of Nerves: Soldiers and Psychiatrists in the Twentieth Century*. Cambridge, MA: Harvard University Press.

Smith, E. G. and Pear, T. H. (1918) *Shell Shock and Its Lessons*. Manchester: Manchester University Press; London: Longmans, Green.

Turner, M. A. (2005) "Acute Military Psychiatric Casualties from the War in Iraq," *British Journal of Psychiatry*, 186: 476–479.

War Office Committee (1922) *Report of the War Office Committee of Enquiry into Shell Shock*. London: HMJ.

Young, A. (1995) *The Harmony of Illusions: Inventing Post-Traumatic Stress Disorder*. Princeton: Princeton University Press.

Further Reading

Binnevald, H. (1997) *From Shell Shock to Combat Stress: A Comparative History of Military Psychiatry*. Amsterdam: Amsterdam University Press.

Chickering, R. and Förster, S. (Eds.) (2002) *The Shadows of Total War: Europe, East Asia and the United States, 1919–1939.* Cambridge: Cambridge University Press.

Cooter, R., Harrison, M., and Sturdy, S. (Eds.) (1999) *War, Medicine and Modernity.* Stroud: Sutton.

Dean, E. (1997) *Shook Over Hell. Post-Traumatic Stress Disorder, Vietnam and the Civil War.* Cambridge, MA: Harvard University Press.

Gabriel, R. and Metz, K. (1992) *A History of Military Medicine from Renaissance through Modern Times.* Westport: Greenwood Press.

Gray, P. and Oliver, K. (Eds.) (2004) *The Memory of Catastrophe.* Manchester: Manchester University Press.

Harrison, M. (2004) *Medicine and Victory: British Military Medicine in the Second Word War.* Oxford: Oxford University Press.

Jones, E., Palmer, I., and Wessely, S. (2002) "War Pensions (1900–1945): Changing Models of Psychological Understanding," *British Journal of Psychiatry,* 180: 274–379.

Micale, M. and Lerner, P. (Eds.) (2001) *Traumatic Pasts: History, Psychiatry and Trauma in the Modern Age, 1870–1930.* Cambridge: Cambridge University Press.

Reid, F. (2010) *Broken Men: Shell Shock, Treatment and Recovery in Britain, 1914–1930.* London: Hambledon Continuum.

Shephard, B. (2008) "Why the Psychiatry of War is Too Important to be Left to Psychiatrists." In Wellcome Collection, Deutsche Hygiene-Museum, Dresden, *War and Medicine.* London: Black Dog Publishing.

Psychological Warfare

STEPHEN BADSEY

The most straightforward description of psychological warfare is propaganda directed against an enemy in wartime in order to gain a military advantage, particularly when directed at his armed forces. More generally, psychological warfare is the institutionalized, deliberate, and systematic generation and use of ideas, words, and images by one side in a war, aimed at lowering the morale of its enemies, especially enemy armed forces, and their ability to fight. Psychological warfare may function solely on the battlefield, or throughout all aspects of an enemy's war effort.

As a term, psychological warfare was first systematically defined and popularized in the United States in the 1950s, although abandoned by the US Armed Forces in the 1960s in favor of "psychological operations" ("psyop" or "psyops").

One often-quoted American definition from the 1950s was that psychological warfare constituted activities, other than physical combat, that communicated ideas and information intended to affect the minds, emotions, and actions of the enemy, for the purpose of disrupting his morale and his will to fight. At various times much broader meanings have been attached to psychological warfare, including the idea that it is warfare conducted by "non-violent means," not with weapons intended to kill or destroy, but with ideas intended to persuade the enemy into defeat. Apart from psychological operations, other associated terms are "combat psychology," "political warfare," "sychwar (or psychwar)," "intellectual warfare," "information warfare," and "information operations," although the last-named term, as first defined in the 1990s, included concepts much broader than psychological warfare as it is traditionally understood.

At various times, some theorists and practitioners have seen psychological warfare as virtually identical to propaganda in wartime, to be aimed at neutral, friendly, and even domestic audiences as well as at an enemy; an analogy employed in the 1950s was that just as peacetime sanctions become economic warfare, so in wartime propaganda becomes psychological warfare. Others have understood psychological warfare as specifically the military aspects of propaganda in peace or war; yet others have seen it as largely distinct from propaganda because of its specifically military nature and purpose. One useful illustration of the nature of psychological warfare is that its most common and characteristic weapon has been the simple mass-produced printed leaflet providing enemy troops with encouragement and information on how to desert or surrender, often augmented by radio broadcasts and by loudspeakers on the battlefield. With antecedents dating back to at least the American War of Independence (1775–1783), surrender leaflets have been used in their millions from World War I (1914–1918) onwards, usually delivered by balloons or aircraft. Some of these leaflets have included overt propaganda in making an emotional or reasoned appeal, but many have provided only practical details on how to surrender safely, without any ideological content. Used in large numbers in such one-sided conflicts as the Gulf War (1990–1991), these leaflets have been instrumental in saving many lives. The use of surrender leaflets is also one of the few cases in which the impact of psychological warfare may be measured or even reasonably assessed.

It is a truism that all war (including killing and wounding the enemy) has a psychological dimension, and that throughout history attempts have been made to damage the enemy's will to fight as well as to inflict physical harm. In this sense ambushes, terror weapons, frightening war masks, triumphal arches, war songs, and many other artifacts and activities have been described as psychological warfare. Indeed, since its first use in the early twentieth century the term has always been in danger of being rendered meaningless by such widely differing interpretations. In 1951, Harold Lasswell (1902–1978), one of the pioneers of modern propaganda studies, argued that "the basic idea is that the best success in war is achieved by the destruction of the enemy's will to resist, and with a minimum annihilation of fighting capacity" (Jowett and O'Donnell 1992: 155). This is a recognizable version of the dictum attributed to the ancient Chinese military writer Sun Zi (Sun Tzu) (*ca.* fourth century BCE), whose work enjoyed a revival in the West from the 1920s onwards, that "supreme excellence consists in defeating the enemy without fighting." But although the roots of psychological warfare may be found in the past, both its conscious practice and its associated theory and vocabulary are relatively modern inventions.

In the middle of the nineteenth century, battle studies, including those by Charles Ardant du Picq (1819–1870), revealed that in most European battles the number of casualties on both sides was only a proportion of the total forces involved, and that the losing side had mostly run away rather than be annihilated. This led to the argument that victory in war depended on non-physical factors. As expressed by Count Leo Tolstoy (1828–1910) in *War and Peace*, "The spirit of an army is the factor which multiplied by the mass gives the resulting force. To define and express the significance of this unknown factor – the spirit of an army – is a problem for science." When coupled with military concerns from the 1880s onwards about the impact of the firepower revolution, and the ability of mass European conscript armies to withstand the stresses of battle, this led before World War I to a cult of the offensive, and exaggerated claims for the

ability of determined and well-motivated troops to overcome heavy losses. The expectation was that high or low troop morale and psychological factors would determine victory, particularly in land warfare. This was the military reflection of an increasing popular awareness of psychology and the theories of such figures as Sigmund Freud (1856–1939) and Carl Jung (1875–1961), and of an increasing interest in both individual and mass human behavior.

Prior to World War I even the term "propaganda" was vague and ill-defined in military usage. Although arguably the practice of propaganda has always existed, it was only in World War I that it was deliberately institutionalized by governments as a weapon of war. Even then, most governments preferred terms such as "information" to propaganda. The first governmental propaganda institutions were created by the British within a month of the war's outbreak, and evolved into their Ministry of Information by early 1918; similar institutions were created by France, while, on its entry into the war in 1917, the United States formed its Committee on Public Information (Creel Committee). In the same year, the United States also coined the term "psychologic warfare," although most belligerents had no specific words for the practice.

In the course of the war, the development of the concepts of total war and of the home front led to the blurring of the distinction between armed forces and civilians, including the extent to which propaganda and psychological warfare overlapped, as leaflets, pamphlets, and even newspapers written in enemy languages were being used to target enemy civilian populations and reserve areas as well as frontline soldiers. This reached a pinnacle in early 1918 with the British creation of a Department for Propaganda in Enemy Countries (known as Crewe House) under Lord Northcliffe (1865–1922), the owner of *The Times*. The early Bolsheviks also made extensive use of psychological warfare techniques to foment discontent and desertion in the Russian army prior to the 1917 Revolution, and against Germany and Austria-Hungary afterwards. Major psychological warfare campaigns were mounted by the British, French, and Italians against Austria-Hungary and Bulgaria in the hope of exploiting national ambitions and ethnic rivalries, by Germany and Austria-Hungary against Italy, and by the British and French against

German frontline troops in 1918, which may have played a significant part in the German defeat on the Western Front.

It was a principle particularly of British official propaganda, laid down in 1914, adopted by other democracies, and largely observed throughout both world wars, that any official statement must be based on the truth as it was known at the time, although information might be withheld or a greater emphasis placed on some facts rather than others; the long-term political and strategic value of truthfulness was rated as much more important than any short-term or tactical advantage to be gained by lying. This also applied to official films, photographs, and any overt officially produced propaganda material. In contrast, psychological warfare often includes deception and the use of misleading information in order to support some immediate military advantage. This led to a convention by the end of World War I that official propaganda, and especially any official institutions dealing with news media, should be institutionally separated from any organizations dealing with deception or psychological warfare. This posed problems particularly for military hierarchies, in which both press relations and deception usually came under the broader heading of military intelligence, but on the whole it was observed. A distinction was also made between "white" propaganda, which was open about its official origins, and both "gray" propaganda, which concealed its official origins, and "black" propaganda, which purported to come from enemy sources, both of which have often been used for short-term tactical advantages or to mislead the enemy.

In the aftermath of World War I much greater attention was paid by theorists to psychological warfare. In the case of Germany this interest was heavily associated with the "stab in the back" myth that appeared at the war's end, by which for political reasons successive governments and military leaders sought to deny that German troops had been defeated militarily, claiming instead that the home front had collapsed under pressure from an Allied psychological warfare campaign. In the case of early British theorists of armored warfare, particularly J. F. Fuller (1878–1966) and Basil Liddell Hart (1895–1970), the interest was linked to two beliefs: that the mass disintegration of an army could be caused by the psychological shock produced by tank attacks; and also that in 1918 the Allied victory over Germany had come about chiefly through the psychological collapse of General Erich Ludendorff (1865–1937, *de facto* commander of the German army 1916–1918), so that the target of any military operation should be the enemy commander's will and perceptions. An interpretation of mass psychological behavior was also implicit in interwar theories of the impact of strategic bombing on civilian populations, notably those of Giulio Douhet (1869–1930). All these theories were based on general and popular notions of psychology, and on a desire to avoid another protracted confrontation like World War I, rather than on any developed reasoning or study of human behavior. Fuller's comment that he envisaged a future era in which physical combat might be "replaced by purely psychological warfare, wherein weapons are not used or battlefields sought" (1920: 328), is a reflection of just how vaguely the term was used.

Although interest in psychological warfare increased greatly after World War I, the wide assumption in democracies was that such activities should be reserved for wars only. But the relationship between war and propaganda became increasingly blurred by the creation in Moscow, in 1919, of the Third (Communist) International or Comintern (disbanded 1943), with its mission to spread revolution around the world, partly through agitation and propaganda or "agitprop." This ideological war between communism and western capitalist democracy lasted in various forms and degrees until the dissolution of the Soviet Union in 1990, and many of its activities on both sides fell into the category of psychological warfare, usually conducted in the case of democratic countries by clandestine or intelligence agencies. In the 1920s, Soviet military thought also developed the concept of "*maskirovka*," a mandatory form of support for all military operations that combined deception, camouflage, propaganda, and psychological warfare. The concept of warfare in which ideas, politics, or psychology would play a greater part than conventional military strength was taken even further in the 1930s by Chinese communists under Mao Zedong (Mao Tse-tung) (1893–1976). The Maoist concept of "revolutionary war" observed almost no distinctions between politics and warfare, placing heavy stress on psychological warfare to wear down the enemy, and on the political and psychological aspects of all military operations. This owed part of its origin to the traditional thinking of Sun Zi and other Chinese military writers, and part to the later nineteenth-century idea of the "propaganda of the deed" popularized by revolutionary anarchists, but in the Maoist case these ideas were applied on a much greater scale and in a systematic manner.

From at least the middle of the nineteenth century to the end of World War II, German military propaganda was triumphalist by tradition, aimed more at intimidating enemies than persuading them. This approach was taken to new levels in the later 1930s by the Nazi state under Adolf Hitler (1889–1945), with a heavy emphasis on psychological warfare evident in the German contribution to the Spanish Civil War (1936–1939), ranging from leaflets to films, and such details as the diving siren fitted to the famous Junkers Ju-87 "Stuka" dive-bomber. This style of psychological warfare continued into World War II (1939–1945). All belligerents employed psychological warfare staffs and techniques, including "black" propaganda, as an accepted part of their war efforts. On the Eastern Front in particular, the ideological nature of the struggle meant that both the Axis and the Soviet forces made great use of psychological warfare techniques.

Among the first acts of World War II was the dropping of propaganda leaflets by British aircraft on Germany. Thereafter the British developed an effective psychological warfare apparatus headed by the Political Warfare Executive (PWE), while the revived Ministry of Information provided information and "white" propaganda. After the entry of the United States into the war in December 1941, the American term "sychwar" (for psychological warfare) came to dominate. While the British Broadcasting Corporation (BBC) was at the forefront of "white" propaganda in the form of radio broadcasts to occupied countries, the PWE (while making use of BBC transmitters) used methods including clandestine radio broadcasts and disinformation to undermine enemy morale. The PWE made a specialty of "black radio" broadcasts in German, appearing to come from within Germany, and promoting views such as the possibility of a compromise peace, in contrast to the official Anglo-American position of unconditional surrender announced at the Casablanca Conference in 1943. The principal American organization for covert warfare including psychological warfare was the Office of Strategic Services (OSS), while "white" propaganda was handled chiefly by the Office of War Information, both created in 1941. The western Allies also set up psychological warfare branches in various theaters of war in order to support their military campaigns, of which the first and largest was in North Africa (1942–1943). This reached its height in the campaign for the liberation of northwestern Europe, for which SHAEF (Supreme Headquarters Allied Expeditionary Force) under General Dwight D. Eisenhower (1890–1969) created its Psychological Warfare Division. Eisenhower believed that psychological warfare played an important part in the campaign, including by encouraging German surrenders at the end of the war. A similar role was played by psychological warfare units at the end of the war against Japan in persuading Japanese soldiers to surrender, notably the Psychological Warfare Section of US Far East Command, which remained in existence after the war.

The United States displayed its greatest belief in the effectiveness of psychological warfare during the height of the early years of the Cold War. This was the military aspect of the contemporary popularity of behaviorism as a scientific discipline, a recognition of the rise in importance of commercial advertising, concerns about the social implications of the new medium of television, and bafflement over the ideological strengths of revolutionary war and the appeal of communism. The prevailing impression was that Hitler and other right-wing demagogues in the 1930s had shaped and won over national publics by sheer force of rhetoric, and that the appeal of communism was based very much on the same psychological skills. It was seriously believed that individual and mass opinion control, or even mind control, by psychological means, would be achievable within the near future.

It is a feature of psychological warfare that many of its practitioners have been civilians rather than members of the armed forces. The older western democratic tradition, first developed by the British and adopted by the United States, is that wartime propaganda is fundamentally a civilian activity and an extension of diplomacy, although with some military aspects. As an extension of the experience of the PWE, British psychological warfare during the Cold War was run principally by the Information Research Department of the Foreign Office from 1948 to 1977. The newer American approach increasingly militarized psychological warfare, seeing it as a branch of armed conflict governed by military imperatives. In 1947, the Central Intelligence Agency (CIA) was formed from the wartime OSS, with responsibility for psychological warfare as part of covert actions around the world. This was followed in 1948 by the Information and Educational Exchange Act (Smith–Mundt Act), which authorized the US government to disseminate propaganda ("information") abroad but made it illegal to direct propaganda toward the American people. The effect of this was largely to exclude the State Department from direct participation in psychological warfare overseas.

In 1947, the Psychological Warfare Section of Far East Command was joined by the US Army's creation of a small psychological warfare unit at Fort Riley, Kansas, known as the Tactical Information Detachment. In 1950, President Harry S. Truman established the Psychological Strategy Board in Washington, and the United States and other countries sent psychological warfare leafleting, loudspeaker, and radio units to the Korean War (1949–1953). One of the most inventive US psychological warfare campaigns of this war was "Operation Moolah," a publicized offer of a financial reward to any enemy pilots flying the latest MiG-15 jet fighters who deserted with their aircraft; although no pilots took up the offer, this obliged the Chinese and North Koreans to temporarily ground and restrict the use of the MiGs. In 1951, the US Defense Department created the Office of the Chief of Psychological Warfare, and in 1952 a Psychological Operations Coordinating Committee was established in Washington, together with the creation at Fort Bragg, North Carolina, of the US Army's Psychological Warfare Center, a name changed in 1956 to the Special Warfare Center. In 1961, the Defense Department was given shared responsibility with the CIA for covert operations, and "political-psychological activities" were made part of the role of the new Special Forces ("Green Berets"). By this period, the preferred US military term was "psychological operations."

At the higher levels of politics and strategy, in 1951 the US State Department created the International Information Administration, and in 1953 President Dwight D. Eisenhower (who had commanded SHAEF in 1944–1945) created the United States Information Agency, with the Voice of America as its overt "white" radio station broadcasting US propaganda to the communist world, in contrast to the CIA's clandestine funding of the "gray" Radio Free Europe and Radio Liberty. But although propaganda was seen as an essential part of the Cold War ideological struggle, and psychological operations as an essential part of CIA and US military covert actions, by their nature their actual extent and impact remain very hard to assess.

Although psychological operations continued to be standard practice in many conflicts around the world, their value was increasingly called into question and their importance downgraded, as ideas of mind manipulation and opinion control turned out to be fanciful. In the United States' involvement in the Vietnam War (1959–1975), attempts to win over the enemy by psychological warfare were largely unsuccessful. Although the United States retained a small psychological operations apparatus within its armed forces, in most other democratic countries covert propaganda was left to civilian agencies and practiced with caution in peacetime. The fact that the Vietnam War was a defeat, and also the first major war of the television era, led to US military claims (in a manner highly reminiscent of the German "stab in the back" myth of 1918) that the country had fallen victim to an enemy propaganda or psychological warfare campaign that had undermined political support for the war. Psychological warfare remained part of Soviet military thought and practice as an aspect of *maskirovka*, and also an important part of Maoist revolutionary war and other forms of insurgency warfare.

Military psychological operations enjoyed a revival in the United States in the mid-1980s under President Ronald Reagan (1911–2004), who saw ideological issues as an important part of the increasing confrontation with the Soviet Union that became known as the "new Cold War" (1979–1985). In the aftermath of the collapse of the Soviet Union in 1990–1991, many Russians complained (also in a manner reminiscent of the German "stab in the back" myth) that they had been victims of an American and western propaganda campaign which had pushed them into a spiraling arms race and eventually bankrupted their economy. In this period, US psychological operations forces underwent considerable expansion, including the addition of aircraft that could transmit television as well as radio broadcasts down into enemy territory. At the same time, the military definition of psychological operations was expanded to the point that it included almost any provision of information by the military, including signposts for shelters during disaster relief or warnings of minefields.

This trend for the definition of psychological operations to expand into areas other than propaganda directed at an enemy further increased after the Gulf War, as a reflection both that psychological operations had played a major part in the Coalition victory and that computerization and electronic networking could provide a considerable military advantage to the side that could develop them as weapons of war, to be known altogether as "information warfare." Although electronic warfare dated back in primitive forms at least to the US Civil War and had been prominent in World War II, this view represented the military version of the belief that a computer information revolution was transforming the world. In 1996, electronic warfare, including the use of computers and space-based systems, was made the center of a new US armed forces concept, "information operations," which also included psychological operations. Although military relations with the news media were notionally excluded from this new concept, they were envisaged as part of the same overarching activity, the objective of which was to defeat the enemy by controlling their access to information in every sense and by every means imaginable.

These developments increasingly eroded the distinctions previously observed by the US government and military between propaganda and media relations, between domestic and overseas audiences, and between psychological warfare activities appropriate to war or peace. In late 2001, after the 9/11 terrorist attacks, the United States announced a Global War on Terror, and as part of this launched a short-lived Office of Strategic Influence, which was closed within a year amid accusations that among its functions was the promotion of propaganda within the United States; instead, an Office of Global Communications was created and operated within the White House from 2003 to 2005. Successive US governments also saw psychological opera-

tions as fundamental to an information strategy as part of the continuing War on Terror, although its importance as a war was progressively downgraded up to 2010.

Psychological operations played an important part in the US-led invasion of Iraq (2003), including the identification of "regime targets" in Iraq such as statues, palaces, and other symbols of government authority, to be captured or destroyed with the maximum attendant publicity. But as the United States' military involvement in Iraq continued, criticisms were increasingly made that the institutions and methods being used, including psychological operations, were not appropriate to a democracy even when at war. In 2006, the United States sought to implement a new counterinsurgency approach in Iraq. But the controversies associated both with information operations and with the relationship between psychological warfare and the news media continued to cause increasing problems, leading to a new US psychological operations doctrine being issued in 2010, the same year that the United States proclaimed the withdrawal of its combat forces from Iraq. The introduction, in 2008, of a counterinsurgency strategy in the continuing war in Afghanistan by the United States, in association with the United Kingdom and other countries, caused similar problems with both the meaning and the implementation of psychological operations.

SEE ALSO: Gulf Wars (1990–1991, 2003–Present); Korean War (1949–1953); Spanish Civil War (1936–1939); Terrorism, War Against; Vietnam War (1959–1975); War Propaganda; World War I: Eastern Front; World War I: Southern Front; World War I: Western Front; World War II: Eastern Front; World War II: War in Asia.

References

Fuller, J. F. C. (1920) *Tanks in the Great War, 1914–1918.* New York: E. P. Dutton.

Jowett, G. and O'Donnell, V. (1992) *Propaganda and Persuasion.* London: Sage.

Further Reading

Armstrong, L. (Ed.) (2004) *Information Operations.* Washington, DC. Brassey's.

Cull, N. J. (2009) *The Cold War and the United States Information Agency*. Cambridge: Cambridge University Press.

Dougherty, W. and Janowitz, M. (1958) *A Psychological Warfare Casebook*. Baltimore: Johns Hopkins University Press.

Garnett, D. (2002) *The Secret History of PWE*. London: St. Ermin's Press.

Lerner, D. (1949) *Sykewar*. New York: George W. Stewart.

Nelson, M. (1997) *War of the Black Heavens*. London: Brassey's.

Roetter, C. (1974) *Psychological Warfare*. London: Batsford.

Taylor, P. M. (1995) *Munitions of the Mind*. Manchester: Manchester University Press.

R

Russian Civil War (1917–1920)

DAVID R. STONE

The Russian Civil War was a war among Russia's competing political movements for control of the country in the aftermath of World War I, ending in the victory of Vladimir Lenin's Bolshevik Party and their supporters (the Reds) over a coalition of military officers, nobles, and others opposed to Bolshevik rule (the Whites).

Faced with a growing domestic crisis provoked by urban food shortages and mismanagement of World War I, the government of Russia's Tsar Nicholas II collapsed in March 1917 and was replaced by dual power, an uneasy balance between a Provisional Government, recognized by Russia's western allies and made up of members of the pre-revolutionary Russian legislature on one hand, and on the other hand a nationwide network of soviets or councils, collective bodies of workers, soldiers, or peasants who enjoyed popular legitimacy without formal legal authority. In this unstable situation various political movements struggled for power; among those, Lenin's Bolsheviks, the more radical wing of Russian Marxism, stood out by their uncompromising rejection of continued Russian participation in World War I and their refusal,

unlike other left-wing parties, to cooperate with or join the Provisional Government. As economic collapse continued over the course of 1917 and social polarization grew, increasing numbers of workers and soldiers gravitated to the Bolsheviks as the most radical alternative available to them, one untainted by the Provisional Government's failures. By November 1917, having obtained majorities in a number of key urban soviets, Lenin's ally Leon Trotsky launched a classic *coup d'état* in the capital Petrograd (St Petersburg's wartime name), overthrowing the Provisional Government and seizing power in the name of Russia's soviets. Victory in Petrograd was quickly followed by similar seizures of power in cities throughout Russia as the revolution spread by rail and telegraph. Lenin proclaimed a new government for Russia, the Council of People's Commissars, with all posts held by Bolsheviks and their allies from the Left Socialist Revolutionaries, a radical pro-peasant party.

The Bolshevik takeover required violence. As yet the Bolsheviks did not muster real armed forces of their own, relying instead on sympathetic units from the tsarist military, particularly the Latvian Rifles, and improvised worker militias called Red Guards. The initial takeover in Petrograd involved relatively little loss of life, but Red Guards had to hold off an attempt by General Peter Krasnov to retake the city with loyal

Twentieth-Century War and Conflict: A Concise Encyclopedia, First Edition. Edited by Gordon Martel.
© 2015 John Wiley & Sons, Ltd. Published 2015 by John Wiley & Sons, Ltd.

Cossacks, the cavalry from Russia's southern borderlands which the regime had relied on for centuries for skirmishing, policing, and riot control. In Moscow, Bolshevik victory required several days of bloody street fighting against military cadets and other opposition.

The Bolshevik coup, commonly referred to as the October Revolution, did not end political conflict, for bitter and long-standing divides within Russian society had not been erased but only exacerbated by Lenin's takeover. Over half the population of the Russian Empire was ethnically non-Russian and took advantage of the breakdown of control in the center to secede. Within ethnically Russian territory, deep splits between conservative elites, moderately liberal parties like the Constitutional Democrats, and radical workers and peasants offered little common ground for compromise. Even within the left, the pro-peasant Right Socialist Revolutionaries saw little common ground with Lenin's Marxist industrial socialism. Even within Marxism, the more moderate Mensheviks resented the dictatorial approach of Lenin's Bolsheviks; leftists of all stripes had generally presumed that any revolutionary government would take the form of a broad coalition of socialist parties. Lenin wanted no part of real power sharing, and the result was a tense and complicated political environment in the midst of ongoing world war.

Russia then began a slide into full-scale civil war. The Bolsheviks rejected an effort by Russia's railway workers' union to broker a settlement with other left-wing parties. Those parties placed their hopes in the impending meeting of a freely elected Constituent Assembly to write a new constitution for Russia and believed that it would force the Bolsheviks into compromise. Elections for the Constituent Assembly, held roughly at the time of the Bolshevik seizure of power, illustrated the political conundrum. The Right Socialist Revolutionaries, drawing on their strength among the peasantry, won a plurality of votes, roughly 40 percent of the total. The Bolsheviks, by contrast, did much better in cities and military units and scored 25 percent of the overall vote. Lenin refused to let what he saw as the irrelevant views of backward peasants derail his revolution. He allowed the Constituent Assembly to meet only once in January 1918 before forcibly dissolving it. At the same time, those on Russia's right wing knew they could not compete in electoral politics given the overwhelmingly leftist sentiments of workers, peasants, and soldiers. They turned instead to organizing armed resistance to the Bolsheviks. As the tsarist army disintegrated, with peasant soldiers walking home from the front lines, many conservative military officers headed south to a nascent counter-revolutionary movement, the first signs of the White armies, in Cossack territory on the Don River. Sheltered by tsarist general Aleksei Kaledin's newly established Cossack state, White forces began to coalesce. An improvised Bolshevik expedition under Vladimir Antonov-Ovseenko in late 1917 succeeded in temporarily dispelling this threat and bringing the Don region under control. Kaledin committed suicide and the White movement barely survived the winter of 1917–1918.

Bolshevik hopes for quick victory were, however, premature. In particular, Lenin's government was still technically at war with Germany. The German high command expected to gather the fruits of victory from the total collapse of Russia's war effort in 1917, including detaching Ukraine from Russia and making it a German puppet state. Lenin and the Bolshevik leadership, still hoping for Europe-wide revolution to rescue them from giving away land and population to Germany, attempted to draw out the peace talks at Brest-Litovsk as long as possible. When German patience ran out and the Bolsheviks were presented with an ultimatum, Trotsky, now acting as the Bolsheviks' commissar for foreign affairs, declared "no war, no peace," and walked out of negotiations in February 1918. The German response was simply to resume advancing into Russian territory with no tsarist army left to resist them. Faced with imminent destruction, Lenin had no choice but to accept a dictated peace. In the Treaty of Brest-Litovsk of March 3, 1918, Lenin surrendered to German control territory in the Baltics, Belorussia, and Ukraine. A large part of Lenin's own party was opposed to these concessions, and the Left Socialist Revolutionaries abandoned their alliance with the Bolsheviks altogether, leaving the Bolsheviks alone against all other political movements in Russia. The German takeover of Ukraine and establishment of a puppet government there also provided welcome respite for anti-Bolshevik Cossacks and Whites in the south, who benefited from weapons transferred from the Germans. With the Cossack resurgence, over the summer and fall of 1918 fighting raged as the Whites attempted to seize from the Bolsheviks the key Volga River town of Tsaritsyn (later renamed Stalingrad, then Volgograd).

The Treaty of Brest-Litovsk also ensured the hostility of Russia's former allies. German assistance and money had enabled Lenin to return to Russia and seize power; when Lenin then took Russia out of the war and ceded enormous territories to Germany, this made him appear to be an evident German agent. Large stocks of Allied war material were still in Russian hands, and so Britain, France, and the United States began moving toward open opposition and finally military intervention against Lenin's new regime. Small parties of Allied soldiers occupied Russian ports in early 1918 to prevent military goods from being transferred to Germany and to prop up local resistance to the Bolsheviks. Their number grew steadily over 1918 and into 1919.

This growing opposition led the Bolsheviks to convert their slapdash partisans and worker militias into a real army. Trotsky gave up his role managing foreign affairs and took over as people's commissar of military affairs, that is, head of the Red Army, in March 1918, imposing discipline and centralized control on Bolshevik soldiers. At least initially, Trotsky could rely on the very real German threat to attract soldiers and, more importantly, trained tsarist officers into the Red Army. Once enlisted to fight Germans, however, many of these men found themselves sent to fight fellow Russians. When voluntary recruitment did not produce the necessary results, Trotsky turned to conscription of former tsarist officers to run his new force. These "military specialists" were often indifferent or hostile to the Bolshevik cause, and Trotsky employed commissars, party activists charged with monitoring commanders for any hint of disloyalty, to guarantee their service. Though this institution had been introduced by the Provisional Government, it became a characteristic aspect of Bolshevik military policy.

Matters became still worse for the Bolsheviks in May 1918. They had inherited from World War I hundreds of thousands of prisoners of war, many of them non-Germans from the multinational Austro-Hungarian army with little enthusiasm for the German-dominated Central Powers. Under the tsar, a substantial number of Czech and Slovak

prisoners had been organized into the Czech Legion, intended to fight on the Allied side for the liberation of their homeland from Austrian rule. When Lenin took Russia out of the war against Germany, the Czech Legion found itself without a role. After tortuous negotiations, the Legion agreed to leave Russia by traveling east across the Trans-Siberian Railway, then heading by ship from Vladivostok to Europe to continue the fight against Germany on the Western Front. This remarkable odyssey was interrupted in May 1918 by a clash between local Bolshevik authorities and the Legion en route across Siberia. The 40,000 soldiers of the Legion then mutinied, seizing control of the railroad and with it all access to the vast region of Siberia. The bulk of Russian territory, albeit mostly sparsely populated Siberian wilderness, was lost to Bolshevik control at a stroke. This created a space in which Siberian opposition to the Bolsheviks, ranging from military officers to moderate socialists, could organize further resistance to Lenin. It also eased Allied intervention, since the Legion represented a large and well-trained force already in control in key territories.

New anti-Bolshevik regimes quickly organized their own armies and waged a see-saw struggle with the Reds for control of the industrial cities of the Ural mountains and the Volga River basin. The Whites of Siberia were notably fractious, however, as the range of viewpoints among them prevented effective unity. Initially, the Czechs and the western allies engineered the creation of a unified government under the title of the Directory, with its capital at Omsk, but the Directory was overthrown in November 1918 by a military coup which set up tsarist Admiral Aleksandr Kolchak as head of the Whites in Siberia.

Even inside central Russia, where the Bolsheviks never lost control, they faced repeated uprisings by their political opposition. The Socialist Revolutionary Boris Savinkov engineered a July 1918 uprising in Yaroslavl. At the same time in Moscow, the Bolsheviks' former allies, the Left Socialist Revolutionaries, assassinated the German ambassador in hopes of restarting the war with Germany. Though their attempt to seize control of Moscow failed, a later assassination attempt on Lenin himself at the end of August 1918 led to a massive Bolshevik crackdown on all political opponents and the execution of thousands of conservatives, liberals, Mensheviks, and

Socialist Revolutionaries in a Red Terror. The town of Izhevsk, a major armaments production center, also rebelled against Bolshevik rule in August 1918.

From the summer of 1918 through the spring of 1919, the contending forces in the ongoing Civil War became increasingly clear. The Bolsheviks consolidated their authority in central Russia and used its large population to build a substantial army. German defeat in World War I in November 1918 removed one key player in the conflict as German troops headed for home. Ukraine plunged into anarchy as the German puppet government, the Hetmanate under Pavlo Skoropadskyi, collapsed. Three chief centers of White resistance emerged around the periphery of Bolshevik territory, along with a number of smaller movements less threatening to the Bolsheviks. In Siberia, Kolchak's regime controlled enormous territories, but the sparsely populated region provided little support to match the resources available to the Bolsheviks. In southern Russia and the northern Caucasus, another White movement, under Anton Denikin, accumulated a large number of former tsarist officers and enjoyed substantial western support. Finally, a smaller White force, under Nikolai Iudenich, based in the Baltics, threatened Petrograd. Little tied those three White armies together, or the White movement as a whole, beyond hostility to the Bolsheviks. The social nature of the White leadership – made up of the old officer corps and largely noble – alienated workers and peasants. The White slogan of "Russia, one and indivisible" likewise alarmed the non-Russian populations of the empire's periphery where White forces were based. The Romanov Dynasty offered little as a political program; even before the execution of deposed tsar Nicholas II by the Bolsheviks in July 1918, monarchism was exhausted as a political force.

Lenin's Bolsheviks, by contrast, enjoyed in Lenin a leader whose position at the head of the party was unquestioned. Though groups within the party opposed Lenin on various points of policy, none opposed his absolutely central role. Only Trotsky, with his charisma and position as head of the Red Army, might have challenged Lenin, but he never displayed any inclination to do that. By comparison to the fractious Whites, the Bolsheviks' very real internecine struggles were

relatively insignificant. Lenin and his party devised a system by which the Bolsheviks' ruling Central Committee set policy that was implemented by the governing Council of People's Commissars – often with the same men serving simultaneously in both bodies. This enabled one-party rule, but provided some illusion of popular control through the system of soviets. Lenin also made tactical concessions to the peasantry, endorsing land seizures and the strengthening of village communes, though those lay far outside orthodox Marxist attitudes. This provided an important edge in the contest with the Whites for peasant loyalty, though the Bolsheviks continually strained this relationship by forcible requisitioning of grain from the peasants in order to feed the Red Army and their power base in the cities.

Despite their political differences, both the Reds and the Whites were forced by Russia's social chaos and economic collapse into very similar policies. Neither side could wholly rely on peasant sympathy, but building armies required conscripting unwilling peasants in massive numbers. The result was an epidemic of desertion, with peasants fleeing the ranks of Red and White armies almost as quickly as they could be put into uniform. Russia's cities depopulated as its industrial economy collapsed and food supplies dwindled, while Russia's old middle classes found themselves suddenly impoverished.

The fighting that settled the outcome of the Civil War began in earnest in the summer of 1918 and continued through the early autumn of 1919. The Whites' disunity – socially, politically, and militarily – gave the Bolsheviks a crucial advantage in the struggle for power. The decisive clashes began in the east. In late 1918, the Bolshevik Reds and the Whites struggled for control of the industrial cities between the Volga River and the Ural mountains to the east. Admiral Kolchak, drawing on supplies from the allies and marshaling what soldiers he could from thinly populated Siberia, launched an offensive in March 1919 that cracked Bolshevik defenses and advanced rapidly to the west. By the end of April, Kolchak's troops were near the Volga River. Though he had succeeded in cutting the link between Lenin's government in Moscow and Bolshevik-held cities in central Asia, Kolchak faced an insoluble strategic dilemma. He lacked the mass of soldiers necessary to sustain his offensive to victory, whether by attempting to link up with Whites in the Russian far north, pushing hundreds of miles further west to Moscow, or by driving southwest to link up with Denikin's forces in the North Caucasus. His supply lines were thinly stretched even as the Reds fell back on their own sources of supplies and manpower. At the end of April, the professional revolutionary Mikhail Frunze, though devoid of real military experience, organized a devastating counter-attack in the far south that smashed through Kolchak's exhausted forces and compelled rapid retreat through the territory the Whites had just conquered.

This victory unleashed an immediate dispute within the Red high command over the proper course of action: pursue and finish Kolchak, or send scarce troops to defend against a rapidly developing new threat – a push from southern Russia by Denikin's White armies aimed at Moscow. Trotsky, along with the Red Army's commander in chief Ioakim Vatsetis, argued for the greater danger from Denikin, given that Kolchak was a spent force. This dispute was resolved only in June, when Vatsetis was dismissed and replaced by S. S. Kamenev, former commander of the Eastern Front against Kolchak. Frunze then rose to fill Kamenev's former position.

Despite Trotsky and Vatsetis's political defeat, their position was proven at least partially correct by the crisis that quickly emerged as Denikin's much more dangerous offensive moved steadily north. Beginning in earnest in May 1919, after Denikin had consolidated his control in the south following the disintegration of the Don Cossacks as an independent force, the White armies rapidly pushed north. The major cities of Khar'kov and Tsaritsyn fell in June, and Denikin continued to drive on Moscow. By the end of September, Denikin had taken Kursk and Voronezh, and in mid-October his troops had reached Orel, only 200 miles from Moscow. Just as the crisis was at its height, another White force under N. N. Iudenich attempted to take Petrograd, pushing east from the Baltics into the city's eastern suburbs.

In both cases, though, the small size of White forces told against them. Though White armies were capable of skillful fighting, overmanned as they were with veteran officers of World War I, greater peasant and working-class hostility toward the Whites, along with the more limited population base in the regions under their control, meant that their armies were much smaller than the Red forces they faced. Attrition and Russia's enormous interior spaces drained White armies of resilience and striking power. Both Denikin and Iudenich stalled well short of victory, and with the loss of momentum their seeming triumphs quickly became ignominious retreat. The remnants of Iudenich's force fled into the Baltic states, and Denikin's Whites withdrew under relentless pressure from Red cavalry into southern Russia and the Crimea. The Reds recaptured Ukraine's major cities in late December. In late March 1920, Denikin's remaining forces were pushed into the Black Sea at Novorossiisk, leaving only the Crimean Peninsula as the final refuge of organized White resistance.

Other centers had collapsed. The White enclave in Russia's far north crumbled when the allies realized that resistance to the Reds was a lost cause. Kolchak's White Siberia was also disintegrating. Even as Denikin neared Moscow in his final offensive, the Reds' rapid pursuit of Kolchak continued in the east. By the end of July 1919, the Reds had passed through the Ural mountains into western Siberia. Lacking substantial mountain ranges or defensible river barriers to help them, Kolchak's troops found any effort to stem the Red tide to be hopeless. Any stand was quickly overrun or outflanked, and only the enormous spaces of Siberia delayed Red victory. Kolchak and members of his regime fled east in an effort to escape, but he was arrested in Irkutsk by the soldiers of the Czech Legion and shot by local Bolsheviks the next month. The pursuing Reds reestablished control over much of Siberia and settled into an uneasy truce with the Japanese and American forces who had occupied the Russian far east. To prevent the outbreak of further conflict when the Civil War was not yet complete, the Bolsheviks created a buffer state, the Far Eastern Republic, until the last Japanese forces finally left Russian territory in autumn 1922.

A final reckoning with the White forces in the Crimea, now commanded by Baron Peter Wrangel in place of the defeated and disgraced Denikin, was delayed by the outbreak of the Russo-Polish War. Once the chance of an actual White victory had passed, with its danger of restoration of the Russian Empire, the newly created Polish state attacked east in spring 1920 to bring as much as possible of the Polish–Russian borderlands in Belorussia and Ukraine under its control. This Russo-Polish War pulled manpower and supplies temporarily away from the Red fight against Wrangel. Though the war ended in serious defeat for the Reds in August and September 1920, Wrangel's available manpower and territory in Ukraine were too limited to maintain long-term resistance to Red pressure. In early November 1920, the Red Army under Frunze smashed through the narrow land bridge that connected the Crimea to the mainland, and eliminated all remaining White resistance in little more than a week. Wrangel and his surviving soldiers evacuated by ship to join a substantial Russian émigré population in Europe, comprising conservatives and socialists but united by their forced exile as enemies of the Bolsheviks.

With Wrangel's defeat, the last major White army was gone, but small-scale fighting continued for several years. Most dangerous was an ongoing rural insurgency by peasants driven to violence by the Bolsheviks' forcible requisitioning of grain and conscripts from the countryside. The Bolsheviks crushed this mercilessly; in the particular case of the massive peasant rebellion in the Tambov region, Red troops under Mikhail Tukhachevskii employed poison gas to clear rural insurgent groups from forests. In an effort to alleviate peasant discontent, the New Economic Policy, introduced by Lenin in spring 1921, replaced forcible seizures of grain with a more moderate tax-in-kind and succeeded in grudgingly reconciling peasants to the new regime. Scattered rural violence, what the Bolsheviks termed "banditism," continued well into the 1920s. In March 1921, sailors at the major naval base of Kronstadt, near Petrograd, rebelled against what they saw as the Bolsheviks' dictatorial message, and the base had to be retaken by storm. In Ukraine, Denikin and then Wrangel's defeat allowed the systematic reimposition of Bolshevik control as peasant rebels and local warlords were brought under control. In central Asia, rural Muslims sustained an ongoing insurgency while urban centers, dominated by Russian industrial workers, remained in Bolshevik hands throughout the Civil War. Bolsheviks in central Asia were cut off from Moscow for most of the war, but Kolchak's defeat in late 1919 reopened communications. Skirmishing with remaining

traditionalist Muslim partisans, the basmachi, lasted several more years. A series of whirlwind campaigns in 1920 and 1921 brought the regions of the Caucasus back under Moscow's control. Only on the western frontier, where Poland, Finland, and the Baltic states established effective governments and enjoyed western support, did the Bolsheviks fail to regain large territories that had been part of the Russian Empire.

Combat in the Civil War had several peculiarities that marked it as quite distinct from World War I, which preceded it, and the interwar developments that followed. Russia's economic and political collapse meant that combat was in many ways more primitive than on World War I's Eastern Front. Aviation played little role, and standards of training and professionalism were far lower in the improvised armies of the Reds and Whites. Harsh but inconsistent discipline combined with the unwillingness of peasant conscripts to produce high levels of desertion. Relatively low unit densities in Russia's enormous physical expanse meant that fronts moved with dizzying speed, particularly by comparison to the stagnation of fighting in northern France and Belgium during the world war. Lines were stretched thin, and so, when troops managed to mass enough force to crack an enemy line, demoralized and poorly trained defenders found it difficult to contain a breakthrough, and might retreat hundreds of miles before exhaustion forced an end to pursuit. Given the centrality of railroads to this mobile warfare, armored trains carrying machine guns and artillery became a key weapons system.

The Russian Civil War had important implications for the later history of the Soviet Union. Industrial production collapsed almost completely, and loss of life totaled between seven and eight million people, several times more than Russia lost during World War I. During the Civil War, unlike World War I, famine and disease accounted for most deaths, and so civilians were far more at risk than they had been in 1914–1917. The ruling Bolshevik Party had possessed only 20,000 members at the beginning of 1917, and more than 200,000 by the end of the Civil War. The result was that the formative experience for the bulk of the ruling party was bloody civil war against not only the Bolsheviks' political opposition but also intervening troops from the capitalist world and Russia's own peasantry. This created a residue of bitterness and xenophobia which contributed greatly to Joseph Stalin's subsequent rise to power. The improvised nature of the Civil War also provoked deep divisions within the Red Army over the shape of future war. Revolutionaries who had been forced into soldiering by the needs of the moment emphasized the importance of revolutionary zeal over technical knowledge. Professional soldiers who remained with the Bolsheviks, by contrast, argued – with Trotsky's support –for the continuing relevance of professional military training.

SEE ALSO: Russo-Polish War (1919–1920); World War I: Eastern Front.

Further Reading

Erickson, J. (1962) *The Soviet High Command: A Military–Political History, 1918–1941*. New York: St. Martin's Press.

Lincoln, B. (1989) *Red Victory: A History of the Russian Civil War*. New York: Touchstone.

Mawdsley, E. (1987) *The Russian Civil War*. Boston: Allen and Unwin.

Swain, G. (1996) *The Origins of the Russian Civil War*. New York: Longman.

Trotsky, L. (1979) *How the Revolution Armed*, 5 vols. London: New Park.

White, D. F. (1944) *The Growth of the Red Army*. Princeton: Princeton University Press.

Russo-Finnish War (1939–1940)

MARY ELIZABETH AILES

The Russo-Finnish War, also known as the Winter War, began on November 30, 1939, when Soviet forces invaded Finland. Beginning in 1938, the Soviet government pressured Finland to allow it to build a military base on the Finnish coast to guard the maritime approaches to Leningrad. The Soviet leadership feared that Germany would invade the Soviet Union through Finland and that the Finnish military could not withstand such an attack. The Finnish government denied this request. It believed that such an action would make it difficult for Finland to resist further Soviet expansion in the future. Throughout 1938 and 1939, the Soviet government continued to make

territorial demands of Finland. The signing of the Nazi–Soviet Non-Aggression Pact in August 1939 led the Soviet government to increase its diplomatic pressure upon Finland as it believed that Germany would not react to a Soviet invasion of its western neighbor.

On November 26, 1939, the Soviets broke off negotiations after alleging an artillery attack along the Finnish–Russian border. The war began on November 30, 1939, when the Soviets launched an invasion into Finland along the entire Finnish–Russian border from Petsamo on the Arctic coast to the Karelian Isthmus in the south.

The Russians advanced on all fronts with tank units followed by infantry regiments. Additionally, the Russian air force began a bombing campaign of Finland's major cities, including Helsinki and Viipuri. Despite possessing a vast numerical superiority in terms of troops and equipment, the Soviets experienced significant difficulties during the invasion's initial stages. Because the Soviet military leaders expected their troops to overrun Finland quickly, Soviet troops wore light-weight uniforms. Additionally, they had insufficient supplies, and no medical staff or field hospitals. The lack of winter gear and supplies became problematic as deep snow blanketed the ground and temperatures constantly fell below zero degrees Fahrenheit. The Soviet commanders' miscalculation was very costly as many soldiers suffered from frostbite and the wounded froze to death where they fell. The weather also created problems with equipment as Soviet tanks experienced difficulties running in the subzero weather. Adding to the Soviet military's problems was a lack of experienced leadership. Earlier in the 1930s, Stalin had purged much of the officer corps. The Soviet military had an inexperienced officer corps that was controlled by political commissars whose objectives were to forward the state's political agenda.

Despite being vastly outnumbered, the Finns successfully repelled the Soviets' initial attacks. In the Karelian Isthmus, they successfully defended the string of fortifications known as the Mannerheim Line. Further north, they made effective use of guerrilla tactics. Working in small groups, the Finns skied around the Soviet forces and attacked the rear and flanks of Soviet columns in order to split the Soviet forces into small groups that could be more easily destroyed. Using such tactics, the Finns destroyed two Soviet divisions at the Battle of Suomussalmi. The Finns also developed ways to destroy Soviet tanks. Anti-tank units would shove logs into the tank tracks, causing them to derail. When the tank crew emerged to fix the problem, snipers would shoot them. The anti-tank units also became adept at using Molotov cocktails, which they tossed into tank air intakes or hatches.

These defeats caused the Soviet leadership to reevaluate its military organization and to commit greater forces to winning the war. The military was reorganized under the leadership of General Semyon K. Timoshenko, who launched a new offensive on February 1, 1940. This invasion concentrated on the Karelian Isthmus, and was supported by numerous aerial bombardments. With the Soviet forces being concentrated exclusively within the peninsula, their numerical superiority over the Finns became a significant advantage. While the Finns initially repelled the Soviet attack, they did not have the manpower, equipment, or ammunition to outlast the invasion. On February 11, 1940, Soviet forces broke through the Mannerheim Line. Throughout the rest of February and into March, the Finnish forces were in retreat.

The Finns entered into negotiations with the Soviets in early March and signed the Peace of Moscow on March 12, 1940. According to the treaty, the Finns relinquished the Karelian Isthmus including the country's second largest city, Viipuri, territory on the western shore of Lake Ladoga, the Arctic port of Petsamo, and some islands in the Gulf of Finland. Additionally, the Finns leased the Hanko Peninsula southwest of Helsinki to the Soviet Union for 30 years. These areas consisted of 22,000 square miles of land, and were home to about one-eighth of Finland's population. The Finns who lived in these territories were resettled within the new borders of Finland.

The Russo-Finnish War held great significance for both Finland and the Soviet Union. For the Soviet Union, its difficulties during the Finnish campaigns pointed out its military deficiencies, which were partly remedied either during or shortly after the war. The Soviets' difficulties also shaped foreign opinion of the state's military capabilities. In particular, the Germans believed that the Soviet Union was very weak militarily and their observations of the Russo-Finnish War shaped Hitler's decision to invade the Soviet Union in 1941. For Finland, the Russo-Finnish War would not end its conflicts with the Soviet Union, as it would become an ally of Germany in 1941 and fight another war, known as the Continuation War, against the Soviet Union between 1941 and 1944. The Russo-Finnish War unified the Finnish population in its determination to maintain its independence. The legacy of this war would continue to shape Finnish–Soviet relations throughout the rest of the twentieth century.

SEE ALSO: World War II: Eastern Front.

Further Reading

Edwards, R. (2008) *The Winter War: Russia's Invasion of Finland, 1939–1940*. New York: Pegasus Books.

Engle, E. and Paananen, L. (1973) *The Winter War: The Soviet Attack on Finland 1939–1940*. Harrisburg, PA: Stackpole Books.

Van Dyke, C. (1997) *The Soviet Invasion of Finland, 1939–40*. New York: Routledge.

Vehvilaínen, O. (2002) *Finland in the Second World War: Between Germany and Russia*. New York: Palgrave.

Russo-Japanese War (1904–1905)

DAVID SCHIMMELPENNINCK VAN DER OYE

This was a major war in Manchuria and the surrounding waters, fought for dominance in Northeast Asia. Although Japan was unable decisively to defeat Russia on land, its naval victories, together with revolutionary unrest in Russia, enabled the island empire to prevail. Japan's victory marked the first significant defeat of a leading European power by a non-European in the modern age.

The conflict's origins lie in the decline of imperial China, which whetted the territorial appetites of more vigorous powers. Russia had already prized large swaths of land on the Amur and Ussuri rivers from the Middle Kingdom in 1860 and considered the rest of Manchuria an area of interest. Japan's easy victory in the Sino-Japanese

War (1894–1895), however, encouraged that nation's expansive designs as well. Russian diplomatic pressure during the peace talks at Shimonoseki in 1895, which forced Japan to retrocede to China the Liaodong Peninsula with its naval base of Port Arthur at the southern tip, thoroughly aggravated its rival. Tensions were hardly eased by Russia's occupation of the same naval base two years later. A clash might nevertheless have been averted had St Petersburg responded to Tokyo's repeated efforts to negotiate respective spheres of influence in the region. However, the former's endless prevarications ultimately convinced Japan to go to war by early 1904.

Japan's armed forces enjoyed a numerical advantage over Russia in the Northeast Asian theater on the eve of the confrontation. Its German-trained army mobilized 375,000 men well equipped with modern Arisaka rifles (based on the German Mauser) and 1,140 guns, including 4.6-inch Krupp howitzers. Facing them in Manchuria and Siberia were 98,000 soldiers and 272 guns, supplemented by 24,000 railway guards. Furthermore, whereas Japan fielded its best troops in the campaign, Russia considered its Far East to be a colonial posting and manned it accordingly. With seven battleships and six armored cruisers at its Port Arthur headquarters and another four cruisers based at Vladivostok, Russia's Pacific Fleet slightly outnumbered the Japanese navy in heavy warships. However, the latter was more modern, better captained, and possessed a larger number of lighter cruisers and torpedo boats. Japanese strategic and tactical military intelligence was also far superior to that of its foe.

Japan's military preponderance in East Asia was only temporary, since the Russian army's total active strength was 1,350,000 men. Most of them were in European Russia and could only be brought to the front on the 8,000-km Trans-Siberian Railway. Not yet complete at the start of the war and with long stretches of single track, it could only transport some 20,000 troops per month. Accordingly, the Japanese strategy was to strike swiftly and boldly to neutralize the enemy fleet. Having gained mastery of the sea, it would land armies both to take Port Arthur and defeat the bulk of Russia's forces on the Manchurian mainland before the numerical balance shifted in the latter's favor. The Russian war plan, which had

last been drawn up in 1903, aimed at defending Port Arthur while concentrating the bulk of its strength at Mukden to the north and waiting until reinforcements from Europe were sufficient to go on the offensive.

Although not unsound, Russia's plan was predicated on two false assumptions: steadiness of purpose and decisive command, neither of which would be forthcoming. Its emperor, Nicholas II, appointed War Minister Aleksei Kuropatkin to be his commander in chief shortly after the war's outbreak. A general of undeniable intellect and integrity, Kuropatkin proved to be notoriously irresolute in the field. Confused lines of authority did not help matters. Kuropatkin was now technically subordinate to Nicholas's viceroy of the Far East, Admiral Evgenii Alekseev, and the two would clash repeatedly about whether priority should be given to the Manchurian interior or Port Arthur.

On February 8, 1904, much as at Pearl Harbor 37 years later (and against China 10 years earlier), the Japanese fleet struck Port Arthur without a formal declaration of war. The assault, by torpedo boats under Vice Admiral Togo Heihachiro's command, caused relatively minor physical damage. But its impact on Russian morale was catastrophic. With the notable exception of Kuropatkin, most tsarist officers thoroughly discounted Japan's fitness for battle and thought it inconceivable the Asians would even contemplate aggression. The shock was compounded by news that another Japanese naval detachment had sunk the Russian cruiser *Variag* at Chemulpo (now Inchon) near Seoul the following day and was busy landing troops on Korean soil.

Spirits at Port Arthur were temporarily lifted when the energetic Vice Admiral Stepan Makarov arrived to take command of the Pacific Squadron. The boost proved short-lived, for on April 13 a mine sunk the admiral's flagship, *Petropavlovsk*, drowning him and most of his crew. Russian captains lapsed into timid passivity and effectively yielded the initiative to their foe. Aside from a few ineffectual sorties and the disastrous Battle of the Yellow Sea on August 10, the Russian navy remained *hors de combat* until the arrival of Rear Admiral Zinovii Rozhestvenskii's Second Pacific Squadron in May 1905.

With its communications to the mainland secure, Japan moved quickly to build up its forces in Manchuria and Korea. Kuropatkin focused entirely on Manchuria's defense, essentially giving the Japanese a free hand in the Hermit Kingdom. The first clash on land came in late April at the mouth of the Yalu River on the Korean–Manchurian border as three divisions under General Kuroki Tametomo advanced against a force roughly half that size led by Lieutenant General Mikhail Zasulich (brother of the former terrorist, Vera). If Kuroki employed reconnaissance, camouflage, and deception to great effect, the Russians neglected even the basic step of hiding their guns. Meanwhile, Zasulich had contradictory orders: Kuropatkin called for a delaying action, while Alekseev insisted that he stop the enemy at all costs. In the event, Zasulich accomplished neither. As their howitzers easily silenced the Russian guns, the Japanese attacked at dawn on May 1, and by the afternoon had succeeded in driving Zasulich's men from the river's left bank.

In the wake of the Battle of the Yalu the land war eventually split into two separate operations: the siege of Port Arthur and the Manchurian campaign. Although Admiral Alekseev decamped for Mukden (Shenyang) some 400 km to the north shortly after the battle, the naval base remained a vital strategic objective. General Oku Yasukata speedily landed his Second Army on the Liaodong Peninsula to the north with orders to isolate the port. Oku achieved his goal on May 26 by capturing the Nanshan Heights, an important defensive feature overlooking the narrow isthmus that separates Port Arthur from the rest of the peninsula. As Oku turned the bulk of his forces back to join the First Army in the Manchurian interior, General Nogi Maresuke's Third Army was now given the task of taking Port Arthur.

Having captured the base once before from the Chinese less than 10 years earlier, Nogi had the right experience. This time he faced a considerably greater challenge. It would take nine months of ferocious combat that cost nearly 100,000 lives and intensive artillery exchanges involving one million shells to convince its commander, Lieutenant General Baron Anatolii Stoessel, to surrender. Even then, his capitulation was premature, and a court martial condemned the timorous baron to death for treason, a sentence subsequently commuted by the tsar. Much like Sevastopol during the Crimean War, Port Arthur's tenacious defense is remembered with pride by Russians. Historians have noted that the siege's real importance lay not in its ultimate success but in the tremendous cost in lives to take a well-defended position, eerily presaging the industrialized carnage in Flanders' fields some 10 years later.

For Kuropatkin, the siege of Port Arthur had been little more than a distraction from his main objective, which was to draw the Japanese up the Liaodong Peninsula into Manchuria until the conditions were right for a counteroffensive, preferably no earlier than autumn. Nevertheless, he reluctantly submitted to Alekseev's badgering to relieve the pressure on his erstwhile headquarters by ordering Lieutenant General Baron Georgii Stackelberg to confront General Oku's Second Army on June 24 at Telissu, 135 km to the north. With superior intelligence, more disciplined lieutenants, and a numerical advantage of 48 battalions to Stackelberg's 32, Oku easily countered by outflanking his foe. It was only because of a providential downpour that the Russian general managed to avoid encirclement and retreat northward.

As the Second Army continued its advance, the newly arrived Fourth Army now joined it. Together they linked up with the First Army in early August near Liaoyang, the last city before the Mukden. Still reluctant to meet the foe, Kuropatkin was once again ordered by Alekseev to go on the offensive in late August. By now Russia's Manchurian Army enjoyed superiority in numbers, with 158,000 troops opposing the 125,000 Japanese under Field Marshal Oyama Iwao's command. Nevertheless, Kuropatkin's faulty military intelligence led him to overestimate his adversary's strength. After less than a week of fighting along a 70-km front, Kuropatkin ordered a retreat to Mukden on September 3. Aside from another indecisive encounter at the Sha River just south of Mukden in mid-October, the opponents stood down for the winter.

The respite brought little relief to the Russians. While fresh troops continued to arrive via the Trans-Siberian Railway, shortly after New Year news of Port Arthur's surrender reached them. There were also ill tidings from the home front. Public opinion had never really supported the distant war and it had little patience for General Kuropatkin's passivity. When troops fired on unarmed workers approaching the tsar's Winter

Palace in St Petersburg on January 22, 1905 ("Bloody Sunday"), revolutionary disturbances erupted throughout the empire over the coming months. The outlook for the Japanese was little better. Despite having chased the Russians nearly 400 km into Manchuria, they were stretching the limits of their manpower and finances. Without a decisive victory, it would be increasingly difficult to carry on.

It was against this gloomy backdrop that Oyama launched an attack on Kuropatkin's forces on February 26, 1905, in what would prove to be the last major battle on land. Its scale was unprecedented in modern warfare: over half a million men faced each other along a 150-km front. The adversaries clashed for nearly two weeks, repeating the dismal pattern of their previous engagements as Kuropatkin's imperfect intelligence and excessive caution once again led him to order a retreat on March 6. The general relinquished his command to the aged General Nikolai Linevich. However, by now both combatants were utterly exhausted and the campaign on land largely came to an end.

The war's most dramatic encounter took place at sea three months later at the Tsushima Straits, the narrowest waterway between Korean and Japanese territory. The Russian admiralty had already ordered Admiral Rozhestvenskii in April 1904 to sail the newly created Second Pacific Squadron on a 5,500-km journey from the Baltic Sea to assist the Pacific Squadron at Port Arthur. Since the base had meanwhile surrendered, Rozhestvenskii proceeded toward Vladivostok, which harbored the Pacific Fleet's remnants. The Japanese proved to be just as adept on sea as they had on land. On May 27, 1905, Admiral Togo confronted the Russians at Tsushima, sinking all but three ships within a few hours in perhaps the twentieth century's most decisive naval engagement.

The Battle of Tsushima effectively ended the Russo-Japanese War. If Russia's morale was shattered, Japan lacked the resources to continue the fighting. Responding to American President Theodore Roosevelt's offer to act as mediator, the adversaries met at Portsmouth, New Hampshire, to negotiate an end to the war. Thanks to the able diplomacy of the chief Russian negotiator, Sergei Witte, the terms were relatively mild: Japan gained control over Korea and the southern half of Sakhalin Island. While St Petersburg agreed to

withdraw its forces from Manchuria, it lost none of its own territory and paid no indemnity.

In the short term, Russia's defeat was disastrous as its public came to equate the military reversal with the Romanov dynasty's shortcomings more generally. Much like after the Crimean debacle half a century earlier, the coming years saw a series of reforms both to liberalize society and to improve the military, although they were not enough to overcome the tremendous stresses of World War I. For Japan, the consequences were arguably worse. Emboldened by its victory, the empire began an increasingly aggressive course in East Asia that ultimately led to Hiroshima and Nagasaki. But the war's significance for the broader sweep of history was even more profound. For the first time in recent memory the white man had been spectacularly beaten at his own game, thereby heralding the beginning of the end of Europe's global hegemony.

Further Reading

Committee of Imperial Defence (1910–1920) *Official History (Naval and Military) of the Russo-Japanese War*, 3 vols. London: HMSO.

Connaughton, R. (1991) *The War of the Rising Sun and the Tumbling Bear*. London: Routledge.

Corbett, J. S. (1994) *Maritime Operations in the Russo-Japanese War, 1904–1905*, 2 vols. Annapolis: Naval Institute Press.

Hamilton, Sir Ian (1905) *A Staff Officer's Scrap-Book during the Russo-Japanese War*, 2 vols. London: Edward Arnold.

Kowner, R. (Ed.) (2007) *Rethinking the Russo-Japanese War, 1904–1905*, 2 vols. Folkestone: Global Oriental.

Kowner, R. (Ed.) (2007) *The Impact of the Russo-Japanese War*. London: Routledge.

Levitskii, N. A. (1936) *Russo-Iaponskaia voina 1904–1905gg [The Russo-Japanese War of 1904–1905]*. Moscow: Gosudarstvennoe voennoe izdatel'stvo.

Menning, B. (1992) *Bayonets Before Bullets: The Imperial Russian Army 1861–1914*. Bloomington: Indiana University Press.

Rossiiskii gosudarstvennyi voenno-istoricheskii arkhiv (2002) *The Russo-Turkish War, 1877–1878*. Woodbridge, CT: Primary Source Microfilm, 168 reels.

Schimmelpenninck van der Oye, D. (2001) *Toward the Rising Sun: Russian Ideologies of Empire and the Path to War with Japan*. DeKalb: Northern Illinois University Press.

Schimmelpenninck van der Oye, D. (2002) "The Russo-Japanese War." In F. Kagan and R. Higham (Eds.), *The Military History of Tsarist Russia*. New York: Palgrave.

Steinberg, J., Menning, B., Schimmelpenninck van der Oye, D, *et al.* (Eds.) (2005–2007) *The Russo-Japanese War in Global Perspective: World War Zero*, 2 vols. Leiden: Brill.

Svechin, A. A. (1910) *Russo-Iaponskaia voina [The Russo-Japanese War]*. Oranienbaum: Izdatel'stvo Ofitserskoi Strelkovoi Shkoli.

Russo-Polish War (1919–1920)

DAVID R. STONE

The Russo-Polish War was unleashed by the end of World War I for control of the eastern European borderlands between Polish and Soviet territory. The war grew out of the collapse of the three empires of eastern Europe at the end of World War I: Russia in 1917, then Germany and Austria-Hungary in 1918. The resulting power vacuum created an opportunity for smaller nations of eastern Europe to create independent states. The new Polish republic emerged from territories and populations previously part of all three empires, with an army cobbled together from multiple sources, including Polish formations of the now-defunct empires, under the leadership of former socialist, now Polish nationalist, Józef Klemens Piłsudski (1867–1935). In Russia, the Bolshevik Party under Lenin seized power in late 1917 and then fought a civil war to establish its own authority over what had been the Russian Empire.

Between territory that was clearly Polish and that which was clearly Russian stretched vast borderlands inhabited by a mixture of peoples, including Lithuanians, Belarusians, Ukrainians, and Jews. Both the Poles and the Soviets strove to solidify their control over this disputed region, leading to spasmodic fighting and intermittent negotiations over 1919. With the Russian Civil War hitting its height in 1919 and drawing Soviet forces to other theaters, Poland was able to extend its control well into present-day Lithuania and Belarus. By spring 1920, with the defeat of most of the Bolsheviks' opponents inside Russia, both sides were preparing for a showdown.

That clash finally came in April 1920 when Piłsudski launched an attack south of the Pripet Marshes into Ukraine, succeeding in capturing Kiev by early May. Mikhail Tukhachevskii, commanding the Soviets' Western Front in Belarus, north of the marshes, saw an opportunity for a counterattack and smashed west toward Warsaw. Soon after, the Soviet Southwestern Front used massed attacks spearheaded by its First Cavalry Army to force Polish withdrawal from Kiev. By mid-summer, Polish forces were in rapid retreat both north and south of the marshes. The Western and Southwestern fronts pushed into Polish territory, but diverged as they advanced; the Western Front headed for Warsaw, while the Southwestern moved towards Lvov. Excited by his successes, Tukhachevskii proclaimed that Soviet troops could carry communist revolution through Poland on to Germany and the rest of Europe, and at the end of July the Soviets created a Polish Provisional Revolutionary Committee made up of Polish communists, expecting an uprising in their favor by Polish peasants and workers. Alarmed at the rapid Soviet advance, the British government warned the Soviets in July 1920 to halt their advance at the Curzon line, named for the British foreign minister. France provided a limited group of military advisors under General Maxime Weygand, including a young Charles de Gaulle. The Poles were disappointed by Weygand's failure to bring any concrete assistance, and ignored his advice. The Soviets likewise ignored the British ultimatum, and pushed on into Poland.

As the Soviets advanced west, their forces became dangerously overstretched. Despite his lengthening supply lines and exhausted troops, Tukhachevskii planned to take Warsaw by sweeping his Western Front around to the north of the city, avoiding a direct attack. This maneuver, however, moved him even further away from the Soviet Southwestern Front, still embroiled in fighting around Lvov. Concerned about Tukhachevskii's overextension, and fearing that the distance between the two Soviet fronts would prevent any mutual support, on August 2, 1920, the Soviets' ruling Politburo ordered the command of the Southwestern Front to send two armies northwest toward Warsaw to assist Tukhachevskii. At this point, Joseph Stalin, military commissar of the Southwestern Front, refused to countersign the necessary orders. Stalin's motivations are unclear; he may have resented the reduced importance of his Southwestern Front and delayed Tukhachevskii's reinforcements in a fit of pique. In any event, the necessary reinforcements remained around Lvov until well after the fight for Warsaw was complete.

The delay turned out to be fateful. While defending Warsaw from Tukhachevskii's attack, Piłsudski massed forces southeast of the city. On August 16, they counterattacked into the gap between the Western and Southwestern fronts, precisely the region intended to be covered by reinforcements from the Southwestern Front, reinforcements which Stalin had blocked. Tukhachevskii's left flank was torn open, and the bulk of his force was threatened with imminent encirclement hundreds of miles inside Polish territory. The Western Front went into disordered retreat. Some units managed to withdraw east to safety; others fled north into German East Prussia and were interned; the Poles captured at least 100,000 Soviet troops.

Peace talks immediately changed their tone when the scope of Polish victory became clear. Polish forces pursued Tukhachevskii through eastern Belarus and managed to take Vilnius but failed to capture Minsk. A ceasefire went into effect in October 1920 and after contentious negotiations the final Treaty of Riga was signed on March 18, 1921, ratifying a Polish–Soviet border that was determined by where fighting stopped, not by any natural or ethnographic boundary.

The war had important consequences for both sides. It ensured the survival of a new Polish state, which had been eliminated from the map of Europe since the end of the 1700s. It enshrined Piłsudski as the central figure in Polish politics until his death in 1935. In the Soviet Union, defeat began to convince the Bolsheviks that world communist revolution was not imminent, and they would have to find some accommodation with capitalist powers. It also created bad blood between Stalin and Tukhachevskii, which persisted until Tukhachevskii was killed in Stalin's purge of the Soviet military in 1937. Polish–Soviet hostility was not resolved by the Peace of Riga, but continued to dominate military and diplomatic thinking for the rest of the interwar period.

SEE ALSO: Russian Civil War (1917–1920); World War I: Eastern Front.

Further Reading

Borzecki, J. (2008) *The Soviet–Polish Peace of 1921 and the Creation of Interwar Europe*. New Haven: Yale University Press.

Davies, N. (1972) *White Eagle, Red Star: The Polish–Soviet War, 1919–1920*. New York: St. Martin's Press.

Fiddick, T. (1973) "The 'Miracle of the Vistula': Soviet Policy versus Red Army Strategy," *Journal of Modern History*, 45 (4): 626–643.

Piłsudski, J. (1972) *Year 1920 and Its Climax: Battle of Warsaw during the Polish–Soviet War, 1919–1920*. New York: Piłsudski Institute.

Ponichtera, R. M. and Stone, D. R. (2002) "The Russo-Polish War." In R. Higham and F. W. Kagan (Eds.), *The Military History of the Soviet Union*. New York: Palgrave.

Zamoyski, A. (2008) *Warsaw 1920: Lenin's Failed Conquest of Europe*. New York: Harper Collins.

Rwandan Genocide

MICHAEL P. INFRANCO

In spring 1994, in the central African country of Rwanda, the Hutu-led government planned and executed the murder of an estimated 800,000 Rwandans in what became the most rapid genocide in human history. The extermination of ethnic Tutsi and moderate Hutu occurred within the span of 100 days, and was carried out in disparate locations from communes to roadblocks, and even inside churches. The roots of the conflict reached back to the colonial period, in which the two major ethnic groups within Rwanda, the Hutu and Tutsi, competed for dominance over the country. When independence came to Rwanda in the early 1960s, the majority Hutu seized power and purged the government of Tutsi. Thereafter, the Tutsi were persecuted sporadically and denied positions in government. The Hutus perceived the Tutsis in a negative, hostile image, in which the latter were depicted as former oppressors with bellicose intentions. The Hutu political elite consciously propagated these negative images of the Tutsi in the media and later directed their extermination. Yet, the genocide must also be viewed within the context of the 1990 war that pitted the Tutsi-based Rwandan Patriotic Front against the Hutu-led government forces. In sum, the history of this human catastrophe was founded in decades of interethnic antagonism and intermittent violence.

The origins of the Hutu–Tutsi ethnic divide remain historically unclear since the groups had lived side by side for many generations, intermarrying along the way. Yet, if ethnicity can be viewed as a social construct (though this has been the subject of scholarly debate), in Rwanda it became the most salient feature of that society. The Tutsis were a Nilo-Saharan people who migrated from the Horn of Africa and over time became associated as the area's aristocracy and ruling caste over the Hutu and Twa peoples. These historical facts, however, were undermined by colonial efforts to depict the Tutsi as lighter-skinned, cultured northerners who brought civilization to central Africa. According to the Hamitic myth, offered up by British colonial agent John Hanning Speke, the Tutsi were a more advanced racial grouping separate from the ordinary and less-civilized Bantu (Hutu) (Melvern 2004: 4). Thus, the Tutsi were really closer to Europeans and Egyptians than sub-Saharan ethnic groups. For the Europeans, the Hamitic myth became the justification for Tutsi rule over the Hutu. In reality, the Hutu were seen as farmers and the Tutsi as cattle grazers. A communal labor system, called *uburetwa*, probably heightened the tension between the groups (Melvern 2004: 4).

The ethnic identity labels became especially hardened during the colonial era. The European powers partitioned most of Africa at the Berlin Conference (1884–1885), in which Rwanda was placed under German control. With military backing from the Bazungu (first the Germans, and then, post-1916, the Belgians), the Tutsis increased their power over the Hutu. Although the Germans were less intrusive than the later Belgians (i.e., ruling more indirectly through the Tutsi mwami or rulers), they helped to reinforce the ethnic divisions. Under colonial rule, the Tutsi chiefs became virtual warlords (Prunier 1995: 25). After World War I, Rwanda became a League of Nations mandate and the territory was put under Belgian supervision, a country that continued the divisive ethnic policies. In the

1930s, the Belgian administration organized a census categorizing the Rwandan population as Hutu, Tutsi, or Twa. Each person received an identity card that demarcated his or her ethnicity. The Belgians initially buoyed Tutsi domination over the country. As independence approached in the late 1950s, however, the Hutu (representing some 85 percent of the population) rose up against Tutsi rule, which led to widespread violence throughout the country. In November 1959, in response to an incident in which a Hutu sub-chief was accosted by several Tutsis, armed Hutu groups plundered and burned Tutsi communities and sporadically killed Tutsi across Rwanda. Belgian authorities were forced to tamp down the hostilities; within a few months, they reversed course and embraced Hutu political ascendancy. As a result of national elections in 1960, the principal Hutu party, Parmehutu, captured over 90 percent of the political offices (Gourevitch 1998: 60). In addition, thousands of Tutsi families were forced off their lands, with many driven out of the country. Under the direction of Rwanda's first president Grégoire Kayibanda, Parmehutu headed the drive for independence (gained in 1962). After 1965, the Hutu from central Rwanda headed up a one-party state that produced tensions not only between Hutu and Tutsi, but also between Hutu factions from the north and central part of the country.

In July 1973, a group of 10 Hutu army officers (from northern Rwanda), who called themselves the Committee for National Peace and Unity, overthrew Hutu leader Kayibanda in a classic military *coup d'état*. The coup was spearheaded by former general Juvenal Habyarimana, who established a veritable one-party state in Rwanda (Gourevitch 1998). During the 1970s and 1980s, Habyarimana was intent on creating stability within the country, but his efforts were impeded by a severe economic recession, endemic rural poverty, and mounting international fiscal obligations. These factors combined with a population explosion (the country's density becoming among the highest in Africa) and competition for resources to create an untenable political environment and a quest for scapegoats. In 1990, the expatriate Rwandan Patriotic Front (RPF), a Tutsi-dominated political and military organization, invaded Rwanda from its bases in Uganda in an attempt to topple Habyarimana's oppressive regime and create a power-sharing government. The RPF was led by Major-General Paul Kagame, a Tutsi from Gitarama, whose family was chased out of Rwanda in the late 1950s. The Hutu extremists perceived any deal with the RPF as treason, believing that only a total victory was acceptable. The RPF invasion triggered a fanatical response from the Hutu extremists. Henceforth, no distinctions were made between RPF guerrillas and the civilian Tutsi population within Rwanda. The Hutu extremist paper *Kangura* (or Wake It Up) spread a virulent anti-Tutsi message imploring Hutu to do their work, which meant to kill Tutsis. The lead militia, the *Interahamwe* ("those who attack together"), was supported by the Hutu extremists (Gourevitch 1998: 93).

By 1993, Habyarimana was under intense international pressure to sign a peace accord with the RPF. On one hand, he dared not antagonize the Hutu extremist leadership, yet he was pressured from abroad to accept the peace deal. Habyarimana eventually signed the Arusha Accords, which established a power-sharing arrangement between the two political factions. The agreement theoretically brought the war to a close, but this was far from the reality on the ground. The Accords addressed the return of Rwanda's Tutsi refugee communities in adjacent states, proposed merging the armed forces of the belligerents, and set up a government in which all political parties could participate. Hutu leaders accused the president of treason. In February 1993, it was reported that Rwanda's Hutu government had created bands of "death squads" whose purpose was to exterminate Tutsi (Melvern 2004: 41). The *Réseau Zéro* (or Zero Network), a militant Hutu extremist group tied in with Habyarimana's clan, was responsible for organizing killing units under the auspices of Hutu public duty. Moreover, the Hutu extremists were ready to sacrifice Habyarimana. On April 6, 1994, the Rwandan president's private jet was mysteriously shot down over Kigali by an unidentified missile. This attack killed the Rwandan president along with his counterpart, Burundi President Cyprien Ntaryamira, and provided the impetus for the Hutu extremists to begin the genocide. The Hutu extremists blamed the Tutsis for the murders. Using both radio and newspapers, they broadcast depictions of Tutsis as *inyenzi*

(or cockroaches) who wanted to destroy the Hutus. Hutu citizens were encouraged to slaughter Tutsi in the streets. The death of Habyarimana signaled a *de facto coup d'état* for the Hutu Power leadership. Leading the way was former colonel Théoneste Bagasora, who after the president's murder chaired a meeting of the so-called "crisis committee" composed of Hutu Power military officers (Gourevitch 1998: 114). By the time the meeting adjourned, the capital Kigali was teeming with presidential guard units, soldiers, and *Interahamwe* units ready to carry out the killings of those who had been placed on lists – both important Tutsis and "accomplice" Hutus. Moderate Hutu were targeted because they supported the Arusha Accords and were amenable to resolving the long-standing conflict. Hence, they were deemed accomplices. Rwanda's Prime Minister Agathe Uwilingiyimana, a moderate Hutu, was assassinated within 24 hours of the downing of the presidential airplane. The genocide had begun.

The United Nations Assistance Mission for Rwanda (UNAMIR) had been sent to Rwanda to oversee the implementation of the Arusha Accords, but the mission had largely failed to stop the violence. The UNAMIR force was given an unclear mandate, there was little political will on the part of the Security Council member states for substantive military action, and the United Nation's (UN) bureaucracy was reluctant to intervene more aggressively in the conflict. As an illustration, UNAMIR Commander Roméo Dallaire had learned of the Hutu genocide plan when in early 1994 a Hutu informer, who maintained contacts in the upper echelons of the Rwandan government, provided UNAMIR with information about the arming of extremist militias. Dallaire also discovered that Hutu militias throughout the country were identifying Tutsis for extermination. He quickly relayed this information to the UN headquarters in New York, but was directed not to take action. In fact, in January 1994, UN headquarters denied a request to raid weapons caches. The UNAMIR commander continued to press for more troops, but his requests were turned down. Rwanda's story became a sad commentary on the miscalculations of the UN hierarchy. Thousands of Tutsi were under the direct protection of UNAMIR before the force was ordered to withdraw. Even as

Dallaire was pleading for more troops, the UN Department of Peacekeeping Operations ordered that UNAMIR "should not, repeat not, extend to participating in possible combat except in self-defense" at a time when the killing of Tutsis was escalating (Powers 2001: 8). In the end, the Security Council elected to withdraw the bulk of the troops, leaving a smaller force behind with substantially less military capability.

In retrospect, the Hutu *génocidaires* had calculated that if they killed a small group of UNAMIR soldiers, the Security Council would remove the force, because the institutional body feared a repeat of the Somalia debacle one year earlier. At the onset of the genocide on April 7, 1994, Rwandan army units confronted and outnumbered a platoon of 10 UN Belgian soldiers. These troops were taken into custody, tortured, and subsequently murdered in what were planned atrocities to scare away the international community. By this time, Rwandan army units, militias, and even Hutus in provincial communes were engaged in the widespread killing of Tutsis. The *Interahamwe* began slaughtering Tutsis at roadblocks, schools, and church sanctuaries. The genocide was also supported by the Rwandan media. In 1993, the *Radio Télévision Libre des Milles Collines* (RTLM) was created by extremist Hutu Ferdinand Nahimana to incite ethnic hatred. Several months prior to the violence, the radio station was airing Hutu "folk songs, slogans, speeches, and inaccurate news reports [that] demonized the Tutsis" (Kressel 1996: 110). During the genocide, RTML directed militias to specific locations, in which innocent Tutsis were exterminated.

While the genocide was ongoing, the RPF had made steady military progress in taking control of Rwanda. In the first week of July 1994, the RPF seized the capital Kigali; however, most remnants of the outgoing genocide government had fled with the national treasury into eastern Zaire (now Congo). Approximately two million people fled Rwanda at the insistence of the RTLM, which claimed that the RPF would murder all Hutus who were still left in the country. In the meantime, RPF forces had been driving into the northwestern heartland of the former Hutu extremists. By July 13, the city of Ruhengeri was under RPF control. This incident sparked the mass exodus of about half a million Hutus

into Zaire. The Hutu killers were among the refugees. The situation in Zaire had begun to deteriorate quickly as thousands of Rwandans were huddled in refugee camps. The camps were set up near Goma. Within a short time cholera had spread throughout the population due to the unsafe sanitary conditions. Estimates suggest that up to 3,000 refugees were dying each day. News coverage told of the plight of the exiled Hutus in the camps, but little was done to apprehend the actual genocide killers who were running and terrorizing the refugees. International relief agencies were dumping tons of food shipments into eastern Zaire with little aid going into Rwanda, the country that had been devastated by four years of war and genocide. The presence of Hutu extremists in eastern Zaire marked the beginning of years of conflict in the border region.

In sum, the genocide was carried out with extraordinary speed, which seemed to imply that it was planned and coordinated well in advance. Alan Kuperman reports that "the majority of Tutsi gathering sites were attacked and destroyed before April 21, only 14 days into the genocide," and perhaps 250,000 people were annihilated in the first two weeks of the bloodbath (2000: 98). By the time the RPF seized the capital Kigali (and forcibly ended the genocide), at least 800,000 Rwandans had been murdered. The Rwandan genocide stands as a reminder of the destructive power of intergroup hatred and violence. In its aftermath, the United Nations Security Council established the International Criminal Tribunal for Rwanda (ICTR) under Resolution 955 to punish those who had organized and committed genocide and crimes against humanity.

SEE ALSO: Peacekeeping.

References

Gourevitch, P. (1998) *We Wish to Inform You That Tomorrow We Will Be Killed With Our Families: Stories From Rwanda*. New York: Farrar, Strauss, and Giroux.

Kressel, N. J. (1996) *Mass Hate: The Global Rise of Genocide and Terror*. New York: Plenum Press.

Kuperman, A. J. (2000) "Rwanda in Retrospect," *Foreign Affairs*, January/February: 94–118.

Melvern, L. (2004) *Conspiracy to Murder: The Rwandan Genocide*. London: Verso.

Powers, S. (2001) "Bystanders to Genocide," *Atlantic Monthly*, September: 1–21.

Prunier, G. (1995) *The Rwanda Crisis: History of a Genocide*. New York: Columbia University Press.

Further Reading

Dallaire, R. (2004) *Shake Hands with the Devil: The Failure of Humanity in Rwanda*. New York: Carroll and Graf.

Des Forges, A. (1999) *Leave None to Tell the Story: Genocide in Rwanda*. New York: Human Rights Watch.

Gourevitch, P. (1995) "Letter from Rwanda: After the Genocide," *The New Yorker*, December 18: 78–94.

Lemarchand, R. (1996) *Burundi: Ethnic Conflict and Genocide*. Cambridge: Woodrow Wilson Center Press and the University of Cambridge Press.

Mamdani, M. (2001) *When Victims Become Killers: Colonialism, Nativism, and the Genocide in Rwanda*. Princeton: Princeton University Press.

Peterson, S. (2000) *Me Against My Brother*. New York: Routledge.

Staub, E. (1989) *The Roots of Evil: The Origins of Genocide and Other Group Violence*. Cambridge: Cambridge University Press.

Straus, S. (2008) *The Order of Genocide: Race, Power, and War in Rwanda*. Ithaca, New York: Cornell University Press.

Uvin, P. (1998) *Aiding Violence: The Development Enterprise in Rwanda*. West Hartford, CT: Kumarian Press.

S

Somalia Civil War (2006)

GERVASE PHILLIPS

In June 2006, a coalition of local Sharia courts (responsible for the implementation of the Islamic code of law) seized control of the Somali capital Mogadishu, driving out the rival forces of feuding warlords. This alliance, known as the Islamic Courts Union (ICU), brought a measure of peace and stability to the war-torn city unknown since the government of Siad Barre had been overthrown in 1991. Yet their success would bring further conflict. As the ICU's sphere of influence expanded across southern and central Somalia, its militia clashed with the forces of the internationally recognized (but weak) Transitional Federal Government (TFG). To the north, the semi-autonomous region of Puntland and the *de facto* independent state of Somaliland were both militantly resistant to any notion of reintegration into a unified Somali state. Furthermore, although the ICU contained a broad spectrum of religious opinion, the presence within its ranks of committed fundamentalists attracted the anxious attention of the United States and the foremost regional power, Ethiopia, leading to military intervention by both countries.

Sharia courts had first been established in Mogadishu in 1993, working with clan and secular authorities in an attempt to establish a degree of stability and law enforcement. Following the exodus of US and United Nations (UN) peacekeepers from the Somali capital (1994–1995), the challenge facing them had become ever greater as local warlords competed for control of territory, key infrastructure (such as airports and harbors), and the lucrative trades in arms and the narcotic *qat*. The warring factions were largely kinship based. There are six main Somali clans, all claiming Arabian ancestry: the pastoralist Darod, Isaq, Dir, and Hawiye and the more settled "agro-pastoralist" Digil and Rahanweyn. Beyond these divisions, however, were a host of sub-clans and feuding families, engaged in shifting and transient coalitions whose complexities largely baffled outsiders. Often commentators merely dismissed the situation as anarchy, symptomatic of intractable tribal conflict or rampant criminality. Yet the clans were essentially rational political actors, competing or cooperating as necessary to gain control of resources. To the north, in Somaliland (the area of the former British Protectorate) the clans had worked together, their elders forming a *gurti* (national committee) in 1993, which implemented a successful demilitarization program and went on to create a functioning state, with a

Twentieth-Century War and Conflict: A Concise Encyclopedia, First Edition. Edited by Gordon Martel.
© 2015 John Wiley & Sons, Ltd. Published 2015 by John Wiley & Sons, Ltd.

disciplined army, police force, schools, and hospitals. Somaliland's neighboring province Puntland attempted, with less success, to follow this model.

In central and southern Somalia, the clans fought. Mogadishu was dominated by General Muhammad Farah Aideed until his death in a skirmish in August 1996. His son Hussein Aideed, raised in the United States and a Marine Corps veteran, took over his interests, finally emerging as the central figure in a coalition of American-backed warlords: the Alliance for the Restoration of Peace and Counter-Terrorism (ARPCT). The ARPCT, alongside the violent pursuit of its own local interests, also acted against suspected terrorists, based in Somalia and associated with the radical Islamist organization al-Qaeda. Thus, when the ICU, under Sharif Sheikh Ahmad, finally drove the ARPCT from Mogadishu in June 2006, it was perceived, in Washington and Addis Ababa, as being itself committed to the global *jihad* (Holy War). This impression was reinforced in July when al-Qaeda's Osama bin Laden called upon Somalis to support the ICU and oust the western-backed transitional government. Although prominent ICU members publicly distanced themselves from bin Laden, many, such as Sheikh Hassan Dahir Aweys, were indeed closely tied to political Islamist movements such as Al-Itihad Al-Islamiya (Unity of Islam). The ICU's insistence on the veiling of women, the public flogging of criminals, the banning of public singing and dancing, and the suppression of the local cult of Muslim saints soon led to comparisons with Afghanistan's Taliban.

Militarily, the ICU enjoyed some striking early successes. Twenty-nine TFG ministers resigned from their posts as ICU pressure mounted. On July 19, 2006, the ICU's well-disciplined and highly motivated militia seized the town of Burkakaba, just a few miles from Baidoa, where the TFG's interim president, Abdillahi Yusuf, was based. By November, ICU forces had pushed into Puntland in support of a Sharia court established by local clerics in Galka'ayo. Meanwhile, the leaders of Somaliland were condemned as apostates who had turned their backs on Islam to work for the Jews and the Americans. However, the Ethiopians had now become actively involved. Already fighting an ethnic Somali independence movement in their own troubled Ogaden province, they wished to install a grateful and acquiescent TFG regime in Mogadishu. The first supplies and military advisors were reaching Baidoa as early as July; on October 25, Ethiopian President Meles Zenawi declared his country "technically at war" with the ICU. Somali "technicals" (civilian pick-up trucks converted to military use) proved little match for Ethiopian air strikes and armor and by late December the ICU was in full retreat. Besides sharing intelligence with the Ethiopians, the United States also launched air strikes of its own, against suspected terrorist training facilities. The internationalization of the conflict continued apace, with Eritrea pursuing a proxy war against Ethiopia by supplying the ICU. Yet they could not halt the Ethiopian/TFG advance; Mogadishu was taken on December 28, 2006, and a TFG government was in place in the capital by January 8, 2007.

The outcome of the 2006 fighting did not bring stability to Somalia. Without the influence of the ICU, banditry and piracy in coastal waters flourished once more. Ethiopian forces were unable to withdraw until January 2009, as two insurgent groups swiftly emerged: the Alliance for the Re-liberation of Somalia (ARS), under Sharif Sheikh Ahmad, and a more militant Islamist faction, Shabaab, bolstered by foreign mujahideen fighters and headed by Sheikh Hassan Dahir Aweys. The TFG and ARS were able to engage constructively in talks, leading to Ahmad becoming president in December 2008. Shabaab fought on, establishing control over much of south-central Somalia from its stronghold in Kismayo. The human cost of the conflict had been staggering, a fact, perhaps, best illustrated by the estimated two million refugees granted asylum worldwide by 2008.

Further Reading

Duyvesteyn, I. (2004) *Clausewitz and African War: Politics and Strategy in Liberia and Somalia*. London: Routledge.

Elmi, A. A. (2010) *Understanding the Somalia Conflagration: Identity, Political Islam and Peacebuilding*. New York: Pluto Press.

Fergusson, J. (2013) *The World's Most Dangerous Place: Inside the Outlaw State of Somalia*. London: Bantam Press.

Hansen, S. J. (2013) *Al-Shabaab in Somalia: The History and Ideology of a Militant Islamist Group, 2005-2012*. London: C Hurst & Co.

Harper, M. (2012) *Getting Somalia Wrong?: Faith and War in a Shattered State*. London: Zed Books.

Healy, S. (2008) *Lost Opportunities in the Horn of Africa: How Conflicts Connect and Peace Agreements Unravel*. London: Royal Institute of International Affairs.

Lewis, I. (2008) *Understanding Somalia and Somaliland*. London: Hurst.

Menkhaus, K. (2004) *Somalia: State Collapse and the Threat of Terrorism*. Oxford: Oxford University Press.

Shay, S. (2008) *Somalia between Jihad and Restoration*. London: Transaction.

Soviet War in Afghanistan (1979–1992)

ARTEMY KALINOVSKY

The Soviet–Afghan war was one of the bloodiest episodes of the Cold War. In 1979, fearing that the radical Marxist regime of Hafizullah Amin would destabilize the country to the point where it might prove tempting for the United States to infiltrate, Soviet troops entered the country to install a more moderate leader, Babrak Karmal, and to support the Afghan military in its fight against a growing insurgency. The result was a 10-year war that cost the lives of over 14,000 Soviet soldiers and anywhere between 800,000 and 1.2 million Afghans, a refugee crisis, enormous economic damage, and the long-term political instability of Afghanistan itself.

Prior to 1978, Afghanistan had a long and largely successful history of neutralism. During the "Great Game" it served as a buffer between two encroaching great powers: Britain on the Indian subcontinent and Russia as it took over central Asia. During the Cold War the country received aid from the United States as well as from the USSR, while Afghans were sent to study abroad in both countries. (Crucially, though, it was the Soviet Union that was the key supporter of the Afghan military, while the United States largely refrained from arms sales for fear of antagonizing Pakistan.) Under King Zahir Shah the country continued a cautious modernization program. At the same time, pressure for more radical reform was growing and was one of the reasons for the king's overthrow by his cousin, Prime Minister Mohammed Daoud, in 1973.

Daoud moved the country closer to the USSR and ruled with the support of a number of leftist groups, among them the two factions of the communist movement. Founded in 1965, the People's Democratic Party of Afghanistan (PDPA) soon split into two factions: Khalq and Parcham, named after their respective newspapers. Parcham, led by Babrak Karmal, preferred to work with the Daoud regime; Khalq pressed for more radical reforms and increasingly criticized the existing order. Both groups looked for support among the country's intellectuals and within the army, although it was Khalq that was more successful in the latter case. In 1977, the two factions reunited, following pressure from Indian communists as well as Soviet advisors.

Although Daoud's reforms and closeness to the USSR evoked criticism from more traditional Afghan politicians and some sectors of society, it was the growing confidence of the left wing that worried Daoud most. In the spring of 1978 he prepared to move against the communists. Following the assassination of a Parchami ideologue, Mir Akbar Khaibar, a public demonstration against Daoud's rule broke out in Kabul. The government's subsequent attempt to arrest PDPA leaders backfired, for they were quickly able to rally their supporters in the military and stage a coup. The Saur (April) Revolution, as it came to be known, had ushered a communist government into power.

The new rulers formed a government led by Khalqi leader Nur Muhammad Taraki as president and premier and with Karmal as deputy premier. The Khalqis in particular aimed at nothing less than the wholesale reconstruction of Afghan society. A number of radical measures were quickly announced, including equal rights for women and the redistribution of land. They went much further than anything attempted by Daoud and it soon became clear that the old divisions within the party had never healed: a mass purge of Parchamis took place, with some arrested and others sent into diplomatic exile. Soviet pleas to slow down the reforms and to avoid internal strife fell on deaf ears.

In March 1979, the communist leadership faced its first massive uprising in the mostly Tajik city of Herat. Anger at the government and its reforms led to a massacre of Soviet advisors and their families. A panicked Taraki begged for

Soviet troops to help restore order. The Soviet leadership considered his request but held firm: the introduction of Soviet troops, they reasoned, would not be accepted by the Afghan population, would worsen relations with the West, and could lead to a situation where Soviet soldiers were fighting ordinary Afghans.

In the event, the Afghan army was able to restore order, but the regime had not learned its lesson. Soon a conflict was brewing between its top figures: Taraki and Hafizullah Amin. In September, Taraki traveled to Moscow, where Soviet leaders assured him of their support and urged the removal of Amin. But Taraki's attempt to have Amin assassinated backfired. Amin escaped and had Taraki arrested and executed.

The Soviet relationship with Amin was tense. Although he publicly proclaimed fealty to Moscow, privately he feuded with the Soviet ambassador and ignored Soviet advice. He asked for Soviet troops to come help him fight off the emerging rebellion. At the same time, he seemed to be moving closer to Washington, meeting secretly with the ambassador outside Kabul. By December, the Soviets had decided that he would have to be replaced. Soviet special forces would eliminate Amin, and troops would be sent in to help the Afghan army stabilize the country and return it to order.

The Soviet decision to intervene needs to be seen in the context of détente's collapse at the end of the 1970s. Soviet gains in the Third World throughout the 1970s had angered many politicians in the United States, who felt that Moscow was simply taking advantage of stability in Europe to make gains elsewhere. President Jimmy Carter and his National Security Advisor, Zbigniew Brzezinski, shared this view. While they continued to work with Moscow on arms control, they also felt it was important to demonstrate the limits of US tolerance in the Third World and on issues of human rights within the USSR. The result was confrontations by proxy in places like the Horn of Africa and an increasingly tense bilateral relationship. The rejection of the Strategic Arms Limitation Talks II agreement by Congress in the summer of 1979 and the placement of Pershing missiles in Germany that autumn convinced Soviet leaders that Washington was moving toward confrontation. They also feared that, following the toppling of the

pro-United States Shah of Iran earlier that year, Washington would look to Afghanistan as a new foothold in the region.

If the decision to intervene was taken in the context of a deteriorating United States–Soviet relationship, the intervention itself destroyed whatever was left of détente and helped bring on what became known as the "second Cold War." Concerned that it was, in fact, Moscow taking advantage of the sudden US weakness in the Persian Gulf, President Carter announced his administration's new policy, stating that "An attempt by any outside force to gain control of the Persian Gulf region will be regarded as an assault on the vital interests of the United States of America, and such an assault will be repelled by any means necessary, including military force." The United States also committed to aiding the mujahideen, primarily by working with the Pakistani Inter-Service Intelligence. Under President Ronald Reagan, this aid expanded as support for the "freedom fighters" battling communism and foreign intervention became an increasingly popular cause in Congress. Most Third World states were also highly critical of the invasion and voted year after year to condemn it in the United Nations (UN). One of the few exceptions was India, whose officials feared the expansion of Pakistani influence and its acquisition of US weaponry more than they did Soviet expansionism and therefore tempered their criticism of the Soviet intervention, even offering Moscow support in the UN.

Soviet leaders originally hoped that their soldiers would primarily be used for training and garrisoning duties, thus freeing the Afghan army to quell uprisings and restore order. Faced with Afghan army mutinies in a number of regiments, violent protests against the regime, and repeated requests from the Afghan leadership that Soviet troops take an active part in the fighting, the leadership in Moscow relented and instructed the 40th Army to participate in counterinsurgency efforts. From the spring of 1980, Soviet forces took a lead in fighting the opposition, which over time coalesced around a number of groups whose leaders were based in Peshawar, Pakistan.

The Soviet military strategy in Afghanistan was, naturally, quite typical for counterinsurgency warfare: protect main routes, cities, air bases, and logistic sites; support the Afghan forces with superior air, artillery, intelligence, and logistic capabilities; and strengthen Democratic Republic of Afghanistan (DRA) forces so that they could fight without Soviet help. A key challenge was stemming the flow of supplies to the opposition fighting the government, which primarily came across the mountainous and porous border with Pakistan. Soviet and Afghan military units, secret police detachments, and border patrol all took part in the effort to secure the border. Numerous gaps still remained, and arms continued to flow to the insurgents, completing a long supply chain that included US and Saudi funding and weapons, sometimes acquired from countries such as China, Egypt, and Israel.

The 40th Army tried to compensate for its inability to close the Pakistani–Afghan border by working to interrupt the supply lines on Afghan territory. Fixed-wing aircraft provided were employed against mujahideen convoys, often accompanied by attacks from helicopter gunships. Mines were dropped from the air along supply routes. As with other cases when mines were used in warfare, they became a lasting hazard for civilians, yet another of the tragic legacies of the war. (They were not, however, deliberately disguised as toys, as much anti-Soviet propaganda at the time had it.)

One of the 40th Army's key tasks was protecting lines of communication, crucial for supplying Soviets and DRA forces as well as Afghan cities. The only reliable overland route was a highway that ran from Termez to Kabul and connected that city with urban centers like Jalalabad and Herat. Not only were Soviet soldiers vulnerable to attacks along the route, they often found it difficult to attack mujahideen who could quickly disappear into the mountains. According to some estimates, guarding these crucial roads alone required some 35 percent of Soviet troops in the country, thus limiting the number available for operations or patrols.

To clear areas of insurgents, the 40th Army employed "hammer and anvil" operations. Massive attacks from the air were accompanied by sweeps conducted by mechanized forces on the ground. Over time the Soviets began relying more on helicopter gunships, which could drop bombs from a lower altitude (and thus with greater precision) than fixed-wing aircraft and could also strafe rebel fighters. The 40th Army also increased its use of special forces (*voiska spetsialnogo*

naznachen'ia, or *Spetsnaz*), which could be used for targeted attacks against bands of fighters. Throughout the war, airpower remained a key feature of Soviet combat tactics as well as a way to supplement transport by road. The introduction of CIA-supplied Stinger missiles from 1986, which for the first time provided the mujahideen with a reliable way to counter Soviet airpower, complicated Soviet strategy in several ways. Most importantly, it made close air support difficult, and it also put cargo and passenger planes in danger during descent and take-off. Pilots adopted a corkscrew pattern for take-off and landing, and the Soviets limited their use of helicopter gunships. The Stingers did not play a role in the Soviet decision to withdraw their troops.

The Soviet military was geared toward conventional warfare in central Europe, not the counterinsurgency it encountered in Afghanistan. Over time, however, it adjusted to the requirements of mobility that came with a guerrilla war in a mountainous terrain. In the first two years of the war, officer training changed little and was still designed to prepare soldiers for conventional war. In 1982, however, a new training program for officers and sergeants was introduced to take into account new requirements imposed by terrain, logistics issues, and the kinds of engagement likely with mujahideen forces. Privates being sent to Afghanistan underwent a special two-month course in central Asia before continuing their training with regiments in-country. Training for officers and privates was constantly updated and restructured to take account of the requirements of counterinsurgency on the Afghan terrain.

The larger dilemma that confronted Soviet generals was how to use force against the insurgents without alienating the Afghan population. Attacks from the air inevitably hit civilians as well as fighters, but a significant decrease in the use of airpower would have necessitated the introduction of more ground troops. More boots on the ground could have created political difficulties within Afghanistan as well as within the USSR. (It should be noted that Soviet leaders avoided deepening their commitment beyond a certain level. There were never more than about 108,000 troops in the country, for example, and the war was never expanded into neighboring Pakistan. This limited the war's impact domestically and internationally, giving Moscow some freedom of maneuver and allowing Soviet leaders to put off decisions about withdrawal. Throughout the conflict, Moscow faced domestic pressure from parents of soldiers and dissidents as well as international criticism of the war, but not at a level that necessitated an immediate change of course.)

The battle fought by the Soviet military was only one side of the effort. To stabilize the government and broaden its base of support, the Soviet Union sent thousands of advisors and technical specialists to Afghanistan, adding to the significant number already in the country before the intervention. Besides those attached to the military and security services, Soviet party workers were sent as advisers to Kabul and the provinces, where they entered factories, businesses, and universities. They were sent to help the government spread its influence and to assist in bringing economic improvements to the country, and thus to win the population over to the Kabul regime's side.

The use of advisors on such a large scale, however, brought its own problems. Many were poorly prepared for the politically sensitive and complex work they were asked to carry out, and as a result they sometimes did more to insult local customs even as their bosses in Moscow were encouraging the regime to make peace with traditional society. Most had no special preparation for the kind of work they were sent to do. Many party advisors proved doctrinaire in their suggestions and insensitive to local customs. Further, rather than providing training and aid, they sometimes simply took over the functions of their "advisees." The presence of Soviet troops and advisors seemed to cause paralysis among Afghan politicians.

Soviet leaders had begun looking for ways to withdraw their troops as early as 1982, but they needed a guarantee that the regime they installed would not collapse soon after their departure. As Soviet troops and advisors continued their nation-building and counterinsurgency within the country, diplomats met with US, Afghan, and Pakistani officials under UN auspices. Under Mikhail Gorbachev these talks were continued with renewed determination. Frustrated at the stalemate within Afghanistan and determined to build on his improving relationship with Washington, Gorbachev abandoned some of the preconditions for withdrawal. The Geneva

Accords, signed in April 1988 by Pakistan, Afghanistan, the United States, and the USSR, stipulated a withdrawal with a nine-month time frame. The United States, however, reserved the right to keep supplying the mujahideen and Moscow the Kabul regime.

The Soviet withdrawal began in May 1988 and was completed February 15, 1989. The Soviets negotiated with the mujahideen commanders, most notably the Tajik leader Ahmad Shah Massoud, to secure safe passage as they made their way north. Supplies and bases used by Soviet troops were turned over to the Afghan military. The withdrawal itself was completed in good order.

Contrary to the expectations of many western observers (and Soviet officials), the Kabul regime did not collapse once Soviet troops left. It managed to hold its own, with funds and supplies from Moscow, for over three years, in part by relying on semi-independent militias. Once the Soviet Union collapsed and its supplies dried up, however, the regime's supporters (including militias that had received subsidies) turned on it, and Kabul fell in April 1992. The mujahideen, who had been barely united even while fighting the Soviets and the PDPA regime, now turned on each other. Kabul itself, which had up to that point been spared the effects of war, now felt its full impact. The fighting and disorder continued to escalate after 1992 and helped lead to the rise of the Taliban, who in turn took Kabul in 1996.

Further Reading

Bennett, A. (1999) *Condemned to Repetition? The Rise, Fall, and Reprise of Soviet-Russian Military Interventionism, 1973–1996*. Cambridge, MA: MIT Press.

Braithwaite, R. (2011) *Afgantsy: The Russians in Afghanistan 1979–1989*. London: Profile Books.

Coll, S. (2004) *Ghost Wars: The Secret History of the CIA, Afghanistan, and bin Laden, from the Soviet Invasion to September 10, 2001*. New York: Penguin.

Crile, G. (2003) *Charlie Wilson's War*. New York: Grove Press.

Dorronsoro, G. (2005) *Revolution Unending: Afghanistan 1979–Present*. New York: Columbia University Press.

Feifer, G. (2009) *The Great Gamble: The Soviet War in Afghanistan*. New York: HarperCollins.

Giustozzi, A. (2000) *War, Politics and Society in Afghanistan*. London: Hurst.

Gregorian, V. (1969) *The Emergence of Modern Afghanistan: Politics of Reform and Modernization, 1880–1946*. Stanford: Stanford University Press.

Kalinovsky, A. (2011) *A Long Goodbye: The Soviet Withdrawal from Afghanistan*. Cambridge, MA: Harvard University Press.

Maley, W. (2002) *The Afghanistan Wars*. Basingstoke: Palgrave Macmillan.

Urban, M. (1990) *War in Afghanistan*. Basingstoke: Macmillan.

Spanish Civil War (1936–1939)

JOSÉ MARÍA HERRERA

The Spanish Civil War was a prelude to the coming conflict of World War II. The hard ideological differences between the combatants, the heavy loss of life, and the extent of material destruction would mirror that which Europe would experience only a few months after the war's conclusion.

The causes of the Spanish Civil War were rooted in several problems that afflicted Spain at the beginning of the twentieth century. The nineteenth century witnessed the erosion of the Spanish Empire. By 1898, the Spanish–American War had whittled Spanish possessions down to a couple of enclaves in Africa. This loss was symptomatic of the impoverishment and general backwardness of Spain.

A constitutional monarchy, Spain could not escape the general political radicalization evident in the rest of Europe. The tensions between conservative and liberal groups became a volatile mix by the 1920s. On one side were arrayed those who wanted to maintain the monarchy and the traditional privileges that had been enjoyed by certain groups in Spanish society. The church, for instance, was sponsored by the state; it controlled education and held considerable economic interests. Critics believed that the only way that Spain could begin to modernize would be by the suspension of the church's privileges and by the confiscation of its considerable assets within Spain. In addition to the church, the army's officer class held a vested interest in the status quo. The ranks of the Spanish officer corps were bloated beyond the needs of an army its size. Any change

or reform in the structure was regarded as a threat to their livelihood.

Economically, Spain was an agricultural nation. Most of the land was concentrated in the hands of fewer than 10,000 owners. Vast numbers of landless, ill-paid migrant workers (many from Andalusia) worked these farms, causing considerable class resentment. The industrial contribution to the economy was minor compared to that of agriculture. Most of the industry was located in two cities: Barcelona and Bilbao. The economic discrepancies in turn fueled separatist movements in the parent regions of these two cities: Catalonia and the Basque country. Both regions spoke a different native language and had divergent cultural traditions.

Starting in the early 1900s, the Spanish began to extend their influence into Morocco. This sparked a series of wars against local tribesmen. The Rif Wars became a quagmire that exposed the corruption, inadequate training, and poor quality of the Spanish army. Most of the soldiers were conscripts from the laboring classes who resented fighting a war for the benefit of the wealthier classes. The experiences of the war helped shape a new generation of Spanish officers, including Francisco Franco, the commander of the elite Spanish Legion.

The poor performance of the army at the start of the Rif War, together with labor unrest, prompted a military coup by General Miguel Antonio Primo de Rivera. Primo de Rivera immediately engaged in a series of reforms to help modernize Spain. Beyond successfully concluding the Rif War, he began to reform Spain's transportation infrastructure, built hydroelectric dams, and provided incentives for industrial development. He also co-opted the labor movements by directly intervening in labor negotiations. Although well intentioned, Primo de Rivera was unable to tackle the three elements within Spain that needed to be reformed: the church, the army, and the agrarian sector. The coming of the Great Depression undid much of the good his economic policies had engendered and in 1930 he was forced to resign. King Alfonso XIII was forced to abdicate a year later as a consequence of having sided with the dictator against his own constitutional government.

Spain was reconstituted as a republic. The new left-leaning government immediately tackled the problems of the church and the army. The church's monopoly on education and marriage was dissolved and the Jesuits were disbanded. Divorce was made legal and the separation of church and state was passed into law, ending the government subsidies that the church had traditionally enjoyed. Thousands of military officers were forced into retirement, prompting a failed military revolt in 1932. In addition, Catalonia was granted some degree of autonomy. While the reforms were popular among the left, the conservative right saw the measures against the church as an attack on the soul of Spanish culture and civilization. Land reform efforts were seen as inadequate by the rural poor, while landowners were angered by this attack on their privileges. Others feared that the granting of autonomy to Catalonia signaled the future dissolution of Spain.

The elections of 1933 brought a conservative coalition government into power. This government immediately canceled the land reform efforts and the measures against the church. It also ended Catalan autonomy. The reversal of the reforms led labor parties to call on their confederates to engage in a strike. Anarchist miners in Asturias took this call a step further and led a violent revolt that included a takeover of the regional capital of Oviedo. General Franco was sent with an army and brutally crushed the revolt, earning the undying hatred of organized labor.

The unpopularity of the conservative coalition prompted leftists to set aside their differences and join with centrists to score a victory in the 1936 elections. The new administration immediately reinstated the earlier reforms, repolarizing Spanish society. Civility began to disintegrate as elements on both sides of the political divide resorted to street violence and murder. Certain military officers, whose loyalty was in question, were reassigned by Prime Minister Manuel Azaña (including Franco, who was exiled to the Canary Islands). By the summer of 1936, a cadre of officers including Franco, Emilio Mora, and José Sanjurjo were plotting with rightist groups for a military coup.

The murder of prominent monarchist José Calvo Sotelo left little doubt of the direction of Spanish politics and on July 18, 1936, Franco flew out to Morocco and reestablished command over the Spanish Legion. He issued a manifesto calling for a revolt against the government. Spain immediately splintered between those who supported the government and those who were in sympathy with the rebellion. Arrayed on one side were the Nationalists, a collection of monarchists, fascists, and center-right groups supported by most of the church, landowners, and a large percentage of the military. On the other side were the Republicans, composed of anarchists, socialists, communists, labor unionists, and pro-government centrists as well as Catalan and Basque separatists.

The coup attempt was only partially successful. In the regions where Nationalist sentiment was particularly strong, like western Andalusia, Galicia, Leon, and Navarre/Aragon, the plotters and their supporters were able to take immediate control. They failed, however, to take Madrid and the important industrial cities of Barcelona and Bilbao. In addition, the Republicans began to arm their citizens and take firm control of the regions where sentiment was in their favor. Two days after the coup commenced, Sanjurjo, the nominal Nationalist leader, was killed in a plane crash. This death and the fact that Franco directly commanded the largest contingent of available troops placed the leadership of the coup firmly in his hands and would in time render him the undisputed leader of the rebellion.

At the start of the rebellion, Franco requested and received aid from both Germany and Italy. Adolf Hitler supplied Franco with transport planes, which allowed him to quickly ferry troops to Spain. In addition, both Hitler and Mussolini provided a considerable number of troops and arms to the Nationalists. Both would be crucial in the early days of the war, as German planes (the Condor Legion) would guarantee Nationalist air superiority and the Italian navy would provide an effective sea blockade of Republican ports.

The Republicans were also able to count on foreign aid, but it was considerably less useful than that received by the Nationalists. Several units of volunteers were organized to fight for the Republicans, the vast majority by foreign communist parties. These International Brigades would provide between 25,000 and 30,000 soldiers. The Soviet Union provided planes and other military equipment as well as advisors to the Republicans. Even though the Spanish Communist Party was rather small (and dwarfed by the much larger anarchist and socialist movements), its association with this major benefactor would increase its importance within the Republican fold. By the end of the war its domination of the Republican side would weaken the government and play a key role in its collapse.

The Initial Madrid Campaigns

Upon arriving in Spain, Franco initiated an offensive to capture Badajoz in order to connect Nationalist territory in the south with Nationalist gains in the north. His forces succeeded in August 1936 and then turned east toward Toledo to relieve a besieged pro-Nationalist force. Republican forces failed to capture Toledo, leaving the western and southwestern approaches to Madrid open for Nationalist penetration. Before beginning the operation toward Madrid, Franco was recognized by the Nationalists as the undisputed leader of the rebellion. This unity of command would add a further impetus to the eventual success of the Nationalist cause.

On November 6, 1936, the Nationalists commenced their siege of Madrid. In anticipation of the collapse of the capital, the Republican government moved to Valencia that same day. Anarchists and the first International Brigades joined the local militia in the defense, repulsing an assault on November 8. Checked for the moment, Nationalist forces headed toward the northeast of Madrid in an effort to surround the city. The assault was blocked at the Coruña road, momentarily stabilizing the Madrid front. Franco, concerned over his mounting losses, halted direct frontal attacks and ordered a bombardment of Madrid.

The effort did not soften Republican resolve and by the start of 1937 Franco was forced to revise his plans. He turned toward the south of Madrid and attempted to cut off the capital from Valencia. On February 6, 1937, the Nationalist forces crossed the Jarama River and began an assault upon its heights. Once again the Republicans fiercely resisted and by the end of the month the Nationalist offensive stalled. Franco redirected his attention northward; using large numbers of Italian troops, he ordered an offensive upon the city of Guadalajara, northeast of Madrid. The purpose was to effect a pincer movement on the Republican forces defending the Jarama line while at the same time encircling Madrid. The attack commenced on March 8, 1937, and the Nationalist forces had initial success in capturing key towns in the region. Poor weather, however, grounded the Nationalist air force and bogged down its tanks. The Republicans were able to take advantage and knocked out many of the Italian armored units. They then proceeded to counterattack and nearly routed the Italian troops, who were forced to retreat from their earlier gains. By March 23, the Republican forces had stabilized their lines northeast of Madrid.

The Northern Campaign

Simultaneously, Nationalist General Mola conducted a campaign in northern Spain to isolate both the Basque separatists and the pro-government areas of Cantabria and Asturias from the rest of Republican Spain. He captured the strategically important province of Guipuzcoa after the Battle of Irun on September 5, 1936, cutting off Asturias and Cantabria from the Basques. By the summer of 1937, Nationalist forces had surrounded the city of Bilbao. A Republican defector provided the Nationalist commander with the defensive plans of Bilbao, allowing for the quick capture of the strategically valuable city on June 18, 1937. During the Basque campaign, elements of the Condor Legion conducted an aerial bombardment of the cities of Durango and Guernica, the latter becoming the subject of the famous Picasso painting.

After the fall of the Basque country, the Nationalists turned westward toward Cantabria and Asturias. In a two-week campaign, the Republican forces were battered and overwhelmed and Cantabria fell on August 26, 1937. By the end of the summer of 1937, only Asturias remained as the last Republican stronghold in the north. Surrounded on three sides, the Republican forces defended the mountainous region tenaciously, but when the pass at El Mazuco fell to the Nationalists on September 22, the defenses collapsed. By October 21, Republican resistance had ceased in the north. The only consolation for the Republicans was that Mola had died in a plane crash on June 3, 1937.

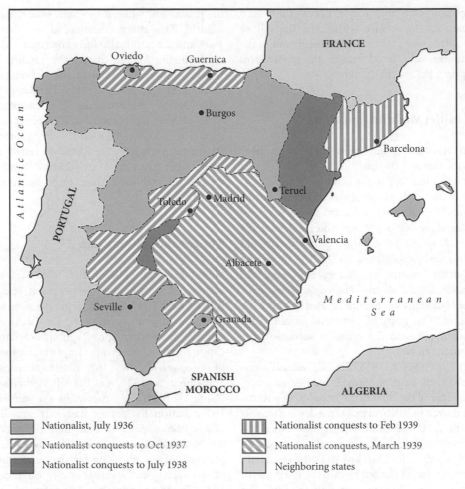

Nationalist, July 1936

Nationalist conquests to Oct 1937

Nationalist conquests to July 1938

Nationalist conquests to Feb 1939

Nationalist conquests, March 1939

Neighboring states

Map 15   Spanish Civil War, 1936–1939.

Republican Offensives

The impending collapse of the north motivated Republican planners to engage in two offensive campaigns. The objective was to regain the initiative, to cut off the Nationalist forces besieging Madrid, and to draw off Nationalist forces from the northern campaign.

The first effort was conducted west of Madrid in July 1937. On July 6, the Republicans launched an assault on the town of Brunete. The initial assault was effective and the town fell, but the Nationalists reconstituted their forces south of the city and halted the advance. Attacks and counterattacks would continue in and around the surrounding villages, blunting the offensive's momentum.

On July 18, the Nationalist forces mounted a counteroffensive and by July 25 the battle lines restabilized.

After the failure of Brunete, the Republican command initiated a second diversionary offensive southeast of the city of Zaragoza. The main strategic goal was to capture Zaragoza and disrupt the operations of the Nationalist forces in the eastern end of their northern offensive. As at Brunete, the Republicans managed to take key points but were eventually bogged down by stiff Nationalist resistance in the town of Belchite. This allowed the Nationalist forces to mount a counteroffensive. By September 6, 1937, the lines had stabilized and the offensive failed to achieve any of its goals.

Although the north was lost, the Republicans attempted another offensive south of Belchite in December 1937. The attack was aimed at capturing the provincial capital of Teruel. The Republicans brought overwhelming force on the town and, in spite of a solid defense and air attacks by the Condor Legion, the Nationalist garrison surrendered after two weeks. By the start of January 1938, Franco had concentrated sufficient force to mount a counterattack. His army steadily whittled away the Republican forces and on February 7, 1938, his attack north of Teruel collapsed the Republican right flank. By February 20, Teruel was surrounded and the remaining Republican defenders either fled or surrendered.

Aragon Offensive

Although Franco was forced to cancel a new offensive toward Madrid and Guadalajara, his victory at Teruel marked the final turning point of the war. The losses sustained by the Republicans were irreplaceable and encouraged Franco to engage in an offensive toward Barcelona.

The new offensive began on March 7, 1938. The attack was so successful that the Republican forces disintegrated in the face of the advancing Nationalists. Political dissensions within Republican ranks exacerbated the retreat. By March 17, the Nationalists had driven a wedge that left them less than 100 miles from the Mediterranean coast. They paused to reform their lines and reinitiated the attack on March 22. Nationalist troops captured the eastern portions of Aragon and reached the coast on April 8. Catalan resistance stiffened considerably and halted the offensive but by April 19 the Nationalist strategy had split Catalonia from the rest of Republican Spain.

Toward Valencia and the Battle of the Ebro

Franco turned his attention southward after the Aragon offensive. His objective was to capture Valencia and the resident Republican government. Standing in his way was a system of fortifications dubbed the XYZ Line. Starting on July 18,

1938, Franco hurled his forces against the lines. The Republicans gave way at first, but their resistance stiffened until the Nationalists were halted in the rough mountainous terrain 70 miles north of Valencia.

Immediately afterwards, the Republicans initiated their final major offensive of the war in the direction of the Ebro River, north of Valencia. The hope was to reconnect Catalonia to Republican Spain and perhaps prolong the war sufficiently to allow for a peace settlement. On July 25, the Republicans launched a surprise attack across the Ebro River. They made modest gains at the beginning but did not have sufficient airpower, armor, or artillery to dislodge Nationalist strongpoints or appropriately consolidate their gains. The battle bogged down into a stalemate. The Republican leadership was aware that the attack was a failure but was unwilling to call off the operation. The remnants of the Republican army were destroyed and this reality ended the offensive on November 16, 1938.

The Fall of Barcelona and Madrid

Franco rested his forces for a month before launching the final two campaigns of the war. On December 23, 1938, he began the invasion of Catalonia. Infighting between communists and anarchists within Catalonia had severely weakened the defenses of the Republican forces and by 1939 they were in no position to successfully defend themselves against Franco. By the end of January, Barcelona had fallen and, by the middle of February, the last pockets of resistance in Catalonia had been subdued.

By 1939, Madrid and Valencia were the sole enclaves held by the Republicans. On March 26, Franco made his final offensive toward Madrid. Republican resistance quickly collapsed and on March 28 the Nationalists took possession of the city. The next day, Valencia capitulated and the last Republican forces in Spain surrendered on April 1, 1939.

The end of the war completed the reunification of Spain under an ultra-conservative government. Franco restored most of the privileges of the Catholic Church and eventually set up Spain to once again become a monarchy. Reprisals had taken place on both sides during the war and continued under Franco, prompting a large-scale emigration of leftists and intellectuals from Spain. Franco suppressed liberal and leftist parties and essentially outlawed non-government-sponsored trade unions. In addition, Franco endeavored to erase Catalan, Basque, and other regional separatist movements by creating a Spanish nationalist identity. This included the appropriation and Hispanicization of some regional customs, the promotion of Castilian as the national language, and the suppression of minority languages. He also commissioned and built a gigantic monument to the victims of the war. This monument, *El Valle de los Caídos*, entombed the remains of both Nationalists and Republicans and was intended by Franco to be a project of national reconciliation. Franco would serve as dictator until his death in 1975. Spain sat out World War II and would remain a pariah state until the Cold War made it a useful ally to the United States.

SEE ALSO: War Crimes.

Further Reading

Beevor, A. (1982) *The Battle for Spain: The Spanish Civil War 1936–1939*. London: Penguin.

Forrest, A. (2000) *The Spanish Civil War*. London: Routledge.

Preston, P. (2007) *The Spanish Civil War: Reaction, Revolution, and Revenge*. New York: W.W. Norton and Co.

Preston, P. (2012) *The Spanish Holocaust: Inquisition and Extermination in Twentieth-Century Spain*. New York: W.W. Norton and Co.

Thomas, H. (2001) *The Spanish Civil War*. New York: Modern Library.

Sri Lankan Civil War

DAVID R. STONE

The Sri Lankan Civil War originated in religious and ethnic divides among the Sri Lankan population. Under British colonial rule, Sri Lankan society was dominated by English-educated Christians who were disproportionately Tamil. With independence in 1948, the Sinhalese, the Buddhist ethnic majority comprising approximately 70 percent of the population, asserted their own identity, making Sinhalese the official language, establishing Buddhism as the official religion, and disenfranchising Tamil migrants who had moved to Sri Lanka from India under British rule to work on tea plantations. This created resentment among the largely Hindu Tamil minority. Tensions between Buddhist Sinhalese and Hindu Tamils grew steadily.

Though significant numbers of Tamils lived in Colombo, the capital, and in the central highlands, the bulk of the Tamil population lived along the island's east coast and especially in the north. Tamil militancy centered around the Jaffna Peninsula, a small but densely populated region approximately 70 km east–west and 25 km north–south. Tamil activism was supported by the much larger Tamil population of India and even the Indian government. These links made the Sinhalese majority wary of concessions for fear of being swamped by Sri Lanka's massive neighbor. Over time, Sinhalese intransigence and Tamil radicalism fed one another. Sinhalese nationalism and the Buddhist faith became increasingly linked. Split among Hindus and smaller populations of Christians and Muslims, the Tamil population's political organizations moved from the pursuit of civil rights or regional autonomy to advocacy of full independence for a Tamil homeland: Eelam.

Political conflict degenerated into isolated violence and ethnic riots. This became full-scale civil war in July 1983, when the small, radical Liberation Tigers of Tamil Eelam (LTTE, or Tamil Tigers) ambushed and wiped out a Sri Lankan army patrol in Jaffna. This triggered massive anti-Tamil riots in Colombo, beginning an escalating cycle of ethnic violence and vicious reprisal. Ethnic cleansing began, as Sinhalese and Tamils alike fled areas where they were suddenly an endangered minority. The Tamil diaspora in India and the West provided substantial material and financial support to enable the LTTE to sustain an insurgency despite the overwhelming Sinhalese advantage in numbers.

Over the course of the 1980s, the Tamil movement became dominated by its most radical and ruthless faction: the Tamil Tigers. The LTTE eliminated or suppressed other less radical Tamil parties. Under the leadership of Velupillai Prabhakaran, the Tigers evolved into an organization of remarkable capacity. While maintaining a full-scale insurgency, the Tigers performed quasi-state functions in areas under their control, particularly the Jaffna Peninsula where Sri Lankan military forces were confined to their bases or expelled altogether. The LTTE drafted soldiers (including children), collected taxes, and provided rudimentary social services. In addition, the Tigers built a military force capable of matching the Sri Lankan army, a tiny navy and air force, and a terrorist organization of exceptional discipline and fanaticism. Indeed, it was the Tamil Tigers who perfected the technique of suicide bombing. The group also experimented with the use of chemical weapons against Sri Lankan soldiers. The Tigers' uncompromising stance produced one of the war's characteristic features: the seeming impossibility of an enduring negotiated settlement. Repeated efforts at a federalist compromise for the Tamils failed, either not going far enough to satisfy the Tigers or going too far to be acceptable to the Sinhalese majority.

By 1987, the Sri Lankan army lost control of most of the Jaffna Peninsula. Its bloody efforts to regain control resulted in public pressure on Indian Prime Minister Rajiv Gandhi to intervene on behalf of Sri Lanka's Tamils. Gandhi compelled Sri Lanka to accept the Indian Peace Keeping Force (IPKF) in Jaffna and along the east coast. Though initially welcomed by the LTTE, the IPKF's relations with the Tigers swiftly deteriorated. After a disastrous attempt to capture the LTTE's leadership in October 1987, the IPKF found itself in a full-scale war with the Tigers. After suffering over 1,000 soldiers killed, India withdrew in early 1990. The Tigers assassinated Gandhi in 1991 in retaliation for his intervention.

The 1990s saw continual fighting interrupted by occasional ceasefires as Sri Lankan governments fluctuated between military efforts to end the war and attempts at compromise and accommodation. The war centered around the fight for control of a number of key areas: the Jaffna Peninsula and the city of Jaffna itself; Elephant Pass, the narrow isthmus that provided the sole link between the Jaffna Peninsula and the main island; and bases and strongpoints in Tamil regions. Small LTTE forces routinely defeated or evaded offensives by Sri Lanka's much larger army. As Jaffna and Elephant Pass changed hands in bloody battles, the war seemed no closer to an end. The sophistication and resources of the LTTE made the war as much conventional as guerrilla. The Tigers captured a major military post at Kilinochchi in 1998, mauled a Sri Lankan army attempt to expand its control of Jaffna in 1999, and finally captured Elephant Pass in 2000, forcing nearly 40,000 Sri Lankan soldiers in Jaffna to be supplied by sea and air.

By the fall of 2001, Sinhalese war weariness produced the parliamentary victory of Ranil Wickremesinghe and his United National Front, who agreed to a Norwegian-brokered ceasefire with the Tigers. Though the LTTE operated as a *de facto* government in much of northern and eastern Sri Lanka, its hold now began to slip. In 2004, the LTTE commander in the east broke with Prabhakaran, halving the Tigers' forces. In addition, the inflow of foreign aid into LTTE hands after the December 2004 Indian Ocean tsunami made its leadership overconfident in its ability to achieve full independence.

The result was the breakdown of the ceasefire in 2006. A newly militant government under President Mahinda Rajapaksa launched a renewed offensive against the LTTE under the leadership of General Sarath Fonseka. The Sri Lankan government regained control of the island's eastern regions in 2007 then systematically reduced territory under Tiger control in the north. The last remaining LTTE forces were destroyed in May 2009, and Prabhakaran was killed. The human catastrophe of full-scale warfare in a densely populated region with atrocities and war crimes on both sides, however, means that Sinhalese–Tamil relations are still fraught with potential for further conflict.

SEE ALSO: Chemical Warfare.

Further Reading

Hashim, A. S. (2013) *When Counterinsurgency Wins: Sri Lanka's Defeat of the Tamil Tigers*. Philadelphia: University of Pennsylvania Press.

Hoffman, B. (2009) "The First Non-State Use of a Chemical Weapon in Warfare: The Tamil Tigers' Assault on East Kiran," *Small Wars and Insurgencies*, 20 (3–4): 463–477.

Mampilly, Z. (2009) "A Marriage of Inconvenience: Tsunami Aid and the Unraveling of the LTTE and the GoSL's Complex Dependency," *Civil Wars*, 11 (3): 302–320.

Nieto, W. A. S. (2008) "A War of Attrition: Sri Lanka and the Tamil Tigers," *Small Wars and Insurgencies*, 19 (4): 573–587.

Submarine Warfare

MICHAEL STURMA

While underwater craft were the subject of fantasy and experimentation for centuries, submarine warfare only became a reality in the twentieth century. Although some designers promoted their commercial potential, submarines were conceived primarily as weapons. With the ability to attack from beneath the sea, they created a new dimension in naval warfare. During both world wars, submarines posed a huge threat to both warships and commercial shipping. In more recent years, submarines have become capable of missile attacks on targets both at sea and on land.

The first documented attack by a submersible dates back to the American War of Independence, when on September 4, 1776, the *Turtle*, designed by American David Bushnell, unsuccessfully tried to sink a British ship in New York harbor. The actual sinking of an enemy ship by a submarine had to wait until February 17, 1864, when the Confederate *Hunley* blew up the Union ship *Housatonic* off Charleston, South Carolina. The *Hunley* disappeared itself a short time after the attack, and was eventually raised from Charleston harbor in August 2000.

Despite these early experiments with the military application of underwater craft, submarines only became a regular part of navies in the twentieth century. A series of innovations over many decades was needed before the submarine became an effective weapon. Whereas initial submarine attacks involved attaching mine-like explosives to an enemy ship's hull, the English engineer Robert Whitehead developed the first powered torpedoes in the 1860s. In the 1880s, a Spanish naval lieutenant, Isaac Peral, made another important breakthrough when he designed an underwater craft powered by storage batteries.

At the end of the nineteenth century, the Irish-American John P. Holland developed a craft using a gasoline engine and rechargeable batteries capable of 8 knots on the surface and 5 knots submerged. The USS *Holland*, commissioned by the US Navy in 1900, became the world's first fully operational, as opposed to experimental, submarine. The British launched the 63-foot *Holland 1* a year later. Germany launched its first submarine, *U-1*, in 1906. The Imperial German Navy's *U-9*, commissioned in 1910, became the first submarine equipped with a gyrocompass and capable of submerged navigation.

For nations with weak navies, submarines offered a relatively inexpensive alternative to battleships. The increasing importance of aircraft also gave them the further advantage of being less easily detected than other warships. The destructive potential of submarines, however, meant that the major powers endeavored to put strict limitations on their use from the early twentieth century. International law at the time specified that warships should not attack merchant shipping unless the vessels were first searched for contraband and their crews assisted to safety, measures that posed obvious risks to submarines.

World War I

Although previously perceived as largely a defensive weapon for protecting harbors and coasts, the submarine's status quickly changed during World War I. For the first time, submarines engaged in a strategy of naval attrition. On September 5, 1914, the *U-21* commanded by Otto Hersing became the first submarine to sink a warship during the conflict. Its victim, the cruiser *Pathfinder*, sank in the Firth of Forth in less than four minutes with all but 11 of its 350 crew. The same month, the British *E-9* sank the German light cruiser *Hera*. While losses to submarines were initially small, they caused considerable anxiety to fleet commanders. Eventually, German submarines were responsible for sinking five of the 13 British battleships lost during the war.

World War I also witnessed Germany conduct the first concerted submarine campaign against merchant shipping. In England, the writer Arthur Conan Doyle was apparently one of the few to anticipate the use of submarines for commerce raiding. Although German submarines initially made efforts to ensure the safety of passengers and crew on merchant ships in line with international law, the complexion of the war quickly changed. In February 1915, Germany declared a blockade of the British Isles and announced that merchant ships in the area would be sunk without warning. Germany's use of submarine warfare became central to the decision of the United States to enter the war. The sinking of the *Lusitania* by a U-boat on May 7, 1915, created outrage in America, while President Woodrow Wilson deplored the death of non-combatants including merchant seamen. Germany declared a policy of "unrestricted" warfare by its U-boats from January 9, 1917, in large part prompting the United States to declare war on April 16, 1917.

During the course of the war some 320 U-boats carried out 3,274 operations, and sank 5,282 merchant ships totaling 12,284,757 tons. Although German submarines sank some vessels off the American and Canadian coasts in 1918, the anti-submarine war remained focused in European waters. By the end of 1916, the British deployed nearly 3,000 patrol craft to counter the U-boat threat but with relatively little success. In 1917, however, the Admiralty adopted several measures to combat more effectively the U-boat threat, including building faster merchant vessels, extensive mining, but most importantly the introduction of convoys. Although previously eschewed as a purely defensive measure, convoys in fact gave anti-submarine vessels more opportunities to take the offensive. Thereafter German attacks came at a heavy cost to the submarine service, with U-boats most commonly sunk by gunfire or ramming. The first U-boat claimed by a depth-charge attack was in July 1916, but for most of the war depth charges proved unreliable and in short supply. By the end of the war the Germans lost 178 U-boats at sea (19 due to accidents) with 5,410 crewmen, while Britain lost 54 submarines.

Interwar Years

As described by Herwig (1996: 261), "ambivalence and confusion" characterized the submarine policies of major powers during the interwar period. Allied propaganda had cast submarine warfare as largely a form of piracy. Despite the success of U-boats against merchant shipping during World War I, the German naval high command remained committed to strategies involving decisive battle-fleet actions. British, American, and Japanese naval planners similarly focused on battleships, viewing submarines as mainly an auxiliary to fleet actions.

Most nations considered the threat of unrestricted submarine warfare eliminated by international agreements. The Washington Naval Conference of 1922 and the London Naval Conference of 1930 specifically addressed the issue of submarine warfare, and under the London Submarine Protocol of 1936 the major naval powers agreed that submarines could attack merchant ships only if they refused search, and only when the safety of passengers and crew was ensured. The British also believed, mistakenly, that they could counter any submarine threat with the use of asdic (the sound navigation and ranging system known today as sonar).

Nevertheless, some important developments in submarine tactics took place during the interwar years. The Germans experimented with night surface attacks, and in 1935 such attacks became part of U-boat doctrine. The introduction of short-wave radio meant that U-boats could be centrally directed from shore or a command ship, a technique first tested in 1937, which helped shape the later thinking of Admiral Karl Dönitz. In America, a Submarine Officers Conference was formally constituted in 1926. This included many of the submariners who would assume leading roles in World War II. They pushed for the development of larger and more habitable fleet submarines capable of remaining at sea for two months or more.

World War II: Atlantic

Attempting to avoid the type of backlash that resulted from unrestricted warfare during World War I, German skippers were initially issued elaborate rules of engagement. However, the policy began to unravel from the first day of the war, September 3, 1939, when Fritz-Julius Lemp of the *U-30* sank the British passenger liner *Athenia*. The British subsequently began arming merchant ships, thus affording a pretext for U-boats to attack without warning. British submarines also later followed suit in attacking enemy merchant shipping without warning.

German U-boats fought a so-called tonnage war, attempting to sink as much Allied shipping as possible for the smallest loss of submarines. Much of the German submarine campaign was fought on the surface. Admiral Dönitz (Doenitz 1958: 127) described German U-boats as functioning primarily as "diving-vessels," that is, mainly acting as surface vessels but capable of disappearing when advantageous. Although submarine patrol lines had been used during World War I, the "wolf pack" concept was named and developed in World War II. The wolf packs primarily prowled routes in the North Atlantic, where convoys were beyond the range of land-based Allied air cover.

The Allies suffered their worst shipping losses in November 1942, when German U-boats claimed 743,000 tons. In mid-March 1943, wolf packs of up to 20 U-boats attacked convoys and claimed the sinking of 21 ships without a loss. It wasn't long, however, before the German submarine service realized that British–American shipbuilding outstripped their ability to sink ships. By May 1943, so-called Black May when over 40 of the 420 U-boats in operation were lost, it became equally clear that Allied anti-submarine forces had gained the upper hand in the Atlantic.

Technological innovations as well as convoys aided Allied anti-submarine forces. High frequency direction finders (HF/DF or "Huff Duff") allowed vessels to detect the direction of short-wave radio signals used by U-boats. More effective radar helped counter night surface attacks. With the forward-throwing "Hedgehog," depth-charge attacks became more accurate. Once British cryptanalysts broke the U-boat Enigma settings, convoys could be routed away from U-boat concentrations. Codebreakers also made it increasingly difficult for U-boats to meet supply vessels at sea. The use of small escort aircraft carriers allowed the Allies to cover the air gap previously exploited by submarines.

Despite fitting U-boats with "schnorkels," which allowed diesel engines to be run while submerged, and asdic "foxers" to deflect sonar, the German submarine service never recovered. During the war, 593 U-boats were lost to anti-submarine forces, and at the war's end 156 U-boats surrendered while another 221 were scuttled by their crews. Germany commissioned 1,171 submarines between 1935 and 1945. During World War II, U-boats conducted 3,000 operations and sank 2,927 ships totaling 14,915,921 tons.

World War II: Pacific

During World War II, President Franklin D. Roosevelt, like President Woodrow Wilson during World War I, denounced German unrestricted submarine warfare as a threat to American freedom of the seas and as a crime against humanity. While the United States previously supported strict protocols for submarine warfare, the Japanese attack on Pearl Harbor elicited an immediate change of policy. Within hours of the attack, chief of naval operations Admiral Harold Stark ordered "unrestricted air and submarine warfare against Japan." Particularly in light of the destruction of US battleships, submarines offered the primary means of taking the fight to the enemy.

Before the war, American submarines trained almost exclusively by making submerged attacks, but during the war effective night surface tactics evolved taking advantage of the submarines' camouflage and high speed. These tactics were greatly facilitated by surface-search SJ radar generally available by the end of 1942. During the course of the war, the capability of US submarines improved with sturdier hull construction allowing them to operate at greater depths. The warheads of torpedoes were made more lethal. By early 1943, the breaking of Japanese codes and dissemination of intelligence known as "Ultra" allowed submarines to frequently intercept enemy ships.

The greatest drawback of the American submarine campaign was defective torpedoes, which frequently exploded prematurely or failed to detonate at all. Early in the war, Germany had been plagued by similar problems, but these were sorted out relatively easily compared to those of the Americans. Anticipating attacks on armored battleships, the US torpedoes incorporated an exploder mechanism intended to be triggered by an enemy ship's magnetic field, detonating under its keel. The magnetic exploder proved unreliable, as did the contact exploders and depth settings; it took nearly two years of war before all of the faults of the American torpedoes were corrected.

As Japan belatedly implemented a convoy system from late 1943, US submarines adopted their own version of the wolf pack – the coordinated search and attack group, as the Americans preferred to call them. These typically consisted of three submarines which traveled together from port, contrasting the German practice of summoning large numbers of U-boats once a convoy was located. In the Pacific, approximately 300 US submarines conducted some 1,500 war patrols, sinking 200 Japanese warships and over 1,000 merchant ships. Japan's dependence on imported oil, raw materials, and foodstuffs rendered them especially vulnerable to the submarine campaign. Japan began the war with approximately 1,600 ships totalling six million tons, and because of limited shipbuilding capacity, Allied submarines were able to inflict massive damage. By the latter stages of the war, as larger vessels disappeared from the seas, Allied submarines increasingly used their deck guns to destroy smaller craft such as schooners, sampans, junks, and fishing trawlers used for moving troops and supplies. During 1945, American, British, and Dutch submarines in the Far East attacked over 1,000 small craft using their deck guns.

By comparison, the Japanese submarine campaign proved relatively ineffectual. Although Japanese submarines periodically attacked freighters and troop ships, they were largely employed providing fleet screens and, as the war progressed, used in desperate supply operations and evacuations of beleaguered troops. American anti-submarine warfare also proved much more effective than its Japanese counterpart.

In contrast to U-boats in the Atlantic, American submarines were able to transit to their patrol areas in relative safety. Even so, the US submarine service suffered substantial losses, with a total of 52 submarines lost during the war, most without survivors. The 3,500 US submariners lost represented 15 percent of the total operational force. The Japanese lost 131 submarines during the war, but even these losses were modest when compared to the loss of German submarines and crews.

Cold War and Beyond

In the post-World War II period, submarines acquired a range of new capabilities. In 1946,

the US Navy's Bureau of Ships moved to increase the underwater speeds of submarines. Between 1947 and 1951, 50 US fleet boats underwent conversion to "Guppy" (Greater Underwater Propulsion Program), with high-capacity battery plants. In 1951–1952, six *Tang* class electroboats were completed, and in 1953 the hull design of the *Albacore* was optimized for underwater speed. These developments, along with improved sensors, helped recast the submarine as an effective anti-submarine weapon.

Under the direction of Admiral Hyman G. Rickover (1900–1986), the US Navy began development of a nuclear submarine, and in 1954 the USS *Nautilus* became the world's first ship with a nuclear propulsion plant. Submarines could now remain submerged indefinitely and afford greater space for personnel than before. The *Skipjack* combined a new hull design with nuclear propulsion in 1959, giving submarines sufficient speed to operate with or against battle fleets. The *Thresher* became America's first deep-diving attack submarine in 1960, but it also became the first nuclear boat lost when it disappeared in 1963.

US submarines first experimented with firing rockets against Japanese targets during World War II, but in the post-war period submarines gained the capacity to strike targets using guided missiles. Cruise missiles were first deployed on submarines in 1957, allowing them to hit targets several hundred miles inland. In the post-nuclear age, the deployment of submarines armed with ballistic missiles and nuclear warheads played a key role in strategies of deterrence through assured destruction between the major powers. In November 1960, the *George Washington* became the first ballistic missile submarine to go on active patrol. It carried 16 intermediate-range (1,200 nautical miles) Polaris missiles, becoming the world's first "boomer," as the submarines were nicknamed.

Britain's first nuclear submarine, the HMS *Dreadnought*, was commissioned in 1963. The choice of the name "Dreadnought" was significant, calling to mind the powerful battleships that so altered naval warfare at the beginning of the twentieth century. The nuclear submarine had arguably replaced the battleship as the apex of technological power and national prestige. In 1968, the HMS *Resolution*, armed with 16 US Polaris missiles, became the first British ballistic-missile submarine on patrol. Whereas Britain's nuclear submarines usually operated under the auspices of the North Atlantic Treaty Organization, the French remained independent and produced their first nuclear submarine, the *Redoubtable*, in 1971.

In the mid-1970s, America introduced the *Los Angeles* class, the first fast-attack submarines. They first carried a variety of weapons, including cruise and anti-ship missiles. The 1970s also saw the development of the *Ohio* class, strategic missile submarines some 560 feet long. They first entered active service in 1981, armed with 24 of the new multiple-warhead Trident intercontinental ballistic missiles (ICBMs).

The Soviet Union commissioned its first nuclear submarine, *Leninsky Komsomol*, in 1958. In the 1980s, the Soviets introduced the huge nuclear-powered *Typhoon* class submarines armed with ICBMs. From the 1980s, Soviet and US submarines were also armed with anti-ship cruise missiles capable of being launched from underwater and hitting targets hundreds of miles away. Submarines further developed "quieting" and "silencing" stealth technologies to maximize their invisibility.

During the Vietnam War, submarines focused on reconnaissance, surveillance, and clandestine missions. The HMS *Conqueror* made the first attack by a nuclear submarine when it sank the heavy cruiser *General Belgrano* during the Falklands War of 1982. Whereas during the world wars submarines played a relatively minor role in anti-submarine forces, this has since become a major function. Equipped with long-range acoustic sensors, they are effective in locating other submarines. Anti-submarine capabilities have also increased with the adoption of seabed sensor arrays, towed sonar arrays, and anti-submarine warfare helicopters.

The current trend is toward the production of increasingly sophisticated submarines in smaller numbers. Today, both nuclear submarines and conventionally powered submarines can be used to attack enemy naval forces or land installations using anti-ship and cruise missiles. In the opening offensive against Iraq on January 17, 1991, for example, US attack submarines launched Tomahawk missiles against Iraqi naval bases. From once being depicted as an equalizer for relatively weak navies and morally suspect nations, the submarine today is viewed by many as the ultimate weapon system. The loss of the Russian submarine *Kursk* in August 2000, though, underlines the continued fragility of life on a submarine.

SEE ALSO: Falklands War (1982); Vietnam War (1959–1975); World War I: Western Front.

References

Doenitz, K. (1958) *Memoirs: Ten Years and Twenty Days*. London: Weidenfeld and Nicolson.

Herwig, H. H. (1996) "Innovation Ignored: The Submarine Problem, Germany, Britain, and the United States, 1919–1939." In W. Murray and A. R. Meillett (Eds.), *Military Innovation in the Interwar Period*. Cambridge: Cambridge University Press.

Further Reading

Ben-Yehuda, N. (2013) *Atrocity, Deviance and Submarine Warfare: Norms and Practices during the World Wars*. Ann Arbor: University of Michigan Press.

Blair, C. (1975) *Silent Victory: The US Submarine War against Japan*. Philadelphia: J. B. Lippincott.

Blair, C. (1996) *Hitler's U-Boat War: The Hunters 1939–1942*. New York: Modern Library.

Blair, C. (1998) *Hitler's U-Boat War: The Hunted 1942–1945*. London: Cassell.

Gannon, R. (1996) *Hellions of the Deep: The Development of American Torpedoes in World War II*. University Park: Pennsylvania State University Press.

Holwitt, J. I. (2009) *"Execute Against Japan": The US Decision to Conduct Unrestricted Submarine Warfare*. College Park: Texas A&M University Press.

Lautenschlager, K. (1986–1987) "The Submarine in Naval Warfare, 1901–2001," *International Security*, 11 (3): 94–140.

Parrish, T. (2004) *The Submarine: A History*. New York: Viking.

Redford, D. (2010) *The Submarine: A Cultural History from the Great War to Nuclear Combat*. London: I. B. Tauris.

Sturma, M. (2011) *Surface and Destroy: The Submarine Gun War in the Pacific*. Lexington: University Press of Kentucky.

Vego, M. (2009) *Operational Warfare at Sea: Theory and Practice*. London: Routledge.

T

Terrorism, War Against

SEUMAS MILLER

The phenomenon of terrorism is not new: any authoritative history of terrorism (e.g., Laqueur 1977) would include, for example, references to anti-state terrorism of groups such as the Narodniki (Populists) in nineteenth-century Russia (e.g., assassination attempts on the tsars), the state terrorism of the Committees of Public Safety and General Security during the so-called Reign of Terror in the late eighteenth-century French Revolution, and anti-colonialist terrorism in Africa (e.g., Algeria) and elsewhere in the post-World War II period (Whittaker 2003). Moreover, counterterrorism, including police and military counterterrorism strategies, is a well-developed field of study (Hewitt 1984). However, the idea of a war against terrorism is quite recent. It has come into vogue primarily, it seems, as a consequence of the September 11, 2001, attacks on the World Trade Center in New York and the Pentagon in Washington, DC, by al-Qaeda operatives. The person most famously associated with prosecuting what he called a "war against terrorism" was US President George W. Bush in the aftermath of 9/11 (Coady and O'Keefe 2002). The idea brings together two prior notions, that of war and that of terrorism, both of which are somewhat vague and subject to ideological manipulation.

Post 9/11 there have been a number of specific terrorist bombings of civilians that have made international headlines, including in Bali in 2002, Madrid in 2004, London in 2005, New Delhi in 2005, and in Mumbai in 2006. In addition, there have been ongoing terrorist attacks in a number of theaters of internecine war, including in Iraq, Afghanistan, Kashmir, and in the Israeli–Palestinian conflict in the Middle East. These specific and ongoing attacks have ensured that terrorism remains a major international concern.

No one denies the reality and impact of terrorism in the contemporary world. But when it comes to defining terrorism there is much disagreement, including among philosophers and politicians, and among international lawyers and policymakers seeking to draft legislation so as to mobilize international support to combat terrorism (Wellman 1979; Whittaker 2003; Primoratz 2004; Wilkinson 2006; Saul 2008; Coady 2009; Miller 2009). If al-Qaeda is a paradigm of a terrorist network, what of the African National Congress (ANC) in the 1960s, 1970s, and 1980s? The ANC was branded a terrorist organization by the South African apartheid government. However, the ANC and its supporters claimed that they were not a terrorist organization, but

Twentieth-Century War and Conflict: A Concise Encyclopedia, First Edition. Edited by Gordon Martel.
© 2015 John Wiley & Sons, Ltd. Published 2015 by John Wiley & Sons, Ltd.

rather a liberation movement engaged in an armed struggle. State actors (e.g., the US government) often deny the existence of state terrorism (Whittaker 2003: 3; Primoratz 2004). Terrorism, they claim, is an activity only undertaken by non-state actors. This is, of course, consistent with claiming (as the US government, for example, does) that some nation-states *sponsor* terrorist groups – for example, by providing them with weapons, finance, or safe havens. But some theorists (Primoratz 2004: Part 3 State Terrorism) argue that state actors engage in terrorism and, indeed, that there can be and have been terrorist states. For example, the Soviet Union under Stalin was, on this view, a terrorist state. Certainly, Stalin routinely used a great many of the methods of terrorism.

Moreover, many allegedly non-state terrorist groups claim that the state actors against which they are fighting are the terrorists. Consider the Israeli–Palestinian conflict. On the one hand, many Israelis will argue that when Israeli forces engage in targeted assassinations of members of Hamas and the like, they are not engaged in terrorism but rather are using morally justified counterterrorist tactics (Hewitt 1984). On the other hand, many Palestinians proclaim these and other acts of the Israeli state to be acts of terrorism perpetrated against the Palestinian people.

Historically, terrorist organizations and campaigns have been identified not simply by their political motivations but also by their methods (Whittaker 2003). The methods they use to achieve their political ends are ones deployed in order to instill fear: quite literally to terrorize. These methods include assassination, indiscriminate killing, torture, kidnapping and hostage taking, and ethnic cleansing. Here a distinction can be made between terrorist actions *per se* (e.g., indiscriminate killing of civilians) and acts that are related to terrorist acts but are not in themselves terrorist acts (e.g., weapons procurement or passport forgery).

So terrorism is the use of violence in order to terrorize or otherwise instill fear in a target population for the purpose of achieving some political end. However, according to many influential accounts, what especially distinguishes terrorism from other forms of political violence is its favored method of the deliberate killing of innocent civilians by, for example, detonating bombs in crowded buses, trains, marketplaces, and the like (Primoratz 2004; Meggle 2005; Coady 2009; Miller 2009). A complication here is that there are some categories of civilians (e.g., collaborators) who some have argued are legitimate targets in armed conflict and, therefore, deliberate killing of them might not constitute terrorism (Primoratz 2004; Miller 2009). Be this as it may, here as elsewhere, the existence of hard cases does not remove the fundamental distinction. It is plausible, therefore, that deliberately killing innocent children in the service of political ends should count as terrorism, but that deliberately killing enemy soldiers in self-defense should not count as terrorism. A typical definition of terrorism to be found in the academic literature is the following one (Primoratz 2004: 24): "the deliberate use of violence, or threat of its use, against innocent people, with the aim of intimidating some other people into a course of action they otherwise would not take."

What of the notion of war in play in the war against terrorism (Walzer 1977; Gilbert 2003)? If there is a war against terrorism then presumably there is at least armed conflict between two or more protagonists, at least one of whom is engaged in terrorism. Some theorists have sought to restrict the notion of war to armed conflict between states. On this view, armed conflicts involving a nation-state and a terrorist non-state actor would not be a war.

However, this notion of war as restricted to armed conflict between states would rule out civil wars (e.g., the American Civil War that was waged by massed armies led by generals) and wars of revolution (e.g., the various wars of independence fought against colonial powers); that is, it would rule out armed conflict in which at least one of the protagonists is not a state actor (Gilbert 2003; Coady 2009). Arguably, therefore, the notion of war should not be restricted to armed conflict between states; non-state actors can, and sometimes do, engage in wars. If non-state actors can engage in wars then there seems no good reason why some terrorist groups could not wage war. Indeed, the Tamil Tigers in Sri Lanka, for example, evidently did just that. The Tigers trained and organized large numbers of combatants who engaged in ongoing armed combat with the Sri Lankan army for many years using many of the standard weapons of war such as guns, bombs, and the like.

Whether or not terrorist groups can engage in wars, it is evident that a minimal condition for being the sort of entity capable of waging war is to be an organized armed force. Thus lone individuals and ideological movements that do not possess an armed organized wing cannot engage in wars. Moreover, war in its primary sense is a form of political conflict. So war is armed conflict waged between or, at least, by or against a nation-state, city-state, tribe, or like political entity.

From our discussion of the relevant history and history of ideas in respect of the notion of the war against terrorism the following three (contested) propositions have emerged. First, state actors (e.g., the Soviet Union under Stalin), and not simply non-state actors (e.g., al-Qaeda), sometimes engage in terrorism. Secondly, non-state actors (e.g., the Tamil Tigers), and not simply state actors, sometimes engage in wars. Thirdly, a war against terrorism is not necessarily a war waged by a non-terrorist, state actor (e.g., a liberal democratic state such as the United Kingdom) against a terrorist non-state actor (e.g., the Irish Republican Army (IRA)). Thus ANC supporters claimed that the ANC was a non-terrorist, non-state actor fighting a war against a terrorist apartheid government which routinely tortured and killed innocent African school children who sought to exercise their human rights and which did so in part in order to terrorize them into submission. In claiming that the ANC was not a terrorist group, ANC supporters contrasted the official policies of their organization with those of other political organizations such as the Pan African Congress who did endorse the killing of innocent white civilians (e.g., by planting bombs in crowded restaurants).

Thus far we have discussed the notion of the war against terrorism in its literal sense. However, perhaps President Bush's pronouncements on the war against terrorism are not to be taken literally but rather figuratively. After all, the United States is not literally at war with terrorism *per se*, for terrorism *per se* is not an organization; nor is a terrorist ideological movement necessarily an organization. Moreover, there are some terrorist groups (e.g., the Oklahoma City bombers) which are not the sort of entities that are able to conduct

a war. Further, there are many terrorist groups – whatever their military capacity might be – that are simply not engaged in a war with the United States. It is surely false that the United States is at war with all the dozens of disparate terrorist groups all over the world, Islamic and otherwise, and at war also with numerous nation-states that engage in terrorism (e.g., Robert Mugabe's government in Zimbabwe).

If the notion of the war against terrorism is not taken literally but only figuratively, then a question arises as to its implicit meaning. One suggestion here is that implicit in the use of the term "the war against terrorism" in much contemporary western media is the idea that terrorism is the preserve of non-state actors and that liberal democratic states, in particular, are the ones who are fighting the war *against* terrorism. This general view is, as we have seen, directly or indirectly, at variance with much theoretical work on terrorism, as well as with the history of terrorism. A further additional historical claim is that liberal democracies do not have an entirely clean historical record when it comes to terrorism. Consider, for example, the bombing of civilian areas in Lebanon conducted by Israel in recent times (in response to Hezbollah terror bombings of civilian areas in northern Israel); or the bombing of civilian areas of Dresden and other German cities by Britain during World War II, apparently principally in order to terrorize the Germans into submission (there being few important military targets in these areas). Many have argued that these bombings were acts of terrorism. Thus Igor Primoratz says, "The bombing of German cities and towns also needs to be seen in the context of the history of terrorism: as a major and historically important campaign of state terrorism" (2010: 5). (For a contrary view, see Rosenbaum 2003.) Evidently, they meet the above-mentioned definitions of terrorism in terms of methods used, such as the deliberate killing of civilians.

Terrorism as Crime and Terrorism as War

Theoretically, and in practice, some terrorist acts can be regarded as ordinary crimes and subject to domestic criminal law. Accordingly, such terrorists should presumably be investigated, arrested and charged, and tried and punished in accordance with the principles and processes of the criminal justice system in the same way as an ordinary murderer or other criminal would be. This terrorism-as-crime approach would need to abide by human rights laws (domestic and international), such as presumption of innocence, rights of silence, requirement for proof beyond reasonable doubt, and so on. On the other hand, some terrorist acts are perpetrated in the context of wars. Being acts of war, they may take place outside the sphere of domestic criminal law. The terrorists operating in theaters of war are *de facto* military combatants: so they can be referred to as terrorist-combatants. Moreover, if these terrorists are combatants, then presumably they can justifiably be shot at, bombed, ambushed, and either captured or killed in the manner of combatants.

Here we need to invoke the notion of a socalled unlawful combatant. This term is controversial. We need to distinguish between the legal notion of an unlawful combatant and a non-legal one. On one view international law admits only of combatants and civilians, and defines combatants in such a way that they must meet certain criteria such as wearing a uniform and bearing arms openly. Accordingly, many resistance fighters, guerrillas, and terrorists are not combatants. This view is disputable since legally speaking the term "unlawful combatant" has been used to refer to combatants such as mercenaries whose activities contravene international law.

Whatever the legal situation, we can use the term "combatant" in a non-legal sense to refer to members of organized groups who carry weapons and engage in ongoing armed conflict with like armed groups. Consider Hamas fighters engaged in armed conflict with Israeli soldiers. The fact, if it is a fact, that legally speaking combatants might be defined in such a way that they must wear uniforms and bear arms openly, provides very weak grounds for refraining from regarding Hamas fighters as combatants in contexts of internecine war, such as the Israeli–Palestinian conflict. Arguably, persons who are trained in military techniques, are armed, and are engaged in killing combatants (as well as civilians) for military and political purposes are, for all intents and purposes, combatants, notwithstanding the fact that they do not wear uniforms and do not bear arms openly.

For our purposes here – using the term "combatant" in its non-legal sense – we need to distinguish between terrorist-combatants (e.g., members of al-Qaeda fighting US forces in Afghanistan), on the one hand, and lawful combatants that have, nevertheless, engaged in war crimes (e.g., a US soldier who tortures enemy prisoners). Lawful combatants who engage in war crimes typically breach the legal and ethical principles that govern the conduct of war. These principles include the impermissibility of torturing enemy combatants and of deliberately killing civilians. They are collectively referred to as the principles of *jus in bello*.

It could be argued that terrorist-combatants are *by definition* unlawful combatants since the definitive mode of combat of the military organization of which they are members is terrorism (e.g., murdering innocent civilians). It is not simply a matter of some individual combatants from time to time breaching the laws of war (the *jus in bello*), as in the case of a few rogue soldiers committing atrocities against civilians (e.g., the atrocities of US soldier Lieutenant Calley in 1968 at My Lai in Vietnam). On this view, terrorist-combatants, once determined to be such by an appropriately constituted, judicial body, ought to be subject to a criminal justice process analogous to that to which ordinary criminals are subject.

Contra the former Bush administration, David Luban (2002: 9; May 2007: ch. 14) and others hold that terrorists should not be subjected to a hybrid framework under which they are both ordinary criminals and simultaneously military combatants. However, in some conflict situations – for example, internal armed struggles such as Northern Ireland in the 1970s or Indian-controlled Kashmir at this time – it may be difficult to know which framework to apply; that is, whether to apply the criminal justice framework or the framework of war.

How are we to adjudicate between these competing conceptions of terrorism in such contexts: should terrorist attacks be regarded as crimes to be dealt with by the criminal justice system or as acts of war to be responded to by a military intervention?

In practice there have been a number of responses to terrorism, some essentially responses of the criminal justice system and some military in character. Some terrorist acts have been treated simply as crimes committed by criminals who are not also military combatants. For example, the Red Brigades' terrorist acts of the kidnapping and murder of Aldo Moro, president of the Christian Democrats, in 1978 in Rome were regarded as ordinary crimes (Whittaker 2003: 220). On the other hand, the US intervention in Afghanistan against al-Qaeda is essentially a military response.

However, there remains the issue of inconsistency raised by Luban and others. Presumably there is no inconsistency in regarding some terrorist acts as war crimes. War crimes are both acts of war and crimes; there is no inconsistency here. However, it might be inconsistent to treat a terrorist act as an ordinary crime outside a war setting and simultaneously treat it as a war crime. The question that now arises is how to differentiate terrorist acts that are war crimes from terrorist crimes that are simply ordinary crimes to be dealt with by the domestic criminal justice system. One way to do so is to attend both to the context in which terrorist acts are perpetrated and also to the types of institutional actors who commit acts of terrorism.

Terrorist acts take place in a variety of contexts. We can make the following threefold distinction in relation to such contexts (Miller 2009): (1) well-ordered (non-totalitarian) nation-states in peacetime: specifically, well-ordered, liberal democratic states at peace; (2) theaters of war in the context of wars between nation-states; and (3) theaters of war in the context of wars involving non-state actors (e.g., a civil war or an armed insurgency between a government's security forces and some other armed and organized military force). The attack on the World Trade Center took place in a type-1 context, the World War II bombing of Dresden took place in a type-2 context, and the terrorist attacks on Iraqi civilians during the current US armed forces occupancy of Iraq is taking place in a type-3 context. Note that from the fact that two states (or for that matter a state and a non-state actor) are at war it does not follow that all or, indeed, any of their respective territories are theaters of war. A theater of war is a *de facto* battlefield in which military combatants are engaged in combat. In World War II the US mainland (as opposed to, for example, Pearl Harbor in Hawaii) was not a theater of war.

Terrorist acts are performed by a variety of different sorts of institutional actors. Here we can distinguish two different types of terrorist, namely, *military* combatants (including the leaders of military combatants) and non-combatants (ordinary civilians).

Other things being equal, terrorists functioning in type-1 contexts (well-ordered, liberal democratic states) can be regarded as non-combatants and, therefore, as ordinary criminals, irrespective of how they regard themselves. Thus members of the Red Army Faction in Germany or the Red Brigades in Italy engaged in assassinating corporate and political leaders and security personnel in the 1970s should be regarded as (terrorist) non-combatants who are, therefore, ordinary criminals.

On the other hand, terrorists functioning in type-3 contexts (theaters of war) can be regarded as military combatants, specifically terrorist-combatants and, therefore, as unlawful combatants and war criminals. Presumably al-Qaeda operatives in Afghanistan are unlawful combatants and war criminals. As already mentioned, it is important to distinguish *unlawful* combatants who are war criminals from *lawful* combatants who are, nevertheless, war criminals. Thus the US airmen who bombed Hiroshima and Nagasaki were lawful combatants functioning in a type-2 context (theater of war being waged between nation-states); however, if their acts were acts of terror, then they were war criminals.

As already noted, on the view under discussion here a terrorist who is not a terrorist-combatant is a terrorist who is either not a member of a terrorist organization fighting a war, or is someone who is perpetrating acts of terrorism outside a theater of war. Accordingly, on this view, Timothy McVeigh was a terrorist but he was not a terrorist-combatant because he was not a member of a terrorist organization fighting a war. Again, the members of terrorist organizations who detonated bombs in the London Underground are not terrorist-combatants because the UK is a well-ordered, liberal democracy at peace.

Most theorists would accept that the conception of terrorism-as-crime is appropriate in the context of a well-ordered, liberal democratic state at peace in which non-combatant citizens of that state are performing acts of terrorism within the territory of that state and directed at that state and its citizens. However, even terrorist acts rightly dealt with under the terrorism-as-crime framework have properties that most other crimes to do not have. First, being actions in the service of some political or military end that is antithetical to the liberal democratic state – indeed, being actions that often constitute direct attacks on the state – terrorist actions are, other things being equal, potentially more destabilizing of law and order in a well-ordered, liberal democratic state than ordinary crimes.

Secondly, they involve not only the violent crime at the core of the terrorist act (e.g., murder), but also the intentional inculcation of fear in a population. By virtue of this fear-inducing feature, terrorist actions are, other things being equal, potentially more destabilizing of law and order in a well-ordered, liberal democratic state than many ordinary crimes. In this respect terrorist actions in a well-ordered, liberal democratic state are not to be equated to those performed by an authoritarian state against its own citizens; the latter may well contribute to the preservation of the authoritarian political order.

Thirdly, being organized actions, as opposed to, say, a one-off crime committed by an individual acting alone, or even a pattern of crimes committed by an individual acting alone, they are, other things being equal, potentially more destabilizing of law and order in the context of a well-ordered, liberal democratic state. In this respect they are akin to organized crime.

Presumably the terrorism-as-crime model – as opposed to the terrorism-as-war model – is the preferred and, therefore, default framework when a liberal democratic state is suffering lethal attacks from a terrorist organization. More precisely, it is plausible that the terrorism-as-war framework should be applied only under the following general conditions (Miller 2009):

1. The terrorism-as-crime framework cannot adequately contain serious and ongoing terrorist attacks.
2. The application of the terrorism-as-war framework is likely to be able adequately to contain the terrorist attacks.
3. The application of the terrorism-as-war framework is proportionate to the terrorist threat.

4. The terrorism-as-war framework is applied only to an extent (e.g., with respect to a specific theater of war but not necessarily to all areas that have suffered, or might suffer, a terrorist attack) and over a period of time that is necessary.
5. All things considered, the application of the terrorism-as-war framework will have good consequences in terms of security, and better overall consequences (e.g., in terms of lives lost, freedoms curtailed, economic impact, institutional damage) than the available alternatives.

Accordingly, it is only when the liberal democratic state cannot adequately contain the terrorist activity of a specific terrorist organization that the terrorism-as-war model might need to be applied – for example, in a theater of war involving ongoing, large-scale terrorist attacks and military counter-strikes by government security forces. The Israeli–Hezbollah conflict is arguably a case in point. Moreover, even if the terrorism-as-war model is to be applied in a given theater of war it would not follow that it should be applied outside that theater of war. Thus, even if it is desirable and necessary to apply the terrorism-as-war model to the armed conflict between al-Qaeda combatants and US forces in Afghanistan seeking to destroy al-Qaeda military bases and personnel, it would not follow that it was desirable or necessary to apply it to al-Qaeda operatives functioning in the US homeland.

This way of proceeding presupposes that the distinction between civil societies at peace and theaters of war can adequately be drawn. The concept of war is, of course, somewhat vague; the point at which a violent attack, or set of attacks, on one military organization by another military organization constitutes a war is indeterminate. Moreover, the concept of war is especially vague in its application to armed conflict between nation-states and non-state actors. Nevertheless, it is difficult to avoid the proposition advanced earlier that a nation-state and *a fortiori*, a liberal democratic nation-state, can engage in wars with non-state actors – for example, a civil war, a revolutionary war, or a war against an armed, organized, belligerent, external, non-state entity. Presumably Israel, for example, is engaged in a war with the terrorist organizations Hamas and

Hezbollah. Again, the United States is at war with the Taliban and al-Qaeda in Afghanistan. On the other hand, as noted above, from the fact that two states (or a state and a non-state actor) are at war, it does not follow that all or any of their respective territories are theaters of war.

If war is not necessarily a conflict between states and if terrorist organizations can wage war, then wars between terrorist organizations and liberal democratic states can be either external or internal wars. Presumably, the United States is fighting an external war against al-Qaeda in Afghanistan. On the other hand, India is fighting an internal war in India-controlled Kashmir against a variety of terrorist and separatist groups. In this conflict India is deploying hundreds of thousands of military and police personnel (Sen 2005: 65) and tens of thousands of civilians, soldiers, police, insurgents, and terrorists have lost their lives (Dhillon 2005: ch. 13).

There are a number of problems of application posed by terrorism for this dual (terrorism-as-crime or terrorism-as-war) approach. Some of these are discussed in Kretzmer (2005) who, in effect, offers a version of the dual approach. Moreover, there are alternative approaches – for example, the terrorism-as-crime (but not as war) favored by some governments who are confronting terrorist groups, and the terrorism-as-war (but not as crime) favored by many terrorist groups. Clearly, many governments do not want to be seen to be legitimizing terrorists by giving them the status of combatants engaged in war; they prefer to present them as criminals. For the same reason, terrorists seek legitimacy by presenting themselves as combatants engaged in war and reject the idea that they are merely criminals.

I now turn to a discussion of some of the problems of application for both the terrorism-as-crime and the terrorism-as-war frameworks. As such, they are problems for the dual approach as well as the alternative approaches.

Terrorist Attacks, Disasters, and States of Emergency

The first problem concerns large-scale, one-off, lethal terrorist attacks by non-state actors against, and within the territorial jurisdiction of, a well-ordered, liberal democratic state during peacetime – for example, the September 11, 2001, attack on the World Trade Center in New York and the Pentagon in Washington in which more than 3,000 people were murdered. Such a large-scale attack ought to be distinguished from ongoing, small-scale, lethal terrorist attacks of the kind perpetrated by, for example, the Red Brigades in Italy in the 1970s. For not one of the latter terrorist attacks taken by itself constituted a disaster as such; rather, each individual terrorist attack could be equated to, say, the murder of a public official by the mafia (e.g., the bombing of Judge Falcone in Italy in 1984). The point here is that such small-scale killings can be readily accommodated within the terrorism-as-crime model. However, large-scale terrorist attacks, including (potentially) chemical, biological, radiological, and/or nuclear terrorist attacks, are not ordinary crimes, but nor are they military attacks undertaken in theaters of war.

In some respects such attacks, given their one-off character, the large-scale loss of life, and the fact that they take place outside theaters of war, are more akin to disasters, such as the Indian Ocean tsunami in 2004 (in which approximately 200,000 lost their lives) or the flooding of New Orleans in 2005, than they are to ordinary small-scale murders. On the other hand, they are intentional lethal attacks; they are not simply natural disasters.

At any rate, perhaps some lessons can be learned from the way disasters are dealt with by governments (Miller 2009). Disasters typically call for the imposition of a legally circumscribed, geographically limited state of emergency during the period of the disaster and its immediate aftermath, but not beyond, and certainly not for a prolonged period. Moreover, if the terrorist actions in question are perpetrated outside a theater of war then presumably they should be treated as crimes, that is, the most appropriate framework to apply is the terrorism-as-crime framework – as opposed to the terrorism-as-war framework. So they are disasters as well as being crimes.

Let us now consider the possibility that the one-off, large-scale terrorist attack is perpetrated by a non-state actor based in some state outside the jurisdiction of the liberal democratic nation-state under attack. Here there are two salient possibilities. First, the state in which the terrorist group is based is itself well-ordered, and is willing and able successfully to apply the terrorism-as-crime framework (under its domestic law or derivatively under international law) to the terrorist attack. If so, then there is no need to apply the terrorism-as-war framework; the terrorism-as-crime framework will suffice (Kretzmer 2005).

Secondly, and alternatively, let us assume that the state in which the terrorist group is based is itself not well-ordered, and/or is unwilling or unable successfully to apply the terrorism-as-crime framework. In these circumstances the liberal democratic state that had suffered the one-off, large-scale terrorist attack could reasonably regard itself as the victim of an act of war by an external aggressor – albeit a non-state actor – and respond accordingly. The point here is that the non-state actor is not only a belligerent actor, it is a belligerent actor that is operating outside the authority and control of any state actor. An example of an external war between a liberal democratic nation-state and a non-state actor is the recent conflict between Israel and Hezbollah. The terrorist attacks against Israel perpetrated by Hezbollah (e.g., rocket attacks on Israeli settlements), and Israel's response in bombing parts of Lebanon (including civilian areas), constitutes such a war. However, this is not an example of a response to a single, large-scale terrorist attack. On the other hand, the US attack on al-Qaeda bases in Afghanistan following September 11, 2001, is such an example.

The general points to be extracted here are fivefold. First, territories under a state of emergency should not be equated to theaters of war; although some areas declared to be under a state of emergency (e.g., some regions under martial law) are theaters of war, many are not. Specifically, some contexts involving a one-off, large-scale terrorist attack (e.g., the al-Qaeda attack on the World Trade Center) warrant the declaration of a state of emergency but nevertheless are not theaters of war.

Secondly, disastrous occurrences in liberal democratic states in peacetime, including large-scale, one-off terrorist attacks, do not necessarily justify an increase in the *standing* powers (as opposed to the *emergency* powers granted for the limited period of the disastrous occurrence) of governments to order the use of, or security personnel to use, deadly force against offenders,

terrorists, or otherwise; and even disasters do not justify the granting to governments and/or security personnel of a legal power to deliberately kill innocent citizens.

Thirdly, any imposition of a state of emergency should presumably be comprehensively legally circumscribed in respect of: (i) the geographical area in which it is in force and the time period; (ii) the conditions under which it can be imposed (and the conditions under which it must be terminated); and (iii) the precise powers granted to government and security agencies during the state of emergency. Moreover, the imposition of states of emergency, and the granting and use of emergency powers, arguably ought to be subject to some form of independent scrutiny (e.g., be subject to judicial oversight).

Fourthly, notwithstanding the granting of emergency powers, it is plausible that the default framework to be applied domestically by well-ordered, liberal democratic states to large-scale, one-off terrorist attacks is the terrorism-as-crime – not the terrorism-as-war – framework. For the terrorist attack and the security response to it do not constitute an internal war within the liberal democratic state. (This is consistent with the application of the terrorism-as-war framework in the case of externally based terrorist groups to which the terrorism-as-crime framework has not been successfully applied by relevant external states.)

Fifthly, unlike in war, decisions in peacetime – including under a state of emergency – that will potentially result in large-scale loss of life are to be made (wherever possible) by the government, and not by the police (or military) leadership.

Terrorism, Internal Armed Struggles, and Theaters of War

Let us now focus on an additional theater of terrorist attacks, namely (liberal democratic) societies in which the political violence taking place has led to a substantial breakdown of law and order, that is, the state is not well ordered. Examples of this kind of context would include Northern Ireland in the 1970s, parts of South Africa at various times under apartheid rule (e.g., the so-called Independent States and some townships within the "official" South African state), and, at the present time, the West Bank in the Middle East, and Indian-controlled Kashmir.

In these kinds of contexts martial law or a state of emergency is typically declared. However, such contexts are not necessarily theaters of war in the normal sense. For one thing, the protagonists are not nation-states. For another thing, the combatants are not members of armies engaged in conventional warfare. Nor are they contexts in which essentially well-ordered, liberal democratic nation-states at peace are suffering a degree of political violence. I take it that the present-day mainland UK is an instance of the latter kind of context; the UK is a well-ordered, liberal democratic nation-state at peace, but one which has recently suffered political violence, that is, the London terrorist bombings in 2005 in which approximately 50 people lost their lives. Moreover, I take it that many (but by no means all) states within the contemporary nation-state of India that have experienced political violence nevertheless constitute well-ordered, liberal democratic societies at peace – for example, the state of Maharashtra, notwithstanding the Mumbai bombings in 2006 and the Mumbai bombings and shootings of 2008.

There are two salient conceptualizations of liberal democratic nation-states undergoing a substantial breakdown of law and order as a consequence of political violence and operating under emergency rule. The first is that the state is facing an extraordinary crime problem. An example of an indisputably extraordinary crime problem – albeit not one that arose initially from political violence – is that posed by Pablo Escobar in Colombia in the 1980s (Bowden 2001). Escobar was a major drug dealer whose crime organization was able to threaten the Colombian state as such. Accordingly, there were grounds for declaring a state of emergency and increasing judicial and police powers for a limited period to deal with the criminal threat to the state. Perhaps Northern Ireland in the 1970s should be included in this model; IRA operatives should have been held to be criminals (not combatants in a war) and the IRA itself a criminal organization, albeit one that was threatening the state as such in Northern Ireland. (I don't mean to dispute the proposition that the IRA's ultimate motivation was a political one, unlike Escobar.) On this conception, terrorist acts performed in a polity in

which a state of emergency has been imposed can, nevertheless, be regarded as ordinary crimes and, as such, be subjected to domestic criminal law, that is, the terrorism-as-crime framework prevails.

A second salient conceptualization is one in which the state is facing a civil war or at least is in the midst of internecine warfare. Perhaps the ANC's armed struggle in apartheid South Africa eventually reached the status of a low-level civil war, given the ongoing ungovernability of many of the townships in the context of domestic and international financial and other pressures, including sanctions.

Internecine warfare, including actual or potential civil wars, provides grounds for the government to put its armed forces on a war footing, albeit in relation to an internal armed group that is threatening the authority of the state. Legally speaking, it might do so within provisions for emergency rule or martial law. However, the substantive point here is not a legalistic one; rather, it pertains to *de facto* control. The government has lost, or is in danger of losing, control over the contested area. Moreover, to the extent that it has or can retrieve control, it is essentially relying on military force. Perhaps Kashmir should be included in this model. That is, perhaps Lashkar-e-Toiba operatives in Kashmir should be held to be terrorist-combatants (and, therefore, unlawful combatants, but not ordinary criminals) and the organization itself a military force engaged in a war (albeit a terrorist organization and, as such, an unlawful organization). On this conception, and notwithstanding the legal situation under emergency rule or martial law, certain terrorist acts, namely ones perpetrated by terrorist-combatants in theaters of war, should probably be regarded as acts of war, indeed as war crimes, and therefore as acts that take place outside the sphere of ordinary domestic criminal law. The reason for this is that the context is a *de facto* theater of war.

In relation to armed internal struggles we can make use of the threefold distinction adumbrated above, namely, that between terrorist-combatants, lawful combatants guilty of war crimes, and non-combatant terrorists. In *de facto* theaters of war in internal armed struggles involving terrorist non-state actors, the terrorist operatives are terrorist-combatants and, therefore, unlawful combatants.

Let us now turn to a consideration of counter-terrorism measures on the part of states confronting internal armed struggles by non-state actors. In so doing we need to keep in mind the distinction between terrorist-combatants and terrorist-non-combatants. In order to focus our discussion, I consider one salient counterterrorist measure, namely, the ambush. My assumption here is that a person performing acts of terrorism can, at least in principle, either be regarded as an ordinary civilian perpetrating a crime (terrorist-non-combatant), or as a terrorist-combatant perpetrating a war crime, but not as both simultaneously.

In wartime, killing the enemy in the context of an ambush is legally and morally acceptable. Now consider the ambushing and killing of IRA operatives in Northern Ireland. During the 1969–1994 period, the police of the Royal Ulster Constabulary and Britain's armed forces, including the Special Air Service (SAS) and the 14th Intelligence Company, conducted anti-Provisional IRA ambushes. Having located an arms cache, security forces would stake out and attempt to arrest terrorist suspects who came to collect the weapons, knowing that in doing so they would provoke a fire-fight in which the suspects would be killed; in short, a military-style operation was being conducted. The alternative strategy of confiscating the weapons, or rendering them inoperable and arresting the unarmed suspects, would normally be required of police operating under civilian rule. In short, the Northern Ireland context of the time was one in which offenders and security forces were engaged in a form of urban guerrilla warfare, notwithstanding the British government's insistence that the IRA was essentially a criminal organization, and the fact that members of the SAS could be convicted of murder for such acts. Similarly, ambushes, or so-called fake encounters, are a feature of anti-terrorist operations conducted in Indian-controlled Kashmir and parts of India by the Indian security forces, including police.

The question that is a matter of dispute between, for example, human rights advocates and security personnel, is whether or not police and other security personnel ought to treat a group of terrorists as if they are a criminal gang committing their crimes in peacetime, or as military combatants (albeit terrorist-combatants) fighting a war. Here we need to get clear on the difference between theaters of war and conditions of peace in well-ordered, liberal democracies. In the latter the presumption is that one is among one's fellow citizens and that, therefore, one's right to life will be respected; this is so whether one is an ordinary citizen, a police officer or, for that matter, a member of the armed services. Naturally, this presumption can be offset by, for example, the escape of a dangerous, armed offender or the existence of a terrorist cell. However, the point is that there is a presumption to be offset. However, in theaters of war the presumption is the reverse; one's life is presumed to be under threat. In the case of combatants, it is kill or be killed. And even in the case of non-combatant civilians there is a presumption of insecurity in theaters of war. On the one hand, the lives of non-combatants are at risk when caught in the crossfire between combatants. On the other hand, in theaters of war there is no effective, organized security agency, such as the police, to guarantee their safety; rather, citizens must seek to preserve their own lives as best they can.

This distinction between theaters of war and well-ordered, liberal democracies in peace-time is mirrored in the difference between the role of military combatants and that of police officers. The role of police is to apprehend suspected criminals in order that they can be tried by the courts, and, if found guilty, punished. Accordingly, police – as we argued above – are only entitled to use deadly force in limited conditions and as a last resort (e.g., in self-defense or in defense of the lives of others). Police are not legally or morally entitled to ambush and kill criminals, as would be the case if they were fighting enemy soldiers on the battlefield. Even if the only moral and legal justification for waging war is self-defense, a particular military unit conducting a specific military operation does not necessarily have to meet the criterion of acting in its own self-defense with respect to the particular group of enemy combatants being engaged in that operation at that time. This is in part because the presumption in war is the reverse of that in a well-ordered, liberal democratic state at peace.

The difficulty that arises at this point is that Lashkar-e-Toiba, Naxalities, the IRA (in, say, the 1970s), and like groups are, in effect, operating as soldiers fighting a war; indeed, they regard themselves as such. Accordingly, they have the practice of ambushing, bombing, shooting at, and otherwise killing police in the manner of soldiers fighting a war against enemy soldiers. In light of this, it might be unrealistic to expect police to respond to Lashkar-e-Toiba, Naxalites, or IRA terrorists in the manner in which they would respond to ordinary armed criminals; further, it might be difficult to enforce any policy that required police so to respond. Indeed, the practice that is likely to emerge among police is one of treating terrorists as enemy combatants being confronted in a theater of war. Moreover – and notwithstanding the legal situation – this practice appears to have a readily available, even if not decisive, moral justification, namely, self-defense; for all intents and purposes the police are confronting organized enemy soldiers hell-bent on trying to kill them.

One response to this kind of problem has been to impose emergency rule or martial law in the disputed territory – for example, Indian-controlled Kashmir has at various time been under one or other of these legal impositions. On pain of ceasing to be a liberal democracy, a liberal democratic government can impose martial law only for a definite and limited period, and only once the security situation has seriously deteriorated, that is, when the domestic criminal justice system is unable to provide security to the citizenry. In this context members of terrorist groups can be designated as military combatants (albeit terrorist-combatants) rather than ordinary criminals. Nevertheless, combatants can be tried and punished for war crimes, including terrorism. Accordingly, this is tantamount to the application of the terrorism-as-war-crime model, notwithstanding the difference between an unlawful combatant committing a war crime and a lawful combatant committing a war crime. For example, in Assam in India martial law was declared in January 2007. Following the slaughter of dozens of Hindi-speaking migrant workers by a separatist terrorist organization, the United Liberation Front of Asom (ULFA), a curfew was imposed by authorities and shoot-on-sight orders issued to security personnel. There have been similar attacks in the past – for example, in 2000, ULFA militants killed 100 migrants.

A closely related alternative to martial law is the imposition of a state of emergency in which the military remain, nevertheless, under the authority of the civil authorities, including the police. This was the situation during the IRA's armed struggle in Northern Ireland in the 1970s. This solution stops short of the application of the terrorism-as-war model; it remains an application of the terrorism-as-crime model. It is essentially an extension of the state of emergency concept discussed above in relation to well-ordered, liberal democratic states at peace confronting one-off disasters. As is the case with the imposition of states of emergencies in the context of disasters, it involves significant restrictions on civil and other rights of a kind that is inconsistent with liberal democracy; hence the plausibility of the argument that the imposition of emergency powers should be only for a definite and limited period, and should be comprehensively legally circumscribed.

References

Bowden, M. (2001) *Killing Pablo: The Hunt for the World's Greatest Outlaw*. London: Atlantic Books.

Coady, C. A. J. (2009) *Morality and Political Violence*. New York: Cambridge University Press.

Coady, C. A. J. and O'Keefe, M. (Eds.) (2002) *Terrorism and Justice: Moral Argument in a Threatened World*. Melbourne: Melbourne University Press.

Dhillon, K. (2005) *Police and Politics in India: Colonial Concepts, Democratic Compulsions: Indian Police 1947–2002*. New Delhi: Manohar.

Gilbert, P. (2003) *New Terror, New Wars*. Edinburgh: Edinburgh University Press.

Hewitt, C. (1984) *The Effectiveness of Anti-Terrorist Policies*. Lanham: University Press of America.

Kretzmer, D. (2005) "Targeted Killing of Suspected Terrorists: Extra-Judicial Executions or Legitimate Means of Defence?" *European Journal of International Law*, 16 (2): 171–212.

Laqueur, W. (1977) *Terrorism*. London: Little and Brown.

Luban, D. (2002) "The War on Terrorism and the End of Human Rights," *Philosophy and Public Affairs Quarterly*, 22 (3).

May, L. (2007) *War Crimes and Just War*. Cambridge: Cambridge University Press.

Meggle, G. (2005) *Ethics of Terrorism and Counter-Terrorism*. Frankfurt: Ontos.

Miller, S. (2009) *Terrorism and Counter-Terrorism: Ethics and Liberal Democracy*. Oxford: Blackwell.

Primoratz, I. (2004) *Terrorism: The Philosophical Issues*. New York: Palgrave Macmillan.

Primoratz, I. (Ed.) (2010) *Terror from the Sky: The Bombing of German Cities in World War II.* New York: Berghahn Books.

Rosenbaum, A. S. (2003) "On Terrorism and Just War," *International Journal of Applied Philosophy*, 17 (2).

Saul, B. (2008) "Attempts to Define 'Terrorism' in International Law," *Legal Studies Research Paper No. 08/115*, http://ssrn.com/abstract=1277583 (accessed January 27, 2014).

Sen, S. (2005) *Law Enforcement and Cross Border Terrorism.* New Delhi: Concept Publishing.

Walzer, M. (1977) *Just and Unjust Wars.* New York: Basic Books.

Wellman, K. (1979) "On Terrorism Itself," *Journal of Value Inquiry*, 13 (4): 250–258.

Whittaker, D. J. (Ed.) (2003) *The Terrorism Reader*, 2nd ed. London: Routledge.

Wilkinson, P. (2006) *Terrorism versus Democracy: The Liberal State Response*, 2nd ed. London: Routledge.

Further Reading

Walzer, M. (1973) "Political Action: The Problem of Dirty Hands," *Philosophy and Public Affairs*, 2 (2): 160–180.

Turco-Italian War (1911–1912)

BRUCE VANDERVORT

The Italian invasion of Ottoman-ruled Libya, which comprised the provinces of Tripolitania, with its capital at Tripoli, and Cyrenaica, with its capital at Benghazi, in October 1911, was, in the words of Italian historian Angelo del Boca, "a project nurtured for 30 years." Although Italian designs on Libya can be traced back to the early years of the nineteenth century, actual planning for the conquest of the region only began in earnest in November 1884, when the Italian government came to believe that the French, who had just established a protectorate over Tunisia, were about to seize Morocco, which would have given them control over all of North Africa, save for Egypt and Libya. Rome feared both for Italy's maritime security, as the Mediterranean risked becoming a French lake, and for Italy's future as an imperial power, a future already darkened by the French occupation of Tunisia, where many Italians lived and Italy had played a leading economic role for decades. Some Italians also cast covetous eyes on what they believed, quite erroneously as it turned out, was a rich caravan trade across the desert from sub-Saharan Africa to the Libyan port of Tripoli, and feared its diversion to entrepots in Tunisia or Algeria controlled by France.

Italy's motives for acquiring Libya differed in some particulars from those espoused by other imperial powers. Italians liked to portray their attempt to seize Libya as the reconquest of a lost colony. The region had been part of the Roman Empire in ancient times. Also, the Italian government saw Libya – and Eritrea and Ethiopia – as places in which to settle the country's surplus population. The loss of so many citizens to new allegiances in the Americas was a burning issue in Italian politics in the early twentieth century. This led some Italian politicians and journalists to make exaggerated claims about the agricultural and commercial potential of Libya. Some Italian politicians and statesmen coveted Libya for strategic reasons. They believed Italy needed ports and naval bases in North Africa in order to keep control over the central Mediterranean in the hands of Italy's new and formidable navy. These people tended to be Sicilians or southern Italians, for whom Libya was a short voyage away.

The Italian invasion of Libya was preceded by a successful diplomatic campaign to secure approval of the venture from the major European powers. The only power that might have posed obstacles to the Italian scheme was France, but she was won over by Italian support for her position in the Moroccan Crises of 1905 and 1911. The pretext used by the government of Prime Minister Giovanni Giolitti to justify launching an invasion of Libya was alleged Turkish discrimination against Italian businesses in Libya and the presumed inability of the Ottoman authorities there to guarantee the security of foreign residents. An ultimatum delivered to the Sublime Porte on September 28, 1911, gave the Turkish government 24 hours to agree to Italian military occupation of Libya. Although the Turkish response was conciliatory, Rome declared it unsatisfactory and ordered its fleet into action. The army was mobilized, but since Italy used regular army conscripts, not a purpose-built colonial army like France, for example, to fight its wars in Africa, precious time had to be spent assembling the approximately

45,000 soldiers assigned to the invasion force and equipping them for tropical warfare.

The war that ensued was almost solely a product of the machinations of the Italian government, particularly of Foreign Minister Antonino di San Giuliano and Prime Minister Giolitti, and its conduct stayed very largely in the same civilian hands. The armed forces remained pretty much in the dark about the government's intentions until the final weeks before the war began and, once the fighting started, the advice of the generals and admirals was only rarely sought and even less often listened to. Although the Italian Constitution, or *Statuto*, placed the military under the direct control of the king, in actual fact the nation's armed forces marched to the orders of their civilian superiors.

The first Italian soldiers came ashore at Tripoli, Libya's largest city, on October 9, by which time the city already had been occupied, following a short bombardment, by 7,000 sailors. The scratch force had set up a defensive arc around the city, well within range of naval gunfire. The small Turkish garrisons in the main cities of Libya, meanwhile, had withdrawn to the interior, where they joined forces with Arab militia and tribal levies to mount a resistance to the Italian invasion. The Italian army and its civilian masters had believed that the Turks would give up and return home, but Rome had done almost everything in its power to assure that this did not happen. Prior to the war there had been some discussion in Italian government circles about declaring a protectorate in Libya, as the French had done in Tunisia and the British in Egypt. This would have permitted the Turks to retain nominal sovereignty, while ceding the actual running of the country to the occupying power. Mainly on the insistence of Prime Minister Giolitti, this idea was dropped, on the pretext that such an arrangement would be too complicated for the Libyan masses to comprehend. The real issue, it would seem, was Giolitti's fear that the increasingly nationalistic Italian population would settle for nothing less than full sovereignty over Libya. Thus, on November 5, 1911, a decree was issued by the Italian government formally annexing Libya. In retrospect, this appears to have been a big mistake.

The Italian government and military had also concluded that because of their dislike for their Turkish overlords, the Arab and Berber populations of Libya would greet the Italians as liberators.

The fact that this supposition proved false and that the shared faith of ruler and subject outweighed all other considerations, when added to Turkey's unexpectedly firm military commitment, made the conflict in Libya very rough going for Italy.

On October 23, 1911, a mixed force of Turkish soldiers and Arab irregulars launched a surprise attack on a weakly defended sector of the Italian defense cordon around Tripoli. The subsequent massacre of Sciara Sciat, in which some 500 Italian soldiers were killed, provoked severe reprisals by the Italian army, including large-scale summary executions and the opening of concentration camps in Libya and Italy. The Italian response to the massacre stirred up considerable anti-Italian sentiment in Europe, in particular in Britain.

From October 1911 well into 1912, Italian forces made little headway against Turkish–Arab opposition, despite receiving reinforcements in November 1911 and enjoying a lopsided advantage in weaponry, including aircraft and dirigibles used to bomb enemy positions. This was the first time that aircraft were used in a combat role, rather than simply for reconnaissance. The Italian army in Libya also pioneered the use of armored cars and developed a system of battlefield wireless communications. Toward the end of the conflict, the Italians brought in a battalion of *ascaris*, African colonial troops from Eritrea on the Red Sea coast, in the twin hopes that these soldiers, presumably more acclimated to desert warfare, could spearhead an advance into the interior, and that their Muslim background would impress the local population. The latter hope faded when it was discovered that some of the Eritrean troopers were Christian.

Lack of progress in the war stemmed in part from the difficult terrain and climate and the low morale of the largely conscript force, but also was a product of the army's lingering fear of being drawn into "another Adowa." This Italian defeat at the hands of the Ethiopians in 1896, the bloodiest encounter in the whole of the European colonial wars, had brought down a government, and fears of a repetition were only made more intense by the Sciara Sciat massacre. Many of the generals who served in Libya, including the commander, General Carlo Caneva, had fought in East Africa earlier in their careers. Turkish leadership proved somewhat more inspired, although, even with mass Arab support, Turkish regular troops were consistently outnumbered in the field and were seldom able to take the offensive. The Turkish officers who served in Libya included Kemal Atatürk, who would become the first president of the new Turkish Republic in 1923, and Enver Bey, who served as Ottoman minister of war during World War I.

Enver played a particularly important role in effectively liaising with the powerful Sufi brotherhood, the Sanusiya, who served as the spiritual and, to some extent, political leaders of the Bedouin of the desert interior of Libya, particularly in the province of Cyrenaica. The orthodox Sanusi traditionally had carried on an arm's-length relationship with the Turks, not considered very good Muslims, and this had been seen by Italian officials as an indication that the brotherhood might rally to Italy or at least remain neutral in case of an Italian invasion. Agents of Prime Minister Giolitti, beginning in 1908 when he was interior minister and continuing down to the eve of the war, had used pledges of money and arms to try to win over the Sanusi. As it turned out, however, after a short period of inactivity following the Italian landings, the Sanusi, on the urging of Enver Bey, took the leadership of Bedouin reinforcements for the Turkish regulars in Cyrenaica, with the result that Italian troops were unable to penetrate into the interior of that province for the duration of the war.

The fighting between Italy and Turkey could only be brought to an end when the Italians decided to expand the war to the eastern Mediterranean. A naval raid on the Dardanelles was followed by the occupation by Italian troops of Rhodes and other islands in the Dodecanese chain in the Aegean Sea. This, plus anticipation of renewed conflict in the Balkans over what remained of European Turkey, brought the Turks to the peace table. On October 18, 1912, a settlement was reached at Lausanne in Switzerland, granting Italy sovereignty over Libya. The Italians also agreed to remove their troops from the Dodecanese Islands as soon as the Turks evacuated Libya, but Turkish participation in World War I on the side of the Central Powers allowed Italy to continue to occupy the islands down into World War II.

The consequences of the Turco-Italian War, the only war between European powers from 1878 to World War I, proved ominous. For Italy, the war was costly, not so much in blood as in treasure. More Italian soldiers died of disease than enemy bullets – 1,948 to 1,432 – but what many of them were calling a "war for a desert" by the end of the conflict had cost Italy around 527 million lire and had drawn off a large portion of its army and modern military equipment. Worse, the fighting in Libya did not end with the Peace of Lausanne. An Arab insurrection continued until 1932, when Mussolini's army used scorched earth tactics to finally bring it to an end. In 1916, when the Italian army entered its second year of heavy fighting in the Alps against the Austrians during World War I, over 40,000 of its soldiers were still battling guerrillas in Libya. The Arab struggle against the Italians in Libya, which gained support, mostly moral, from Muslim peoples around the world, has been called the first pan-Islamic mass resistance movement against western colonialism and has been credited with providing modern Libya with the necessary credentials to declare itself an independent nation-state. Defeat in the war seriously weakened the Ottoman Empire, a development which quickly led to the Second Balkan War, casting Turkey into a losing battle against the newly independent states in the Balkans and raising the long-dreaded specter of the collapse of the Ottoman Empire, followed by war among the European powers eager to get their share of the spoils. In this way, the war between Italy and Turkey over Libya added significantly to the tension in Europe that would help produce World War I.

SEE ALSO: Balkan Wars (1912–1913); Italo-Abyssinian Wars.

Further Reading

Askew, W. C. (1942) *Europe and Italy's Acquisition of Libya, 1911–1912.* Durham, NC: Duke University Press.

Del Boca, A. (1986) *Gli Italiani in Libia. Volume 1: Tripoli, bel suol d'amore, 1860–1922.* Bari-Rome: Laterza.

Gooch, J. (1989) *Army, State and Society in Italy, 1870–1915.* New York: St. Martin's Press.

Herrmann, D. G. (1989) "The Paralysis of Italian Strategy in the Italian–Turkish War, 1911–1912," *English Historical Review,* 104 (411): 332–356.

Labanca, N. (2012) *La guerra italiana per la Libia, 1911–1912.* Bologna: Il mulino.

Malgeri, F. (1970) *La guerra libica (1911–1912)*. Milan: Bompiani.

Maltese, P. (1968) *La terra promessa: la guerra italo-turca e la conquiste della Libia 1911–1912*. Milan: O. Mondadori.

Romano, S. (1977) *La quarta sponda: La guerra di Libia 1911–1912*. Milan: Bompiani.

Simon, R. (1987) *Libya between Ottomanism and Nationalism: The Ottoman Involvement in Libya during the War with Italy (1911–1919)*. Berlin: Klaus Schwarz.

Vandervort, B. (2012) *To the Fourth Shore: Italy's War for Libya (1911–1912)*. Rome: Stato Maggiore dell'Esercito. Ufficio Storico.

V

Veterans

MICHAEL D. GAMBONE

Introduction

Throughout history, the military has been a permanent component of civilization. With each new era, from the most primitive to the contemporary modern world, the need for social groups to survive has been paramount and individuals have fought to pursue that goal. While success has varied across the centuries, as civilizations have increased in size and complexity, militaries accordingly have grown in size and scope.

The survivors of military service are defined as veterans. Produced in concert with military institutions and their wars, generations of veterans occupy the historical timeline in the aftermath of conflict. In uniform and as returning members of greater civil society, they have exercised an influence on events far greater than their physical numbers.

Veterans have been, and will continue to be, the foundation upon which viable militaries are built. Old soldiers are institutional memory. In peacetime, they are the mentors for enlisted soldiers and young officers, imparting the traditions

and good practices that are the glue holding together individual units and whole branches of the service. In wartime, this same experience provides the hard-won lessons that mark the difference between life and death.

When veterans return to civilian society, it is arguable that their influence is even more important. The veteran is a yardstick that civilizations use to measure legitimacy, whether this means the righteousness of a war's cause, or a specific policy decision, or the simple definition of what it means to be a citizen. By presenting the ultimate sacrifice for the collective good, both the principle and the flesh-and-blood reality of a veteran create a context for public discourse.

In another sense, veterans have also provided critical leadership in times of peace and war. Throughout history, military service has been a particular litmus test for legitimate decision-making. Whether applied to medieval kings or American presidents during the Cold War, this basic quality has transcended time and place with its durability.

More ominously, veterans have at times proven to be a threat to public order. In more than a few instances, the veteran has simply failed to completely reassimilate back into normal society. Representing a surplus of martial talent and

Twentieth-Century War and Conflict: A Concise Encyclopedia, First Edition. Edited by Gordon Martel.
© 2015 John Wiley & Sons, Ltd. Published 2015 by John Wiley & Sons, Ltd.

aggressiveness, veterans have often proven to be an anathema to the very societies they pledged to protect. History is littered with the bitter remnants of former armies cast out and alienated by their obsolescence. Peace has often been defined by larger efforts to find a place for these men on a new, landed frontier or in a modern-day college classroom.

Veterans and the Great War

The industrial era significantly altered both society and the art of war, interweaving individuals with the process of production and distribution, while vastly increasing the lethality of modern conflict. Millett and Maslowski have noted the integration of industrial society with increasingly complex weapons systems. Steel dreadnoughts were the product of technological leaps forward as well as the industrial capabilities of steel and railroad corporations. Once industrial nations took this step, "armed forces modernization bound together the public welfare, private interest, and national security" (Millett and Maslowski 1994: 265–270).

Improvements in public schooling and the imposition of mandatory periods of education also created a literate populace more ready to accept the concept of nationalism. The advent of the telegraph and the penny press provided readers with information on a global scale. Consequently, the citizen of the period possessed both a greater sense of duty to the state and a better understanding of its policies at home and abroad.

The Briton of Victorian England, the prototype of a modern, industrial nation in the nineteenth century, was a joiner who saw public service as a civic duty. Public charities flourished during the day, attempting to circumvent the many social and economic problems suffered by industrial England. However, in a country largely separated from the campaigns of imperial conquest, distance tempered the lengths to which civilian duty might translate into military service. At the turn of the century, the British military was again a separate and distinctly lower class in society, embodying a function that Kipling captured at the end of his famous poem "Tommy":

> For it's Tommy this, an' Tommy that, an'
> "Chuck him out, the brute!"

> But it's "Savior of 'is country" when the
> guns begin to shoot;
> An' it's Tommy this, an' Tommy that, an'
> anything you please;
> An' Tommy ain't a bloomin' fool –
> you bet that Tommy sees!
> (Kipling 1909: 9)

Great Britain's treatment of its veterans reflected this ambivalence. Former service members suffered under a poorly structured military pension system that often left them heavily dependent on private charities. A 1909 report of the Commission on the Poor Law noted that: "it is the men who have left the permanent situation afforded by the Army, and who, after more or less interval, have abandoned hope of getting employment of a permanent character, who furnish the largest contingent of the floating population of the casual wards" (Barr 2005: 10).

This state of affairs changed after the outbreak of World War I. Enthusiastic patriotism guided the armies that mobilized to fight throughout most of Europe. The heroic ideal was embodied in the Ersatz Corps of German students who volunteered to serve their Kaiser and the hundreds of thousands of British men who volunteered for Minister of War Kitchener's "New Army" in 1914. Even the United States, long suspicious of overseas conflicts, joined the fray singing and offering full-page newspaper ads in thanks for Woodrow Wilson's declaration of war.

However, as the world geared up for the greatest conflict in human history to that time, it universally failed to provide veterans with facilities equal to the war effort. The sheer scale of service quickly overwhelmed even well-functioning state systems designed to assist veterans returning home. In Britain, for example, approximately one-quarter of World War I veterans, or 1.2 million men, suffered from various disabilities. After four years of war, 5.7 million German soldiers were wounded and as many as 2.7 million left with some type of permanent disability (Barr 2005: 120–121).

In relatively short order, the British veterans' pension system collapsed under the weight of new demands. National agencies proved to be underfunded, antiquated, and totally overwhelmed. Even after the Ministry of Pensions was created in 1917, it failed to allay the problems of medical care, job placement, and housing that plagued veterans during and after the war. Despite additional resources, demand far outran the state's ability to keep pace. The tens of thousands of applications for benefits stored in the ministry's Lost Files Room attested to the breadth of the failure.

British cultural mores compounded the problem of bureaucratic ineptitude. Michael Roper has argued that social welfare as a concept flew in the face of Edwardian standards that defined "manliness." For thousands of veterans suffering from the period's post-traumatic stress disorder, "shell shock," an admission of need was a profound departure from a society that mandated "muscular Christianity" and stoicism among its men. Oscar Wilde's son, who died on the Western Front in 1915, captured the moment in a letter to his father: "first and foremost, I must be a *man*. There was to be no cry of the decadent artist, of effeminate aesthete, of weak-kneed degenerate" (Roper 2005: 348). Consequently, veterans would struggle with both their maladies and a conventional wisdom that branded them as cowards.

As these personal and social tragedies unfolded in Europe and the United States, private organizations attempted to reform the veterans' welfare and pension system. Many of these were composed of returning servicemen who wanted a more effective means to lobby for both veterans' rights and broader social recognition of their military service. The British Legion, for example, sponsored the first Poppy Day in 1921 to commemorate the Great War and made the event a national tradition thereafter. Organizations such as the American Legion, the Veterans of Foreign Wars, the Canadian Legion, the French *Union Fédérale*, and the *Reichbund* in Weimar Germany were intended not only to win new state allotments for veterans, but also to counter the potentially negative impact of state policies upon them. While all of these organizations sought medical and economic assistance that was critical to recovery, none wanted or expected a lifelong dependency upon the benefice of the state. The *Union Fédérale* and the *Reichbund* represented disabled veterans and sought a reasonable degree of personal autonomy for their memberships. Historian Robert Wheldon Whalen placed the problem in proper context:

> The dead finally escaped the need to confront death; it was the living and especially the wounded who had to confront it. Disabled soldiers faced a desperate problem. Touched by grotesque death, they discovered to their horror that they had become grotesque. (Whalen 1984: 47)

For many, this basic dilemma made recovery a long path. However, once it had begun, the hope was that the veteran – whether disabled or not – would eventually return to civilian normalcy.

Still, despite both official and informal advocacy, millions struggled with the post-war peace. Generically described as the "lost generation," this cohort of veterans retained a basic division between the military and civilian spheres of life for years. In *All Quiet on the Western Front*, Erich Maria Remarque explained the source of this barrier in the military training millions received for the war:

> We became hard, suspicious, pitiless, tough – and that was good; for these attributes had been entirely lacking in us. Had we gone into the trenches without this period of training most of us would have certainly gone mad. (Remarque 1958: 25)

But training and experience proved hard to shed. Too many veterans flatly refused to cooperate with society. In fact, signs of this behavior appeared during the war and were sometimes the bizarre product of official policy. The 1916 German Auxiliary Service Law included provisions to employ disabled veterans in war industries. However, once a disabled veteran was declared "fit" for factory work, he immediately lost his pension. Consequently, shirking became a chronic problem, to the point where wounded soldiers would refuse medical treatment so that they could avoid returning to military service or losing their meager benefits.

Other types of separation from society were subtler. A French veteran recounted what the war had taught him in Antoine Prost's *In the Wake of War*: "I learnt to appreciate better the joy of being alive. I eat, I drink, I breathe, I sleep with pleasure. Through this precious good humor, I am inclined not to worry much about minor matters" (Prost 1992:17).

In matters of personal association, veterans preferred a form of self-segregation, not only from general society, within which they formed a distinct subculture, but also from other veterans who had not shared the experience of combat. Non-participants found themselves privately excluded by cliques that had witnessed bloodshed. Publicly, combat veterans poured their derision upon parades, rallies, and other overt demonstrations of patriotism and nationalism for their insincerity and ignorance.

The outcomes produced by this large plurality of veterans varied across Europe. Deborah Cohen has noted that, "In Great Britain, the state escaped the wrath of its veterans, whereas in Germany, a newly founded republic bore its heroes' full fury" (Cohen 2001: 3). Ironically, where British policy largely failed the millions of veterans produced by the Great War, there was no critical mass of resentment that turned against London. The various private organizations that sprung up after 1918, particularly the British Legion, provided an effective buffer between veterans and civil society in the 1920s and 1930s.

Post-war Germany proved to be another story entirely. Disgruntled veterans flocked to the ranks of fringe organizations and later served as the fulcrum that eventually destroyed the Weimar government. Many German veterans organized to recreate the sense of camaraderie established during the war. However, many of these organizations also served as vehicles to express discontent with either veterans' benefits or the general absence of law and order in the country. One component of the "national opposition" was Stahlhelm, which comprised 300,000 members by the end of the 1920s. Although considered too conservative by Nazi Party leaders, right-wing organizations like Stahlhelm clearly contributed to the decline of a civil political process in Germany (Jones 2006: 484). Groups like it were later absorbed into Nazi *Sturmabteilung* (Storm Troopers) after Hitler's ascent to power in 1933.

Veterans and World War II

World War II was distinct as a twentieth-century conflict not only by virtue of its titanic size and scope, but also for the attitudes of its combatants from the start. It is clear that when the fighting broke out in September 1939, the broad disillusionment produced by the Great War had left its mark on the generation destined to fight World War II. Most of the romantic notions that accompanied soldiers into the trenches were gone, along with the poetry that had expressed their enthusiasm. Replacing this ardor was cynicism at worst or, as Paul Fussell noted in *Wartime*, a prolonged silence about the war that most veterans embraced for decades. Lacking a clear link between their personal sacrifices and platitudes such as the "Four Freedoms" expressed by Roosevelt and Churchill, they commonly turned inward and kept their own counsel. Fussell notes that Kurt Vonnegut, who witnessed the destruction of Dresden, waited 23 years to write *Slaughterhouse-Five* before expressing the horrors he witnessed in Europe. Most men were embodied by John Bradley, the subject of the 2000 bestseller *Flags of Our Fathers*, in that he simply avoided contact with the war even though he was a legitimate hero in it.

Despite the fact that veterans globally numbered in the tens of millions after World War II, they did not coalesce into a distinct movement. As was the case after 1918, most sought normalcy in peacetime and focused on reconstructing the basic pillars of civilian life: family, work, and education. In the United States, where 16 million men and women rapidly exited the service, loyalties were anchored to family and the hope for a better future. It is a testament to the genius of the Servicemen's Readjustment Act of 1944, more commonly known as the "GI Bill," that millions successfully and peacefully reassimilated back into mainstream society and participated in one of the greatest peacetime booms in American history.

The GI Bill proved to be one of the most successful social welfare programs of the twentieth century. When it was first crafted, the policy was intended to stave off the possibility of social and economic trouble in post-war America. Facing the prospect of millions of workers returning from military service, lawmakers worried about the possibility of a second Great Depression. Other pundits, such as Willard Waller in his popular 1944 book *The Veteran Comes Back*, speculated that returning veterans would form the catalyst for a fascist movement in the United States.

Neither result came to be. Instead, the GI Bill offered a broad spectrum of programs that both occupied returning veterans in the short term and, more importantly, provided them with the means to achieve long-term success. For entrepreneurs already prepared to enter the marketplace, the law offered small business loans. For veterans interested in burnishing their skills or striking out in a new direction, the GI Bill offered vocational job training as well as tuition and stipends for college. While millions attended American universities and permanently opened the doors of higher education to the public at large, a larger proportion of American veterans (3.5 million overall) participated in job training programs or used federal assistance to attain a high-school equivalency certificate. In doing so, they rapidly improved their earning power and provided an enormous reservoir of skilled labor for the American economy (Gambone 2005: 32, 68–69, 74).

After the war, many states also created their own versions of the GI Bill. Florida provided unemployment compensation for veterans. Louisiana offered homestead land. A number of southern states waived the poll-tax requirement for veterans, a decision that had immediate implications for the post-war civil rights movement. Overall, veterans' entitlements became an embedded part of American public policy and popular expectations (Gambone 2005: 32).

Although publicly celebrated and lavishly subsidized in many western nations, veterans in other parts of the world experienced a much harsher post-war transition. In defeated Nazi Germany, the treatment of millions of veterans varied according to occupation zone. France tended to treat military veterans relatively leniently, while the harshest sanctions were reserved for Soviet-dominated eastern Germany.

Interestingly, a consensus among the Allies did emerge that a national system of veterans' benefits in Germany should be deliberately dismantled. The primary objective of this policy was to actively discredit the military caste system that prevailed in Germany and prevent the return to extremism that had prevailed in the 1920s and 1930s. At the same time, however, Allied leaders realized that it was impossible to ignore the millions of former military personnel and civilians directly affected by the war. Consequently, occupation authorities allowed assistance for "war victims" that was exclusively governed by civilian rather than military authorities. When West Germany gained its initial autonomy, one of its first actions was to pass the Federal War Victims' Benefits Law in 1950 (Diehl 1993: 72–83, 109).

The treatment of veterans in post-war eastern Europe proved to be even more problematic. Mark Edele's account of returning Soviet veterans is a fascinating and perverse story of a group numbering in the millions that was celebrated by official policy, yet suffered the same privations of a ruined country governed by an incompetent and dangerous bureaucracy. Assistance for returning soldiers almost always failed to meet even the most basic needs. In the autonomous republic of Bashkiria, for example, 12 in 1,000 received shoes and six in 1,000 one piece of clothing. It is arguable that these individuals suffered perhaps even more than the average Soviet citizen because the state tended to view veterans' organizations as a potential political threat. Soviet paranoia made the treatment of returned prisoners of war particularly brutal and delayed homecomings for thousands of Red Army soldiers for years in some cases (Edele 2008: 40, 59–71, 102–114).

Veterans and the Cold War

The Cold War replenished the ranks of veterans with millions who served in the United States, Soviet, and Allied militaries. The gargantuan size of the conflict normalized the military draft for male citizens in a specific demographic. Service became a routine milestone after secondary school not only for the average young man, but also for athletes and entertainers. Even an iconic figure such as Elvis Presley surrendered his freedom for a few years in uniform.

The Cold War also produced new generations of combat veterans and augmented the experiences of existing service members. Korea was famous for its "retreads" from World War II. Other conflicts soon beckoned to soldiers throughout the world, in the Middle East, Southeast Asia, Africa, and Southwest Asia. It was during wars fought in the so-called "Third World" that veterans gained new notoriety as mercenaries prepared to fight for the highest bidder. In the 1960s and 1970s, the "dogs of war" led by men such as "Mad" Mike Hoare and Bob Denard became famous for their role in toppling African governments and attracting the ire of the continent.

In a broader social context, veterans established a baseline for conservative values during the Cold War. When the discharged service members of World War II re-entered civilian life, they brought ingrained military habits and practices into the corporate world, classrooms, and volunteer groups. In the United States, millions of sons and fathers flocked to play American Legion Junior League baseball. Still other veterans participated in fraternal societies and ran for public office. As the decades progressed after 1945, military service became a litmus test for political leadership in many countries.

The veteran also became a straw man for social conflicts centered on the post-war generation gap. Baby boomers found easy targets in the post-war regimentation that they perceived permeating their lives. Students in the United States fought the lecture-style pedagogy embraced by their GI Bill professors. Hair length dominated many kitchen table conversations between fathers and sons. Similarly, military symbols such as the North Vietnamese Army flag raised during campus protests or the ubiquitous surplus field jacket worn in the service of "radical chic" became touchstones in the cultural wars that raged during the 1960s and 1970s.

Twenty-First-Century Trends

The conclusion of the Cold War against the Soviet Union in 1991 profoundly changed the world in ways unforeseen at the time. When George H. W. Bush declared a "New World Order," many assumed a new age of stability and growth was finally possible. In the United States, the new conventional wisdom shifted to a debate on spending the newly won "peace dividend." For the world's sole remaining superpower, Bill Clinton's election – and his mantra of "it's the economy, stupid" – marked a critical shift in basic priorities.

Worldwide, as many as seven million military personnel demobilized in the decade following the destruction of the Berlin Wall (Singer 2003: 53). The 1990s were characterized by a massive surplus in military talent (and weaponry) suddenly unlinked to standing militaries. The skill set of this group covered the spectrum from basic combat training to highly technical expertise in communications and weapons systems.

What has happened to these millions of veterans? Thousands of former Cold War combatants found employment outside the law, in organized crime in the former Soviet Union, as security for narcotics traffickers in South America, or as mercenary proxies for the ethnic factions that dominated warfare in the Balkans. These individuals were, and continue to be, the source of instability and lawlessness throughout the world.

Conversely, Cold War veterans also gravitated toward a host of embryonic private security firms that emerged to combat skyrocketing global crime rates. As newly minted security contractors, they provided both military and police expertise for intelligence gathering, threat assessment, physical security, and training. Private military companies ran the gamut from loosely run organizations that were little more than hired guns to highly organized and professional corporations fully endorsed by their host governments. Between 1994 and 2002, the US Defense Department signed some 3,000 contracts with private contractors worth an estimated $300 billion (Macomber 2004: 26–30).

Veterans serving as private contractors have proven extremely popular in the past decade. Nations, like the United States, that are unwilling to expand standing armies have increasingly relied upon a pool of readily available talent to act as agents of foreign policy and deflect the cost of conflict from a public grown hostile to overseas deployments. Industry growth has reflected this value. Estimated profits from the global security market were $55.6 billion in 1990. In 2010, earnings were projected to rise as high as $200 billion (Singer 2003: 21).

However, countries that have become increasingly reliant upon contractors have also invited controversy. While useful, military contractors have been until only recently very poorly regulated throughout the world. The absence of sufficient oversight has invited activity covering the spectrum from questionable (as was the case of Executive Outcomes in Sierra Leone) to blatantly illegal (such as DynCorp in the Balkans). Iraq and Afghanistan have proven to be a magnet for both contractors and a range of abuses. The 2008 Status of Forces Agreement between Iraq and the United States placed the former nation specifically in charge of contractors in an attempt to alleviate this problem. One of Baghdad's first actions was to ban the firm Blackwater from the country for multiple violations of state and international humanitarian law.

Conclusions

When observing the course of veterans' affairs in the modern day, a number of factors emerge. Military service is becoming more and more rarefied in the western world. Where once it was a filter to distinguish citizenship in World War I, today those who serve in uniform rarely represent more than 1 percent of any given country. In 2009, the total active duty US armed forces stood at approximately 1.1 million personnel, a fraction of the total national population. Individuals distinguished by service in the Middle East or real combat experience represented an even smaller number.

Military service in the underdeveloped world has followed the opposite trend. In the aftermath of the Cold War, as whole regions were engulfed in the instability that came with "failed states," increasingly larger elements of societies in Africa, Asia, and Latin America have been drawn into war. The "child soldiers" of Africa's many conflicts are emblematic of a new generation of fighters exposed to the horror of war without the prospect of benefits commonly enjoyed in the modern, industrialized nations. However, the world's future will likely be shaped by the untold numbers of these individuals.

SEE ALSO: Gulf Wars (1990–1991, 2003–Present); Post-Traumatic Stress Disorder; Vietnam War (1959–1975).

References

Barr, N. (2005) *The Lion and the Poppy: British Veterans, Politics, and Society, 1921–1939*. Westport: Praeger.

Cohen, D. (2001) *The War Come Home: Disabled Veterans in Britain and Germany, 1914–1939*. Berkeley: University of California Press.

Diehl, J. M. (1993) *The Thanks of the Fatherland: German Veterans after the Second World War*. Chapel Hill: University of North Carolina Press.

Edele, M. (2008) *Soviet Veterans of the Second World War: A Popular Movement in an Authoritarian Society, 1941–1991*. New York: Oxford University Press.

Gambone, M. (2005) *The Greatest Generation Comes Home: The Veteran in American Society*. College Station: Texas A&M University Press.

Jones, L. E. (2006) "Nationalists, Nazis, and the Assault against Weimar: Revisiting the Harzburg Rally of October 1931," *German Studies Review*, 29: 483–494.

Kipling, R. (1909) *Barrack-Room Ballads: And the Story of the Gadsbys*. New York: A. L. Burt Company.

Macomber, S. (2004) "You're Not in the Army Now," *American Spectator*, 37: 26–30.

Millett, A. R. and Maslowski, P. (1994) *For the Common Defense: A Military History of the United States of America*, 2nd ed. New York: Free Press.

Prost, A. (1992) *In the Wake of War: "Les Anciens Combattants" and French Society*, trans. H. McPhail. Providence: Berg.

Remarque, E. M. (1958) *All Quiet on the Western Front*. Boston: Little, Brown.

Roper, M. (2005) "Between Manliness and Masculinity: The 'War Generation' and the Psychology of Fear in Britain, 1914–1950," *Journal of British Studies*, 44: 343–362.

Singer, P. W. (2003) *Corporate Warriors: The Rise of the Privatized Military Industry*. Ithaca: Cornell University Press.

Whalen, R. W. (1984) *Bitter Wounds: German Victims of the Great War, 1914–1939*. Ithaca: Cornell University Press.

Further Reading

Bell, D. A. (2001) *The Cult of the Nation in France: Inventing Nationalism, 1680–1800*. Cambridge, MA: Harvard University Press.

Clarke, J. (2007) *Commemorating the Dead in Revolutionary France: Revolution and Remembrance, 1789–1799*. New York: Cambridge University Press.

Gerber, D. A. (2003) "Disabled Veterans, the State, and the Experience of Disability in Western Societies, 1914–1950," *Journal of Social History*, 36: 899–916.

Millis, W. (1956) *Arms and Men: A Study in American Military History*. New Brunswick: Rutgers University Press.

Pash, M. L. (2012) *In the Shadow of the Greatest Generation: The Americans Who Fought the Korean War*. New York: New York University Press.

Vietnam War (1959–1975)

EDWIN MOÏSE

The Vietnam War was primarily a struggle for control of South Vietnam, which began gradually in 1959 and 1960, and ended in 1975. It pitted Vietnamese communist forces, both southern and northern, against the Republic of Vietnam and the United States.

It was in many ways an outgrowth and continuation of the First Indochina War (1945–1954), in which the Vietminh, a Vietnamese nationalist organization under communist leadership, had fought against France and a French puppet government, the State of Vietnam. By 1954, the Vietminh were clearly winning, but in July 1954 a peace conference in Geneva, Switzerland, produced agreements, the Geneva Accords, that ended the war and divided Vietnam at the 17th parallel. The forces of the French and of the State of Vietnam regrouped to the South, and the Vietminh armed forces regrouped to the North, giving up control of the very large areas they had controlled in what became South Vietnam. The Final Declaration of the Geneva Conference stated that an election was to be held in mid-1956, after which the two halves of Vietnam were to be reunited under whoever had won the election.

When Ngo Dinh Diem became prime minister of the State of Vietnam in mid-1954, this position carried almost no power. But by mid-1955, with American assistance, Diem had become the effective ruler of most of South Vietnam. He rejected the all-Vietnam elections called for by the Final Declaration of the Geneva Conference. Late in 1955, the State of Vietnam was renamed the Republic of Vietnam (RVN), with Diem as president.

In the North, the Democratic Republic of Vietnam (DRV) had its capital at Hanoi. It was controlled by the Lao Dong Party (Workers' Party – the Communist Party of Vietnam), headed by Ho Chi Minh. For several years the division of Vietnam between the RVN and the DRV appeared stable. But neither accepted the legitimacy of the other, or of the division of Vietnam. Each regarded itself as the legitimate government of all Vietnam.

For several years the communist leaders in Hanoi forbade their followers in the South to use large-scale violence to defend themselves against government forces seeking to arrest or kill them. Some small-scale violence was permitted, but it was not allowed to grow to the point of becoming a guerrilla war, which meant that in most areas it was not adequate to defend the communist organizations against government repression. By 1959, they were down to a fraction of their 1955 membership.

The communist leaders in Hanoi, many of whom were southerners by birth, finally decided early in 1959 to authorize a guerrilla war in the South. This decision was not announced publicly; the communists in the South learned of it gradually over a considerable period. In most areas, serious guerrilla warfare did not begin until 1960. At first the guerrillas, whom the government called the "Vietcong" (short for Vietnamese communists), were few and poorly armed. But the government was very weak and its rural administration collapsed in wide areas, even under the rather modest attacks the Vietcong was able to carry out.

The National Liberation Front (NLF) was formally established in December 1960 as the official leadership of the insurgency that was already well underway. It claimed to be an independent South Vietnamese organization, including communists but not dominated by them, and independent of North Vietnam. But this was a pretense. The NLF was firmly controlled by its communist members, who took their orders from the Lao Dong Party leaders in Hanoi.

On the other hand, the actual Vietcong guerrillas, its combat personnel, were essentially all South Vietnamese. Most had never been outside of South Vietnam; a minority had gone to the North in 1954 and 1955 under the terms of the 1954 Geneva Accords, and then returned to the South, by what came to be called the "Ho Chi Minh Trail," beginning in 1959. The officers who commanded and led them also were essentially all South Vietnamese. The supreme command that ultimately controlled them was the leadership of the Lao Dong Party, a mixed group of North and South Vietnamese. Le Duan, the general secretary of the Lao Dong Party, was a southerner. So was DRV Prime Minister Pham Van Dong.

On the government side, the soldiers of the Army of the Republic of Vietnam (ARVN) were a mixture of North and South Vietnamese. (Many northerners, having supported the French in the First Indochina War, had come south under the terms of the Geneva Accords.) The officers who led the ARVN were a mixture of North and South Vietnamese, as was the supreme command in Saigon. Overall, while the NLF was not so purely a South Vietnamese organization as it claimed to be, it was more South Vietnamese than was the government against which it rebelled.

The essence of guerrilla warfare is that a weaker force, which could not survive a head-on confrontation with the main forces of its enemy, evades such confrontations. If the stronger force keeps its troops bunched up in large formations, those large formations will only be in a few locations at any one time, and the guerrillas will be able to evade contact with them. If the stronger force spreads out in many small groups, the guerrillas may be able to win fights against some of those small groups. The Vietcong was so badly outgunned that it had no choice but to use such tactics. It could concentrate forces for a surprise attack on a government outpost at night. In daylight, its forces might ambush or snipe at government forces moving through the countryside, or they might simply conceal themselves, either hiding their weapons and blending in with the local population or hiding themselves in the forest or in holes in the ground.

In 1960, when the insurgency was first beginning, it was very weak. It used assassinations to create an impression that it was stronger than it actually was, and to drive government officials and policemen out of many rural areas. Having done so, it could establish its own administrative structures in the villages and recruit more members. It became less reliant on assassination as its real strength increased.

When John Kennedy was inaugurated president of the United States in January 1961, there were fewer than 1,000 American military advisors in South Vietnam. He soon decided that the growing communist strength in South Vietnam represented a serious threat. He rejected suggestions that he put in regular ground combat troops, but by the end of the year he had more than tripled the number of American military personnel in South Vietnam. There was still a public claim that these were just advisors, but in reality, by 1962, some were functioning in a variety of combat roles. When the US Air Force pilots of Project Farmgate flew air strikes against the Vietcong, they always had to have a Vietnamese in the co-pilot's seat to maintain the pretense that the Americans were advisors. But no such rule applied to US Army and Marine pilots flying armed helicopters. US Army Special Forces personnel were the *de facto* combat commanders of Civilian Irregular Defense Groups, military forces made up mostly of Montagnard tribesmen in the Central Highlands,

established under the sponsorship of the US Central Intelligence Agency (CIA).

The United States provided large quantities of weaponry for the ARVN and the various irregular forces associated with the Saigon government. The rifles, machine guns, and mortars ended up equipping both sides, since the Vietcong was able to capture large quantities of them. Even though the Vietcong was overwhelmingly outgunned overall, and had to avoid confrontations with large ARVN units, it could easily concentrate enough forces to capture a small outpost and take its weapons. The ARVN maintained a monopoly on artillery, tracked vehicles, and aircraft.

During 1962, it became more difficult for Vietcong regular units to evade battle. ARVN troops could appear suddenly in an area, dropping by parachute, landing in helicopters, or churning across rice fields in armored personnel carriers with caterpillar treads. If Vietcong troops tried to flee, they were vulnerable to attack by fixed-wing aircraft and by helicopter gunships armed with rockets and machine guns. But the Vietcong was building larger, more heavily armed units that might be capable of facing the ARVN in serious battles. At the beginning of 1963, a Vietcong force of about 350 held an entrenched position against ARVN troops, supported by American aircraft, in a day-long battle at Ap Bac, southwest of Saigon. Greatly outnumbered and even more overwhelmingly outgunned, the Vietcong took maximum advantage of the tactical defensive and of the indecisiveness and ineptitude of their attackers. Encouraged by this victory, the Vietcong continued building larger and stronger units. These were armed mostly with weapons captured from small government outposts, but some came from North Vietnam. From late 1962 onward, small ocean-going cargo vessels made clandestine voyages to South Vietnam, approaching the coast at night and concealing themselves inside river mouths to unload. Weapons also came down the Ho Chi Minh Trail. This originally had run directly across the Demilitarized Zone (DMZ) separating North from South Vietnam. But in 1961 it was shifted west to run through southeastern Laos; this meant that traffic could enter South Vietnam across the long border with Laos rather than across the short border with North Vietnam.

President Diem was determined to hold ARVN casualties to a minimum. He urged his generals to avoid battles, even battles in which they would enjoy a substantial superiority, if there was a danger the Vietcong might inflict significant casualties on ARVN forces.

General Paul Harkins, head of the United States' Military Assistance Command, Vietnam (MACV), maintained that the war against the Vietcong was going well under Diem's leadership. Some US military advisors in the field, as well as some reporters, believed that the war was going badly (and in retrospect it appears clear they were correct). There were also disagreements over Diem's pacification program, based on gathering peasants into "strategic hamlets." This program did have considerable success in separating the peasants from the Vietcong, making it difficult for the Vietcong to propagandize and tax them. But critics pointed out that peasants bitterly resented being uprooted from their previous homes and moved forcibly to much less desirable quarters.

Officials in Washington were divided. Diem's supporters had the edge until the spring of 1963, when a conflict broke out pitting Diem, a Catholic, against large sections of the Buddhist community in Vietnam. In a country where Buddhists greatly outnumbered Catholics, this was a political disaster. The United States government gave rather cautious and hesitant encouragement to ARVN officers to stage a military coup. These officers overthrew and killed Diem in early November.

The ARVN generals who replaced Diem were themselves overthrown less than three months later, in a second coup by a different set of generals. More coups and attempted coups followed. This distracted the ARVN from the war against the Vietcong. Meanwhile, in Hanoi, the Lao Dong Party Central Committee decided in December 1963 on a major expansion of the war in the South. During 1964, the Ho Chi Minh Trail was expanded to facilitate larger munitions shipments. Significant numbers of North Vietnamese began going down the trail to join the war in the South; until this time, those sent down the trail had overwhelmingly been southerners, returning to the South after a few years in the North. At the same time, the Vietcong, which had relied mostly on volunteers in earlier years, increasingly used conscription to expand its forces, creating units far stronger than those that had fought at Ap Bac. At the Battle of Binh Gia, from late December 1964 into early January 1965, Vietcong forces deliberately sought combat with elite government units only about 60 km east of Saigon, inflicting crippling losses on them.

Lyndon Johnson, who became president of the United States after the assassination of John Kennedy in November 1963, wanted to reduce American military spending to make more money available for his domestic programs. But he feared the consequences, both strategic and political, of losing South Vietnam. Many Americans believed, and President Johnson at least took seriously, the "domino theory," which stated that if South Vietnam fell to communists, then numerous other countries would quickly fall also. By early 1965, it seemed obvious that South Vietnam would fall quite soon if the United States did not intervene with direct military force.

At the beginning of 1965, there were fewer than 24,000 US military personnel in South Vietnam, with the pretense still being maintained that they were there not to fight, only to train and advise Vietnamese forces. But in late February, Air Force pilots flew the first openly American bombing missions in South Vietnam. In early March, the United States began systematic bombing of North Vietnam (Operation Rolling Thunder) and sent US Marine battalions to guard the airfield at Danang. More ground troops followed; total US military strength in Vietnam reached 184,000 by the end of the year, and 385,000 by the end of 1966. But escalation of the war occurred gradually, a step at a time. President Johnson did not want the public or Congress to understand how large the war was expected to become.

When President Harry Truman put the United States into the Korean War in 1950, he had not asked Congress for a declaration of war, but he had declared a national emergency. Top military leaders expected President Johnson to do the same for Vietnam in 1965. They were shocked when he decided not even to issue a declaration of national emergency. Such a declaration would have enabled the military to hold onto trained soldiers, by extending their enlistments, and to obtain more trained soldiers by calling up reservists. Lacking the power to do this, the army had to rely heavily on conscription. This caused a significant decline in quality; there were too many draftees, and not enough soldiers (especially sergeants) with years of experience to train, lead, and discipline those draftees.

MACV, under General William Westmoreland, showed little interest in seizing territory. Instead, it focused on attrition of communist forces, especially the largest and best-armed enemy units, those capable of fighting conventional battles. American forces would sweep through an area on a "search-and-destroy" operation, and then leave. If communist forces then returned (or emerged from concealment, never having left), the Americans might sweep through the area again a few months later. Some of these operations were in unpopulated jungles, but others, in the populated areas near the coast, devastated Vietnamese villages.

In I Corps, the northernmost part of South Vietnam, US Marine commanders wanted to place more emphasis on counterinsurgency. They put Combined Action Platoons (CAPs) – mixed units of US Marines and local Vietnamese troops – in villages for extended periods to keep Vietcong forces out. But Westmoreland would not permit the Marines to devote much manpower to the CAP program.

Westmoreland expected to win a war of attrition because he had overwhelmingly superior firepower. His forces had plentiful artillery. Communist forces in most of South Vietnam, having no artillery, used mortars, and to some extent rockets, as inadequate substitutes. The Americans had armored personnel carriers and sometimes tanks; the communist forces in South Vietnam had no tracked fighting vehicles at all until 1968, and almost none until 1972. Most of all, the United States used airpower on a huge scale, and in many forms. B-52 s at high altitudes dropped much heavier bomb loads than the heavy bombers of previous wars. At the other end of the scale, helicopter gunships firing rockets and machine guns could apply firepower more precisely than fixed-wing aircraft could have managed. The greatest weight of American airpower was applied to the communist forces in South Vietnam, which directly threatened US troops. South Vietnam became the most heavily bombed country in history. American bombing of the Ho Chi Minh Trail made Laos the second most heavily bombed. Even in North Vietnam, where anti-aircraft guns, radar-guided missiles, and fighter aircraft made bombing much more difficult and dangerous than in South Vietnam or Laos, the Americans dropped a bomb tonnage comparable to that they had dropped on Germany in World War II.

Complaints that the United States fought an unreasonably limited war often refer to the limits on bombing of North Vietnam, especially the northern part of North Vietnam. The United States feared, for good reason, that if it went too far against North Vietnam, it might trigger a war with China. But there was no way to tell how far would be too far. From 1965 to 1968, President Johnson permitted hardly any air strikes in the areas of North Vietnam closest to the Chinese border, and exercised tight personal control over air strikes within about 150 miles of that border. President Richard Nixon did hardly any bombing of North Vietnam from 1969 to 1971, though he bombed quite heavily in 1972. Complaints about limited war also sometimes refer to the fact that American attacks on Vietnamese communist base areas in Laos and Cambodia were limited mostly to aerial bombing, with little use of ground troops, and that the base areas in Cambodia were not even bombed significantly until 1969.

The government of Laos, under Prince Souvanna Phouma, was nominally neutral but *de facto* allied with the United States. The United States had supported a genuinely neutral government under Souvanna Phouma until 1958, but then turned against him, preferring a rightist, anti-communist government. At the end of 1960, Souvanna Phouma was driven into an alliance with the Pathet Lao (the Laotian communist movement) and the People's Army of Vietnam (PAVN). Agreements signed in Geneva in 1962 stated that Laos was to be neutral once more, and returned Souvanna Phouma to office as prime minister. But in the months that followed, the PAVN significantly violated Laotian neutrality, especially along the Ho Chi Minh Trail. Souvanna Phouma drifted into an alliance with the United States, but he defined its terms. He allowed massive use of US airpower against communist forces in Laos from 1965 onward, but he did not want US ground troops. The United States found him so much more useful as an ally than the rightists had been that it was not willing to risk offending him by ignoring his wishes.

There were two wars in Laos. In the North, PAVN and Pathet Lao forces fought the Royal Laotian Army and the "Secret Army" of Hmong tribesmen, armed and supported by the CIA. In the South, American aircraft attacked the PAVN forces along the Ho Chi Minh Trail. Air strikes were supplemented only by very small covert operations on the ground, small enough that American officials could reasonably hope Souvanna Phouma would not find out about them.

Cambodia, under the rule of Prince Norodom Sihanouk, was nominally neutral but *de facto* was increasingly allied with the Vietnamese communist forces. A clandestine channel was opened in 1966 by which munitions were transported by sea to Sihanoukville, a port on the south coast of Cambodia, and shipped by truck across Cambodia to the border of South Vietnam. Sihanouk allowed the PAVN and Vietcong to use base areas in Cambodia, relatively safe from US and ARVN attack, as long as they kept those bases small and did not support the Cambodian communists commonly known as the Khmer Rouge.

In South Vietnam there was a bloody war of attrition. The Americans and the communist forces each hoped to win by inflicting a level of casualties that the other side would not be able to endure. Each pushed relatively hard, willing to suffer casualties in order to inflict them. The communists lost far more personnel, but they were willing to lose far more, since Vietnam was much more important to them than it was to the United States. Beginning in mid-1966, there were some fairly conventional battles near the northern and western borders of South Vietnam. PAVN troops would build fortified positions, and then wait for the Americans to find and attack them. The Americans were willing to attack because their advantage in weaponry was so great that they could inflict far more losses than they suffered, even when attacking PAVN troops in fortified positions. The PAVN was willing because defending fortified positions gave it better odds than were available in most other circumstances, and because these battles drew American troops out to the borders of South Vietnam, away from the populated areas near the coast.

The government in Saigon, which had been in continual turmoil since the overthrow of Ngo Dinh Diem, began to stabilize in 1965 when a group of generals headed by Nguyen Cao Ky and Nguyen Van Thieu took control. The last serious challenge to this group ended in mid-1966. Thieu outmaneuvered Ky and made himself president

of the Republic of Vietnam in 1967. He remained firmly in control until 1975.

The intensity of combat increased steadily as the forces on both sides expanded. By 1967, with 700–800 US personnel and thousands of communist personnel being killed per month, both sides were feeling the strain. The US government responded with a public relations campaign to convince the American public that victory was near. American spokesmen announced late in 1967 that the strength of the communist forces in South Vietnam had peaked in late 1966, and had been declining since that time.

The communists, meanwhile, were planning to change the war with a dramatic surprise attack. Both sides had in past years declared ceasefires to allow the celebration of Tet, the Vietnamese New Year, by far the most important holiday in Vietnamese culture. Many soldiers left their units to celebrate Tet with their families. The communists announced a ceasefire as usual for Tet of 1968, but instead launched a massive wave of attacks against cities and military bases. They hoped that the ARVN would collapse under the unexpected shock and that there would be a "general uprising" of the South Vietnamese population.

This was a far more complex operation than the communist forces had ever attempted before, and they proved unable to coordinate it properly. The plan called for a simultaneous wave of attacks before dawn on January 31, 1968. But a significant number of units attacked one day ahead of schedule, while others were late by a day or more. The offensive brought them out into the open, often in unfamiliar terrain, where the Americans' superior firepower inflicted very heavy casualties. But they persisted, pushing the fight, for months. January 1968 to June 1969 was by far the bloodiest period of the war for US forces, with an average of over 1,000 men per month killed in action. By mid-1969 the communist forces, especially the Vietcong, had been severely weakened. But the prolonged heavy casualties had eroded American public support for the war.

In March 1968, a leak to the media revealed that US military commanders had requested substantial reinforcements for the US forces in Vietnam. This undermined public belief in the military's claims that the Tet Offensive had been an American military victory and had weakened enemy forces. President Johnson announced at the end of March that the United States would stop bombing the northern part of North Vietnam and attempt to negotiate a settlement of the war. At the end of October, he halted bombing of all of North Vietnam. Richard Nixon, who won the presidential election of 1968, continued to restrict bombing of North Vietnam for the next several years.

Preliminary talks in 1968 led to formal peace negotiations in 1969, held in Paris, France. These negotiations produced no result for years. The essential problem was that the war could not be compromised. Someone was going to end up in control of South Vietnam. The Republic of Vietnam and the Vietcong (who by this time had formally created the Provisional Revolutionary Government of the Republic of South Vietnam) were each determined utterly to destroy the other's power. The only way either could achieve safety was to destroy the other. The real negotiators in Paris were representatives of the United States and the DRV. For an agreement between them actually to end the war, it would have to take one of two forms: either the United States would betray the RVN and consign it to destruction, or the DRV similarly would betray the Vietcong.

By 1969 and 1970, the war in South Vietnam was going better for the United States and the ARVN in some important ways. The Vietcong military forces had been critically weakened (though not, as some authors claim, essentially destroyed). A program called Operation Phoenix was inflicting significant damage on the "infrastructure," the political and administrative apparatus of the Vietcong. In 1970, President Thieu initiated a serious land reform campaign; for the first time the Republic of Vietnam was genuinely bidding against the communists for the allegiance of poor peasants. Most of the rural population came under government rule, partly by the extension of government control over more and more villages, and partly by bombing and shelling that forced peasants to flee areas still under communist control.

At the same time, the decline in American public support for the war had major effects on American policy. After the bloody battle of "Hamburger Hill" in May 1969 led to a public controversy, American units were ordered to be less aggressive in ground combat, to hold casualties down. Soon after, President Nixon began with-drawing American forces from Vietnam, handing responsibility for the war over to the ARVN in a policy called "Vietnamization." A sense that the American public was not behind the war effort contributed to a serious decline in the morale and discipline of American units. Stories about widespread drug abuse, and significant numbers of armed attacks ("fraggings") against unpopular officers, contributed to a further decline in public support.

In early 1969, President Nixon decided he could no longer afford to leave unmolested the Vietnamese communist base areas in Cambodia. He began Operation Menu, an extremely secret program of B-52 air strikes. In March 1970, a military coup led by General Lon Nol overthrew Prince Sihanouk and put Cambodia into the war on the anti-communist side. In the short run this was extremely beneficial to the United States and the RVN. Munitions shipments through Sihanoukville to the communist forces ceased. US and ARVN forces went into eastern Cambodia and severely disrupted communist base areas there. The American forces withdrew in mid-1970, but ARVN units continued operating in parts of eastern Cambodia for much longer.

The results for Cambodia were very bad. PAVN forces spread widely across the country, attacking Lon Nol's army. The United States gave Lon Nol some weapons and financing, and a lot of air support, but hardly any American personnel on the ground after mid-1970, not even advisors. The PAVN did a remarkably effective job of training and arming Khmer Rouge forces. By the end of 1972, the PAVN was able to withdraw most of its forces from Cambodia, handing over the war there to the Khmer Rouge, which had grown significantly stronger than Lon Nol's army.

American military personnel in South Vietnam had peaked at 543,000 in April 1969. By the end of 1971, the number was down to 158,000, and dropping rapidly. The remaining American forces hardly participated in ground combat. The communist forces were preparing what became the Easter Offensive of 1972. There were major thrusts in three areas: in the extreme north, where PAVN forces came straight across the DMZ from North Vietnam; in the Central Highlands; and in the area just north of Saigon. This was the first time the PAVN had used surface-to-air missiles against aircraft in South Vietnam; it also used artillery and tanks on a much larger scale than ever before. With heavy American air support, the ARVN was able – barely – to hold on. By June, the ARVN was counterattacking and retook some, though not all, of the territory it had lost.

President Nixon responded to the Easter Offensive by resuming large-scale bombing of North Vietnam. His Operation Linebacker did not involve much heavier bomb tonnages than President Johnson's Operation Rolling Thunder, but it was more effective. A laser-guided "smart bomb," which had been tested in Laos in 1971, made it easy to destroy crucial bridges that had been much harder to attack from 1965 to 1968. Also, the range of permissible targets was broader than during Rolling Thunder. Nixon, who was opening up friendlier relations with the Soviet Union and especially with China, was less worried that they would react violently to what America did in North Vietnam.

In October 1972, the US and DRV negotiators in Paris finally hammered out an agreement, and the Americans stopped bombing the northern part of North Vietnam. After they had agreed on the text, the Americans showed it to President Thieu, who reacted with horror; it called for an American withdrawal from Vietnam, which seemed to him likely to doom the RVN. The Americans returned to the negotiations, asking for major changes in the draft agreement. This led to a deadlock. In December, Nixon launched Operation Linebacker II, commonly called the "Christmas Bombing," for the first time risking B-52s in the areas of the strongest North Vietnamese air defenses. But this was not nearly so brutal and ruthless a campaign as many thought it was. Most of the targets were on the edges of Hanoi, not in the city center, and civilian casualties were not huge. After 11 days of bombing the peace talks resumed, quickly producing an agreement very similar to the draft that had been negotiated the previous October.

The agreement that was signed in Paris on January 27, 1973, despite anguished protests from President Thieu, called for a ceasefire. After this the remaining American military personnel, as well as troops of other countries allied with the United States (primarily South Korea), were to withdraw from South Vietnam. No matching withdrawal by North Vietnamese forces was specified, but the neutrality of Laos and of the DMZ was to be respected; implementation of these clauses would have closed the Ho Chi Minh Trail and cut off the PAVN forces in South Vietnam. The agreement did not resolve the question the war was about: who would end up in control of South Vietnam. This was to be settled by peaceful political processes that were described only vaguely, and seemed obviously incapable of being implemented. It appears very unlikely that either side signed in good faith.

Combat among the Vietnamese forces continued after the agreement supposedly went into effect, but the Americans were no longer participating and stopped bombing Laos soon after. President Thieu hoped, and the communists feared, that a rapid collapse of the ceasefire might draw the Americans back into the war. So the ARVN went on the offensive in the months immediately after the Paris Agreement supposedly became effective, while PAVN and Vietcong forces were more cautious. However, by the second half of 1973, the communist forces were less worried about the Americans and were fighting more vigorously.

In the United States, the Watergate scandal was weakening the Nixon administration and opponents of the war in the US Congress were becoming more assertive. In August 1973, Congress actually passed a law forbidding US military personnel from operating in Vietnam, Laos, or Cambodia; this ended US bombing of Khmer Rouge forces in Cambodia. The willingness of Congress to continue providing munitions and financial support for ARVN operations was also declining. Congress did not, as some authors have claimed, cut off aid to the ARVN. But by late 1974, with Nixon no longer in office and his successor, Gerald Ford, politically very weak, Congress cut US military aid to Saigon to a level not much greater than that US intelligence agencies said China and the Soviet Union were providing to North Vietnam. The ARVN was trained and organized to fight a war in which it enjoyed vastly greater firepower and much more lavish supplies than its enemies. It did not adjust well to losing this advantage.

By the end of 1974, the PAVN was ready to test its advantages. It took a whole province, though a relatively unimportant one, Phuoc Long on the Cambodian border. The ARVN was unable to reinforce Phuoc Long significantly, and it fell in

January 1975. Communist leaders at this point still expected the war to last another year, but they were beginning to hope that the Republic of Vietnam might collapse more rapidly. They launched a major offensive in the Central Highlands in March and quickly took the important town of Ban Me Thuot. President Thieu decided that the other major centers in the Highlands had become untenable, and ordered the ARVN forces there to retreat to the coast. He also pulled the elite Airborne Division out of I Corps to reinforce the area around Saigon.

The withdrawal of the Airborne Division triggered panic and disintegration in I Corps. PAVN forces had occupied three provincial capitals, against little resistance, by March 24, and took the major cities of Hue and Danang on March 26 and 30. This triggered a similar disintegration farther south, and PAVN forces entered Saigon on April 30. There were units of the Vietnamese Marine Corps that had stood and fought in I Corps, and ARVN units that had fought closer to Saigon, but they had not been numerous enough seriously to slow the PAVN advance.

The war in Cambodia had ended with a Khmer Rouge victory about two weeks before the fall of Saigon. Pathet Lao and PAVN forces brought Laos under full communist control toward the end of 1975.

SEE ALSO: First Indochina War (1945–1954); Post-Traumatic Stress Disorder.

Further Reading

Allen, G. (2001) *None So Blind: A Personal Account of the Intelligence Failure in Vietnam*. Chicago: Ivan R. Dee.

Caputo, P. (1977) *A Rumor of War*. New York: Holt, Rinehart, and Winston.

Catton, P. (2002) *Diem's Final Failure*. Lawrence: University Press of Kansas.

Deac, W. (1997) *Road to the Killing Fields: The Cambodian War of 1970–75*. College Station: Texas A&M University Press.

Duiker, W. (2000) *Ho Chi Minh*. New York: Hyperion.

Elliott, D. (2003) *The Vietnamese War: Revolution and Social Change in the Mekong Delta*. Armonk, NY: M. E. Sharpe.

Hallin, D. (1986) *The "Uncensored War": The Media and Vietnam*. New York: Oxford University Press.

Hickey, G. (1993) *Shattered World: Adaptation and Survival among Vietnam's Highland Peoples during the Vietnam War*. Philadelphia: University of Pennsylvania Press.

Isaacs, A. (1983) *Without Honor: Defeat in Vietnam and Cambodia*. Baltimore: Johns Hopkins University Press.

Karnow, S. (1983) *Vietnam: A History*. New York: Viking.

Kimball, J. (1998) *Nixon's Vietnam War*. Lawrence: University Press of Kansas.

Littauer, R. and Uphoff, N. (Eds.) (1972) *The Air War in Indochina*, rev. ed. Boston: Beacon Press.

Moïse, E. (1996) *Tonkin Gulf and the Escalation of the Vietnam War*. Chapel Hill: University of North Carolina Press.

Moore, H. and Galloway, J. (1992) *We Were Soldiers Once... and Young*. New York: Random House.

Prados, J. (1999) *The Blood Road: The Ho Chi Minh Trail and the Vietnam War*. New York: John Wiley & Sons, Inc.

Pribbenow, M. (2002) *Victory in Vietnam: The Official History of the People's Army of Vietnam, 1954–1975*. Lawrence: University Press of Kansas.

Race, J. (1972) *War Comes to Long An*. Berkeley: University of California Press.

Sheehan, N. (1988) *A Bright Shining Lie: John Paul Vann and America in Vietnam*. New York: Random House.

Spector, R. (1983) *United States Army in Vietnam: Advice and Support: The Early Years, 1941–1960*. Washington, DC: Center of Military History, United States Army.

Thayer, C. (1989) *War by Other Means: National Liberation and Revolution in Viet-Nam*. Cambridge, MA: Unwin Hyman.

Thompson, W. (2000) *To Hanoi and Back: The US Air Force and North Vietnam, 1966–1973*. Washington, DC: Smithsonian Institution Press.

Turley, W. (2009) *The Second Indochina War*, 2nd ed. Lanham: Rowman and Littlefield.

Veith, G. (2012) *Black April: The Fall of South Vietnam, 1973–75*. New York: Encounter.

Wiest, A. (2008) *Vietnam's Forgotten Army: Heroism and Betrayal in the ARVN*. New York: New York University Press.

Zhai, Q. (2000) *China and the Vietnam Wars, 1950–1975*. Chapel Hill: University of North Carolina Press.

A much more complete bibliography is online at http://www.clemson.edu/caah/history/FacultyPages/EdMoise/bibliography.html

War and Cinema

JAMES CHAPMAN

Cinema has been the dominant mass medium of the twentieth century and has played a vital role in shaping popular perceptions of war. Cinema has been employed both as a medium of war propaganda to mobilize popular support for particular conflicts and as a commentary on the "horrors" of war in films such as *All Quiet on the Western Front* (dir. Lewis Milestone, 1930) and *Apocalypse Now* (dir. Francis Ford Coppola, 1979). It has served both as a vehicle for recruitment to the armed services and as a means of showing the "reality" of war to those who have not experienced it at first hand. It has popularized the romantic idea of war as an adventure and has promoted the cult of heroism. But it has also examined the dehumanizing effects of war on combatants and has aided in the social and psychological rehabilitation of ex-servicemen. It has documented the genocidal conduct of "total war" and has been a key medium for exploring the historical memory of the Holocaust. And, while cinema has done much to influence attitudes toward war, the medium itself has also been shaped by war.

The Cinematograph Goes to War

Until the advent of photography no one who had not experienced war at first hand could have known what it was really like. The Crimean War (1854–1856) is the first for which photographic evidence is available, though even so it was the dispatches of William Howard Russell of *The Times* that had more public impact than the efforts of royal photographer Roger Fenton. There is a substantial photographic record of the American Civil War (1861–1865), where Alexander Gardner was the official photographer for the Army of the Potomac. It was only at the turn of the century, however, that visual records of war received wider dissemination due to the invention of the cinematograph in the 1890s. The Spanish–American War (1898) and the South African War (1899–1902) were the first to be covered by cinematographers and short "actualities" of war scenes were one of the first types of genre film.

Pierre Sorlin (1994: 359) calls the cinematograph "the younger sibling of photography." In the early history of the medium the appeal of film was that it offered, or at least seemed to offer, images of the real world. In 1898, for example, the pioneer Polish cinematographer

Twentieth-Century War and Conflict: A Concise Encyclopedia, First Edition. Edited by Gordon Martel.
© 2015 John Wiley & Sons, Ltd. Published 2015 by John Wiley & Sons, Ltd.

Boleslas Matuszewski declared: "The cinematograph may not give a complete history, but what it gives is incontestably and absolutely true…. One could say that animated photography has a character of authenticity, accuracy and precision that belongs to it alone" (Matuszewski 1995: 323). It is only to be expected that early filmmakers would make such claims for their work: they were first and foremost businessmen who wanted to sell their films. Yet it is now apparent that many of the early "topicals" purporting to show historical events were in fact dramatic reconstructions. The French pioneer Georges Méliès, for example, produced films of the sinking of the battleship USS *Maine* (1898) and the assassination of President William McKinley (1901) that were entirely reconstructed in the studio. The first known example of battlefield reconstruction passed off as the real thing was *The Battle of Santiago Bay* (1898). The cinematographer Alfred E. Smith had traveled to Cuba to cover the US intervention there, but when his footage proved insufficiently dramatic Smith and his partner J. Stuart Blackton restaged the battle in a water tank using model ships and smoke from their cigars.

It was during World War I that the cinematograph came of age as a medium of war reporting. Most of the belligerent nations allowed cinematographers access to the front, though initially at least they were often unwelcome. The antipathy of the War Office toward the film industry meant there was no official film of the British Army during the first 18 months of the war. It was not until late in 1915 that a Topical Committee for War Films was set up, following much lobbying from the trade, to meet the public demand for films from the front. In Germany, too, the military authorities were initially hostile toward filmmakers, and it was not until 1916 that a film and photography unit was established. No less a figure than General Ludendorff was converted to the view that "the war has demonstrated the paramount power of images and of film as a means of enlightenment and influence" (quoted in Jelavich 1999: 360). When the United States entered the war in 1917 it learned from the British and German experience: it immediately designated the US Army Signal Corps as its official film unit.

While there is an extensive film record of World War I, however, its quality is patchy. Sorlin contends that much actuality footage "is tediously repetitive, mostly parades, long lines of prisoners, or tracking-shots of the seemingly inexhaustible build-up of supplies accumulated before offensives" (1994: 360). This also seems to have been the response of audiences who saw the films: they were disappointed that there were no films with close-up shots of actual fighting (Reeves 1999: 31). This changed in 1916 with the release of *The Battle of the Somme*. It is difficult to exaggerate the historical importance of this film in shaping the popular image of war and in establishing the conventions of the combat documentary. *The Battle of the Somme* was compiled from actuality footage shot at the front by two official cameramen, Geoffrey Malins and J. B. McDowell. When the rushes were shown to the Topical Committee in London it decided they should be edited into a full-length film. *The Battle of the Somme* was released in London on August 21 and a general release across the country followed a week later.

The reception of *The Battle of the Somme* was been well documented: it evidently had an enormous impact on the British public and there are reports of hundreds of thousands of people flocking to see it (Badsey 1981; Reeves 1997). It received what effectively amounted to an official endorsement when King George V had it shown for him at Windsor. Reviews in both the national press and the trade papers were much impressed by its vivid and authentic pictures of the front. One sequence in particular was much commented upon: where a platoon of soldiers go "over the top" and two fall dead. Among those who saw the film was the author Sir Henry Rider Haggard, who recorded in his diary that it "does give a wonderful idea of the fighting." "The most impressive to my mind," he went on, "is that of a regiment scrambling out of a trench to charge and of the one man who slides back shot dead. There is something appalling about the instantaneous change from fierce activity to supine death" (quoted in Smither 1993: 149).

As film archivist Roger Smither has conclusively demonstrated, however, this sequence was staged for the camera behind the lines. There are numerous visual clues. The trench is too shallow for the front line and there is no barbed wire on the parapet; the troops are lightly equipped and are not wearing field packs; the position of the camera is too exposed for this to have been taken under enemy fire; and the clinching detail is that one of the "dead" soldiers who falls can be seen crossing his legs. How far does this compromise *The Battle of the Somme* as a historical record? Smither (1993: 150) points out that "the proportion of such film to the whole work is actually quite small" and that the vast majority of *The Battle of the Somme* is indeed the real thing. Perhaps the chief value of *The Battle of the Somme*, however, is that it shows something of the effects on combatants: many of the troops returning from the front look dazed and exhausted, and, while some of them look at the camera, there is none of the waving and cheering that characterized the newsreels marking the outbreak of war in 1914.

The success of *The Battle of the Somme* prompted the making of two further films in the same vein: *The Battle of the Ancre and the Advance of the Tanks* (1916) and *The German Retreat and the Battle of Arras* (1917). *The Battle of the Ancre* was almost as successful as its predecessor, perhaps because it contained shots of the new tanks, but by the time that *The Battle of Arras* was released in June 1917 it seems that the public's appetite for war films was on the wane. At the instigation of Lord Beaverbrook, the press baron, film taken at the front was thereafter incorporated into a newsreel, *War Office Official Topical Budget*, which was produced twice weekly until the end of the war. By this time there were seven official cameramen in different theaters of war: four on the Western Front, one in Mesopotamia, one in Egypt, and one with the Royal Navy. Among the events that *Topical Budget* reported were General Allenby's entry into Jerusalem (December 11, 1917) and the signing of the peace treaty in the Hall of Mirrors at the Palace of Versailles (June 28, 1919).

Cinema and the Memory of the Great War

Cultural historians such as Jay Winter have shown how, following the Armistice of 1918, a culture of commemoration and mourning emerged through which populations decimated by the war "tried to find ways to comprehend and then to transcend the catastrophes of war" (1995: 1). Cinema played an important role in this process. As early as the mid-1920s there were films commemorating the war from most of the combatant nations. These were not necessarily all anti-war films in their ideological orientation. The American films *The Big Parade* (dir. King Vidor, 1925) and *What Price Glory?* (dir. Raoul Walsh, 1926) were melodramas that did not shy away from depicting loss but at the same time suggested that the war had been necessary in order to halt the spread of German militarism. Paramount Pictures' aviation epic *Wings* (dir. William Wellman, 1927) was the first film to win the Academy Award for Best Picture: with its stirring scenes of aerial combat it was the first truly spectacular war film. Early talking pictures such as *Hell's Angels* (dir. Howard Hughes, 1930) and *The Dawn Patrol* (dir. Howard Hawks, 1930) also celebrated the figure of the aviator: a type of heroic individualism that seemed like a throwback to a more chivalrous age of warfare. A more documentary-style treatment was exemplified by a series of battle reconstructions produced by Harry Bruce Woolfe for British Instructional Films: *The Battle of Jutland* (1921), *Ypres* (1925), *Mons* (1926), and *The Battles of the Coronel and Falkland Islands* (1927). These were made with the cooperation of the War Office and Admiralty and represent an official view in so far as they "presented the War as a national achievement – an adventure in which brave young Britons won immortality" (Paris 1999: 56).

It was a cycle of films produced between 1928 and 1932, however, which did most to establish the enduring cinematic image of the war. These included films from the United States – *All Quiet on the Western Front* – France – *Verdun* (dir. Léon Poirier, 1928) – Germany – *Westfront 1918* (dir. G. W. Pabst, 1930) and *The Other Side* (dir. Heinz Paul, 1931) – and Britain – *Journey's End* (dir. James Whale, 1930) and *Tell England* (dir. Anthony Asquith, 1931). The internationalism of the cycle is significant in that it suggested a shared experience that crossed national boundaries. The most successful of these films critically and with the public was *All Quiet on the Western Front*, an American film of a novel by German author Erich Maria Remarque directed by a Russian immigrant to the United States (Lewis Milestone). When the film was shown in Britain, the British Board of Film Censors described it as a "wonderfully realistic representation [of] war with minimum national bias" (quoted in Kelly 1998: 113).

Collectively these films were responsible for establishing a visual iconography of the Western Front that persists to the present day. The recurring images are devastated landscapes with ruined buildings and dead trees, tangled fences of barbed wire and, above all, mud: one could be forgiven for thinking that World War I was fought entirely in the rain. They also demonstrate a consistent psychological response to the war. Their recurring theme is that "war is hell." It is a catastrophic experience that leaves its combatants traumatized physically and mentally. Most of the films show how idealistic young volunteers arriving at the front find their dreams of martial glory shattered by the experience of combat. The protagonists of *Journey's End* and *Westfront 1918* are alcoholics: drink is a metaphor for their descent into madness. There is no hatred for the enemy in these films: *Westfront 1918* ends with a French soldier in a military hospital reaching out for the hand of the dying German in the next bed saying "Moi comrade, pas enemie" (My comrade, not enemy). The overriding impression of the films is of the futility and waste of war: most end in the deaths of one or more of their protagonists.

These films need to be understood as part of a wider anti-war movement that arose a decade or so after the Armistice. This was the time when anti-war literature flourished, with a range of fictional and factual accounts including Ernest Hemingway's *A Farewell to Arms* (1929), Richard Aldington's *Death of a Hero* (1929), Robert Graves's *Goodbye To All That* (1929), Siegfried Sassoon's *Memoirs of an Infantry Officer* (1930), and Vera Brittain's *Testament of Youth* (1933). *Journey's End* was originally a play by R. C. Sherriff, *Westfront 1918* a memoir by Ernst Johannsen, and *Tell England* a novel by Ernest Raymond. *The Other Side* was a German film of *Journey's End* that maintained the play's British characters. The appearance of this anti-war movement in film and literature at this time prompts Sorlin to remark that "knowledge of the horrors of the war was a grim secret whose communication was delayed" (Sorlin 1994: 362). Its ascendancy, however, was brief. The Nazi accession to power in Germany led to the banning of anti-war films and the promotion of the *Dolchstosslegende* (stab-in-the-back legend). Films such as *All Quiet on the Western Front* had no place within National Socialist propaganda.

World War II: Cinema and Propaganda

When World War II broke out in 1939, military authorities had learned their lessons from previous experience. The British and German armies had their own film units that were attached to the services. German PK Units (*Propaganda Kompanie Einheiten*) accompanied troops into the field in Poland and France and the film from these early campaigns was put to highly effective use in the documentaries *Baptism of Fire* (1940) and *Victory in the West* (1941). *Baptism of Fire* was an early example of "shock and awe" tactics: the film was shown to frighten neutrals and soften up future targets with its mesmerizing images of the might of the Luftwaffe. The British Army Film and Photographic Unit (AFPU) grew from four cameramen at the start of the war to 80 by 1943. Its early efforts were disappointing – most of the footage of the evacuation of Dunkirk, for example, came from commercial newsreel rather than service cameramen – but it achieved good results later with the three "Victory" films: *Desert Victory* (1943), *Tunisian Victory* (1944), and *Burma Victory* (1945). The Americans, following the disappointing results of their cameramen in North Africa in 1943, entirely reorganized their film organization so that by 1944 they had 400 cameramen in the European theater. D-Day was not only the greatest strategic and logistical undertaking in modern warfare, it was also "the most lavishly equipped and planned photographic operation in history" (Bull 1945: 90).

World War II saw the widespread adoption of cinema as an instrument of propaganda. One of the particularly noteworthy features was the influx of filmmakers from the commercial film industry into the services. British directors David Macdonald and Roy Boulting both joined the AFPU. Carol Reed made *The New Lot* (1943), a training film for new recruits, for the Army Kinematograph Service, and then expanded it into the commercial feature film *The Way Ahead* (1944) starring David Niven, who was temporarily released from the army to star. Several prominent Hollywood studio directors, including John Ford,

Frank Capra, William Wyler, and John Huston, joined the US Army Signal Corps. Ford's *The Battle of Midway* (1942) and Wyler's *The Memphis Belle* (1943) are two of the finest combat documentaries: both are notable for their use of color actuality footage. Capra was tasked by the Office of War Information with producing a series of instructional films to help explain to servicemen why America was at war. The *Why We Fight* series proved so effective that several were also released in cinemas. Huston courted controversy with his film of the Italian campaign, *The Battle of San Pietro* (1944), which was suppressed until after the war due to its controversial use of voice-overs from "dead" soldiers. The British and Americans collaborated on the production of *The True Glory* (1945), an account of the war in Europe from D-Day to VE-Day, which marks the culmination of the combat documentary form that had begun with *The Battle of the Somme*. *The True Glory* is highly effective in that it contrasts an "official" view of the war, in the form of a triumphalist commentary by playwright Robert E. Sherwood, with an "unofficial" view from below that uses the anecdotes and experiences of ordinary servicemen that are by turn matter-of-fact, tragic, humorous, and poignant. However, its production was hampered by inter-service and inter-allied rivalries as everyone involved staked their claim for their share of the glory (Chapman 1996).

The commercial studios were also active in supporting the war effort. Hollywood mythologized the British home front in the sentimental *Mrs. Miniver* (dir. William Wyler, 1942) and, controversially, the Soviet ally in *Mission to Moscow* (dir. Michael Curtiz, 1943). Fictional treatments of war extended from the blatantly melodramatic heroics of *A Yank in the R.A.F.* (dir. Henry King, 1941) to the realism of films such as *They Were Expendable* (dir. John Ford, 1944) and *Objective: Burma!* (dir. Raoul Walsh, 1945). A similar process is evident in British cinema. Ealing Studios, for example, shifted from the early-war melodramas *Convoy* (dir. Pen Tennyson, 1940) and *Ships With Wings* (dir. Sergei Nolbandov, 1941), criticized for their focus on such irrelevancies as marital strife and heroic redemption, to documentary-style films such as *Nine Men* (dir. Harry Watt, 1943) and *San Demetrio, London* (dir. Charles Frend, 1943), praised by critics for their realism and emotional restraint. Perhaps the archetypal British war film was *In Which We Serve* (dirs. Noël Coward & David Lean, 1942) in which the destroyer HMS *Torrin* – inspired by Mountbatten's HMS *Kelly* during the Battle of Crete – represents a microcosm of the nation in which the hierarchies of class and rank are mapped onto one another. *The Life and Death of Colonel Blimp* (dir. Michael Powell, 1943), however, courted controversy in its fictional dramatization of a British officer based on David Low's cartoon character: Prime Minister Winston Churchill threatened to ban the film on the grounds that it was "propaganda detrimental to the morale of the Army" (Chapman 1995).

The war also saw a cycle of expensive costume epics to provide inspirational lessons from history. This narrative strategy can be seen in different national cinemas, where stories of heroic achievements from the past were used explicitly to draw parallels with the present. Shakespeare was pressed into war service in *Henry V* (dir. Laurence Olivier, 1944), released following D-Day and the Battle of Arnhem and dedicated "to the Commandos and Airborne Troops of Great Britain – the spirit of whose ancestors it has humbly been attempted to recapture in some ensuing scenes." The last major German film of the war was *Kolberg* (dir. Veit Harlan, 1945), which used an incident from the Napoleonic Wars to attempt to inspire the German nation to resistance in the closing stages of the war. In the Soviet Union the same purpose was served by *Alexander Nevsky* (dir. Sergei Eisenstein, 1938) – produced before the war but shelved due to the Nazi–Soviet Pact – and *Ivan the Terrible* (dir. Sergei Eisenstein, 1944–1946).

Cinema and the Memory of World War II

The events of 1939–1945 have continued to fascinate filmmakers and audiences long after the war itself. Whereas films of World War I presented it as a universal experience that was not defined by nationality, films of World War II have been intimately related to the national experience of war and have contributed to dominant myths. In Britain, for example, cinema promoted the narrative of the "finest hour" by focusing almost exclusively on the British war effort in such films as *The Cruel Sea* (dir. Charles Frend, 1953),

The Dam Busters (dir. Michael Anderson, 1955), *The Battle of the River Plate* (dir. Michael Powell, 1956), *Dunkirk* (dir. Leslie Norman, 1958), and *Sink the Bismarck!* (dir. Lewis Gilbert, 1960). The popularity of the war film has been related to Britain's post-war decline and the retreat from empire. In reconstructing past glories they created "an imaginary present in which we can go on enjoying our finest hours" (Whitebait 1958). Nevertheless, there is evidence of some ideological import to these films. They have been understood as an assertion of a more meritocratic social order where the emphasis is on leadership by ability rather than class (Ramsden 1998).

For the Soviet Union, in contrast, the narrative of the Great Patriotic War continued into postwar films such as *The Fall of Berlin* (dir. Mikhail Chiaureli, 1949) that represented an ideological project to promote a theme of national unity in which Stalin is portrayed as the savior of the Russian people (Taylor 1999: 99–122). Following Stalin's death and the decline of the doctrine of Socialist Realism – a mode of representation that enforced an idealized image of the heroic proletariat – Soviet filmmakers shifted away from glorifying the leadership and examined the effects of the war on ordinary Russians. The more humanist narratives of *The Cranes Are Flying* (dir. Mikhail Kalatozov, 1957) and *Ballad of a Soldier* (dir. Grigori Chukrai, 1959) were accompanied by greater levels of visual stylization and formal experimentation. It was not until the remarkable *Come and See* (dir. Emil Klimov, 1985), however, that Soviet cinema produced an account of the war marked by its unflinching realism in the representation of both German atrocities and the reprisals of partisans. Klimov's direction deliberately makes the viewing experience uncomfortable for the viewer through disorienting devices and shocking images.

The Polish representation of the war was conditioned by historical circumstances: the imposition of a communist puppet government in 1945 meant that Polish filmmakers had to tread warily. *Border Street* (dir. Alexander Ford, 1948), for example, was an account of the Warsaw Uprising that does not identify the partisans as either nationalists or communists. A trilogy of films by Andrzej Wajda – *A Generation* (1954), *Kanal* (1956), *Ashes and Diamonds* (1958) – demonstrates how Polish cinema negotiated its response to political

circumstances. *A Generation* is an ideologically correct narrative of resistance to Fascism, but *Kanal* is more sympathetic to the nationalist Home Army and implicitly critical of the Soviets for allowing the suppression of the Warsaw Uprising. *Ashes and Diamonds*, set in the days following the German surrender in May 1945, is decidedly anti-heroic in tone, suggesting that the idealism of the wartime resistance fighters has been betrayed at the altar of political expediency.

The representation of the war in German cinema was even more problematic due to the post-war division of Germany into two states. In the German Democratic Republic, the state film organization DEFA (*Deutsche Film Aktiengesellschaft*) maintained a rigorous level of control over form and content. *The Adventures of Werner Holt* (dir. Joachim Kunert, 1965) and *I Was Nineteen* (dir. Konrad Wolf, 1968) were commentaries on the legacy of National Socialism and employed a range of discursive strategies to account for the historical conditions that allowed Hitler into power. The ideological project of the cinema of the German Federal Republic, in contrast, was to distance Germans from National Socialism. Thus there were films focusing on German resistance to Hitler such as *The Jackboot Mutiny* (dir. G. W. Pabst, 1955) and *The Devil's General* (dir. Helmut Käutner, 1955). The other recurring strategy was the resort to the conventional theme of war is hell. *Punishment Battalion 999* (dir. Harald Philipp, 1959) and *Stalingrad* (dir. Frank Wisbar, 1958) focus on the brutality of the war on the Eastern Front and present a narrative in which Germans can be portrayed as victims too. *Stalingrad*, for example, differentiates between Nazis and "good" Germans, and lays the blame for the German defeat at Stalingrad squarely at the door of Hitler's misguided strategy. While the films of the 1950s can be seen in the context of Germany's political rehabilitation, later films could afford a more detached perspective. *Das Boot* (dir. Wolfgang Petersen, 1981) was a major international hit for West German cinema: the fact that the protagonists are German is almost irrelevant as the conventions of the submarine film are common to other national cinemas.

The problematic relationship of the war film to national identity is nowhere better demonstrated than in France. On the one hand films such as *The Battle of the Rails* (dir. René Clément, 1946) and *Is*

Paris Burning? (dir. René Clément, 1965) project a Gaullist narrative of the resistance as a national movement. On the other hand, however, films that challenge the myth of the resistance have been hugely controversial. *Lacombe Lucien* (dir. Louis Malle, 1974) was a fictional story about a disaffected youth who, turned down by the Maquis, instead joins the Gestapo as an informer. Malle saw the film as a way of exploring "the ambiguities and contradictions in behavior that belonged to that period" (quoted in French 1993: 103). The controversy that ensued forced Malle to leave France and work in America for the next decade.

Cinema and "Virtual War"

The representation of war in cinema is a form of spectacle: it invites the audience to "come and see" war at first hand. This is true both of documentaries such as *The Battle of the Somme* and of entirely fictional treatments. There has long been a tradition of representing war as an epic visual spectacle. This was evident as early as *The Birth of a Nation* (dir. D. W. Griffith, 1915) – one of the foundational films of American cinema – and persists in the digitally enhanced Ancient World battlefields of *Gladiator* (dir. Ridley Scott, 2000) and *Troy* (dir. Wolfgang Petersen, 2004). Most of the major campaigns of World War II have been restaged for the cinema in a cycle of international epics: *The Longest Day* (dir. Andrew Morton, 1962), *Battle of the Bulge* (dir. Ken Annakin, 1965), *Battle of Britain* (dir. Guy Hamilton, 1969), and *A Bridge Too Far* (dir. Richard Attenborough, 1977).

The increasingly sophisticated methods of representing war in film and on television have led some cultural theorists to argue that the distinction between war as it is experienced and war as it is represented has become increasingly blurred. Terms such as virtual war, cyber war, and spectator-sport war indicate an epistemological shift in the way in which war is understood. Arising from the television coverage of the first Gulf War of 1991 and the North Atlantic Treaty Organization's aerial campaign over Kosovo in 1999, and lent intellectual ballast by theorists such as Jean Baudrillard and Paul Virilio, the concept of virtual war refers to changes both in the conduct of modern warfare and in the media's representation of it. Following the lessons of the Vietnam War,

where the up-close television coverage was believed to have played a major part in turning public opinion against the war, military authorities now adopt a much more proactive approach to "managing" the media. One tactic is the resort to obtuse jargon: "material degradation" (bombardment) and "collateral damage" (a euphemism for civilian casualties). Another is the emphasis on so-called smart weapons such as laser-guided bombs and cruise missiles able to "take out" their targets with pinpoint accuracy. There is now an overriding imperative on the part of the military to demonstrate that modern warfare is a "clean" and "surgical" enterprise conducted with absolute precision in order to minimize casualties. Baudrillard believed that, during the Gulf War, the techniques used to represent the campaign in Pentagon simulations and computer graphics had become indistinguishable from the coverage of the real thing. This led to his infamous remark that "The Gulf War Did Not Take Place:" not, as some critics willfully misrepresented it, a conspiracy theory akin to the Moon landings, but rather an assertion of the poststructuralist idea that we experience the world not through actuality but through its representation (for the best discussion of this area, see Norris 1992).

The theoretical debate around reality versus representation is illustrated by *Saving Private Ryan* (dir. Steven Spielberg, 1998). This is a hugely important milestone in the representation of war. *Saving Private Ryan* was an enormous popular success (it grossed over $480 million at the box office worldwide) and won a clutch of prizes, including Spielberg's second Academy Award as Best Director (following *Schindler's List* in 1993). It is widely held to have set new standards of realism in the representation of combat in a fiction film. The sequence of the American landings on Omaha Beach on June 6, 1944, was greeted as "Hollywood's most grimly realistic and historically accurate depiction of a World War II battlefield" (Landon 1998). It was not just film critics, but, crucially, veterans and historians who praised the film for its realism. Stephen E. Ambrose, for example, felt that it was "the most accurate and realistic depiction of war on screen that I have ever seen" (quoted in United International Pictures' press book for the film).

Yet this "most realistic" of combat movies is, of course, entirely fictitious (contrary to some accounts it is not based on a true story) and its sequence of the Omaha beach landings is the work of a master filmmaker with all the technical resources of Hollywood at his disposal. The publicity material for *Saving Private Ryan* emphasized the lengths to which Spielberg and his crew went to achieve the impression of realism. In order to simulate the noise of bullets ripping into bodies the sound editor recorded rounds being fired into meat carcasses wrapped in cloth, while cinematographer Janusz Kaminski used desaturated colors and out-of-focus shots to replicate the "look" of actuality combat footage such as *The Battle of Midway* and *Report from the Aleutians*. Archivist Toby Haggith has shown that, in fact, Spielberg over-egged the pudding, creating effects that would have been impossible for a cameraman to achieve under combat conditions: for example, shots taken from outside the landing craft looking back. Haggith concedes that "the Spielberg version of D-Day is a more impressive account" than the actuality footage of the landings, but nevertheless points out "the artificial and manipulative technique with which the battle has been recreated" (Haggith 2002: 348).

It might be useful, in conclusion, to compare *Saving Private Ryan* with *The Battle of the Somme*. While, obviously, the films are poles apart technically, they raise similar issues. The aim of both films was to make the audience feel they had witnessed – even experienced – war at close quarters. The contemporary response to the films is remarkably similar: viewers were impressed by their graphic and realistic images of the battlefield. We might say that *The Battle of the Somme* is the more authentic of the two films in that most of it is compiled from actuality footage, whereas *Saving Private Ryan* is the more realistic (understanding realism to mean an impression of the real thing) but is not authentic (as its visual and aural realism is created through artifice). And both films mobilize the war for ideological ends: *The Battle of the Somme* was a propaganda film produced to help explain the war to the general public, while *Saving Private Ryan* can be seen as part of a cultural project to reclaim the memory of World War II as "the good war" following the trauma of Vietnam for Americans. What they each demonstrate, in their different ways, is the power of cinema as a medium for projecting images of war to the public.

SEE ALSO: Combat Film; War Photography; War Poetry; War Propaganda.

References

Badsey, S. D. (1981) "*The Battle of the Somme*: British War-Propaganda," *Historical Journal of Film, Radio and Television*, 3 (2): 99–115.

Bull, D. (1945) "Filming D-Day," *Documentary News Letter*, 6 (2): 90.

Chapman, J. (1995) "*The Life and Death of Colonel Blimp* (1943) Reconsidered," *Historical Journal of Film, Radio and Television*, 15 (1): 19–54.

Chapman, J. (1996) "'The Yanks are shown to such advantage': Anglo-American Rivalry in the Production of *The True Glory* (1945)," *Historical Journal of Film, Radio and Television*, 16 (4): 533–554.

French, P. (Ed.) (1993) *Malle on Malle*. London: Faber and Faber.

Haggith, T. (2002) "D-Day Filming – For Real: A Comparison of 'Truth' and 'Reality' in *Saving Private Ryan* and Combat Film by the British Army's Film and Photographic Unit," *Film History*, 14 (3–4): 332–353.

Jelavich, P. (1999) "German Culture in the Great War." In A. Roshwald and R. Stites (Eds.), *European Culture in the Great War: The Arts, Entertainment and Propaganda, 1914–1918*. Cambridge: Cambridge University Press.

Kelly, A. (1998) *Filming All Quiet on the Western Front: 'Brutal Cutting, Stupid Censors, Bigoted Politicos.'* London: I. B. Tauris.

Landon, P. (1998) "Realism, Genre and *Saving Private Ryan*," *Film and History*, 28 (3–4): 58–63.

Matuszewski, B. (1995/1898) "A New Source of History," trans. L. Marks and D. Koszarski, *Film History*, 7 (3): 322–324.

Norris, C. (1992) *Uncritical Theory: Postmodernism, Intellectuals and the Gulf War*. London: Routledge.

Paris, M. (1999) "Enduring Heroes: British Feature Films and the First World War, 1919–1997." In M. Paris (Ed.), *The First World War and Popular Cinema*. Edinburgh: Edinburgh University Press.

Ramsden, J. (1998) "Refocusing 'the People's War': British War Films of the 1950s," *Journal of Contemporary History*, 33 (1): 35–63.

Reeves, N. (1997) "Cinema, Spectatorship and Propaganda: *Battle of the Somme* (1916) and Its Contemporary Audience," *Historical Journal of Film, Radio and Television*, 17 (1): 5–28.

Reeves, N. (1999) *The Power of Film Propaganda: Myth or Reality?* London: Continuum.

Smither, R. (1993) "'A wonderful idea of the fighting': The Question of Fakes in *The Battle of the Somme*," *Historical Journal of Film, Radio and Television*, 13 (2): 149–168.

Sorlin, P. (1994) "War and Cinema: Interpreting the Relationship," *Historical Journal of Film, Radio and Television*, 14 (4): 357–366.

Taylor, R. (1999) *Film Propaganda: Soviet Russia and Nazi Germany*, rev. ed. London: I. B. Tauris.

Whitebait, W. (1958) "Bombardment," *New Statesman*, April 4: 432.

Winter, J. (1995) *Sites of Memory, Sites of Mourning: The Great War in European Cultural History*. Cambridge: Cambridge University Press.

Further Reading

Basinger, J. (2003) *The World War II Combat Movie: Anatomy of a Genre*, rev. ed. Middletown, CT: Wesleyan University Press.

Chambers, J. W. and Culbert, D. (Eds.) (1996) *World War II, Film and History*. New York: Oxford University Press.

Chapman, J. (2008) *War and Film*. London: Reaktion.

Fox, J. (2007) *Film Propaganda in Britain and Nazi Germany: World War II Cinema*. Oxford: Berg.

Kelly, A. (1997) *Cinema and the Great War*. London: Routledge.

Koppes, C. R. and Black, G. D. (1987) *Hollywood Goes to War: How Politics, Profits and Propaganda Shaped World War II Movies*. Berkeley: University of California Press.

Manvell, R. (1974) *Films and the Second World War*. London: J. M. Dent.

McKernan, L. (1992) *Topical Budget: The Great British News Film*. London: British Film Institute.

Virilio, P. (1989) *War and Cinema: The Logistics of Perception*, trans. P. Camiller. London: Verso.

War and Sexuality

SUSAN R. GRAYZEL

Why War and Sexuality Matter

Even without accepting ideas popularized by Sigmund Freud at the turn of the twentieth century that human beings are driven by drives toward sexual pleasure (the life instinct or *Eros*) and deadly violence (the death instinct or *Thanatos*), an understanding of war and sexuality sheds light on every type of military conflict: local, civil, and international. All wars have involved both men and women to some extent and the actions of most militaries have had an effect on sexual behavior. By suggesting that the warrior is the epitome of manhood, ideas about the relationship between military valor and human sexuality have varied. Ideas have circulated that abstinence makes for better fighters, who can channel sexual urges into those toward violence, but so too have notions that better fighters demand and require satisfaction of sexual appetites beyond the norm. The study of war provides ample examples of the core significance of gender cross-culturally and cross-chronologically (Goldstein 2001).

Violent intergroup conflict also repeatedly exhibits the disturbing intertwining of sexuality and brutality. Wars have been waged over sexual honor, have been accompanied by horrific and indiscriminate sexual violence, and have employed women and men as objects for the sexual gratification and thus pacification of military forces. Groups and states waging war have tried to regulate both the sexual behavior and, in the modern period, the sexual identity of members of militaries (both formal and informal). Along with the taking of slaves from vanquished foes, warfare has also led to (again largely but not exclusively) women becoming the physical spoils of war. In the case of the sexual abuse or conquest of women, this has had the added perceived advantage of eradicating one's enemy by genetically supplanting him through impregnating his women.

Given the wide range of topics that fall under the rubric of war and sexuality, this chapter focuses on a few of the most salient matters for understanding both historical and contemporary practices in wartime. First, it investigates sexual behavior as warfare, examining the sexual violence accompanying military conflicts and especially the evolution of the concept of rape, particularly mass rape, as a war crime, notably in late twentieth-century conflicts in Bosnia-Herzegovina and Rwanda. This section of the chapter includes a discussion of sexual violence and the sexual slavery of women for the use of militaries, looking in particular at the "comfort women" exploited by the Japanese army during World War II as a separate kind of war crime from more conventional wartime rape. Secondly, it traces a few of the state efforts to regulate the sexual behavior of members of the armed forces, focusing especially on the role of state-sanctioned prostitution and brothels for the military, and policies developed to contain the spread of venereal diseases among members of the military forces. Thirdly, the chapter examines sexual behavior and identity within organized armed forces, particularly how militaries have addressed issues raised by the modern presence of openly gay and lesbian troops. All of these issues merit the further attention of those interested in any aspect of warfare.

War and Sexual Violence

Rape in warfare has a history as old as warfare itself. Both the threat of sexual violence against the women of one's own population and the promise of unfettered access to sexual partners among a vanquished enemy have thus served as a rallying cry for men to wage war. Other explanations proffered for the prevalence of sexual violence accompanying military conflict include the notion that rape is a "natural" part of warfare; that shared abuse of (in particular) women contributes to male bonding among warriors; that wartime culture both embraces and elevates a masculine ethos that associates manhood with violence; and that warfare allows for a broader social contempt for all things and persons deemed "feminine" to become embodied. Early feminist interpretations of wartime rape offered the explanation that war and rape were interchangeable, but more recent historical and theoretical studies have insisted on issues both of commonality and specificity to understand better the precise forms of sexual violence that have accompanied modern warfare (Scully 2009).

The treatment or rather mistreatment of civilians confronting invading and occupying armies continued to be an aspect of modern wars. In this regard, the scale of World War I dwarfed anything that had gone before, and in this conflict rape became a powerful tool of war efforts in two distinct senses. First, given the rise of mass media and literacy in participant states, accounts and representations of the allegedly mass and brutal rape of innocent civilians became a pronounced part of propaganda in the first great war of the twentieth century. The invasion of neutral Belgium in 1914 by the German army cast as the "Rape of Belgium" and the subsequent invasion and occupation of portions of France were portrayed vividly and literally as sexual assaults in a range of Allied media. Atrocity propaganda highlighted the depravity of German "Huns" who abused women and children, purportedly engaging in orgies of sexualized violence. For instance, in one poster, under the heading "Destroy this Mad Beast," a gorilla in a spiked German helmet clutches a half-clad female. The actions of the German army are thus shown as instinctively bestial. Secondly, while individuals in the armies of World War I committed rape in all theaters, the widespread and seemingly calculated acts of violence portrayed in Allied propaganda exaggerated the extent of the sexualized violence. Rape also accompanied the Ottoman Empire's deadly attacks on the Armenian population in 1915, but media saturated with tales of wartime rape from western Europe were less interested in paying attention to this latter case. Moreover, the discrediting of such Allied propaganda in the war's aftermath made accounts of atrocities that emerged in conflicts in the 1930s less likely to lead to international outrage or action. The return of warfare to European soil in the Spanish Civil War was also accompanied by acts of sexual violence, but the next war's equivalent to the "Rape of Belgium" would be found in Asia (Grayzel 2002).

Like the 1914 "Rape of Belgium," the 1937 "Rape of Nanking" must be understood both as metaphor and description. Among the damages inflicted in the early years of the conflict that became World War II were the sexual abuses committed by the Japanese in its conquests in Asia in the late 1930s. When Japanese forces attacked the then Chinese capital of Nanking, a wave of brutal violence followed, lasting from mid-December 1937 until February 1938. During this span of time, rapes of over 20,000 women occurred. Most documented cases record rapes by two or more soldiers – this was at core group rather than individual assault. Moreover, the sexual violence associated with this and other abuses by Japanese troops in China and elsewhere in Asia was part of an ethos whereby these soldiers had come to see Chinese civilians as less than human and therefore not worth being treated according to the usual codes of behavior (Chang 1997; Vikman 2005).

In addition to its sexual assaults against civilian women, Japan's military also used women, primarily from Korea, as sexual slaves. These so-called comfort women serviced "comfort stations" or military brothels, providing sexual outlets for Japanese soldiers. Making use of local networks that already trafficked in women, the Japanese military demanded large numbers of women to service the presumed sexual needs of troops. Many of these women were recruited locally from rural areas and promised work opportunities in Japan only to find themselves imprisoned in comfort stations and repeatedly raped. During the course of the Asia–Pacific War, tens of thousands of women from Taiwan, China, the Philippines, and Indonesia, including Dutch women colonists, were subject to systematic sexual exploitation and violence. What remains striking about the comfort women system was its scale, duration, and scope in terms of the time period, geographic locations, and numbers involved. In December 1991 (the symbolic fiftieth anniversary of the Japanese bombing of Pearl Harbor), a group of former comfort women filed a class action suit against the Japanese government, and following upon this in 1992, a group of South Korean women who survived this wartime horror began to organize protests and called upon the Japanese government to issue a formal apology and offer compensation for their suffering. To date, these women, whose numbers continue to dwindle, are still protesting and still waiting for both a formal admission of full responsibility and financial recompense, an issue that continues to mar Japanese and Korean relations (Soh 2001; Tanaka 2002; Ford 2013).

One of the most widespread and well-documented occurrences of more conventionally understood mass rape in World War II took place when the Soviet army swept into Germany in 1945. In addition to other motives usually attributed to soldiers enacting such abuses, the brutality of the war waged against Soviet civilians seems to have prompted a desire to take specific revenge on German ones. As was the case with other acts of mass rape by invading and occupying forces, the subjugation of German women through sexual violence was also seen as the ultimate humiliation for defeated German men. For this reason, among others, the mass rape of the women of Berlin remained a kind of open secret until the 1980s (Grossman 1995; Naimark 1995).

Attempts to reform aspects of international law led to the Geneva Convention of 1949, wherein rape by militaries was prohibited. Making this an aspect of international law was part of an effort to take sexual assaults more seriously than had previous national military laws, which might condemn rape by their troops but made punishments for such behavior relatively lenient. Despite the 1949 Geneva Convention, and as with the failure of previous national efforts, mass rape by troops continued to exist as a grisly component of wars in the second half of the twentieth century, including outbreaks of organized violence in such states as El Salvador, Guatemala, Kuwait, Liberia, Somalia, Sudan, and Uganda. While the widespread occurrence of rape in each of these examples must be contextualized in terms of particular circumstances, rape functions in most such instances to "intimidate, degrade, humiliate, and torture the enemy." In undermining the morale of local populations via extensive sexual violence, a group can cause its enemy to take flight, turning rape into a form of "ethnic cleansing," and in some genocidal instances rape has served as a prelude to the more extreme "cleansing" of death (Weitsman 2008: 563).

It took two large-scale occurrences of mass rape in separate late twentieth-century conflicts – the wars accompanying the break-up of Yugoslavia, notably in Bosnia-Herzegovina, and the genocidal events that erupted in Rwanda in 1994 – to bring renewed international attention to rape as an instrument of war. The events in Bosnia-Herzegovina drew special attention because of the systematic and calculated nature of the attacks: the setting up of "rape camps" where Muslim women were imprisoned and, in many instances, forcibly impregnated by brutal gang rapes conducted by Bosnian Serb militias. In these instances, charges of rape against perpetrators of this violence came before the International Criminal Tribunal for the former Yugoslavia and the International Criminal Tribunal for Rwanda. Moreover, the international community via the United Nations (UN) Security Council passed Resolution 1325 in 2000 (in the aftermath of these events) noting that women and children constitute a special category of victims of war. In 2008, Resolution 1820 expanded the previous one by directly focusing on sexual violence against women and girls as threatening peace and security. Such legislation represents a new legitimating of rape as a war crime, but it ignores the reality that men and boys may also fall victim to wartime sexual violence (Scully 2009).

Ongoing, extremely high levels of rape associated with violence in the Democratic Republic of Congo (DRC) have also led to new efforts to address rape as a particular war crime, one that demands both prosecution and careful treatment of survivors. In February 2010, in the aftermath of a UN Population Fund report that showed more than 8,000 women had been raped in the past year in the DRC and thus recognized the serious nature of ongoing mass rape, the UN secretary general appointed Margot Wallström as the first ever "Special Representative on Sexual Violence in Conflict," a position that provides an international focal point for combating sexual violence during wartime and its aftermath. One of Wallström's first statements was to declare that sexual violence in wartime "is not cultural, it is criminal. It is a crime under international law and it is also a war crime" (IANSA 2010).

Alongside taking seriously the psychological, physical, and social damage inflicted by the rapes that accompany armed conflict, scholars have also begun to investigate the exceptions – conflicts where sexual violence is uncommon. This is all part of an effort to treat rape not as a "normative" part of war and indeed of masculinity, but as a deviant, criminal act committed by individuals and by groups of armed men during specific contexts. Given that it is only relatively recently that international law has prosecuted mass rape as a war crime, it has yet to be determined that legal sanctions will act as a deterrent. In the meantime, ongoing international non-governmental organizations (NGOs) and the UN have made strides in recognizing the needs and rights of victims of this crime.

What has received even less attention and certainly less legal action than wartime rape has been sexual or domestic violence committed by soldiers and veterans after their active duty service has ended. The traumas of total war in particular have been associated with fears of post-war sexual disorder; this was the case for both men and women after World War I (Mosse 1985; Doan 2006; Crouthamel 2008). However, the issue of domestic violence by veterans has remained largely hidden from historical view. The silence surrounding this issue is slowly lifting as the news media publicize, and the military begins to react to, violence that comes home; for instance, a new level of openness on the issue of veterans and domestic violence has emerged in the United States during the conflicts in Iraq and Afghanistan (Alvarez 2009).

As it has been in all recorded wars, sexual violence thus continues to be a factor in modern conflicts. What is new is a willingness on the part of individual states and the international community to make strides toward defining it as an unacceptable part of warfare. Rather than seeing rape as somehow inevitable during wartime, new international law seeks to make it unthinkable, and perhaps, far more uncommon.

Regulating Sex with Soldiers

Groups engaging in organized violence need to maintain their readiness to fight. Historically, when such groups contain all-male units isolated from regular ties to lovers or spouses, their fitness for combat becomes linked to satisfying or sublimating their sexual needs. This can be done within armies, but modern states have been more concerned with regulating the behavior of those providing sexual outlets to military men. If the oldest profession is prostitution, perhaps the oldest consumer of commercial sex is the soldier.

In the twentieth century and especially during World War I, state agents were just as concerned to halt the behavior of "amateur" girls of their own nations who were seen as falling victim to what Britain deemed "khaki fever" – the desire for men in uniform that led to sexual interactions that proved impossible to regulate. Officials were also deeply agitated about possible interactions between European women, perhaps acting as nurses, and troops composed of colonial non-white subjects. There was fear that wartime liaisons romanticized in popular culture meant that bourgeois standards of behavior could fall by the wayside with potentially frightening consequences for society and, in the case of colonial troops, the prestige of imperial powers. Fear about the spread of disease led, for example, to the reemergence of aspects of Britain's Contagious Diseases Acts in the Defence of the Realm Regulations that again punished women for "infecting members of His Majesty's Forces" with venereal disease (Grayzel 2002). When the United States entered the war, part of the provision of the statute instituting the draft in 1917 was a measure granting the secretary of war extraordinary powers to prohibit prostitution near army and naval bases. Such anti-vice measures attempted to control all sexual behavior, not just that of the commercial variety, for reasons of both physical and "moral" health.

At the time that states tried to control the sexual behavior of their militaries in order to control disease and morale, the larger popular culture surrounding twentieth-century total war promoted certain types of heterosexuality in order to "sell" the war to men, such as the pin-up girl. This was especially true in nations that relied on voluntary conscription, such as Great Britain. The mass media in both world wars walked a fine line between encouraging women to step out with soldiers and keep them happy and yet simultaneously avoid catching the "khaki fever" that would turn them into promiscuous dangers to these men and their national war efforts.

During World War II, concern about rampant immorality also expressed itself in racialized terms. While the militaries of all participant states made some effort to reorganize or control prostitution, commercial sex thrived in outposts from Hawaii to Paris to Bombay to Cairo – essentially any place where soldiers congregated in large numbers. Within the United States itself, public campaigns focused on convincing women to be patriotic "good girls" rather than promiscuous "patriotutes" (Hegarty 1998). If sexually promiscuous women were seen as dangerous on the home front, sexual encounters between "white" soldiers and "native" women in colonial or imperial brothels caused relatively little concern, which makes the intense focus on the sexual behavior of African American troops, especially in Britain, noteworthy. When African American soldiers interacted with local women in Britain, public attention focused on the "deviant" behavior of the young women in question and on efforts to curtail their interaction with such troops (Rose 1997).

In the conflicts that followed World War II, the flourishing presence of prostitution around military bases continued. During the Vietnam War, Bangkok became a prominent center of commercial sex, as military prostitution led to sex tourism. Where the United States maintained such bases in the Philippines, South Korea, and Japan, the presence of prostitution has remained high and has led to increased tensions between members of the US military and the local population, as US servicemen have been accused of sexual assaults against non-prostitutes. While wars do not lead inevitably to upsurges in the numbers of prostitutes or to the spread of venereal disease, there is no doubt that war alters the sexual climate in the locations where it occurs, and this contributes greatly to the exploitation of women in these locales (Enloe 1993; Goldstein 2001).

Sexuality and Homosexuality within the Military

In February 2010, in anticipation of the overturning of the "Don't Ask, Don't Tell" policy that allowed closeted gays and lesbians to serve in the US military, the Palm Center at the University of Santa Barbara issued a report on the contemporary military service of gay and lesbian personnel around the world. It found 25 nations that allowed gays and lesbians to participate in their countries' militaries; these include most of Europe (Austria, Belgium, the Czech Republic, Denmark, Estonia, Finland, France, Germany, Ireland, Italy, Lithuania, Luxembourg, the Netherlands, Norway, Slovenia, Spain, Sweden, Switzerland, and the United Kingdom) and Australia, Canada, Israel, and New Zealand, but only one African state (South Africa) and one Latin American nation (Uruguay). In its summation of its findings, the report stated definitively: "Research has uniformly shown that transitions to policies of equal treatment without regard to sexual orientation have been highly successful and have had no negative impact on morale, recruitment, retention, readiness or overall combat effectiveness. No consulted expert anywhere in the world concluded that lifting the ban on openly gay service caused an overall decline in the military" (Frank 2010: 2).

The contentious debates at the dawn of the twenty-first century over the military service of gay and lesbian troops are only the latest thoughts in a long history of (homo)sexuality and military forces. In the *Symposium*, Plato envisaged the ideal army as follows:

> if there were only some way of contriving that … an army should be made up of lovers and their loves, … when fighting at each other's side, although a mere handful, they would overcome the world. For what lover would not choose rather to be seen by all mankind than by his beloved, either when abandoning his post or throwing away his arms? He would be ready to die a thousand deaths rather than endure this. Or who would desert his beloved or fail him in the hour of danger? The veriest coward would become an inspired hero, equal to the bravest, at such a time; Love would inspire him. (Crompton 1994: 25)

This model was realized by the so-called Sacred Band of Thebes, a unit comprised of paired same-sex lovers that thrived for some 40 years until Thebes's defeat by Philip of Macedonia. Given other examples of the valorization of same-sex lovers as warriors, according to scholar Louis Crompton, one can conclude that in Ancient Greece,

> love between men owed its high prestige primarily to one consideration – its perceived ability to inspire heroic self-sacrifice in men, especially in some military cause. In this respect it supported one of the society's pre-eminent male ideals – that of the courageous warrior, an ideal required by the fact that a city or state that failed to produce such men might face subjugation or even enslavement by its rivals. (Crompton 1994: 29)

Given the all-male nature of militaries until the modern period, attitudes toward male homoerotic and homosocial behavior tacitly allowed these to continue even if civil or military law punished overt acts of homosexuality (such as statutes against "sodomy" or "buggery" or "gross indecency"). Prior to World War II, the US military prohibited "sodomy," defined as anal or oral sex between men. After World War II, "homosexuals" were excluded as a class of persons. Homophobia became part of how the modern military defined itself.

With the increasing entry of women into the armed forces in the late twentieth century, the all-male nature of the military changed. Prior to this,

female combatants were the truly exceptional, like Joan of Arc, or were able to fight because they disguised themselves as men. With women called upon to participate in more modern militaries in significant numbers, assumptions about the sexuality of servicewomen came to fall into two distinct stereotypes. Either women who joined the military were sexually voracious camp followers who had found the ideal means by which to chase men in uniform, or they wanted to be "men," emulating virile soldiers in all things, including their sexual preference for women. Rumors about the immorality of members of the first women's army auxiliary, the Women's Army Auxiliary Corps created in Britain in 1917, centered on scandalous heterosexual behavior, suggesting that such women acted as prostitutes and became pregnant with soldiers' illegitimate offspring. Countering such rumors required a construction of women in uniform as exemplars of morality; they might wear khaki but underneath it these women were domestic, heterosexual creatures longing for marriage and family.

The 1917 creation of the Women's Battalions of Death by Russia's provisional government offered another contemporary view of female soldiers. In this case, since these women were quite exceptional in assuming combat roles, all traces of femininity had to be eradicated. Publicity stills showed these women cutting off their long hair, so that with their close-cropped hair and military uniform, they looked virtually indistinguishable from their male counterparts. They were "honorary" men, and beyond this, allegedly asexual beings, but still controversial.

When women once again actively joined the military during World War II, renewed anxiety about their sexuality returned. In the United States, debates over how to control the sexual behavior of members of the Women's Army Corps (WAC) grew quite heated, especially when rumors swirled about the unit being created solely to provide prostitutes for the army or that such an environment would create a breeding ground for lesbians. The official response was to construct a model of female soldiers as embodying middle-class values of chastity, restraint, and respectability. Despite prohibitions on sexual behavior, WACs formed both heterosexual relationships with men in uniform and same-sex relationships with one another within the services (Meyer 1992).

Wartime created a climate in which some gay and lesbian relationships could flourish within the military, but the sanctions against gay men remained much stronger than against lesbians. On the other hand, the treatment of gay men in the British and American militaries varied depending on their status (officer or enlisted) or value; there was a tendency to excuse the behavior of soldiers and sailors with a demonstrated ability, but to punish or expel those less skillful at fighting. The influence of the mobilization of gay men during World War II led paradoxically to greater awareness for gay men of their collective identity, a certain degree of tolerance by heterosexuals exposed to gay relationships, and post-war homophobia (Costello 1985; Bérubé 1990).

In post-1945 western society – and especially where the sexual revolution and gay liberation movements took root – the issue of gays and lesbians openly serving in their nations' militaries became an increasingly contentious issue. Marked resistance to the entrance of both non-whites and females as full members of the military and, to an extent, antagonism to gay and lesbian troops, mirrored earlier fears that a military accepting of difference would be a compromised one. In wartime, especially during the world wars, militaries mostly tolerated the presence of homosexuals. The outright ban in the US military on gays and lesbians as categories of persons did not occur until 1950 under the Uniform Code of Military Justice (prior statutes against "sodomy," prohibiting oral or anal sex with partners of either sex, are also incorporated into this legal code). While the enforcement of this policy varied, between 1980 and 1990 for instance, nearly 1,500 members of the US armed forces were dishonorably discharged for "homosexuality" (Scott and Stanley 1994). The issue rose to greater public attention in 1992 when president-elect Bill Clinton announced that he would end the military's ban on gays and lesbians.

However, instead of overtly doing so, Clinton shifted to a policy enshrined in 1993 legislation that became known as "Don't Ask, Don't Tell." This meant that gays and lesbians could serve as long as they did so invisibly; they could not be overtly asked about their sexual orientation but they had to remain closeted. This continued effectively to ban openly gay and lesbian troops from serving by making it impossible for them to do so and live free and open lives. The debates that have followed the implementation of this policy have argued on the one hand that this is unacceptable because it allows the military to deny basic civil rights to gay and lesbian citizens. On the other hand, those defending the need for a heterosexual-only military argue that such rights are far less important than combat readiness, and thus national security, which are presumably compromised by openly gay troops. Throughout discussions of the policy, it is the presence of gay men that seems to threaten the normative, heterosexual male bonding that underlies good morale and camaraderie – the very association of the military with manhood itself (Cohn 1998; Goldstein 2001).

As evidence continued to mount that having gay and lesbian members of the military in no way compromised military effectiveness, a new assault on the policy of excluding them arose. Given the size and global presence of its military, the United States became the touchstone for the issue of gays and lesbians in uniform. In May 2010, the US House of Representatives voted to allow the Defense Department to repeal the ban, and so too did the Senate Armed Services Committee (Herszenhorn and Hulse 2010). A formal change in policy awaited a Pentagon report on the effect of openly gay and lesbian troops, which concluded that ending the policy would have little impact on military preparedness. As a result, after passage by the Senate, the repeal of "Don't Ask, Don't Tell" was signed into law by US President Barack Obama in December 2010 (Stolberg 2010).

One sideline to debates about the dangers posed by having gay and lesbian troops is the presence of sexual abuse of members within militaries, such as that of the US. As women became fully integrated into the US military and military service academies, the incidence of sexual harassment, including physical abuse, and rape climbed. In two investigations conducted in 1988 and 1996, the majority of US servicewomen reported experiencing some form of sexual harassment. The sexual violence discussed earlier in this chapter can also be found operating among those serving in the same militaries, an issue that remains an ongoing concern for both servicemen and servicewomen as well as for military leaders in the US (O'Neill 1998; Dao 2013).

War and Sexuality

The study of sexuality is integral to the study of warfare and vice versa. Sexual violence has long accompanied military actions in a variety of contexts. Rape as a form of warfare has long-range damaging consequences that the international community has slowly been coming to address. In addition, political and military leaders as well as individuals have tried to harness and control the sexual impulses of troops with mixed results. Providing sexual outlets for military men has led to the enslavement and abuse of women that again has only recently become subject to international sanction. War-making relies on normative ideas about masculinity and femininity, including assumptions about military valor and manhood that have often contained homophobic assertions. The presence of women in modern militaries and of openly gay and lesbian troops has challenged many of these assumptions, but not eroded fears about compromising the stature and/or effectiveness of militaries. As the above discussion suggests, understanding the role played by sexuality in warfare sheds light on past, present, and future conflicts.

SEE ALSO: Ethnic Cleansing; Psychological Warfare; Rwandan Genocide; War Crimes; War Propaganda; Women and War; World War II: War in Asia.

References

Alvarez, L. (2009) "A Focus on Violence by Returning GI's," *New York Times*, January 1.

Bérubé, A. (1990) *Coming Out Under Fire: The History of Gay Men and Women in World War Two*. New York: Free Press.

Chang, I. (1997) *The Rape of Nanking: The Forgotten Holocaust of World War Two*. New York: Basic Books.

Cohn, C. (1998) "Gays in the Military: Texts and Subtexts." In M. Zalewski and J. Parpart (Eds.), *The "Man" Question in International Relations*. Boulder: Westview Press.

Costello, J. (1985) *Love, Sex and War, 1939–1945*. London: Pan.

Crompton, L. (1994) "'An Army of Lovers:' The Sacred Band of Thebes," *History Today*, 44 (11): 23–29.

Crouthamel, J. (2008) "Male Sexuality and Psychological Trauma: Soldiers and Sexual Disorder in World War I and Weimar Germany," *Journal of the History of Sexuality*, 17 (1): 60–84.

Dao, J. (2013) "In Debate over Military Sexual Assault Men are Overlooked Victims," *New York Times*, June 23.

Doan, L. L. (2006) "Topsy-Turvydom: Gender Inversion, Sapphism, and the Great War," *GLQ: A Journal of Lesbian and Gay Studies*, 12 (4): 517–542.

Enloe, C. (1993) *The Morning After: Sexual Politics at the End of the Cold War*. Berkeley: University of California Press.

Ford, P. (2013) "Korea to Japan: Time Running Out for 'Comfort Women' Resolution." *Christian Science Monitor*, October 20.

Frank, N. (2010) *Gays in Foreign Militaries 2010: A Global Primer*. Santa Barbara: Palm Center Blueprints for Sound Public Policy.

Goldstein, J. S. (2001) *War and Gender: How Gender Shapes the War System and Vice Versa*. Cambridge: Cambridge University Press.

Grayzel, S. R. (2002) *Women and the First World War*. Harlow: Longman.

Grossman, A. (1995) "A Question of Silence: The Rape of German Women by Occupation Soldiers," *October*, 72: 42–63.

Hegarty, M. E. (1998) "Patriot or Prostitute? Sexual Discourses, Print Media, and American Women during World War II," *Journal of Women's History*, 10 (2): 112–136.

Herszenhorn, D. M. and Hulse, C. (2010) "House Votes to Allow 'Don't Ask, Don't Tell' Repeal," *New York Times*, May 27.

IANSA Women's Network (2010) "Action on UN SCR 1888: Margot Wallstrom appointed as UN Special Representative," January 21.

Meyer, L. D. (1992) "Creating GI Jane: The Regulation of Sexuality and Sexual Behavior in the Women's Army Corps," *Feminist Studies*, 18 (3): 581–602.

Mosse, G. (1985) *Nationalism and Sexuality: Respectability and Abnormal Sexuality in Modern Europe*. New York: Howard Fertig.

Naimark, N. (1995) *The Russians in Germany: A History of the Soviet Zone of Occupation, 1945–1949*. Cambridge, MA: Belknap Press.

O'Neill, W. L. (1998) "Sex Scandals in the Gender-Integrated Military," *Gender Issues*, 16 (1/2): 64–86.

Rose, S. O. (1997) "Girls and GI's: Race, Sex, and Diplomacy in Second World War Britain," *International History Review*, 146–160.

Scott, W. J. and Stanley, S. C. (1994) "Introduction: Sexual Orientation and Military Service." In W. J. Scott and S. C. Stanley (Eds.), *Gays and Lesbians in the Military: Issues, Concerns and Contrasts*. New York: de Gruyter.

Scully, P. (2009) "Vulnerable Women: A Critical Reflection on Human Rights Discourse and Sexual Violence," *Emory International Law Review*, 23: 113–124.

Soh, C. S. (2001) "Japan's Responsibility Toward Comfort Women Survivors." Working Paper No. 77. San Francisco: Japan Policy Research Institute.

Stolberg, S. G. (2010) "Obama Signs Away 'Don't Ask, Don't Tell.'" *New York Times*, December 22.

Tanaka, Y. (2002) *Japan's Comfort Women: Sexual Slavery and Prostitution during World War II and the US Occupation*. London: Routledge.

Vikman, E. (2005) "Modern Combat: Sexual Violence in Warfare, Part II," *Anthropology and Medicine*, 12 (1): 33–46.

Weitsman, P. A. (2008) "The Politics of Identity and Sexual Violence: A Review of Bosnia and Rwanda," *Human Rights Quarterly*, 30: 561–578.

Further Reading

Bailey, B. and Farber, D. (1992) *The First Strange Place: The Alchemy of Race and Sex in World War II Hawaii*. New York: Free Press.

Bristow, N. K. (1996) *Making Men Moral: Social Engineering during the Great War*. New York: New York University Press.

Buss, D. E. (2009) "Rethinking 'Rape as a Weapon of War,'" *Feminist Legal Studies*, 17: 145–163.

Haskell, J. D. (2009) "The Complicity and Limits of International Law in Armed Conflict Rape," *Boston Third World Law Journal*, 35: 35–84.

Levine, P. (2003) *Prostitution, Race and Politics: Policing Venereal Disease in the British Empire*. New York: Routledge.

Noakes, L. (2006) *Women in the British Army: War and the Gentle Sex, 1907–1948*. London: Routledge.

Stockdale, M. K. (2004) "'My Death for the Motherland is Happiness': Women, Patriotism, and Soldiering in Russia's Great War, 1914–1917," *American Historical Review*, 109 (1): 78–116.

Trustam, M. (1984) *Women of the Regiment: Marriage and the Victorian Army*. Cambridge: Cambridge University Press.

United States General Accounting Office (1993) *Homosexuals in the Military: Policies and Practices of Foreign Countries*. Washington, DC: United States General Accounting Office.

Wood, E. J. (2009) "Armed Groups and Sexual Violence: When Is Wartime Rape Rare?" *Politics and Society*, 37 (1): 131–162.

Woollacott, A. (1994) "'Khaki Fever' and Its Control: Gender, Age, Class and Sexual Morality on the British Homefront in the First World War," *Journal of Contemporary History*, 29: 325–347.

War Crimes

SEAN MCGLYNN

It is no easy task to define a war crime with absolute clarity, authority, and unanimity. What constitutes a war crime has meant different things to different people in different cultures in different times. Thus our current interpretations of the term should not be deemed fixed and immutable; indeed, revisions in international law are continuously adopted to meet with changing circumstances. Thus, in the late twentieth century, the accusation of a war crime might attempt to be sidestepped simply by the avoidance of declaring an act of war while engaging in what is, by any definition, warring activity; international lawyers now employ terms such as "armed conflict" or "force" to vitiate such circumambulations. The loosest definition – that war crimes are crimes committed in times of war – fails to separate the military sphere from the civil one. A modern, consensual definition of a war crime may be a violation of international law regulating the legality and conduct of war, especially in relation to non-combatants (civilians, prisoners of war, the wounded). It should be noted, however, that the issue then becomes the preserve of specialist international lawyers; many would also argue that victor's justice still prevails, and that in the twenty-first century the defeated still cannot expect a fair trial.

The legalistic element is, of course, essential to the process of establishing war guilt, but the admirable attempt to do so cannot always penetrate the fog of war or even necessarily achieve much in the way of curtailing war's worst excesses. The military commander and strategist Clausewitz, writing in the nineteenth century at a time when war was becoming increasingly formalized and the international laws on war began their process of codification, stated: "War is an act to force or compel our enemy to do our will. … Attached to force are certain self-imposed, imperceptible limitations hardly worth mentioning, known as international law and custom, but they scarcely weaken it" (Clausewitz 1976: 75). This rightly suggests that the military imperative takes precedence over all other concerns, including restraints. When states commit their vast resources to armed conflict in which perhaps hundreds of thousands of people, even millions – soldiers and civilians alike – are expected to be casualties of the pursuit of final victory, the fate of the individual victim is easily overlooked. War is the ultimate environment of violence in which peacetime norms of morality are suspended. Cicero recognized this in the first century BCE, declaring, "Laws are silent in times of war" (Cicero 1991: 121).

The philosopher Larry May has argued that "the best way to understand war crimes is as crimes against humaneness ... they are violations of the principle requiring that soldiers act humanely, that is with mercy and compassion, even as these same soldiers are allowed to kill enemy soldiers" (May 2007: 1–2). This may sound a very modern view, with little relevance to the depredations of the Vikings or to the European wars of religion in the early modern era, when this principle was seemingly not so evident; in fact, it is a useful approach in identifying war crimes. For as long as writers have written of war, they have also addressed its sufferings with compassion. In the formative era of the laws of war in the Middle Ages, the late twelfth-century writer Gerald of Wales wrote: "When the turmoil of battle is over ... ferocity too should be laid aside, a human code of behaviour should once more be adopted, and feelings of mercy and clemency should be revived in the spirit that is truly noble" (Gerald of Wales 1978: 61). Thus, while there have been many changes as to what constitutes a war crime throughout history, there have also been consistencies.

Twentieth Century to the Present

Treaties on restraining excesses in war punctuated the twentieth century, but arguably the most significant development was the eventual emergence of international war tribunals to try suspected war criminals. In 1907, the landmark Hague Conference, drawing heavily on the Lieber Code, produced 13 treaties, 10 of which were concerned directly with the laws of war; taken with those of 1899, they form the most comprehensive number of conventions and declarations on constraining the conduct of warfare to date. In just 50 years the laws of war had been transformed from general principles and customs, many based on religious teaching, to formal and, in law, binding codification. More practically, as with Lieber, the conventions found themselves incorporated into military manuals in the expectation that they would determine conduct in the field. As ever, theory, even when bound by law, soon succumbed to practice and military imperative in the first major test of Hague in World War I: atrocities in Belgium (no longer considered as anti-German propaganda myth); submarine warfare against non-military shipping; the naval blockade of Germany to starve the civilian population; the killing of prisoners in all areas of conflict: all highlighted the limitations of law. On the periphery of advanced states, the deaths of over a million Armenians at Turkish hands and most of the Herero population in Africa at German hands serve only to underline the murderous intent of armed conflict in the twentieth century in cases where conquest for negotiated settlements was replaced by the objective of absolute imposition of rule.

Reaction to World War I stimulated more international efforts to restrict war through legal punishment. Article 231 of the Versailles Treaty of 1919 established Germany's guilt in causing the war; the preceding four articles established the arraignment of German war criminals to be tried by a court presided over by judges from the victorious powers. Squabbles over extradition resulted in the cases being heard in Germany at the Leipzig trials of 1921, a notable development in that the defeated country took responsibility, albeit under coercion, for its own war criminals. A handful of defendants were imprisoned for the ill-treatment of prisoners and submarine warfare. The optimistic but desperate Kellogg–Briand Pact of 1928, signed by 63 states, outlawed war as an instrument of policy other than for self-defense. The 1925 Geneva Gas Protocol prohibited poisonous gases and bacteriological warfare, while the Geneva Conventions of 1929 focused on the sick, wounded, and prisoners of war. Much hope was also placed in the League of Nations to curtail war, but this was largely misplaced: the interwar years witnessed British bombing of Iraqi tribes people; Italy waging brutal war in Abyssinia (Egypt), with many non-combatant fatalities; and the unbridled slaughter and savagery of the Rape of Nanking in 1937 when Japanese forces massacred over 300,000 victims, one of the most appalling atrocities of the twentieth century.

Ideas on race and eugenics were advanced to their ultimate exploitation in World War II: demonization of "barbaric" Slavs and "evil" Jews provided Nazi Germany with their perverse justification for a war of annihilation (*Vernichtungskrieg*) in Russia and industrial slaughter of Europe's Jews: of some 5.7 million deaths in the Jewish genocide, over two-thirds were Russians and Poles; three million Russian prisoners died of disease or starvation in German camps. The war saw innovation in killing objectives and a return to a form of the ancient practice of slavery: military units such as the *Einsatzgruppen* were formed with the sole intention of killing non-combatants, unequivocally violating international law by any interpretation, while occupied territories were exploited to feed what had become a "slave labour economy" (Mazower 1998: 179). Only defeat of Germany curtailed the losses: the Nazi *Generalplan Ost* had envisaged the elimination of 50 million people. War and conquest was the prerequisite for such extensive slaughter; politically motivated murder in Stalinist Russia through starvation, forced labor, and executions could claim "only" five million victims in the period 1928–1953. (In Mao's more populous communist China the figure rose to tens of millions.)

The aftermath of war saw the establishment by the victorious powers of the International Military Tribunal in Nuremberg in 1945–1946, where sentences of imprisonment and execution were passed on major war criminals: justices from the main Allied powers found 19 civil and military leaders guilty of war crimes, including Hermann Goering. Twelve defendants were sentenced to death by hanging and three to life imprisonment. The tribunal relied heavily on the fourth Hague Convention of 1907 and hence judgments reflected the understanding that the laws and customs of war mirrored customary international law. The trials stressed charges of atrocities, but emphasis was also placed on the German hierarchy's culpability in initiating an aggressive and therefore unjust war: the war itself

was illegal, compounding the crimes against humanity it had led to. Nuremberg established the precedent for the similar war crimes tribunal set up in Japan between 1946 and 1948, where crimes against peace took precedence over atrocities on the charge sheet. Of 29 defendants standing trial, many of them high-ranking officials, seven were sentenced to death by hanging and 16 to life imprisonment. Many individual states also held their own war crimes trials. International law recognized the gravity of these crimes against humanity by allowing no time limits for their prosecution.

A concerted legal effort was therefore made not only to uphold international law but to expand it. In 1948, the United Nations (UN) passed its convention recognizing genocide as a separate crime and in 1949 four Geneva Conventions listed "grave breaches" of law, summed up by an explicit statement that the killing of civilians and willfully causing great suffering were war crimes. The latter was added to in 1977 with the first Protocol, clearly designating various attacks on civilians as punishable violations. This came in the wake of many well-documented atrocities of the Vietnam conflict, which led, however, to only one American war crimes trial, against Lieutenant William Calley in 1971 for the indiscriminate My Lai massacre of 1968. While notable in that the proceeding was undertaken by the defendant's own side (showing some similarity to the Leipzig trials in 1921), it was done so very reluctantly; the sentence of life imprisonment for Calley resulted in less than a week in prison and three years under house arrest. Circumventions of the proliferation of twentieth-century legalities are evident in the reluctance of many powers to actually declare war (thus the conflicts in Abyssinia, Manchuria, Korea, Suez, Afghanistan, the Falklands, and Iraq were not technically wars, just as the instigating belligerents intended). Article 2(4) of the UN Charter from 1945 attempted to counter this by substituting the term "force," while the Geneva Conventions apply to armed conflicts.

In this nuclear, legalistic age, jurists struggle to deal with the new technology just as the ancient and medieval world did with crossbows and poisoned arrows. UN General Assembly Resolution 1653 of 1961 condemned the use of nuclear weapons, but Russia was the only nuclear power to support it. There remains a lack of clarity: "Despite many international agreements and significant domestic legislation relating to nuclear arms, the overall legal framework for nuclear constraints is fragmentary and subject to conflicting interpretations. Existing legal restrictions were and are hardly specific enough to promise much efficacy in constraining actual operations" (Rosenberg 1994: 162). Unsurprisingly, therefore, when, in 1963, a Japanese court case (*Shimoda v. Japan*) deemed the atomic bombing of Hiroshima and Nagasaki illegal, they did so in the context of the 1907 Hague Convention against bombardment of civilians and also referred back to the 1868 St Petersburg Declaration.

The proportion of non-combatant fatalities has climbed through the twentieth century from approximately 10 percent in World War I, to an estimated 70 percent in Vietnam, and perhaps as high as 90 percent in the 2003 Iraq conflict. It can be argued that accountability for war crimes has done little to stem atrocities: in the 1990s and early twenty-first century, massacres and genocide in Yugoslavia, Rwanda, and Sudan have led to a proliferation of legal proceedings and the setting up of the International Criminal Court (ICC) in 2002, but existing laws did not prevent atrocities on a massive scale. It remains to be seen whether the trend to pursue heads of states has an impact: former Liberian president Charles Taylor was put on trial at The Hague in 2006 for war crimes and President Omar al-Bahir of Sudan was indicted by the ICC in 2008 for war crimes and crimes against humanity, and again in 2010 for genocide. It is hoped that such high-profile cases will deter such acts in the future. Meanwhile, many known war criminals are not brought to trial: a report from the special war crimes unit of the UK Border Agency identified nearly 400 suspected war criminals living freely in the UK in 2011; not one faced prosecution.

In 2002, Carla del Ponte, chief prosecutor at the war crimes tribunal at The Hague, accused Slobodan Milošević, the ex-leader of Serbia, of "medieval savagery" for his part in the atrocities committed in the former Yugoslavia in the 1990s, such as the massacre of up to 8,000 men and boys at Srebrenica. Medieval times in turn looked back to the Old Testament for their benchmark of atrocity and to the book of Deuteronomy for guidance on restraint. With the twentieth century being the worst in world history for the perpetration of war crimes, it is no easy thing to be optimistic that the raft of historically recent legal developments to protect non-combatants will usher in a new age of "civilized" warfare; indeed, they may prove to be a temporary aberration. The problem lies with war itself.

SEE ALSO: Ethnic Cleansing.

References

Cicero (1991) *Pro Milone*. Bristol: Bristol Classical Press.

Clausewitz, C. von (1976) *On War*, trans. M. Howard and P. Paret. Princeton: Princeton University Press.

Gerald of Wales (1978) *Expugnatio Hibernica*, ed. and trans. A. B. Scott and X. Martin. Dublin: Royal Irish Academy.

May, L. (2007) *War Crimes and Just War*. Cambridge: Cambridge University Press.

Mazower, M. (1998) *Dark Continent: Europe's Twentieth Century*. London: Penguin.

Rosenberg, D. (1994) "Nuclear War Planning." In M. Howard, G. Andreopoulus, and R. Shulman (Eds.), *The Laws of War: Constraints on Warfare in the Western World*. New Haven: Yale University Press.

Further Reading

Best, G. (1980) *Humanity in Warfare: The Modern History of the International Law of Armed Conflicts*. London: Weidenfeld and Nicolson.

Browning, C. (1992) *Ordinary Men: Reserve Battalion 101 and the Final Solution in Poland*. London: Harper Collins.

Chang, I. (1998) *The Rape of Nanking*. London: Penguin.

Chirot, D. and McCauley, C. (2006) *Why Not Kill Them All? The Logic and Prevention of Mass Political Murder*. Princeton: Princeton University Press.

Drakulic, S. (2004) *They Would Never Hurt a Fly: War Criminals on Trial in the Hague*. London: Abacus.

Grimsley, M. and Rogers, C. J. (Eds.) (2002) *Civilians in the Path of War*. Lincoln: University of Nebraska Press.

Howard, M., Andreopoulus, G., and Shulman, R. (Eds.) (1994) *The Laws of War: Constraints on Warfare in the Western World*. New Haven: Yale University Press.

Johnson, J. T. (2000) "Maintaining the Protection of Non-combatants," *Journal of Peace Research*, 37 (4): 444–447.

Jones, A. (Ed.) (2004) *Genocide, War Crimes and the West: History and Complicity*. London: Zed Books.

Jones, A. (2008) *Crimes Against Humanity*. Oxford: One World.

Neier, A. (1998) *War Crimes: Brutality, Genocide, Terror, and the Struggle for Justice*. New York: Random House.

Owen, J. (2007) *Nuremberg: Evil on Trial*. London: Headline.

Ramsay, P. (1983) *The Just War: Force and Political Responsibility*. Lanham: University Press of America.

Robertson, G. (2006) *Crimes Against Humanity*. London: Penguin.

Roseman, M. (2003) *The Villa, the Lake, the Meeting: Wannsee and the Final Solution*. London: Penguin.

Synder, T. (2010) *Bloodlands: Europe Between Hitler and Stalin*. New York: Basic Books.

War Photography

LAURA BRANDON

Introduction

Photographic images that range from dead, fly-infested US Civil War casualties to napalmed Vietnam War victims and to the bloodied survivors of the "War on Terror" form part of our visual understanding of war. War photographs enable us to be spectators to conflict and to empathize with or react to its worst horrors and greatest successes. As a result, both the protagonists and the protestors of war use photographs to document, promote, and justify their actions and attitudes to the public. Photographers themselves are complicit in these activities. In the twenty-first century, however, more than at any other time, the boundaries between professional and amateur photography (photography is here defined as both the act of taking a photograph and the photograph itself), photojournalism, and photographic art are blurred. Amateur photographs achieve worldwide distribution through the Internet, artist–photographers participate in official military art programs, and photojournalists exhibit their photographs in art galleries. Furthermore, for the public and for photographers themselves, photography increasingly is about the spectacle of war as much as it is about its documentation. Perhaps one of the most compelling recent links between war, art, photography,

and spectacle was when the shocking photographs taken by American military personnel of Iraqi prisoners in Abu Ghraib jail were printed straight off the Internet and exhibited at the International Center of Photography in New York in October and November 2004.

With these developments in mind, and in the context of a historical trajectory, this chapter briefly and variously examines five areas of war photography as process and product, namely its role as art, document, propaganda, tool and inspiration, and its technological evolution. There are four kinds of war photography associated with the military. First, there are the photographs taken on an official basis by both military and civilian photographers with the intention of releasing them to the public for the purposes of information or propaganda. Secondly, there are the photographs taken by the armed services for their own needs – equipment use, fortification construction, reconnaissance photographs, and such like – that they, or others, might eventually distribute publicly, often as archival documents. Thirdly, there are the photographs taken by military and civilian personnel for their own private use, which also, especially today, they may make available to the public over the Internet. Then, fourthly, there are artists' photographs produced under military sponsorship or independently in response to conflict, usually with immediate public dissemination as the goal. The division between civilian and military photography is a fluid one in that a civilian photographer may hold a military commission while a military photographer may take photographs for personal use.

The technical history of war photography began in France in 1839 with the advent of the medium as we know it. All those involved in conflict swiftly understood the documentary possibilities of this new tool. For the military authorities, a photograph could capture a battle site, a formation or unit, a commander, a fortification, or the aftermath of conflict in a way that a war artist, lacking the apparently swift and objective eye of the camera, could not. Indeed, in the face of this new technology many artists turned to photography. For the soldier, a photograph could confirm his presence in particular places, or at specific events. Not only could such photographs document, but the relevant authorities could use the documentary evidence the images provided to develop strategy or determine the future best use of men and matériel. For the military and the public at large in those early days, a photograph was a neutral medium equivalent to a picture caught by the eye's retina. What many understood less well was that while photographers could manipulate their images through technical means including cropping and pasting, they and their employers could also influence what was, and was not, photographed. This made it possible for the military authorities actively to seek out images that would benefit recruitment efforts – pictures of happy wounded soldiers, for example, or those showing enemy destruction, thereby engendering ill-feelings toward the foe. Especially after World War II, when it came to photography's widespread use in propaganda, the combination of technical trickery combined with the medium's link to veracity to help convey questionable truths about the conduct and consequences of war both from the point of view of its practitioners and from that of its opponents. Over time, the photographer's ability to frame, light, crop, stage, and manipulate an image became not only more practiced but more publicly familiar, leading to questions as to photography's reliability as an unmediated image.

Further complicating any idealistic view of photography as unvarnished truth is the fact that war photography's aesthetic dimensions are founded in war art, whose history, particularly as propaganda, stretches back to the ancient kingdoms and empires of the Middle East many thousands of years ago, if not earlier. While there are discernable differences between art and photography that are associated mainly with technology, viewed through a wide lens over time and only in terms of image making, there are significant interrelated areas of common ground.

The vexing issue of fakery sometimes ensured iconic status for a photograph. A combination of distribution, accessibility, and availability through a wide variety of media including the broadcast and print kind, not to mention books, postcards, and albums, facilitated public response to photographs leading to discussions about their veracity. Sometimes this questioning alone was enough to ensure widespread renown. Whether manipulated or not, however, the ability of a photograph to represent a significant and meaningful event or a tragedy of war to a wide audience helped ensure

iconic status nationally and sometimes internationally. For the most part, because the public can still see and appreciate historic iconic images through the ever-widening variety of media available to photographic reproduction, such photographs remain well known.

The public cannot see and evaluate photographs that did not make it through conflict, that battle destroyed before they left the field, or that never entered into military collections, magazine archives, and newspaper vaults. Without access to an established distribution network, a photographer's work remains unrecorded and his or her contribution to war photography largely unknown. Unidentified photographs remain almost equally invisible. Survival as an identified image or not, furthermore, requires the photograph's creator, sponsor, user, historian and, sometimes, subject to agree that it constitutes a part of the photographic war record. In other words, what we understand as war photography is the result of a selective process. For those images that no longer exist, that researchers and the public even know the names of their photographers, if not these people's birth and death dates, is because surviving exhibition catalogues and news magazines of the time document their existence. Censorship is another issue. It existed formally on the part of most militaries for a large part of photography's history in all countries, but self-censorship remains a private matter, conditioned by personal moral codes. This, too, determines what survives.

Late Nineteenth-Century Technical Innovations

If photography increasingly recorded nineteenth-century conflicts as varied as the Crimean War, the Indian Mutiny, and the US Civil War, it also documented technical innovations. More famous, perhaps, for his images of human and animal motion, and prompted undoubtedly by his interest in locomotion, Eadweard Muybridge (1830–1904) photographed Native American warriors in action in the early 1870s. Unlike his predecessors, Muybridge had a significant advantage. In this period, along with the invention of the half-tone process for use in the reproduction of photographs in newspapers, a number of technical improvements had begun to expand photography's range. Dry-plate negatives, faster lenses and shutter speeds, and the folding camera presaged the invention of the portable Kodak box camera in 1888 and the folding pocket Kodak camera 10 years later. Pre-prepared dry-plate negatives freed the photographer from his traveling darkroom, but for good images a tripod was still required. Nonetheless, a war photographer could now seek out an event and function more as a war correspondent than as a studio artist. Furthermore, by the time of the Spanish–American War (1898), the Anglo-Boer War (1899–1902), and the Russo-Japanese War (1904–1905), the ordinary soldier equipped with a relatively inexpensive camera could shoot an image of a battle in which he was participating. Some argue amateur photographers achieved this as early as the 1870–1871 Franco-Prussian War and the 1885 Canadian North West Rebellion. Print quality was poor, however, and this sort of photography remained largely in lay hands, even if growing media demand made the requirement for battle photography more urgent, leading to the establishment of organizations like Underwood & Underwood, which purchased photographs both amateur and professional to sell.

Twentieth Century

Widespread debate as to what art is began in the twentieth century and, concomitantly, photography began to challenge its own status as a mechanical means of reproduction and to view itself as an art form. Composition became as important as subject. For the public, however, war photography retained for far longer its perceived documentary value.

At the beginning of the century there were four main kinds of equipment in use: the handheld folding plate, the single lens reflex, the panoramic, and the field camera. While handheld cameras had come into wider use, they were not widely adopted by professional photographers, who preferred the quality that came with larger negatives, which required tripod support for the camera. Color photography using the autochrome system developed by the French brothers Auguste and Louis Lumière in 1904 was available but color reproductions were not possible until the 1940s with the introduction of color photographic paper. Equipment challenges aside, undermining any developing photographic freedom brought about by improved technology was the continuing, if self-inflicted, form of censorship against atrocity images, driven undoubtedly by a post-Victorian public more interested in sentimental depictions of death. Photographing the 1912 Balkan War, British photographer and later Australia's first Great War official photographer Herbert Baldwin (1880–1920) elected to avoid photographing the unpleasant scenes he came across. In so doing, he reaffirmed a moral dimension to the work of the war photographer that diluted any notions of its objectivity.

World War I

By World War I, photography was ubiquitous but still limited by the nature of the apparatus. Official photographers would occasionally arrange men and equipment in order to create images that showed more than the endless featureless tracts of no-man's land. In this period, photography was also subject to military censorship. In its published or album form, a great deal of text accompanied each image that explained what was going on, often for propaganda purposes. This need for control resulted in British, Canadian, and other Allied powers' attempts to ban previously acceptable amateur photography so that repeats of the Christmas 1914 images of German and Allied troop fraternization never occurred again. For the Australians in particular, private photography had been essential for record-keeping initially, and the first official Australian war correspondent Charles Bean's carefully collected amateur images of events in Gallipoli (1915) form a critical visual testimony. Many of the 100,000 New Zealand soldiers, journalists, and medical staff who went overseas carried cameras. Thomas Frederick Scales (dates unknown) was New Zealand's official war photographer in Britain during World War I.

The number of surviving World War I photographs is astounding – literally tens of millions – and it includes new subjects such as aerial reconnaissance images. Flight provided the camera mobility denied to photographers on the ground. The concept of using photography to identify people and act as a record of whole populations also became common. The Germans, for example, photographically documented two million people in the former Russian Poland using 60 clerks who produced 30,000 photos a day.

Following the establishment in 1916 of an official photography program, 16 British official photographers (double that for France and triple that number for Germany) found employment. The British photographers did not all work at the same time; at most there were no more than between two and four photographers on the Western Front at once. The first British Army official photographer was Ernest Brooks (1878–?), appointed in March 1916, who was renowned for his distinctive use of the silhouetted soldier and who, like many Allied photographers, although he denied it, was accused of occasionally staging his images. The US Signal Corps was notable for the number of photographers it employed, and for the fact it developed, censored, and titled all the resultant images. One of its most famous photographers was Edward Steichen (1879–1973), who went on to direct the Naval Aviation Photographic Unit in World War II. On the opposing side, famed modernist photographer André Kertész (1894–1985) briefly served in the Austro-Hungarian forces and captured images of soldiers at leisure and civilian scenes. Germany established the Picture and Film Bureau (*Bild- und Filmamt*) in 1916 in the interests of propaganda, but amateur photography more effectively documented life behind the front lines, especially when compiled in albums.

The Canadian experience exemplifies how the Allied combatant nations organized their official photography programs. In 1916, the Canadian War Records Office (CWRO) appointed British official war photographers to work at the front, recruiting half from a single newspaper, the *Daily Mirror*. The best known was William Rider-Rider (1889–1979) who, for most of his assignments, used glass plates and a German Goerz 4×5-inch camera fitted with a German Zeiss lens. The authorities forbade the photographing of dismembered and gruesomely dead Canadians but were less concerned about dead Germans. This resulted in a rather sanitized record of the conflict. The lack of visual evidence of war's more exciting moments encouraged at least one photographer to stage some of his

images. Ivor Castle (1877–1947) achieved notoriety in Britain and Canada for his image *Over the Top*, which he constructed from rehearsal attacks at a British training school in France. The authorities censored all officially produced images if these images made it to safer areas without the challenging circumstances of war destroying or damaging them. The CWRO program's intention was variously information, propaganda, and historical document, the organization arranging for the publication of many of the images in exhibitions, newspapers, and commemorative books. Indeed, as is still the case today, what was publishable, sellable, and appropriate to exhibit drove a not insignificant part of the photographic record. Profits from photographic sales and exhibitions contributed to the fees paid to official war artists who, indeed, relied on war photography for their compositions. British artist William Nicholson's (1872–1949) *Canadian Headquarters Staff* (1918), for example, not only uses an aerial reconnaissance photograph for its background but an official group photograph of a number of generals for its main subject matter.

Paralleling the Canadian commercialization of war photography, the British sold images through the Ministry of Information Photographic Bureau. This is not surprising since Sir Max Aitken (from 1917, Lord Beaverbrook), who was Canadian-born, was involved heavily in both British and Canadian propaganda schemes. By playing one country off against the other he rose to become not only head of the Canadian War Records but also, in 1918, the British minister of information. Elsewhere, French photographer Jules Gervais-Courtellemont's (1863–1931) lantern-slide show of the Battle of Verdun (1916) showed 50 times to packed Paris audiences. If French war photography was emotive, picturesque, and patriotic, in contrast the Australian Frank Hurley (1885–1962), who had earlier accompanied explorer Ernest Shackleton to the Antarctic, used multiple Paget plates (the alternative to the Lumière system) to produce a number of gritty images, considered by some, notably Charles Bean, to be fake because they were composites. George Hubert Wilkins (1888–1958), multi-talented like so many early photographers, was a polar explorer, ornithologist, pilot, soldier, and geographer, as well as an official Australian war photographer. Almost invariably, such photography became museum or archival property, ensuring that the official view of war became the national view. For museums, the intellectual issue is often identification. Soldier–photographers rarely titled their images and the authorities frequently labeled official photographs to relay a positive narrative at odds, sometimes, with the actual subject.

At the end of the war, shocking images of wounds began to circulate in all the combatant countries. It was not until 1924, however, that the German conscientious objector Ernst Friedrich (1894–1967) compiled *War against War!* (*Krieg dem Kriege!*). Published in several languages, his album of more than 180 previously unpublished photographs of terrible injuries drew upon German military and medical archives and went through 10 editions by 1930.

Spanish Civil War

While photographers recorded the Russo-Polish War (1919–1920), the 1922 Irish Civil War, the Italian invasion of Abyssinia (1936), and the Sino-Japanese War beginning in 1937, these records faded from public memory when compared to the images from the Spanish Civil War (1936–1939). These marked the first time photographs had an agenda of their own as opposed to one rooted in the tradition of illustration. In this conflict the photograph was the story. This development was helped by the 1924 invention of the small, mobile, high-resolution 35-mm German Leica, which enabled the tight action close-up but also could mimic the by-now established snapshot. High-quality images of battle scenes rather than their aftermath became possible. Increasingly, photography rather than line engravings from photography dominated magazine and newspaper illustration. This is the era of *Vu* and *Paris Match* in France, *Life* in the United States, *Picture Post* in Britain, and the *Berliner Illustrierte Zeitung* in Germany. Photography was also easy to transmit over the newly established wire services of organizations such as Associated Press dating from 1935. In this era the public understood their world visually before they read about it. Bias was rampant, however. While a new social-realist aesthetic approach generally dominated all photography of the time, the media not only selected, cropped, and erroneously captioned photographs but photographers themselves staged images that they could sell.

The best-known war photographer in this period was the Hungarian-born Robert Capa (1913–1954). Capa's famous photograph entitled *Loyalist Militiaman at the Moment of Death, Cerro Muriano, September 5, 1936* remains hotly debated in terms of its truthfulness. Was it photographed near the front lines or was it staged many miles away? At the time, it made Capa's name (and ensured him financial security) while revolutionizing attitudes toward photographers in a way that emphasized their creative motivations as opposed to their technical skills. Capa later photographed the US landing on Omaha Beach in northern France on D-Day (1944). He always maintained that the supposed camera shake apparent in his celebrated photographs was the result of overdeveloping and not his hand trembling. However, even Capa's work pales in impact after high-speed shutters and improved light-sensitive paper enabled a new level of close-up and detail, exemplified in emotive images from the Korean War and World War II.

World War II

Photographs were ubiquitous during World War II, both amateur and professional. The processes and records of war varied from country to country depending on the political circumstances, but some degree of censorship was a given, particularly in the more authoritarian countries. Throughout the war, Allied military censors allowed the publication of images of dead bodies, for example. Official images did not tell the whole story, however. Amateur photography was critical, providing additional information, especially after the war, on what had really gone on, and, through the still-prevalent interest in making albums, ensuring the existence of personally meaningful souvenirs of war experiences.

The British alone produced at least two million official photographs and even Canada's official artists received cameras as part of their equipment. In the United States, the best-organized country in terms of photography, both military and civilian personnel produced powerful images that continue to shape that nation's memory of the conflict as well as ideas about warfare and its impact. There, as in other nations, photographers served in all services and in all terrains at war and on the home front. The photographer's role was threefold: to provide accurate and detailed pictures in order to design effective military tactics and strategy, bolster home front morale and, by showing what was happening overseas, demonstrate why civilian help in the war effort was essential. Furthermore, as in World War I, the authorities expected their official photographs to serve as historical documents of the conflict and thus they provided their photographers with manuals on how to shoot good images. Established civilian photographers such as Margaret Bourke-White (1904–1971) produced exceptional work. Lee Miller (1907–1997), originally a fashion photographer, captured the horrors of the Nazi concentration camps at Buchenwald and Dachau among other subjects. Both these women demonstrated that sex could not be a barrier to war journalism. W. Eugene Smith's (1918–1978) photographs stressed the personal. Issues of fakery abounded. Joe Rosenthal's (1911–2006) Pulitzer Prize-winning 1945 photograph of the raising of the US flag on Iwo Jima is still the subject of debate as to whether it was staged. Rosenthal's work influenced Russian photographer Yevgeny Khaldei (1917–1997), whose 1945 image of three Russian soldiers holding a flag aloft on the captured German Reichstag in Berlin was a pre-planned imitation. Indeed, his uncle had made the flag from a red tablecloth. The Allies censored photography. Bourke-White's images did not go straight to *Life* but had first to pass through the American military censorship process. The same applied to any collected amateur photography. The US military authorities also recaptioned photographs to meet the needs of Allied propaganda. In a conflict that mobilized civilians in unprecedented numbers, New York's Museum of Modern Art staged photographic exhibitions in support of the war effort.

The Nazis required all German photographers to be government-registered, thus ensuring that photography could be put fully into the hands of its propaganda machine run by Joseph Goebbels, resulting in millions of message-driven images. Heinrich Hoffmann (1885–1957) was Hitler's favorite photographer. Hoffmann portrayed the Führer both as a leader and as a man of the people. His photographs appeared in albums, newspapers, and other media and were widely available as postcards. Even before the outbreak of the war, the Nazis forced artists who used photography to criticize the growing power of Hitler – such as John Heartfield (1891–1968) – to flee the country. Although the German authorities essentially banned amateur photography, it was not entirely discouraged as they largely, and erroneously as it turned out, assumed it innocuous. After the war, atrocity photographs found on the bodies of dead or captured German fighters became evidence in the trials against German war criminals in the Soviet Union and later at the trials of Nazi war criminals. Recently, wartime official photography has helped resolve restitution issues stemming from Nazi looting.

In Japan, military photographer Yosuke Yamahata (1917–1966) made 119 images of Nagasaki one day after an American atomic bomb leveled the city on August 9, 1945. He later died from his exposure to radiation. The tail gunner in the American bomber the *Enola Gay*, however, took the familiar photographs of the mushroom cloud rising from the ground. Elsewhere, French photographer Robert Doisneau (1912–1994) joined the French Resistance in 1940, where he took photographs of resistance fighters. Polish Jew Henryk Ross (1910–1991), a photographer appointed by the Jewish Council in the Lodz Ghetto in Poland, took thousands of photographs documenting life there. After the war, cataloguing Allied official photographs of Bergen-Belsen after its liberation by the British for the Canadian army so traumatized British-born Canadian artist Jack Shadbolt that the subject dominated his post-war art for a decade.

Korean War and Vietnam War

Many of the photographers who covered the Korean War (1950–1953) for the Americans were veterans of World War II. They included the British-born Larry Burrows (1926–1971) and the Americans Margaret Bourke-White, David Douglas Duncan (b. 1916), and Carl Mydans (1907–2004) who were on assignment for *Life* and focused on portrayals of individual suffering. In all, 19 nations sent a total of 270 correspondents and photographers to this war.

A decade later, in 1960, Cuban Alberto Korda's (1928–2001) image of the Cuban revolutionary Che Guevara began its journey toward being the most iconic of all photographs associated with conflict both for and against, reimaged repeatedly in many media – from tattoo to embroidery.

While television undoubtedly influenced public opinion during the Vietnam War (1959–1975), individual photographs dominated the public sphere, especially in the West. Between 1961 and 1972, *Life* published more than 1,200 photographs from the war zone and a further 600 from the home front. Following on the Korean War photographic example, imagery focused on the ordinary soldier. Larry Burrows, unrestricted by censorship, produced some of the most dynamic and visceral photographs to emerge from any war, although he died there, as did 134 other war photographers. The wrenching reality of British war photographer Don McCullin's (b. 1935) work was painfully memorable. Others, such as the Welshman Philip Jones Griffiths (1936–2008), chose more unusual subjects, photographing the war with the aim of capturing the suffering of Vietnamese peasants. Notably, women photographers such as the French-born Catherine Leroy (1945–2006) made important contributions. More noticeably than before, perhaps, the public began to question the authenticity of newly iconic images.

Like the protestors at home, many war photographers sought to influence public opinion in their work, but it is likely that they simply reflected it. In the United States protest was rife and celebrated images resulted from infamous acts. John Paul Filo's (b. 1948) photograph of a young woman screaming over the body of a student killed by a member of the Ohio National Guard during the Kent State University protest as if lamenting the dead body of Christ provoked visceral reaction in the United States. This response also demonstrated that traditional and familiar images depicting death and loss deriving from Christian iconography visually grounds much powerful photographic war imagery. The most infamous picture to come out of the war, however, was Eddie Adams's (1933–2004) 1968 photograph of General Loan executing a Vietcong suspect. For many in the western world, it symbolized the injustice of the war and the indifference of the protagonists to human suffering. Yet,

this image, too, has been subject to debate over the years as to its authenticity. Vietnamese citizens also photographed. Huynh Cong (Nick) Ut (b. 1951) took the now-famous 1972 image of a naked young Vietnamese girl fleeing a napalm attack alongside other children. Such photographs fed the work of artists. American Martha Rosler (b. 1943) created photomontages from war photographs and pictures taken from design and architectural magazines to create a series called *Bringing the War Home* (1967–1972). She later reworked the concept in connection with the 2003 war in Iraq. An artists' collective transformed US Army photographer Ronald H. Haeberle's (b. 1944) photograph of a particularly distressing scene from the My Lai massacre into an iconic 1969 anti-war poster *Q. And babies? A. And babies.*

The End of the Century

Photographs of the skeletal inmates of the liberated concentration camps at the end of World War II and the charred bodies in Hiroshima and Nagasaki in Japan after the August 1945 bombings remind us that war is terrible for civilians. Uniquely, one use of photography for identification purposes has yielded a record of a notable civilian consequence of conflict. A government-sponsored photographic project that involved mug shots of people who were jailed documents the death by disease, starvation, and murder of two million Cambodians during the cruel regime of Pol Pot during the civil conflicts in Cambodia beginning in 1970. Five thousand recovered unidentified images from Tuoi Sleng prison now are stored in the Tuoi Sleng Museum of Genocide in Cambodia. Yale University has put these and other photographs and documents from the genocide on a website called the Cambodian Genocide Program. In this instance, photographs that have no inherent activist ability of their own transform themselves not only into weapons of protest but also into historical documents for a country that under Pol Pot would never have allowed this. Furthermore, the Internet has made the sharing of this information global.

After the Korean War and the ending of strict censorship with its requirement for a prior security review backed by legal sanctions, two distinct kinds of photographer appeared to emerge. On one side was the military official photographer whose seemingly more heavily controlled work authorities could provide to the media to mold public opinion and use as an internal document of events and practices. On the other was the ostensibly independent and rather glamorous photojournalist who worked for the media rather than the military. In truth, there was little difference thanks to the pool system. In 1975, the United States had adopted this approach, which was the result of negotiation and agreement between its government and major media institutions. Working together with the military, the media designated a number of people including one or more photographers who would be available to join a pool in the event of a military deployment. Photographers made their results available to the media as a whole rather than exclusively to their employers. Some photographers and media outlets considered the Gulf War (1990–1991) a particularly trying experience in this regard, believing that any system enabled the military to control more effectively what was photographed, and when and where. Certainly, during this conflict, critics argued that the American authorities strove to present it to the public as a casualty-free, color-saturated and technologically advanced light show. Actual events do not necessarily substantiate this.

At the end of the twentieth century, those who created images of war increasingly challenged the boundaries between art and photography. Contemporary British and American photojournalists drew attention to this fact with authored work that appeared on websites, and in books, museum collections, and the media. The American photographer Susan Meiselas (b. 1948), who works for the internationally renowned Magnum photo agency co-founded by Robert Capa, published her work widely in coffee-table books. Her dramatic and graphic images of the 1979 Nicaragua insurrection are her best-known images. A subsequent commission took her to Kurdistan where she photographed the devastation of Kurdish villages and the mass graves that resulted, publishing these images in 1997. She also took photographs in 2001 of the devastation after 9/11 at Ground Zero, the site of the former World Trade Center towers in New York. French photographer Gilles Peress (b. 1946) worked

similarly and exhibited, representing a breed of photojournalist who then as now saw his work as transcending several genres and markets.

There were also photographers who did not need to be in the battlefield to make images of war. Krzysztof Wodiczko (b. 1943) spent half his life in Poland and half in Canada and the United States. His projects involved the projection of carefully selected photographic images on to national sites to make points about power and repression. Just days after the outbreak of the Gulf War, he projected a pair of skeletal hands, one grasping an M-16 machine gun, the other a gas-pump nozzle, onto the triumphal arch in Madrid, Spain, that celebrates the victory in the 1936–1939 Spanish Civil War of fascist Generalissimo Francisco Franco. At the top of the arch he beamed the question *¿Cuantos?* (How many?). French artist–photographer Sophie Ristelhueber (b. 1949) published her extraordinarily beautiful photographs of the desert following the Gulf War in a book entitled *Fait: Koweit, 1991* (published in English as *Aftermath: Kuwait, 1991*). A typical image is the desert taken from a great distance, its features reduced to a pattern resembling a close-up of a dried and pebble-strewn riverbed. Ristelhueber followed *Fait* with *Everyone* (1994), again a book based on photographs. Ostensibly about the hostilities in the former Yugoslavia in the early 1990s, the images are actually of anonymous scarred bodies taken into Paris hospitals.

Photographic artists whose subject is war usefully questioned photographic truth in this period. Canadian Jeff Wall's (b. 1946) *Dead Troops Talk (A Vision after an Ambush of a Red Army Patrol, near Moqor, Afghanistan, Winter 1986)* (1992) is an extraordinary essay on what war photography is and is not. Much like a World War I official artist commissioned to reconstruct a battle on canvas after the fact, Wall had at his disposal the necessary elements – models, accoutrements, still-life elements, and photographs – to compose his work. However, he did not reconstruct an event that happened, but rather one that he had imagined. Dead men do not talk but here the 13 sometimes severely wounded Russian soldiers lounge around a shell crater and pass the time of day chatting and relaxing. Here, war is seemingly normal but, in undertaking the exercise, Wall shows us how abnormal it really is.

Twenty-First Century

The first decade of the twenty-first century saw the beginnings of a photographic revolution as the amateur photographer came into his or her own through the ubiquity of digital technologies. The televised media became increasingly reliant on ordinary people caught up in extraordinary circumstances to relay on-the-spot reports and photographs so that they could keep their news bulletins completely up to date. While official military photographers and photojournalists continued to work overseas, particularly in connection with the War on Terror, military personnel, within limits, were able to record their personal views of the war, which they uploaded onto Internet sites.

To overcome the restrictions of the pool approach, in 2003, with the onset of the Iraq War, the notion of the embedded journalist or photographer took hold. The embed system is an expansion of the pool system and was used first by the United States in Bosnia in 1995. In this system the military arranges for particular photographers to follow specific units as they perform their various tasks. While no authority literally prevents an individual from taking pictures of the dead or wounded, there are policies in place that help prevent the publication of images that might endanger the troops or make public classified information. These restrictions, of course, do not apply to photographers who have no agreement with the military.

If it was the burgeoning new and influential digital technologies that made it possible for anyone to be a war photographer, it was its partnership with conflict's inherent violence that enabled another worldwide view of the Iraq War in the form of the burnt and abused bodies of the four US security guards killed on March 31, 2004. After dragging them through the streets of Fallujah, the insurgents hung their blackened remains on a bridge over the Euphrates River. They made their own video of the attack, broadcasting the images around the world the next day. Newspapers and magazines, and the broadcast media, of course, made extensive use of them. One Canadian artist has made an artwork out of a tragedy that occurred on air. Stephen Andrew's artwork *Friendly Fire* (2003) reworks in paint that looks digital the occasion when British journalist John Simpson's translator was killed mid-broadcast in 2003, his blood splashing onto the camera's lens.

For war photographers and war artists, photography in its still, moving, and digitized formats still brings home the horrors of conflict today. More graphically violent than in any previous era, it is a reflection of its own time and tastes. Since World War I and its aftermath, photography remains hugely influential even if selective processes on the part of the authorities and the public all too often define what survives. Artists and photographers have engaged with one another since the invention of the medium, some photographers defining themselves as artists rather than photojournalists although they may make photographs that fall into both camps. The reworking of iconic war photographs proves that photographers engage with the history of war photography as well.

Official military art programs in Canada and Great Britain and elsewhere now commission civilian artists who work in photography and exhibit the results. In 2002, the Art Commissions Committee of the Imperial War Museum commissioned Paul Seawright (b. 1965) as a photographer in Afghanistan. Aware of photographic precedent, and interested in notions of memory, his large-format washed-out color images of the war-torn Afghan landscape quietly describe that country's contrasting states of remote beauty and extensive devastation. *Valley* (2002) unequivocally echoes Roger Fenton's *The Valley of the Shadow of Death*. In Seawright's image a similarly flattened dry path wends its way into the distance toward the crest of a hill with only sky beyond. Seawright has replaced the cannonballs of Fenton's image with spent shells – possibly placed there by the photographer himself in a conscious echo of Fenton's presumed addition.

On June 20, 2009, Iranian Neda Agha-Soltan was en route to protest the recent Iranian presidential elections. Her car's air-conditioning was not working well, so she stopped it some distance away and got out to cool down. An unidentified assailant shot her in the chest. An anonymous bystander captured her subsequent death with a camera video recorder and uploaded the footage onto the Internet. Within hours the moving image and stills from it had circled the globe in private and public fora. This powerful image of protest featuring a previously unknown woman by a still-unknown photographer using relatively new technology represents the new face of war photography. The era of the war photographer as such may be over, but the era of war photography is not.

SEE ALSO: Balkan Wars (1912–1913); Falklands War (1982); Gulf Wars (1990–1991, 2003–Present); Italo-Abyssinian Wars; Korean War (1949–1953); Russo-Japanese War (1904–1905); Russo-Polish War (1919–1920); Spanish Civil War (1936–1939); Vietnam War (1959–1975); War Propaganda; World War I: Western Front.

Further Reading

Apel, D. (2012) *War Culture and the Contest of Images*. New Brunswick: Rutgers University Press.

Barfield, T. (Ed.) (2005) *War Photography: Images of Conflict from Frontline Photographers*. London: Magpie.

Bolloch, J. (Ed.) (2004) *War Photography*. Milan: 5 Continents.

Brothers, C. (1997) *War and Photography: A Cultural History*. London: Routledge.

Carmichael, J. (1998) *First World War Photographers*. New York: Routledge.

Fabian, R. and Adam, H.-C. (1985) *Images of War: 130 Years of War Photography*. Sevenoaks: New English Library.

Fairchild Camera and Instrument (1944) *Focusing on Victory: The Story of Aerial Photography at War*. Jamaica, NY: Fairchild Camera and Instrument Corp.

Fralin, F. (1985) *The Indelible Image: Photographs of War-1846 to the Present*. Boston: Abrams.

Howe, P. (2002) *Shooting Under Fire: The World of the War Photographer*. New York: Artisan.

Lakin, S. (2006) *Contact: Photographs from the Australian War Memorial Collection*. Canberra: Australian War Memorial.

Lewinski, J. (1978) *The Camera at War: A History of War Photography from 1848 to the Present Day*. New York: Simon and Schuster.

Moeller, S. D. (1989) *Shooting War: Photography and the American Experience of Conflict*. New York: Basic Books.

Musée de l'Armée (1986) *Soldat et Société*. Paris: Musée de l'Armée.

Robertson, P. (1973) *Relentless Verity: Canadian Military Photographers since 1885*. Toronto: University of Toronto Press.

Roeder, G. (1993) *The Censored War: American Visual Experience during World War II*. New Haven: Yale University Press.

Sontag, S. (1977) *On Photography*. New York: Farrar, Straus and Giroux.

Sontag, S. (2003) *Regarding the Pain of Others*. New York: Farrar, Straus and Giroux.

Taylor, J. (1998) *Body Horror: Photojournalism, Catastrophe, and War*. New York: New York University Press.

Wilkes Tucker, A. and Michels, W. (2012) *War/Photography: Images of Armed Conflict and Its Aftermath*. New Haven: Yale University Press.

Williams, V. (1994) *Warworks: Women, Photography and the Iconography of War*. London: Virago.

Zelizer, B. (1998) *Remembering to Forget: Holocaust Memory through the Camera's Eye*. Chicago: University of Chicago Press.

War Poetry

JAMES A. WINN

The use of poetry to celebrate military victories, praise heroic acts, and mourn the slain is much older than alphabetic writing. The Hebrew Bible, the Greek *Iliad*, and the Sanskrit *Bhagavad-Gita* provide famous examples of oral poetry concerning war, and the literary tradition arising from those oral roots – including the *Aeneid* of Virgil, *The Song of Roland*, and a host of Renaissance chivalric epics – is rich and strong. Some later poets, such as Rudyard Kipling, in his influential *Barrack-Room Ballads* (1892), moved away from the heroic tradition by using the actual idioms of modern soldiers, and in the twentieth century, those who responded to the unprecedented slaughter of the World Wars did so with a necessary awareness of the tension between ancient poetic traditions, especially those portraying warriors as chivalric knights, and the shocking horror of modern warfare.

In the justly famous lyric poems composed during World War I, we hear the voices of men who fought, and in many cases died, in the conflict. To their amazement, Robert Graves, Siegfried Sassoon, Ivor Gurney, and Edmund Blunden survived the war, but Rupert Brooke, Alan Seeger, Charles Hamilton Sorley, Isaac Rosenberg, and Wilfred Owen did not. In "The Soldier," written early in the war, Brooke imagines his English dust as *richer* than the surrounding earth of a foreign grave:

> If I should die, think only this of me:
> That there's some corner of a foreign field

That is forever England. There shall be
In that rich earth a richer dust concealed;
A dust whom England bore, shaped,
made aware, ...
(Brooke 1970: 24)

In a nationalistic gesture, Brooke emphasizes the fact that the dust is *English*, and therefore richer than anything else in the *foreign* field. Violence has no place in this sentimental and nostalgic poem. Others used chivalric imagery to camouflage the bloodshed of the present. In "The Volunteer," the minor poet Herbert Asquith, son of the Prime Minister, imagines a "clerk ... Toiling at ledgers" while dreaming of "horsemen, charging under phantom skies." His death is described in chivalric clichés:

From twilight to the halls of dawn he went;
His lance is broken; but he lies content
With that high hour, in which he lived and died.
(Marsh 1918: 181)

Cavalry units were issued lances in 1914, but machine guns soon demonstrated the futility of edged weapons or mounted troops in modern war. Trenches, barbed wire, and poison gas were the realities, and after the Battle of the Somme and the Battle of Verdun in 1916, each of which cost the Allies more than 600,000 casualties, it became difficult to pretend that the mechanized slaughter had anything to do with knighthood, honor, or glory.

By 1916, over a million combatants were dead, and poets began to reject the stock vocabulary of chivalric terms and abstract nouns that had seemed so apt a few years earlier. In a sonnet called "The Poet as Hero," Sassoon explained why he was now "scornful, harsh, and discontented, / Mocking and loathing War":

You are aware that once I sought the Grail,
Riding in armour bright, serene and strong;
...
But now I've said good-bye to Galahad,
And am no more the knight of
dreams and show.
(Sassoon 1961: 320)

For Sassoon, chivalric myth is no longer an adequate motive for fighting. Brutalized by combat and disillusioned with knightly honor, he now takes pleasure in "lust and senseless hatred." Poetry, which once served to glorify combat, is now a way of seeking "absolution."

Wilfred Owen's "Anthem for Doomed Youth," written in 1917, combines the traditional language of elegy with the harsh realities of the modern battlefield:

What passing-bells for these who die as cattle?
– Only the monstrous anger of the guns.
Only the stuttering rifles' rapid rattle
Can patter out their hasty orisons.
No mockeries now for them;
no prayers nor bells;
Nor any voice of mourning save the choirs, –
The shrill, demented choirs of wailing shells;
And bugles calling for them from sad shires.
(Owen 1983: 99)

Unlike Brooke or Asquith, Owen acknowledges the reality of guns, rifles, and shells, but he brings these realistic details into a metaphorical relationship with the older practices of religious ritual. The rattle of the rifles is a hasty orison, a rapidly spoken prayer, and the wailing shells are a choir, albeit a *demented* choir. Owen avoids the false nostalgia of those who deny the suffering of the present by describing it with glorious hazy images from a past imagined as heroic fantasy. With a compact, painful lyricism, he shows how present realities overwhelm the rituals of the past. A year later, he was dead, machine-gunned on the eve of the Armistice.

World War II produced far fewer poems than World War I, for reasons succinctly expressed by the British poet C. Day-Lewis. "Where are the War Poets?" an editorial writer asked in 1943. Taking that question as his title, Day-Lewis answered crisply:

It is the logic of our times,
No subject for immortal verse –
That we who lived by honest dreams
Defend the bad against the worse.
(Day-Lewis 1992: 335)

Although he took part in the war effort by joining the Home Guard and working in the Ministry of Information, Day-Lewis was a severe critic of his own government. To treat the war as a subject for immortal verse seemed to him an act of bad faith, a betrayal of the honest dreams of true poetry. In the face of the Nazi threat, it may have been logical, even imperative, to defend the bad against the worse, but it was not a subject for poetry.

Still, refusing to provide traditional patriotic verses did not mean that poets were required to be silent, and World War II produced some compelling poems, including fine work by Keith Douglas, a British tank commander. In a poem entitled "Aristocrats," Douglas deftly deplores the traditional language of chivalry:

> The noble horse with courage in his eye,
> clean in the bone, looks up at a shellburst:
> away fly the images of the shires
> but he puts the pipe back in his mouth.

Fighting on horseback was the original marker of knightly nobility, so Douglas, with comic affection, turns his comrade into a noble centaur – part horse, part man – who absurdly displays his courage by smoking his pipe as shells fall nearby. Mortally wounded, "crawling on the sand, he said / It's most unfair, they've shot my foot off." By describing his mortal wound as "most unfair," the dying man echoes the cherished notion that noblemen fight by fixed and generous rules, playing the game as if it were cricket or polo. Douglas recognizes the folly and obsolescence of such attitudes, but is man enough to admit being moved:

> How can I live among this gentle
> obsolescent breed of heroes, and not weep?
> Unicorns, almost,
> for they are fading into two legends
> in which their stupidity and chivalry
> are celebrated. Each, fool and hero,
> will be an immortal.
>
> (Douglas 1951: 38)

The poet finds a way to praise the dead man's heroism and unconcern while honestly recognizing his outdated stance as a form of stupidity. His own death in the Normandy invasion, at the age of 24, was a great loss for poetry.

In "Soldiers Bathing, " the South African intelligence officer F. T. Prince admires

> the freedom of a band
> Of soldiers who belong to me. Stripped bare

> For bathing in the sea, they shout and
> run in the warm air.

After comparing his naked soldiers to those in Renaissance paintings, Prince reaches an astonishing conclusion:

> Because to love is frightening we prefer
> The freedom of our crimes. Yet, as I drink the dusky
> air,
> I feel a strange delight that fills me full,
> Strange gratitude, as if evil itself were beautiful,
> And kiss the wound in thought, while
> in the west
> I watch a streak of red that might have issued from
> Christ's breast.
>
> (Prince 1993: 55–57)

The poet's sense of propriety – his official responsibility for the soldiers who belong to him, his educated impulse to interpret their bodies in terms of art or religion – is in constant tension with the love he evidently feels for them, a love both great and frightening. These lines admit of many readings, but I think the central one is this: because we are afraid to acknowledge loving other men, an emotion forbidden by the ordinary rules of Prince's society, we prefer war, in which we are free to commit acts that would normally be crimes, including killing other men. War, Prince implies, licenses both. By enacting within the poem the difficulty of facing his own erotic feelings, Prince transforms the tension between reticent propriety and passionate desire into art, and links that personal tension to the larger, more public tension between violence and love.

Writing more compactly, the American poet Randall Jarrell compresses years of suffering into a few lines in "The Death of the Ball Turret Gunner":

> From my mother's sleep I fell into the State,
> And I hunched in its belly till my wet fur froze.
> Six miles from earth, loosed from its
> dream of life,
> I woke to black flak and the nightmare fighters.
> When I died they washed me out of the turret with a
> hose.
>
> (Jarrell 1969: 144)

Unborn, unchristened, the speaker has no name. From his mother's sleep he falls into another womb, the airplane turret to which the State consigns him. He hunches like a fetus in the belly of the State, here imagined as the airplane, and his death looks like an abortion.

More recently, the conflict in Vietnam produced a rich harvest of poetry, much of it in the form of protest songs. Phil Ochs, Bob Dylan, and Country Joe McDonald used the power of rhyming language and music to dramatize their outrage. In the years after the war, poetry without music has served as one way for Americans to grapple with their feelings about Vietnam. In "Waiting for the Fire," for example, Philip Appleman insists that we need the wisdom of losses to prevent us from repeating our evil deeds:

> But forgetfulness will never walk
> with innocence; we save our faces
> at the risk of our lives, needing
> the wisdom of losses, the gift of despair,
> or we could kill again.
>
> (Ehrhart 1989: 6)

Though intensely aware of daily losses, the soldier-poets writing about Iraq have not yet mounted a political attack on the politicians responsible for the war. Their moral sensibility tends to be local and personal, not yet global. In a poem addressed to the infantry team he led in Iraq, Brian Turner attempts to counter their habit of keeping up their courage by boasting of their desire to kill:

> It should make you shake and sweat,
> nightmare you, strand you in a desert
> of irrevocable desolation, the consequences
> seared into the vein, no matter
> what adrenaline
> feeds the muscle its courage, no matter
> what god shines down on you, no matter
> what crackling pain and anger
> you carry in your fists, my friend,
> it should break your heart to kill.
>
> (Turner 2005: 56)

This admirable and moving plea for retaining an awareness of the cost of war should remind us of the continuing importance of poetry as a medium for dealing with war. Turner's idiom is not that of Virgil or Tennyson or Owen, but his is nonetheless an authentic and urgent poetry.

References

Brooke, R. (1970) *The Poetical Works*. G. Keynes (Ed.). London: Faber and Faber.

Day-Lewis, C. (1992) *The Complete Poems of C. Day Lewis*. London: Sinclair-Stevenson.

Douglas, K. (1951) *The Collected Poems of Keith Douglas*. J. Waller and G. S. Fraser (Eds.). London: Editions Poetry.

Ehrhart, W. D. (Ed.) (1989) *Carrying the Darkness: The Poetry of the Vietnam War*. Lubbock, TX: Texas Tech University Press.

Jarrell, R. (1969) *Complete Poems*. New York: The Noonday Press.

Marsh, E. (Comp.) (1918) *Georgian Poetry, 1916–1917*. New York: G. P. Putnam's Sons.

Owen, W. (1983) *The Complete Poems and Fragments*. J Stallworthy (Ed.). London: Chatto & Windus.

Prince, F. T. (1993) *Collected Poems: 1935–1992*. Manchester: Carcanet.

Sassoon, S. (1961) *Collected Poems: 1908–1956*. London: Faber & Faber.

Turner, B. (2005) *Here, Bullet*. Farmington, ME: Alice James Books.

Further Reading

Kipling, R. (1992) *Selected Poetry*. Craig Raine (Ed.). London: Penguin.

Paris, M. (2000) *Warrior Nation: Images of War in British Popular Culture, 1850–2000*. London: Reaktion Books.

War Propaganda

RANDAL MARLIN

Derived from the Latin "propagare," meaning "to propagate," the word "propaganda" can be interpreted broadly to apply to purposeful dissemination of ideas, spreading of information, or inculcation of attitudes with the aim of advancing some cause of the propagator. On this understanding it is neither good nor bad in itself, but derives its goodness or badness from the nature of the messages or attitudes communicated and the purpose of the disseminator. So understood, propaganda is, with certain qualifications, itself morally neutral. It would be wrong, though, to assume that contemporary English speakers will understand the word in this neutral sense. On the contrary, it is commonly understood in a narrower, pejorative sense. Reference to another's communications as "propaganda" is ordinarily treated as an accusation of manipulation, deceit, disingenuousness or suchlike, and can be expected to elicit some attempt at rebuttal.

How is "propaganda" defined in this narrower sense? The central idea is that of manipulation. The propagandist communicates in such a way as to direct a target audience to believe things, or have emotional attitudes and dispositions to act, in ways that suit the propagandist's aims. While an ethical communicator has as a main concern not to mislead an audience, the propagandist in this narrower sense typically has no compunctions about doing so. There are many means for deceiving people and propaganda can be effective in the absence of straightforward lies. G. K. Chesterton once referred to the "blackest of all lies" as consisting entirely of truths, but so selected as to give a false impression.

Systematic recklessness as to truth in advancing a cause may for the same reason qualify as propaganda. In an age of opinionated radio and television talk shows, the word "truthiness" has come into use to describe the kind of statements that are likely to seem true to a given audience, whether or not they are in fact true. Such statements derive a spurious air of veracity from frequent repetition. It has been argued that lack of adequate warrant for one's truth claims, so-called "epistemic defectiveness," should be treated as central to a reconstructed idea of propaganda (Cunningham 2002). Others have emphasized the aspect of control. A leading French propaganda theorist, Jacques Ellul (1912–1994), has defined propaganda as manipulative communication for the purpose of gaining or maintaining power over others.

Propaganda is of the greatest importance for the successful waging of war. As Carl von Clausewitz recognized, morale is a strong factor in the willingness of soldiers to fight. If they don't believe that their cause is just, or if they think that they are doomed to defeat, they are less likely to succeed. Thus the use of what Shakespeare termed "paper bullets" – propaganda to persuade an enemy that their cause is wrong or hopeless. A classic example of this is in *Henry V*, where King Henry wins a bloodless victory over the French at Harfleur (Act III, Scene iii). Propaganda of this sort against the enemy is commonly described as "psychological warfare" and such things as the use of leaflets in wartime are appropriately discussed under that heading.

As defined above, propaganda can be found in all ages, but the twentieth century brought with it new mass media and such pervasive use of social and psychological techniques as to amount arguably to a difference in kind. To wider circulating and photographically enhanced print media were added radio, cinema, and, in the latter half-century, television. War toys and space-age video games encourage militarism among children. An army of lobbyists, public relations advisors, consultants on "perception management" and "event management" has arisen to guide power-holders on how to affect public opinion. Not without reason has our modern period been called the "age of propaganda." Wide use of the Internet in the twenty-first century has provided many opportunities for resistance to propaganda, but traditional power-holders have also learned to make use of this medium, and its overall impact has yet to be determined.

Taxonomy

War propaganda can be classified and analyzed under a wide variety of categories. The following list is not intended to be exhaustive:

1. Propaganda can be directed to one's own country, to allied countries, to neutral countries, to an enemy country, or to an occupied country.
2. Propaganda can be classified according to the kind of motivation sought: whether, for example, to motivate people to go to war, buy war bonds, keep secrets, recycle scrap metal, grow "victory gardens," or the like.
3. Propaganda can emanate from government, private corporations, media, public relations firms, think tanks, or from other organized groups.
4. Propaganda may use many different media: news reports, articles, commentary, books, pictures, speeches, leaflets, films, videos, radio, music, monuments, bumper stickers, flags, clothing, posters, maps, coins, postage stamps, symbolic acts (including those of violence), YouTube, Twitter, and text

messages. Virtually any form of communication can be used for propaganda.

5. Propaganda is termed "black" when its source is deliberately misrepresented, as when a radio station is presented as one operated by the enemy, in order to confuse the enemy. The term is sometimes used for propaganda that is grossly repugnant on other grounds. "White" propaganda is honest about its source. "Gray" propaganda does not deceive as to its source, but neither does it reveal the source. In overlapping terminology, "covert" propaganda deliberately keeps the source hidden, while "overt" propaganda reveals the source.

6. Propaganda can be analyzed according to the techniques employed. These can involve appeals to powerful emotions, such as fear or anger. They may employ devices such as tendentious framing of questions, repetition, use of misleading terminology, bold assertion, suppression of relevant facts to give a false impression, misleading juxtaposition or association of people or ideas … the list is very long.

7. At a more rarefied level, propaganda may be analyzed in terms of its making use of certain background, all-encompassing beliefs that Ellul termed "myths," which vary from culture to culture. Examples of such myths include those of race, the Führer (leader), the hero, the nation, progress, and work (treated as salvific). Ellul's categorization of propaganda into four contrasting pairs – political/sociological; vertical/horizontal; agitation/integration; and rational/irrational – has also been useful and influential for classification purposes. Integration propaganda refers to symbols, stories, flags, pictures, and so on, that promote group cohesion, such as patriotic pride.

History

The following account is intended only to illustrate war-related propaganda techniques as found mainly in European-based history, and selected for their interest and instructiveness for understanding current propaganda. A "history of war propaganda" as such would require reference to Egyptian, Indian, Chinese, Japanese, Latin American, African, and other important sources.

An early example of the use of propaganda to gain power is found in the case of Pisistratus (sixth century BCE), who faked an attack on himself and his mules. As a respected military leader, he asked for, and obtained from the Athenian people, bodyguards that he then used to build up a power base, eventually becoming a tyrant of Athens. The technique of faked, provoked, or exaggerated victimization to justify war is a common one throughout history, and has been dubbed "victim hegemony."

Expelled by united opposition, Pisistratus regained power in Athens, by first biding his time and then returning with a tall and beautiful woman dressed in armor and mounted on a chariot. His claim that she was the goddess Athena and that he was under her protection met with success. This was an early example of "God is on our side" propaganda, a kind that has persisted through the millennia, against the same claim in different languages, as "*Gott mit uns*," or "*Dieu avec nous*."

Pericles, as described by Thucydides, used his funeral oration in 431 BCE to laud the Athenian soldiers who had lost their lives fighting in the Peloponnesian War, thereby encouraging living Athenians to honor their sacrifices by continuing the fight. He encouraged a patriotic spirit by extolling the superiority of Athenian society, with its democracy, nobility, spirit of caring, and the like, thus motivating new recruits. Similar claims of racial or cultural superiority, but for different nations, have been a staple of imperial war propaganda through the ages.

Aristotle (384–322 BCE) studied how successful rhetorical persuasion works. Rhetoric, the art of speaking effectively, can be one form of propaganda, but the principles he describes are often applicable to other forms as well. The propagandist will need to know his or her audience, and should project a good ethos, or character. A propagandist should appear simple and unmanipulative for this reason. The propagandist should excite and harness the pathos, or emotions of the crowd, and ensure that the argument, the logos, is clear and simple, without obvious detectable flaws. Among the emotions Aristotle lists, fear and anger have been prominent for fomenting hatred and war.

Caesar Augustus (63 BCE–14 CE), with his successful launching of imperial Roman rule lasting for centuries, clearly understood certain basics of war propaganda. He projected an image of himself as victorious, powerful, competent, a "son of a god" (being the adopted son of the deified Julius Caesar, his great uncle) who nevertheless was not striving for power but was concerned to provide security for those subject to his rule.

Tracing the history of war-related propaganda in western Europe is a complex undertaking, intertwined with the spread of Christianity and subsequent challenges to its institutional power. The Wars of the Crusades, starting in the twelfth century, were largely fueled by the belief, on the part of both Muslims and Christians, that they were fighting a Holy War on God's side, for which their death would bring them an eternal reward. As reported by Robert the Monk, Pope Urban II made use of vivid, hatred-inducing atrocity stories to motivate Christians to fight the advancing Seljuq Turks.

The Thirty Years' War (1618–1648), with its widespread anarchic violence in Europe, led to a strong desire for restoration of order. Supported by King Louis XIII, the cartoonist Jacques Callot produced a series of cartoons in 1632, titled "The Miseries of War," lauding the king for bringing order. At the same time his gruesome portrayal of the war also conveyed a powerful message against war in general.

In all wars, the need for justification exists, because soldiers need to believe in the rightness of what they are doing. Theologians developed a theory called "Just War Theory" with early emphasis on when it would be right, and when wrong, to go to war. Only a proper authority could declare a just war. As roles and powers of kings, lords, popes, and emperors shifted, so did the application of this principle in justifying a given war (Russell 1975).

The French Revolution created a need for a new sense of identity, with the traumatic effect of regicide and upheaval of the traditional order. Propaganda on a large scale helped to meet this need. Engravings, pamphlets, medals, songs, posters, crockery, and even playing cards carried revolutionary messages such as liberty, equality, and fraternity. Festivals attracted huge crowds, contributing to the forging of a new mass consciousness. Napoleon (1769–1821) exercised unprecedented power over opinion, largely through censorship, control over media, theater,

and the arts, and indoctrination in the schools. "I shall never allow the papers to say or do anything contrary to my interests," he said (Holtman 1950).

Patriotic history and literature were emphasized in the school curriculum. The Catechism proclaimed that to honor and serve the emperor was to honor and serve God himself. He would greatly exaggerate his victories and minimize his losses with a view to sustaining morale when needed, believing victory to be the best form of propaganda. He knew how to inspire loyalty through military decorations ("trinkets" or "baubles" as he once described them).

Imperial propaganda flourished in nineteenth-century Europe. The ideas of progress, national, racial, and cultural superiority and the like gave impetus to the drive for domination over "primitive" countries. These ideas were reinforced in elite schools through the reading of the Greek and Roman classics. Ideas of cultural or other superiority are not necessarily deliberately disseminated with a view to causing people to act in some definite way. But once they are in existence, they are easily exploited, as in the case of World War I.

World War I

British propaganda was well organized and unprecedented in its scope and reach. Early activities, prior to January 1917, took place under the direction of Charles F. G. Masterman, in a building called Wellington House, after which his department was named. Three official reports on "Work Conducted for the Government at Wellington House" provide a very detailed review of these activities up until September 1916. Operations were continued under the more aggressive Department of Information and later the Ministry of Information under Lord Beaverbrook.

The very important function of supplying news to daily newspapers of the world was carried out separately by the News Department of the Foreign Office. The department frequently used telegraphic means for speedy access to target audiences, believing that those who got their side of the story across first would have a distinct advantage.

One of the main jobs of Wellington House was to recruit recognized authors to write books, articles, and pamphlets that would then be published and widely circulated without any indication of their being subsidized by the British government. The need for secrecy is frankly avowed in the reports. By contrast, German written propaganda in the United States appeared with acknowledgment of the source. By September 1916, Wellington House had published a total of 207 books and pamphlets such as Max Aitken's (later Lord Beaverbrook's) "Canada in Flanders." German film propaganda made inroads in advance of the British, but by 1916 the British also became active in that medium. Wellington House also handled opinion articles and photographs for insertion in the foreign press, with the United States a main target. It dealt in personal propaganda, reaching influential people in foreign countries, particularly those in the media, hosting them in England and France and sending recognized British personalities abroad to spread pro-British sentiment. Classics Professor Gilbert Murray was cited as one among others whose influence could have "a propagandist effect without his presence having a propagandistic purpose" (Parker 1916). Wellington House regularly produced pictorial magazines, translated into many languages, for worldwide distribution.

Atrocity Propaganda

Depicting an enemy as guilty of atrocities has long been a staple of war propaganda. British propaganda in World War I pressed this theme incessantly, with the idea that nothing less than civilization itself depended on defeating the Germans. In H. G. Wells's widely circulated phrase, this was "the war to end all wars."

A. J. Mackenzie (1938) wrote that effective war propaganda requires a kernel of truth, lots of repetition, and color to stimulate the imagination. It should be built around a slogan, and should be directed to a specific objective. It should be carefully timed, and its source should be concealed.

All of these features were present in the sum total of different atrocity stories, starting with the catalogue of outrages in the Bryce Report (1915) widely reproduced and disseminated by Wellington House, which added to the text its own call to arms.

Much was made of German barbarity in torpedoing the Cunard liner *Lusitania* on May 7, 1915, though along with its passengers it was clearly carrying munitions, and the Germans had warned passengers that it would be targeted.

An atrocity story in 1917 about how Germans allegedly boiled down their own dead soldiers to make useful war products is in a class by itself and deserves to be studied carefully for what it can teach us.

What was called the "corpse utilization plant" story became anchored in British and world consciousness with the simultaneous publication of it April 17, 1917, by two British newspapers owned by Lord Northcliffe: the authoritative *Times* and the widely circulating *Daily Mail*. The newspapers juxtaposed a supposed eyewitness account, from inside an installation where Germans were purportedly boiling down their own dead soldiers, with the translation of a report in an official German newspaper that seemed to confirm the existence of such a plant.

In truth, there were indeed installations for extracting materials from the many dead horses on the battlefield at the time, killed by shells and machine guns. The deception came when it was alleged that human corpses were used rather than horse carcasses.

The eyewitness account was taken from the French-language newspaper, the *Indépendance belge*, of April 10, 1917. It was detailed and gruesome. The German newspaper, the *Lokal-Anzeiger*, also of April 10, 1917, carried a dispatch by Karl Rosner dated April 5, in which he reported seeing from a distance a "*Kadaververwertungsanstalt*" ("carcass utilization plant"), which the Northcliffe papers translated as "corpse utilization plant."

There were two key mistranslations of the German text. The word "*Kadaver*" should have been translated as "carcass" instead of "corpse." The German word for corpse is *die Leiche*. Rosner also spoke of a dull vapor in the air as if "*Leim*" (the German word for glue) were being boiled. The Northcliffe papers translated this as "lime" that was "burnt." Since rendering superannuated horses to make glue was a well-recognized practice in those days, the mistranslation assisted in a deception. Lime (quicklime) would easily be associated with the disinfection of diseased corpses.

Rosner had made a passing reference of a few lines in a much larger story, but by taking his remarks out of context and introducing the mistranslations, the Northcliffe press made Rosner's account appear to confirm the other, unsubstantiated report. The daily newspaper *Indépendance belge* claimed to have taken the story from another publication, *La Belgique* (no date given), supposedly published in Leiden, Holland. This made verification next to impossible. The newspaper *Indépendance belge* existed, but it was edited in London, where close cooperation in propaganda is known to have taken place between Belgians and British. Frederic Wile of the *Daily Mail* acknowledged joint responsibility for what he called the "body-boilers" revelation with J. E. Mackenzie, of *The Times*, in an article "Why I Believe the Germans are Ghouls," published in *The War Illustrated*, May 19, 1917.

The special significance of this story lies not only in the power it had to generate hatred and contempt for Germans, thereby encouraging the war effort, but also in the special technique used to gain credibility for the story: namely, the faking of credentials by making it seem as if the story were accepted by the Germans. The corpse utilization plant story was endlessly repeated, with the recurrent slogan "Germans are ghouls." It was deeply resented by the Germans, as an editorial in the *Frankfürter Zeitung*, "Moral Insanity," April 29, 1917, made clear at the time. Memory of the deception, and official discrediting of the story by the British in the House of Commons in 1925, contributed to early skepticism in World War II concerning the Nazi gas ovens and the Holocaust.

Other key aspects of British propaganda during World War I were the exposure of the Zimmerman telegram and Lord Northcliffe's efforts, as director of enemy propaganda, to encourage the breakaway of Germany's allies in Austria-Hungary, with the help of Woodrow Wilson's Fourteen Points, in particular the principle of self-determination for nations.

Nazi War Propaganda

Principles of propaganda were spelled out in Adolf Hitler's *Mein Kampf*. Simplicity, appeal to emotions, repetition, and endless reversion to a few simple themes were at the core of his blueprint for persuasion. In the early 1920s, he resolved to make Jews a scapegoat for German resentment, exploiting these feelings for his own rise to power. He linked Jews to capitalist exploitation in the West and to communist ideology in the East.

In the early years following 1919, the Nazi Party made extensive use of posters. During elections and after coming to power in 1933, the Nazis used posters to disseminate their anti-Semitic messages, both directly and by encouraging people to buy cheap radio sets, read party newspapers, view certain movies, and the like.

Both Hitler and Josef Goebbels, who became Minister for Propaganda and People's Enlightenment, were dramatic and mesmerizing speakers. Goebbels cultivated the public image of Hitler as someone with special, almost superhuman, characteristics, who could be relied on to express the will of the German nation, and to whom allegiance was personally owed. Willingness to die for Nazi ideals was inculcated at an early age, and Goebbels was able through passionate speechmaking to turn the defeat at Stalingrad into a reason for even greater sacrifices from the German people.

Hitler's invasion of Poland in 1939 was preceded by a staged attack on Germany supposedly by Poles. In that way it was presented to the German people as a response to aggression, rather than aggression itself. Hermann Goering said in an interview at the time of the Nuremberg trials that the technique could be used by democracies as well. "[T]he people can always be brought to the bidding of the leaders. That is easy. All you have to do is tell them they are being attacked, and denounce the peacemakers for lack of patriotism and exposing the country to danger. It works the same in any country" (Gilbert 1947).

Wartime propaganda against France and Britain was skillfully handled with the help of articulate and witty native speakers such as Paul Ferdonnet, known to the French as "*le traître de Stuttgart*," and later Philippe Henriot. Early in World War II, Ferdonnet would broadcast slogans to the French such as "Why die for Danzig?" or "Englishmen will fight Germany down to the last Frenchman." Henriot was superbly entertaining, but his accurate reports of damage done by Allied bombings of French towns seriously undermined French morale.

Posters conveyed the idea that Europe had become an impregnable fortress under the Nazis and that resistance was futile. Following Dunkirk, occupied France was subjected to the sight of posters depicting British forcibly preventing French from embarking. This was selective presentation of truth, inasmuch as many tens of thousands of French were later picked up under direct orders from Churchill. William Joyce, taking over the name Lord Haw-Haw from Norman Baillie-Stewart, broadcast to Britain amusing skits, jibes, and information with a view to encouraging distrust of the British leadership. His reports could interfere with production, as when he said about a munitions factory in the Midlands employing 5,000 workers that it would be bombed in a few days: "Don't trouble to finish the new paint shed, you won't need it." This bit of local knowledge gave credibility to his prediction and there was a drop in production (Cole 1964: 155).

Art

Art has played a large role in fostering a warlike spirit, in lionizing state leaders, and in demonizing enemies. Church, kings, and nobility have all commissioned artworks contributing directly or indirectly to favorable regard from the people. Paintings and monuments emphasizing bravery and glory, reminding people of past heroes and victories, have assisted in recruitment.

Jacques-Louis David made notable contributions to revolutionary France, among them the depiction of the assassinated Jacobin Jean-Paul Marat with a beatific expression. He repaid Napoleon with favorable portraits, such as the heroic depiction of him at the St Bernard Pass with billowing cloak, mounted on a powerful white horse. Napoleon's beckoning hand summons followers to join him in adventures ahead.

Illustrated newspapers were well established at the time of the Franco-Prussian War and with accompanying commentary helped to shape judgments on the war (Martin 2006: 52).

World War I British artists such as Muirhead Bone produced largely sanitized pictures from the front, showing devastation but not mass slaughter, chaos, misery, and the sense of futility.

The iconic "I Want You" recruitment posters began with the World War I British depiction by Alfred Leete of Lord Kitchener pointing his finger at the viewer. Montgomery Flagg copied the idea in a famous World War I poster of Uncle Sam

recruiting young Americans. A similar, more modernized poster of Uncle Sam was widely circulated in World War II.

Soviet posters were often brilliant in design. The 1943 portrayal by the Kukryniksy Group of Hitler ordering German soldiers to march east to their graves is especially poignant. When the Nazis began their 1941 Barbarossa invasion, Irakli Toidze represented a stern-faced woman in red, with piercing eyes and one hand raised, bayonets in the background. The words, "The Motherland Calls You," appear at the top.

Art has also served the anti-war cause. Goya's depiction of a Spanish peasant about to kill one of Napoleon's fallen troops shows horror on his face rather than triumph. Picasso's celebrated *Guernica* conveys the dreadfulness and consternation following the bombing of that Basque town by German and Italian planes in 1937. The covering up of a replica of *Guernica* outside the United Nations (UN) Security Council in New York when US Secretary of State Colin Powell made his Iraq war-promoting representations on February 5, 2003, was seen by many as a move to suppress a powerful anti-war icon.

John Heartfield used techniques of photomontage to ridicule Nazis in a magazine called *AIZ*, published in Prague in the 1930s. Posters have used the "I Want You" theme for ironic purposes. In the Vietnam War the recruiting Uncle Sam was depicted as having his face blown off, and during the build-up to the 2003 war against Iraq, a portrayal of Osama bin Laden announcing "I Want You – to Invade Iraq" was widely circulated on the Internet.

Photographs can have a powerful influence on attitudes. The image of the US Marines raising the flag at Iwo Jima gave Americans cause for pride. By contrast, the 1972 image of crying and naked Kim Phuc fleeing the napalm attack on her village produced intense revulsion against the Vietnam War.

Music

Napoleon said that of all the liberal arts, music has the most impact on the emotions, and that the chorus of a song has a greater affect leading to action than a moral treatise. He instructed his Minister of the Interior in 1803 to compose a song for the invasion of England, to the tune of "*Le Chant du Départ*" (Cronin 1994: 292). Bagpipe music and drums have for centuries spurred on Scots in battle, and unnerved their enemies. Among national anthems the French "Marseillaise" is arguably the most stirring. The US Civil War pitted the northern "Battle Hymn of the Republic" against the southern "Dixie." The lively "Caisson Song" was widely played in the United States during World War II, as was "Over There." The Nazis produced their own songbook and alternative anthem, the "Horst Wessel Song." Wagnerian music, with its celebration of German mythology, was also widely played on radio. The Allies appropriated the opening bars of Beethoven's Fifth Symphony to announce their victory in 1945. The three short notes followed by a long note represented V for victory in Morse code.

Music can also give solace in adversity, as with the German "*Ich hatt' einen Kameraden*" ("I had a comrade"), and many bagpipe laments. It could also boost morale in the case of numerous World War I songs, such as "Pack Up Your Troubles," "It's a Long Way to Tipperary," "Keep the Home Fires Burning," and "Alexander's Ragtime Band." The sprightly "Colonel Bogey March" in its World War II version cheered up Allied marchers with insulting references to Nazi leaders.

Among anti-war songs, the Australian "And the Band Played Waltzing Matilda," by singer-songwriter Eric Bogle, is memorable. Bob Dylan's "Blowin' in the Wind" of the early 1960s has been frequently sung at war protest gatherings, beginning with the Vietnam War. Phil Coulter's "The Town I Loved So Well" describes the effects of conflict in Northern Ireland.

Film

In the pre-television years of World Wars I and II, cinema played a large role in developing sympathies, motivating recruits, and encouraging war efforts. World War I coincided with the creation of large film audiences, and hundreds of films dealing with war themes were released in the United States. The British Ministry of Information estimated weekly home audiences at 20 million, with about the same proportion in other countries. The ministry invented two-minute "film tags" – messages attached to news résumés and carrying a moral such as "Save Coal" or "Buy War Loans" (Marlin 2002: 69).

Newsreels were popular in both world wars, and were carefully censored. After 1935, Goebbels controlled the flow of news in Germany, and during World War II cameramen were part of specific propaganda companies whose work was to reveal "that side of the truth that it is necessary to propagate in the interest of the German people" (Dolezal 1984: 5).

Hollywood came to the aid of British efforts in World War II with films such as *Mrs. Miniver* (1942) depicting a woman from the privileged class pulling her weight with ordinary people in the war effort. *The Sullivans* (1944) allowed mothers who lost a son the consolation that at least they did not lose five, as with the mother in the film. US war films presented the toughness of the conditions GIs had to endure, but the determined faces of actors like John Wayne left no doubt that the United States would ultimately prevail. Japanese were portrayed as treacherous, for example, falsely surrendering with a concealed machine gun and opening fire on trusting American soldiers.

Soviet filmmaking benefited from the genius of Sergei Eisenstein. His classic *Battleship Potemkin* (1925) served as integration propaganda to remind post-revolutionary audiences how bad things had been under the tsar. His *Alexander Nevsky* (1938), incorporating a carefully synchronized score by Sergei Prokofiev, served an important role in tapping into deep roots of pre-revolutionary consciousness to develop patriotic feeling against the German invaders. Any explicit reference to religion would have been at odds with official communist ideology, but the film allows those who are so predisposed to see divine intervention when it shows the Teutonic knights foundering in breaking ice.

Like Lenin, Goebbels was a great believer in the power and utility of the film for propaganda. He also thought that the primary goal was to seize the attention and imagination of the audience and introduce propaganda themes indirectly. Films such as *Jud Süss* (1940) and *The Eternal Jew* (1940) reinforced well-entrenched anti-Semitic themes in 1940, while Leni Riefenstahl's *Triumph of the Will* (1935) presented an idealized picture of Hitler, the Nazi

Party, German workers' dignity, and the power and order of disciplined marching troops.

Among anti-war films, director Lewis Milestone's *All Quiet on the Western Front* (1930), based on Erich Maria Remarque's novel, is a recognized classic.

Ethics and Jurisprudence

The ethics of war propaganda is partly connected to war ethics. Propaganda in both the neutral and the bad sense of the term will be wrong if it is supporting a war of aggression. But if it is mobilizing people for a just war, and is not engaged in deception, propaganda in the neutral sense would appear to be justifiable.

Controversially, even deceptive propaganda can arguably be justified for a good cause, particularly in emergency situations; the problem is recognizable as an example of a "dirty hands" situation where a wrongful act is justified as a way of avoiding even greater wrongs.

A long-standing division of opinion about the ethics of deception pits the ideas of St Augustine against those of Machiavelli. The latter was concerned with effects and appearances, and countenanced deception when it would be likely to produce good results. The former advocated truthful speaking, even when lying would appear to lead to a better outcome.

So-called "realists" tend to support Machiavelli's view. You engage in propaganda to all parties, including your own people, whenever it appears necessary to do so to save the nation from serious harm. But opponents of such "realism" tend to be alarmed at the anti-democratic potential of such a philosophy. When leaders see the need to deceive their own people for the latter's supposed benefit, they may easily interpret their own political party fortunes as bound up with the people's ultimate good. Such thinking can lead to the kind of deceptions associated with the administration of US President Richard Nixon and the attempted cover-up of its illegal actions at Watergate in the early 1970s.

Concerns have also been expressed about the false "incubator babies" story used to gain acceptance of the United States-led attack on Saddam Hussein's Iraq in 1991 (Marlin 2002). Emotional testimony by a young Kuwaiti woman persuaded the world to believe that Iraqi soldiers had taken babies from hospital incubators, leaving them to die. It was not revealed at the time that the woman was the Kuwaiti ambassador's daughter. The story gained further credence when Amnesty International confirmed December 19, 1990, that 312 incubator babies had died that way. Later Amnesty admitted that it had been duped.

Another kind of deception occurred with the 2002–2003 build-up in the US media for war against Iraq, culminating in Colin Powell's representation of Saddam Hussein as having weapons of mass destruction and connections with al-Qaeda. The thinking under the George W. Bush administration appears to have been that selling war to the public required a simple reason such as that the United States was in danger of attack. The reasons given were later discredited, but they served their purpose.

A current-day problem for the "realist" is that deceptions may be less easy to pull off successfully today than in previous generations, because of the Internet and the facility with which a whistleblower can reach wide audiences. Daniel Ellsberg required great knowledge and skill to pull off his Pentagon Papers revelation about the Vietnam War. With today's technology, deceptions can be readily exposed on the Internet. Attempts to make heroes out of Pat Tillman and Jessica Lynch very soon conflicted with the news, disseminated on the Internet, that he was killed by friendly fire and that she was unconscious when she was supposedly fighting the enemy.

Augustinian believers, resolving to stick with the truth, have a different problem. What a person says or reveals takes place in a context. In the context of a highly emotional and misinformed crowd, stating some truths and not others could spark violence and injustice. Every statement is situated, and proper moral evaluation of speech acts cannot ignore context and likely effects. To the question of the truth of a statement has to be added that of truth about the rightness or wrongness of making that statement in a particular context, where one could be inciting injustice.

Modern-day wars of insurgency are closely linked with propaganda because the aim is to win over the "hearts and minds" of the people among whom the insurgents thrive. Those fighting the insurgents in an asymmetric war have to show restraint, because however successful their propaganda toward their own people may be, the people among whom insurgents operate know all too well the existence of those innocent people killed by "collateral damage." Deceptions about these matters are likely to discourage those people from standing up against the insurgents. Given the utter horror of war, and the difficulty of containment to one geographical area, those who would engage in propaganda for war have an enormous burden of proof to discharge. Many countries have the capability to deliver weapons of mass destruction. In times of heightened tension, errors, misapprehensions, and mistakes could trigger a spiral of violence ending in catastrophe. The range of situations where propaganda for war could be justifiable would have to be limited to the clearest cases of defense against aggression, where victory would be attainable and where the risks of a worldwide conflagration would be next to zero.

Propaganda in war would also have to be subject to strong constraints. Creation of negative stereotyping and dehumanization of the enemy, such as the British portrayal of Germans in World War I, Hitler's characterization of Jews up to and during World War II, and American depictions of Japanese in World War II, all encouraged barbarous actions. Systematic use of communications in Rwanda to depict Tutsis as subhuman "cockroaches" threatening the lives of Hutus led to the massacre of Tutsis by the hundreds of thousands in the 1990s (Thompson 2007).

The appalling fallout from dehumanizing propaganda has produced a strong movement to make it illegal. The UN International Covenant on Civil and Political Rights (ICCPR), Article 20(1) provides: "Any propaganda for war shall be prohibited by law." Little effect has been given to this provision in practice, for four reasons: (i) power politics; (ii) use of this provision domestically by dictatorial regimes to suppress legitimate dissent, and the opposing tradition of free speech in western democracies; (iii) the legitimacy of some types of propaganda for mobilizing people against a war of aggression; and (iv) the difficulty of defining "propaganda" (Kearney 2007).

The strong tradition of freedom of expression in western democracies has been cited as standing in the way of giving effect to prohibition of propaganda for war, but as with other conflicts between rights, the judiciary may be able to suitably define "propaganda" and take account of context so as to balance the rights of those affected by war against rights to express one's opinions on any matter.

When Canada's hate propaganda law was challenged in the courts, the term "hate" became judicially defined in a much narrower way than the accepted meaning in ordinary language. Similar refinements can be expected concerning the meaning of "propaganda" in ICCPR 20(1).

Agitation on behalf of giving effect to ICCPR 20(1) can serve as a focal point for democratic forces to counteract in a timely way the propensities of countries with imperial ambitions to dominate others through illegal use of superior military power. Such efforts, even if they do not succeed in the courts, can at least draw attention to the problem of war propaganda and alert people in a more timely way to threats to peace as they arise.

SEE ALSO: Terrorism, War Against.

References

Cole, J. A. (1964) *Lord Haw-Haw and William Joyce: The Full Story*. London: Faber and Faber.

Cronin, V. (1994) *Napoleon*. London: HarperCollins.

Cunningham, S. (2002) *The Idea of Propaganda*. Westport: Praeger.

Dolezal, S. (1984) *German Newsreels 1933–1947*. Munich: Goethe-Institut München.

Gilbert, G. (1947) *Nuremberg Diary*. New York: Farrar, Straus.

Holtman, R. (1950) *Napoleonic Propaganda*. Baton Rouge: Louisiana State University Press.

Kearney, M. G. (2007) *The Prohibition of Propaganda for War in International Law*. Oxford: Oxford University Press.

Mackenzie, A. J. (1938) *Propaganda Boom*. London: John Gifford.

Marlin, R. (2002) *Propaganda and the Ethics of Persuasion*. Peterborough, ON: Broadview Press.

Martin, M. (2006) *Images at War: Illustrated Periodicals and Constructed Nations*. Toronto: University of Toronto Press.

Parker, G. (1916) "The United States." In *Third Report on the Work Conducted for the Government at Wellington House*. Introduction by Charles F. G. Masterman. London: Secretary of State for Foreign Affairs.

Russell, F. H. (1975) *The Just War in the Middle Ages.* Cambridge: Cambridge University Press.

Thompson, A. (2007) *The Media and the Rwanda Genocide.* London: Pluto Press.

Further Reading

Balfour, M. (1979) *Propaganda in War 1939–1945.* London: Routledge and Kegan Paul.

Barburina, B. (1985) *The Soviet Political Poster.* Harmondsworth: Penguin.

Campbell, C. W. (1985) *Reel America and World War I.* Jefferson, NC: McFarland.

Chakotin, S. (1971) *The Rape of the Masses.* New York: Haskell House.

Chesterton, G. K. (1987) "Distortions in the Press." In *The Collected Works of G. K. Chesterton.* Volume 28: *The Illustrated London News 1908–1910.* Ft. Collins, CO: Ignatius Press.

Chomsky, N. (1991) *Deterring Democracy.* London: Verso.

Crossman, R. (1958) "The Creed of a Modern Propagandist." In William Daugherty (Ed.), *A Psychological Warfare Casebook.* Baltimore: Johns Hopkins University Press.

Cull, N., Culbert, D., and Welch, D. (2003) *Propaganda and Mass Persuasion: A Historical Encyclopedia, 1500 to the Present.* Santa Barbara: ABC-CLIO.

Dutton, P. (1986) "'Geschäft über Alles': Notes on Some Medallions Inspired by the Sinking of the Lusitania," *Imperial War Museum Review,* 1.

Ellsberg, D. (2002) *Secrets.* New York: Viking.

Ellul, J. (1965) *Propaganda: The Formation of Men's Attitudes,* trans. K. Kellen and J. Lerner. New York: Knopf.

Ellul, J. (1976) *Histoi re de la propagande.* Paris: Presses Universitaires de France.

Hitler, A. (1971) *Mein Kampf,* trans. R. Mannheim. Boston: Houghton Mifflin.

Howe, E. (1982) *The Black Game: British Subversive Operations Against the Germans During the Second World War.* London: Michael Joseph.

Jackall, R. (Ed.) (1995) *Propaganda.* New York: New York University Press.

Knightley, P. (1975) *The First Casualty.* London: André Deutsch.

Lakoff, G. (2009) *The Political Mind.* New York: Penguin.

Lasswell, H. (1927) *Propaganda Technique in the World War.* New York: Alfred Knopf.

Miller, D. (1994) *Don't Mention the War: Northern Ireland, Propaganda and the Media.* London: Pluto Press.

Neander, J. and Marlin, R. (2010) "Media and Propaganda: The Northcliffe Press and the Corpse Factory Story of World War I." In R. Marlin (Ed.), *Global Media Journal – Canadian Edition,* 3 (2). http://www.gmj.uottawa.ca/1002/v3i2_neander%20 and%20marlin_e.html

Nobécourt, R. G. (1962) *Les Secrets de la propagande en France occupée.* Paris: Fayard.

Osgood, K. A. (2002) "Propaganda." In *Encyclopedia of American Foreign Policy.* The Gale Group, Inc. Encyclopedia.com, www.encyclopedia.com

Ponsonby, A. (1928) *Falsehood in Wartime.* London: George Allen and Unwin.

Pronay, N. and Spring, D. W. (1982) *Propaganda, Politics and Film, 1918–45.* London: Macmillan.

Rampton, S. and Stauber, J. (2003) *Weapons of Mass Deception: The Uses of Propaganda in Bush's War on Iraq.* New York: Jeremy P. Tarcher/Penguin.

Rhodes, A. (1976) *Propaganda: The Art of Persuasion: World War II.* New York: Chelsea House.

Ross, S. H. (1996) *Propaganda for War: How the United States Was Conditioned to Fight the Great War of 1914–1918.* Jefferson, NC: McFarland.

Saunders, M. L. and Taylor, P. (1982) *British Propaganda During the First World War, 1914–18.* Basingstoke: Macmillan.

Simpson, C. (1974) *Lusitania.* Harmondsworth: Penguin.

Taylor, R. (1979) *Film Propaganda: Soviet Russia and Nazi Germany.* London: Croom Helm.

Thomson, O. (1999) *Easily Led: A History of Propaganda.* Stroud: Sutton.

Walzer, M. (1977) *Just and Unjust Wars: A Moral Argument with Historical Illustrations.* New York: Basic Books.

Welch, D. (2002) *The Third Reich: Politics and Propaganda.* London: Routledge.

Whitton, J. B. and Larson, A. (1964) *Propaganda: Toward Disarmament in the War of Words.* Dobbs Ferry, NY: Oceana Publications.

Women and War

JENNIFER GAYLE MATHERS

Women have played vital and sometimes pivotal roles in wars throughout the twentieth century, although societies tend to be selective in their memories of the extent and significance of women's participation in war. Most societies – and many women as well – are comfortable with the notion that women are inherently peace-loving and that they only come into contact with war either when they oppose it or become its victims. Women's relationships with war are far more complex, however. Women perform a wide range of roles in times of conflict, from providing various forms of support

for war economies, militaries, and militias to serving as combatants and war leaders. It would not be
possible to wage war without the active involvement of women, but women's contributions to war
are often viewed as fundamentally different from
the wartime actions and responsibilities of men.
This is the main reason why women's involvement
in war has been relatively neglected by those who
study wars and why it tends to be overlooked or
downplayed by political leaders, popular culture,
and ordinary citizens, especially in times of peace.
The home and the family are often regarded as the
appropriate and natural sphere of women's activities and the place where they make their contribution to society, through bearing and raising children
and supporting their husbands, fathers, brothers,
and sons when they go to war. Wars and militaries,
in the same way, are usually seen as the places
where men demonstrate their masculinity by fighting to protect and defend their homeland and their
families. When wars break out, however, societies
often undergo a process of rediscovering and recognizing women's past wartime achievements. This
serves the dual purpose of identifying those roles
that might be appropriate for women to adopt in
the current or coming conflict, as well as giving
women permission to step outside their everyday
activities and take on less conventional roles for the
duration of the war.

Women in World War I

World War I was the first "total war" of modern
times and involved the mobilization of the civilian populations of the combatant countries for
the war effort. Certain activities were regarded as
suitable for women to engage in during wartime,
even though these included work in sectors, such
as heavy industry and the armed forces, which
had previously been exclusively or predominantly
male. In spite of the pressing need to involve
women in new roles, the fact that women were
heading households, wearing men's clothing,
earning their own wages, and engaging in male
behavior such as smoking and drinking in public
caused concerns about the possible breakdown of
the family, of traditional relations between men
and women, and of society itself.

Thousands of women filled the roles of nurse
or ambulance driver during World War I. The

need for large numbers of nurses led to the use of
volunteers to supplement the relatively small
numbers of professional civilian and military
nurses. In Britain, women joined organizations
such as the First Aid Nursing Yeomanry and the
Voluntary Aid Detachment. In other countries,
such as Germany, religious orders provided a supply of women who were willing to nurse the
wounded. Organizations such as the Red Cross
provided basic instruction in first aid and nursing
for those without medical training and permitted
middle-and upper-class women, who could
afford to work without wages, to gain firsthand
experience of the war. The introduction of so
many volunteers with rudimentary skills created
tensions with professional nurses, however.

While women in the higher socioeconomic
classes may have had the luxury of choosing
whether and how they would support their country's war effort, the nature and scope of most
other women's involvement in the war was dictated by sheer necessity. The large numbers of
working-class men who were serving in their
national armies meant that many families who
could least afford it found themselves suddenly
without their main – or only – source of regular
income and could expect little or no financial
support from the state. The war provided some
women with their first experience of paid employment, while it allowed others to move from low-
paid work such as domestic service into jobs in
munitions, which offered much higher wages
although it exposed them to dangerous chemicals
and industrial accidents. The movement of
increasing numbers of women into paid employment was a trend in all combatant countries, but
there were national variations. Britain had the
highest numbers of women entering the factories
during the war. In France the expansion was more
modest, largely because there was a higher pre-
war rate of women's employment in industry,
while in Germany the combination of govern-
ment-paid family allowances and strong trade
unions meant that the terms of employment
offered to women were not very attractive
(Grayzel 2002).

Most combatant countries were reluctant to
permit women to join their armed forces,
although some, such as France, employed women
to provide support services in a civilian capacity.
Late in the war, however, both Britain and the

United States formed separate women's services within their militaries. In Britain approximately 90,000 women served in Queen Mary's Army Auxiliary Corps, the Women's Royal Naval Services, and the Women's Royal Air Force. The United States allowed women to join the US Naval Reserve as Yeoman (F) or Yeomanettes and the US Marines Reserve as Marine (F) or Marinettes, although the number of American women serving in the armed forces was much smaller, around 34,000 including nurses. Efforts were made to ensure that the women soldiers would be able to retain their femininity. British women wore uniforms made of khaki, like their male counterparts, but they were decorated with flowers instead of the crowns, crosses, and bars that appeared on the men's uniforms (Noakes 2006). Both British and American women were placed in a narrow range of jobs, such as clerks, cooks, and drivers. Although some of these women were exposed to danger in the performance of their duties, there was no question of them serving in combat roles.

Things were very different on the Eastern Front, where there were several cases of women serving in uniform alongside men. Perhaps the most famous of these was Flora Sandes, a British woman who fought with the Serbian army. Although Sandes went to Serbia in order to be a nurse, once there she decided to support the Serbian cause by taking up arms. She was welcomed into the ranks, was wounded, decorated, and reached the rank of captain by the time she was demobilized. Another nurse-turned-soldier was Ecaterina Teodoroiu, who is venerated in Romania as a national heroine. Teodoroiu joined the Romanian army after her two brothers were killed in the war and during her military career was captured by enemy forces and escaped, although she later died in battle (Grayzel 2002).

One combatant country, Russia, experimented with recruiting women into all-female units with the intention of sending them into battle. Several such units were created after the February 1917 Revolution by the new provisional government in an effort to stem the flow of desertions from a war-weary army. Only one of these units saw service on the front lines: the First Russian Women's Battalion of Death led by Maria Bochkareva engaged German forces and took several hundred of them prisoner. Bochkareva believed that in order for women to become proper soldiers they needed to dress and act like men and so she not only imposed strict discipline on her soldiers but also banned girlish behavior such as giggling as well as makeup, long hair, and even toothbrushes (Stoff 2006).

The consequences of World War I for women were very mixed. In some respects it marked the entry of women into the realm of modern political citizenship: many countries extended the right to vote to women (or to certain women) during or shortly after the war, although women in France had to wait until 1944 for the vote. A select group of women also found it easier to enter professions such as law or medicine. For most women, however, the end of the war marked the end of opportunities to earn high wages in non-traditional areas. Many of the jobs women had occupied during the war disappeared along with the need to produce large numbers of armaments, and those women who had been employed by militaries were demobilized. Civilian employers preferred to give jobs to returning war veterans rather than to women. The war did, however, establish precedents for women's involvement in wartime that were built upon when war broke out again in 1939.

Women in World War II

Like World War I, World War II was a conflict in which civilian populations were mobilized in support of their country's war efforts. But while the distinction between the front lines and the rear was blurred in many previous wars, the enormous expansions of battle zones and the extensive use of aerial bombing by both Allied and Axis powers meant that civilians on both sides of the conflict had far greater direct exposure to the dangers of war than had previously been the case for those living outside the battle zones. Women were encouraged to do their part on the "home front" to help their countries win the war. This encompassed a wide variety of activities, from planting "victory gardens" to entering the work place to replace the men joining the armed forces. In the United States Rosie the Riveter became an iconic figure, celebrating the willingness of American women to undertake dirty and difficult jobs in industry in order to help win the war. Several combatant countries created land armies staffed predominantly or exclusively by women to minimize the disruption to agricultural production caused by the departure of male workers.

During World War II, many of the Allied countries recruited women into their armed forces to serve primarily areas such as clerical, medical, transport, and communications in order to release men for service in combat units. The United States revived and expanded the women's forces that were created in World War I and introduced the Women's Army Corps, the Navy Women's Reserve (WAVES or Women Accepted for Voluntary Emergency Service), the Marine Corps Women's Reserve, and the Coast Guard Women's Reserve. The Americans also formed the Women's Airforce Service Pilots who performed a range of flying duties within the United States, such as testing military aircraft and delivering planes to their destinations, in order to free male pilots for combat duties overseas. African American women struggled to be accepted into the armed forces: the navy refused to accept black women until near the end of the war and the Marine Corps refused to accept them until 1949. Those African American women who did manage to gain admittance found that their housing, meals, and social activities were completely segregated.

In Britain women served in the Auxiliary Territorial Service (ATS), the Women's Royal Naval Service (WRNS), and the WAAF (Women's Auxiliary Air Force). Many British women who served in uniform were volunteers, although Britain was one of the few Allied countries to conscript women for military service. Britain used its ATS women in anti-aircraft units, where they performed very well and helped to defend the country from attack from the air. The daughter of Prime Minister Winston Churchill served in one such unit. The regulations, however, prohibited women from firing the weapon, so every anti-aircraft unit had to include at least one man. This meant that the women were formally regarded as non-combatants and so were not eligible for the service medals awarded to their male colleagues or the higher wages paid to those performing combat service. Their non-combatant status did not, of course, protect them from injury or death while on duty, and ATS women suffered more than 300 casualties (Noakes 2006). Women

in Britain also served in units of the "Home Guard" which were tasked with civil defense responsibilities, although women's formal membership in these groups was resisted in the early years of the war.

Of all the combatant countries it was the Soviet Union that made the most extensive use of women in combat situations. The Soviets also conscripted women for military service and as many as a million women served in uniform, many in the front lines. In fact, in the USSR certain wartime roles became associated with women, such as sniper, anti-aircraft operator (Soviet women *were* permitted to pull the trigger), and pilot. Unlike the Americans, the Soviets permitted their women pilots to fly combat missions and three all-female regiments were created early in the war, including the 46th Guards Night Bomber Aviation Regiment, known as the "night witches" by the German troops whose nights were disrupted by their missions (Pennington 2001). More than 100,000 Soviet women received medals for their military service during the war, including 91 who were awarded the highest possible honor: Hero of the Soviet Union.

Some countries, by contrast, kept women out of their armed forces for as long as possible, in some cases for the duration of the war. The Vichy government in France discharged all women from the military in October 1940, just a few months after taking power. Some Frenchwomen served in military (including medical) roles outside France, for example in North Africa and Syria, while others who remained in Nazi-occupied France made important contributions to the war effort through their support for the Resistance. The leaders of Nazi Germany were also opposed to women doing "men's" jobs and encouraged German women to marry and stay at home to raise the next generation of Aryans. As the war continued and began to strain Germany's economic and military capability, however, the regime reluctantly accepted the necessity of employing some women in industry and even in women's auxiliaries in the armed forces. Distinctions between men and women in the military were maintained, though: members of the women's auxiliaries were regarded as civilians and were not permitted to fire weapons. In the final weeks of the war, Hitler did approve a plan to create a trial women's combat battalion inspired by the Soviets' use of women at the front, but Germany was defeated before the experiment could take place. In Japan women served in Home Guard units, where they learned to fire weapons, dig bomb shelters, and create booby traps on the beaches. In the summer of 1945, large numbers of civilian women were trained to use bamboo staves against attack from an invading enemy in an operation known as the Spirit of Three Million Spears. But although there is anecdotal evidence of individual Japanese women dressing as men and serving in combat roles or as kamikaze pilots, the Japanese military used women chiefly as nurses and as prostitutes. "Comfort women" was the euphemistic term for the women and teenage girls who were lured or abducted from the territories defeated by Japanese forces, such as China, the Philippines, Indonesia, and Korea, and forced to work in military brothels. As many as 200,000 women and girls were effectively enslaved in this way during the war and many died of venereal disease or were murdered by soldiers.

During World War II, women also worked for intelligence agencies and joined resistance movements and partisan groups. Women had been involved in espionage during World War I also – famously in the case of Mata Hari, the stage name of Dutch exotic dancer Gertrud Margarete Zelle, who was executed by the French for spying – but during World War II women's roles in intelligence expanded significantly. Women were employed extensively by intelligence agencies in clerical roles – for example, members of the WRNS worked the deciphering machines and provided secretarial support for the codebreakers at Bletchley Park in England. A small number of women became agents. Under the guidance of the British intelligence organization MI5, Nathalie Sergueiev (codename Treasure) played a role in the successful efforts to deceive German intelligence about the planned location of the D-Day landings. Both the British Special Operations Executive and the American Office of Strategic Services trained women agents and sent them into territories occupied by the Axis powers, where they worked with local resistance movements. Most of the women who supported resistance movements, however, did not have secret identities or live underground. Instead, they did their resistance work, such as carrying messages or transporting weapons, while engaging in typical female behavior such as shopping or visiting family members, which did not arouse the suspicions of enemy soldiers (Weitz 1995). Many Jewish women participated in resisting the Nazis, whether through the actions of youth groups in ghettos in central and eastern Europe, by joining armed partisan groups, or by sabotaging the armaments they were required to build for the German war effort in concentration camps. But the very invisibility that allowed many women to engage in resistance without being detected by the enemy during the war meant that their contributions were overlooked later when the work of resistance was celebrated publicly. Instead, the emphasis in published histories and official commemorations has been on activities that were carried out predominantly by men, such as occupying leadership roles, living underground, and fighting in armed groups, such as the Maquis. In France, for example, the highest honor given by the state for resistance activities, the *Compagnon de la Libération*, was awarded to 1,059 people, only six of whom were women. In some countries, though, women did join armed groups and fight, especially where there was an ideological commitment among the partisans to equality for men and women. In Yugoslavia women are estimated to have made up approximately 100,000 of the 800,000 who joined the National Liberation Army and some 25,000 of these women were killed in the fighting. The Greek National People's Liberation Army trained women to use weapons and some women commanded units. Women comprised about 10 percent of partisans in Italy and in Nazi-occupied territories of the Soviet Union. The Soviet Communist Party recruited and trained young people and sent them behind enemy lines to carry out a variety of sabotage and combat operations. Although there was pressure on female partisans to concentrate mainly or entirely on domestic roles within the camp, Soviet women did carry out missions and the lives and deaths of several female partisans were celebrated by the Soviet state in the years after the war (Furst 2000).

Women in Civil Wars and Wars of National Liberation

The tendency for peacetime norms governing the appropriate roles and behavior of women to be relaxed in times of war is especially pronounced in civil wars and wars of national liberation. Women's participation in such conflicts most frequently involves providing food, shelter, and other forms of support for male combatants, but in many cases women and girls also adopt non-traditional roles including combat roles. The fact that many armed groups involved in such conflicts have less formal structures than state militaries may make it easier for women to be accepted in a wider range of roles. Movements with an ideological commitment to equal rights for men and women are also often more open to women's active participation in fighting roles (and are particularly appealing to women), as are those groups that are under pressure to make use of all available forms of support.

In the Spanish Civil War (1936–1939) women briefly served as combatants but quickly returned to more traditional methods of supporting their sides' war efforts. In the first few weeks of the conflict, small numbers of Republican women enrolled in the militia to fight against the Fascists. These women, known as *milicianas*, were predominantly young and unmarried and while many were motivated by their political and ideological convictions, others were attracted by the prospect of participating in an exciting adventure. The wartime adventure of the *miliciana* only lasted for a few months, however, and even at the height of this phenomenon in the summer of 1936, fewer than 200 women are believed to have served at the front. Although the women in the militia received praise for their bravery and their contribution to the Republican cause from their male comrades and from foreign journalists, by the autumn of 1936 there was a growing consensus within Spanish society that women should support the war effort in more traditional ways. The slogan used by the Catalan Communist Party, "Men to the War Fronts, Women to the Homefront," encapsulates the predominant mood. This sentiment was apparently shared by many of the *milicianas* themselves, who began voluntarily leaving the militia on the grounds that they would be able to make a more significant contribution to the war in other ways (Nash 1993).

The conflict in Vietnam in the late twentieth century provides an excellent example of the ways that women participate in national liberation struggles and civil wars. Women living in both North and South Vietnam supported the communist forces (Vietminh, later the National Front for the Liberation of South Vietnam) in order to achieve the independence and reunification of their country and to expel foreign troops from their homeland. Many such women combined their wartime activities with their daily lives and their responsibilities to their homes and families. Women were well placed to spread the message of resistance within their communities and to encourage family and friends to join Ho Chi Minh's forces, as well as to gather and pass along information. Women played a key role in the defense of their villages, building fortifications, digging shelters, and participating in fighting enemy forces, including shooting down American planes and capturing the pilots. Women helped to build, maintain, and protect the network of paths and tunnels known as the Ho Chi Minh Trail, which became the vital supply line between North and South, as well as carrying supplies of food, weapons, and equipment that sustained the communist forces fighting in the South. The women who took a more active part in the fighting are known as the "long-haired warriors" or the "long-haired army" and became famous in Vietnam. These were predominantly young, unmarried women and teenage girls who had fewer domestic responsibilities and were more easily able to leave their homes and effectively become full-time soldiers (Taylor 1999). It is striking, however, that women soldiers were more commonly found in the local and regional guards than among the national forces, which, as time went on, became more formally organized, hierarchical, and in general came to resemble a state military rather than a revolutionary force.

It is not uncommon for revolutionary forces to use the image of the woman fighter, sometimes depicted as holding a rifle in one hand and a baby in the other, as a symbol of the unity of the people. The celebration of the woman revolutionary's participation in the conflict that defines the new nation can continue long after the fighting is over and the post-revolutionary state has been consolidated. But while such official recognition for women may appear empowering, it is often at odds with the realities of their lives under the new regime. While some post-revolutionary regimes do introduce greater equality for women, it is far more common for the aspirations of gender equality to remain unfulfilled and for women to discover that their lives are not significantly improved as a result of the conflict. Women who fought in such conflicts side by side with men often struggle to return to ordinary, peacetime life. In addition to suffering from the physical and emotional wounds of war as do their male counterparts, these women veterans can find themselves shunned by their communities for their unfeminine behavior during the conflict.

The glorified image of the woman revolutionary fighter may give the impression that women will have a significant presence in the ranks of the new state militaries that are constructed from the wartime armed groups, but this is rarely the case. Instead, women's roles as fighters are usually seen as exceptional and temporary. In Israel women are conscripted alongside men, partly in recognition of women's participation in the Haganah, the Jewish paramilitary organization operating during the British Mandate of Palestine, but it is much easier and more common for Israeli women to gain exemptions from service on the grounds of marital status, parenthood, and religious objections than for men. As a result, women only comprise about 30 percent of the force, rather than the 50 percent that one might expect. Those women who do enter the Israeli Defense Force (IDF) serve for shorter periods, both initially and in the reserves. And although in 1995 the IDF began to integrate women into some combat roles, they are still excluded from infantry, armor, and reconnaissance units and from positions that provide pathways to promotion to the highest ranks (Sasson-Levy 2007).

Many Nicaraguan women were attracted to the Sandinista National Liberation Front by the group's commitment to women's equality. Women made up approximately one third of those who fought for the Sandinistas against the US-supported Somoza regime during the 1960s and 1970s, and filled many leadership posts in the guerrilla army (Gonzalez-Perez 2008). In some respects, however, the Sandinistas took a very traditional approach to women's participation in war. The movement appealed to women to join the group in order to protect their children, and encouraged them to think of themselves as "patriotic wombs" whose primary responsibility was to raise children who would

fight for the cause. The picture for women in Nicaragua was also mixed after the Sandinistas' victory in 1979. Although the new regime gave many women the opportunity to enter the public sphere, most of the women who had served in the armed units were demobilized, and all-female units were created for the small numbers who remained.

Women's Opposition to War

Although many women support the war efforts of their own societies and many men campaign against war, there is a strong relationship between women and opposition to war both in history and in the public imagination. Some women peace activists embrace this identification of women with opposition to war and make use of it in their campaigns, for example by organizing women-only groups or activities or by emphasizing their position as women or as mothers in their appeals for peace to warring factions. One of the earliest examples of this association between women and opposition to war can be found in a cultural artifact of the ancient world: *Lysistrata*, the play by Aristophanes set during the Peloponnesian War, in which the women of Sparta and Athens refuse to perform their domestic duties (including having sexual relations with their husbands) until a ceasefire is declared. There have been several real-life examples of women adopting a similar strategy in their efforts to persuade the men of their communities to bring an end to conflict, including a sex strike declared in 1963 by women in what was then Rhodesia in order to halt political violence in that country.

In the late nineteenth and early twentieth centuries a number of women's peace organizations were founded in Europe and North America that campaigned for women's rights, particularly full citizenship and the right to vote, alongside their calls for international disarmament and an end to war. The outbreak of World War I divided the international movement for women's suffrage. Some women decided to suspend their anti-war activism in order to support their countries' war efforts, placing national loyalties above solidarity with fellow women of other nations and hoping that such a public demonstration of patriotism in wartime would strengthen the case for expanding women's civic rights when peace resumed. Others rejected this course of action and the logic of linking citizenship with militarism and war. Representatives of the latter came together in The Hague in 1915 to found the Women's International League for Peace and Freedom (WILPF), one of the most famous examples of women organizing for peace (Berkman 1990). One of the founding members was the American social reformer Jane Addams, who led a delegation to the United States to meet with President Woodrow Wilson. Wilson was so impressed with the anti-war resolutions put forward by WILPF that he adopted several of them in his own proposals to bring an end to World War I.

During the early 1980s, a series of women's peace camps was established in North America and Europe to protest against the nuclear arms race between the United States and the Soviet Union that was a central feature of the Cold War. The camp at Greenham Common in England was established in 1981 outside a Royal Air Force base where American cruise missiles were deployed. The women protesters were not persuaded by the arguments of the British and American governments that the presence of these weapons would deter a Soviet attack, believing instead that the deployment made conflict more likely and therefore increased the threat to themselves and their families. Tactics used by the women included surrounding the perimeter of the base and blocking its entrances with their bodies, as well as trespassing onto the facility and attempting to deface and damage the missiles themselves (Book and Kirk 1983).

In Northeast India a group known as the Naga Mothers launched a "shed no more blood" campaign in the mid-1990s in response to the violent conflict between Indian government forces and militant separatist factions, and on a number of occasions the women played a crucial role in the peace process (Manchanda 2001). In Russia the publicity generated by the Committee of Soldiers' Mothers about the widespread brutality in the armed forces significantly diminished society's tolerance of conscription. During Russia's conflict with Chechnya in 1994–1996, a group of mothers traveled to Chechnya under the Committee's auspices to search for their sons who were missing in action while serving in the Russian army. In exposing the incompetence of the Ministry of Defense and making common cause with grieving Chechen mothers, these Russian women helped to fuel public opposition to the war.

The anti-war campaign organized in Liberia by the Women in Peacebuilding Network (WIPNET) very effectively used the activists' identities as women to gain attention and ultimately victory for their cause. In 2003, WIPNET began a campaign of mass action for peace that mobilized women to protest against the continuation of the civil war that had begun in 1989 and created thousands of refugees and child soldiers. Wearing a uniform of white t-shirts to emphasize their unity of purpose as women and to eliminate visible signs of class or tribal differences, day after day the women occupied public spaces, sang, prayed, and called for peace. The persistence of the WIPNET women gained them a great deal of support in Liberia which, together with the moral authority they commanded as women and especially as mothers, ensured that the leaders of the warring factions could not ignore their demands for peace.

SEE ALSO: Chechnya Wars (1990s–Present); Peacekeeping; Spanish Civil War (1936–1939); Vietnam War (1959–1975); War and Sexuality; World War I: Eastern Front; World War II: Battle of Britain; World War II: Eastern Front; World War II: The Defeat and Occupation of France; World War II: War in Asia.

References

Berkman, J. (1990) "Feminism, War, and Peace Politics: The Case of World War I." In J. B. Elshtain and S. Tobias (Eds.), *Women, Militarism, and War: Essays in History, Politics and Social Theory*. Savage, MD: Rowman and Littlefield.

Book, A. and Kirk, G. (1983) *Greenham Women Everywhere: Dreams, Ideas and Actions from the Women's Peace Movement*. Boston: South End Press.

Furst, J. (2000) "Heroes, Lovers, Victims: Partisan Girls during the Great Fatherland War," *Minerva: Quarterly Report on Women and the Military*, 18 (3–4).

Gonzalez-Perez, M. (2008) *Women and Terrorism: Female Activity in Domestic and International Terror Groups*. New York: Routledge.

Grayzel, S. R. (2002) *Women and the First World War.* Harlow: Pearson Education.

Manchanda, R. (Ed.) (2001) *Women, War and Peace in South Asia: Beyond Victimhood to Agency.* New Delhi: Sage.

Nash, M. (1993) "Women in War: Milicianas and Armed Combat in Revolutionary Spain, 1936–1939," *International History Review,* 15 (2): 269–282.

Noakes, L. (2006) *Women in the British Army: War and the Gentle Sex 1907–1948.* New York: Routledge.

Pennington, R. (2001) *Wings, Women, and War: Soviet Airwomen in World War II Combat.* Lawrence: University Press of Kansas.

Sasson-Levy, O. (2007) "Contradictory Consequences of Mandatory Conscription: The Case of Women Secretaries in the Israeli Military," *Gender and Society,* 21 (4): 481–507.

Stoff, L. S. (2006) *They Fought for the Motherland: Russia's Women Soldiers in World War I and the Revolution.* Lawrence: University Press of Kansas.

Taylor, S. C. (1999) *Vietnamese Women at War: Fighting for Ho Chi Minh and the Revolution.* Lawrence: University Press of Kansas.

Weitz, M. C. (1995) *Sisters in the Resistance: How Women Fought to Free France 1940–1945.* New York: John Wiley & Sons, Inc.

Further Reading

Al-Ali, N. and Pratt, N. (Eds.) (2009) *Women and War in the Middle East: Transnational Perspectives.* New York: Zed Books.

Alison, M. H. (2009) *Women and Political Violence: Female Combatants in Ethno-National Conflict.* New York: Routledge.

Benedict, H. (2009) *The Lonely Soldier: The Private War of Women Serving in Iraq.* Boston: Beacon Press.

Burke, C. (2004) *Camp All-American, Hanoi Jane, and the High-and-Tight: Gender, Folklore, and Changing Military Culture.* Boston: Beacon Press.

Campbell, D. (1993) "Women in Combat: The World War II Experience in the United States, Great Britain, Germany, and the Soviet Union," *Journal of Military History,* 57: 301–323.

Cohn, C. (Ed.) (2013) *Women and Wars.* Cambridge, UK: Polity.

D'Amico, F. and Weinstein, L. (1999) *Gender Camouflage: Women and the US Military.* New York: New York University Press.

DeGroot, G. J. and Peniston-Bird, C. (Eds.) (2000) *A Soldier and a Woman: Sexual Integration in the Military.* Harlow: Pearson Education.

De Pauw, L. G. (1998) *Battle Cries and Lullabies: Women in War from Prehistory to the Present.* Norman: University of Oklahoma Press.

Enloe, C. (2000) *Maneuvers: The International Politics of Militarizing Women's Lives.* Berkeley: University of California Press.

Feinman, I. R. (2000) *Citizenship Rites: Feminist Soldiers and Feminist Antimilitarists.* New York: New York University Press.

Goldstein, J. S. (2001) *War and Gender: How Gender Shapes the War System and Vice Versa.* Cambridge: Cambridge University Press.

Hegarty, M. (2008) *Victory Girls, Khaki-Wackies and Patriotutes: The Regulation of Female Sexuality during World War II.* New York: New York University Press.

Higate, P. (2007) "Peacekeepers, Masculinities, and Sexual Exploitation," *Men and Masculinities,* 10 (1): 99–119.

Higonnet, M. R., Jenson, J., Michel, S., and Weitz, M. C. (Eds.) (1987) *Behind the Lines: Gender and the Two World Wars.* New Haven: Yale University Press.

Koonz, C. (1988) *Mothers in the Fatherland: Women, the Family and Nazi Politics.* London: Methuen.

Lee, J. (2008) "Sisterhood at the Front: Friendship, Comradeship, and the Feminine Appropriation of Military Heroism among World War I First Aid Nursing Yeomanry (FANY)," *Women's Studies International Forum,* 31 (1): 16–29.

Leiby, M. L. (2009) "Wartime Sexual Violence in Guatemala and Peru," *International Studies Quarterly,* 53 (2): 445–468.

Meyer, L. D. (1993) *Creating GI Jane: Sexuality and Power in the Women's Army Corps during World War II.* New York: Columbia University Press.

Moore, B. L. (1991) "African American Women in the US Military," *Armed Forces and Society,* 17 (3): 363–384.

Ness, C. D. (Ed.) (2008) *Female Terrorism and Militancy: Agency, Utility, and Organization.* London: Routledge.

Pankhurst, D. (Ed.) (2008) *Gendered Peace: Women's Struggles for Post-War Justice and Reconciliation.* London: Routledge.

Proctor, T. M. (2003) *Female Intelligence: Women and Espionage in the First World War.* New York: New York University Press.

Rehn, E. and Sirleaf, E. J. (2002) *Women, War and Peace: The Independent Experts' Assessment on the Impact of Armed Conflict on Women and Women's Roles in Peace-Building.* New York: UNIFEM.

Skaine, R. (1999) *Women at War: Gender Issues of Americans in Combat.* Jefferson, NC: McFarland.

Summerfield, P. and Peniston-Bird, C. (2007) *Contesting Home Defence: Men, Women and the Home Guard in Britain in the Second World War.* Manchester: Manchester University Press.

Tanaka, Y. (2002) *Japan's Comfort Women.* New York: Routledge.

Weber, C. D. (2008) "Navigating Gender Boundaries Inside and Outside the Wire," *Minerva Journal of Women and War*, 2 (2): 8–25.

Whitworth, S. (2004) *Men, Militarism and UN Peacekeeping: A Gendered Analysis*. Boulder: Lynne Rienner.

World War I: Afro-Asian Theaters

MATTHEW HUGHES

During World War I, fighting spread to Africa and Asia as Entente forces attacked the Ottoman (Turkish) Empire in the Middle East, and German colonies in Africa and the Far East (in China and the Pacific islands). The heaviest fighting was in the Middle East, where by 1918 British-led forces had occupied all of what would become, after the war, the states of Palestine, Transjordan, Syria, Lebanon, and Iraq. What remained of the Turkish rump of the Ottoman Empire became the Republic of Turkey in 1923. In Africa, the Belgians, British, and French invaded and occupied the German colonies of South-West Africa (Namibia), Togoland, Cameroons, and German East Africa (Tanganyika/Tanzania) (Strachan 2001; Anderson 2004; Paice 2008). In 1916, Portugal joined the war but her forces in Africa did little beyond defending Portugal's African colonies. In the Far East, Japan took German territory in China at Kiaochow (Jiaozhou in Pinyin spelling) and Australian, Japanese, and New Zealand forces did the same in the Pacific islands of Micronesia (the Mariana, Marshall, and Caroline islands), northern Papua New Guinea, Nauru, the northern Solomon islands, and Samoa. Before, during, and after these conquests, the attacking powers – the British and French but also local powers such as Australia, Japan, New Zealand, and South Africa – made a series of arrangements, commitments, and promises, both among themselves and with local peoples, regarding the future status of captured enemy territory, that shaped the post-war world.

The conquering powers wanted to establish traditional colonies in captured territory but under pressure – not least from the United States, opposed to European imperial expansion – they were forced to accept a new system of imperial control known as the League of Nations Mandates system. The Mandates threatened traditional desires for imperial expansion at the expense of the German and Ottoman empires. Britain proposed that colonies be graded by their stage of development into A, B, and C Mandates, a classification that was eventually adopted. A Mandates were to have eventual independence and were applied in the Middle East; B Mandates differed little in practice to the A Mandates and were applied in Africa (except South-West Africa); C Mandates were to be administered as integral parts of the territories of the mandatory power and were established in the Pacific and South-West Africa. The Mandates were empire in all but name. States such as Britain and France wanted to reduce the degree of international League of Nations control on the Mandates and aimed for (and achieved) *de facto* if not *de jure* imperial rule after the war.

Africa

Africa was dragged into World War I because it was almost completely controlled by European powers. While militarily Africa was a sideshow, there was fighting there as Entente armies conquered Germany's African colonies. Moreover, both sides mobilized Africa's resources and manpower, thus affecting the lives of vast numbers of Africans, and proving the value of empire as a strategic resource. Because of the difficulty of communications, the major military difficulty was not defeating the enemy but bringing him to battle. The war in Africa involved small company-sized columns operating with little artillery support, the machine gun being the heaviest weapon used in most engagements. Locally recruited black soldiers and porters (and some local white troops, notably from South Africa) played a vital part in these campaigns, supporting the Entente forces assaulting Togoland, Cameroons, South-West Africa, and East Africa. British Empire troops from India also fought in Africa.

Togoland was weakly defended and fell by the end of August 1914. The Germans had their most powerful wireless station at Kamina in Togoland and its loss severed radio communications with

Berlin. Victory in Cameroons was not so easy. On September 25, 1914, the British commander, C. M. Dobell, arrived off Cameroons in charge of an Anglo-French force of some 13,000 soldiers, largely locally recruited, the majority of whom were French. The port city of Duala fell without a shot fired on September 27, German forces retreating inland. Meanwhile, other British- and French-led troops advanced across the borders from Nigeria and French Equatorial Africa. This was not a war of large battles, and the major enemies were disease, poor communications, and rough terrain. Short of men, in March 1915 Dobell reported that he had only two battalions fit for service – poor health was a major problem – and so London signaled Dobell to sit on the defensive. Although in overall charge, Dobell had great difficulty controlling his diffuse force, divided as it was between France and Britain (and Belgium), four governor generals, six independent commanders in chief, and eight column commanders. The war dragged on into 1916, ending only when the last German forces retreated after a protracted and difficult campaign in neutral Spanish-run Muni. Britain and France then expanded their African empires by dividing Togoland and the Cameroons. Interestingly, German authorities in West Africa suggested to the British that they should arrange a local armistice to spare black Africans the unseemly spectacle of Europeans killing one another. It was rejected.

Meanwhile, South African forces attacked German South-West Africa. In September–October 1914 a revolt of pro-German white Afrikaners in South Africa, led by a South African officer, S. G. Maritz, delayed the invasion. Eventually, loyal South African forces quelled the revolt, after which they invaded South-West Africa by land and sea across the Orange River, from Lüderitz and from Walvis Bay. The last German forces surrendered at Tsumeb in July 1915. Casualties were low: more South Africans died in Maritz's revolt than in fighting the Germans. South Africa's conquest of South-West Africa was an example of local empire building: she remained in charge in the country until 1990.

The major campaign of the war in Africa was in German East Africa against askaris – local black troops commanded by Germans.

Under the overall command of Paul-Emil von Lettow-Vorbeck, 218 Europeans and 2,542 askaris were divided into some 21 companies, each with 150–200 askaris and 16–20 German officers and NCOs. A small police force plus the guns and crew of the German light cruiser SMS Königsberg – wrecked off East Africa at the start of the war – augmented this force. The Germans repulsed a bungled British-led Indian Expeditionary Force amphibious landing at Tanga (Anderson 2004). Thereafter, Lettow-Vorbeck kept his force in being until the war's end, tying down Entente troops that could have been elsewhere. He avoided major battles, instead invading at different times Portuguese Mozambique, Northern Rhodesia (Zambia), and British Nyasaland (Malawi). While Lettow-Vorbeck kept fighting until after the war in Europe was over, his command in East Africa is not as impressive as it might seem. His sustained defense of the colony only lasted from March 1916 to November 1917 – comparable in length to the German defense of the Cameroons – and he had no theory of guerrilla war, preferring classic German theories of envelopment and the decisive battle. On November 25, 1918, two weeks after the war had ended in Europe, the last German-led forces in East Africa surrendered at Abercorn in British-run Northern Rhodesia. Britain took charge of German East Africa after the war, with Belgium receiving the heavily populated northwestern part of German East Africa that would become Rwanda and Burundi. Finally, Portugal and Italy received some minor territorial gains: Kionga, a coastal strip of German East Africa added to Mozambique; the Juba Valley in East Africa and some minor adjustments along the Algeria–Libya border for Italy.

Some two million Africans served in the war as a whole, either as soldiers or laborers, and an estimated 200,000 died or were killed in action. Africa was used as a vast pool of manpower by the Entente, with hundreds of thousands of men from Belgian, British, French, German, and Portuguese Africa employed as porters and soldiers, many dying from disease, especially malaria (as did many white troops). The war dented European racial superiority in Africa. Recent scholarship on black Africans' experiences of the war is expanding our understanding of this traditionally neglected theater of combat (Morgan and Hawkins 2004; Vandervort 2009).

The Far East

While Germany was no danger to Japan, the latter – allied to Britain in 1902 – wanted the German-controlled territory of Kiaochow and its main port of Tsingtao (Qingdao in Pinyin spelling) on the Chinese coast. Japan also had designs on Germany's extensive island colonies in the Pacific. Britain was keen for Japan to join the war, assuming that her armed forces, especially her navy, would help in the fight against Germany. Indeed, there was even talk of Japanese troops being sent to support British forces fighting in the Middle East. Thus, the Entente promised support for Japan's claims to Kiaochow and to Germany's Pacific islands so as to get Japan into the war (Strachan 1998: 208). If Japan remained neutral and Britain concentrated on the war in Europe, Germany stood a reasonable chance of defending Tsingtao. Once Japan entered the war on August 23, 1914, German forces in the region were doomed. Without naval support, the German governor of Tsingtao, C. F. Meyer-Waldeck, prepared for a siege against 60,000 Japanese troops plus a small Anglo-Indian contingent. The first contact was on September 18, 1914; the main advance began on September 25 against the German garrison of 184 officers and 4,390 men. The Japanese employed a gradual siege warfare approach – also the innovative use of airpower for bombing – and, running out of ammunition, Meyer-Waldeck surrendered on November 7.

Australia, Japan, and New Zealand also occupied Germany's island colonies in the Pacific and New Guinea. There was little or no actual fighting. Japan took the Micronesian islands in October 1914 – the Marianas, Carolines, and Marshalls. To the south, New Zealand took German possessions to the east of longitude 170° while Australia got those to the west. This meant that by late November 1914 New Zealand had Samoa, while Australia had Germany's New Guinea possessions. In the Pacific, the equator became the dividing line between Japanese-controlled German islands to the north and Australian and New Zealand ones to the south.

While the collapse of Germany's empire in the Pacific freed up British and Entente forces for the war in Europe, it also represented the rise of Japan as a major regional power whose aim was to expand her empire across the Pacific and into China. Australia and New Zealand were also showing that they had regional power ambitions.

World War I was an opportunity for Japan to realize expansionist foreign policy aims. Her taking over Germany's central Pacific islands transformed the regional strategic position, as she now had a commanding position in Pacific waters, something that she had not had before. Japan's conquests of Germany's Pacific island colonies led the United States to transform its war plan against Japan to take into account the need to drive through these Japanese-controlled islands if there was a war between the two countries. This was known as US War Plan Orange and during World War II the former German central Pacific islands were the site of heavy fighting between US and Japanese forces (Miller 1991).

More immediately, in 1915, Japanese aggression manifested itself in a series of demands made against China (known as the 21 Demands) that tried to extend further Japanese influence over that country. The 21 Demands comprised five sections. These five sections demanded the following: (i) that Japan assume Germany's position in Kiaochow; (ii) that Manchuria and Mongolia be reserved to Japan for exploitation and colonization; (iii) that Japan control the main coal deposits of China; (iv) that the other powers be excluded from further territorial concessions; and (v) that Japan guide China's military, commercial, and financial affairs. The demand for control of Chinese affairs was dropped, partly at the insistence of the United States. After the Japanese threatened to attack China, Chinese president Yüan accepted the remainder of the demands. As a symbol of Japan's intent, she made (and presented to the Chinese) the 21 Demands on paper watermarked with warships and machine guns. Put simply, the 21 Demands, if fully implemented, "would have virtually turned China into a Japanese protectorate" (Macmillan 2001: 337).

The 21 Demands set a pattern for Japanese attempts at domination over China, but the treaties were not ratified by the Chinese legislature. The Japanese reinforced their claims in 1917 and forced a second agreement from the Chinese in 1918. At the Paris Peace Conference in 1919, Japan was awarded the German possessions in Kiaochow despite strong Chinese protest. China refused to sign the Versailles Treaty, and there were widespread anti-Japanese demonstrations across China (the May 4, 1919 movement). At the Washington Conference (1921–1922), Japan agreed to restore full sovereignty to China but this was only a stopgap measure as, in the 1930s, Japan renewed her aggression against China by occupying Manchuria and then launching an all-out invasion in 1937 that led to a Sino-Japanese war that lasted until 1945.

At the Paris peace talks in January 1919, the leaders of Australia, New Zealand, and South Africa tried to convince US President Woodrow Wilson that the Pacific islands (south of the equator) and southwestern Africa were so essential to the security of the British Empire that the Mandates system should not be applied to them. At the same time, Japan demanded the outright annexation of the northern Pacific islands and recognition of her acquisition of Germany's former rights in Kiaochow (Dockrill and Douglas Goold 1981: 64). On January 27, 1919, Wilson agreed to the establishment of Mandates but rejected Australasian, Japanese, and South African annexationist demands. The Australian prime minister, William Hughes, led the opposition to Wilson; Hughes only changed his position after British leader David Lloyd George and the South Africa statesman Jan Smuts convinced him that the Mandates were annexation in all but name. The Mandate system was then accepted by the British Empire. Annoyed at Hughes's opposition, Wilson delayed making a decision on the Mandates until May 1919 when Australian, Japanese, and New Zealand conquered territory was given to them as Mandates. Japan refused to agree to the Mandate system being extended to cover Kiaochow and threatened to walk out of the Paris talks, so a face-saving gesture was arranged whereby Japan promised that sovereignty of Kiaochow would eventually revert to China. But no time limit was imposed on this transaction. Without support from France and Britain, Wilson had been forced to accede to Japanese demands and when the Mandates were finally divided in May 1919, Japan got everything that she wanted (Macmillan 2001: 322, 325).

The Middle East

British or British Empire troops did most of the fighting in the Middle East during World War I; in some Middle Eastern campaigns, British or imperial troops did all of the fighting. The imperial troops came in the main from Australia, India, and New Zealand, but included small contingents from Canada, Rarotonga, South Africa, the West Indies, Hong Kong, and Singapore. In Mesopotamia (Iraq), Britain completely dominated the fighting, while in Palestine small token French and Italian units fought alongside the British (Barker 2009; Hughes 1999; Erickson 2001, 2007; Gardner 2004). On the Gallipoli Peninsula, France contributed about 12 percent of overall troop strength, with many of France's troops also coming from her empire (Hughes 2005). The exception was the Caucasian Front, one of the least-studied theaters of the war, where Russian forces drove back the Ottomans, before themselves collapsing in 1917 following the Russian Revolution, after which Ottoman forces invaded the Russian Caucasus area, taking the city of Baku in September 1918 (Allen and Muratoff 1953).

As the major military power in the Middle East, Britain dominated political events in the region during and after the war. Power on the ground meant power at the negotiating table. Britain restricted French and Italian military contributions and made sure that the British Army controlled the region by the war's end, thus greatly helping Britain's politicians and diplomats negotiating at the 1919 Paris Peace Conference for the future status of captured enemy territory.

The Middle East: Palestine

Before 1916, British-led forces in Egypt were on the defensive, keeping open the vital Suez Canal and repelling a Turkish attack across the canal in February 1915. In 1916, this strategy changed, as the British commander, General Archibald Murray, went on the offensive, pushing forces into the Sinai Peninsula toward Palestine. His advance met with several setbacks before halting at Gaza town in early 1917. In March and April 1917, Murray launched two assaults on Gaza, both of which the Turks comprehensively defeated. Murray's biggest achievement was to put in place the logistical infrastructure of railroads, roads, and water pipelines across the Sinai that would permit a British advance into Palestine.

After these defeats, Britain's war leader, Lloyd George, dismissed Murray. Looking for a fresh, dynamic commander for the Palestine theater, he chose General Edmund Allenby, a Western Front army commander. Allenby was unhappy at going to Palestine, seeing it as demotion, but independent command in a peripheral war theater would make his name. In 1919, he would become a field marshal and a viscount in recognition of his success in Palestine.

Allenby's arrival in Palestine in June 1917 revitalized the British-led force at Gaza, the Egyptian Expeditionary Force (EEF), whose morale had plummeted under Murray's command. Keen to push on in peripheral war theaters and to get Jerusalem as a Christmas present for the nation, Lloyd George sent Allenby the reinforcements he needed for a new offensive. Men and matériel poured into Palestine, augmenting Allenby's force to 10 divisions. It was a remarkable mixture of nationalities: as well as British troops, there were Australian, Indian, and New Zealand cavalry (or mounted) divisions, Jews, Arabs, and contingents from the British West Indies, the French Empire, and Italy.

Having reorganized the EEF into two infantry corps (20th and 21st) and a cavalry corps (Desert Mounted Corps), Allenby began the third battle of Gaza on October 31, 1917. While he had a massive preponderance of artillery, Allenby eschewed another assault on the heavily defended town of Gaza, in favor of a cavalry attack on the less well defended Beersheba at the eastern extremity of the Turkish lines. Allenby wanted to roll up the Turkish lines from the east. A dramatic Australian Light Horse cavalry charge took Beersheba on October 31. A few days later, the infantry assaulted Gaza. Forced to retire, the Turks retreated north toward Junction station, hoping to stabilize the line south of Jerusalem. Allenby kept up the pressure, rotating his units so that fresh infantry was available for the assault on Jerusalem. After much hard fighting west of Jerusalem, the Turks withdrew from the city on December 9, 1917. Two days later, Allenby walked through the Jaffa Gate into the city, read out a brief proclamation of martial law, and left. For the first time since 1187, Jerusalem was back in Christian hands. The world press made much of the capture, turning Allenby into a modern-day Crusader, and it was a welcome propaganda boost for the Entente powers at a difficult time in the war.

The need to send the bulk of his infantry and some of his cavalry to France as reinforcements after Germany's March 1918 "Ludendorff Offensives" scuppered Allenby's plans to renew the offensive into northern Palestine. Instead, he sent his men on two "Trans-Jordan" raids across the Jordan River, March–May 1918, to capture Amman, break the Hejaz railroad, and link up with the pro-British Hijazi Hashemite Arab forces of the Northern Arab Army (NAA) – attached to which was the British liaison officer T. E. Lawrence ("of Arabia") – that was fighting a guerrilla-style war against the Turks along the railroad. Both raids – the official nomenclature for multi-divisional attacks – failed, lowering British prestige among wavering Arab tribes in the region.

Allenby spent the summer of 1918 reorganizing and training the raw troops – mostly Indian – sent to replace the men who had gone to France. He was not able to go back on the offensive until September 19, 1918, when his force of 11 divisions (four cavalry, seven infantry) attacked along the coastal plain of Palestine. The result was tremendous. After an infantry and artillery assault, the Turkish line crumbled and three cavalry divisions (one Australian and two Indian) poured through the ruptured line to exploit the victory, while "Chaytor's force" of one division (a mix of Australians and New Zealanders) pushed on Amman. Typically cautious, Allenby did not anticipate the extent of the Turkish collapse. Once aware of this, he ordered an advance on Damascus and beyond. Damascus fell on October 1 to Indian and Australian mounted troops. The cavalry – suffering badly from endemic malaria – then pushed on to Aleppo. The infantry, meanwhile, advanced up the coast, taking Beirut on October 8. Helping the British from the desert flank, Arab troops of the NAA joined British forces at Dar'a (Deraa) for the push on Syria. The attacking force had passed by the ancient mound of Megiddo in northern Palestine, the site of many battles, and this lent its name to Allenby's final battle. The victory at the Battle of Megiddo should be set against the poor state of the Turks in Palestine in September 1918. The Turkish high command denuded Palestine of troops and the Turks in Palestine in September 1918 were in no state to offer a protracted defense.

Allenby's victories in 1917 and 1918 were a welcome alternative to the mud and misery of France. His cavalcade through the Holy Land captured the imagination of the British public, and gave Britain a commanding position when it came to negotiating the political settlement in the Middle East after the war, as British troops were in control of the whole region. While cavalry was used after 1918 in the Russian Civil War (and in World War II), the Palestine campaign was the real swansong of cavalry – the last time that it acted as a decisive weapon of war.

The Middle East: The Dardanelles and Gallipoli

In 1915, the Entente launched naval and land operations to knock the Ottoman Empire out of the war with a single decisive blow. The brainchild of the mercurial British First Lord of the Admiralty Winston Churchill, the initial plan took advantage of the Entente's naval superiority. Obsolescent Entente warships were to force the narrow Dardanelles Straits, after which warships could threaten the Turkish capital, Constantinople (Istanbul). An Anglo-French fleet assembled off the Gallipoli Peninsula and in February–March 1915 it fought its way up the Dardanelles, in the face of fixed and mobile Turkish and German shore batteries, three shore-mounted torpedo-tubes, and minefields. While the larger ships engaged the shore batteries, trawlers swept for mines. This was a slow process, with the capital ships retiring at dusk to return the following day. The naval assault made some progress, passing the outer forts, and was approaching the final set of defenses at the Chanak (Canakkale) narrows on March 18, 1915, when the ships hit a recently laid undetected minefield, a fiasco neatly described by Prior (2009). The French battleships *Bouvet* and *Gaulois* and the British *Ocean*, and the British battle cruisers *Irresistible* and *Inflexible*, were sunk, beached, or badly damaged. The British admiral, John de Robeck, withdrew his fleet and on March 22 he met Ian Hamilton, in charge of land forces,

to tell him that a naval assault was impossible. While bolder spirits pointed out how close they were to breaking through the Straits, with the Turks demoralized and low on ammunition, de Robeck's cautious counsel prevailed and the British and French planned an amphibious assault on the Gallipoli Peninsula.

For the difficult task of launching an amphibious assault, Hamilton had at his disposal six divisions: the British 29th Division and Royal Naval Division, two divisions of the Australian and New Zealand Army Corps (ANZAC), and two divisions of the French *Corps expéditionnaire d'Orient*. From March 22 to April 25 these units gathered on the island of Lemnos, while Hamilton devised a hasty plan to assault Gallipoli. With poor intelligence on the Turks, and eschewing a landing at Bulair to the north, Hamilton decided to make his main assault on the relatively flat tip of Cape Helles, with French forces making a diversionary landing at Kum Kale. The ANZACs would land at the one practicable landing site on the seaward side of the peninsula (Anzac Cove), while the 29th Division landed at five sites from west to east around Cape Helles: Y, X, W, V, and S beaches. Hamilton's plan made little sense. His force was inadequate to clear the peninsula, but without doing this, the Turkish shore forts remained to bar the naval route to Istanbul. A landing at Bulair might have cut off the peninsula, but Hamilton's force was too weak to advance across the rough terrain separating Bulair from Istanbul. Only if the Turks chose to do nothing could Hamilton succeed. But forewarned of the preparations for an amphibious assault the Turks busied themselves building defensive works on Gallipoli, under the command of a German general, Otto Liman von Sanders.

On April 25, the invasion armada gathered off Gallipoli. After a naval bombardment, steam-powered pinnaces towed ashore boats full of troops, casting them adrift close to the shore to be rowed to the beach. There was only one specialized landing ship with holes cut in her bows for landing troops, the old collier *River Clyde*, to be landed at V beach. The ANZAC troops got off to a bad start, landing a mile north of the planned landing site (for reasons which have never been properly explained) below steep, tangled bluffs. Unless the ANZACs could reach the crest of the high ground they ran the risk of being hemmed

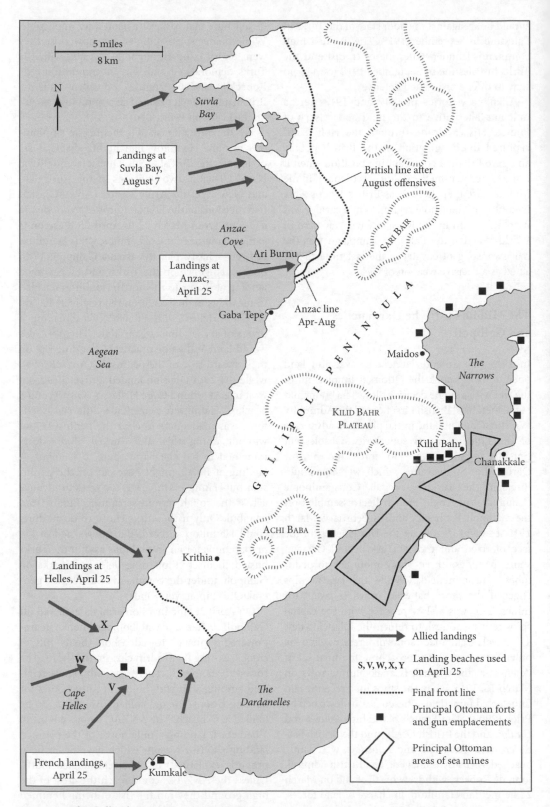

Map 16   The Gallipoli Campaign, 1915–1916.

in, dominated by an enemy holding the high ground. In the dense gullies above their landing site, the ANZACs proved unable to dominate the high ground and were forced to establish a shallow defensive perimeter overlooked by the enemy.

While the landings at Kum Kale and Y, X, and S beaches at Cape Helles were largely unopposed, at W and V beaches the few Turks present put up fierce resistance, raking the landing beaches with concentrated machine-gun fire with devastating results. But by the evening of the April 25, men were ashore at all the beaches. The Turks rushed the 19th Division to the area, under the command of Mustafa Kemal (Atatürk), to take up positions on the high ground. Helped by Hamilton's lack of offensive momentum, Kemal's men held the ANZACs, but were unable to push them off their beachhead. At Cape Helles, the 29th Division, reinforced by the French and the Royal Naval Division, attacked the village of Krithia, 4 miles inland. Soon Western Front-style trench deadlock set in as the British struggled unsuccessfully to take Krithia.

To break the deadlock, Hamilton devised a new amphibious assault at Suvla Bay for August 6/7 that would link up with an attack from Anzac Cove. But the new landing at Suvla Bay achieved little, a hastily assembled force led by Kemal blocking the dilatory British advance. After the Suvla Bay fiasco, Charles Monro replaced Hamilton and he recommended withdrawing from a lost battle. The British evacuated Suvla/Anzac Cove and Cape Helles (December 10, 1915–January 8, 1916) without a man being lost, the one successful part of the ill-fated campaign. Turkish casualties numbered some 300,000 to Entente losses of 265,000. Although their casualties were relatively slight, for the ANZACs, Gallipoli became a symbol of their coming of age as nations; for the Turks, Gallipoli was a material triumph that saved their country; for the British, it was one of the most poorly mounted and ineptly controlled operations in modern British military history.

The Middle East: Mesopotamia and the Caucasus

The war in Mesopotamia began in November 1914 when India sent a naval expedition to Basra to protect British interests – notably British-run oil facilities in southern Persia – at the head of the Persian (Arabian) Gulf. Under the control of the Indian government, British and Indian land forces at Basra pushed into southern Mesopotamia, using the Tigris and Euphrates rivers for their lines of advance. Initial success spurred the Mesopotamia force into thinking that it could capture Baghdad, 250 miles upriver (in a straight line) from Basra. Although London had reservations about an advance to Baghdad, it did nothing to stop the Mesopotamia force, under the overall command of General John Nixon, from advancing inland. Nixon's force was ill-equipped for the task ahead. He failed to build up the logistical infrastructure necessary for taking an army deep into hostile territory. Docking facilities at Basra were poor; thereafter, supply to the front relied on limited numbers of small riverboats that negotiated the Tigris and Euphrates rivers in the face of intense heat and a hostile local population. Nixon's failure to realize that the Mesopotamia campaign depended on proper logistical support ruined his operations. (Nixon retired on the grounds of ill-health in early 1916.)

Having captured An Nasiriyah and Al Amarah (May–July 1915), thus clearing southern Mesopotamia, in September 1915 the 6th Indian Division (with nine Indian and three British battalions), spearheading Charles Townshend's "Expeditionary Force D," raced up the Tigris. It defeated the Turks at Es Sinn just south of Al Kut (Kut al Amara) before advancing on Baghdad. The Turks checked Townshend's overextended force at the Battle of Ctesiphon, 19 miles south of Baghdad, in November 1915. Ctesiphon was the high-water mark of Townshend's advance, after which Townshend's exhausted men fell back on Al Kut, where a bend in the river offered a suitable defensive line. In early December, the Turks surrounded and invested Kut. The fear of losing the besieged 6th Division galvanized the British and Indian governments into deploying three new divisions to relieve Kut. But the chaotic supply arrangements in Mesopotamia delayed the deployment of this force, giving the Turks time to tighten their hold on Kut and build defensive works south of the town to block any relief force.

Townshend issued erroneous statements that he could only hold out for two months, forcing the hand of the relief force. In a series of bloody battles ending in April 1916, the Turks held the hastily assembled and deployed relief force. After suffering 23,000 casualties, the relief force got to within 7 miles of Kut but no further. Townshend failed to introduce rationing until it was too late, and on April 29, 1916, his starving garrison of some 10,000 men surrendered – 4,000 died in Turkish captivity. Townshend spent his time as a prisoner in some comfort, worried about his post-war reputation.

Kut was a tremendous blow to British imperial prestige and once the garrison surrendered the recriminations began. The lack of proper medical services was one area of concern, many wounded soldiers having suffered terribly because of this. The British government assumed direct control over the Mesopotamia campaign in the summer of 1916, appointing General (Frederick) Stanley Maude as commander in chief in the theater. By the autumn of 1916, Maude had at his disposal some 150,000 troops.

Maude's first task was to expand the port facilities at Basra and reorganize the logistical system that took supplies to the front line. Having revolutionized his supply lines, Maude set out to avenge the defeat at Kut, advancing against an outnumbered and outgunned enemy. He attacked in December 1916, defeating Turkish forces at Kut, before advancing on Baghdad, which he took on March 11, 1917. Maude died in November 1917 from cholera. His replacement was the commander of III Indian Corps in Mesopotamia, William Marshall, who launched a final offensive in October 1918 that cleared the Turks from all of northern Mesopotamia, capturing Mosul (and its potential oil reserves) on November 2, 1918.

The Caucasian Front is one of the least-studied campaigns of World War I. Russia and the Ottomans had traditionally clashed in the Caucasus, and so once the latter entered the war the two sides deployed troops for a confrontation in the mountainous mass of eastern Asia Minor. Keen to expand east into the Caucasus, the Ottoman minister of war, Enver Pasha, gathered two armies at Erzurum, which he personally led in an offensive toward Ardahan and Sarikamish (Sarikamiş). The result was a disastrous defeat in battle on December 29, 1914. At high altitude and in mid-winter, thousands of Turks died of cold in Enver's ill-fated expedition. The Russians repulsed another Turkish attack in the summer of 1915.

In 1916, the Russians counterattacked and were spectacularly successful. Fighting in harsh terrain and with limited logistical support, the Russians nevertheless took the fortress of Erzurum in February 1917. Using naval forces to support the advance, the Russians then switched the offensive to the coast, taking Trabzon in April 1917. The Russian Revolution in March 1917 put a halt to large-scale Russian operations. By then the Russians had pushed deep into eastern Turkey, past Lake Van (Van Gölü). The Bolshevik Revolution in November 1917 led to the collapse of Russian forces in the Caucasus as Russian soldiers deserted en masse. With Russia's collapse, Turkish forces reoccupied territory lost in 1916 and 1917 before launching an offensive into the Trans-Caucasus region, capturing the port of Baku in September 1918. In 1915 and 1916, as part of the war in the Caucasus region, the Ottomans targeted the local Christian Armenian population, whom they considered pro-Russian, and the resulting genocide by the Ottomans led to the deaths of around one million Armenians, a portent of the Nazis' Final Solution of World War II.

The Political Settlement in the Middle East

At the peace talks in Paris in 1919, the British extended their zone of control to include all of Palestine and Mosul in northern Iraq, the latter being important because of its potential oil deposits. After considerable diplomatic infighting, France eventually got Britain to agree to her having Lebanon and Syria and in 1922–1923 the League of Nations formally agreed that Britain should get Palestine, Transjordan, and Iraq as Class A Mandates, while France received Syria and Lebanon, also as A Mandates. What of the Arabs? Britain established and sponsored Arab regimes in Transjordan and Iraq led by the sons of the Hashemite Emir Husayn of the Hijaz, Abdullah and Faysal, but there was no Arab independence and this left a sense of betrayal, exacerbated by Britain's support for Jewish immigration to Palestine, exemplified in the

Balfour Declaration of November 1917. The Mandate document for Palestine also embodied the right of Jewish immigration. The status of Class A Mandates meant that these territories should have got independence fairly quickly, something that did not fully happen until after World War II (although Iraq got nominal independence in 1932).

Conclusion

In the Middle East, World War I saw the end of the Ottoman Empire and the rise of the modern Middle East boundary system based on the Mandate boundaries. Thus, the war established the basic political framework that has endured to this day, notwithstanding subsequent revolutions and coups in the 1950s and 1960s. In this sense, the war was significant. In Africa there were some minor boundary adjustments after the war, but the main change for Africa was the transfer of colonial power from one European power to another (or to South Africa in the case of German South-West Africa). It was not until the 1950s and 1960s that Africa threw off colonial rule. It was in the Pacific that World War I had the biggest immediate impact, as it signaled the continuing rise of Japanese power that would reach its apogee in the long war Japan fought in China and then with the United States from 1937 to 1945.

SEE ALSO: War Crimes; World War II: War in Asia.

References

Anderson, R. (2004) *The Forgotten Front: The East African Campaign, 1914–1918*. Stroud: Tempus.

Barker, A. J. (2009) *The First Iraq War*. London: Enigma.

Dockrill, M. and Douglas Goold, J. (1981) *Peace without Promise: Britain and the Peace Conference, 1919–23*. London: Batsford.

Erickson, E. (2001) *Ordered to Die: A History of the Ottoman Army in the First World War*. Westport, CT: Greenwood Press.

Erickson, E. (2007) *Ottoman Army Effectiveness in World War I: A Comparative Study*. London: Routledge.

Gardner, N. (2004) "Sepoys and the Siege of Kut-al-Amara, December 1915–April 1916," *War in History*, 11 (3): 307–326.

Hughes, M. (1999) *Allenby and British Strategy in the Middle East, 1917–19*. London: Frank Cass.

Hughes, M. (2005) "The French Army at Gallipoli," *Journal of the Royal United Services Institute*, 150 (3): 64–67.

Macmillan, M. (2001) *Peacemakers: The Paris Peace Conference of 1919 and Its Attempt to End War*. London: John Murray.

Miller, E. (1991) *War Plan Orange: The US Strategy to Defeat Japan, 1897–1945*. Annapolis: Naval Institute Press.

Morgan, P. and Hawkins, S. (Eds.) (2004) *Black Experience and the Empire*. Oxford: Oxford University Press.

Paice, E. (2008) *Tip and Run: The Untold Tragedy of the Great War in Africa*. London: Orion.

Prior, R. (2009) *Gallipoli: The End of the Myth*. New Haven: Yale University Press.

Strachan, H. (1998) *The Oxford Illustrated History of the First World War*. Oxford: Oxford University Press.

Strachan, H. (2001) *The First World War: Volume 1*. Oxford: Oxford University Press.

Vandervort, B. (2009) "New Light on the East African Theater of the Great War: A Review Essay of English-Language Sources." In S. Miller (Ed.) *Soldiers and Settlers in Africa, 1850–1918*. Leiden: Brill.

Further Reading

Allen, W. E. D. and Muratoff, P. (1953) *Caucasian Battlefields: A History of the War on the Turco-Caucasian Border, 1828–1921*. Cambridge: Cambridge University Press.

Bruce, A. (2003) *The Last Crusade: The Palestine Campaign in the First World War*. London: John Murray.

Carlyon, L. A. (2000) *Gallipoli*. Sydney: Pan Macmillan.

Crowder, M. (1985) "The First World War and Its Consequences." In A. Adu Boahen (Ed.), *General History of Africa, Volume 7: Africa Under Colonial Domination 1880–1935*. London: Heinemann.

Grainger, J. (2006) *The Battle for Palestine, 1917*. Woodbridge: Boydell.

Hickey, M. (1995) *Gallipoli*. London: John Murray.

Horne, J. (Ed.) (2010) *A Companion to World War I*. Oxford: Wiley-Blackwell.

James, R. R. (1999) *Gallipoli*. Parkville: Melbourne University Press.

Macleod, J. (2004) *Reconsidering Gallipoli*. Manchester: Manchester University Press.

Macleod, J. (Ed.) (2004) *Gallipoli: Making History*. London: Routledge.

Page, M. (Ed.) (1987) *Africa and the First World War*. London: Macmillan.

Steel, N. and Hart, P. (2002) *Defeat at Gallipoli*. London: Papermac.

Townshend, C. (2011) *Desert Hell: The British Invasion of Mesopotamia*. Cambridge, MA: Harvard University Press.

Travers, T. (2004) *Gallipoli*. Stroud: Tempus.

World War I: Eastern Front

RICHARD L. DINARDO

World War I was fought on many fronts, none more enormous than the Eastern Front. The geographic scale alone was mammoth, and the casualties inflicted and losses in equipment were equally immense. In its conduct, the war on the Eastern Front was quite different from that on the Western Front; while operations on the Western Front assumed a stationary character between the mobile campaigns of 1914 and the return of mobility in 1918, in the East the war remained mobile throughout, with large swaths of territory (and the people inhabiting them) changing hands on a regular basis. Finally, in a political sense, the war on the Eastern Front was far more destructive than that on the Western Front. Of the three political regimes that went to war on the Eastern Front in 1914, none remained by the end of 1918.

As on the Western Front, coalition warfare played an important part in the course of events on the Eastern Front. In the case of the Eastern Front, however, relations between Germany and Austria-Hungary were far less transparent than those between Britain and France. Relations between the chiefs of the general staffs of Germany and Austria-Hungary had gone through fair and foul stretches since the signing of the Dual Alliance in 1879. Helmuth von Moltke (the Elder) kept his Austro-Hungarian counterpart informed of various changes in German war planning during the 1880s. Communication was critical as plans called for Germany and Austria-Hungary to act in concert against Russia in the large salient that was Russian Poland. This state of affairs did not continue, however, after Moltke's retirement in 1888.

This was especially true after Alfred von Schlieffen became chief of the German General Staff in 1894. For a variety of reasons, Schlieffen shifted the focus of German war planning to the West. None of this was communicated to the Austro-Hungarians. In fact, by the last years of Schlieffen's tenure, contact between the two general staffs was limited to the most perfunctory forms of communication.

After Schlieffen's retirement in 1905, his successor, Helmuth von Moltke (the Younger), sought a relationship with his Austrian counterpart, Franz Baron Conrad von Hötzendorf, that was more open. Nonetheless, neither officer was fully honest with the other. While the Austro-Hungarians were aware of the Schlieffen Plan in its broad concept, they would not become fully informed of the details of the plan until after the onset of war. The Austro-Hungarians continued to believe that the Germans would launch an offensive into Poland even after Moltke had told Conrad in a 1913 letter that Austria's fate would be settled on the Seine River, not the Bug.

Russian war planning was based on the expectation that a war against Germany would be difficult at best, but that Austria-Hungary could be dealt with successfully. In any case, the Russians regarded it as imperative that an offensive be launched to aid France in a war with Germany. The one matter over which there was much concern was how quickly the Russian forces could be mobilized. In the actual event, Russian mobilization was executed far more quickly and effectively than the Germans thought possible.

As on the Western Front, all the war plans of the powers on the Eastern Front miscarried to one degree or another. *Stavka*, the Russian supreme headquarters headed by Grand Duke Nicholas (the uncle of Tsar Nicholas II), divided the forces mobilized between the Northwest Front facing Germany and the Southwest Front facing Austria-Hungary. The Russians took the offensive in both sectors.

The Northwest Front launched a two-pronged offensive into East Prussia with Pavel Rennenkampf's 1st Army and Alexander Samsonov's 2nd Army. The 1st Army defeated part of Max von Prittwitz's German 8th Army at Gumbinnen on August 20, 1914. The Russian victory triggered a crisis in the German high command (*Oberste Heeres Leitung*, or OHL). Moltke relieved Prittwitz and his chief of staff and replaced them with one of the most famous military marriages in German history, Colonel General Paul von Hindenburg and Colonel Erich Ludendorff.

Hindenburg and Ludendorff, arriving in East Prussia on August 23, 1914, quickly adopted a plan formulated by the German 8th Army staff.

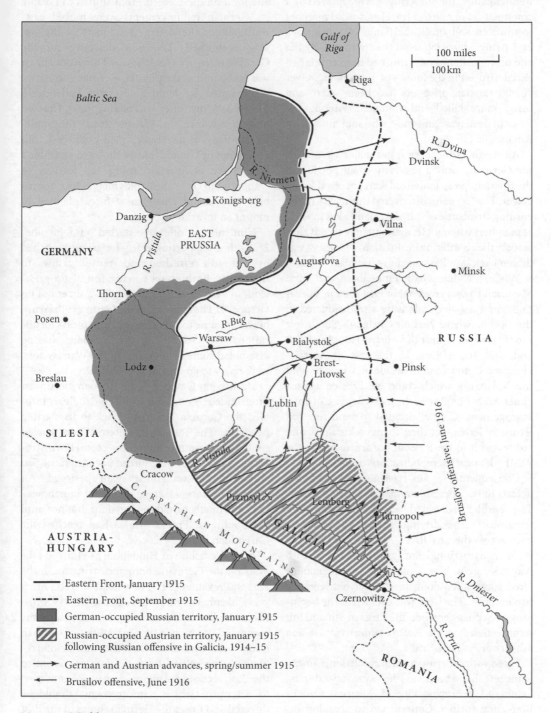

Baltic Sea

Gulf of Riga

100 miles
100 km

Riga

R. Dvina

Dvinsk

Königsberg

Danzig

EAST
PRUSSIA

R. Niemen

GERMANY

R. Vistula

Vilna

Augustova

Minsk

Thorn

R. Bug

Posen

Warsaw

Bialystok

RUSSIA

Lodz

Brest-
Litovsk

Pinsk

Breslau

Lublin

SILESIA

R. Vistula

Brusilov offensive, June 1916

Cracow

Przmsyl

Lemberg

GALICIA

Tarnopol

AUSTRIA-
HUNGARY

CARPATHIAN MOUNTAINS

R. Dniester

Czernowitz

R. Prut

ROMANIA

——— Eastern Front, January 1915

- - - - Eastern Front, September 1915

▨ German-occupied Russian territory, January 1915

▨ Russian-occupied Austrian territory, January 1915
following Russian offensive in Galicia, 1914–15

→ German and Austrian advances, spring/summer 1915

← Brusilov offensive, June 1916

Map 17 World War I: Eastern Front.

Leaving a screen of cavalry to confront Rennenkampf, the 8th Army was redeployed by a combination of railroad travel and rapid marches to threaten and attack the flanks of Samsonov's 2nd Army advancing from the southeast. By the end of August, the 2nd Army had been enveloped and destroyed in the forests of Tannenberg. Over 90,000 Russian prisoners had been taken, and many more killed and wounded. Among the Russian dead was Samsonov, who shot himself on August 30.

Although Tannenberg was a major victory for the Germans, only a relatively small portion of the Russian forces mobilized were involved in the defeat. The Germans discovered this reality in the ensuing first battle of the Masurian Lakes in early September, when a German attempt to advance across the border into Russian territory was driven back by a Russian counterattack.

While the dramas of Tannenberg and First Masurian Lakes played out in East Prussia, operations on a massive scale were also conducted in the South, where Nicholas Ivanov's Southwest Front faced off against the Austro-Hungarian 1st, 2nd, and 4th Armies. In the case of Austria-Hungary, Conrad had to decide on where to send the 2nd Army, which could be directed against either Serbia or Russia. In a classic case of mismanagement, Conrad decided to send the 2nd Army to Serbia, but then changed his mind and redirected it to the Russian border, reducing the Austro-Hungarian mobilization to chaos.

Consequently, Austria-Hungary suffered defeats in the opening campaigns on both fronts. The Serbians defeated an Austro-Hungarian invasion of Serbia, driving the Austro-Hungarians back across the Save River. At the same time, the main Austro-Hungarian armies clashed with Ivanov's forces. The contending forces encountered each other along the border between the two empires. The issue was decided at the beginning of September when the Russian 5th and 9th Armies defeated the Austro-Hungarian 1st and 4th Armies at Rava Ruska.

Faced with the prospect of annihilation, Conrad withdrew his armies to the west, abandoning Lemberg, the capital city of Austrian Galicia. Retreating further, Conrad had to abandon his headquarters, the fortress of Przemysl, leaving a strong garrison to withstand a siege. Fortunately for Conrad, the Russians were equally worn out.

As summer turned to autumn, the center of attention on the Eastern Front shifted to Poland. As German reinforcements were moved eastward, an additional army headquarters, the 9th, was established. The new objective for the German offensive was Warsaw. The major thrust was to be undertaken by the German 9th Army, commanded by Hindenburg and Ludendorff. The 9th Army, after assembling near Cracow, was to advance on Warsaw from the south. Interestingly, Hindenburg's plan coincided with an attempt by Grand Duke Nicholas to assemble a large force at Warsaw, using the fortress of Ivangorod to cover the deployment. Once assembled, the Grand Duke's new force planned to mount an invasion of Silesia.

Hindenburg's offensive started on September 28, with a supporting offensive being launched by Conrad's refreshed and refitted armies to the south. Both attacks made initial progress. Conrad's forces were able to relieve Przemysl on October 7. The left wing of the German 9th Army, however, came to a halt before Ivangorod's fortifications. By October 9, the Russians, having assembled some 60 divisions in the Warsaw area, were ready to go over to the offensive.

Starting on October 9, the Russian Northwest Front, aided by rain, snow, and cold, quickly tumbled the German 9th Army back to its starting positions. The Russian counteroffensive spread south to the Southwest Front's sector. The Austro-Hungarian armies were forced back from the San and Przemysl was once again besieged. An Austro-Hungarian tactical success at Limanowa–Lapanov finally halted the Russians, but not until the Southwest Front's armies had reached the Carpathian passes.

After the failure of Hindenburg's effort to take Warsaw, the German command structure in the East was revamped. The new head of OHL, Erich von Falkenhayn, who had replaced Moltke when his health had broken down, decided to alter the command situation in the East. With two German army headquarters in the field and reinforcements being shifted from the Western Front to the East, a coordinating mechanism was needed to determine where reinforcements should be directed and to get the German forces in the East to act in concert. This consideration led Falkenhayn to create *Oberbefehlshaber Ost* (*Ober Ost*), a headquarters that would now direct

German forces in the East. The organization was headed by Hindenburg. Command of the 9th Army went to August von Mackensen, who had distinguished himself as commander of the 17th Corps in the Tannenberg and Warsaw campaigns.

The 9th Army was redeployed to the area between Thorn and Posen. From there it was launched in an offensive against Lodz, the center of the textile industry in Russian Poland. After getting off to a good start on November 11, a Russian counterattack pushed Mackensen's forces back by late November. Undeterred, Mackensen went back over to the attack on December 1. By December 6, the 9th Army had defeated the Russian 1st and 2nd Armies and captured Lodz, an event that marked the effective end of active operations on the Eastern Front in 1914.

When the leaders of Germany and Austria-Hungary met at the beginning of 1915, they faced a situation on the Eastern Front that was fraught with danger. Although Germany was not mortally threatened, part of East Prussia was still occupied by Russian troops. Austria-Hungary's situation was far more serious. Przemysl was besieged by the Russian 11th Army. Worse, the Russian 3rd and 8th Armies were in the Carpathian passes. Any advance to the west would bring the Russians into the Hungarian Plain, an eventuality that could result in taking Austria-Hungary out of the war. A prolonged Russian presence in the Carpathians might also persuade Italy and Romania to join the Entente powers.

The meetings involving Falkenhayn and Conrad resulted in the broad outline of a plan for the Eastern Front. Conrad was to concentrate a force to launch a relief attack to lift the siege of Przemysl. Part of the Austro-Hungarian Front was to be covered by a small German force, the Süd Army. Falkenhayn's attempt to post Ludendorff as commander of the Süd Army foundered on the vehement opposition of Hindenburg. Instead, the appointment went to Alexander von Linsingen. Meanwhile, Mackensen's 9th Army was tasked to make a limited attack toward Warsaw. Ober Ost was to launch an offensive in its sector a bit later.

In the end, none of these operations produced the desired result. Mackensen's attack, launched at the end of January 1915, was marked by the employment of a generous amount of heavy artillery and poison gas. It only brought about limited gains. The freezing weather severely reduced the effectiveness of the gas.

Much less successful and far bloodier was Conrad's first attempt to relieve Przemysl. Like many of Conrad's plans, the expectations did not match realities. Although Conrad had concentrated some 175,000 men and 1,000 guns in the Austro-Hungarian 3rd Army, this force was too small to launch an enveloping attack along a front of almost 100 miles. Once the attack started on January 23, 1915, it ran into trouble quickly. Aside from determined Russian resistance, the elements had to be overcome as well. When the attack began, the temperature stood at minus 13 degrees Fahrenheit. Two weeks later, *Armeeoberkommando* (AOK) was reporting that the 3rd Army had suffered some 89,000 casualties, including a large but indeterminate number of losses from exposure and frostbite.

While Conrad's offensive petered out, *Ober Ost* put its plan in motion. Using three new reserve corps formed in Germany and a corps transferred from the Western Front, *Ober Ost* created the German 10th Army, under the command of Hermann von Eichhorn. Inserted into the front on the left flank of Otto von Below's 8th Army, the combined forces were launched in an attempt to encircle the Russian 10th Army in the Masurian Lakes region.

Launched on February 7, 1915, the offensive made some progress. Like their Austro-Hungarian counterparts in the Carpathians, German troops had to contend with temperatures so low that water in the jackets of machine guns froze, and heavy snow storms made the movement of guns and heavy equipment difficult. The Russians fought back hard, and several places changed hands a few times. Ultimately, after fighting both the Russians and the elements, the German forces drove the Russian 10th Army out of East Prussia. Parts of two Russian corps were encircled and destroyed in the Augustowo Forest. The Russians suffered 100,000 casualties and had a further 92,000 taken prisoner, about half of the 10th Army's original strength. The Germans captured almost 300 guns as well as hundreds of machine guns. The rest of the Russian 10th Army retreated successfully into Poland.

For all of its tactical success, the Second Masurian Lakes campaign was barren of strategic results. Although the Russians had been ejected from German territory (the last time enemy soldiers would be on German territory before the 1918 armistice), the original goal of the offensive, the destruction of the 10th Army, proved beyond German capabilities, especially in the harsh winter environment. The Russians brought up replacements to fill the 10th Army's depleted ranks, and the new 12th Army was assembled in the Northwest Front's sector. A German attempt to press into Poland was quickly brought to a halt by a Russian counterattack and driven back to the Russo-German border. Most importantly, the German offensive failed to draw significant Russian forces away from the Carpathian front.

Undeterred by the failure of his first attempt to relieve Przemysl, Conrad set about organizing a second. Shifting the weight of effort to the Austro-Hungarian 2nd Army, Conrad beefed up the army to more than a 100,000 men. The preparations were not completed, however, until the end of February. Thus Conrad's second offensive began just as the Second Masurian Lakes campaign was winding down. Launched late in February, Conrad's second Carpathian offensive failed for the same reasons his first one did. The terrain was awful, made worse by the weather, marked by heavy snowfalls followed by a thaw. Russian defenses in the Carpathians were stoutly constructed, well manned, and aggressive. Finally, the effectiveness of Austro-Hungarian artillery was severely limited by ammunition shortages.

Despite two failures in the Carpathians, Conrad scraped together his rapidly dwindling manpower for one more attempt to relieve Przemysl. This puny effort, mounted by only one corps, was quickly defeated by the Russians by March 21. A day later Przemysl surrendered, with over 100,000 prisoners and large amounts of equipment and guns falling into Russian hands. Buoyed by Przemysl's capture, Ivanov's Southwest Front went over to the offensive. The Austro-Hungarian front teetered precariously as the fighting extended into April. Finally, much to the relief of the Austro-Hungarians, the Russian offensive ground to a halt, worn down by Austro-Hungarian defenses, problematic terrain, logistical difficulties, and shortages of artillery ammunition.

Realizing the gravity of Austria-Hungary's situation, Falkenhayn, after consulting with OHL's liaison officer at AOK, August von Cramon, resolved to aid Germany's beleaguered ally. Falkenhayn informed Conrad via Cramon that four corps, roughly half of Germany's newly created strategic reserve, were to be sent to Galicia. An attack would be launched to pry the Russians out of the Carpathians.

Further details were settled when Falkenhayn and Conrad met on April 14, 1915, in Berlin. The force, designated as the German 11th Army, was to be inserted into the front between the Austro-Hungarian 3rd and 4th Armies, and attack on a narrow sector between Gorlice and Tarnow. While Conrad was relieved about the prospect of German help, the command arrangements were rankling for him. Command of the German 11th Army was entrusted to Mackensen, with the brilliant Hans von Seeckt as his chief of staff. Mackensen would also be able to exercise some degree of control over the Austro-Hungarian 4th Army. Most annoying to Conrad, Mackensen was subject to orders from either AOK or OHL, but any directive from Conrad had to be approved by Falkenhayn.

The attack was marked by a powerful concentration of artillery. Equally notable was the employment of heavy artillery on a large scale. Of the 11th Army's 400 guns, over one quarter were heavy, that is guns, howitzers, and mortars ranging from 150–305mm. The Austro-Hungarian 4th Army was also lavishly equipped with artillery. Unlike *Ober Ost*'s offensive in the Masurian Lakes region, no great encirclement was envisioned here. Instead, the German 11th and Austro-Hungarian 4th Armies planned simply to tear a hole in the Russian lines and then drive east. Seizure of the road junction of Zmigrod in the south end of the 11th Army's sector would effectively outflank the Russian forces in the Carpathians.

For their part, the Russians spent the early part of 1915 considering their options. *Stavka* convened a strategy conference at Siedlce on January 17, 1915. After considering several alternatives, including another invasion of East Prussia, Grand Duke Nicholas decided on an offensive using the soon to be created 12th Army aimed at Petrikau. A successful offensive might have put the Russians in a position potentially to extend the attack to recover Lodz. The Second Masurian Lakes campaign, however, disrupted this idea and the 12th

Army was deployed to shore up the Russian positions after the battle.

With the first option now moot, the Grand Duke decided to shift his efforts to the south. Buoyed by the surrender of Przemysl, the Grand Duke sought to have the Southwest Front renew its offensive to reach the Hungarian Plain, but that attack also had to wait until logistical challenges, especially shortages of artillery ammunition, were overcome.

Although both sides had offensive plans, the Central Powers struck first. The 11th Army was able to deploy without any notice by the Russians until April 26, when the presence of the new German force was detected. Mackensen's attack began on May 2, 1915. Ultimately, the German and Austro-Hungarian heavy artillery proved devastatingly effective against the field fortifications of General R. D. Radko-Dmitriev's Russian 3rd Army. After four days, the Germans and Austro-Hungarians had torn an enormous hole in the Russian lines and driven forward to a depth of about 10 miles.

With Zmigrod in German hands by May 6, the operational flank of the Russian forces in the Carpathians had been compromised. The rest of the Russian 3rd Army and the 8th Army began to draw back from the Carpathians, gingerly pursued by the Austro-Hungarian 3rd Army. Falkenhayn and Conrad decided to press forward. Mackensen's new objective was the San River, which would include the fortress of Przemysl.

The Germans and the Austro-Hungarians now pressed forward toward the river, reaching the San by the middle of May. After an operational pause, Mackensen and Seeckt directed their forces to the southeast, crossing the San and isolating Przemysl from the north. When the Austro-Hungarian 3rd Army failed to make significant progress against the Przemysl from the west, Mackensen and Seeckt decided to mount a siege type of operation against the northern side of Przemysl.

After another short operational pause to position heavy artillery and bring up the needed ammunition, the bombardment began on May 30. In two days the German and Austro-Hungarian heavy artillery made short work of several of the concrete forts that ringed Przemysl. The Bavarian 11th Division stormed into the rubble

on June 1. After a Russian counterattack was defeated early on June 2, the fortress commander, General Sergei Delvig, decided to abandon Przemysl. The Russian troops who could withdrew to the east, blowing up the last bridge over the San. Przemysl was back in the hands of the Austro-Hungarians.

Although a great victory had been achieved, it proved insufficient to prevent Italy from declaring war against Austria-Hungary. Mackensen's offensive, however, apparently dissuaded Romania from entering the war on the side of the Entente. Conrad, anxious to wreak vengeance on Italy for what he regarded as perfidious behavior, wanted to concentrate forces on the Italian front for an offensive. Falkenhayn, however, would have none of that, and made sure that Conrad would be unable to act on his desires. With the Italian option effectively closed, Conrad and Falkenhayn agreed to continue the attack in Galicia to recover the rest of the territory lost by Austria-Hungary in the opening year of the war.

After a pause to rebuild their ammunition stocks, bring the railroad forward, and conduct a thorough reconnaissance, Mackensen and Seeckt set June 13 as the date for the resumption of the offensive. In accordance with the agreement reached between Falkenhayn and Conrad, Mackensen now exercised operational command over both the Austro-Hungarian 4th and 2nd Armies, the latter taking over the sector formerly held by the 3rd Army.

Once launched, the "Mackensen Phalanx," as the Russian press described it, rolled forward relentlessly. The Russian Southwest Front's defenses crumbled under the pressure of Mackensen's offensive. Ivanov attempted to cobble together a defensive line west of Lemberg around the village of Grodek. The Grodek position, however, proved unable to withstand the power of German and Austro-Hungarian artillery. Once a penetration had been made, the Russian line crumbled quickly. By June 20, the Germans had seized a 25-mile stretch of the rail line between Lemberg and the communications hub Rava Russka. The Russians quickly evacuated Lemberg, which was retaken by the Austro-Hungarian 2nd Army on June 22, a major boost in morale for the beleaguered dual monarchy.

The months of May and June 1915 had completely reversed the situation on the Eastern

Front. The Russians had been driven back from the Carpathians, eliminating the threat to Austria-Hungary. Mackensen's forces had captured over 250,000 prisoners, plus enormous quantities of guns and equipment. Total Russian casualties in the Southwest Front for May 1915 alone were over 400,000. With the Russians in evident disarray, both Falkenhayn and Conrad agreed that offensive operations should continue, in the hope that Russia might be dealt a blow so severe that Tsar Nicholas II might be willing to make peace.

The next phase of operations on the Eastern Front originated with Seeckt. On June 15, 1915, Seeckt, secure in the knowledge that Lemberg would soon fall, wrote a lengthy appreciation of the situation. Regarding any further advance eastward by Army Group Mackensen as unproductive, Seeckt advocated another course of action. He proposed that Mackensen's army group turn north, attacking the southern end of the salient that constituted Russian Poland. This held the promise of a potentially decisive action against the Russian Northwest Front. Both Falkenhayn and Mackensen supported the concept and Conrad, with Falkenhayn's urging, soon came around as well. Falkenhayn also secured the support of Kaiser Wilhelm II.

Ober Ost had its ideas as well. Hindenburg and Ludendorff were still thinking in terms of encirclement on the largest scale possible. Ludendorff envisioned a giant pincer movement with the southern attack taking Brest-Litovsk, while *Ober Ost*'s offensive aimed at taking Kovno and then moving on a further 160 miles to Minsk. This would serve to sever the rail communications of all the Russian forces in Poland, effectively cutting them off.

The issue was definitively settled at a meeting held at Posen on July 2, 1915. Like any successful bureaucrat, Falkenhayn had effectively determined the outcome of the meeting before it even began. Much to the fury of Hindenburg and Ludendorff, the decision taken by Falkenhayn and endorsed by the Kaiser conformed to Falkenhayn's vision of operations. Mackensen's thrust would be supported by an offensive all along *Ober Ost*'s sector. The aim of the attack was to drive the Russians out of Poland, while using the extant logistical resources to support the offensive.

The great offensive began on July 13, 1915. Initial progress was slow, but after a week advances by the German 8th Army and Army Group Gallwitz (later redesignated as the 12th) on the Narew River alarmed *Stavka* sufficiently to authorize the Northwest Front to evacuate Warsaw. The Northwest Front, now headed by General Mikhail Alekseev, ordered the abandoning of the whole of the Polish salient. Large garrisons were left in some of the fortresses in Poland, most notably Novogeorgievsk (present-day Modlin).

Over the course of August 1915, the Russian position in Poland collapsed and the Germans and Austro-Hungarians filled the void. The fortresses in which the Russians had invested so much in resources before the war fell like overripe fruit from trees. Most notable was the fall of Novogeorgievsk. Subjected to bombardment by a German siege train commanded by Hans von Beseler, the conqueror of Antwerp, the fortress quickly collapsed. About 90,000 prisoners fell into German hands, along with some 30 general officers, on August 19, 1915 (DiNardo 2010: 130). Twenty thousand prisoners had been taken a day earlier when the antiquated fortress of Kovno fell. Meanwhile, Warsaw was entered by German forces without fanfare on August 5, 1915.

The great offensive began to wind down in late August. Brest-Litovsk was occupied by the Austro-Hungarian elements of the German 11th Army on August 26, 1915. Makensen's 11th Army was withdrawn from the front and sent to the Serbian border for that now-impending operation. Action continued on the flanks. *Ober Ost* launched a thrust into Lithuania, an operation urged by Ludendorff that fulfilled the dreams of pan-German nationalists. Meanwhile, Conrad, still seeking to score a victory for which Austria-Hungary alone could take credit, launched an ill-conceived effort against the Russian Southwest Front to take the remainder of Galicia and gain Ukrainian territory. The attack produced limited territorial gains accompanied by incommensurate casualties. When the Russians recaptured Lutsk, Falkenhayn had to dispatch two divisions to shore up the Austro-Hungarian front (Herwig 1997: 147).

For the Russians, the Central Powers' offensive into Poland brought about a crisis of command. The loss of Kovno in particular reflected very poorly on the *Stavka*'s conduct of the war. After its fall, Nicholas II dismissed his uncle, Grand Duke Nicholas, as head of *Stavka* and took over the direction of Russia's conduct of the war personally. In addition, the tsar made it clear that, despite the defeats suffered, Russia would remain in the war.

While 1915 had seen the Central Powers on the offensive on the Eastern Front, in 1916 the roles were reversed. With Germany undertaking its battle of attrition at Verdun and Austria-Hungary launching an offensive against Italy in the Trentino, the Central Powers planned simply to remain on the defensive. The Russians, however, had other ideas. Beseeched by the French to launch an offensive to relieve the pressure on Verdun, *Stavka*, now headed by Nicholas II but effectively run by General Mikhail Alexiev, decided to mount an attack. The Russian 2nd Army, headed by the elderly General V. V. Smirnov, was to attack in the Lake Narotch area toward Vilna. Supported by over 900 guns, the Russians planned to commit some 350,000 men to the attack against Eichhorn's heavily outnumbered German 10th Army.

The attack, launched on March 18, was a fiasco. The area chosen for the attack offered terrain that was unsuitable for offensive operations. The weather created conditions very much like those at the Second Masurian Lakes the year before, hindering the movement of troops, supplies, and equipment. The artillery bombardment proved ineffective, as there was almost no coordination between the artillery and the infantry. The guns were poorly organized and the requisite observation posts were lacking, so that the artillery was firing blindly.

With the artillery bombardment ineffective, the infantry struggled forward. At the cost of heavy casualties, the Russian 2nd Army was able to advance a few miles. Ultimately, the battle proved futile. The Russians suffered some 100,000 casualties, including an astonishing 12,000 deaths due to frostbite. Matters were made worse by the fact that the German 10th Army was able to fight off the attack mostly with its own resources. *Ober Ost* had to move only three divisions to Eichhorn's sector. No German troops were drawn from the Western Front. The Lake Narotch debacle reduced much of the Russian army to an utterly passive status.

If the late winter and early spring of 1916 saw the Russian army experience its worst failure, the late spring and summer saw the army achieve its greatest success since 1914. The Southwest Front, now commanded by Alexei Brusilov, arguably Russia's best field commander, launched an attack against the Austro-Hungarians in Volhynia. Brusilov had carefully husbanded his ammunition so that by June 1, 1916, he had about a million artillery shells at his disposal.

On June 4, Brusilov unleashed artillery and infantry of the Southwest Front against the Austro-Hungarian line. The attacks made uneven, if occasionally spectacular, progress. By the middle of June, the Russian 8th Army had driven the Austro-Hungarian 4th Army back to a depth of almost 50 miles and captured Lutsk. After the offensive stalled, Brusilov shifted the weight of his attack to the southern end of the line. The Austro-Hungarian 7th Army was shattered and the German Süd Army was forced to retreat as well. The Russians 9th Army was soon headed toward the Carpathian passes, a development that produced panic at AOK.

Unfortunately for the Russians, Brusilov was unable to sustain the momentum of the offensive. Instead of pressing on to the Carpathians, *Stavka* desired an attack on the key rail junction of Kovel, the capture of which would have split the front between German and Austro-Hungarian sectors. To accomplish this, an army composed of Guards units was created by *Stavka* and committed to the attack. In fact, the Russians had little if any chance of taking Kovel, as *Ober Ost* had dispatched strong forces to defend the town. The Guards Army suffered heavy casualties with little to show for its efforts.

The Brusilov offensive had run its course. Although the territorial gains were considerable, the Russians were not able to attain the positions they had the year before. In a sense, the Brusilov offensive destroyed two armies, those of Russia and Austria-Hungary. The losses inflicted on the Austro-Hungarian armies on the Eastern Front effectively eliminated the Austro-Hungarian army as a major military force. More worrisome to AOK was the increasing number of deserters. At the same time, the Russians suffered a staggering number of casualties in the Brusilov offensive, including as many as a million dead. The Brusilov offensive was the last major effort of the Imperial Russian Army.

Strategically, the Brusilov offensive had two important results. The first was the entry of Romania into the war on the side of the Entente. That in turn brought about the dismissal of Falkenhayn as the head of OHL, and his replacement by the "silent dictatorship" of the Hindenburg–Ludendorff duumvirate. Romania's entry into the war proved a considerable disappointment. Romania's forces were ill-suited and ill-prepared for a relatively mobile war. A well-conducted pair of thrusts was commanded by Falkenhayn, with the German 9th Army, and Mackensen, with a pick-up force with troops from every member of the Central Powers. By the end of 1917, the majority of Romania had been occupied by Germany and Austria-Hungary, a conquest that greatly enhanced Germany's ability to continue the war.

Hindenburg and Ludendorff were "easterners" who believed it was possible to knock Russia out of the war first, thus freeing up forces to defeat Britain and France later. This goal seemed within reach when the March 1917 revolution in Russia toppled the tsarist regime. With the abdication and exile of Nicholas II and the royal family to Siberia, power came into the hands of a shaky provisional government headed by Alexander Kerensky. Although the provisional government pledged to its Entente partners that Russia would remain committed to the war, it was abundantly clear that the Russian army was in no condition to undertake active operations. For their part, Hindenburg and Ludendorff sought to expedite the Russian collapse by facilitating the passage back to Russia of anti-war Bolshevik revolutionary Vladimir Lenin and a number of his associates from exile in Switzerland in April 1917.

In June 1917, in an effort to demonstrate Russia's willingness to fight and show that he had control of the military, Kerensky decided to commit the army to an offensive, and entrusted the task to Brusilov. Brusilov decided that the best place to attack was in eastern Galicia against the Austro-Hungarians, with the capture of Lemberg as the ultimate objective.

The attack on July 1, 1917, enjoyed some initial success against the Austro-Hungarians and gained ground. Swift German countermeasures, however, combined with the typical problems of continued logistical support, brought the offensive to a halt. A German and Austro-Hungarian counterattack triggered a rout of the Russian armies. The offensive spread north, and in September 1917 the Germans, experimenting with newly developed tactics, captured Riga. This was followed up in October 1917 by a hastily mounted German amphibious operation against the Baltic islands of Oesel, Moon, and Dagö. By the autumn of 1917, the only thing that stopped the German and Austro-Hungarian advance was the fact that the supply system had been outrun by the troops.

With the Russian army now in a state of dissolution and the provisional government's authority at a low ebb in the Russian capital of Petrograd (Nicholas II had changed the name from St Petersburg in 1914 because it sounded too German), Lenin and his collaborator Leon Trotsky saw their chance. The Bolshevik coup of November 6–7, 1917, toppled the provisional government, and Kerensky escaped to America. Once in power, Lenin moved immediately to take Russia out of the war. An armistice was reached in December 1917 and after negotiations that were in parts both confusing and tendentious, the Treaty of Brest-Litovsk was signed in March 1918. The terms of the treaty, however, lie beyond the scope of this chapter. World War I on the Eastern Front was over.

German (and to a lesser extent Austro-Hungarian) success and Russian failure can be ascribed to several factors. The first was the ability to improvise in situations. Tannenberg was an excellent example of this. Also the deployment of Mackensen's 11th Army to Galicia was improvised to a great degree, and certainly the landings in the Baltic islands were a masterpiece of improvisation. While the Russians could do well in set-piece scenarios, such as the Brusilov offensive, in fluid situations their command system broke down.

Another trump card for the Central Powers was their ability to employ heavy artillery. Both Germany and Austria-Hungary produced heavy artillery pieces of high quality. By 1915, these were available in sufficient quantity that they could be committed to field operations. At Gorlice, Mackensen used heavy artillery to smash the Russian 3rd Army's field fortifications. Thereafter, the conduct of the 1915 offensive was influenced by the availability of heavy guns and ammunition. Heavy artillery also rendered the huge Russian pre-war investment in fortresses in

Poland irrelevant. In 1914, the Russian fortress of Ivangorod played an important role in foiling Hindenburg's attempt to take Warsaw. In 1915, much more heavy artillery was available. Seeckt, with his experience on the Western Front and the breaking of the Belgian forts in 1914 under his belt, had no doubt that the German and Austro-Hungarian heavy guns would make short work of Przemysl's modern concrete fortifications. His expectations were well justified. In the ensuing phases of the campaign, German artillery easily smashed obsolescent fortresses such as Novogeorgievsk and Kovno.

The superiority of German and Austro-Hungarian artillery was enhanced by close cooperation with the infantry and by aerial reconnaissance. The Germans especially developed very close cooperation between the two branches, so that the infantry could count on artillery support when they needed it. This was rarely the case with the Russians. Too often the artillery, which regarded itself as superior, were willing to leave the infantry in the lurch.

Air superiority was critical to German success is several ways. First, control of the air allowed the Germans and Austro-Hungarians to conduct extensive aerial reconnaissance of Russian positions and rear areas. This was particularly important during the mobile phases of the campaign, as the ability of the Russians to employ swarms of Cossacks severely limited the effectiveness of German and Austro-Hungarian cavalry to conduct reconnaissance. The Germans also employed aerial reconnaissance to enhance the effectiveness of its heavy artillery. This was critically important in the opening phases of the Gorlice campaign and in operations against fortresses. Finally, the Germans used the Eastern Front as an area where they could test new types of aircraft.

The Eastern Front was perhaps the most dynamic theater of World War I. Operations there resulted in advances and retreats over hundreds of miles, and the slaughter of millions. It ended with the destruction of all three political entities that waged the war there, accompanied by millions of deaths from combat, starvation, and disease.

SEE ALSO: World War I: Southern Front; World War I: Western Front.

References

DiNardo, R. L. (2010) *Breakthrough: The Gorlice-Tarnow Campaign 1915*. Santa Barbara: Praeger.

Herwig, H. H. (1997) *The First World War: Germany and Austria-Hungary 1914–1918*. London: Arnold.

Further Reading

Barrett, M. B. (2008) *Operation Albion: The German Conquest of the Baltic Islands*. Bloomington: Indiana University Press.

Dowling, T. C. (2008) *The Brusilov Offensive*. Bloomington: Indiana University Press.

Golovine, N. (1931) *The Russian Army in the World War*. New Haven: Yale University Press.

Menning, B. W. (1999) *Bayonets before Bullets: The Imperial Russian Army, 1861–1914*. Bloomington: Indiana University Press.

Rothenberg, G. E. (1976) *The Army of Francis Joseph*. West Lafayette: Purdue University Press.

Showalter, D. E. (2004) *Tannenberg: Clash of Empires*. Dulles: Brassey's.

Stone, N. (1975) *The Eastern Front 1914–1917*. New York: Scribner's.

Tunstall, G. A. (2010) *Blood on the Snow: The Carpathian Winter War of 1915*. Lawrence: University Press of Kansas.

World War I: Southern Front

BRUCE VANDERVORT

From 1915 down to the end of World War I, some three million Italian soldiers, aided from time to time by British and French troops, fought a little over two million Austro-Hungarian soldiers, backed on occasion by German troops, over control of some of the most unforgiving real estate in western Europe. The war these soldiers waged took place along a 400-mile arc north of Venice, fronted over most of its distance by the highest mountains in Europe, the Dolomites and the Carnic and Julian Alps. But most of the battles were fought along the eastern sector of the front, the some 40-mile stretch along the Isonzo River, which flows to the Adriatic. Across the river, the land rises approximately 2,000 feet to two desolate plateaux, the Bainsizza, etched with steep ridges, and the Carso, or Karst, a treeless limestone waste in what is today Slovenia. The territory the two armies fought over was partially inhabited by Italians who had remained Austrian subjects after the nineteenth-century wars that led to the unification of Italy. Bringing this irredenta, or "unredeemed" region, under the Italian flag was a major reason for Italy's abandonment of its long-standing partnership in the Triple Alliance with Germany and Austria-Hungary and its entry into World War I in 1915 on the side of the Triple Entente.

From Neutrality to Intervention

When World War I began on July 28, 1914, Italy was not among its belligerents, despite over 35 years of participation in the Triple Alliance alongside Germany and Austria-Hungary. Officially, Italy could justify its declaration of neutrality on August 2, 1914, by noting that under the terms of the Triple Alliance it was only bound to come to the aid of its partners if they were attacked. Clearly, this was not the case. Besides, Austria, whose invasion of Serbia had brought on the war, was obliged by treaty to compensate Italy for any gain in the Balkans and had made no effort to do so.

However, although these lapses by its erstwhile allies provided convenient excuses for Italian inaction, there were other, probably more pertinent reasons for it. For one, in a secret agreement in 1902, Rome had promised France that if it came under attack from Germany, Italy would remain neutral. Neutrality was also favored by Italian public opinion, which was opposed to intervention and would remain so until as late as April 1915. Italy's Chamber of Deputies, dominated by partisans of the powerful former prime minister, Giovanni Giolitti, who had declared his opposition to intervention, also backed neutrality. And, while he was more equivocal than Giolitti, his longtime colleague in government, the foreign minister Antonino di San Giuliano, counseled restraint down to his death in October 1914. Finally, of all of Europe's great powers in 1914, Italy was the least prepared to go to war. Even the armed forces of backward Russia operated at a higher state of readiness in 1914 than those of Italy.

Decisions with regard to peace and war in Italy, however, were not dictated by public opinion or even by the representatives of the people gathered in parliament. Just as the decision to go to war against Turkey over Libya in 1911 was made by Giolitti and San Giuliano without prior consultation of the king, Victor Emmanuel III, who served as the head of the armed forces under Italy's Constitution, or the parliament, so the decision to intervene in World War I, when it came in the so-called Radiant May of 1915, was made by *noi due soli* ("we two alone"), as Prime Minister Antonio Salandra wrote to Sidney Sonnino, San Giuliano's successor as foreign minister. Both had come to support intervention, originally if for no other reason than that they feared the international and domestic consequences of neutrality. If the Central Powers won, they reasoned, an Austrian war of revenge, probably abetted by the Germans, was sure to follow. If, on the other hand, the Entente won, they believed Italy would be likely to face isolation, hostility, and contempt. Domestically, they thought that by standing aside the government would risk condemnation by all those who had been weaned on the notion of Italy as one of Europe's Great Powers. Thus, if the war brought a division of the spoils by the victors, a neutral Italy might emerge with clean hands but they would also be empty ones and Italian patriots were unlikely to forgive or forget such an outcome.

But if "we two alone" became more and more convinced that Italy had to abandon neutrality, it was nevertheless unclear for a time on which side they thought the Italians should take their place. For the whole of his long political career Salandra had been a staunch supporter of the Triple Alliance. Foreign Minister Sonnino, however, appears to have favored intervention on the side of the Entente. In the meantime, Italy's new army chief of staff, General Luigi Cadorna (1850–1928), went about making preparations for the possibility of entry into the war on the side of the Germans and Austrians until finally told differently by the prime minister in the spring of 1915, a dramatic indication of just how closely held the power of war-making was in early twentieth-century Italy.

It is easy with hindsight to view Italian entry into World War I on the side of the Entente as a foregone conclusion. Geography would have seemed to dictate it. Italy's long coastline was vulnerable to naval attack, and the British and French fleets dominated the Mediterranean. Her colonies would be largely defenseless against British and French invasion. Despite improved rail connections, around nine-tenths of Italy's imports still came by sea – much of the grain needed to make bread to keep the masses content; nearly all of the fertilizer its farmers required; two-thirds of its iron; 90 percent of its imported coal – and an Entente naval blockade would have reduced them to a trickle. But it appears that contingency trumped this rather obvious long-term perspective in the minds of Italy's leaders. Prime Minister Salandra began to come around to the idea of intervention on the side of the Entente after the German defeat at the First Battle of the Marne. When Foreign Minister Sonnino sat down to negotiate the secret Treaty of London of April 26, 1915, which brought Italy into the war on the side of the western allies, what seems to have been in the forefront of his and Salandra's minds was the expectation of successful operations by the British to knock Turkey out of the war (the Gallipoli landings) and of punishing attacks by Russian and Romanian armies on the Austrian rear that would facilitate a headlong war of movement by the Italian army against enemy troops in the "unredeemed" lands north and east of Venice. A powerful Italian thrust might also forestall further Austrian advances into the Balkans and render superfluous Serbian and Russian joint operations in the peninsula, another area on which Italy had long-standing designs. There was also the expectation, less sanguine perhaps, of an allied naval incursion into the Adriatic to smash the Austro-Hungarian navy and give Italy access to the Dalmatian coast south from Trieste.

The London pact promised Italy the "unredeemed" territories in the Tyrol; the port city of Trieste and its hinterland; the northern part of the Dalmatian coast and most of the islands along it; permanent occupation of the Dodecanese Islands off the Turkish coast, seized by Italy during the Turco-Italian War of 1911–1912; a protectorate over Albania; and an unspecified share of Germany's Asian and African empire. It was also agreed that the Vatican would not be permitted to take part in any eventual peace talks.

Italy's leaders, however, did not foresee a full-blooded integration of Italian arms into the war effort of the Entente. Salandra in particular was adamant that Italy's war should remain *guerra*

nostra ("our war"), a *piccola guerra* ("little war") focused squarely on exclusively Italian objectives, a policy that the prime minister did not hesitate to explain to the Italian public (and ultimately to Italy's Entente allies) as *sacro egoismo* ("holy self-ishness"). Having taken such a stance, it may seem surprising that the Italian leadership looked to their new allies for crucial help in besting the Austrians. There was some concern, in fact, that the British and French had embraced a kind of *sacro egoismo* of their own and were only interested in defeating Germany, that they saw the struggle against the Austro-Hungarian Empire as a secondary theater that could be left to the Russians and their Balkan allies – and now the Italians – to sort out. The British proved willing to provide a much needed war loan to enable Italy to beef up her military, but no British or French fleet ventured into the Adriatic to help the Italian navy defeat the Austrians and stake Italy's claim to the Dalmatian coast. And no British or French troops of any consequence were to be deployed to the southern front until the winter of 1917, in the wake of the catastrophic battlefield defeat at Caporetto, when it appeared that Italy had been knocked out of the war.

A preoccupation of the Italian government that interfered with its ability to give full attention to the war on its borders was the ongoing war in Libya against Arab irregulars, aided by Turkish officers and some Turkish regular troops. Indeed, this conflict, which was a continuation of the Turco-Italian War of 1911–1912 and which would rumble on virtually without let-up until 1932, deserves to be seen as a secondary theater of the Great War for Italy. In late 1914, there were 60,000 Italian troops in Libya. This number fell to 44,000 in 1915, as soldiers were diverted into service on the Southern Front, but the price was a withdrawal of Italian troops from the interior of Libya into enclaves on the coast. In the process, the army suffered another serious colonial defeat at Qasr Bu Hadi in April 1915, on the eve of the decision for intervention. Some 500 Italian troops were killed and there were heavy losses of weapons and ammunition. The Italian retreat to the coast opened the way for the Turks and the Sanusi brotherhood, which led the Arab struggle, to invade Egypt and the French colony of Chad, obliging the British and French to divert troops to North Africa to contain them.

The story of how the Italian war cabinet managed to inject Italy into World War I against the wishes of the majority of Italy's population is a complicated one. Since no one had declared war on Italy and no enemy was clamoring at the gates of the country, it was inevitable that domestic politics would play a major role in the battle over intervention. What most united the foes of neutrality was hatred of Giovanni Giolitti, the Left Liberal politician who had served as prime minister for most of the first decade of the twentieth century and who led the neutralist camp. For the nationalists, whose voices were loudest in favor of intervention, Giolitti was a monster of political opportunism and corruption, a closet bedfellow of socialism, and a faint-hearted patriot. Meanwhile, Benito Mussolini and his comrades of the revolutionary wing of socialism had the knives out for the former prime minister because of his success in forging alliances between his Left Liberals and moderate socialists. And Right Liberals like Salandra were more than happy to paint their old electoral foe and his fellow neutralists as stalking horses for Italy's foreign enemies. (It should also be noted that 30 out of Italy's 50 largest newspapers, led by the prestigious *Corriere della Sera* of Milan, supported intervention, as did a small clutch of liberal political figures, such as Gaetano Salvemini, who saw the war as a struggle for democracy and against Prussian militarism.)

No such thread bound together the anti-interventionist camp. Though Pope Benedict XV had come out against Italian participation in the war, he had stopped short of preaching civil disobedience to the faithful. Thus, despite widespread Catholic support for neutrality, there was no organized Catholic opposition as the Salandra government pushed a motion for war through the parliament in May 1915. Even more important, King Victor Emmanuel III let it be known that he believed that Italy's honor was at stake in its pledge to join the Entente and that repudiation of the Treaty of London might force him to abdicate. When Prime Minister Salandra offered to step down when opposition to ratification of the treaty materialized in the Chamber of Deputies, the king refused to accept his resignation. This announcement convinced Giolitti to retire from politics and, with this, the Left Liberal opposition to intervention collapsed. This left the mainstream of the

Socialist Party as the only neutralist faction still in the field. (The party's revolutionary left had departed on the eve of the war under the leadership of Benito Mussolini and was now ensconced in the interventionist camp, pleased at the discomfiture of the pied piper, Giolitti, and believing that the war could open the way to revolution, not a far-fetched notion, as developments elsewhere during the war would confirm.)

Enter Cadorna

The war policy of Salandra and Sonnino was knocked into a cocked hat almost immediately upon the official entry of Italy into the war on May 24, 1915. For as soon as war began, command of the army in the field devolved upon its chief of staff, General Luigi Cadorna, who had made a name for himself before the war for his fierce opposition to civilian control of the military. Cadorna had very definite ideas about the aims of Italy's war and how it should be fought and he carried on an unrelenting battle against efforts of the "politicians," be they cabinet officials or members of parliament, to interfere in "his war."

Cadorna scorned the notion of the *piccola guerra* pushed by Salandra, whose main focus would be the recovery of the "unredeemed" territory in Austrian hands. He saw himself as a generalissimo of the same stature as the Western Front army commanders, France's General Joseph Joffre and Britain's General Douglas Haig, and thus one of the architects of a unified grand strategy aimed at the defeat of the Central Powers. Cadorna's own strategy, as Italy went to war in 1915, was Napoleonic in its grandeur. He foresaw a quick offensive across the Isonzo River, then northeast toward Vienna, with perhaps a lunge to the southeast to snap up the prized port city of Trieste. The Italian offensive would be coordinated with attacks by the Russians and the Serbs, and, if they could be persuaded to enter the war, the Romanians. There was some logic in Cadorna's plan. An immediate offensive would catch the Austrians off guard and, if launched simultaneously with attacks by Italy's eastern allies, stood a good chance of making major gains if not the breakthrough Cadorna believed was possible. There were two substantial problems with the general's plan, however. First off, the anticipated Russian and Serbian assaults did not take place and the Romanians postponed a decision on entering the war. Secondly, and most importantly, Cadorna did not possess, and would not possess during the whole of his tenure at the head of Italy's armies, the kind of army that was capable of achieving the rapid breakthrough into Austrian territory he forecast.

Cadorna had around 600,000 frontline troops in place in 1915, but they were woefully ill-equipped for the sort of warfare that was taking shape on the Western Front and which would be replicated by his Austrian and German enemies. The Italian army had exhausted much of its stock of ammunition and weapons in the Turco-Italian War of 1911–1912 and still had not substantially replenished it by 1915. The high command had asked parliament for 551 million lire to replace used-up stocks but only 148 million had been furnished. The army had only 595 trucks in 1914 and relied on around 200,000 horses and other draft animals to transport men and matériel. Although the Italians had pioneered in the use of aircraft in combat roles in the war against the Turks in Libya, only 58 aircraft, all venerable French machines, were in Italian service in 1914.

The infantry that would do Italy's frontline fighting was poorly equipped for war in 1915. Only some 2,500 modern rifles were being produced per month in that year; a year later, the army had only around 112,000 rifles to supply its 228,000 conscripts. As a consequence, many infantrymen went into combat in 1915 carrying 1870-model single-shot rifles instead of the new 1891-model magazine-fed weapon. Machine guns also were in short supply. The Italian army in 1915 had just 618 machine guns and thus was able to field only two to six of the weapons per regiment as against two per battalion in the Austrian army. The artillery park of the Italian army was woefully small for a conflict in which the big guns were rapidly becoming the King of Battles. In 1915, the army possessed only 14 artillery batteries, most of them equipped with outdated pieces. An equally grave problem was the severe shortage of small arms ammunition and artillery shells. The situation would begin to improve in the summer of 1915 once the government declared a national mobilization of industry and appointed a competent officer, General

Alfredo Dallolio, as undersecretary for arms to oversee the production and acquisition of weapons and ammunition.

Dallolio carried out a thorough-going mobilization of industry and the industrial labor force. By war's end, his office had brought over 1,900 firms employing 903,000 workers under military control. Some 40 percent of the Italian labor force was formally militarized, many of the workers being obliged to wear uniforms. Labor force militarization meant a ban on strikes and the ability of workers to move from place to place without authorization. Labor contracts agreed prior to the war were suspended for the duration of the conflict. All workers in militarized factories were subject to the military penal code, including women and children. Labor did benefit, however, from implementation of uniform wage scales in the various branches of industry and a ten-hour day.

Frontline soldiers would have envied their blue-collar counterparts. Many of them failed to receive steel helmets until a year into the conflict. They fought year round in heavy woolen uniforms. Many ended up fighting barefoot because footwear contractors produced boots that disintegrated in the water and mud. The almost immediate descent into trench warfare on the Southern Front meant exposure to a variety of deadly diseases, including typhus, cholera, dysentery, malaria, and frostbite. Pay was derisory (half a lire a day) and often late. Mail came irregularly, but this may have been less of a problem since over half of the army's conscript soldiers were illiterate. The bright spot, at least when the supply system functioned regularly, was the rations the troops received. Many of the items provided were luxuries unknown to most of the peasant soldiers: meat, chocolate, tobacco (sometimes even cigars), and cognac.

The Italian army also was riven by class and regional biases. Over half of the common soldiers were originally *contadini* or peasants from the south of Italy. Many could not speak or understand the Tuscan dialect that had been made the standard for language instruction in Italian schools and was the language of command in the army. Most of them had never ventured outside their native Apulia or Basilicata before the war or had much of an idea of what was meant by "Italy." Fewer still could understand why they were being expected to fight and die for the rugged mountains and limestone barrens east of the Isonzo. Their situation was exacerbated by the fact that, while many of the army's junior officers might have come from the professional middle classes of southern cities, senior officers tended to be northerners, often nobles from the Piedmont, home of Italy's kings and known as the "Prussia" of Italy for the martinet qualities of its military men. Their commander, General Cadorna, was a quintessential example of the Piedmontese caste, a stern disciplinarian, as we will see, who did not hesitate to recommend revival of the ancient Roman form of punishment for soldiers who showed weakness in the face of the enemy: decimation, or the summary execution of every tenth man in the offending unit.

In time, as the war dragged on and casualties mounted, the peasant soldiers of Italy's frontline army began to imagine themselves in a new social universe. They were, they said, the *fessi* (literally, "dumb asses"), who inhabited the world of the trenches. Next came the *fissi*, the "fixed" or "immobile" ones, who never ventured near the front lines but shuffled papers in staff jobs out of artillery range. Then, further out still from the hellish center of this universe one found the *italiani* ("the Italians"), still men in uniform like the *fessi* but denizens of the rear areas where life was safe and warm. Last, numerous but proliferating at the remote edge of a nation at war were the *italianissimi* ("real Italians"), civilians who might work in factories or in offices that served the war effort, but who were unlikely to ever hear a shot fired in anger. All of these people, the *contadini*-in-arms came to believe, were *imboscati*, domestic enemies who lay in ambush to the rear, intent on sending them to the front and keeping them there to carry out ever more fruitless attacks on impregnable Austrian positions.

Battles of the Isonzo (1915–1917)

The Austro-Hungarian forces Cadorna's troops would face on the Southern Front were in some ways worse off than their Italian enemies. The Dual Monarchy's armies had already been at war for nearly a year when fighting began on the Italian front and had suffered massive losses in campaigns against Serbia and Russia. An estimated 42 percent of their mobilization strength had been killed, wounded, or captured. Their imperial or professional army component had been particularly hard-hit. By 1915, the Austro-Hungarian troops facing the Italians were almost all conscripts, part of the Landwehr/Honved second tier of the army. There was also a shortage of officers, in part due to the losses suffered in combat, but also a result of the inability to recruit in Germany as the Austrians traditionally had done; German officers now had an army of their own in which to serve. The Dual Monarchy's armies also faced a morale problem that the Italians did not. Some 44 percent of their soldiers were Slavs, who in turn comprised 66 percent of the infantry. There had already been some desertions of Slavic soldiers to the Russians and more disaffection was feared. Fortunately for Vienna, the chances of Slavs deserting to the Italians were probably minimized by knowledge among the troops of Italian designs on Dalmatia and the Balkans. Like its Italian counterpart, the Austro-Hungarian army had been starved of funds in the run-up to the war, with the result that its troops were short of arms and ammunition and its artillery park was badly outdated. And, again like the Italians, the Austrians lacked an industry readily capable of providing their armies with the matériel of modern warfare. However, they had one enormous advantage: their armies had command of the heights along the front. And they were led by a veteran soldier of talent, the Croat General Svetozar von Boroevic.

The Austrian advantage did not seem to unduly concern General Cadorna, the Italian commander. He had been for many years a firm believer in the superiority of shock over firepower on the battlefield and this faith did not desert him through three long years of relentless combat along the Isonzo front. In 1885, a young Cadorna had written a slim volume exalting the will-power of the infantryman as the crucial factor in modern war; exactly 30 years later, on the eve of Italian entry into the Great War, he wrote another book, called *Attacco frontale e ammaestramento tattico* ("Frontal Attack and Tactical Mastery"), which demonstrated that his ideas had not altered, despite nearly a year's worth of primary evidence of the superiority of the defense behind the firepower of machine guns and artillery on both the Western and Eastern fronts.

Cadorna knew that he did not have the kind of long-service professional army that advocates of the primacy of shock such as C. J. J. J. Ardant du Picq believed was necessary to carry the day against defensive firepower. He also knew that he was not at the head of an army with a tradition of victory. Whereas his German counterpart in 1915, Moltke the Younger, was in command of an ever-victorious army, he lamented, he, Cadorna, was "the leader of the army of Custoza and Adua." (Custoza was a lopsided victory of the Austrians over the army of the new Kingdom of Italy in 1866. Adua was a crushing defeat administered to an Italian expeditionary force in Ethiopia 30 years later.) Cadorna believed, and we have to think that this belief was in keeping with the ingrained predilections of this Piedmontese aristocrat, that the only way his peasant conscript army could achieve the breakthrough by frontal assault he sought was through the inculcation of unquestioning obedience. Severe punishment had to be meted out to those who refused to advance, who broke in the face of the enemy, who deserted, or who mutilated themselves to avoid combat. There was no need, he believed, for him or his officers to explain to this army of peasants why they were fighting. If there were to be any explanations, Cadorna thought that they were best left to the corps of chaplains he had brought into being. (Like its French counterpart, the Italian army officer corps of the era was dominated at its higher levels by members of the Masonic lodges. The devout Cadorna, who took a priest, Father Gemelle, as a close personal advisor, was a prominent exception to this tendency. Some have argued that Cadorna's clerical outlook, made manifest in his creation of a corps of chaplains and the preference he showed for like-minded officers, played a role in his dismissal in November 1917.)

Against the advice of his civilian superiors, Cadorna ordered an offensive against Austrian positions on the Isonzo River north of Venice shortly after Italy's entry into the war. The June 7–13 engagement was the first of eleven battles of the Isonzo and, like most of them, its centerpiece was a frontal assault that won little ground at a considerable loss of life. There would be four more offensives on the Isonzo front in 1915, on June 23–July 7; July 18–August 3; October 18–November 4; and finally November 10–December 2.

The first succeeded in crossing the Isonzo in some places but at the cost of 14,950 Italian casualties, as against 10,400 for the defenders. The second battle, a secondary aim of which was to relieve Austro-Hungarian pressure on the Russians, with the aid of a Serb offensive, cost the Italians 10,700 casualties, twice as many as those suffered by the Austro-Hungarians, and again failed to gain substantial ground. The third offensive, launched in part to support a French attack in Champagne, took place in a darkening theater context as the Germans intervened to smash the Montenegrins and Serbs in the Balkans and the Bulgarians entered the war on the side of the Central Powers. No ground changed hands. The final assault of 1915 took place in terrible winter weather and, while it achieved minor gains, casualties were extremely high. In the third and fourth battles of the Isonzo, the Italian troops took some 116,000 casualties, as against around 67,000 for the Austro-Hungarians.

The year 1916 would see five more Italian offensives along the Isonzo, punctuated by an Austro-Hungarian counteroffensive in mid-year that came close to breaking through the Italian defenses. Despite this, Cadorna's armies made their first important territorial gains in this second year of the war for the kingdom, albeit at the price of soaring casualty rates. One of the reasons for this relative success was a rapidly increasing supply of guns, trucks, aircraft, and, especially, artillery pieces. Another was that, as the Italian capacity to wage war grew, that of its Austro-Hungarian enemy declined. The burden of waging a two-front war was becoming unbearable. The problems of supply and troop morale, already serious in 1915, were becoming steadily more grave. By 1917, the Dual Monarchy would become a virtual ward of the German Reich, its economy, such as it was, integrated into that of its powerful and overbearing partner, its army buttressed, to a large extent replaced, on both its Eastern and Italian fronts by German troops.

Cadorna, however, would have insisted that the advances his armies had made were as much the result of his stern imposition of discipline as of the burgeoning supply of the tools of war or the weakness of his enemies. Before he was removed from command, Cadorna's tribunals would convict 170,000 men of various offenses and hand down 4,028 death sentences, of which 728 were carried out (some sources claim 834). If the number of soldiers shot out of hand for refusing or failing to advance is added to this figure, it is clear that the Italian army executed more of its men than any other during World War I. While few officers paid the ultimate price for their failings, Cadorna sacked them in droves during his tenure as chief of staff. In all, he dismissed 220 generals and 255 colonels, some for incompetence, others for refusing to enforce his draconian system of discipline. Nor did Cadorna welcome criticism from officers in his army. The future prophet of strategic airpower, then Colonel Giulio Douhet, for example, spent a year in a military prison for a private memo criticizing Cadorna's way of war which went astray and ended up on the general's desk. The sterner measures to stifle dissent within the officer corps and the increasingly harsh punishment meted out to the troops in the second year of the war reflected the realization by the high command that hopes for a breakthrough and a subsequent war of movement had faded, that what Italy's armies now faced was a grinding war of attrition.

The first Italian offensive of 1916, from March 6 to April 30, again struck Austro-Hungarian defenses on the Isonzo front. At a conference of Allied chiefs of staff in Chantilly, France, in December 1915, Cadorna had agreed to launch the offensive to relieve German pressure on the French at Verdun. Fought in deep mud and snow, the battle registered no significant gain despite some 50,000 Italian casualties. The Austro-Hungarian defenders suffered 40,000 casualties.

The painfully acquired Italian gains on the Isonzo were called into question in the spring of 1916 by an Austro-Hungarian counteroffensive, called the *Strafexpedition* ("punitive expedition") by its architect, the fanatically Italophobic Austrian army chief of staff, General Franz Conrad von Hoetzendorf. The blow fell on May 15, 1916, in the form of a drive southeast from Trent toward Venice, threatening to cut off the Italian 2nd and 3rd Armies on the Isonzo. The Austrians enjoyed complete surprise, as Cadorna, though warned by intelligence of an impending assault, believed nothing would happen. In spite of some gains, the counteroffensive had to be brought to a halt short of its objective on June 4, in order to shift troops to the Eastern Front to counter a Russian offensive in eastern Poland.

While one might have expected that blame for the setback would have driven Cadorna into retirement, it was in fact the prime minister, Antonio Salandra, who paid the price. His government was forced from office on June 10, 1916, and Salandra wandered in the Italian political wilderness for the rest of the war.

Interestingly, it was in the aftermath of the Strafexpedition that Italian forces registered their biggest gains so far in the war. The sixth battle of the Isonzo, on July 7–August 3, resulted in the capture of the city of Gorizia 5 km east of the Isonzo on the Italian border with present-day Slovenia. Although the battle resulted in over 51,000 Italian casualties, as opposed to just under 40,000 for the Austro-Hungarian defenders, Cadorna's armies had scored their first major victory of the war, giving a temporary fillip to the morale of both the public and the troops. One writer has called the capture of Gorizia "the first Italian victory against a foreign army in a major battle since the days of Rome."

Success at Gorizia emboldened the Italian high command to begin speculating once again about the possibility of a breakthrough of Austro-Hungarian lines, this time in the direction of the city of Trieste to the southeast. The tactics chosen to accomplish this were to be different, however. There was a shift from front-wide attacks to concentrated assaults on single targets, what the Italians were to call *spallate* ("pushes"). These assaults would be preceded by massive artillery preparation centered on the point to be "pushed," followed by a large-scale infantry assault. The seventh, eighth, and ninth battles of the Isonzo would stick to this scenario but with limited results. The Italian army improved its tactical position somewhat, but at the usual high cost: 77,000 casualties over the three offensives. Despite the meager gains, however, the Italians had managed to weaken the enemy defenders significantly, imposing 74,000 casualties on an army already heavily outnumbered and increasingly outgunned. The next two Italian offensives, the tenth and eleventh battles of the Isonzo, on May 12–18 and August 17–29, 1917, would push the Austro-Hungarian defenses to the breaking point and finally convince the Germans, hitherto preoccupied with the Western Front, to come to their aid. While the tenth battle produced little gain for the Italians, the eleventh opened the way to a seven-mile advance, the biggest so far by Allied armies. Although Italian losses in the two offensives had been exceptionally heavy – 112,000 casualties in the tenth battle and 143,000 in the eleventh – they could be borne, if only barely, as the available number of conscripts was beginning to dry up. Austria-Hungary, however, although it had suffered only some 185,000 casualties in the two offensives, now had to scrape the bottom of the barrel to find soldiers to send to the front and even these, it was clear, would not be enough.

Caporetto

Although the Italians, as we have seen, took far heavier casualties in the tenth and eleventh battles of the Isonzo than the Austro-Hungarian defenders, it was apparent to both Vienna and Berlin that the Habsburg army would not be able to hold on much longer. A German rescue was agreed, though with great reluctance on the part of the Austrians, who had been smarting from German arrogance and condescension virtually since the beginning of the war and believed, quite correctly, that if the joint assault now being planned was a success, the Germans would take all the credit. The blow that struck Italian lines at 2 a.m. on October 24, 1917, had been choreographed with great thoroughness. For over a month, troops, artillery, and aircraft from the Baltic front had moved into staging areas on the southern slopes of the Julian Alps. Wireless deception and massive air cover had thwarted Italian efforts to trace the troop movements. German troops who had no previous experience of mountain warfare trained assiduously and rehearsed the tactics that the German commander, General Otto von Below, believed would achieve a breakthrough into the Venetian plain and the ultimate destruction of the Italian army. The German troops would employ the new stormtroop assault tactics that had been tested at Verdun and used with great success in breaking the Russian siege of Riga earlier in the year. Known as the Hutier method because the Riga breakthrough had been accomplished by troops under the command of General Oskar von Hutier, stormtroop tactics called for short, sharp artillery barrages on enemy lines, behind which small elite units would penetrate into previously identified weak spots in enemy defenses, their gains to be exploited by so-called assault blocks – battalions of infantry with mortars and machine guns – following hard on their heels. (The German storm troopers should not be confused with the Italian *arditi* formations created in 1917, whose original purpose was similar, but who never really moved beyond raiding in small units, to destroy enemy matériel or to kill or capture enemy personnel. There is, however, a curious symmetry between the two groups in terms of their post-war history. As is well known, the Nazis applied the name "storm troopers" to their street-fighting auxiliaries. Likewise, former *arditi* emerged as prominent toughs in the Italian Fascist movement in the 1920s.)

The German–Austro-Hungarian attack along a 30-mile-wide sector of the Isonzo front was preceded by a murderous gas attack. The gas worked even better than usual in the fog-bound valleys in the mountains; their ineffective gas masks assured that thousands of Italian frontline infantrymen would be killed or incapacitated by the barrage. The gas attack was followed by a four-hour mortar bombardment against the front line of the Italian defenses, where most of their heavy weapons were concentrated, then the second line. Between 8 and 9 a.m. the German and Austro-Hungarian infantry jumped off, behind a creeping artillery barrage. Straight ahead of them lay the village of Caporetto, which would lend its name to the ensuing battle. Some units, such as the Württemberg Mountain Battalion of Lieutenant Erwin Rommel, advanced as far as 10 miles on the first day, taking thousands of prisoners.

A rout followed. By the end of October around one million men from the Italian 1st and 2nd Armies, some with their gear, some without, were in flight from the Isonzo to the Tagliamento River, miles to the south. In just four days all the gains made by Cadorna's armies at such tremendous cost over the two previous years had been forfeited. And the retreat continued, from the Tagliamento to the Piave River, 70 miles south of the Isonzo. Six French and five British divisions were rushed to the front to shore up the Italian defenses, but by this time the Austro-German offensive had lost momentum, as a shortage of motorized transport to bring forward supplies began to make itself felt. Indulgence of the troops in the captured wine stocks of the Italian army also seems to have slowed the advance. Still, for the Central Powers, the battle had been one of World War I's most spectacular operational successes. For the Italians, meanwhile, Caporetto had been one of the war's most staggering defeats. While the victors had suffered 65,000–70,000 casualties, the Italian army had lost 10,000 dead, 30,000 wounded, and 293,000 prisoners of war, as well as some 5,000 artillery pieces. More than 350,000 soldiers who had deserted or lost their units roamed the countryside. Only 33 of 65 Italian divisions had emerged intact from the debacle. Around 14,000 sq km of territory had been lost to the enemy, and an estimated one million Italian subjects had been abandoned.

Blame for the defeat began to be apportioned well before the Italian armies reached the Piave. General Cadorna, predictably, blamed the defeat on the "cowardice" of the soldiers of the 2nd Army. What his armies had suffered, he said, was not a military defeat but a "military strike," a massive dereliction of duty by soldiers whose loyalty had been undermined by civilian defeatists. While blaming the soldiers and the anti-war elements in the civilian population, who presumably had egged them on, won more than a few adherents in the aftermath of the catastrophe (one can still hear them today), there were not enough of them to save Luigi Cadorna, who was sacked on November 9.

The general's relief was not entirely due to domestic pressure. The same alarm that had prompted the dispatch of British and French troops to Italy in the wake of the Austro-German onslaught brought about an emergency conference of Allied heads of state at Rapallo in Italy to decide on measures to better coordinate action among the Entente armies. This was the conference that agreed formation of a Supreme War Council to achieve this purpose. The British and French chiefs of staff who attended the meeting, General William Robertson and General Ferdinand Foch, insisted that Allied support for Italy be made conditional on the sacking of Cadorna. The general was a "defeatist," they said, for having suggested that the defeat at Caporetto might force Italy to leave the war, and morale in the Italian army was not likely to be improved until he was replaced. Vittorio Orlando, the new Italian premier, reluctantly agreed to what he saw as heavy-handed dictation from Italy's allies.

Home from Rapallo, Orlando and his government picked a relatively unknown Neapolitan officer, General Armando Diaz (1861–1928), to succeed Cadorna. It proved to be a sound choice. Diaz, who had been operations chief on the Italian general staff until 1916, had as a frontline corps commander gone on to win and retain the respect of his men throughout the long ordeal on the Isonzo front. He now acted quickly to rebuild the shattered army and restore its morale. The troops were given longer periods of leave, better food, and more frequent rotation from the front lines to rest areas. They were also given promises intended to encourage them to persevere. The largely peasant army was told that after the war there would be land reform, a pledge that proved to be illusory.

A commission of inquiry was formed by the Italian Senate on December 6, 1918, to try to determine the causes of the Caporetto disaster and, in the process, to apportion the blame. Although members of the commission were eager to put the onus elsewhere than on the army itself, it is interesting to note that they rejected the argument that it was the undermining of the soldiers' morale by outside agitators that had led to the debacle. Some critics had laid the blame at the door of the pope, who in August 1917 had issued a "Papal Peace Note" in which he referred to the war as "useless slaughter." Others had made socialist deputy Claudio Treves the culprit for promising "not another winter in the trenches" in a speech in parliament on July 12, 1917. The commission said it could find no proof that these statements had resonated among the troops, or that there was any discernible impact on them of news of the March Revolution in Russia or of August 1917 food riots in Turin. What they did find was that the departed General Cadorna had been guilty of "egocentrism" and that his command style had not been conducive to the good morale of his troops. The inquiry also established that certain senior officers had made serious tactical mistakes that had weakened Italian defenses and permitted the German–Austro-Hungarian breakthrough. What the commission could not bring itself to do, however, was to identify and censure the senior officers most responsible for these lapses. The omission was particularly glaring with respect to the officer then and now considered to have been the most remiss: General Pietro Badoglio, commander of the 27th Corps.

Badoglio's troops were defending a key bridge across the Isonzo when the enemy attacked. Historian Vanda Wilcox has written that "due to a combination of slow responses, poor decision-making and inadequate planning, Badoglio lost his vital position and allowed the enemy to pass more or less unhindered up the valley of the Isonzo to take the town of Caporetto." The general had been accused of negligence after the battle by his superior officer, General Luigi Capello, but, rather than being sacked or demoted, he was promoted to vice-chief of staff of the army. This promotion, Wilcox believes, is what saved Badoglio from being censured by the commission of inquiry. Other writers have cited his Masonic connections. Among the points raised in defense of the latter thesis is the curious reversal of opinion by General Capello, who began as a severe critic of Badoglio in the wake of Caporetto and ended up defending him before the commission of inquiry; Capello was perhaps the highest-profile Mason in the Italian army. (Badoglio, of course, would go on to much greater things, becoming army chief of staff in 1924 and marshal of Italy in 1926, then commander of Italian forces during the conquest of Ethiopia in 1935–1936, and finally head of state in Italy, following the dismissal and arrest of Mussolini, from July 25, 1943, to June 9, 1944.)

Although one continues to read in popular histories of the Great War on the Southern Front that the Caporetto debacle was due to the spread of "defeatism" among the soldiers, the majority of academic historians who have studied the battle today are of the opinion that it was a military defeat brought about by faulty leadership on the Italian side and the superior tactics employed by the enemy. They note that the defeat came on the heels of one of the most significant gains made by the Italian army during the war, rendering it unlikely that defeatism would have been a key motivator.

Endgame: The "Miracle" of Vittorio Veneto

On October 24, 1918, the first anniversary of the catastrophe at Caporetto, the Italian army got its revenge, in the Battle of Vittorio Veneto, the last battle of the war on the Southern Front. The Austro-Hungarian army was completely destroyed in nine days of fighting. On November 3, an armistice was agreed at Villa Giusti, providing for the surrender of what remained on Italian soil of the armies of the Habsburg Empire, itself now crumbling beyond repair. The day before the armistice, the Italian army and navy occupied the city of Trieste, so as to avoid having to haggle over it in post-war negotiations.

Much hyperbole has attended this Italian victory, and this is no doubt understandable after so many years of sacrifice and heavy loss of blood and treasure. But, to begin with, Vittorio Veneto was not a specifically Italian victory, although it is probably true that the Italians could have prevailed unaided. British and French troops still in the country in the wake of Caporetto took part in the offensive and contributed to its success. The triumph at Vittorio Veneto was no "miracle," as was (and is) so often alleged. The Austro-Hungarian army on the other side of the Piave was in desperate straits by October 1918. If there was a miracle at Vittorio Veneto it was that an army so bereft of the tools of war, an army so nearly leaderless, indeed so nearly stateless, should have been able to fight on for nine days. The late British historian Edward Crankshaw described the Battle at Vittorio Veneto as "a superflous operation" (1963: 419).

> The monarchy existed no longer. There was only a monarch. The troops who tried to stem the attack belonged now to half a dozen countries, some of them already bound to the Entente. But the troops did not know this: they thought they were still Austrians, and they tried to fight back. There was nobody to tell them when to stop. In the end they simply broke away, not knowing where to go, or indeed where they belonged.

Some 400,000 of these leaderless men ended up as prisoners of war of the Italians, rounded up in the interim between the signing of the armistice and its implementation a day later. This unusual hiatus has led to controversy, permitting, for example, this malicious description of events by British historian A. J. P. Taylor (1965: 251):

> After the armistice had been signed, but before it came into force, the Italians emerged from behind the British and French troops, where they had been hiding, and captured hundreds of thousands of unarmed, unresisting Austro-Hungarian soldiers in the great "victory" of Vittorio Veneto – rare triumph of Italian arms.

Where hyperbole swirls most intensely around this final battle of the war on the Southern Front is in regard to its role in the winding down of the Great War as a whole and the German decision to seek an armistice. Some Italian historians, quoting General Erich Ludendorff, the German supreme army commander in 1918, have claimed it was the Austro-Hungarian collapse in Italy and the subsequent threat of an Italian offensive north into Bavaria that convinced the Germans to lay down their arms. Whether or not the Italian army could have or would have mounted an offensive across the Alps into southern Germany is one of those historical questions for which there probably is no answer. But those historians who take Ludendorff as their source need to recall how far the general was prepared to go to seek out scapegoats for Germany's defeat. Blame could be fastened anywhere so long as it was not on the German army. The army had not been defeated, according to Ludendorff, it had been "stabbed in the back," by socialists, Jews, and, yes, the feckless Austrians.

The Italian Navy and Air Service in the Great War

At the time of the Turco-Italian War of 1911–1912, Italy boasted the third largest navy in Europe. During World War I it enjoyed a significant edge in surface vessels over its Austro-Hungarian rival (211 ships to 38) in the Adriatic theater, the arena most important to Italy. Because of this disparity, the Austro-Hungarian navy only rarely ventured out of port, making the war at sea in the Adriatic an affair of mine-laying, fire support for land operations,

anti-submarine warfare, and raids on enemy bases. For the latter kind of operations the Italians developed a fleet of torpedo boats, whose Italian acronym was MAS, considered the prototype of the PT-boat of World War II fame. These boats, some 15–16 meters in length, displacing up to 16 tons, and making 22–25 knots, carried machine guns, torpedoes, depth charges, mines, and a crew of eight. On June 10, 1918, two of them sank the *Szent István*, an Austrian dreadnought. Another naval weapon developed by the Italians was a slow-moving torpedo designed to be manipulated by frogmen. On November 1, 1918, the *Viribus Unitis*, a battleship of the new Yugoslav navy, was sunk by one of these units. The Italian navy and its allies had less success in defending Italy's merchant marine from enemy attack. Some 955,000 tons of Italian shipping were lost from 1915 to war's end, almost 50 percent of the tonnage of the merchant marine. This had a considerable negative impact on imports, including coal and oil, the shortage of which put a crimp in some of Italy's naval operations.

The Italian army air service expanded considerably during the war, from just 58 aircraft in 1914 to 1,683 in 49 squadrons in 1918. Whereas most of the aircraft in use early in the war were foreign-built, an Italian aircraft industry developed quickly and by war's end was supplying most of the planes being flown by the army and navy air services. Prominent among the aircraft produced was the Caproni 1–5 series of three-engine biplanes whose prototype had been designed and built by Giulio Douhet and which were manufactured in the Milan factories of industrialist Gianni Caproni. The only bombers specifically designed for strategic missions produced during the war, the craft were employed not only by the Italians, but by the Americans, British, and French, for long-range reconnaissance work and to bomb enemy rear areas. Toward the end of the war, a flight of Caproni bombers dropped leaflets on Vienna. Among the pilots of these bombers was New York congressman (and future mayor of New York City) Fiorello La Guardia, seconded to the Italian air force from the US Army Air Service. It was the experience of employing the Caproni bombers on long-range missions that would convince Giulio Douhet of the viability of strategic airpower. Douhet survived his year in prison for criticizing General Cadorna, noted above, and ended the war as chief of the Italian Air Service.

Post-War

The post-war "wish list" of Italian statesmen and soldiers had grown longer as the list of casualties on the Isonzo had lengthened. The question that would have been foremost in the minds of these worthies as the war came to an end was: What can be gained from this struggle that will recompense the deaths of 461,491 soldiers, sailors, and airmen and the wounding of yet another 953,886 and the languishing in prisoner of war camps of still another 600,000 (and where upwards of 100,000 had died of disease and malnutrition)? There were promises of a better life, to be sure: land to the tiller, higher wages, better working conditions, expanded civil rights. However, for many of the leaders who had directed the war and now would be called upon to shape the peace, at the great conference in Paris where all would be put to rights, the war had not been about bringing forth a better life for Italians but a greater Italy, not just in terms of the victories it had won on the battlefield but in terms of the new lands it would bring under the Italian flag. Meanwhile, raging inflation set against a decline in real wages, the difficulties of making a transition from a wartime economy to a peacetime economy, and the relative impoverishment of the Italian countryside during the war had created an explosive social situation that could only be exacerbated by news of the establishment of a communist state in Russia.

Revelation of the promises made to Italy in the secret London pact of 1915, in the Soviet newspaper *Izvestia* in November 1917, although it may have shocked public opinion in many parts of Europe, seems only to have emboldened the Italian negotiators at the Paris conference. Their list of demands now included new measures intended to ensure Italy's domination of the Adriatic: demilitarization of the Dalmatian coast ruled over by the new Kingdom of Yugoslavia, and the right to establish a naval base at Valona in what was assumed would be the Italian protectorate of Albania. Italy also wanted to play a major role in the eastern Mediterranean. She asked for mandates over portions of the defunct Ottoman Empire, having already established herself in the Dodecanese chain of islands off the coast of Turkey. What must have most taken aback Italy's allies at the Paris conference, however, would have been her greatly expanded list of colonial concessions. Italy wanted French Djibouti and British Somaliland turned over to her, presumably as jumping-off points for a second bid to conquer Ethiopia. Most brash of all, perhaps, was a demand that all German and Austro-Hungarian concessions in China be given to her.

Italy's Entente allies rejected the bulk of her territorial demands, including most of those granted in the secret Treaty of London of 1915. The American president, Woodrow Wilson, who had not been made privy to the terms of the secret treaty until the eve of the Paris conference, made clear that the United States would only be prepared to support cession of the "unredeemed" lands in the Tyrol to Italy. The president was particularly adamant that Dalmatia not be turned over to the Italians, since this was to be part of the new Kingdom of Yugoslavia, which had been created in large part at his insistence, as a showcase example of the "self-determination of peoples." But it was not only the rejection of the bulk of their demands by the "Anglo-Saxons" and French, however, that would so enrage Italian delegates to the Paris conference and ultimately the Italian public, but the manner in which the unwelcome verdict was delivered. It was made clear to the Italian delegates that the real war had been fought on the Western Front, that Italy had been able to defeat the decrepit Austro-Hungarian Empire on the Southern Front only with the aid of her British and French allies, who had rescued her after the debacle of Caporetto and provided the stiffening that had made possible the "miracle" of Vittorio Veneto. In the end, it was the humiliation heaped upon her by her erstwhile allies as much as the dreams of land and glory gone a-glimmering that fueled the myth of the "mutilated victory" that helped so much to bring Fascism to power in Italy in 1922.

SEE ALSO: Turco-Italian War (1911–1912); World War I: Eastern Front; World War I: Western Front.

References

Crankshaw, E. (1963) *The Fall of the Hapsburg Empire*. London: Penguin.

Taylor, A. J. P. (1965) *The Habsburg Monarchy, 1809–1918*. New York: Harper.

Further Reading

Albrecht-Carrié, R. (1938) *Italy at the Paris Peace Conference*. New York: Columbia University Press.

Burgwyn, H. J. (1993) *The Legend of the Mutilated Victory: Italy, the Great War, and the Paris Peace Conference, 1915–1919*. Westport, CT: Greenwood Press.

Hughes-Hallett, L. (2013) *Gabriele D'Annunzio: Poet, Seducer, and Preacher of War*. New York: Knopf.

Kann, R. A., Kiraly, B. K., and Fichtner, P. S. (Eds.) (1977) *The Habsburg Empire in World War I*. New York: Columbia University Press.

Knox, M. (2007) *To the Threshold of Power, 1922–33: Origins and Dynamics of the Fascist and National Socialist Dictatorships*. Cambridge: Cambridge University Press.

Melograni, P. (1969) *Storia politica della grande guerra, 1915–1918*. Bari: Laterza.

O'Brien, P. (2005) *Mussolini in the First World War: The Journalist, the Soldier, the Fascist*. New York: Berg.

Paoletti, C. (2008) *A Military History of Italy*. Westport: Praeger.

Pieri, P. (1968) *L'Italia nella prima guerra mondiale (1915–1918)*. Turin: Einaudi.

Rochat, G. (1976) *L'Italia nella prima guerra mondiale. Problemi di interpretazione e prospettive di ricerca*. Milan: Feltrinelli.

Seth, R. (1965) *Caporetto: The Scapegoat Battle*. London: Macdonald.

Silvestri, M. (1984) *Caporetto: una battaglia e un enigme*. Milan: Mondadori.

Sondhaus, L. (2000) *Franz Conrad von Hoetzendorf: Architect of the Apocalypse*. Boston: Humanities Press.

Sullivan, B. (1994) "Caporetto: Causes, Recovery, and Consequences." In G. J. Andreopolous and H. Selesky (Eds.), *The Aftermath of Defeat: Societies, Armed Forces, and the Challenge of Recovery*. New Haven: Yale University Press.

Thayer, J. A. (1964) *Italy and the Great War*. Madison: University of Wisconsin Press.

Thompson, M. (2009) *The White War: Life and Death on the Italian Front 1915–1919*. New York: Basic Books.

Ungari, A. (2011) "The Official Inquiry into the Italian Defeat in the Battle of Caporetto (October 1917)," *Journal of Military History*, 75 (3).

Vigezzi, B. (1966) *L'Italia di fronte alla prima guerra mondiale. Volume 1: L'Italia neutrale*. Milan: R. Ricciardi.

Wilcox, V. (2009) "Generalship and Mass Surrender during the Italian Defeat at Caporetto." In I. W. F. Beckett (Ed.), *1917: Beyond the Western Front*. Leiden: Brill.

World War I: Western Front

DAVID R. WOODWARD

Modern Armies and War Plans

The general European war that followed Archduke Ferdinand's assassination at Sarajevo (June 28, 1914) soon became global, spreading to other corners of the world, from Africa to Asia to the Pacific. But the war remained an essentially European conflict; and no European front proved more crucial in determining victory for either side than the Western Front in France and Flanders. On this front, the first modern US Army also made its debut.

The strengthening of the nation-state prior to 1914, bolstered by a strong sense of national identity, gave Europe's leaders unprecedented popular support. Patriotic young men from all classes were prepared to make the ultimate sacrifice in defense of their country. The industrial revolution also provided European states with an arsenal of extraordinarily lethal weapons. No previous armies had been better equipped to inflict death and destruction and no previous war produced more casualties: 8.5 million killed and another 20 million wounded. During the course of the war, roughly one-half of French males between the ages of 20 and 32 in 1914 were killed and German soldiers died at the rate of almost one a minute.

Pre-war preparations involved conscription and extensive mobilization and offensive plans. Conscription and military training became a right of passage for most young European males. After active duty of from two to three years, men returned to civilian life as reservists. Mobilization plans focused on rapidly calling up these reservists, forming them into units, and transporting them by rail to the enemy's frontier. No detail was overlooked, from precise railroad timetables to the registration of farmers' horses for possible

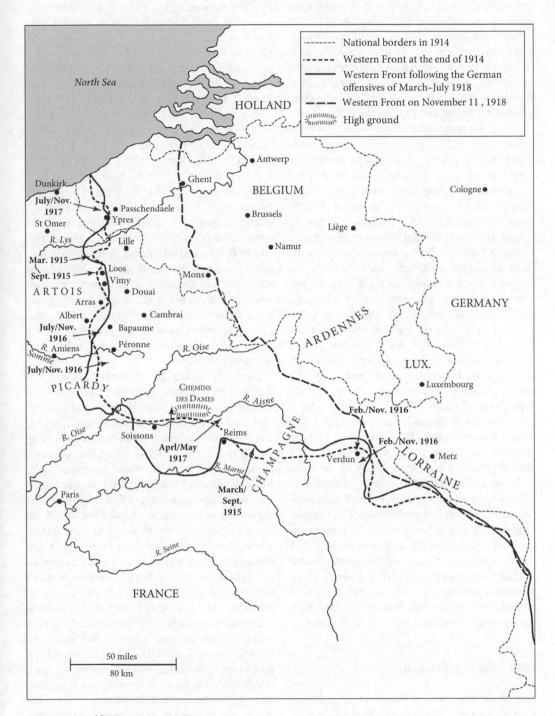

Map 18　World War I: Western Front.

military use. By the end of the war's first month, the warring armies had increased five fold, from four million to some 20 million in the field.

European general staffs expected these formidable conscript armies to achieve quick and decisive victories, with prevailing doctrines focusing on flanks, envelopments, and annihilations. Faced with the unsettling prospect of a two-front war against Russia and France, the German general staff concentrated first on France (with its well-trained and equipped army and superior transportation system), drawing up an extremely ambitious war plan that dispatched most of the German army through the Low Countries in a gigantic wheeling movement to win a decisive victory within six weeks. This plan is popularly described as the Schlieffen Plan after its architect, Count Alfred von Schlieffen, the chief of the German general staff, who died in 1905. His alleged last words, "Keep the right wing strong," were not always followed by his successor, General Helmuth von Moltke (the Younger).

The French general staff developed a more flexible war plan, Plan XVII. General Joseph Joffre, the chief of the French general staff, sought to concentrate his forces before fighting a decisive battle. Doughty consequently viewed Joffre's deployment of the French army as more of a "concentration" plan than a "war" plan (2005: 37). Joffre's favorite option, however, was an all-out offensive in Lorraine if Germany attacked through Belgium and Luxembourg. It remained to be seen, however, if the new generation of weapons, improved mobility through rail transport, and the unprecedented size of the armies would result in a prolonged conflict rather than the brief and decisive clash of arms envisaged by the European general staffs. Was it really possible to destroy a modern army with a single blow? Might not the sheer size of the armies and their formidable armaments prolong rather than shorten warfare and lead to a war of attrition?

1914: War of Movement

Having declared war on Russia (August 1) and France (August 3), Germany invaded Belgium on August 4. Twelve Belgian concrete and steel forts at Liège blocked the German right wing's advance. Blasted by 17-inch siege howitzers, the last of these forts fell on August 16. During the next 16 days the extreme right wing of the German army advanced some 180 miles across Belgium into northern France. The French responded to this German flanking movement in the north with a powerful thrust into Lorraine (August 14), commencing the so-called Battle of the Frontiers (August 14–24). Meanwhile, Great Britain committed its small professional army to the continental war. The first elements of the British Expeditionary Force (BEF) arrived in France on August 7. Initial battles did not go well for either the French or the British. After confronting a vastly superior force at Mons the BEF was forced into a general retreat. Meanwhile, the French offensives proved a dismal failure resulting in approximately 300,000 casualties, roughly 25 percent of the combatants. French infantrymen, bayonets fixed and dressed in their traditional blue coats and red trousers, pressed forward across open country with reckless abandon. Without any artillery support to suppress enemy fire, French infantry's stout hearts proved no match for German artillery, magazine rifles, and machine guns.

Four weeks after the Germans advanced into Belgium it appeared that the Schlieffen Plan (although altered in some important respects by Moltke) was about to eliminate France from the war. The German army had been victorious along its whole front and its right wing had advanced across Belgium into France and threatened Paris. By September 5, 1914, many Parisians, including the French government, had fled the capital. The expanding war map, however, did not tell the full story. The German right wing's rapid and distant advance, with marches of 20 or more miles a day, exhausted German infantry and created a logistical nightmare. A breakdown in communications between the general staff and frontline commanders also created confusion. General Alexander von Kluck, who commanded the First Army on the extreme right of the advancing German forces, altered the axis of his advance to go around Paris on the east rather than the west, which made his forces vulnerable to a counterattack. Now confident that Kluck's entire First Army was moving in a southeasterly direction, Joffre informed his officers on September 5: "Gentlemen, we will fight on the Marne." The resulting battle along a front of around 100 miles destroyed Germany's hopes of a quick victory in the west. German armies, although occupying Belgium and much of northern France, now faced the two-front war that the German general staff had sought to avoid with its Schlieffen Plan.

Following the First Battle of the Marne, both sides attempted to outflank the other. When a Belgian force of some 50,000 men took up a position on the North Sea in mid-October 1914 the so-called Race to the Sea was over. With no flanks to turn, the war of movement that characterized the initial fighting on the Western Front was replaced by the construction of extensive fortifications and the beginning of siege warfare. On a battlefield dominated by magazine rifles, machine guns, and exploding artillery shells, soldiers had to dig to survive. Shovels and other digging implements became an important part of an army's equipment.

Opposing forces constructed an almost continuous series of parallel trenches, separated by a "no-man's land" crisscrossed by barbed wire strung on trestles and stakes to a height of 3–5 feet, from Nieuwpoort on the Belgian North Sea coast to Switzerland. Life in these trenches was miserable. Soldiers had to combat lice, extreme cold in the winter, mud and flooded trenches when it rained, sleep deprivation, the constant danger posed by snipers, frequent shelling, trench raids, iron rations, and rats the size of cats. And then there was the smell that many soldiers never forgot: decaying flesh, unwashed soldiers, and human excrement and urine from the trench latrines. To sustain morale soldiers were allowed extensive time away from the trenches to recuperate in rest camps and granted occasional leave to visit loved ones at home.

1915: Siege Warfare

To escape trench warfare, army commanders and their staffs explored ways to break through the enemy's extensive fortification system and into open countryside. A breakthrough and a return to mobile warfare, however, proved illusory. New rapid-fire weaponry aided the defense more than the offense. A break-*in* was possible if sufficient suppressing fire were available. But this limited success could not be converted into a break-*through* and a resumption of mobile warfare

because the offensive's momentum could not be maintained, certainly not by the cavalry and not even by tanks (unreliable and slow) when they first appeared on the battlefield in 1916. A system of light railroads also made possible the rapid dispatch of reinforcements to any threatened sector of the front before it was completely overrun. Ground might be gained, usually measured in yards rather than in miles, but a dent in the enemy front could not liberate armies from the resumption of trench warfare.

Siege warfare soon evolved into a war of attrition with catastrophic casualties. In 1915, the French and the Germans did most of the fighting and dying on the Western Front in one failed offensive after another. (Britain, the only major European power without conscription before the war, played a limited role while it built a mass army, initially with volunteers.) The weapon of choice for all armies became artillery. Approximately 58 percent of British casualties on the Western Front were inflicted by artillery. In an offensive to capture Vimy Ridge (Second Battle of Artois), French artillerymen in their preliminary bombardment fired 1,813,490 shells; heavy guns expended another 342,372 shells. In five weeks of heavy fighting, the French lost 2,260 officers and 100,273 men killed, wounded, or missing. No ground of any strategic value was gained. To assist the French offensive in Artois, the British First Army attacked Aubers Ridge, suffering heavy casualties. In some instances British soldiers were killed instantly as they left their trenches, some falling back on the bayonets of soldiers waiting to climb out. The British also suffered heavy losses in blunting the German offensive at the Second Battle of Ypres (where the Germans first introduced chemical warfare on a large scale to the Western Front). The Allied 1915 campaign concluded with an autumn campaign (Loos, Artois, and Champagne) that began on September 25.

Despite heavy fighting in 1915 and casualties in the tens of thousands, the Western Front had been little altered, having moved no more than 3 miles in any direction. Despite his lack of success, Joffre, who served as the Allied *de facto* commander in chief on the Western Front, proposed a continuation of the offensive in 1916. His "Plan of Action," which now emphasized wearing down the German army (or attrition) rather than a breakthrough, called for simultaneous offensives against the Central Powers on the Western, Eastern, and Italian fronts. An inter-Allied military conference (December 6–8) at Chantilly, the headquarters of the French army, unanimously accepted this formula.

Of growing concern for the Anglo-French leadership was that Russia in 1915 had almost been knocked out of the war by a powerful Austro-German offensive which had occupied Galicia and overrun the Polish salient, inflicting upon the Russian army as many as two million casualties. Concern that Russia might drop out of the war if not supported by Allied pressure in the west had been an important factor in Joffre's earlier decision to continue offensive action into the autumn. It now encouraged him to resume the offensive in 1916.

1916: Verdun and the Somme

Despite Germany's success on the Eastern Front in 1915, Erich von Falkenhayn, who in 1914 had replaced Moltke as chief of the German general staff, wanted to focus on the Western Front. Although he believed that only in the west could victory be won, he did not believe a breakthrough and rout of Anglo-French forces was possible on the Western Front in 1916. Although he identified Great Britain as Germany's primary enemy, he sought a monster battle of attrition with the French at the fortress town of Verdun. In his words he wanted "to bleed" the French army "to death." Through this bludgeoning of France he believed that Germany would wrest from Britain's "hands" its "best sword," resulting in the collapse of the anti-German coalition (Woodward 2009: 98).

The 10-month Battle of Verdun, which led to some 700,000 French and German casualties, opened at dawn on February 21 with a thunderous nine-hour bombardment, the most powerful bombardment yet seen in warfare. A mortar-like howitzer, "Big Bertha," fired a shell as tall as a man and weighing over a ton. Although the Germans captured Fort Douaumont, considered by some to be the strongest fort in the world, the French rushed reinforcements to Verdun and stood their ground. This, of course, was exactly what Falkenhayn expected and wanted.

Germany's powerful offensive against Verdun created anxiety and uncertainty in London. Great Britain now had the largest army in Europe that it would ever send abroad, but the British civilian leadership was hesitant to commit these new recruits and inexperienced officers to a great offensive, especially before the British munitions industry had produced sufficient heavy artillery and high explosive shells that appeared essential to success in siege warfare. Other British leaders, most notably David Lloyd George, believed that Britain should follow an indirect strategy, committing British military resources to the outer theaters away from the killing fields of France and Flanders. Lloyd George and other "easterners," however, were confronted with the reality that the battle at Verdun might determine Britain's fate as well as France's. Sir Douglas Haig, the new commander in chief of the BEF, moved forward his date for a joint Anglo-French offensive on the Somme originally scheduled for August 15: "We *must* march to the support of the French," he notes in his diary (Haig 2005: 187).

At 7:30 a.m., on July 1, the Anglo-French offensive on the Somme began along a 25-mile front. The more experienced French infantry, with a more realistic tactical doctrine that emphasized artillery superiority and rejected an attack "in mass formation," enjoyed some success, capturing all of their first day's objectives. In contrast, the British assault resulted in the worst single day in British military history. The official figures for British losses on July 1 were 57,470 of the some 100,000 men involved, or 35,493 wounded and 19,240 dead. These appalling casualties were partly a result of Haig's overly ambitious belief in a deep penetration and rapid exploitation of the German defenses.

The Battle of the Somme is often remembered for its bloody first day, but it should be emphasized that the Anglo-French offensive continued until mid-November. Germany was forced to shift men, artillery, and even aircraft to the Somme battlefield and eventually suspended its offensive against Verdun. The Germans also magnified their losses on the Somme with their determination to retake lost ground. For their part, the British developed more realistic tactics and deployed a new weapon: the tank, which did not prove to be a war-winner. Mechanically unreliable and difficult to maneuver, the tank often could not keep up with advancing infantry.

Falkenhayn's policy of bleeding the French white at Verdun cost him his job. With Germany under intense pressure in August on both its Eastern and Western fronts, Kaiser Wilhelm II replaced him with Paul von Hindenburg and Erich Ludendorff. Germany's new high command quickly embraced tactics to reduce German casualties on the Western Front. They turned Falkenhayn's attrition policy on its head, emphasizing defense over the offensive. In the words of a new training manual, "Principles of Conduct for Defensive Battle in Position Warfare," the objective was to allow the enemy "to exhaust itself and to bleed itself" through offensive action (Herwig 1997: 247). The Germans subsequently established an elastic defensive system in depth and shortened their front by constructing a series of strong defensive systems (popularly known as the Hindenburg Line). Ludendorff emphasized the construction of "pill boxes" over deep underground positions which he characterized as "fatal man-traps." Unable to break the deadly stalemate in France, the German high command also pressured the government to resume unrestricted U-boat warfare in an attempt to starve Great Britain out of the war.

1917: Strategic Dilemmas

Although major Allied theaters existed elsewhere, in Italy, the Balkans, Palestine, and Mesopotamia as well as the Eastern Front, the Western Front remained the primary theater. Jerusalem and Baghdad might fall to the British, and operations in the Balkans or on the Italian front might weaken Bulgaria or Austria-Hungary, but these successes could not end the war. "Easterners" might talk about "knocking away the props," but Germany propped up her allies, not the other way around. If Germany were defeated, her allies would quickly collapse.

When Allied generals discussed the next campaigning season, a rift developed between the British and French military leadership. Robert Nivelle, who had replaced Joffre as the French commander in chief, sought victory through a great offensive on the Aisne. Using minutely organized "rolling barrages" he had achieved success in local attacks at Verdun in 1916. He is often credited with the slogan "The artillery conquers; the infantry occupies." Nivelle now promised to rupture the German front in 24–48 hours. Haig, the British commander in chief, was pleased that Nivelle talked of a decisive offensive rather than battles of attrition. But he did not want to continue in the supporting role that had hitherto been assigned the BEF. He favored a British offensive in Flanders to clear the Belgian ports of U-boats and surface raiders, which was also a high priority of his government. Nivelle, however, gained the upper hand when he obtained the support of Lloyd George's new government (Lloyd George had replaced Herbert H. Asquith as prime minister in December 1916). Although Lloyd George remained skeptical of the costly and prolonged offensives that had previously characterized the fighting on the Western Front, he and other British politicians were impressed by Nivelle's confident presentation of his plan. The British also believed that the war-weary French were capable of launching only one more great offensive and must be given strong support, even if that meant subordinating the BEF to Nivelle's command.

In their supporting role to exhaust German reserves, the British (with French support) launched an offensive on April 9 along a 15-mile front at Arras and at Vimy Ridge (Second Battle of Arras). The capture of Vimy Ridge by the Canadian Corps proved to be one of the BEF's greatest accomplishments during the war. Once again, however, this penetration of the German front could not be converted into a breakthrough, as fresh German troops arrived on the battlefield.

On April 16, Nivelle launched his offensive. The primary German defenses had been placed on the rear slope of the Chemin des Dames and were hidden from French ground observers. The French bombardment consequently was much less successful than anticipated. German machine gunners quickly dominated the battlefield, and French infantry failed to keep up with the frantic pace of their "rolling barrages," 100 yards every three minutes. The consequences of Nivelle's failure to achieve his promised breakthrough were especially severe because he had raised expectations so high. From April 16–25 the French army suffered some 134,000 casualties, including 30,000 killed. Nivelle was replaced and his successor Philippe Pétain was soon faced with a serious mutiny in the French army. British losses at Arras (battle ending on May 17) were also heavy, with casualties around 150,000. In fact, judged solely by the daily British casualty rate (4,076 a day), it was the BEF's bloodiest battle of the war.

Following the failure of their spring offensives, the Allies faced a strategic dilemma. Tsar Nicholas II had been overthrown by a revolution, and the Provisional Government that replaced him was weak and unable to revive the waning spirits of Russia's armed forces. The United States, provoked into the war (April 6) by Germany's resumption of unrestricted U-boat warfare in February, could offer no immediate military assistance to balance Russia's headlong decline.

The primary burden of maintaining the Allied position on the Western Front now shifted to the British. Many French leaders wanted to suspend major offensive action and wait until the United States could provide military assistance. But the United States initially could only offer financial and some naval assistance. Building an army from scratch, equipping it, and transporting it to Europe would take months if not years. Although cracks were appearing in the anti-German coalition, Haig insisted that a prudent strategy was to maintain pressure on the German army. To abandon the offensive in the west would hand over the strategic initiative to the Germans. Lloyd George and many other civilian leaders, however, were dubious of initiating another major battle in 1917, especially after the costly failures of the spring offensives. Although Haig promised a cautious step-by-step approach, his strategic objectives remained grand. In his mind, killing Germans (a "battle of attrition") was secondary to the capture of the Belgian ports and perhaps even forcing a German withdrawal from Belgium. After weeks of debate, the government finally (July 20) gave him permission to proceed after he promised that he would terminate his offensive if it became clear that his objectives were unobtainable. But would the famously optimistic Haig ever concede that his offensive had failed?

On the eve of the British offensive in Flanders, the War Office informed the British leadership that three Russian armies comprising 60–70 divisions were in full retreat along a 150-mile front. For their part the French army, paralyzed by mutinies, and the Italian army, also suffering from low morale, remained generally passive. On July 31, Haig initiated the Third Battle of Ypres (popularly known as Passchendaele). Heavy rain immediately turned the battlefield into a quagmire (August had only three days when no rain was recorded). The weather improved in September, but the rains returned before the month was out, once again turning the battlefield into mud and pools of water. Haig, who remained convinced that the enemy would crack if pressure were maintained, continued his offensive into November. With Britain's allies faltering, a case could be made for launching a British offensive during the last half of 1917. But Haig's offensive should have been terminated long before November. German morale declined in Flanders, but British morale declined even more. And with meaningful US assistance in the distant future, the BEF could ill afford its losses. British spirits were initially raised on November 20 when the BEF launched a surprise attack with massed tanks at Cambrai. (The tank had had limited utility in the Flanders quagmire.) Despite this impressive British advance, the Germans launched a counterattack and quickly retook their lost territory.

The fourth year of the war ended on a dismal note for the Allies. The costly Anglo-French offensives on the Western Front had fallen far short of their objectives. A powerful Austro-German offensive in late October had routed the Italian army at Caporetto, sending some one million Italian soldiers fleeing the battlefield. Russia had been knocked out of the war in early November after the Bolsheviks overthrew the Provisional Government and signed an armistice with the Central Powers. With the Eastern Front dormant and the survival of the Italian front in question, US participation in the war offered the best hope for an Allied victory, but American mobilization proceeded slowly after its entry into the war in April. By the end of 1917, the United States had dispatched only 175,000 soldiers to Europe.

A Formula for Success: New Weapons and Methods

The war on the Western Front had evolved from a war of movement in August 1914 to siege warfare fought with weapons of the industrial revolution. Success was often measured in yards and casualties were unprecedented. It is therefore not surprising that popular history usually depicts World War I generals as "butchers" and "bunglers." Certainly generals and their staffs were surprised by and unprepared to wage a war in which the defense quickly came to dominate the offense. Initial attempts to overcome siege warfare were often overly ambitious and lacking in imagination. New techniques and tactics were required. The extraordinary British casualties on the first day of the Somme in 1916 can be explained in part by Haig's flawed utilization of his artillery and his determination to achieve a quick breakthrough as opposed to a more cautious step-by-step approach. But Haig and his staff eventually adapted to the conditions of trench and industrialized warfare, as did other generals and their staffs. A learning curve existed in the command of all the forces on the Western Front, including the US Army in 1918.

The realities of the battlefield spurred both tactical and technical innovations. A coherent combined arms doctrine developed as the infantry was given more firepower that included automatic weapons, trench mortars, and rifle grenades, and supported in their assaults by flame throwers, tanks, aircraft, and armored cars. Soldiers were trained to advance in smaller units and taught to bypass strong positions (the tactics of "infiltration") and to "penetrate quickly and deeply" (a trademark of the German "storm troopers" in 1918). Despite these important technical and tactical advances, artillery continued to dominate the battlefield. Rather than a bombardment that lasted days and gave the enemy advance warning of an attack, guns were now silently registered on their targets (no preliminary shelling to get the range). Massed guns would suddenly unleash a torrent of steel that concentrated on key defensive positions, communications, and the enemy's artillery. Wire was cut and the infantry shepherded across "no-man's land" with "rolling barrages." The new weapons and methods now made it possible to break through the enemy's defenses into open country. There were, however, still limits to an army's advance. The cratered battlefields, crisscrossed with trenches, served as an obstacle in bringing forward the artillery to support a rapid advance. Beyond the reach of their light railroads, an advancing force also soon outran its supplies. Meanwhile, the opposing forces could be rapidly reinforced through a system of light railroads and roads.

As the offensive capabilities of the armies improved, defensive tactics also evolved. In 1917, the Germans developed an elastic defensive system; the French followed suit in early 1918. Pétain, the French commander in chief, advocated a new defensive system: a defensive system in depth that placed a majority of the defenders to the rear so they might be protected from mortars and short-range artillery but still be in a position to repulse an attack. Rather than a continuous line of trenches, Pétain wanted what he called "islands of resistance," strong points to disrupt the enemy's advance and facilitate counterattacks. Pétain's defensive doctrine, however, was not always understood or followed by his subordinates.

1918: German Spring Offensive

Ludendorff and Hindenburg, who had dominated German war policy since the summer of 1916, hoped to win a "victor's peace" before the United States made its presence felt. On January 1, 1918, Ludendorff ordered a powerful offensive (Operation Michael) against the British front which was designed to destroy France's primary ally. Tactically brilliant, Ludendorff's plan included no clear operational objectives other than perhaps driving a wedge between the French and British armies and forcing the British back to the Channel ports. His answer to his critics was as follows: "We will punch a hole into [their line]. For the rest, we shall see. We also did it this way in Russia!" (Herwig 1997: 400).

Germany's spring offensive got off to an astonishing beginning when judged by the standards of previous offensives on the Western Front. On March 21, some 6,000 German guns and howitzers unleashed a massive and well-directed bombardment of high explosive shells, smoke, and poison gas that stunned British defenders. Specially trained German assault troops ("storm troopers"), employing "infiltration" tactics that emphasized deep penetration over reducing every strong point, swept forward. Within 24 hours the Germans captured some 140 square miles. By March 26, the Germans had advanced more than 20 miles and captured Albert. The British Fifth Army disintegrated. It now appeared that German pressure would split the Allied forces, the French falling back to defend Paris, the British to defend their crucial Channel ports. This powerful German offensive, however, lost its momentum as British and French reinforcements arrived on the battlefield. Many German soldiers had also reached the limits of their endurance as supplies and artillery could not keep up as they advanced across the shell-pocked and pulverized countryside of the old Somme battlefield. On May 4, Ludendorff suspended his offensive. New trenches were quickly constructed and the fronts stabilized. Rather than achieving a complete rupturing of the enemy front, Ludendorff succeeded only in creating a deep salient, suffering some 250,000 casualties in the process.

Ludendorff became more desperate as he continued his offensives, one each month, first against the British but eventually on the French front as well. Ludendorff had acquired the necessary manpower for his offensives by transferring German divisions from the moribund Eastern Front. But additional divisions could not be found to keep his army up to strength. This was not the case with the British and French, who had the prospect of American reinforcements.

The Allies responded to the military crisis by establishing unity of command on the Western Front, choosing Ferdinand Foch as generalissimo. Meanwhile, the United States intensified its mobilization efforts. Peyton C. March, the American chief of the general staff, exclaimed: "I am going to get the men to France if they have to swim" (Woodward 2009: 325). Although many US recruits were indifferently trained and their officers inexperienced, their numbers arriving in Europe during the spring and summer of 1918 surpassed all expectations. By the war's end, two million American soldiers had been transported to Europe.

The Germans were running out of time by July when Ludendorff planned a two-pronged offensive, first a diversionary offensive against the French in Champagne and then an offensive to finish off the British in Flanders. Launched on July 15, the first (Second Battle of the Marne) of his planned offensives

established a bridgehead across the Marne. A French counterattack, officially known as the Aisne–Marne Counter-Offensive, which included US soldiers, drove the Germans back, transferring the strategic initiative to the Allies for the remainder of the war.

Following this Allied counterattack the German army found itself in a precarious position. Its five offensives (March–July) had increased the length of its front from 242 miles to 317 miles. Now beyond their formidable system of fortifications, the Germans defended vulnerable salients, often from primitive defenses. Having suffered a million casualties, the German army was now composed of many under-strength divisions, some with fewer than 3,000 men.

Allied Counteroffensive and Germany's Defeat

Both Foch and Haig, although they did not anticipate an end of the war until 1919 at the earliest, eagerly returned to the offensive, concentrating initially on the German salients at Amiens and the Marne. On August 8, the British Fourth Army opened the Battle of Amiens. Spearheaded by masses of tanks, the British advanced some 8 miles in one day. Haig recorded in his diary that the Germans "were blowing up dumps in all directions and streaming eastwards" (Haig 2005: 440). Ludendorff was stunned, later describing August 8 as the German army's "black day."

Foch now recommended converging attacks along the part of the German front that formed a gigantic bulge into French territory from the North Sea to the Meuse (or Verdun). He expected the rapidly expanding American force commanded by John J. Pershing (an independent US Army had been created on August 10) to play a major role in the general offensive. After reducing the St Mihiel salient, the American First Army was assigned the task of cooperating with French forces in an offensive against the right shoulder of this bulge toward Mézières while the British (with French support) attacked the left shoulder toward Cambrai. Meanwhile, the French would maintain pressure between Soissons and Reims toward Laon. On September 26–30, the Allies launched a series of timed attacks along a 200-mile front. At Meuse-Argonne, US troops were engaged in what many consider the greatest, certainly the most deadly battle ever fought by an American army. These converging attacks proved to be a war-winning strategy. On October 6, the German government sent its first peace note to President Woodrow Wilson. Five weeks later, on November 11, the Armistice went into effect and the guns on the Western Front fell silent. By this time Germany's allies had also been driven out of the war.

The costly and prolonged battles on the stalemated Western Front were not the ones that either the generals or politicians expected or wanted to fight. Many generals were slow to adapt new techniques of warfare on battlefields with no flanks to turn. Costly frontal assaults were the only alternative to remaining on the defensive. A cruel truth, however, was that the Western Front remained the primary front throughout the war and neither side could hope to win by remaining in their trenches. Only through costly offensive battles could the strength and morale of the enemy be undermined. In both world wars the defeat of the German army proved an extremely costly endeavor. Unlike in World War I, however, it was the Red Army in World War II rather than the British, French, and American armies that largely paid the human cost in depleting Germany's military strength.

SEE ALSO: Chemical Warfare.

References

Doughty, R. A. (2005) *Pyrrhic Victory: French Strategy and Operations in the Great War*. Cambridge, MA: Harvard University Press.

Haig, D. (2005) *The Haig Diaries: The Diaries of Field Marshal Sir Douglas Haig: War Diaries and Letters, 1914–1918*. G. Sheffield and J. Bourne (Eds.). London: Weidenfeld and Nicolson.

Herwig, H. H. (1997) *The First World War: Germany and Austria-Hungary, 1914–1918*. New York: St. Martin's Press.

Woodward, D. R. (2009) *World War I Almanac*. New York: Facts On File.

Further Reading

Coffman, E. M. (1968) *The War to End All Wars: The American Military Experience in World War I*. New York: Oxford University Press.

Cruttwell, C. R. M. F. (1964) *A History of the Great War, 1914–1918*. Oxford: Clarendon Press.

Ellis, J. (1976) *Eye-Deep in Hell: Trench Warfare in World War I*. New York: Pantheon.

Falls, C. (1961) *The Great War, 1914–1918*. New York: Capricorn Books.

Ferrell, R. H. (2007) *America's Deadliest Battle: Meuse-Argonne, 1918*. Lawrence: University Press of Kansas.

Foley, R. T. (2005) *German Strategy and the Path to Verdun: Erich von Falkenhayn and the Development of Attrition, 1870–1916*. Cambridge: Cambridge University Press.

Griffith, P. (1994) *Battle Tactics of the Western Front: The British Army's Art of Attack, 1916–1918*. New Haven: Yale University Press.

Grotelueschen, M. (2007) *The AEF Way of War: The American Army and Combat in World War I*. New York: Cambridge University Press.

Harris, J. P. (2008) *Douglas Haig and the First World War*. New York: Cambridge University Press.

Hermann, D. G. (1996) *The Arming of Europe and the Making of the First World War*. Princeton: Princeton University Press.

Horne, A. (1963) *The Price of Glory: Verdun 1916*. New York: St. Martin's Press.

Liddell Hart, Captain B. H. (1930) *The Real War 1914–1918*. Boston: Little, Brown.

Ludendorff, General E. (1919) *My War Memoirs, 1914–1918*. London: Hutchinson.

Philpott, W. (2009) *Bloody Victory*. New York: Little, Brown.

Prior, R. and Wilson, T. (1992) *Command on the Western Front*. Oxford: Blackwell.

Prior, R. and Wilson, T. (1996) *Passchendaele: The Untold Story*. New Haven: Yale University Press.

Robbins, S. (2005) *British Generalship on the Western Front 1914–1918: Defeat into Victory*. London: Frank Cass.

Sheffield, G. (2007) *Forgotten Victory: The First World War, Myths and Realities*. London: Headline.

Smythe, D. (1986) *Pershing: General of the Armies*. Bloomington: Indiana University Press.

Stevenson, D. (1996) *Armaments and the Coming of War: Europe, 1904–1914*. New York: Clarendon Press.

Stevenson, D. (2011) *With Our Backs to the Wall: Victory and Defeat in 1918*. Cambridge, MA: The Belknap Press of Harvard University Press.

Strachan, H. (2001) *The First World War. Volume 1: To Arms*. New York: Oxford University Press.

Travers, T. (1987) *The Killing Ground: The British Army, the Western Front, and the Emergence of Modern Warfare, 1900–1918*. Boston: Allen and Unwin.

Woodward, D. R. (2004) *Lloyd George and the Generals*. New York: Frank Cass.

Woodward, D. R. (2007) *America and World War I: A Selected Annotated Bibliography of English Language Sources*. New York: Routledge.

World War II: Battle of Britain

STUART ROBSON

Despite the myths that encrusted it even before it began, and despite the necessary revisions historians have made to our understanding of it, the Battle of Britain mattered. By holding Germany off, Britain was able to become an unsinkable aircraft carrier anchored off the coast of Occupied Europe, the western base for its liberation.

Churchill's "Finest Hour" speech of June 18, 1940, stands in select company. Words alone usually confirm rather than change the course of events. But Churchill was deliberately making a myth. Two weeks before, when he had promised that Britain would never surrender, he had reason to fear that he was speaking mainly for himself. The cabinet Churchill led was much the same that had championed appeasement for two years. Even the Labour representatives in the coalition would probably have preferred peace to catastrophe. Given the bad news from France, Hitler expected the British to come to their senses and seek a peace. Churchill blocked this path, above all in his famous speeches in the Commons. By July, Churchill knew from Ultra intelligence that he could discount the threat of an immediate invasion. But he was trying to make history with his speech, not just record it, and his aim was to lure Hitler into a trap. As early as June 9, he had written to his friend Jan Christian Smuts, "I see only one way through now, to wit, Hitler should attack this country, and in doing so break his air weapon" (Gilbert 1983: 485). Later, when he wrote about home defense, he quoted Dr Johnson: "Depend upon it, when a man knows he is going to be hanged in a month, it concentrates the mind wonderfully."

The Luftwaffe

When Hitler addressed the Reichstag on July 19, he capped his performance by creating a flock of new generals and no fewer than a dozen new field marshals. Included among them were Erhard Milch, the creator of the Luftwaffe and head of the Air Ministry, Albert Kesselring, commander of Air Fleet 2, and Hugo Sperrle, commander of Air Fleet 3. The top airman was Hermann Goering, who was also head of the Four Year Plan and Hitler's anointed successor. Because Goering was already a field marshal, his preeminence was maintained by bumping him up a notch to become the first and only Reichsfeldmarshall, which allowed him to wear a flashy white uniform.

The man who actually built the Luftwaffe was Erhart Milch. He was a bureaucrat; that was his strength and his weakness. As inspector general, he organized the air force and sorted out the personal rivalries that were sprouting under the warm sun of Goering's generosity. But he was not an aviator himself or a student of military theory. Goering of course was a pilot, but little else, and he had a fondness for fellow knights of the air, men like Ernst Udet, another war ace. What the Luftwaffe lacked desperately was the guiding hand of a trained airman who was also an administrator. Actually, such a man was around for a while. As chief of staff, Walther Wever was thoroughly professional, able to balance not only the outlandish types who were infesting the Luftwaffe but also the conflicting doctrines about the best use of airpower. He died in an air crash in June 1936; with him probably went Germany's best chance of winning the war in the air (Murray 1983: 9–12).

In the 1930s, the shapelessness of the Luftwaffe did not matter because it was given its shape by external forces, like a balloon expanding in a box. The strategy of *Blitzkrieg* required the air force to concentrate on the role of ground support. The mixture of fighters and light bombers that Milch developed was what the army needed for this. Wever was starting to work on long-range four-engined bombers when he died, but the program passed away with him. Small and medium bombers were built instead. Because they were cheaper and quicker to build, the Luftwaffe was able to take a shortcut to building a new force that overawed the rest of the world. The inherent excellence of German designers and workers ensured that the technology of the Luftwaffe was state of the art, whatever the shortcomings of amateurs like Goering and Udet. Yet the Luftwaffe was not an air force in the generally accepted current meaning of the term, an independent branch of the armed forces; rather it was the air arm of the army, the *Wehrmacht*. While this gave the ground forces flexibility in handling the added dimension of airpower, it also limited the scope of the air weapon.

On the organization chart, the chain of command ran from the Führer and supreme commander through the Oberkommando Luftwaffe, made up of Goering as commander in chief and minister of air, and General Hans Jeschonnek, chief of Air General Staff. Under the Oberkommando Luftwaffe were the air fleets, of which there were five by 1940. Unlike the British Royal Air Force (RAF), which had organized itself along lines of function into separate commands, the Luftwaffe kept its fighters and bombers together, so that each air fleet was really a miniature air force, attached *en bloc* to an army. Although this proved an advantage in the *Blitzkrieg* of 1940, when the air fleets were able to respond flexibly and quickly to the demands of the battlefield, it was to prove a liability in the Battle of Britain, when the Luftwaffe was on its own. Without the competence of a man like Wever to give it shape, the Luftwaffe fell apart. Each air fleet carried out its own plan, with a minimum of coordination from the top, and the Luftwaffe in the end proved to be all muscle and little brain. Worse still, because of losses in the campaigns in Norway and France, even the muscle was momentarily weakened; one estimate is that the frontline bomber force had dropped from 1,102 at the end of March to 949 when the Battle of Britain began (Terraine 1985: 172). Goering was oblivious to this. Ignoring a Luftwaffe report of the previous year that ruled out defeating Britain through bombing alone, refusing to study the recent campaigns to find out what should have been done better, and dismissing the need for replacement machines, he grandly promised that the Luftwaffe would polish off Britain. Hitler may not have quite believed him, but with no better means to test the British will to carry on, he let Goering loose on the RAF.

When Hitler issued the top-secret Directive 16 on July 16, authorizing preparations for an invasion of Britain as early as mid-August if it proved

necessary, the navy assumed that the Luftwaffe would first conquer the air over the Channel. On that assumption, Raeder proposed a landing west of Dover, the first wave taking 10 days to establish itself. The army, exuberant from its success in France, was aghast; it wanted an invasion of the entire south coast, not a glorified raid. Raeder replied that he could not transport or protect the invasion force along such a wide front, and insisted that the army must pick the best spot within the limits he outlined. While the army and navy passed the buck, Goering did nothing except break security rules by radioing Directive 16 to the air fleet commanders. The British Y Service intercepted the message, the codebreakers at Bletchley Park broke the version of the Enigma cipher used carelessly by the Luftwaffe, and the British government thus learned the gist of the plans for invasion and even the codename for it: Sealion. But they did not know the final plan Hitler imposed at the end of August. Rundstedt would command 13 divisions, with 12 in reserve. He was to push up the Kent promontory to Canterbury within a week. To get the army safely across, the navy would have to mine both ends of the Channel and the Luftwaffe control the air. As Churchill later put it, "each of the three Services involved in the operation … worked upon the hopeful factors in their own theme and left the ugly side to their companions" (Churchill 1949: 309).

Fighter Command of the RAF

There might not always have been an England, despite the claim of the wartime song, because Britain in 1940 would have been hard put to hold off William the Conqueror. Only the Royal Navy and Air Force posed a threat to the Germans, and of the two, it was the RAF and its Fighter Command that was the first line of defense. By the greatest good luck, Fighter Command in 1940 was led by precisely the sort of man the Luftwaffe lacked. Air Chief Marshal Hugh Dowding was both an experienced aviator and a superb administrator. After joining the artillery early in the century, he was captivated by flying, and transferred to the Royal Flying Corps just before the Great War. He stayed with the RAF after 1918, and was one of the few senior officers to question the fad for bombers. Always aloof, inquiring, and dedicated to his work, he played a key role in research and development. With the quiet support of Edward Ellington, chief of the Air Staff, Dowding converted the RAF from canvas-covered biplanes to metal monoplanes, set out the specifications that led to the Hurricane and Spitfire, and worked with Robert Watson-Watt to develop the system of radar defense. When the four separate Commands – Fighter, Bomber, Coastal, and Training – were created in 1938, Dowding's manifest abilities outweighed his lack of tact and influence, and he was made commander in chief of Fighter Command. As his senior air staff officer, he chose Keith Park, a New Zealand ace from the Great War and a professional almost as cool and abrasive as Dowding himself.

Even though money was pumped into the RAF after 1936, and particularly into the fighter defenses after 1938, Dowding's worst problem was the shortage of skilled pilots. So, in 1936, the RAF Volunteer Reserve was set up. Civilians were given the rank of sergeant and paid to learn to fly. For the upper classes, there were also the University Air Squadrons and the Auxiliary Air Force, the so-called "millionaires."

It took a year for a novice to finish basic flight training and another year in a squadron to gain experience. So when the government seemed willing to squander precious men and machines in France in May 1940, Dowding had to forego his usual reticence and step into the limelight. Before he spoke to the War Cabinet on May 15, briefly and professionally, to urge that no more Hurricane squadrons be wasted in France, Churchill and Newall, the chief of Air Staff, had already noted that Fighter Command was down to 36 squadrons, 16 short of the rock-bottom minimum for home defense (Terraine 1985: 138–144). After Newall had heard reports that the fighter pilots in France were completely exhausted and outnumbered, he changed his mind and asked the full cabinet to send the four squadrons across; with the need to encourage France uppermost in mind, Churchill now agreed. The next day he went to Paris. Although he bore Dowding's warning in mind, and refused Reynaud's desperate appeal for more fighters, in private he seems to have transposed the vital minimum of squadrons from 52 to 25, so that he felt able to ask his cabinet to send more Hurricanes. This would have left Dowding with almost nothing to defend Britain, a peril that moved him to write a letter to the Air Ministry pleading that Fighter Command be left intact (Terraine 1985: 150–152). In the end, the extra Hurricane squadrons were allowed to operate from French bases by day only, returning to Britain at night, and with the rapid advance of the Germans, even this operation had to be canceled. Even so, only 66 of the 261 Hurricanes sent to France came back.

The Aircraft

At this point, the aircraft and control systems involved in the Battle of Britain should be introduced. Seven types of aircraft played key roles: the Hurricanes and Spitfires of the RAF, and, for the Luftwaffe, the Messerschmidt 109 fighters; the Junkers 87 dive-bombers (Stukas); the Junkers 88, level medium bombers with a dive-bombing capacity; and the two medium bombers, the Heinkel 111 and the Dornier 17, the "flying pencil." The fighters on both sides were state of the art for 1940. Both the British and the Germans had solved the tough design problems of building wings strong enough to brace against the recoil of machine guns or cannon, deep enough to provide lift, and thick enough to hold landing gear (although the Me 109 undercarriage was mounted on the fuselage, bringing the wheels too close together for the plane to be stable when taxiing). The Me 109 had the advantage of fuel injection, which prevented stalling when climbing and turning; the Spitfire had the advantage of its unique elliptical wing, which allowed eight Browning machine guns to be carried without reducing lift or speed. The Hurricane was a practical machine, designed to make maximum use of existing production facilities and technology. In fact, the first Hurricanes were fabric-covered and had wooden propellers, and many of these were still in use in 1940. The Spitfire, by contrast, was a thing of genius, although the genius involved, Reginald Mitchell, died before his beautiful creation helped to save Britain. By July, Dowding had 19 squadrons of Spitfires and 25 of Hurricanes, plus six with Blenheims and two with Defiants. In all, he had 800 aircraft, 644 of which were available for the battle, and 1,456 pilots, 1,259 of whom were present for duty (Terraine 1985: 174).

Radar and the British Air Defense System

A key advantage the British developed was not radar as such but the way radar was used. By the 1930s, all the major powers were working on long-range detection by radio waves, and, in fact, Germany was well ahead in the sophistication and accuracy of its equipment. So much for the popular myth that radar was a top British secret.

By 1940, the Air Ministry and RAF had secretly built up an elaborate system not only for detecting incoming "bandits" (enemy planes), but also for distinguishing friend from foe, corelating radar reports to ground observations, and getting the information promptly to the operations rooms at all levels of Fighter Command. The system of control was flexible, and it had the added virtue of actually working under pressure. Better still, the Germans had no idea how the system worked. They thought that the radar stations they had noticed were radio transmitters controlling the fighters in the local sector, and never quite realized that they were up against a centrally directed national defense. That was one reason why Dowding was continually able to put up what the dejected German pilots came to call "the last fifty Spitfires."

The Battle of Britain developed in four phases: the battle over the Channel in July; Eagle Attack, which began on Eagle Day, August 12, and lasted a week; the critical phase when the Luftwaffe attacked RAF sector fields and radar stations in the southeast, from August 24 to September 6; and finally, the attacks on London after September 7, climaxing on September 15, since known as Battle of Britain Day.

The Battle Over the Channel

Kesselring's Air Fleet 2 planned and carried out Phase One, the attack on British shipping in the Channel. Kesselring's aim was to set up a double bind for the British: if the RAF covered the Channel, it would be shot down, and if it did not, the shipping in the Channel would be sunk. Realizing this, Dowding committed as few fighters

as possible to the defense of Channel shipping, but as the tonnage sunk increased, so did the pressure on him to take action. The trouble was that the Luftwaffe could reach the Channel quicker than the RAF could scramble, and, with their limited fuel and range, the British fighters could not stay in the air as long as the German bombers. Moreover, the RAF was still using the tight "Vee" formation, suicidal when compared to the looser German "swarm," in which two pairs of fighters gave each other mutual protection. The close Vee formation was supposed to maximize firepower when attacking bomber formations, but the Hurricane squadrons in France were often bounced before they encountered enemy bombers. Because the leader was the only one on the look-out for the enemy and all the others were concerned just to stay in formation, those in the rear were sitting ducks. If the formation somehow ran into a force of bombers, it simply fell apart in the chaos of an air battle. In addition, the pattern of fire of the machine guns, which had been "harmonized" to focus at 400 yards, rendered the fighters almost useless at close range. Individual squadrons began to adopt the German formation, calling it the "finger-four" because of its appearance like fingers on a hand, while more experienced pilots customized their fighters, resetting their cone of fire, installing armor in the back of their seats, anything that would give them a vital edge. Fighter Command was learning, but it took time (Johnson 1980: 107–130).

Indeed, the battle over the Channel was a learning experience for both sides. The Germans had the initial aim that Kesselring had set, but once Dowding refused to take the bait, the Luftwaffe was left without any clear direction. By the third week in July the Germans had also learned to respect the Spitfires, so much so that their supposedly unbeatable long-range escort fighters, the Bf 110s (often mistakenly referred to as Me 100s), themselves had to be escorted. With all types of bombers endangered, the German fortunes rested on the Me 109 fighters, the limited range of which dictated where and how the Battle of Britain was fought. In particular, the RAF learned to use the one obvious advantage they had: as the battle moved over the coast, it was fought over home soil, so that both pilots and aircraft could be saved if they were shot down.

In 1938, after the Munich Crisis, the automotive industrialist Lord Nuffield had started the Civilian Repair Organization (CRO) to help the RAF in maintenance and repair. When the newspaper owner Lord Beaverbrook took over the Ministry of Aircraft Production in 1940, he gobbled up the CRO. He gave Fighter Command almost everything it needed. By late summer, that meant over 500 new Spitfires and Hurricanes a month, fully a third of which were actually damaged aircraft that the CRO had salvaged. The more sedate Air Ministry wanted to build up an inventory of spare parts, but Beaverbrook pointed out that the Luftwaffe was doing a fine job of producing spare parts in the form of crashed British fighters. Without Beaverbrook and the CRO, the increasing stream of new fighters might not have been enough to make the difference.

By the end of July, Dowding was uneasy. He guessed that he had lost 145 planes in July, or about what Beaverbrook could supply in a week. So he was able to restore his squadrons to their normal strength of 20 fighters each plus two in reserve. But the German raids over the Channel were costing Fighter Command its best men and denying their replacements sufficient time to train. Dowding begged the Air Ministry and Admiralty not to send convoys through the Channel. The cargoes could just as well move by train. But the administrators insisted that, simply as a matter of prestige, Britain could not be chased out of the *English* Channel. The loss of four-fifths of a convoy sailing from London ended that nonsense. Kesselring was thus able to drive the Royal Navy and merchant shipping from the Dover Straits. He believed, wrongly, that he had also bled the RAF white. What led him to this error? There were few RAF prisoners to interrogate; the Luftwaffe had no idea of the prodigies of production and repair radiating from the civilians; and it had no idea either of the system of fighter control that let Dowding use his fighters sparingly and keep back his main reserve.

Eagle Attack

As a preliminary to the second phase, Eagle Attack, the Germans decided to attack four of the radar stations in the south. The Luftwaffe had picked up enemy radio activity on the 12-meter band, heard calm female voices guiding the fighter interceptors, and noticed the buildings with the tall masts. They naturally concluded that the buildings were radio stations controlling the fighters in a sector. That being so, the RAF should not be able to bring in fighters from several sectors on short notice, because each sector, it was assumed, worked on its own. Why did the Luftwaffe miss the real function of the stations, and above all the way they were linked into a system integrating sector, group, and command? It was partly because the German scientists and technicians working on radar were not in touch with the Luftwaffe staff officers; the chaotic regimentation and status-mongering of Nazi Germany ruled out the sort of informal liaison between soldiers and scientists that the British achieved, as with Dowding and Watson-Watt, or at Bletchley Park, where a growing team of mathematicians, chess players, historians, literary scholars, cipher experts, soldiers, and oddballs, most of them young, were starting to crack the Enigma codes. In fact, Bletchley Park's civilian specialists deduced the coming of the Eagle Attack from the reports of the Luftwaffe weather aircraft and the sheer volume of German onboard radio sets getting trial runs. So Dowding was ready (Hinsley 1979: 176–182).

The great Eagle Attack starting August 12 was a botch from start to finish. Goering gave the air fleets nothing more than a shopping list of targets. When the weather was overcast in the morning, the attack was canceled, but orders to this effect did not reach Bomber Wing 2, which used slow Dornier 17s. It thus took off blissfully alone to hit Stepney near London, and was bounced first by 74 Squadron and then by 111 Squadron. When the weather cleared in the afternoon, the main attack was finally launched, aimed at the air fields of Fighter Command in the south. But the Germans did not know which air fields were part of Fighter Command's jurisdiction, and their main success, a Stuka attack on Detling that caught the aircrew in the mess and killed 65, hit a base outside Dowding's control. When Fighter Wing 53 tried to lure Fighter Command to the west of the Isle of Wight, the RAF controllers could see the trick shaping up on their map tables and refused the bait. Instead, they sent interceptors to hit the main bombing force from above. By the end of Eagle Day, August 12, the RAF had bagged 46 bandits, losing only 13 fighters in the air but 47 on the ground.

After a lull, the Luftwaffe decided to test what was left of Fighter Command by hitting it from all sides. In effect, the Germans were going to keep staging Eagle Days until they got it right. The Luftwaffe had in fact inflicted deep wounds on Fighter Command, but did not know what kinds of wounds they were. The British, on the other hand, were single-minded. Their goal was simply to hang on. In this, it helped when Dowding got Ultra information on the German tactic of attacking in waves. Knowing this, he could parcel out his fighters carefully rather than sending them all against the first wave.

Goering began August 13 by cancelling the attack because of the weather. Again, one group did not learn of the cancellation and flew off on its own. The feint from the north sent in by Air Fleet 6 was shot to pieces by a fighter group that the Germans thought had been destroyed in the south. A second feint from Denmark was stopped by 12 Group. Both of these disastrous probes were made by bombers not escorted by Me 109s. The Luftwaffe realized that the modern British fighters could outrun their bombers and henceforth provided fighter escorts. But because of the limited range of the Me 109s in escort, this meant that the bombers' targets had to be confined to the south.

In the south, the German escorts could not stop the fighters from 11 Group getting at the Stukas and Me 110 s, 75 of which were shot down against a loss of 34 British fighters in the air and 16 on the ground. By the end of August 15, Goering decreed that Stukas would in future need an escort of three fighters, and that the attacks on the "radio" stations were pointless, because obviously the British had not been blinded.

Up until August 15, Fighter Command had sent Hurricanes against bombers and Spitfires against fighters. But by the end of the day, pilots reported that the German fighter escorts were flying at the same height as the bombers, alongside or ahead. So Fighter Command ordered all the squadrons to ignore the fighters wherever possible and send everything, including the Spitfires,

against the bombers. This meant operating between 12,000 and 20,000 feet, the best range of altitude for the Spitfires.

The Attack on the Fighter Command Sector Fields

After a few days of fierce German attacks on the radar stations and airfields of 11 Group, culminating on the black day of August 18 when Fighter Command lost 33 aircraft, the weather forced both sides to take stock on August 19. Park, on whose 11 Group the weight of the battle was falling, discussed tactics with his sector commanders and controllers. He stressed the need to defend the sector fields and to attack bombers rather than fighter escorts. This meant scrambling as early as possible and hitting the enemy forward, which ruled out the sort of "big wings" of massed fighters that Park's bitter rival, Trafford Leigh-Mallory, commander of 12 Group, was pushing. The idea of the big wings actually came from the remarkable ace with the artificial legs, Douglas Bader, by now the commanding officer of 242 Squadron, the all-Canadian squadron.

Goering also met his commanders on August 19. He released the air fleets to select their own targets, but stressed the need to take out the sector fields and to avoid London, which Hitler wanted to save if a big finish were needed. Goering admitted that the Stukas were too slow and vulnerable, particularly after completing their dives, and he started to pull them out of the battle. He also conceded that his idea of using Me 110s as fighter escorts was wrong and ordered that they too must be escorted. Above all, he stressed the need for close escort. By doing so, he wasted the Me 109s advantage of superior height and speed, and by tying his fighters so closely to his bombers, which were plodding along on predictable set courses, he handed the initiative back to the RAF. It was at this meeting that Goering asked Werner Mölders and Adolf Galland, his two key fighter commanders, what else they might want. Mölders asked for stronger engines, and Galland, a droll fellow, asked for Spitfires. When Goering said that the RAF had only around 300 fighters left, the two experienced pilots disagreed. They knew they were not up against a failing enemy. Indeed, by the end of August, Beaverbrook told Dowding that there were 1,000 fighters available and 500 more under repair.

What worried Dowding was the supply of pilots. In a speech on August 20, Churchill reckoned that "Never in the field of human conflict was so much owed by so many to so few." The unromantic Dowding would have preferred a few more. In the first week of the Eagle Attack, he had lost 80 percent of his squadron leaders. The replacements coming in, except for the experienced Poles, had no more than two weeks of flying high-speed fighters.

The Germans came closest to victory in the third phase of the Battle, the attacks on airfields after August 24. The close escort Goering had ordered, while hampered by the way the fighters could only shoot forward, did protect enough bombers to wreak havoc on the sector fields, particularly Biggin Hill. An angry row between Park and Leigh-Mallory erupted when 12 Group repeatedly failed to protect the fields of 11 Group while it was attacking the bomber formations. Leigh-Mallory repeated his argument for big wings, even though they would have been useless in the sort of fast-breaking emergency Park was facing.

The Attack on London

On August 25, Kesselring decided to hit the sector fields near London with a feint attack up the Thames Estuary. That night, however, one bomber got lost and bombed Central London by mistake. Considering the pounding the suburbs had been taking, this was nothing new to Londoners, but it alarmed the War Cabinet. Churchill ordered Bomber Command to retaliate, and 82 bombers set off to hit Berlin. Legend has it that this was the turning point in the Battle, the point at which the Luftwaffe gave up a successful tactic and turned to blitzing cities in retaliation instead. Not so. Far from turning in favor of Britain on August 25, the Battle turned much, much worse. By August 30, the Luftwaffe had adjusted its tactics and come within a hair's breadth of destroying the bases so vital to Fighter Command. By noon on August 30, the whole of 11 Group had

scrambled to ward off attacks on Biggin Hill, Kenley, Tangmere, and Shoreham. By the afternoon, a chance hit knocked out the power along the south coast and left the radar dead, and a third wave of bombers, close on the heels of the second, hit the sector fields again. By the end of the day, the RAF had shot down 36 enemy bombers and lost 25 fighters, but it faced a cruel bind. How could the fighters refuel and rearm if their bases were under constant attack? Sooner or later they would be caught on the ground.

Everything went right for Kesselring on August 31. Biggin Hill was hit again and the radar stations were knocked out momentarily. Both sides lost 39 aircraft, but it was Dowding who suffered more. He could no longer rotate squadrons away from the cauldron of 11 Group and instead had to bring squadrons in from quieter sectors. Over the previous two weeks he had lost 200 more fighters than Beaverbrook could replace and 231 of his 1,000 pilots, with 103 killed and 128 badly wounded. Six of the seven key sector fields of 11 Group had been devastated. The Luftwaffe was winning, even though, as Admiral Raeder complained, it was fighting an absolute air battle for its own sake and not to help Sealion.

Kesselring knew he was winning. So did Dowding, yet at no time did his nerve fail him. He seemed to expect that something would turn up. And something did. Had Kesselring concentrated on flattening the two remaining usable sector fields 11 Group had, Tangmere and Kenley, he might have won. But the shopping list Goering had given him at the start now distracted him, and he started to send his formations, three-quarters of which were now made up of fighters, against aircraft factories. So it was not the chance bombing of London and British retaliation against Berlin that let Park draw breath; rather, what foiled the Germans was the dithering that had muddled their attack from the start. Dowding had a system for defense; the German system of airpower, such as it was, was keyed to ground support, not strategic bombing, and so an iron law of war now applied: it not only takes a system to beat a system, but a purpose-built system usually beats an improvised system. If the Luftwaffe let its attention wander from the sector fields, this was because it had lacked a clear strategy from the start and was thus prone to opportunism.

On September 3, Goering, Kesselring, and Sperrle conferred. Goering and Kesselring were certain that the RAF was almost out of fighters and wanted to polish off the remainder. They did not realize that Dowding was short of pilots and airfields, not aircraft. An attack on London seemed just the thing to lure the tag end of the RAF into the air and shoot it down.

Goering later claimed that he had wanted to keep hitting the sector fields, but he was being wise after the event. On September 7, he not only announced that he was taking over command of the Battle of Britain, but he personally watched an armada of 1,000 bombers and fighters roar overhead to smash London. The destination of this air fleet, which covered 800 square miles in formation, was not clear to the RAF until the last moment, and so London took a terrible beating. The Blitz had begun. But finally Park had the respite he needed to repair his sector fields. Now he knew where the Germans would be going, so he could organize his defense. Moreover, the agitation of Leigh-Mallory finally paid off. Although 12 Group still failed to protect the bases of 11 Group, it did assemble some big wings and chew up the German bomber stream. The climax came on September 15. Aided by Ultra intelligence, Dowding and Park knew that the Germans would be sending two waves, so Fighter Command would have time to rearm and refuel its fighters after engaging the first wave.

The RAF fought the Luftwaffe from the Channel to London and back again. Dowding had only 80 Hurricanes and 47 Spitfires left in reserve. But everything was sent to help 11 Group. Kesselring had increased the ratio of fighters to bombers in hopes of applying the final blow. But Park and Leigh-Mallory had all their weapons in the right place and it seemed to Londoners watching the contrails of the aircraft in the clear blue sky that everything coming down was German. At the end of September 15, the RAF claimed 185 enemy planes destroyed, rather more than the actual total of 50–60. But the Battle that had begun with Churchill's rhetorical challenge had been a contest of will, morale, and propaganda all along, and simply by surviving to exaggerate its success, Fighter Command had won.

Overall, from July to October, Fighter Command lost 915 fighters and destroyed 1,733 German aircraft (according to the German records) for a 2:1 ratio; not the 3:1 (2,698) claimed at the time but still impressive and decisive. On September 17, Hitler quietly put Sealion on hold. Bletchley Park and thus Churchill found out. Although the fear of invasion did not entirely pass away until Hitler turned eastward the following spring, the British were able to breathe a collective sigh of relief.

References

Churchill, Sir Winston S. (1949) *Their Finest Hour*. Boston: Houghton Mifflin.

Gilbert, M. (1983) *Finest Hour: Winston S. Churchill 1939–1941*. Toronto: Stoddart.

Hinsley, F. H. (1979) *History of British Intelligence*. Cambridge: Cambridge University Press.

Johnson, J. E. (1980) *Full Circle*. New York: Bantam.

Murray, W. (1983) *Strategy for Defeat: The Luftwaffe, 1933–45*. Maxwell Air Force Base, AL: Air University Press.

Terraine, J. (1985) *A Time for Courage: The Royal Air Force in the European War, 1939–1945*. New York: Macmillan.

Further Reading

Barley, M. P. (2004) "Contributing to Its Own Defeat: The Luftwaffe and the Battle of Britain," *Defence Studies*, 4 (3): 387–411.

Bungay, S. (2009) *The Most Dangerous Enemy: A History of the Battle of Britain*. London: Aurum Press.

Cumming, A. J. (2007) "Did Radar Win the Battle of Britain?" *The Historian*, 69 (4): 688–705.

Deighton, L. (1977) *Fighter*. London: Cape.

Gelb, N. (1986) *Scramble: A Narrative History of the Battle of Britain*. London: Joseph.

Hough, R. and Richards, D. (1989) *The Battle of Britain: The Greatest Air Battle of World War II*. London: Norton.

Orange, V. (1984) *A Biography of Air Chief Marshal Sir Keith Park*. London: Methuen.

Orange, V. (2008) *Dowding of Fighter Command: Victor of the Battle of Britain*. London: Grub Street.

Overy, R. J. (2001) *The Battle of Britain: The Myth and the Reality*. New York: Norton.

Overy, R. J. (2005) *The Air War: 1939–1945*. Washington, DC: Potomac Press.

Preston, D. L. (1994) "The Key to Victory: Fighter Command and the Tactical Reserves during the Battle of Britain," *Air Power History*, 41 (4): 18–29.

Puri, S. (2006) "The Role of Intelligence in Deciding the Battle of Britain," *Intelligence and National Security*, 21 (3): 416–439.

Robinson, D. (2005) *Invasion, 1940: The Truth about the Battle of Britain and What Stopped Hitler*. New York: Carroll and Graf.

Wright, R. (1969) *Dowding and the Battle of Britain*. London: Macdonald.

World War II: Eastern Front

DAVID M. GLANTZ

The Eastern Front of World War II – called the Great Patriotic War by Russians – refers to the Soviet–German War during which Hitler's Third German Reich attempted to defeat and subjugate Stalin's Soviet Union. The war began on June 22, 1941, when Germany's *Wehrmacht* (armed forces) invaded the Soviet Union in accordance with Plan Barbarossa, a military operation designed to defeat the Soviet Union's Red Army, overthrow its communist government, and dismember and exploit its territories for the benefit of Germany. The war resulted from political and ideological competition between Nazi Germany and the communist Soviet Union.

The war consisted of seven distinct campaigns; specifically, military operations conducted in the summer and fall periods of 1941, 1942, 1943, and 1944 and the winters of 1941–1942, 1942–1943, and 1944–1945, with the final winter campaign ending at war's end on May 9, 1945. The seven campaigns, in turn, formed three distinct "periods of war," distinguished from one another by virtue of which country controlled the strategic initiative. The first period of war, which lasted from June 22, 1941, to November 18, 1942, was characterized by the *Wehrmacht*'s control of the strategic initiative. The second period of war, from November 19, 1942, to December 31, 1943, was a transitional period during which the strategic initiative fluctuated between the two sides. In the third period of war, from January 1, 1944, to May 9, 1945, the Red Army seized and held the strategic initiative.

Operation Barbarossa, the war's initial campaign in the summer and fall of 1941, consisted of four successive offensive operations conducted by German Army Groups North, Center, and South

and ended with German defeats at Leningrad and Rostov in November and at Moscow in early December. The Barbarossa offensive pitted three million German troops with 3,350 tanks, reinforced by about a million Finnish, Romanian, Italian, and Slovakian soldiers, against 2.7 million Red Army troops equipped with 12,683 tanks in the western Soviet Union, backed up by over 600,000 troops and 3,160 tanks in strategic reserve.

During Barbarossa's initial stage in late June and early July, the three army groups penetrated the Red Army's strategic defenses in the western Soviet Union, encircled and destroyed three Soviet armies and severely damaged eight more, and advanced rapidly eastward along the Leningrad, Moscow, and Kiev axes to reach the western Dvina and Dnepr rivers. While planning Barbarossa, Hitler had assumed the Soviet Union would collapse if German forces destroyed all Red Army forces west of this line. Contrary to this assumption, Barbarossa's first stage ended abruptly in early July when advancing German forces encountered six new Soviet armies manning defenses along the two rivers.

After Hitler's assumption proved incorrect, during the second stage of Operation Barbarossa in July and August, Army Group North cleared Red Army forces from the Baltic region and advanced into Soviet territory south of Leningrad, Army Group Center conducted a two-month long battle for the Smolensk region, and Army Group South defeated Red Army forces in the Ukraine and advanced eastward to the Dnepr River at Kiev. Although the Germans encircled and destroyed or severely damaged five more Soviet armies during this period, Red Army resistance proved far stronger than anticipated. Along the Leningrad axis, the Red Army's Northwestern Front launched twin counterstrokes against Army Group North at Sol'tsy and Staraia Russa, which delayed the German advance on Leningrad for roughly two weeks. Similarly, along the Moscow axis, the Red Army's Western, Reserve, and Briansk Fronts conducted combined counteroffensives against Army Group Center in August and early September, which inflicted heavier than anticipated losses on the army group and halted its advance by forcing it to conduct several operations to clear Soviet forces from its flanks. Ultimately, the

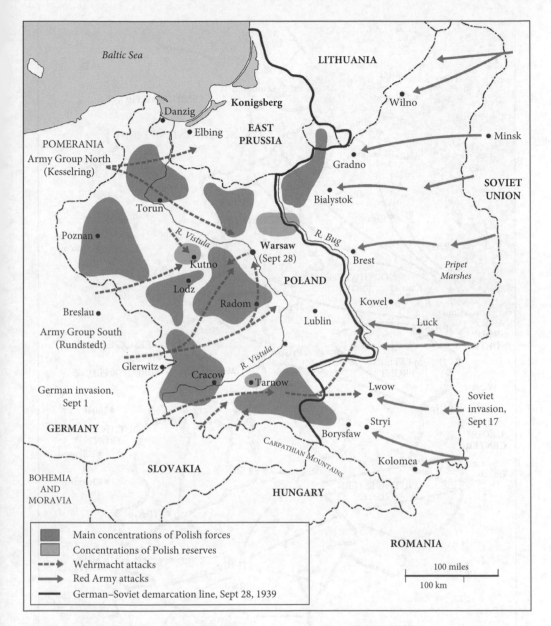

Map 19   German invasion of Poland, 1939.

damage done to Army Group Center contributed to its near collapse at the gates of Moscow in early December. Along the Kiev axis, Army Group South conquered most of the Ukraine from the Red Army's Southwestern and Southern Fronts, but failed to capture Kiev. Despite its heavy losses during this stage, the Red Army managed to field eight new armies to replace those lost in previous encirclements.

During the third stage of Barbarossa in September, because of Hitler's concerns for the security of Army Group Center's flanks and heavier than anticipated Soviet resistance in the Smolensk region, the three German army groups moved to seize Leningrad and Kiev before moving east to capture Moscow. In the *Wehrmacht*'s most dramatic victory of the war to date, Army Groups Center and South jointly encircled and

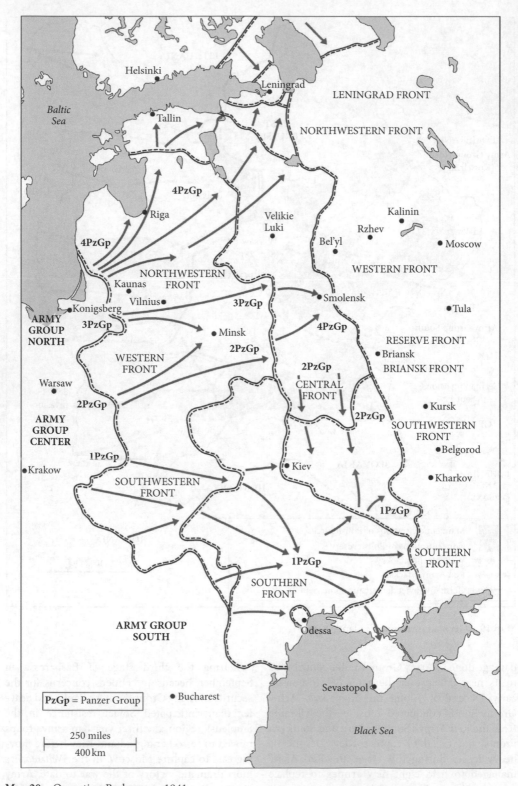

Map 20 Operation Barbarossa, 1941.

destroyed the Red Army's Southwestern Front, eliminating between four and five armies and over 600,000 soldiers from the Red Army's ranks. Further north, however, the Red Army's Leningrad Front thwarted Army Group North's attempt to seize Leningrad. This failure compelled the Germans to settle for a prolonged siege of 900 days which, by January 1944, when the Red Army broke the siege, cost the army and Leningrad's civilian population well over a million human lives.

The final stage of Operation Barbarossa began on September 30, when Army Group Center and three of the *Wehrmacht*'s four panzer groups advanced on Moscow. During its spectacular eastward advance in early October, the army group encircled and destroyed six more Soviet armies and killed or captured more than 600,000 soldiers in the Viaz'ma and Briansk regions. Then, as the Soviet High Command (*Stavka*) frantically reinforced its Western Front's depleted ranks, the German advance bogged down only 100 km from Moscow in late October because of heavy fall rains, the dispersal of its forces over too broad a front, and increasing resistance by Red Army troops manning prepared defenses west of Moscow. Once cold weather froze the ground in early November, Army Group Center resumed its advance and, grinding its way forward against strengthening resistance, reached the immediate approaches to Moscow in early December.

On December 5, with German forces within 10 km of the city's outskirts, the Red Army suddenly struck back with four reserve armies Stalin released to General Georgii Zhukov's Western Front. To his amazement, the counterattacks by the Western Front not only halted the German advance but also obliged German forces, exhausted in the previous fighting, to retreat. Zhukov's desperate counterattacks became, first, a genuine counterstroke and, soon after, with Stalin's approval, a full-fledged counteroffensive.

To the Soviets' amazement and the Germans' chagrin, by mid-December the Barbarossa offensive was replaced by the Red Army's Moscow counteroffensive, as all four Soviet reserve armies went into action. With their front collapsing, but ordered by Hitler to "stand fast," Army Group Center's forces withdrew a bit, dug in, and, somehow, held. Enthusiastic over the unexpected success, as deputy supreme commander to Stalin,

Zhukov steadily expanded the offensive in the Moscow region until, by early January 1942, it encompassed the entire front from Leningrad to the Black Sea. Thus, beginning with a single stroke on the northern outskirts of Moscow, within days Operation Barbarossa's summer and fall campaign became the second campaign of the war – the Soviet winter offensive of 1941–1942. Several weeks before Operation Barbarossa culminated in the battle for Moscow in December, Army Groups North and South suffered similar fates. In the north, Army Group North's northward advance in October to link up with Finnish forces at Tikhvin ended in defeat in November and withdrawal to its original positions east of Leningrad in December. In the south, Army Group South's First Panzer Army drove eastward and captured Rostov in November only to find itself enveloped and defeated by Soviet forces and forced to retreat westward over 100 km before its front stabilized.

Operation Barbarossa failed because Hitler's assumptions regarding the Red Army proved incorrect. Specifically, Hitler's belief that the war would end successfully if the *Wehrmacht* could destroy the bulk of the Red Army west of the Dvina and Dnepr rivers proved erroneous, and the Führer seriously underestimated the Soviet Union's capacity for raising and fielding fresh forces. Compounding these mistakes, the *Wehrmacht* tried to accomplish too much with far too few forces and attempted to operate in the Eastern Theater with techniques learned in and more suited to the West. While learning that traversing a kilometer in the East was far more taxing, logistically, than doing the same in the West, they also failed to take into account the woefully underdeveloped road network in the Soviet Union. As for Army Group Center's advance on Moscow, it faltered because its forces became overextended, its logistical system functioned ineffectively in so underdeveloped a theater of operations, because of the heavy losses it suffered during the fighting in the Smolensk region, and because of the Red Army's ability to mobilize fresh armies to replace those the Germans destroyed. The Red Army survived the first campaign despite losing over 4.3 million soldiers by December 31, 1941, including three million killed, captured, or missing, roughly 80 percent of the pre-war army. Although its mobilization base of about 10 million men compensated for these losses, the army had to fight through most of 1941 and early 1942 with partially trained reservists and poorly or utterly untrained conscripts. The *Wehrmacht*, which included Europe's best-trained soldiers and units, suffered over 830,000 casualties, including 170,000 killed and 35,000 missing, or roughly 26 percent of the 3.2 million men fighting on its Eastern Front, losses Germany could ill afford without quick victory. As for its impact on the war, together with the defeats at Tikhvin and Rostov, the Battle of Moscow was the first turning point in the war because it vividly demonstrated that Germany could not achieve the objectives called for in Hitler's Plan Barbarossa.

During the Barbarossa campaign the German and Soviet sides both exhibited patterns of behavior, some quite brutal but others far more positive for their cause, that would endure to war's end. On the positive side of the Soviet ledger, although the Germans captured immense quantities of military and industrial equipment, the Soviet government exerted Herculean efforts to evacuate the most vital parts of its industrial facilities to the safety of the Ural mountains and beyond. Together with Allied Lend-Lease deliveries of war materials to the Soviet Union, primarily via Arkhangel'sk, the Persian corridor, and the Alaska–Siberian route, these evacuations enabled Soviet military industry to provide its Red Army with the necessary implements of war. These measures, together with Soviet decisions to concentrate on mass production of the simplest and less costly but most powerful types of tanks, artillery, and aircraft, enabled the Soviet Union to out-produce their German counterparts from late 1942 through war's end. On the other hand, the Soviet government's decision to implement a scorched earth policy by destroying all industrial and agricultural facilities of value in territory occupied by the enemy, a policy the Germans, too, pursued as they withdrew westward after mid-1943, laid waste to the territories reconquered by the Red Army in 1944 and 1945.

Similarly, exploiting the immense number of Red Army soldiers left isolated in the *Wehrmacht*'s rear during its rapid and deep advances in 1941 and, once again, in 1942, enabled the Soviet government and Red Army to create large partisan forces capable of conducting guerrilla war in German-occupied territories. Coupled with ideologically motivated harsh treatment of local populations by German forces occupation authorities and officially sanctioned German policies to liquidate "Bolsheviks" in the Red Army (such as the infamous "Commissar" order), the ferocity and excesses generated by this guerrilla warfare spread to the conflict along the front, producing a vicious cycle of atrocities and reprisals on the part of both sides that endured through war's end. As a result, the Soviet–German War became a brutal cultural struggle or *Kulturkampf*, during which neither side often sought or offered quarter. Because of the ideological and ethnic nature of the war and the totalitarian nature of Hitler's and Stalin's regimes, the war was also characterized by widespread collaboration by people on both sides, frequent desertions from the ranks of the opposing armies, and draconian disciplinary measures, such as penal units and blocking detachments, employed by both sides to ensure the loyalty and continued service of their soldiers.

Although the strategic initiative shifted into the Red Army's grasp during the winter campaign of 1941–1942, this was only temporary. Propelled by optimism generated by the victory at Moscow, in January 1942 Stalin ordered all eight of the Red Army's operating fronts to conduct a general offensive from the Leningrad region to the Black Sea. During this offensive, which lasted until late April 1942, the Red Army's Kalinin, Western, and Briansk Fronts organized successive operations aimed at defeating German Army Group Center and recapturing the city of Smolensk. However, because the army lacked large armored and mechanized formations (the largest tank force was the tank brigade with about 50 tanks), it was forced to rely on fragile cavalry and airborne corps to sustain operations into the Germans' rear areas. The frenzied Soviet counteroffensives in the Moscow region placed enormous pressure on the defending Germans but also resulted in heavy Soviet losses. As a result, by the time the attackers reached the approaches to Vitebsk, Smolensk, Viaz'ma, Briansk, and Orel in late February, they lost much of their offensive punch. Nevertheless, by April, Soviet forces carved huge gaps in the *Wehrmacht*'s defenses west of Moscow, creating a crazy patchwork quilt of overlapping forces that took months of fighting to sort out.

A similar pattern existed elsewhere along the front during the winter campaign. In the north the Leningrad and Volkhov Fronts penetrated Army Group North's defenses south of the city, but 2nd Shock Army, which reached the German rear, was itself encircled and destroyed several months later. The 2nd Shock's final commander, General Alexander Vlasov, reacted to the army's tragic and, in his view, senseless destruction by shifting his allegiance to the German side. Likewise, in the south, the Southwestern and Southern Fronts wedged into the Germans' defenses south of Khar'kov, only to see their offensive stall in early February, leaving their forces lodged in a large bridgehead jutting into the Germans' defenses. These operations indicated that, while the Red Army could successfully penetrate German defenses, without large armored forces it was not capable of exploiting these penetrations.

During the summer–fall campaign of 1942, Hitler tried to seize the strategic initiative by conducting Operation Blau [Blue], the Wehrmacht's second strategic offensive of the war, while Stalin decided to conduct limited offensive operations in southern Russia while preparing to defeat an expected German advance on Moscow. Because Stalin misread German strategic intentions, his offensive in the Khar'kov region in May 1942 ended as a catastrophe, with three armies encircled and 270,000 soldiers captured, because it struck German forces preparing for Operation Blau. Likewise, the Red Army's offensive in the Crimea failed with staggering losses because Lev Mekhlis, one of Stalin's political cronies and Stavka representative to the Crimean Front, meddled with the conduct of the operation.

In sharp contrast with these Soviet defeats, the Wehrmacht's summer offensive, Operation Blau, which sought to reach and conquer the oil-rich Caucasus region, achieved spectacular initial success. This offensive began on June 28, 1942, when Army Group South (divided into Army Groups A and B in early July), supported by Italian and Romanian armies, attacked eastward across the southern Soviet Union. This offensive pitted about a million German troops, along with another 300,000 Italian and Romanian, fielding 1,635 tanks, 17,000 artillery pieces, and 1,640 combat aircraft against roughly 1.7 million Red Army soldiers equipped with 2,959 tanks, 16,500 artillery pieces, and 758 combat aircraft.

During the first stage of Blau, from June 28 through July 12, German Sixth and Fourth Panzer Armies and Hungarian Second Army shattered three Soviet armies, advanced eastward to the Don River at Voronezh, and then wheeled southward to seize the eastern Donbas region. In the second stage, July 9–24, German First Panzer and Seventeenth Armies joined the eastward advance and captured the city of Rostov-on-the-Don, destroying six more Soviet armies and paving the way for a subsequent invasion of the Caucasus region. Elated by these successes, Hitler divided his forces, sending Army Group B's Sixth and Fourth Panzer Armies toward Stalingrad and Army Group A's First Panzer and Seventeenth Army deep into the Caucasus region. In Blau's third stage, from July 24 to early September 1942, Army Group A's forces decimated Soviet forces defending the Caucasus region, advanced to the foothills of the High Caucasus mountains, and prepared to cross the mountains to seize the oilfields at Baku. To the north, Army Group B's Sixth Army fought a costly four-week battle to reach the Don River and the approaches to Stalingrad against the newly formed Soviet 62nd and 64th Armies, reinforced by two new tank armies. After Hitler reinforced Sixth Army with Fourth Panzer Army, the two German armies finally overcame the Soviet resistance and drove eastward, reaching the Volga River north and south of Stalingrad in the third week of August and isolating 62nd Army in Stalingrad and 64th Army in a bridgehead on the Volga's western bank south of the city.

During the climactic fourth stage of Operation Blau, from August 21 to November 18, Sixth Army and roughly half of Fourth Panzer Army fought a battle of attrition against Soviet 62nd Army in Stalingrad city, in grueling urban combat that sapped the strength of attacker and defender alike. Simultaneously, Army Group A's forces in the Caucasus region failed to penetrate the High Caucasus mountains and suffered defeat on the approaches to the city of Groznyi in early November. By mid-November Army Groups A and B had lost their offensive punch and were unable to advance further. Furthermore, an acute shortage of German troops because of the attrition in Stalingrad forced Army Group B to assign Romanian and Italian armies frontline positions on German Sixth Army's flanks.

Capitalizing on the attrition battle in Stalingrad, on November 19, 1942, the *Stavka* began a major counteroffensive, code-named Operation Uranus, in the Stalingrad region. Spearheaded by a new tank army and multiple tank corps, a force of over 600,000 Red Army troops struck and penetrated Romanian defenses northwest and south of Stalingrad and, after several days of fighting, destroyed two Romanian armies and encircled all of German Sixth and part of Fourth Panzer Army in the massive pocket around Stalingrad. The Red Army's successful counteroffensive at Stalingrad ended the summer–fall campaign and the first period of the war. This offensive, coupled with another Soviet counteroffensive, code-named Operation Mars, which pummeled German forces occupying the Rzhev salient, west of Moscow, but ultimately failed, abruptly shifted the strategic initiative into the Red Army's hands and marked the beginning of the winter campaign of 1942–1943, during which the Red Army expanded its Stalingrad counteroffensive to encompass the entire southern half of the German–Soviet front.

During the initial stage of the Red Army's winter offensive, the Soviet Don Front, with six armies, besieged German Sixth Army in Stalingrad, the Stalingrad Front, with four armies, defeated German attempts to rescue their forces encircled in Stalingrad, and the Southwestern and Voronezh Fronts, with four armies, expanded the offensive toward the west, in the process destroying or severely damaging Italian Eighth, German Second, and Hungarian Second Armies. In the midst of the winter offensive, German Sixth Army in Stalingrad surrendered on February 2, 1943, bringing Axis losses during the course of the Blau campaign to over 500,000 men, including 200,000 Germans, at a cost of roughly 600,000 Red Army casualties. The German defeat at Stalingrad was a second turning point in the war because it indicated the Soviet Union would win the war. With Stalin determined to vanquish his fellow dictator, the only remaining question was: "How badly would Germany lose?"

In early February 1943, the *Stavka* expanded its winter offensive by ordering its Southwestern, Voronezh, and Southern Fronts to mount two new offensives, the first toward Khar'kov and Kursk, and the second to clear German forces from the Donbas region. After the twin offensives developed successfully, with the Southwestern Front approaching the Dnepr River at Zaporozh'e on February 18 and the Voronezh Front capturing Kursk and Belgorod on February 8 and 9 and Khar'kov on February 16, an overly optimistic *Stavka* expanded the offensive's scope by ordering its new Central Front, formed from the Don Front's "Stalingrad armies," to attack westward from the Kursk region to capture Orel and Briansk and split the Germans' Eastern Front in two. After attacking in mid-February, however, the Soviet forces outran their logistical support, became seriously overextended, and bogged down because of the *rasputitsa* (rainy season). In the midst of this expanded Red Army offensive, General Erich von Manstein, the commander of Army Group South, orchestrated a counteroffensive which defeated Soviet forces in the Donbas region, recaptured Khar'kov and Belgorod, and restored stability to German defenses in the southern Soviet Union by early March 1943, thus ending the winter campaign. The legacy of combat during this period was the infamous Kursk Bulge, which protruded westward into German defenses in the central sector of the Soviet–German front.

German military strategy in the East during the summer–fall campaign of 1943 was shaped by the fact that the *Wehrmacht* was now waging war in multiple theaters, including the war in the East, the U-boat war in the Atlantic, a ground war in Italy, and the battle in the skies over Germany. Moreover, it had already lost the struggle in North Africa and now faced the grim reality of defending the coasts of western Europe against the threat of a "second front." Since Hitler now believed success in the war, as a whole, depended on exhausting the Red Army and forcing the Soviet Union to negotiate a separate peace, he decided to conduct his third major strategic offensive in the East, an operation code-named Zitadelle (Citadel), toward a limited objective, specifically, the destruction of Red Army forces defending the Kursk Bulge. From the Soviet perspective, since the Red Army's previous successes occurred only in the winter months, the *Stavka* sought to prove the Red Army could defeat the *Wehrmacht* in the summer. Therefore, Stalin decided to begin the summer–fall campaign of

1943 by conducting a deliberate defense of the Kursk Bulge, the point where he expected the Germans to attack, and, after the Germans were halted, to conduct successive counteroffensives to drive the Germans back to the Dnepr River line, the same objective as in early 1943, and begin to liberate Belorussia and the Ukraine.

Given these competing strategies, the summer–fall campaign occurred in three distinct stages: first, the battle for the Kursk Bulge; secondly, the Red Army's advance to the Dnepr River; and, thirdly, the struggle for bridgeheads across the Dnepr River and attempts to liberate Belorussia and the Ukraine. During the first stage, July 5–23, the Red Army's Central and Voronezh Fronts and part of the new Steppe Front defeated German forces conducting Operation Citadel, specifically, Army Group Center's Ninth Army and Army Group South's Fourth Panzer Army and Army Detachment Kempf. On July 12, before the fighting around the Kursk Bulge ended, the Soviet Western, Briansk, and Central Fronts launched Operation Kutuzov, during which the three fronts defeated Army Group Center's Second Panzer Army and captured the city of Orel on August 18. Then, on August 3, before the fighting around Orel ended, the Soviet Voronezh and Steppe Fronts conducted Operation Rumiantsev, during which the two fronts defeated Army Group South's Fourth Panzer Army and Army Detachment Kempf and liberated the cities of Belgorod and Khar'kov by August 23.

After its victories in the Orel and Khar'kov regions, the *Stavka* unleashed a series of successive offensives further to the north and south. On August 7, the Soviet Kalinin and Western Fronts began Operation Suvorov, an offensive which drove German Army Group Center's Third Panzer and Fourth Armies westward and liberated the cities of Spas-Demensk, El'nia, Roslavl', and Smolensk by October 2. Before the fighting ceased in the Smolensk region, the Briansk Front had defeated Army Group Center's Ninth Army in the Briansk region and captured the city of Briansk on August 17. Simultaneously, the Southwestern and Southern Fronts smashed Army Group South's defenses in the Donbas region on August 13 and cleared German forces from the Donbas region, advancing to the outskirts of Zaporozh'e and Melitopol' by September

22, and, at the same time, the North Caucasus Front drove German forces in the northern Caucasus region back to the Taman' Peninsula.

During the second stage of the summer–fall offensive, on August 26, the Central, Voronezh, and Steppe Fronts launched multiple offensives known collectively as the Chernigov–Poltava operation, during which Army Group South's Second, Fourth Panzer, and Eighth Armies were forced to withdraw to the Panther Defensive Line (Eastern Wall) along the Dnepr River by late September. By the time this "race to the Dnepr River" ended, Soviet forces seized multiple small bridgeheads across the river from Gomel' southward to Kremenchug.

When the third stage began in October, 1st Baltic (former Kalinin), Western, and Belorussian (former Central) Fronts attempted to liberate Belorussia, and 1st, 2nd, and 3rd Ukrainian (former Voronezh, Steppe, and Southwestern) Fronts cleared German forces from the eastern bank of the Dnepr, seized bridgeheads on the river's western bank, and captured the cities of Dnepropetrovsk and Zaporozh'e. Although 1st, 2nd, and 3rd Ukrainian Fronts conducted multiple offensives aimed at expanding their bridgeheads across the Dnepr and capturing Kiev and Krivoi Rog, all of these attempts failed with heavy losses. Meanwhile, 4th Ukrainian (former Southern) Front seized Melitopol' and the territory between the Dnepr River and the approaches to the Crimea.

In early November, however, 1st, 2nd, and 3rd Ukrainian Fronts finally managed to expand their bridgeheads across the Dnepr. Attacking from the Liutezh bridgehead, north of Kiev, on November 3, 1st Ukrainian Front captured Kiev, Fastov, and Zhitomir from Army Group South's Fourth Panzer Army by November 13, thus seizing a strategic-size bridgehead west of the Ukrainian capital, which it successfully defended by repulsing a series of strong German counterstrokes from November 13 through December 23. To the south, 2nd and 3rd Ukrainian Fronts expanded their bridgeheads but failed to capture Krivoi Rog from Army Group South's defending Eighth and First Panzer Armies, while 4th Ukrainian Front also failed to dislodge the German Sixth Army from its bridgehead on the Dnepr's eastern bank at Nikopol'. Capping this stage of the campaign, but also marking the beginning of the winter campaign, on Christmas day, 1st Ukrainian Front smashed the defenses of Army Group South's Fourth Panzer Army west of Kiev, seizing the city of Berdichev and reaching the outskirts of Vinnitsa in an offensive that continued well into the new year. All the while, throughout November and December, 1st Baltic, Western, and Belorussian Fronts persisted in vain in their attempts to capture Vitebsk and liberate Belorussia.

During the winter offensive of 1943–1944, the Red Army conducted simultaneous offensive operations along the entire front to drive Army Group North from the Leningrad region, Army Group Center from Belorussia, and Army Groups South and A from the Ukraine and the Crimea. In the north the Leningrad and Volkhov Fronts penetrated Army Group North's defenses south of Leningrad in early January, driving the Germans away from the city and back to the Panther Line defenses protecting the Baltic region by late February. However, multiple Soviet attempts to penetrate German defenses at Ostrov, Pskov, and Narva in March and April ended in failure. In Belorussia, 1st Baltic, Western, and Belorussian Fronts tried once again to penetrate Army Group Center's defenses and capture the cities of Vitebsk, Minsk, and Bobruisk in January and February. Although General Konstantin Rokossovsky's Belorussian Front achieved modest success in southern Belorussia, multiple assaults by the 1st Baltic and Western Fronts against German defenses at Vitebsk and Orsha ended as bloody failures.

In the Ukraine, beginning in January 1944, the Red Army's 1st, 2nd, and 3rd Ukrainian Fronts conducted eight separate but interrelated offensives in two distinct stages to expel German forces from the entire Ukraine. In the first stage, 1st Ukrainian Front reached the outskirts of Vinnitsa in early January before being halted by counterstrokes orchestrated by Army Group South's Fourth and First Panzer Armies and 2nd Ukrainian Front captured Kirovograd from Army Group South's Eighth Army. However, 3rd and 4th Ukrainian Fronts were once again halted by German forces short of Krivoi Rog. Then, from mid-January to mid-February, 1st and 2nd Ukrainian Fronts pinched off a salient defended by Army Group South's Eighth Army in the Korsun'-Shevchenkovskii region, killing or capturing as many as 30,000 German troops in three

weeks of heavy fighting, while 1st Ukrainian Front's right wing attacked westward and seized the Rovno and Lutsk region south of the Pripiat' Marshes. Further south, from late January through late February, 3rd and 4th Ukrainian Fronts defeated Army Group A and captured Nikopol' and Krivoi Rog.

During the second stage of its offensive in the Ukraine, in March the Red Army's 1st, 2nd, and 3rd Ukrainian Fronts conducted virtually simultaneous offensive operations, which, for the first time in the war, continued right through the *rasputitsa* without a halt, in a concerted attempt to destroy German Army Group South. Simultaneously, 4th Ukrainian Front sought to destroy Army Group A's forces, by now isolated in the Crimea. Attacking on March 4, 5, and 6, respectively, 1st, 2nd, and 3rd Ukrainian Fronts conducted coordinated offensives spanning the entire width of the Ukraine from northwest to southeast (the Proskurov–Chernovtsy, Uman'–Botoshany, and Bereznegovatoe–Snigirevka offensives), which lasted through late April 1944. In addition to collapsing Army Group South's defenses and propelling Soviet forces westward to the eastern border of Poland and the foothills of the Carpathian mountains and southward to the approaches to northern Romania, these offensives encircled German First Panzer and Sixth Armies and forced the Germans to split Army Group South into two new army groups, Northern and Southern Ukraine.

During the summer–fall campaign of 1944, for the first time in the war, the *Stavka* organized five successive offensive operations, each aimed at defeating an entire German army group. The *Stavka* began its offensives in the north by attacking Finnish forces on the Karelian Isthmus in early June and subsequently expanded the effort to encompass Belorussia in late June, central and southern Poland in mid-July, and Romania in late August in hopes of projecting the Red Army's forces westward to Riga, Minsk, L'vov, and Bucharest by the fall of 1944.

In the first offensive, the Leningrad Front defeated Finnish forces on the Karelian Isthmus and captured Vyborg in late June, forcing Finland to sue for peace. Within days after the fall of Vyborg, on June 22–23, the Red Army's 1st Baltic and 3rd, 2nd, and half of 1st Belorussian Fronts assaulted German defenses in Belorussia. This massive offensive collapsed Army Group Center's defenses, encircled and destroyed most of German Third Panzer, Fourth, and Ninth Armies in Vitebsk, Mogilev, Bobruisk, and Minsk, and drove the army group's remnants from most of Belorussia by late August. Virtually without a halt to rest and regroup, 1st Baltic Front attacked westward toward East Prussia, and 2nd and 3rd Baltic Fronts joined in by attacking westward through the Baltic states toward Riga.

Exploiting the success in Belorussia, on July 18, 1st Belorussian Front's left wing shattered the defenses of Army Group Southern Ukraine's Fourth Panzer Army west of Kovel' and exploited westward toward Lublin and the Vistula River south of Warsaw, where it seized bridgeheads at Magnuszew and Pulavy on August 2. When the Polish Home Army staged an insurrection in Warsaw during 1st Belorussian Front's advance, the *Stavka* dispatched the front's 2nd Tank Army toward Warsaw to exploit the situation. However, German Ninth Army organized a counterstroke east of Warsaw that decimated 2nd Tank Army and delayed the Red Army's advance on the city. Stalin's inability or unwillingness to alter his strategic plans by moving significant forces to the Warsaw region permitted the Germans to extinguish the insurrection in a brutal bloodbath.

Days before 1st Belorussian Front's offensive, on July 13, 1st Ukrainian Front assaulted the defenses of Army Group Northern Ukraine's Fourth Panzer Army in the L'vov region of southeastern Poland. After penetrating the Germans' defenses, the front's forces, spearheaded by three tank armies, encircled and destroyed a German corps and advanced rapidly westward to the Vistula River, where they captured a large bridgehead at Sandomierz. Thus, the twin Soviet offensives into central and southern Poland propelled Red Army forces to the Vistula River and severely damaged Army Group North Ukraine.

The Red Army's summer offensive culminated in late August, when 2nd and 3rd Ukrainian Fronts pulverized Army Group South Ukraine's defenses in Romania. In roughly 10 days, the two fronts encircled and destroyed German Sixth Army, forced the Romanian Third and Fourth Armies to surrender, seriously damaged German Eighth Army, and captured Bucharest, forcing Romania to join the Allies in the war. Soviet forces then advanced westward into the plains of eastern Hungary in October, capturing Belgrade in late October and besieging Budapest in December. Completing this offensive mosaic, in September and October, the Red Army's Northern Front defeated German forces at Petsamo in northern Norway, and the Leningrad and 2nd and 3rd Baltic Fronts overcame Army Group North's Panther Line defenses and liberated the bulk of the Baltic region. Thus, during the summer–fall campaign of 1944, the Red Army advanced westward over 500 km, in the process shortening its front from 1,600 to less than 1,255 km, enabling it to concentrate its forces to a far greater extent than before in the ensuing offensive operations.

In the winter campaign of 1944–1945 the Red Army conducted both simultaneous and successive strategic offensives. These operations actually began in Hungary in November and December 1944, when 2nd and 3rd Ukrainian Fronts attacked to draw German forces away from the Warsaw–Berlin axis. Then, on January 12–13, 1945, five Red Army fronts mounted major offensives against German forces defending East Prussia and Poland. In the most powerful of these offensives, on January 13, 1st Belorussian and 1st Ukrainian Fronts, each spearheaded by two tank armies, attacked Army Group A's forces defending central Poland. After completely shattering the Germans' defenses, the two tank armies spearheading 1st Belorussian Front advanced westward over 450 km in 16 days to reach the Oder River less than 60 km from Berlin by February 1 and immediately captured a bridgehead across the river. To the south, the two tank armies of 1st Ukrainian Front kept pace, reaching and crossing the Oder River north and south of Breslau. In their wake thousands of *Wehrmacht* troops remained helplessly encircled in numerous pockets and bypassed cities and towns.

A day after 1st Belorussian and 1st Ukrainian Fronts struck, on January 13, 3rd and 2nd Belorussian Fronts, assisted by 1st Baltic Front and spearheaded by a tank army, assaulted Army Group Center's defenses in East Prussia. After penetrating the Germans' forward defenses with ease, the two fronts drove westward over 240 km in 12 days, isolating the army group's remnants in a pocket around the city of Konigsberg by the end of January. The twin Soviet offensives virtually destroyed German Army Groups A and Center, leaving only scratch *Wehrmacht* units and

Volksturm (German Home Guards or militia) to defend Berlin.

In early February, Stalin abruptly postponed further attacks toward Berlin, ostensibly because of logistical problems, threats to the two fronts' flanks, and German forces encircled but not yet liquidated in the Soviet rear. However, it seems more likely that Stalin's decision to postpone a direct advance on Berlin in February resulted from political decisions taken at the big-three conference at Yalta, which granted the Soviet Union post-war dominance over eastern Germany but left jurisdiction over Austria and the Danube basin unresolved. Thus, throughout February the bulk of the *Stavka's* strategic reserves, in particular the powerful 9th Guards Army, flowed into Hungary. Thereafter, while 1st Belorussian and 1st Ukrainian Fronts conducted local operations in Silesia and Pomerania, the focal point of Red Army offensive operations shifted to Hungary. There, in the Budapest region, 2nd and 3rd Ukrainian Fronts built up their forces for an offensive to capture the remainder of Hungary and Austria.

Although the Germans tried to preempt the Soviet offensive by conducting a counterstroke of their own from March 6–15 with Sixth SS Panzer Army in an attempt to capture the Balaton oil-fields, in the midst of the German counterstroke, 2nd and 3rd Ukrainian Fronts launched an offensive which sent the SS army reeling westward in disorder, liberated the remainder of Hungary, and captured Vienna on April 13, 1945. Three days later, 1st and 2nd Belorussian and 1st Ukrainian Fronts commenced their climactic assault on Berlin.

The ensuing Berlin operation involved a combined offensive by 1st and 2nd Belorussian and 1st Ukrainian Fronts attacking from bridgeheads on the western bank of the Oder River. Spearheaded by four tank armies tasked with enveloping the city from the northeast and southwest, the three fronts attacked on April 16. After considerable difficulty overcoming German defenses east of Berlin, Red Army forces entered the city, where they captured the Führer bunker and Reichstag by April 30 and accepted the city's surrender on May 8, the same day that Allied and Soviet forces linked up along the Elbe River. While the Berlin offensive unfolded, 2nd and 3rd Ukrainian Fronts completed conquering Austria

and southern Czechoslovakia, 1st and 2nd Baltic Fronts destroyed Army Group North's remnants in Courland, and 3rd Belorussian Front liquidated Army Group Center's remnants in a pocket west of Konigsberg.

The final Soviet offensive of the Soviet–German War began on May 6, 1945, when 1st, 4th, and 2nd Ukrainian Fronts began a rapid advance toward Prague to defeat the *Wehrmacht's* last operational force, Army Group Center. The forward elements of 1st Ukrainian Front's 3rd and 4th Guards Tank Armies captured Prague on May 9, and, two days later, Red Army forces accepted the surrender of more than 600,000 German troops of Army Group Center. The Red Army's field operations ended on May 11, 1945, when the lead elements of 4th Guards Tank Army linked up with the forward elements of US Third Army east of Plzen, Czechoslovakia.

Because it was a conflict dominated by two competing ideologies, with strong racial overtones, unlike other struggles in World War II the Soviet–German War was a virtual *Kulturkampf*, or war of cultures, characterized by extreme brutality and numerous atrocities on both sides. As a result, during the fighting, quarter was often neither asked for nor granted, the human and material cost of the war to both sides was staggering, and the immense quantity of prisoners of war (POWs) captured by both sides suffered unprecedented attrition while in POW and labor camps. While its early victories permitted Germany to avoid total mobilization until later in the war, the Soviet Union's catastrophic defeats in 1941 and 1942 forced it to mobilize its entire economy and society for war in order to withstand defeat and emerge victorious. In terms of the human cost of war, the Soviet armed forces suffered over 29 million casualties, including over 10 million military dead, captured, or missing in action, while the *Wehrmacht* suffered almost 3.9 million dead, over 80 percent in the war in the East. Although incalculable, civilian casualties in the Soviet Union numbered at least 20 million and perhaps as many as 35 million. Because over half of the European Soviet Union became a battlefield subject to scorched earth policies on both sides, the economic costs of the war to the country were catastrophic. In retribution, the Red Army and Soviet government responded in kind as its troops liberated eastern Europe and marched into Germany in 1945. In the end, the war's ferocity and terrible consequences fundamentally shaped popular attitudes and governmental policies of both Germany and the Soviet Union, in the post-war years and probably forever.

Further Reading

Bellamy, C. (2007) *Absolute War: Soviet Russia in the Second World War*. London: Macmillan.

Erickson, J. (1975) *The Road to Stalingrad*. New York: Harper and Row.

Erickson, J. (1983) *The Road to Berlin*. Boulder: Westview Press.

Glantz, D. M. and House, J. (1995) *When Titans Clashed: How the Red Army Stopped Hitler*. Lawrence: University Press of Kansas.

Mawdsley, E. (2006) *Thunder in the East: The Nazi–Soviet War, 1941–1945*. Oxford: Oxford University Press.

Overy, R. (1997) *Russia's War*. London: Ian Allen.

Ziemke, E. F. (1968) *Stalingrad to Berlin: The German Defeat in the East*. Washington, DC: Office of the Chief of Military History, United States Army.

Ziemke, E. F. and Bauer, M. (1987) *Moscow to Stalingrad: Decision in the East*. Washington, DC: Center of Military History, United States Army.

World War II: Invasion of Normandy to the Surrender of Germany

JOHN C. MCMANUS

Invasion of Normandy: Western Allied Second Front

The Normandy invasion, codenamed Operation Overlord, was the beginning of the end for Nazi Germany. Since 1941, the Germans had been able to concentrate primarily on their war against the Soviet Union. The invasion, carried out on June 6, 1944, opened up a bona fide second front in Europe, thus placing maximum pressure on the already hard-pressed German army, which by early 1944 had constructed powerful beach defenses along the northern coastline of occupied France. This operation was the product of more than two years of intensive planning and prepara-

tion by a coalition of nations known as the Western Allies or, more precisely, the Allied Expeditionary Force. The supreme commander of the invasion, and of the ensuing campaign in Europe, was American General Dwight D. Eisenhower. His status as commander hinted at the leading role the United States would soon play, not only in World War II, but as a world power thereafter. Even so, his key subordinates were British: General Bernard Law Montgomery had command of Allied ground forces; Air Marshal Sir Trafford Leigh-Mallory commanded the air forces; Admiral Sir Bertram Ramsey controlled the Allied naval flotilla.

In order to repel the invasion, the Germans had over 60 divisions in place, comprising an "Atlantic Wall," according to Nazi propaganda. There was no wall, though. Divisions of varying quality were sprinkled along the coastlines and, in the case of the best panzer and panzer grenadier units, inland where they could react to any landings. At the coastline, the Germans used a mixture of slave and hired labor to construct a formidable network of bunkers, pillboxes, casements, minefields, beach obstacles, and the like. Field Marshal Gerd von Rundstedt, commander in chief of the German Army in the West, and Field Marshal Erwin Rommel, commander of Army Group B, which defended France's northern coast, could not agree on a plan to defeat the Allied invasion. Rommel believed that, if the Allies succeeded in getting ashore, their superiority in planes, ships, men, and matériel would inevitably overwhelm the Germans. Therefore, he insisted upon a coastal defense strategy designed to stop the invasion right at the water line, where the invaders were most vulnerable. Rundstedt took it as a given that the Allies would make it ashore, no matter how strong the German coastal defenses. So he advocated a mobile, inland defense designed to counterattack the invading forces and either throw them into the sea or pen them into a stalemated beachhead. The two field marshals never reconciled their differences; thus the German defensive plan was generally lacking in coherence.

In the months leading up to the invasion, the Allies conducted an effective disinformation campaign, known as Operation Fortitude, whose purpose was to deceive the Germans about the time and place of the landings. One element of the operation, known as Fortitude North, peddled the bogus idea that the British were planning to invade Norway. The other, more successful component, called Fortitude South, propagated the notion that a massive US Army under Lieutenant General George Patton would invade Calais, whose beaches and ports were ideal spots for any invasion. Dummy radio traffic and bogus orders emanated from fake headquarters such as the British Fourth Army and the First US Army Group (nominally under Patton). Double agents sent seemingly inside, but often useless, information to their German handlers. Artfully constructed but fake planes, tanks, jeeps, and ships deceived German photo reconnaissance pilots about the whereabouts and strength of Allied armies. This operation was effective enough to keep the Germans guessing about Allied intentions and even to fool some of them into thinking after the Normandy landings that a larger invasion of Calais would follow.

On D-Day, the United States, Britain, and Canada led the way into German-occupied France with amphibious and airborne landings, disgorging over 150,000 troops. The invasion armada consisted of over 6,500 ships, ranging in size from small landing craft to mighty battleships. On D-Day alone, the Allies employed a total of 12,500 bombers, fighters, transport aircraft, and gliders.

In total, there were five invasion beaches. At Utah Beach, on the Cotentin peninsula, elements of the US Army's 4th and 90th Infantry Divisions succeeded in securing a beachhead against scattered resistance. Their biggest peril was heavy artillery lobbed onto the beach from German batteries farther up the coast. Behind the beaches, paratroopers and glider troops from the 82nd and 101st Airborne Divisions captured bridges, cut roads, secured causeways, and, in general, harassed the movement of German units. To the east, on the Calvados coast, American soldiers from the 1st and 29th Infantry Divisions, augmented by Army Rangers, duplex drive amphibious tanks, and special engineer units, assaulted Omaha Beach, the most heavily defended portion of the Norman coast. Soldiers from the German army's 352nd Infantry Division turned the beach into a slaughterhouse, raking the Americans with mortar, artillery, machine gun, and rifle fire. The presence of thousands of mines along the beach

and the high ground inland only added to the carnage. Aided greatly by supporting fire from US Navy destroyers, small groups of men steadily and bloodily fought their way off Omaha Beach. By early afternoon, the Americans had carved out a shaky lodgment, but at the cost of nearly 2,500 casualties.

The British and Canadian landings went more smoothly. At Gold Beach, near Arromanches, the British 50th Infantry Division quickly overwhelmed the defenders, some of whom were eastern Europeans pressed into service in the German army. Likewise, at Sword Beach, the eastern end of the British landing area near the Orne River, the British Army's 3rd Infantry Division, with outstanding assistance from the British 6th Airborne Division, secured a major beachhead by late morning. In the middle, at Juno Beach, near Courseulles, the Canadian 3rd Infantry Division ran into the most stubborn resistance. Here, at times, the fighting was as bloody and desperate as at Omaha Beach, but the Canadians nevertheless succeeded in their mission.

By nightfall, 175,000 Allied soldiers were firmly ashore in Normandy, making the landings an unqualified success and a rather dramatic one at that. However, the invasion was only the first battle in a nearly year-long campaign of bloody battles the Allies would have to fight to defeat Germany.

The Battle of Normandy

The timing and location of the invasion took the Germans by surprise, but in the days following June 6, they reacted quickly. Several top-tier infantry, mechanized infantry, and panzer divisions counterattacked the various Allied beachheads, but none of these attacks was strong enough to achieve Adolf Hitler's goal of pushing the invaders back into the sea. What followed was a slow, incremental campaign in which the Allies linked up their five invasion beaches, forming one continuous front, and steadily slugged their way inland against ferocious German resistance.

In general, the British were opposed by the best enemy units, such as the 12th SS Panzer Division, as well as the 2nd and 21st Panzer Divisions. Montgomery hoped to capture the inland port of Caen on D-Day (a fact he later disingenuously denied). Instead, throughout all of June and the first week of July, he found himself enmeshed in a slow-moving contest of attrition with the powerful German formations arrayed around the northern approaches to the city. The Canadian 3rd Division, for instance, squared off with 12th SS Panzer, a formation composed of combat-experienced veterans and fanatical Hitler Youth alumni. The SS behaved with customary barbarity, executing Canadian prisoners. The Canadians at times responded in kind. Over the course of several weeks around Caen, 12th SS fought to complete destruction against its Canadian adversaries.

Without control of the roads that snaked through Caen and led to the excellent tank country south and east of the city, Montgomery had little hope of maneuvering his army out of Normandy. In early July, he employed heavy bombers to clear the way for his troops. This helped him capture Caen, but at the price of reducing it to ruins. Even with control of Caen, the British and Canadians found themselves stalemated as the Germans soon established strong positions along a prominent ridge line south of the city. Once again, in an operation codenamed Goodwood, Montgomery utilized heavy bombers in an attempt to smash through the German defenses. He gained only 3 miles and lost 4,000 men and 500 tanks.

In the meantime, to the west, the Americans were inching through Normandy's vexing bocage country. For nearly two millennia, Norman farmers had built up earthen hedgerows, often reinforced with trees and stones, to mark the borders of their fields. These hedgerows proved to be ideal natural defensive positions for German machine gunners, self-propelled gun crewmen, and riflemen. Under the extreme conditions of combat, the Americans developed combined arms teams of tanks, infantry, and engineers to punch holes through the hedgerows and assault dug-in German defenders. In this way, three US divisions – the 4th, the 9th, and the 79th – fought their way up the Cotentin to capture Cherbourg, a key supply port, on June 27. However, the Germans had skillfully destroyed most of the port facilities, rendering Cherbourg useless for supply purposes until early September.

At the same time, as July began, the rest of the US Army in Normandy was pushing south, at first in the direction of Coutances, but then, by the middle of the month, for the vital crossroads market town of Saint-Lô. From July 10 through July 18, the 2nd, 35th, and 29th Infantry Divisions slugged their way against fierce German resistance, through the thick hedgerows that honeycombed the countryside around Saint-Lô. Among them, the divisions suffered over 7,000 casualties to gain a few miles and whatever remained of the destroyed town.

Having been stalemated in Normandy all summer, the Allied commanders were desperate to break through the German front and fight the sort of fast-moving maneuver campaign that played to Allied strengths. Possession of Saint-Lô afforded Lieutenant General Omar Bradley, commander of the US First Army, the sort of road mobility he needed to plan a major offensive designed to punch a permanent hole in the German lines. Impressed by the damage that heavy bombers had inflicted on Caen, Bradley decided to use the better part of the Eighth Air Force to carpet bomb a 3-mile section of the German line held by the Panzer Lehr Division southwest of Saint-Lô. Codenamed Operation Cobra, Bradley's plan called for the B-24 and B-17 bombers to drop their loads on top of the German dugouts, within 2,000 yards of the American lines. On July 24 and 25, hundreds of planes unleashed a maelstrom of explosive death on the Germans. But they also, on both days, mistakenly bombed their own troops, killing 135 Americans and wounding hundreds more. The short bombings claimed the life of Lieutenant General Lesley McNair, commander of Army Ground Forces, and the highest-ranking US officer to be killed in World War II. In spite of these grisly friendly fire incidents, Bradley's combined tank–infantry teams battered their way through the stunned Germans who manned the forward positions. Once the Americans broke through the initial defenses, they found little to oppose them in the chaotic German rear areas. While heavy bombers were not well suited to support ground operations, medium bombers and fighters proved to be ideal. Throughout the Normandy campaign and during the breakthrough, the Allies employed their superior airpower with devastating effectiveness. Low-flying planes, bombing and strafing with near impunity, wreaked havoc on enemy supply columns and armor, sowing terror in the heart of many a German soldier. The Allies had finally achieved their long-awaited breakthrough in Normandy.

The Breakout, the Liberation of Paris, and the Chase Across France

By August 1, the German position in Normandy verged on the catastrophic. With the lines permanently ruptured, American armored divisions were fanning out, all over Normandy, pushing for Avranches and the ports of Brittany. In several instances, they surrounded and annihilated stranded German units. The US Army of 1944 was the most heavily mechanized in the world. Thus it was designed for just this sort of mobile warfare. American tanks, half-tracks, self-propelled guns, and jeeps roared like avenging angels along the roads, ripping through disjointed German columns and shooting them up mercilessly. Overhead, the ubiquitous fighter bombers provided outstanding close air support, freezing terrified German soldiers in place, and shredding them with machine gun fire and 500-pound bombs. "We could not possibly have gotten as far as we did, as fast as we did, and with as few casualties, without the wonderful air support," Major General J. Lawton Collins, the US VII Corps commander, said.

In early August, Bradley ascended to command of Twelfth Army Group. Under his command was his old First Army, under Lieutenant General Courtney Hodges, and the newly activated Third Army, under Lieutenant General Patton, the ultimate practitioner of offensive-minded maneuver war. Patton's columns roared west, into Brittany, and east in an attempt to encircle the entire German army in Normandy.

At the same time, just south of Caen, Montgomery's Twenty-First Army Group pushed relentlessly toward Falaise, against the remains of the German lines. Canadian, British, and Polish soldiers dealt with heavy resistance from the stubborn defenders, who fought with the desperation of soldiers facing extinction. Time was not on the Germans' side, though. By August 7, they faced the very real possibility that Montgomery's spearheads would link up with Patton's at Falaise and encircle them. Most in the German high command urged Adolf Hitler to withdraw his

armies from Normandy while he still could. Having recently survived an attempt on his life by rebellious generals, he was in no mood to listen to other generals who were ostensibly more loyal to him. Instead, he decided to counterattack. From August 7 to August 12, three German panzer divisions pushed west at Mortain, with the goal of capturing Avranches and cutting off Patton. The brunt of the attack fell on the 30th Infantry Division, which steadfastly held off the German armor while US reinforcements counterattacked and contained the German drive. Mortain was a dismal failure.

After Mortain, the Germans had no choice but to retreat from Normandy. In mid-August, the shattered remnants of their divisions fled east, hounded all the way by Allied fighter bombers. The Allies were slow to link up their pincers in and around Falaise, allowing 20,000 to 40,000 German soldiers to escape (and provoking much post-war finger pointing among the British and Americans). In essence, Bradley blamed Montgomery for failing to close the pocket more rapidly. Montgomery, in turn, blamed Bradley. Historians have generally held both responsible. On August 19, American and Polish soldiers linked up at Chambois, effectively sealing the Falaise pocket. A combination of artillery, mortars, small arms, tanks, and air strikes killed some 10,000 German soldiers within the pocket. The stench of their burned and decaying flesh was so overwhelming that fighter pilots, flying thousands of feet above, could smell it. Another 50,000 exhausted survivors surrendered. Overall, at Normandy, the Germans lost 400,000 men and any remaining chance of winning the war.

To make matters worse for them, the Allies unleashed another invasion of France, this time in the south, along the Riviera. Prime Minister Winston Churchill and the British bitterly opposed the invasion as a wasteful diversion from operations in Italy and, potentially, the Balkans. The Americans, most notably Eisenhower, favored the invasion as a vital feint to support Allied operations in the rest of France. They also coveted the supply ports of Toulon and Marseilles. By this time in the war, the Americans were clearly the leaders of the Western Allied coalition because of their superior manpower, combat power, and resources, so they got their way. On

August 15, the US 3rd, 36th, and 45th Infantry Divisions assaulted the sandy Riviera beaches from Cape Cavaillaire in the west to Saint-Raphaël in the east. They were supported by inland parachute drops of the Allied First Airborne Task Force and over 130 bombarding warships. Codenamed Operation Dragoon, the landings succeeded dramatically against mostly weak German opposition. Seven divisions of the French First Army, composed largely of North African colonials under French leadership, subsequently landed and captured, throughout late August, Toulon and Marseilles. The campaign in southern France quickly degenerated into a rout, with this multinational Allied army chasing the remnants of the German Nineteenth Army north, up the Rhône River valley. The Americans focused mainly on the task of destroying the retreating German formations. The focus of the French was on more than just operations. As their divisions advanced north, liberating town after town, they inspired many local men to join them. Some of these new soldiers had previously served with one or more of the myriad clandestine groups (generally known as "The French Resistance") that opposed the German occupation. Victories in battle, and the swelling ranks of the First Army, began the process of solidifying the Gaullist Free French leadership as major players in post-war French politics.

With the success of Operation Dragoon, the German position in France was hopeless. By the end of August, Allied armies had liberated most of the country. The Germans, reeling under the blows of a massive Soviet offensive in the east, thought of little else now besides recovering sufficiently to defend their own borders. Sensing the collapse of German power in France, resistance groups in Paris rose up against the hated occupiers on August 19. For several days, sporadic fighting raged throughout the city. Hitler ordered General Dietrich von Choltitz, the German commander, to destroy Paris, but the general disobeyed the dictator's vengeful edict. Although fighting did continue, Paris remained largely unscathed as soldiers of the French 2nd Armored Division, along with the US 4th and 28th Infantry Divisions, liberated the city on August 24 and 25. The population responded with spontaneous joy, crowding the streets, celebrating in every fashion imaginable. The liberation of Paris presaged a new post-war France and the end of the Nazi empire.

On September 10, troops from Lieutenant General Jacob Devers's Sixth Army Group, advancing from the south, joined hands with soldiers of Patton's Third Army, moving from the north, thus fusing together the two major Allied fronts in France. On the same day, American soldiers liberated Luxembourg. The British and Canadians of Montgomery's Twenty-First Army Group were already besieging many of the northern ports around Calais. They had also liberated Brussels, Antwerp, and most of Belgium. To their south, American patrols of Hodges's First Army had even begun to breach Germany's western border. Farther south, American divisions from Devers's army group were plunging into Lorraine and the Vosges. In the process, a continuous north-to-south Allied front was fused together under the daily grind of operations. These dramatic successes gave rise to a giddy optimism, even among the generals, that the war might be over by Christmas. But the heady days of late summer soon gave way to the sober realities of the fall.

Market Garden

By the middle of September, two major factors had conspired to slow the Allied advance to a virtual halt. First, the Germans, demonstrating incredible resilience, had patched together their shattered armies, reinforced them, re-equipped them, and had set up a new defensive line along their western frontier. They anchored their front along the Siegfried Line, a series of concrete bunkers, casements, anti-tank traps, fire trenches, barbed wire, minefields, and machine gun pits that stretched mainly along the Luxembourg and Belgian borders. Before the war, Hitler had ordered these fortifications built to protect the vital industrial Ruhr, which lay to the east. Now they served as a major impediment to any Allied advance into Germany.

Second, the Allies were now experiencing serious supply problems. The issue was not a lack of matériel. The problem was transporting it from the invasion beaches several hundred miles to the fighting fronts. In the weeks before the Normandy invasion, British and American bombers had destroyed French railroads, bridges, and cross-roads in an effort to paralyze German reinforcements and keep them from counterattacking the beachhead. Now these same transportation nodes had to be repaired and used to move supply-laden locomotives and trucks to the front. All of this took time. The most nettling issue, though, was the dearth of deep-water ports in which to unload freight. As of September the vast majority of Allied supplies were still arriving over the Normandy beaches, hardly an ideal situation. Anticipating this, the Americans and British had constructed artificial harbors, known as "mulberries," but they proved to be of limited value. The American harbor was destroyed by a powerful storm on June 19. The British mulberry also sustained storm damage. It survived, though with limited capacity. What the Allies needed more than anything by September was control of deep-water ports. Knowing this, Hitler wisely ordered the garrisons of various ports to hold out indefinitely and, when resistance was no longer possible, to destroy the port installations. This forced the Allies to earmark numerous divisions to besiege and assault Saint-Malo, Lorient, and Brest in Brittany (for the Americans) as well as Boulogne, Calais, and Dunkirk (for the British and Canadians). In general, none of these ports contributed much to the Allied supply situation during the fall. The same could not be said for Marseilles and Toulon, which both accounted for thousands of tons of badly needed supplies. The Allies did use transport aircraft to ferry supplies to their leading divisions, but they did not have the capacity to sustain themselves primarily by air. So, by mid-September, most Allied divisions were running dangerously low on food, ammunition, and especially fuel.

As the logistical situation worsened, latent disagreements and rivalries among the Allied commanders began to harden. Montgomery, Bradley, and Patton all lobbied Eisenhower for priority of supply to keep their armies advancing. Patton claimed that the Siegfried Line was undermanned and could be overrun quickly by the Third Army, but only with proper supplies. Montgomery, newly promoted to field marshal, proposed to flank the Siegfried Line to the north, capture the Ruhr, and dash for Berlin. More than anything, the British commander advocated a single thrust into Germany, preferably by his Twenty-First Army Group, to conquer Berlin and end the war

in 1944. He knew that Britain was near the end of its strength – and certainly its manpower – and he believed that a powerful single thrust in Germany could end the war quickly, sparing his country another nightmarish wartime winter. He argued, in his uniquely persistent way, that the supply situation only allowed for one major effort and that his troops, positioned along the Belgian–Dutch border, were in the best position to unleash it. During one meeting, he was so strident in his efforts at persuasion that Eisenhower reached out, touched his knee, and said, "Steady, Monty, you can't talk to me like that. I'm your boss." Chastened, Montgomery graciously apologized. Nonetheless, he devised a daring operation, codenamed Market Garden, to carry out this single thrust. The plan called for three airborne divisions – one British and two American – to drop behind enemy lines on September 17 in Holland. Once on the ground, they were to seize key bridges, including one at Arnhem over the Rhine River. Tanks from the British XXX Corps would then slash through the German lines and fight their way approximately 60 miles northeast along the main roads, linking up with the paratroopers at such places as Son, Eindhoven, Grave, Nijmegen, and Arnhem and then sweep into Germany. To pull off Market Garden, Montgomery would of course need priority of supply.

Eisenhower largely favored a broad front advance into Germany of the sort that would favor the Allied advantages in manpower and matériel (once supplies could be brought forward). These advantages were the product of American abundance, so, to him, it made perfect sense to pause, regroup, and overwhelm Germany with broad front attacks. If that took more time, then so be it. He understood that the American public would expect their own troops to take the lead role for the invasion of Germany. Nonetheless, he departed from his broad front blueprint and authorized Market Garden. This, of course, robbed his American armies of supplies, slowing their advance to a veritable crawl. He was, in essence, gambling that Market Garden could succeed well enough to administer a death blow to Nazi Germany, rendering Allied logistical problems irrelevant.

The gamble was not a wise one. From the beginning, Market Garden had problems.

German resistance, especially in the British sector around Arnhem, was much tougher than anticipated. Actually, in the days before the operation, Montgomery and other British commanders had willfully dismissed photo reconnaissance images that indicated the presence of two refitting SS panzer divisions near Arnhem. Predictably, this caused serious problems for the British paratroopers, as did the fact that their drop zone was too far away from the Arnhem bridge, costing them precious time just fighting their way to the bridge. Radio communication was spotty, creating ignorance among senior commanders about the gravity of the situation in Arnhem. The tanks of XXX Corps ran into a deadly thistle of German anti-tank guns near the start line on the Belgian–Dutch border, slowing the armored advance. The Americans encountered bitter resistance around Son, St Oedenrode, Nijmegen, and the Groesbeek heights. The Germans were quite surprised by the operation, but quick to react, rushing reinforcements into Holland. These troops, along with scratch units on the scene, repeatedly counterattacked the vital road (quickly dubbed "Hell's Highway" by the Americans), forcing the Allies to fight ferociously just to keep the road open. This cost them valuable time. The longer the fighting raged inconclusively with no Allied bridgehead over the Rhine, the stronger the Germans became, and the better their chances of foiling the Allied objective.

Realistically, success in Market Garden could only happen if everything went right and, needless to say, it did not. The weather was often poor, hindering aerial resupply and reinforcement efforts. In the initial fighting, the Germans blew a key bridge at Son, necessitating a laborious effort by British engineers to construct a Bailey bridge substantial enough to support heavy vehicles, costing XXX Corps crucial time. These were just two examples of a flawed plan that had, within the first couple of days of the operation, gone very bad. As a result, the Allies found themselves ensnarled in a bitter struggle just to maintain control of the highway. The tanks of XXX Corps made it through Nijmegen but could not reach Arnhem, where the British 1st Airborne Division was cut off. On September 25, Montgomery ordered an evacuation of Arnhem, effectively conceding the failure of Market Garden. About 10,000 troopers of the 1st Airborne Division had gone into Arnhem. Only 2,398 made it out. In the final analysis, the operation was a dismal failure. Moreover, the Allies, having driven a wedge into the German lines, were now forced to defend it. British and American soldiers spent the rest of the fall manning stalemated frontline positions in Holland. The two American airborne divisions, designed to fight quick battles as shock troops, instead found themselves used as regular infantry in waterlogged trenches. They were not pulled off the line until well into November. By then, they had suffered over 50 percent casualties.

The Gloomy Fall

The failure of Market Garden guaranteed that the war would continue into 1945. To a great extent, this was because of the Allied supply situation. Eisenhower's broad front invasion of Germany could not proceed if he did not have access to deep-water ports in northern Europe. Marseilles and Toulon were helping sustain Devers's Sixth Army Group (comprising the US Seventh Army and the French First Army) in the Vosges. But Bradley's growing Twelfth Army Group (which now included the US First, Third, and Ninth Armies) and Montgomery's Twenty-First Army Group could not maintain continuous offensive operations without more supplies. Basically, Antwerp, the greatest port on the northern coast of Europe, was the solution to the whole problem. On September 4, British troops had captured the city, the docks, and the port facilities intact. But, in order to make use of Antwerp, the Allies needed control of the Scheldt River estuary, a 60-mile waterway leading from the city to the English Channel. The Scheldt was studded with narrow islets, canals, and low country islands, all of which could be fortified to prevent the passage of ships.

With a stunning lack of foresight, the Allies failed to clear the estuary and cut off the entire German Fifteenth Army in early September when the Germans were in complete disarray. Fixated on Market Garden, Montgomery failed to appreciate the importance of the Scheldt. He assigned the job of clearing it to the undermanned Canadian First Army, which was, at that point, heavily involved in the effort to capture other Channel ports. The Germans took great advantage of this mistake. Some divisions of the Fifteenth Army escaped to fight in Holland against the Market Garden salient. Others entrenched themselves along the Scheldt in such places as Walcheren and South Beveland. They also mined the waters. As a result, a combined force of Canadian, British, and American soldiers spent nearly six weeks, from late September to early November, fighting a nightmarish, watery campaign to dislodge the Germans. The Scheldt's many canals and raised roads made ideal defensive ramparts for the Germans with excellent fields of fire over the flat polder land. Casualty rates were devastating for the manpower-impoverished Canadians and British. The 2nd Canadian Division alone suffered 3,650 casualties, sapping nearly 40 percent of its original strength. Losses in the British 52nd (Lowland) Division were similar. A lone US division, the 104th, fought in the latter stages of the campaign and lost 1,300 men in about a week's worth of fighting. Overall, the Allies lost close to 13,000 men at the Scheldt, almost half of whom were Canadian. The Germans lost 41,000 captured and almost 12,000 killed and wounded. Even though fighting on the ground had petered out by November 8, it took Allied ships another three weeks to clear the estuary of mines, finally opening up mighty Antwerp for supply operations. On December 1 alone, the port handled 10,000 tons of supplies.

In the meantime, throughout October and November, the Allies were slowly pushing east with limited offensives. In the Vosges the French and Americans were advancing slowly against stubborn resistance, with the ultimate objective of capturing Strasbourg on the Rhine. Patton was bogged down in Lorraine, uncharacteristically involved in a brutal siege of Metz. Troops from Hodges's First Army were eating away at the Siegfried Line and, in October, took Aachen in a house-to-house, basement-to-basement battle. With control of the Aachen plain, General Bradley grew concerned that the Germans might open up the nearby Ruhr River dams and flood the entire area, essentially swamping the First Army. So, Bradley and Hodges ordered a push through the well-defended Hurtgen Forest, a thick nest of fir and pine trees, west of the Ruhr. This questionable decision led to one of the worst, most fruitless – and costly – American battles of the war. For

several weeks, American divisions bled away to nothingness in the forest, with few, if any, results. Artillery tree bursts multiplied the fragmentation effect of shells and led to horrendous casualties. Rain and snow added to the misery of the soldiers. Morale in the rifle companies plummeted to near hopelessness. The Americans lost 33,000 men at Hurtgen, yet by December they had not even come close to the dams.

The Battle of the Bulge

In spite of Allied disasters like the Hurtgen, even Adolf Hitler understood that World War II had evolved into a war of attrition he would eventually lose. As of December, the Western Allies were growing stronger every day on his western border, especially now that they controlled Antwerp. In the east, the Soviets had plunged into Romania and Hungary. They had overrun parts of East Prussia, half of Poland, and were girding themselves for a massive push into Germany.

Desperate to turn the war around, Hitler decided, under strict secrecy, to scrape together his best remaining troops and unleash a last-ditch offensive against a thinly held sector of the American line in the Ardennes Forest. He clandestinely built up three armies – the Seventh, the Fifth Panzer, and the Sixth SS Panzer – on the east side of the Our. For more than three years, the Allies had benefited from outstanding intelligence that came from their ability to read many German military radio signal codes. This process, known as Ultra, was the war's most closely guarded secret. In this instance, Ultra intelligence provided little inkling of the impending offensive because Hitler ordered his units to maintain complete radio silence. The American front was protected by four and a half under-strength divisions, one of which was brand new. Two others had been shattered in the Hurtgen and were recovering in this ostensibly quiet sector.

The German objective was to smash through the American front, wheel north, cross the Meuse River, press on to Antwerp, and forge a split between Montgomery's army to the north and his American ally to the south. All of this, Hitler expected, would take place under a protective veil of winter weather, negating Allied air superiority. He hoped that this stunning turnaround would force the Americans and British to sue for peace with a newly invigorated Germany and perhaps even join him in his war against the communist Soviet Union. Thus, his ultimate target in the Ardennes was the Allied coalition.

At dawn on December 16, the Germans struck. In some places they preceded their attack with a monumental artillery barrage. In other spots, they simply infiltrated no-man's land and attacked the American defensive positions at close range. By and large, Hitler's legions achieved total surprise, creating a sizable bulge in the US lines (hence the name of the battle). What's more, for the first week or so, the weather in the Ardennes was indeed poor, with rain, snow, and cloud cover. This did, as Hitler had anticipated, ground most American and British planes, negating the Allies' formidable air superiority. However, the Ardennes was composed of large tracts of forest, deep ravines, and rolling plateaus. This challenging terrain, combined with winter mud, made it difficult for the overstretched German columns to advance with the necessary speed. Small crossroads towns such as Hosingen, Houffalize, St Vith, Krinkelt-Rocherath, Clervaux, and, most famously, Bastogne turned into choke points for the German advance. At these towns and elsewhere around the Ardennes, small, disembodied groups of American soldiers resisted with fierce desperation, wreaking havoc on the tight German timetable and inflicting heavy casualties on the Germans. In one typical instance, at Antoniushaff and Allerborn, heavily outnumbered tank crews and infantrymen of Combat Command R, 9th Armored Division fought to extinction but held up the 5th Panzer Army for more than half a day, buying time for American commanders to scramble reinforcements into Bastogne, a town the Germans besieged but never took.

To the north, where the Germans hoped for a quick push to the Meuse, they annihilated the 106th Infantry Division, capturing two entire regiments. But they made little other headway, running into an impregnable line along Elsenborn Ridge. By December 26, when the 4th Armored Division broke the siege of Bastogne, relieving the hard-pressed 101st Airborne Division, the battle had entered a new phase. The Germans no longer had any hope of crossing the Meuse and achieving the objective of their offensive. In essence, they had done little else besides drive a 60-mile bulge into the American line. Eisenhower rushed reinforcements to the Ardennes and, in this second phase of the battle, his soldiers simply counterattacked the Germans, steadily pushing them eastward. It took nearly six weeks of bloody attacks, amid a thick layer of snow, for the Americans to push them back to the original start line. The Germans lost over 100,000 soldiers in the Ardennes. These were losses Hitler could never replace. Thus, the battle probably did hasten the end of the war. Although a few British troops fought along the northern shoulder, the Bulge was almost completely an American struggle. Winston Churchill referred to it as "an ever famous American victory." Indeed, it was the largest battle in US history, and one of the costliest. The United States lost close to 90,000 men, including over 23,000 missing or captured.

The Bitter End

With the failure of the Ardennes offensive, Hitler's demise was now just a matter of time, but he hardly acknowledged defeat. In January 1945, he launched another ill-advised attack against the American Seventh Army front in Alsace. This offensive, codenamed Operation Nordwind, was much smaller than the Ardennes offensive and no more successful. In three weeks of bitter winter fighting, the Germans pushed the American front back a couple of dozen miles and inflicted nearly 12,000 casualties on the Seventh Army. But the advance soon ground to an ignominious halt while 23,000 more German soldiers became casualties. In late January and February, the Americans and French counterattacked and overran the Colmar Pocket, the last slice of German-controlled territory in Alsace.

Since early 1943, the Allies had agreed among themselves that they would only accept unconditional surrender from Germany as a precondition to any cessation of hostilities. Knowing this, Hitler was determined never to surrender.

Germany, he decreed, must fight to the bitter end. If this meant the destruction of Germany and its people, then so be it. He and his Nazi cronies could envision no future Germany without themselves. So, the first few months of 1945 featured more bloody fighting east and west, as the Allies invaded and overran Germany. Casualty rates for both sides were as high as they had been during the summer battles of 1944, but the outcome of the war was obvious to all but the most ardent Nazi fanatics.

In the east, the Soviets launched in January a giant offensive that, by March, took them all the way to the Oder River, within 60 miles of Berlin. In the west, Patton's Third Army fought a vicious battle to clear the Saar and reach the Rhine. Hodges finally took the Ruhr dams. Hitler still hoped that the western armies would be unable to breach the great Rhine. However, in March, the British and Americans both forged successful crossings, the first of which occurred by luck at Remagen on March 7 when the US 9th Armored Division and 99th Infantry Division took advantage of the German inability to blow up a railroad bridge. In the weeks that followed, the other armies forced their own crossings, including, most notably, a joint airborne–amphibious operation, codenamed Operation Varsity, launched by Montgomery on March 24.

At this point, the Allies administered the final death blows. Bradley's Twelfth Army Group and Montgomery's Twenty-First Army Group enveloped the Ruhr (from the south and north respectively) and joined hands on April 1, encircling Army Group B. This forced the surrender of 325,000 German soldiers. Patton's Third Army and Lieutenant General Alexander Patch's Seventh Army smashed into southern Germany. In northern Italy, where the lines had been stalemated for many months, the Allies finally achieved a major breakthrough, overrunning the northern plains, capturing Milan, Verona, and Venice. The Soviets took Hungary, Slovakia, parts of Yugoslavia, Austria, eastern Germany, and smashed their way into Berlin. Soviet leader Joseph Stalin considered the German capital to be the greatest prize of all, and he was willing to spend many lives to take it. Eisenhower decided to halt his armies at the Elbe River, about 40 miles west of Berlin, rather

than suffer the heavy casualties implicit in city fighting. He also did not want to risk any friendly fire incidents with the Soviets. So, American and Soviet troops first joined hands on April 25, at Torgau on the Elbe, not in Berlin.

From April 16 through May 2, the Soviets fought a classic urban battle amid the ruins of a capital city that had already been bombed extensively by the Western Allies. The Soviets lost 81,000 killed and another 280,000 wounded. German losses, civilian and military, approached one million. The most famous casualty of the battle was the German dictator himself. Trapped inside of a bunker complex in downtown Berlin, with Soviet troops only a few blocks away, Hitler elected to commit suicide on April 30 rather than risk capture. He designated Admiral Karl Donitz, head of the German Navy, as his successor. Far to the south in Bavaria, Allied soldiers hustled to take the other great Nazi prize, Hitler's mountain complex at Berchtesgaden. Eisenhower made sure to send plenty of divisions in this direction to negate any possibility that Nazi fanatics would take to the mountains and continue the war. Advance patrols from the 7th Infantry Regiment, 3rd Infantry Division took Hitler's Berchtesgaden complex on the afternoon of May 4. Three days later, Donitz's government surrendered unconditionally to the Western Allies and a Soviet representative at Rheims. The agreement was formalized again, at Soviet insistence, the next day in Berlin. The war in Europe was over.

Further Reading

Ambrose, S. (1994) *D-Day*. New York: Simon and Schuster.

Ambrose, S. (1997) *Citizen Soldiers*. New York: Simon and Schuster.

Beevor, A. (2003) *The Fall of Berlin, 1945*. New York: Penguin.

Beevor, A. (2009) *D-Day: The Battle for Normandy*. New York: Viking.

Blumenson, M. (1961) *US Army in World War II: Breakout and Pursuit*. Washington, DC: Department of the Army.

Bradley, O. (1951) *A Soldier's Story*. New York: Henry Holt.

Bradley, O. (1983) *A General's Life*. New York: Simon and Schuster.

Clarke, J. and Smith, R. R. (1993) *US Army in World War II: Riviera to the Rhine*. Washington, DC: Department of the Army.

Cole, H. (1950) *The US Army in World War II: The Lorraine Campaign*. Washington, DC: Department of the Army.

Cole, H. (1965) *The US Army in World War II: The Ardennes*. Washington, DC: Department of the Army.

Eisenhower, D. (1948) *Crusade in Europe*. New York: Doubleday.

Eisenhower, J. (1969) *The Bitter Woods*. New York: G. P. Putnam's Sons.

Evans, D. (2010) *The Third Reich at War*. New York: Penguin.

Hargreaves, R. (2008) *The Germans in Normandy*. Mechanicsburg, PA: Stackpole Books.

Harrison, G. (1951) *Cross-Channel Attack*. Washington, DC: Department of the Army.

Hastings, M. (1984) *Overlord*. New York: Touchstone.

Hastings, M. (2004) *Armageddon*. New York: Vintage.

Keegan, J. (1982) *Six Armies in Normandy*. New York: Penguin.

Lewin, R. (Ed.) (1970) *The British Army in World War II*. New York: William Morrow.

Lewin, R. (1978) *Ultra Goes to War*. New York: Hutchinson.

MacDonald, C. (1963) *US Army in World War II: The Siegfried Line*. Washington, DC: Department of the Army.

MacDonald, C. (1973) *US Army in World War II: The Last Offensive*. Washington, DC: Department of the Army.

MacDonald, C. (1984) *A Time for Trumpets: The Untold Story of the Battle of the Bulge*. New York: Bantam.

McManus, J. (2004) *The Americans at D-Day*. New York: Forge.

McManus, J. (2004) *The Americans at Normandy*. New York: Forge.

McManus, J. (2007) *Alamo in the Ardennes*. New York: John Wiley & Sons, Inc.

Montgomery, B. (1958) *The Memoirs of Field Marshal Montgomery*. New York: World Publishing Company.

Neillands, R. (2004) *The Battle of Normandy, 1944*. New York: Cassell.

Pogue, F. (1954) *US Army in World War II: The Supreme Command*. Washington, DC: Department of the Army.

Ryan, C. (1959) *The Longest Day*. New York: Simon and Schuster.

Ryan, C. (1966) *The Last Battle*. New York: Collins.

Ryan, C. (1974) *A Bridge Too Far*. New York: Touchstone.

Stacey, Colonel C. P. (1948) *The Canadian Army, 1939–1945*. Ottawa: Minister of National Defence.

Toland, J. (1959) *Battle: The Story of the Bulge*. New York: Random House.

Wilmot, C. (1952) *The Struggle for Europe*. New York: Harper and Brothers.

Zuehlke, M. (2007) *Terrible Victory: First Canadian Army and the Scheldt Estuary Campaign*. Toronto: Douglas and McIntyre.

Zumbro, D. (2006) *Battle for the Ruhr: The German Army's Final Defeat in the West*. Lawrence: University Press of Kansas.

World War II: Mediterranean Campaign

COLIN F. BAXTER

World War II came to the Mediterranean on June 10, 1940, when Italy's Benito Mussolini declared war on Britain and France. For the next five years, the Allied and Axis powers would struggle for control of that ancient sea and its shores: a maritime highway, and a geographical link between continents and oceans. The Mediterranean campaign was and is the subject of intense debate and controversy. "What in the world are we doing in the desert? Who would fight over sand?" Not an unreasonable question posed by some of those who found themselves in North Africa. At the time, US Army Chief of Staff General George C. Marshall strongly opposed the 1942 Anglo-American invasion of French North Africa, codenamed Operation Torch, on the grounds that the Mediterranean theater was "fundamentally unsound," a mere sideshow that delayed a cross-Channel invasion, the "Second Front" that would divert German forces. Some historians regard the Mediterranean campaign as barely worth an "extended footnote," a strategic mistake that led to the so-called "blind alley" of the Italian campaign.

The Mediterranean campaign, however, is not without its defenders: it is argued that an Axis victory in the Mediterranean theater would have threatened the southern flank of the Soviet Union and made possible a German–Japanese junction in the Indian Ocean. It is also argued that the Mediterranean campaign greatly assisted the war on the Eastern Front, and that each campaign assisted the other: Hitler's forces could not be used in *both* Tunisia and Stalingrad at the *same time*. A year later, in 1944, the large German forces committed to the Mediterranean theater were unavailable to reinforce the German army fighting in Normandy. Furthermore, Allied attacks in the Mediterranean theater seriously impacted the Axis oil supply. The Axis had to ship oil from Ploesti in Romania through the Black Sea, the Turkish Straits, the Aegean, and across the Adriatic to Italy. On the other hand, the British fought the war with American, not Middle Eastern, oil (shipping Iranian oil 18,000 miles around the Cape of Good Hope to Britain was prohibitively expensive). The British forces in the eastern Mediterranean, however, were awash in oil shipped from the Anglo-Iranian oil complex at Abadan on the Persian Gulf; in fact, the plentiful supply of oil led British soldiers in the desert to clean their uniforms with petrol rather than use precious water.

With the collapse of France in 1940, Benito Mussolini's Fascist Italy loomed menacingly all through Africa and the Mediterranean. Nearly 500,000 Italian forces were massed in Libya and in East Africa. The Mediterranean world and points east appeared to be the verge of becoming an Italian-dominated region. At the end of June 1940, with the new Vichy French government led by Marshal Philippe Pétain seeking an armistice, and a strong Italian air force and navy ranged against the British, First Sea Lord Admiral Sir Dudley Pound proposed to his fellow chiefs of staff that they consider the evacuation of the British Mediterranean fleet from the eastern Mediterranean. Churchill would have none of it. He was resolved to fight it out at both ends of the Mediterranean. Furthermore, Admiral Andrew Cunningham, who commanded the British Mediterranean fleet, warned that the fleet's removal would mean "the loss of Egypt and Malta" (Woodman 2000: 39). Determined to hold the Mediterranean and the Middle East, Churchill dispatched half of Britain's few remaining tanks to Egypt. This action had been taken at the height of the Battle of Britain as invasion threatened.

Churchill was also determined that the French Fleet based at Mers-el-Kébir, near Oran, Algeria, not fall into German hands, which would tip the naval balance in the Mediterranean against the Royal Navy. Negotiations failed, and on July 3, 1940, British warships opened fire on the French ships, their allies two weeks earlier, when they refused to sail to British ports, demobilize, or sail to the French West Indies. Almost 1,300 French sailors lost their lives in the attack, which made the Vichy government even more vehemently pro-German and anti-British. But the ruthless and determined action taken at Mers-el-Kébir undoubtedly demonstrated to the world that Britain intended to fight on. Mussolini's son-in-law, Count Ciano, was awestruck that "His Majesty's fleet" still had "the aggressive ruthlessness of the captains and pirates of the seventeenth century" (Ciano 1946: 273).

Mussolini had gambled that the war would be over within weeks. Before the outbreak of war, he had rushed troops to Libya to defend it against a British force in Egypt that was wrongly thought to be large. When the weakness of the British became obvious, Mussolini demanded that his army attack. A reluctant General Rodolfo Graziani advanced, and at last an Italian flag flew over an Egyptian town, Sidi Barrani, 20 miles inside Egypt. In the hope of another easy victory, Mussolini's forces crossed from Albania into Greece. Within days, the Greeks launched a counterattack that pushed Italian troops off their soil and invaded Albania.

Further humiliation came in December when General Archibald Wavell launched a brilliant offensive with a small force of two divisions, made up of British, Indian, and New Zealand troops, under the field command of General Richard O'Connor. Sidi Barrani was recaptured and Wavell's forces kept moving west against Marshal Graziani's Tenth Army of nine divisions, which surrendered at Beda Fromm on February 7, 1941. O'Connor signaled to Wavell, "Fox killed in the open." In all, over 130,000 Italian troops had been taken prisoner. Another Fox was already on his way to the desert: Lieutenant General Erwin Rommel was about to leave Germany for Tripoli with the task of saving the Italians in western Libya.

At sea, Admiral Cunningham decided, like General Wavell, to go on the offensive when Royal Air Force crews flying US Glenn Martins from Malta provided aerial photographs that showed the Italian fleet anchored in their strongly defended home port of Taranto – "the Pearl Harbor of the Med," located in the arch of the Italian boot. On November 11, 21 elderly

Swordfish biplane torpedo-bombers of the Fleet Air Arm from the aircraft carrier *Illustrious* attacked the Italian warships. Half the Italian battle fleet was put out of action at least temporarily. The fleet was moved to Italy's Tyrrhenian coast, which allowed the British to sail convoys to Malta and Greece. Hitler castigated Mussolini for his premature attack on Greece and the failures of his naval forces in the Mediterranean and his troops in Libya. Hitler began to give serious thought to intervening in the Mediterranean. On March 28, Cunningham struck again. Using intelligence provided by Ultra (obtained through breaking the German Enigma code), Cunningham surprised an Italian naval force off Cape Matapan, in Greek waters, when it tried to interfere with British convoys to Greece. The Royal Navy sank three heavy cruisers and two destroyers. Matapan exposed the difficulties under which the Italian Navy operated, which included the lack of radar, aircraft carriers, and air–naval cooperation.

Matapan consolidated British naval dominance of the eastern Mediterranean, but on April 6, German armies invaded both Greece and Yugoslavia. British and Dominion troops were transferred from North Africa to aid the Greeks, but another whirlwind German campaign ended with the swastika flag flying over the Acropolis in Athens. Controversy has surrounded the decision to aid Greece since it weakened British forces in Libya. Although Churchill had reservations about the Greek venture, he has been the main target of critics.

The British evacuations, first from Greece, then from the island of Crete, were conducted under circumstances in which the enemy had complete control of the air. The Aegean Sea became a "happy, killing time" for German aircraft. In one 24-hour period they sank over 20 ships that were trying to evacuate British and Allied forces. The Battle of Crete in May 1941 was reckoned the costliest British naval engagement in World War II. The British evacuations, however, might have been a disaster had the Italian Navy been free to interfere with them, which it was not owing to its earlier losses at Matapan. Crete was a flawed victory, however, since the picked troops of Germany's one existing parachute division were almost destroyed on the island.

The attempt to aid the Greeks had serious repercussions for the British in North Africa,

particularly with Rommel's arrival in Libya. Hitler was alarmed that if Mussolini lost Italy's Libyan colony then Fascist Italy might withdraw from the war. Rommel, Hitler's favorite general, was sent to block any further British advances into western Libya. Neither Hitler nor the German General Staff intended that Rommel should strike a decisive blow in Africa in the near future. Hitler could understand *Lebensraum* (living space) and race war, but, in the words of Douglas Porch, the Mediterranean "bored and exasperated him" (Porch 2004: 69). The main German effort would be in the east, the destruction of the Soviet Union in Operation Barbarossa.

The audacious Rommel, however, ignored Berlin's orders, trusting that Hitler would forgive success, and proceeded to exploit the thinly held British line in Libya. On March 31, Rommel, with relentless energy, drove his *Deutsches Afrika Korps*, together with Italian forces, eastward so that by the end of April they were on the Egyptian frontier. Barely two months later, all of Wavell's earlier gains had been lost, except for a foothold which they retained at the small port of Tobruk.

The subsequent siege of Tobruk by the Germans would last for 242 days from April 10 to November 1941, the longest in British military history. A thorn in Rommel's side, Tobruk blocked the coast road, popularly called the Via Balbia, Rommel's route to the Nile delta. Australian, British, Indian, Polish, and Czech forces defeated repeated efforts by Rommel to take Tobruk. To the statement that "Tobruk can take it!" General Leslie Morshead, commander of the 9th Australian Division, reacted angrily: "We're not here to take it – we're here to give it!" (Moore 1976: 28). Rommel's, and Germany's, failure to take Tobruk lifted British morale in the grim summer of 1941.

Rommel's stunning advance had dangerously stretched his line of supply from Tripoli, but an attempt by Wavell to relieve Tobruk in June was a costly failure. In Operation Battleaxe, British tanks had been unable to overcome dug-in German 88-mm guns that could destroy a tank 2,000 yards away.

In July, a tired Wavell was replaced by General Sir Claude Auchinleck, who had been army commander in chief in India. Auchinleck appointed General Alan Cunningham (a brother of the admiral) field commander of the newly named

Eighth Army, and on November 18, Operation Crusader was launched with the aim of lifting the siege of Tobruk and driving Rommel out of Libya. Crusader brought near disaster to both sides. Rommel, convinced that victory was within his grasp, made what came to be known as "the dash for the wire," the Egyptian frontier. Cunningham lost his nerve and prepared to withdraw the Eighth Army behind the Egyptian frontier. Auchinleck flew to the battlefront, restored order, and continued the offensive. Cunningham was replaced by General Neil Ritchie. Rommel, lacking logistical support, was fortunate to withdraw westward after his reckless "dash for the wire." On December 10, the siege of Tobruk was lifted and Rommel evacuated Cyrenaica (eastern Libya). During Crusader, the British lost some 18,000 men killed and wounded, the Axis army 38,000 men.

The pause ended abruptly when a reinforced and resupplied Rommel struck again on January 21, 1942. The British were 500 miles west of Tobruk and their supply line was now overextended. In addition, the Eighth Army was weakened by the loss of two Australian divisions transferred to the Far East – with the Japanese attack on Pearl Harbor, war had come to the Pacific. The British were forced back to the Gazala Line.

Before the British could launch their own offensive, Rommel struck on May 31, 1942. The Battle of Gazala that followed marked the highpoint of German military professionalism in the desert war, and the nadir of British fortunes. Courage and gallantry were squandered by incompetent generalship. On the British desert flank, at Bir Hacheim, General Pierre Koenig and his Free French Brigade made an epic stand until forced to surrender. Gazala culminated in Rommel's capture of Tobruk on June 21, and the surrender of the 2nd South African Division, together with one British and one Indian brigade, a total of 33,000 men. Auchinleck fired Ritchie on June 25 and assumed direct command of the Eighth Army. The surrender of Tobruk shocked the Allied world. It was a bitter blow to Churchill, who was then in Washington to confer with President Roosevelt on plans for a Second Front. A jubilant Hitler promoted Rommel to field marshal. By the end of June the British had withdrawn into Egypt, manning their last defense line at a place called El Alamein, a tiny train station on the coast. The Egyptian capital lay only 150 miles to the east.

Malta

In World War II, the island of Malta, which is located almost exactly in the center of the Mediterranean (like a cork centered in the hourglass between the eastern and western Mediterranean), took on enormous significance as the only British naval base in the 2,000-mile stretch of sea between Gibraltar and Alexandria. The island barred the north–south route across the Sicilian Narrows that connected Mussolini to his African empire. Early on the morning of June 11, 1940, the Italian air force, the Regia Aeronautica, carried out the first of 3,340 Axis air raids on the island over the next three years, when it became the most bombed place on earth. Initially the island was defended by three obsolete Gloster Gladiator biplanes known to the Maltese people as *Faith*, *Hope*, and *Charity*. On August 1, 1940, 12 modern Hurricane fighters landed at Malta from the small carrier *Argus* to reinforce the island's air defense. Potentially, Malta posed a serious threat to the Axis, but in the first six months of the war the few submarines based there rarely sighted an enemy ship, and scarcely knew where to look for one. As a result, in the second half of 1940 the Italian Navy escorted almost 300,000 tons of supplies to their Libyan ports with a loss of only 2 percent of the ships sent.

As Churchill had dreaded, Mussolini's military debacle in Libya led Hitler to intervene in the Mediterranean. On December 10, 1940, *Fliegerkorps X*, a balanced force of 350 aircraft trained in anti-shipping attack, arrived in southern Italy, its primary task to gain air control over the central Mediterranean and to attack British shipping. Its power was dramatically shown on January 10 the following year when the aircraft carrier HMS *Illustrious* was badly damaged while escorting a convoy through the Sicilian channel. *Illustrious* was subjected to further heavy attack while undergoing emergency repairs in Valletta Harbor before it escaped to Alexandria. This attack heralded the first German blitz on Malta. The island managed to hold out until, in April 1941, *Fliegerkorps X* was diverted from southern

Italy to prepare for Operation Barbarossa, the invasion of the Soviet Union. Toward the end of June, codebreakers at Bletchley Park (northwest of London) broke the new Italian cipher machine referred to as C38m. This gave details of all planned convoys from Italy to Libya. A second advantage was the development of airborne radar (ASV), which could locate surface ships at night. In the last seven months of 1941, Malta's air and naval forces waged an increasingly powerful campaign to restrict the flow of supplies to Rommel's forces in North Africa.

But for the welcome news that the United States was now an ally in the war, the winter of 1941 was a cruel month at sea for the British. Three days after Pearl Harbor, Japanese planes sank the *Prince of Wales* and the *Repulse* off the Malay coast. In the Mediterranean, German U-boats transferred from the Atlantic sank the carrier *Ark Royal* and the battleship *Barham*. Four British cruisers hit Italian deep-water mines off Tripoli, sinking two of the ships instantly. The most spectacular Italian naval operation came when Italian two-man human torpedo teams sank, in the naval harbor at Alexandria, the last two remaining British battleships in the Mediterranean, *Queen Elizabeth* and *Valiant*.

A weakened British Mediterranean Fleet was grim news for Malta, but even more serious was Hitler's transfer of an entire air corps from the Eastern Front to Italy and North Africa to regain control over the sea route to Tripoli. German Field Marshal Albert Kesselring boasted that he would "pound [Malta] to dust." The 400 German and 200 Italian aircraft in Sicily were only 10 minutes' flying time away from Malta, whose position became desperate. Convoys could not get through, nor could the Royal Navy operate from Valletta. Food supplies dwindled, while dysentery, tuberculosis, and polio were rampant. The Axis siege of Malta was one of the longest and grimmest in the struggle to control the Mediterranean.

In March 1942, the first 15 British Spitfires were flown to Malta from the aircraft carrier *Eagle* and on April 1, Churchill asked Roosevelt to loan the large American carrier *Wasp*. Two days later the president agreed and on April 20 *Wasp* flew off 47 Spitfires. Churchill made a second request and on May 10 *Wasp* and *Eagle* flew more planes on to the island. The Axis could no longer

take air superiority for granted. An elated Churchill telegraphed Roosevelt: "Many thanks for all your timely help. Who said that a wasp couldn't sting twice?" The climax of Malta's war for survival came between August 11 and 13, 1942, when Churchill organized a 14-ship convoy around the fast oil tanker *Ohio*, loaned by the United States. Once through the Straits of Gibraltar, the convoy ran a four-day gauntlet of Axis naval and air attack. No fewer than 784 Axis aircraft attempted to stop the convoy. The famous Operation Pedestal convoy had started with 14 merchant ships, of which nine were sunk along with the aircraft carrier *Eagle* and several warships damaged or sunk. The remaining merchant ships, bringing the largest cargo since the previous year, arrived at Valletta to be greeted by the Maltese people with tears of joy. The *Ohio* crawled into port the next day, lashed between two destroyers to keep her from sinking. The courage shown by the Maltese people and the garrison was an inspiration to the Allied cause in a time of crisis. Saved from a calamity on the scale of Singapore and Tobruk, Malta was restored as a serious threat to Axis supply lines to North Africa. Nevertheless, the naval effort to sustain Malta, involving as it did the loss of many British ships sunk or damaged, has not gone unquestioned. The costly battle for Malta has been called the "Verdun of Maritime War."

El Alamein

A mere 10 days after the fall of Tobruk on June 21, Rommel's forces were only 60 miles from Alexandria. In the enthusiasm of the moment, the earlier agreement between Hitler and Mussolini to seize Malta before Egypt was postponed, and Hitler now supported Rommel's request to drive on Cairo first. In Egypt, King Farouk and some of his ultra-nationalist army officers imagined that the Germans would soon rid them of the British occupiers. By the end of August 1942, the German general had the most powerful force he had ever commanded in North Africa, and both he and his men were raring to go east.

In this crisis, Churchill and his Chief of the Imperial General Staff, General Alan Brooke, flew to Cairo. Auchinleck was replaced as Commander in Chief, Middle East, by Churchill's favorite general, Harold Alexander. Churchill's first choice to command the "brave but baffled" Eighth Army was General "Strafer" Gott. When the aircraft with Gott aboard was shot down, and the general killed, Churchill appointed Brooke's first choice for the Eighth Army command, Lieutenant-General Bernard Law Montgomery. The change was momentous.

The Eighth Army was disposed in a loosely held defensive line that stretched for nearly 40 miles, anchored in the north by the Mediterranean and in the south by the impassable Qattara Depression. The key to the whole line was the Alam Halfa Ridge, which anchored the British right flank. A confident Rommel was happy with his plan of attack for the upcoming battle, which called for the usual feint to decoy the enemy into defending the coast road, while he launched a hook into the desert to take the British defensive position on Alam Halfa Ridge from the south.

The arrival of a new British commander at the battlefront made no impression on the German field marshal, who counted for success on continued incompetent enemy generalship. Only a day after his arrival in Egypt, however, Montgomery had reconnoitered the virtually undefended Alam Halfa Ridge and at once appreciated the vital importance of holding the position – which would be the object of Rommel's main attack. Within hours he had asked for and got a division to garrison the ridge. That same evening he told his subordinate commanders that he would tolerate no retreat: Eighth Army would do the same, if need be, as the Spartans had done, defending to the death the pass at Thermopylae. In the days that followed, Montgomery infused the multinational Eighth Army with a sense of purpose and self-confidence. Before Rommel's attack on August 31, Montgomery told his commanders to dig in their tanks in protected reverse-slope positions, and on no account were they to rush out into the desert on a wild goose chase onto the waiting muzzles of German anti-tank guns as Rommel had managed to make the British do so often in the past. Fighting a defensive battle from their entrenched position, the Eighth Army defeated Rommel's attack, which had nothing to show for its efforts but burned-out tanks. The Battle of Alam Halfa was a tipping point in the desert campaign and the first unequivocal victory of a British commander over Rommel.

Montgomery's own offensive at El Alamein began on the night of October 23, 1942, with the largest barrage of the war. Some 195,000 British Empire troops, together with French and Greek units, and 1,000 tanks faced off against Rommel's Panzerarmee Afrika, numbering just over 104,000 men with nearly 500 tanks. The argument has been made that Rommel faced a "hopelessly unequal struggle," and that Montgomery "could not miss" (Ellis 1990: 388). To contemporaries, however, a victory by Montgomery was by no means inevitable. There had been too many defeats – Dunkirk, Singapore, Burma, Greece, Crete, Tobruk – to speak of a foregone conclusion. Montgomery's initial thrust failed, and attacks elsewhere suffered repeated checks. Churchill grew angry with the slow progress of the offensive, while Brooke, Montgomery's chief supporter, wondered whether "I was wrong and Monty was beat" (Danchev and Todman 2001: 336). Even Montgomery privately confessed that the battle might have to be broken off in the face of tougher resistance than he had expected. The gloom was about to lift, however, and by November 4, the extent of the Eighth Army's victory began to emerge. Hitler's "fight to the death" order was eventually disobeyed as the remnants of Panzerarmee Afrika fled to the west, only to stop 2,000 miles later in southern Tunisia. The British had won a decisive victory at last, one in which Montgomery displayed tactical adaptability and versatility, belying his stubborn insistence that everything had gone according to plan. Rommel's losses were staggering, nearly 12,000 killed, wounded, or missing and 30,000 captured. Montgomery's losses were 13,560.

Operation Torch

A new stage in the Mediterranean campaign began on November 8, 1942, with Operation Torch, when Anglo-American forces had landed in what was then French North Africa.

The landings, one in Morocco near the Atlantic port of Casablanca, and two in Algeria near the ports of Oran and Algiers, ended several months of Allied debate over grand strategy, at least for the time being. They agreed on a strategy of "Germany First," but the question of where exactly to fight the Axis led to disagreement. Churchill called for an Anglo-American assault on French

North Africa, which would link up with the Eighth Army moving west and clear the Axis Powers from the whole southern shore of the Mediterranean. Roosevelt's military advisors urged a cross-Channel invasion of France that would lead to a direct attack on Germany, and regarded anything less as a diversion. US Army Chief of Staff General George C. Marshall believed that a cross-Channel invasion was the quickest way to defeat Nazi Germany so that America could concentrate its full power on Japan. Secretary of War Henry Stimson did everything short of resigning to prevent action in the Mediterranean, which he dismissed as the "wildest kind of dispersion debauch," and "the President's great secret baby" (Stimson 1948: 425). In making his decision in favor of Operation Torch, the president went against the unanimous advice of his military advisors. Roosevelt, aware of the American public's growing impatience with inaction, not to mention Stalin's demand for a Second Front to assist the Soviet Union, insisted that US ground forces begin fighting the Germans somewhere, and in a place where the Western Allies had a chance of winning. With a do-nothing policy out of the question, and a premature cross-Channel invasion of France a likely disaster, the Allied offensive in North Africa was logical and compelling. Roosevelt's decision was a defining moment after America's entry into World War II.

Churchill, after his momentous August 1942 shake-up of the British command in Egypt, flew on to Moscow to break the unwelcome news to Stalin that there would be no Second Front in 1942. "It was like carrying a large lump of ice to the North Pole," Churchill wrote of his first meeting with Stalin (Churchill 1949: 475). In his effort to sell Stalin on Torch, Churchill declared that it was the intention of the British and Americans to attack "the soft belly of the crocodile as we attacked his hard snout." Stalin's anger that there would be no Second Front in 1942 softened, and he closed with the words, "May God prosper this undertaking" (Churchill 1949: 481).

Under the command of the relatively unknown Lieutenant-General Dwight D. Eisenhower, over 100,000 Allied troops were committed to Torch. Led to expect that the Allies would be greeted as deliverers, Eisenhower commented that French sentiment in North Africa did not "remotely" agree with those expectations. Instead Eisenhower heard, "Why did you bring this war to us? We were satisfied before you came to get us all killed" (Chandler 1970: 677). The Allies had hoped to install General Henri Giraud, an escaped French prisoner of war, as head of French forces in North Africa, but they soon discovered that he had no influence with anyone when the Vichy French opened fire on their liberators. Local French commanders with very few exceptions led their men in resistance to the Americans and British. The danger that Allied forces would become bogged down in French North Africa was averted when Admiral Jean Darlan, head of the French Navy, by chance happened to be in Algiers to see his polio-stricken son. When the opportunistic Darlan realized the size of the Allied invasion, he ordered a ceasefire based on an agreement with Eisenhower, who recognized Darlan as "head of the French state." Eisenhower's agreement with the former Vichy leader caused a political furor in both America and Britain since it appeared to indicate that similar "deals" might be made in the name of expediency. The Darlan deal also enraged the Free French and its leader, General Charles de Gaulle. The embarrassment was removed on Christmas Eve 1942 when the admiral was shot by a young monarchist.

Tunisia, November 1942–May 1943

Allied failure to land further east than Algiers enabled Hitler to rush German and Italian forces across the 100-mile strait between Sicily and Tunisia and to land on Tunisian airfields, as well as to seize the ports of Tunis and Bizerta. Five hundred and sixty miles separated the Allies in Algiers from Tunis. The Allies hoped that Torch would clear North Africa of Axis forces so that in the late summer of 1943 the Allies could launch a cross-Channel invasion. This became impossible when Hitler decided to make a massive commitment of German forces to the Tunisian theater. Earlier he had kept the German Mediterranean commitment to a minimum, but now Hitler saw Germany itself threatened from the south.

By late November, Hitler was pouring troops into Tunisia, declaring that Tunisia would be "decisive," "the cornerstone of our conduct of the war on the southern flank of Europe" (Porch 2004: 371). Weak Allied spearheads, inadequately covered by air forces without forward bases, were checked by German forces. The Allied line extended over a vast front of more than 250 miles. The British were in the north, along the coast; in the center were Free French troops under General Alphonse Juin; and to the south, guarding the right flank, was the US II Corps commanded by General Lloyd Fredendall.

The German counterstroke, under Rommel's command, came on St Valentine's Day, 1943, when two panzer divisions attacked elements of the US 1st Armored Division at the village of Sidi Bou Zid, thus beginning a series of engagements collectively known as the Battle of Kasserine Pass. American forces were driven back 85 miles in a week, suffering more than 6,000 killed and wounded, and 3,000 missing, most captured. The defeat came as a wake-up call to the inexperienced Americans, and a reminder that defeating the Germans would not be easy. Eisenhower relieved the commander of the US II Corps and replaced him with General George Patton. The Allies soon made good their losses and barely two months elapsed between Kasserine Pass and victory in Tunisia. General Omar Bradley would later write, "In Africa we learned to crawl, to walk – then run" (Bradley 1983: 159). When, on May 13, 1943, Tunis fell to the British, 275,000 German and Italian soldiers walked, drove, or rode donkeys into Allied captivity. It was the largest haul of Axis prisoners in the war to date. News of the fall of Tunis led Hitler to send 10 new German divisions to the Balkans and seven to Greece. The Mediterranean "ulcer" would continue to drain German strength so that by the summer of 1944, 24 Germans divisions were in Greece, the Balkans, Bulgaria, and the Aegean. Hitler's worst forebodings were an Allied "third front" in the rear of the German–Soviet front, which would interrupt the supply of bauxite, copper, and chrome from the Balkans and, most precious of all, oil from Romania.

Casablanca Conference, January 14–23, 1943

In January 1943, Churchill, Roosevelt, and the first full meeting of the Combined American–British Chiefs of Staff took place in Casablanca, where they argued honestly about what they should do after the Axis Powers were driven out of North Africa. General Marshall once again argued in favor of a cross-Channel invasion in

1943. British General Alan Brooke pushed for an invasion of Italy, which he regarded as an essential preliminary to an Allied landing in northwestern Europe. Americans doubted the British commitment to a cross-Channel invasion, and the British suspected the strength of the American commitment to the Germany First strategy. However, it was clear that they had to launch a big operation in 1943 if Stalin was to accept – grudgingly – a further delay of the Second Front when the Red Army was bearing the brunt of the ground war in Europe. The Western Allies agreed to invade Sicily, codenamed Operation Husky. No decision was taken at Casablanca on what would follow after Sicily, but with the Tunisian campaign not yet won, a decision did not seem urgent.

Sicily, July 10–August 17, 1943

The invasion of Sicily would be the largest amphibious operation of World War II – the seven divisions in the assault wave were two more than would land at Normandy in 1944. Among the deception schemes preceding Husky was the use of a human corpse – "The Man Who Never Was" – bearing fabricated documents indicating the Allies intended to land either on Sardinia or in Greece. Hitler responded by diverting troops to Greece. He had already sent reinforcements to Sardinia. Ultra – the codename given to the information gained from deciphered German radio traffic – quickly alerted Allied leaders that Berlin had taken the bait. Ultra also provided Eisenhower, who, as Mediterranean theater chief, had overall command of the Sicilian operation, a great deal of information about the enemy's strength and dispositions on the island. Under Eisenhower, British General Harold Alexander led 15th Army Group made up of two armies, the British Eighth commanded by Montgomery, and the American Seventh under General George Patton. The Allied landings on Sicily were preceded by the first major Allied airborne night operation; a combination of strong winds, friendly fire from Allied ships, and inexperienced aircrews resulted in heavy losses for elements of the American 82nd and British 1st Airborne Divisions. Of 147 gliders, 69 crashed into the sea.

The seaborne landings, however, launched on July 10 were successful as only light opposition was encountered from Italian coastal defenders. The US Seventh Army under Patton landed along the Gulf of Gela, where it soon faced an Axis armored counterattack. A valiant stand by the 45th Division and deadly naval gunfire drove off the attackers. Montgomery's Eighth Army landing enjoyed complete surprise and quickly captured the port of Syracuse. But a key operation by British paratroopers on the fourth day of the operation to seize the Primosole bridge leading to the plain of Catania suffered a costly check when the German 1st Parachute Division counterattacked.

When the British stalled in the Catania plain – the most direct route to Messina, separated by only about 3 miles of water from mainland Italy – Patton's forces moved west then north, capturing Palermo on July 22. On August 17, Patton entered Messina, but his triumphal entrance was anti-climactic. In a skillful withdrawal and evacuation, almost unmolested by Allied naval and air forces, 40,000 Germans and 70,000 Italians escaped to the mainland. The Germans also got safely away with 10,000 vehicles. Axis forces, however, were badly battered in Sicily, suffering 164,000 casualties; most of those were surrendering Italians, but about 32,000 were Germans who were captured, killed, or wounded. Most important, the invasion of Sicily led to the downfall of Mussolini, who was overthrown in a coup. The next day Eisenhower was authorized to invade mainland Italy.

The Italian Campaign, September 9, 1943–May 2, 1945

The long and difficult Allied campaign in Italy is one of the most controversial of World War II. Detractors have denounced the Italian campaign as "absurd," "marginal," "a sideshow," "a huge mistake," "a wasteful peripheral strategy," and "the most senseless campaign of the whole war" (Fuller 1977: 535). Other historians have argued that as Italy grew weaker, the campaign imposed a growing drain on limited German resources. Moreover, in July 1943, with the Allies on the doorstep of Mussolini's Italy, it was impossible simply to walk away: the cross-Channel invasion of France, codenamed Operation Overlord, was several months away, and the Western Allies could not remain idle while titanic battles were taking place on the Eastern Front. Allied public opinion would have regarded a suspension of fighting in the Mediterranean as a betrayal of its Russian ally, besides the possibility of a separate Soviet peace with Hitler.

Operation Avalanche

The first major Allied landing on the European mainland occurred on September 9, 1943, when the US Fifth Army, commanded by General Mark Clark, landed at Salerno, about 30 miles south of Naples. To those who observed the countless ships that massed in the sea, Operation Avalanche appeared irresistible. General Eisenhower's broadcast only hours before the assault that Italy had signed an armistice with the Allies was greeted with jubilation by the troops. But the landings took place roughly where German General Albert Kesselring anticipated an assault since Salerno was at the maximum range of Allied fighters operating out of Sicily. Instead of friendly Italians, the Allies encountered ferocious counterattacks from the veteran German 16th Panzer Division. On September 3, British and Canadian troops of Montgomery's Eighth Army had landed on the toe of Italy, 250 miles away from Salerno. Montgomery, who was never enthusiastic about an invasion of Italy, had argued that the US Fifth and British Eighth armies should land side by side, as during Husky. The lack of sufficient landing craft to transport the two armies simultaneously ruled out this option.

On September 11, high-altitude German planes dropped radio-controlled glider bombs that flew at over 600 miles per hour, sinking 13 Allied ships, including a hospital ship. The crisis of the nine-day Battle of Salerno came on September 13 when a German counterattack came within about half a mile of the beaches, where it was stopped by devastating naval gunfire from destroyers. On September 16, Kesselring ordered his forces to withdraw northward. On October 1, Clark rode in triumph into Naples. The British seized the Foggia airfields near Italy's Adriatic coast. From the Foggia airfields many of the most important targets of the German and German-controlled aircraft industry could be reached by Allied bombers. In the subsequent Italian campaign, the Fifth and Eighth armies would fight on the left and right sides respectively of the Apennine mountain range that runs down the center of Italy. Optimists believed the Allies would be in Rome by Christmas 1944, perhaps sooner.

The Road to Rome

Initially, Hitler intended to withdraw his forces to the northern Apennines. Rommel warned that unless such a plan was adopted, German forces in the south risked being outflanked and encircled by amphibious operations. Perhaps, but such operations depended on landing ships of which there were never enough. Kesselring, who disagreed with Rommel, convinced Hitler that Italy could be held. Hitler was determined "to block the enemy's bridge to the Balkans." By September 9, when Italy surrendered to the Allies, Hitler had moved 14 German divisions into Italy and sent reinforcements to the Balkans, Greece, and the Aegean. In November, Hitler placed all the German forces in Italy under Kesselring's command. The Italian theater was about to become a large secondary front for Hitler's Germany with its limited manpower and material resources.

Salerno did bring the Germans time to establish fortified lines across the Italian peninsula, the most famous of which was the Gustav Line north of Naples, and along the Garigliano, Rapido, and Sangro rivers, anchored in the west by the heavily fortified town of Cassino. Above the town, on top of a mountain mass, lay the monastery founded by Saint Benedict – Monte Cassino – which had been destroyed and rebuilt several times in earlier wars. Monte Cassino overlooked Highway 6, the main road to Rome. The Allies battered against the Gustav Line for nearly five months. In January 1944, Clark tried to outflank the Cassino position from the south by an attack across the deep and fast-running Rapido River by the 36th Division (Texas National Guard). The Rapido earned the nickname "Bloody River" when 36th Division suffered heavy casualties in what was a costly failure. Clark shrugged off accusations of "mass murder" and blamed the 36th Division's senior officers.

Direct assaults on Cassino made by American, British, Indian, New Zealand, and Polish troops all failed to dislodge the soldiers of the 1st German Parachute Division. On February 15, in one of the most controversial actions of the campaign, Allied bombers together with artillery destroyed Monte Cassino. German troops did not occupy the monastery, but enemy positions were hardly separate from the building itself. The German paratroops continued to resist. The Gurkhas got to within 200 yards of the monastery, only to be withdrawn when supplies could not reach them even by air. In March there were renewed attacks preceded by bombing and artillery fire, but the few paratroops who survived were able to check any advance.

On May 11, 1944, the Allied armies launched their great spring offensive. Five days later, the Germans withdrew from Cassino. General Alphonse Juin, commander of the French Expeditionary Corps (CEF), outflanked German positions using his Moroccan Goumiers, who scaled almost vertical mountains aided by mules to carry munitions to the remote ridges and peaks. The fourth Battle of Monte Cassino ended when Polish troops hoisted their red and white flag over the ruins of the monastery. The battle had cost the Poles almost 4,000 casualties. Polish troops under General Wladyslaw Anders continued to win many laurels during the long advance to the Po River.

Meanwhile, along the Adriatic coast, Montgomery's Eighth Army of British, Canadian, Indian, and New Zealand divisions pushed back the Germans along a 40-mile front stretching from the coast, advancing from one river to the next, toward the Sangro in front of the Gustav Line. The weather grew worse week by week, but on November 23, the British 78th Infantry Division crossed the Sangro, widened from 100 to 400 feet and more by the almost continuous winter rains. The 1st Canadian Infantry Division now relieved the exhausted British 78th Division, which had suffered 10,000 casualties in the second half of 1943. Between December 20 and 28, the Canadians fought one of the fiercest battles of the Italian campaign at the seaport town of Ortona, which became a "miniature Stalingrad" as the Canadians fought elements of the German 1st Parachute Division in the first large, pitched urban battle in the Mediterranean. After block-to-block, house-to-house, room-to-room combat, the Canadians captured what was left of Ortona.

In the last week of December, with no hope of breaking through to Rome from the Adriatic as long as the Allies were hampered by winter weather,

Montgomery recommended a halt to the Adriatic campaign, and General Alexander agreed. On December 30, Montgomery handed Eighth Army over to General Oliver Leese, and returned to Britain to prepare for the cross-Channel invasion.

Anzio

On January 22, 1944, an attempt was made to out-flank the Gustav Line. A British–American amphibious force of two infantry divisions assisted by special units, commanded by the cautious and pessimistic General John Lucas, landed at Anzio about 35 miles south of Rome. Codenamed Operation Shingle, the landing achieved complete surprise. But then Lucas stopped, and confined himself to securing the small bridgehead. Later Churchill, who had pressed for Anzio, made the remark that he had expected to be hurling a wildcat on shore, but instead had a stranded whale. Within hours of the landing the fast-acting Kesselring had divisions from northern Italy, Germany, the Balkans, and France on the move to Anzio. He massed almost 120,000 men around the beachhead. A massive German attack on February 16 failed to throw the Allies back into the sea as American and British troops fought bravely to save the beachhead. A renewed attack against the Americans failed when US 3rd Division commander General Lucian Truscott, alerted by Ultra intelligence, confronted the enemy with massed firepower. Nevertheless, the beachhead remained under German artillery fire, which included two monster 218-ton railroad guns – "Anzio Annie" and "Anzio Express" – that lobbed 280-mm shells before retreating to cover. The four-month stalemate at Anzio and Cassino was broken by the Allied spring offensive in May.

In one of the most controversial decisions of the campaign, General Mark Clark, with the Gustav Line crumbling after the Allied breakout at Anzio (May 23–24, 1944), ordered the Fifth Army to race for Rome rather than head east and cut off the German retreat. The German forces successfully escaped north of Rome, which Clark's troops entered on June 4, 1944. Two days later came the D-Day landings and the decisive campaign in Normandy. In Italy, 27 German divisions were fighting the Allies, and about 40 German and German-controlled divisions

were in Greece and the Balkans to prevent any Allied invasion from Italy.

Operation Anvil/Dragoon

On August 15, 1944, when the US Seventh Army (one American and one French corps) commanded by General Jacob Devers landed on the southern coast of France, another Allied strategic debate was resolved. At the earlier Teheran Conference in 1943, the Allies had agreed to launch the cross-Channel invasion in May 1944 and to assist that invasion by a landing in the south of France, codenamed Operation Anvil. After the Normandy invasion, however, the British suggested that Anvil (renamed Dragoon) be canceled. The Americans disagreed at once, pointing out that there would be 30–40 American divisions in the United States at the end of July ready to fight in the European theater, and they needed French ports from which to bring their strength to bear. General Charles de Gaulle also insisted that French forces in Italy participate in the liberation of France. General Marshall urged that Anvil be the main Allied effort in the Mediterranean.

Doubting that Anvil would help the fighting in Normandy, hundreds of miles to the north, the British defended the Italian campaign on the grounds that it diverted German forces away from the decisive theaters in the east and west. The Allied wrangling was further aggravated by Prime Minister Churchill's proposal for action in the Aegean. In this case, however, British General Alan Brooke, while a strong advocate of the Italian campaign, opposed what he termed Churchill's "wild schemes." A frustrated Churchill deplored what he viewed as Mediterranean opportunities "flung on one side, like the rind of an orange" (Parker 1997: 192).

Once ashore, American and French troops took the major ports of Marseilles and Toulon and pushed northwards. The bulk of the German troops escaped to help build up a new front along the Franco-German border and along the Alpine passes into Italy.

The End in Italy

Two days after the fall of Rome on June 4, General Alexander ordered the Allied armies in Italy to make all possible speed for Pisa and Florence. Some 170 miles separated the Allies from the next German fortifications, the formidable Gothic Line, but many rivers and hills lay in between. Hitler, instead of freeing up German divisions to fight in Normandy, persisted with his no-withdrawal policy in Italy. The German Gothic Line proved every bit as tough as the Gustav Line, and there always seemed to be another defensive line. The cartoon characters of "Willie and Joe" by American cartoonist Bill Mauldin, with their unshaven, bleary-eyed look, were the enduring symbols of a million soldiers. Heavy rains and casualties in the fall halted the Allied drive toward the Po River. The Allied armies in Italy now comprised troops from 29 nations, including Brazilians, Belgians, Cypriots, and Palestinian Jews. In the spring of 1945, the Fifth and Eighth armies finally left the mountains behind and entered the fertile plains of the Po Valley. On May 2, the Germans in Italy surrendered. For the Italian people, total war had brought destruction and suffering. In reprisal for every German soldier killed by Italian partisans, Kesselring ordered the deaths of 10 Italian civilians.

The Mediterranean was not the decisive theater of World War II, but it was the pivotal theater, a prerequisite until the Allies were ready to launch the Second Front. The Italian campaign was, after all, a peripheral theater, not the main front; its purpose was to support, not rival, the main front. By committing one-tenth of German ground forces, or 50 divisions, to defend the eastern Mediterranean, which would otherwise have been deployed on the Eastern Front or in Normandy, Hitler had "played into the Allied hands" (Howard 1968: 44). In no small measure, the Italian campaign had assisted in bringing about the downfall of the Third Reich, a result for which so many gave their lives.

SEE ALSO: World War II: Battle of Britain; World War II: Invasion of Normandy to the Surrender of Germany.

References

Bradley, O. N. and Blair, C. (1983) *A General's Life: An Autobiography by General of the Army Omar N. Bradley*. New York: Simon and Schuster.

Chandler, A. D., Jr (Ed.) (1970) *The Papers of Dwight David Eisenhower: The War Years: II*. Baltimore: Johns Hopkins University Press.

Churchill, W. S. (1949) *Their Finest Hour*. Boston: Houghton Mifflin.

Danchev, A. and Todman, D. (2001) *War Diaries 1939–1945: Field Marshal Lord Alanbrooke*. Berkeley, CA: University of California Press.

Ellis, J. (1990) *Brute Force: Allied Strategy and Tactics in the Second World War*. New York: Viking.

Fuller, E. F. (1977) *The Mediterranean Theater of Operations: Cassino to the Alps*. Washington, DC: Center for Military History.

Gibson, H (Ed.) (1946) *The Ciano Diaries 1939–1943*. New York: Doubleday.

Howard, M. (1968) *The Mediterranean Strategy in the Second World War*. London: Weidenfeld and Nicolson.

Moore, J. H. (1976) *Morshead: A Biography of Lieutenant-General Sir Leslie Morshead*. Sydney: Haldane.

Parker, R. A. C. (1997) *The Second World War: A Short History*. New York: Oxford University Press.

Porch, D. (2004) *The Path to Victory: The Mediterranean Theater in World War II*. New York: Farrar, Straus, and Giroux.

Stimson, H. L. (1948) *On Active Service in Peace and War*. New York: Harper and Brothers.

Woodman, R. (2000) *Malta Convoys 1940–1943*. London: John Murray.

Further Reading

Atkinson, R. (2002) *An Army at Dawn: The War in North Africa, 1942–1943*. New York: Henry Holt.

Atkinson, R. (2007) *The Day of Battle: The War in Sicily and Italy, 1943–1944*. New York: Henry Holt.

Ball, S. (2009) *The Bitter Sea: The Struggle for Mastery in the Mediterranean, 1935–1949*. London: HarperCollins.

Barnett, C. (1991) *Engage the Enemy More Closely: The Royal Navy in the Second World War*. New York: W. W. Norton.

Baxter, C. (1996) *The War in North Africa, 1940–1943: A Selected Bibliography*. Westport: Greenwood Press.

Blumenson, M. (1969) *Salerno to Cassino: United States Army in World War II*. Washington, DC: United States Army.

Churchill, W. (1949, 1950) *The Second World War. Volumes 2 and 3*. Boston: Houghton Mifflin.

Clark, L. (2006) *Anzio: Italy and the Battle for Rome*. New York: Atlantic Monthly.

D'Este, C. (1988) *Bitter Victory: The Battle for Sicily, July–August 1943*. New York: E. P. Dutton.

D'Este, C. (1991) *Fatal Decision: Anzio and the Battle for Rome*. New York: HarperCollins.

D'Este, C. (2008) *Warlord: A Life of Winston Churchill at War 1874–1945*. New York: HarperCollins.

Hastings, M. (2011) *Inferno: The World at War, 1939–1945*. New York: Alfred A. Knopf.

Molony, C. (1973) *The Mediterranean and Middle East. Volume 5: The Campaign in Sicily and the Campaign in Italy. History of the Second World War*. London: Her Majesty's Stationery Office.

Raugh, H. (1993) *Wavell in the Middle East, 1939–1941*. New York: Brassey's.

Roberts, A. (2009) *Masters and Commanders: How Four Titans Won the War in the West, 1941–1945*. New York: HarperCollins.

Sadkovich, J. (1994) *The Italian Navy in World War II*. Westport: Greenwood Press.

Weinberg, G. (1994) *A World at Arms: A Global History of World War II*. Cambridge: Cambridge University Press.

World War II: The Defeat and Occupation of France

CHALMERS HOOD

The Fog of Memory

In the decades after 1945, French lips were as sealed as were their archives on what happened during the war. This continued for two generations. Only historians with special access got in early but even they were severely constrained because they could not cite their sources. Said Robert Paxton, the American expert on Vichy in 1970 when denied access to the archives, "It will be a long time before those most sensitive materials are opened up to research" (Paxton, 1972: 394). Even so, his book hit like a bombshell, relying heavily on the only open primary sources; the captured German archives. Even now, works on wartime France reflect very different national perspectives about the events of 1939–1945. Recently, the door has begun to crack open, first at the local level where municipal and county-level files about everyday life reside and later at national levels where freedom of information laws are forcing a balance to the German view of the war in France.

A Battle Lost

The shock of defeat in only six weeks of the great victor of 1918 has been the longest studied of France's experiences in the war of 1939–1945. Explanations fall into two general categories. First, there is a military explanation: France and Britain were not militarily prepared to fight a new-era mechanized campaign. Parallel with this is the second school of thought – that this was not so much a tactical battlefield loss as the result of a kind of moral and political decadence that had set in among the western democracies, assuring defeat before the first shots were fired. Both arguments have survived and evolved with conclusions stemming from the kind of evidence authors have found most plausible. Equipment, training, and joint planning were simply not enough. A clever and more flexible enemy who had learned better from mistakes in the last war soundly defeated Allied armies on the battlefield. The French military, knowing itself to be weaker both industrially and demographically than its German rival, prepared for another long war of attrition. It rebuilt a large conscript army protected by an elaborate string of underground defenses, which were presumed to be impenetrable. This left the Franco-Belgian frontier open: it was there the French planned for a conventional defense against an anticipated German onslaught.

Allies were needed against an enemy one-third larger in population. France was slow to accept the new concepts of maneuver and mechanized warfare, and in the summer of 1939 she did not have many of the necessary tools available for her soldiers. In her war industries, France had continued her tradition of emphasizing technical perfection over mass production, which placed her far behind Germany when war was declared. The so-called Phony War of September 1939 through April 1940 was seen as an opportunity to catch up. In May 1940, French defense strategy was built on a framework of weaknesses. Mechanization of the army was only partly complete with the emphasis placed on using light tanks for reconnaissance and scouting instead of in a main tank battle. France could only put 1,200 warplanes in the air against Germany's 3,500 and the alliance with Britain only added another 400 planes to the Allied fleet. The greatest deficiency was in bombers.

French attempts to reach agreement with Britain for a peripheral campaign to cut off Germany from her supply of Scandinavian raw materials and siphon *Wehrmacht* units away from the Western Front failed. Disagreements about the operation delayed an invasion of Narvik, Norway, until April, just as Germany launched her own sudden invasion from the south, nullifying the surprise element of the Anglo-French maneuver.

Belgium chose the neutral path so that any contingencies envisioning another German invasion, as in 1914, could not be rehearsed in peacetime. Nevertheless, French planning anticipated a kind of repeat of the 1914 Schlieffen Plan, requiring French entry into Belgium early in the campaign to stop the German advance earlier than they had in World War I. Britain had agreed to place troops on the ground, but the numbers were small. Only in the summer of 1940, just before the German invasion, did the full British contingent of 10 divisions take positions in the line. At dawn on May 10, 1940, General Maurice Gamelin ordered an advance into Belgium in response to the German invasion of the Low Countries. If all went well, the long Allied line of 135 divisions would stretch from the Swiss frontier through the Maginot Line across Belgium to the Dutch coastline.

German planning had anticipated this reflex action by France and, as a result, focused on a rapid and risky campaign pushing a mechanized force through the weakly defended sector to the northwest of the Maginot Line in the Ardennes forest, which was considered unsuitable for modern maneuver warfare. The Manstein Plan, so-called for the German general who urged its adoption by Hitler, envisioned a quick breakthrough and a move west and then north, the reverse of the 1914 Schlieffen Plan. Upon reaching the Channel coast, this advance would cut off the main body of French and Allied troops, which German planners believed would not be able to react to the swift mechanized blitz. The risk was high but it worked even better than the German planners had expected.

After just two days in the Ardennes, the German tanks reached the Meuse River near Sedan at the critical angle in the French defense line. The next day, Heinz Guderian's Panzer corps of three divisions crossed the river, facing only light opposition from two French reserve infantry divisions that were made up of men between 30 and 40 years of age. By day's end, the Meuse had been crossed at two other points to the north by two other Panzer corps on a front of approximately 50 miles. This placed seven German tank divisions on the west bank of the Meuse, facing very little immediate resistance. On May 14, far to the north, two French light mechanized divisions operating east of Brussels engaged in the first tank battle of the war. These units were equipped only with the lighter Souma and Hotchkiss reconnaissance tanks. Though the French fought well, the German Panzers retained control of the battlefield and were able to recover and repair most of their vehicles damaged in this engagement. The two German tank divisions were not part of the Ardennes offensive, so the engagement did not impede the advance of the seven other Panzer divisions now breaking out from the Sedan area.

On May 12, General Gamelin had decided to send six of his reserve divisions to assist generals André-Georges Corap and Charles Huntziger, who commanded the two French armies in the threatened sector. This was done without any sense of urgency. In this deployment were France's three heavy tank divisions that had only been formed after the war began. Unfortunately, there were not enough of the B1-bis heavy tanks to fully equip these heavier divisions: half the tanks in these units were of the light, reconnaissance variety. The 3rd DCR (*Division Cuirassée de Réserve*), or heavy tank division, arrived south of Sedan but was not ready to attack on May 14, the critical day when the three German Panzer divisions under Guderian were just starting to break out. Allied air attacks on the bridgeheads at Sedan had been weak and failed to destroy any of the German pontoon bridges, which their tanks depended upon to cross the Meuse. The French units spent the day, instead, refueling and deploying in small groups for an attack the next morning. No one on the French side knew that the battle had been a sideshow for Guderian, who had moved the bulk of his armored forces west and away from any French resistance.

On the same day, to the north, the 1st DCR deployed far to the north near the Belgian town of Charleroi. They too had arrived earlier but were dispersed and not ready for action until the afternoon of May 15, when a limited engagement with Erwin Rommel's 7th Panzer division broke out while the French tanks were still refueling. With the Rommel action in the north and the Guderian action in the south attracting all the attention of French commanders, the XLI Panzer Corps advanced unnoticed in the center at a village named Monthermé. Far ahead of it were elements of the only remaining French armored division, the 2nd DCR, which were spread across a 25-mile front, unloading and refueling at the time General Reinhardt's Panzer Corps passed through the area. By the afternoon, his tanks had advanced over 40 miles, had faced little French opposition, and were free to head west with no enemy forces between them and the English Channel, roughly 150 miles away. This was the day that the French premier, Paul Reynaud, nervously contacted Winston Churchill to say that France had lost the battle.

What was called the tortoise head of the German tank advance was only just then starting to develop. On May 16, Rommel took the extreme risk of moving out in advance of his infantry and artillery support with two battalions of tanks in a rush toward the sea. The next morning, he was halfway to the coast. What this meant was that, if unchecked, the seven German Panzer divisions would split the Allied armies in half, with the British Expeditionary Force, the Belgian army, and the most mobile of the French forces isolated to the north. Well to the south was the slower and non-mechanized remainder of the French army trying to maintain a defensive line between the German forces and Paris.

The last significant attempt by heavy French armored forces to engage the German armor thrust occurred on May 17 near Laon. There, Colonel Charles de Gaulle, the outspoken French proponent of mechanized warfare, had command of what was called the 4th DCR but in fact was a collection of troops hastily thrown together with no radios, no air support, no anti-tank weapons, and fewer than 100 tanks. He tried twice to advance north against the German units but both times was easily pushed back. On the next day, General Gamelin was sacked and replaced by Maxime Weygand.

Weygand's only hope of stopping the German advance to the sea came to an end between May 21 and 25. A combined Anglo-French attack on Rommel's forces at Arras was pushed back, while a desperate plan to break out of isolation in the north was called off. This began the rush to Dunkirk and the successful evacuation of over 300,000 British and French troops to England. While the men were saved, their equipment was abandoned on the beaches, leaving Britain with

no chance of projecting power abroad for an indefinite time. In the midst of this, Belgium withdrew from the war on May 28.

On June 10, Paris was declared an open city and the government stumbled south and west away from the ever advancing German forces, to the Loire River Valley by mid-June and finally to Bordeaux, where a new government under Marshal Pétain sought terms for an armistice with Germany. The struggle between the factions about continuing the war from overseas had ended with Reynaud's resignation on June 16. On June 20, Admiral Darlan told a French journalist he still did not know if his fleet would flee to Britain or not. Two days later, the Armistice was signed in the same railroad carriage used to end World War I 22 years earlier. The blame game between France and Britain, and between civilian and military factions, began soon after the line was breached west of Sedan.

On July 3, a large battle squadron of the Royal Navy arrived offshore at the French naval anchorage near Oran, Algeria with orders to neutralize the French warships anchored and partly demobilized there. Offers to sail to Britain were declined by the French admiral, as was an option to scuttle. Late in the afternoon, in obedience to orders from the British cabinet, the Royal Navy opened fire on the French squadron. After a short bombardment, one French battleship was sunk at anchor, another seriously damaged, and a destroyer hit while attempting to leave harbor. The total loss of French life was 1,297 against negligible losses to the Royal Navy. A second strike was ordered three days later, this time by naval aircraft, which attacked while funeral services were underway for the Frenchmen killed in the first engagement. The attacks on Mers-el-Kébir, designed to keep the French warships out of German hands, had been resisted by the British Admiralty during planning stages in the belief that France would not let Germany gain control of her ships. In documents released years later, we see the decision made by Churchill came at a delicate moment when solidifying the new War Cabinet of the Conservative and Labor parties was in the balance. There was also great anger among some ministers that France had accepted an armistice.

Delayed and incomplete telegrams, the refusal of the French admiral to negotiate terms with a

British liaison officer until late in the afternoon, the British cabinet's refusal to accept a last-minute offer from the French admiral, and the absence of the French naval chief of staff who was in transit with his staff between Bordeaux and Vichy that day, all contributed to the disaster.

Two later attacks by British forces on another French colonial naval base at Dakar, West Africa, were repulsed with only modest damage to the French warships in port. That France and Britain did not move to open declarations of war against each other was one of the surprise outcomes of these actions. A dangerous hair-trigger relationship developed between London and Vichy, leading to enhanced American presence as a friendly buffer between the two.

The tragedies of Mers-el-Kébir and other flash points where Frenchmen actually fought other Frenchmen grew out of these unresolved bitter feelings. Had interwar planning been adequate? Were the defensive weapons and plans of Britain and France sufficient in this new era of mechanized warfare and combined air–ground tactics? What if there had been no Munich deal and war had been declared in 1938?

Four eyewitness accounts give us snapshot views of the last months of peace and perhaps the psychological readiness for another war. The British journalist Alexander Werth covered France for the *Manchester Guardian* for six years through the June 1940 collapse. In addition to his daily coverage, he published his diaries in five books. He was endlessly stunned by what he saw. Would the extremes of Left and Right make the country ungovernable? After the failure to back Czechoslovakia in 1938, would they permit another Polish-style Munich? He saw the French defeat as the collapse of the greatest civilization in Europe. In late 1937, a US Marine major attending the French École de Guerre for two years wrote his after-action report to US Naval Intelligence. After spending three months in the field with the French army, he concluded that the tactics of "method and prudence" which had been sufficient for victory 20 years earlier would probably not suffice in the next modern war. Three years earlier, General Weygand had made the conscious decision not to fully mechanize the French army. The French political writer Jacques Benoist-Méchin had been seduced by the masculinity of National Socialism during his many visits

when he befriended men like Otto Abetz and wrote adoringly of the interwar German army. For him, the theme of French decadence was indisputable. Finally, in November 1939, at the height of the so-called Phony War, the American correspondent for the *Herald Tribune*, Walter Lippman, wrote to a friend explaining how General Gamelin saw only a limited window for French success against Germany. Another "pyrrhic victory" would turn France into a third-rate power. The declining French birth rate, said Lippman, was the governing factor in Gamelin's philosophy of war.

Occupation

The Armistice divided metropolitan France into an occupied zone amounting to the northern two-thirds of the country, including the Atlantic ports, and a free zone administered by a rump French regime under the war hero Marshal Pétain, from the spa town of Vichy. This free region included the Mediterranean coast and the Massif Central up to the Italian border and Swiss border. Vichy was allowed to maintain a small peacetime army and retained administrative control of the fleet and French Empire. Somehow the French military intelligence services continued to function and by August 1940 they were providing ominous reports of German intentions in France. The country would be permanently dismembered, the port cities and large zones in the east peeled off and given either to Germany or made into a new Flemish state. French industry would become fully subservient to a European economy run from Berlin. Otto Abetz, the newly appointed German ambassador in Paris, told Vichy that the Armistice could be repealed whenever Hitler saw fit. Plans by the *Wehrmacht* and the *Abwehr* for the invasion of French North Africa were uncovered that summer as well. With this knowledge in hand, the Vichy approach was to attempt to preserve the mantle of sovereignty with the hope that direct German rule under a Gauleiter could be avoided. Already, the German authorities were pushing France to comply with German racial laws. French military attachés serving in eastern Europe provided accurate reports of what occupation meant in Poland and the former Czechoslovakia. Pétain met with Hitler that autumn and started the talk of what collaboration between the two countries would become. Getting word that his nominal prime minister, Pierre Laval, was conducting secret talks behind his back, Pétain fired him in December 1940, replacing him with Admiral Darlan and his cabinet of technocrats. The policy of collaboration had been established by Pétain and the next months would add meaning to this.

France from June 1940 to June 1944 was a collection of very different stories. The German occupation regime included at least two competing authorities that vied for control of French resources and territory. In the summer of 1942, the *Schutzstaffel* (SS) and the *Sicherheitsdienst* (SD) had taken the lead over the German military in the administration of occupied territories. There were also several separate economic organizations seeking control of French industrial and agricultural resources and, by 1943, for access to manpower for the expanding and competing German war industries. Italy's share of the occupation began with a small border strip in the Alps, which grew to the whole southeastern corner of France as well as Corsica, with further claims in North Africa. The United States maintained an embassy at Vichy through November 1942 as well as a growing semi-independent organization of consuls and attachés in Morocco, Algeria, and Tunisia. As the Armistice of 1940 was not viewed as a betrayal of trust in the United States, the relationship between America and Pétain's regime remained cordial. In coordination with Britain, the United States took as its prime responsibilities the oversight of the French navy, which Germany had not grabbed, and pressing Vichy to hold firm to the terms of the Armistice. From early on, the American envoys could see that the North African colonies were important sources of food and manpower should France return to the war. Keeping this territory out of German hands was the overriding concern.

As for Britain, a twin agenda emerged once Churchill formed a wartime coalition with Clement Attlee's Labour Party. While the grander strategy of fighting Germany and returning eventually to Europe was the public side of the British war, there was a semi-secret economic war conducted in France, which at times took on a life of its own. The desire to support Charles de Gaulle's small band of exiles, along with a plan to encourage a kind of guerrilla war from within occupied France, were wartime goals of a portion of the British government which at times conflicted with Churchill and Roosevelt's larger scheme for the European theater. Unfortunately, the British work with the French popular classes and the American support for the rump regime and its military forces was poorly coordinated. For us to understand today what was happening in France and to the French people in this period of occupation and exploitation, we need to see the multiple policies conducted by all the participants.

Though technically in control of the local administration in the two zones, the Vichy government found itself largely cut off from direct contact with local administrators in the German occupied zone. But the pretense of maintaining sovereignty was essential. If Vichy openly acknowledged defeat, Nazi laws and police would follow. Would Vichy switch alliances and join the Axis in the war? In the spring of 1941 there was fear that this would happen, after Darlan conducted secret negotiations with the German military, potentially opening up the French colonies for German military use.

The Protocols of Paris, a series of written accords made in May 1941, offered Germany access to French colonial ports and landing rights to Iraq via Syria, in the next potential stage of collaboration. There were intense debates in Vichy, pitting Darlan against General Weygand, the administrator of French North Africa. The accords were largely nullified but Churchill authorized British and Gaullist troops to invade Syria when German aircraft passed through. At the same time, Abetz pushed again for a more openly French anti-Semitic policy, telling Darlan that if France did not implement a system, Germany would do it for her. The response was the appointment of Xavier Vallat, a French war veteran, anti-Semite, and Germanophobe, to an office that was to be handled under French law. This continued the idea of preserving French sovereignty and limiting further German incursion. Darlan's two greatest fears were the appointment of a Gauleiter over unoccupied France and a German takeover of French North Africa. The concept of Gauleiter, in French eyes, meant the expansion of Gestapo and SS powers over the French police in Vichy. This was to be avoided at all costs. There were several times when a German invasion of French North Africa seemed imminent long before America could intervene.

Slowly but surely, Vichy found itself cut off from direct contact with the French prefects in the north who administered local government and had oversight of the police. The issue, in Darlan's mind, was whose law would prevail on French soil and whose police would be in control. He passed instructions to his prefects to hold the line against expanded German power. Gradually during 1941, administrative and police authority passed into German hands. There was an attempt to keep the administration of the occupation in military hands but by early 1942 that failed as well. In Berlin, the SS and SD had won the bureaucratic war for control of the rear areas in all occupied territory at the same time as they had secretly obtained authority to organize the Holocaust. Assassinations of German military personnel had triggered an ever-growing campaign of terror and reprisals that continued for the rest of the war. Daily life in the occupied zone went downhill rapidly. Who would try the perpetrators? French civilian courts were set up in both zones. In the north, French police were co-opted to assist in the rounding up of foreign Jews, but in the process French Jews were caught as well. By the end of the year, Abetz believed that a new wave of pro-Nazi Frenchmen could be placed in charge to facilitate the switch of alliances on which he had staked his reputation. Abetz had tried to control French policy through a string of secondary appointments at Vichy, but even these could not force the flip in alliances he sought. The big change came in the late spring of 1942 when Darlan was ousted and an SS general arrived with a mandate to control all of the policing in France.

With Laval's return to power in mid-1942 came the increased pressure on three elements of the French and foreign underclasses: Jews, Freemasons, and communists. In addition, there were the growing demands for forced French labor in German factories from several competing Nazi organizations. Persecuted individuals were left with three choices. They could drop low, stay in France, and possibly join a resistance organization. If not, they could seek escape to North Africa where enforcement of racial laws was less severe and where they might join the army. For the daring few, who were usually young and had no job or family concerns, there was always the slim chance of escaping to America or Britain. Few Vichy officials understood that persecutions at home were the source of manpower for resistance movements abroad. De Gaulle's men like Jean Moulin did see this and strove to unite the disparate factions. While their effectiveness is debated, their determination and sophistication are the basis of many legendary tales.

Comparing experiences is difficult because of the varying conditions in each zone and the local nature of occupation policy. Having parallel stories of all 90 departments would make the picture more complete. Relations between occupier and the occupied likewise varied, depending on the zone, the pressure applied by the German authorities, and the skill or attitude of the prefect and his local staff. New evidence suggests that in the occupied zone prominent local citizens managed daily life more than French officials. Gathering and hoarding of food were issues of growing importance as German requisitions grew in both zones. Open resistance was often shunned in the occupied zone until 1943, when the forced labor drafts for work in Germany potentially threatened every adult Frenchman. Prior to that, accommodation was sought, with the average citizen hoping to survive by disappearing into the crowd. Those in the north were rather envious of conditions in the free zone, a difference that largely disappeared in November 1942 when the occupation was made complete. The grabbing of foreigners, especially Jews, by the Germans was something that was officially tolerated in the hope that French Jews would be spared. German agents in North Africa reported in late 1942 that ships arriving from France were carrying as many as 400 Jewish refugees. The relative mildness of the free zone and later Italian occupation came to an abrupt end in October 1943 when Italy backed out of the war. A special SS *Einsatzgruppe* (task force) swept through, grabbing Jews who had run out of places to hide. A French prefect in a former free zone department was told one day by the regional SS commander that failure to control local law and order would be viewed as connivance with the enemy which would incur unspecified German reprisals. This prefect fled to Switzerland.

An amazing Who's Who of people assisting in the rescue of Jews and other persecuted groups emerges from the testimony of witnesses at the post-war collaboration trials in France. The depositions for the prosecution and defense tell countless stories of survival and tragedy under the occupation. Efforts were largely uncoordinated but if there was a common thread, it was a mask of silence. To avoid direct confrontation with German authorities, the roles of resistor and collaborator had to overlap. Even after the war, many of those who helped were reluctant to come forward and say what they had done.

After the US and British invasion of French North Africa, German forces occupied all of Vichy, Gestapo and SS units operating in areas that had been blocked to them earlier. French police were asked to help and new pro-Nazi pseudo-police forces were formed to round up the undesirables of society. The *Waffen* SS recruited 10,000 French boys into a unit called the Charlemagne Division which went down almost to the last man defending Berlin against the Russians in 1945. The *Milice*, an SS-style police force of 6,000 Frenchmen, joined their German counterparts in the capture and transport of Jews, Freemasons, and communists to the concentration camps. Though full police collaboration was worse in other occupied countries, the outrage in France was more intense and long lasting.

The aftermath of the Anglo-American Torch landings in November 1942 finally brought the French back into the war on the Allied side with a 300,000-man Colonial Army, but another incident occurred which could have derailed a developing Allied war strategy. On Christmas Eve 1942, Admiral Darlan, who had taken over administration of North Africa and arranged the shift of France from neutrality to co-belligerency, was assassinated in his office. This was just days before the hugely important Roosevelt–Churchill conference at Casablanca which would publicize their combined plan for the rest of the war. Though proof at that time could not be established, Roosevelt believed that the assassination of Darlan was done under British direction by men loyal to Charles de Gaulle. For the rest of the war, American counter-espionage watched the de Gaulle organization for repeat attempts against other high French or American officials. If there were any one incident that convinced the American president that he would not recognize de Gaulle as provisional leader, it was the Darlan affair. His mind was changed after D-Day, facing

a possible French communist rising and advice from the Office of Strategic Services that only de Gaulle could control this.

Liberation came late but fast. Once the Allied armies in Normandy broke out of the beachhead in the summer of 1944, they proceeded almost unimpeded to the Rhine River frontier, where they would wait until spring 1945 for the final assault on Germany. To everyone's surprise, the landings in the south of France on August 15, 1944, met almost no resistance and these troops joined up with the Normandy force in just one month. Something like a delayed Bastille Day parade took place in liberated Paris in August, with Charles de Gaulle and his entourage of followers leading the march down the Champs-Élysées. A full-fledged French civil war never materialized.

Did all the underground work of Britain's Special Operations Executive make any difference or would resistance have happened anyway? In British historical circles this debate has not ended, with conventional military historians believing the impact of the Resistance has been overstated, while those who like the peripheral strategy reach the opposite conclusion. American troops were happy to call them all Resistance, hoping the various armed bands would guide the liberating troops on safe paths to the German frontier. So, in the end, who resisted and who collaborated? The Gaullist legend was so very different from the story told in Marcel Ophüls's powerful documentary *The Sorrow and the Pity* (1969), and different again from Robert Paxton's trend-setting *Vichy France: Old Guard and New Order* (1972), which helped force open the doors of many national archives and began the widespread study of France under occupation.

The Final Tally

Upwards of 600,000 Frenchmen died in World War II, the majority of whom were civilians. These figures, along with the 1.5 million French prisoners of war and slave laborers held in Germany, are less troubling than the fate of the 300,000 French and foreign Jews living in France when the war began. In percentage terms, four times as many French Jews survived as did Dutch Jews but none of this was immediately discussed in the aftermath of the war. Then, Holocaust studies awakened the public interest.

Slowly, we came to see that Vichy domestic policy was based on protecting French citizens first. In 1940–1941, prominent French Jews endorsed these policies before the full German agenda was understood. To defy the Germans openly would have led to disaster so the plan was to buy time through obfuscation and conceal-ment in hopes of an early Allied liberation. From Germany's perspective, Vichy was dragging its feet and protecting French Jews. Survival came down to local politics. Would a police chief help round up French Jews or not? Would priests offer fake documents showing that Jewish children had been baptized? In the dirty game of ethnic cleans-ing, 70 French prefects – those famous career local administrators – were sent off to concentra-tion camps for resisting German orders. Half of them were exterminated. After the war, 140,000 Frenchmen were tried for collaboration before French civil and military tribunals. Of those accused, about 1,600 were executed for treason.

The very latest declassified papers shed new light on the divided French cause. Through 1943, de Gaulle's closest advisors secretly urged American and British officials to neutralize the general's totalitarian inclinations by backing other leaders. His own military staff was strongly opposed to a "politics before war" strategy which they felt would lead to a civil war. In later life, wartime friends and enemies tended to forget or say nothing of their wartime efforts. Rather than discuss his refusal to support the Free French cause, the French diplomat and poet Alex Saint-Léger remained in exile and in silence until de Gaulle was dead. In those years of waiting, Saint-Léger spoke of his exile in metaphor through his poems for which he received a Nobel Prize. "Save the originals, don't save copies. A poet's writings follow his official words" (Saint-John, 1946: 6). We had to wait another 50 years to know what this meant.

References

Paxton, R. (1972) *Vichy France: Old Guard and New Order, 1940–44*. New York: Knopf.
Saint-John, P. [alias Alexis Saint-Léger] (1946) *Vents*. Paris: Gallimard.

Further Reading

Alexander, M. S. (2004) "The Fall of France, 1940." In G. Martel (Ed.), *The World War II Reader*. New York: Routledge.
Aron, R. (1958) *The Vichy Regime, 1940–44*. London: Putnam.
Bloch, M. (1953) *Strange Defeat*. Oxford: Oxford University Press.
Bowles, B. (2004) "'La Tragédie de Mers-el-Kébir' and the Politics of Filmed News in France, 1940–44," *Journal of Modern History*, 76 (2): 347–388.
Burrin, P. (1993) *La France à l'heure Allemande, 1940–44*. Paris: Editions du Seuil.
Christofferson, T. R. and Christofferson, M. S. (2006) *France during World War II: From Defeat to Liberation*. New York: Fordham University Press.
Comité d'Histoire de la Deuxième Guerre Mondiale (1979) *Français et Britanniques dans la drôle de guerre*. Paris: CNRS.
Couteau-Bégarie, H. and Huan, C. (1992) *Lettres et notes de l'Amiral Darlan*. Paris: Economica.
Doulut, A. (2005) *La Spolation des biens Juifs en Lot-et-Garonne*. Agen: Editions d'Albret.
Foot, M. R. D. (1966) *SOE in France, 1940–44*. London: HMSO.
Foot, M. R. D. (1973) "L'Aide à la Résistance en Europe," *Revue d'Histoire de la Deuxième Guerre Mondiale*, 90: 39–52.
Fox, J. (1992) "German Bureaucrat or Nazified Ideologue? Ambassador Otto Abetz and Hitler's Anti-Jewish Policies, 1940–44." In M. Graham (Ed.), *Power, Personalities and Politics: Essays in Honor of Donald Cameron Watt*. London: Frank Cass.
Gildea, R. (2002) *Marianne in Chains: Everyday Life in the French Heartland under the German Occupation*. New York: Holt.
Hinsley, F. H. (1993) *British Intelligence in the Second World War*. Cambridge: Cambridge University Press.
Jäckel, E. (1966) *Frankreich in Hitlers Europa: Die Deutsche Frankreichpolitik im Zweiten Weltkrieg*. Stuttgart: Deutsche Verlags-Anstalt.
Jackson, J. (2001) *France: The Dark Years, 1940–44*. Oxford: Oxford University Press.
Jackson, J. (2003) *The Fall of France: The Nazi Invasion of 1940*. Oxford: Oxford University Press.
Lamb, R. (1991) *Churchill as a War Leader*. New York: Carroll and Graf.
Lambauer, B. (2001) *Otto Abetz et les Français ou l'envers de la Collaboration*. Paris: Fayard.
Lambert, R. (1985) *Carnet d'un témoin, 1940–43*. Paris: Fayard.
Langer, W. (1947) *Our Vichy Gamble*. New York: Knopf.
Marrus, M. and Paxton, R. (1983) *Vichy France and the Jews*. New York: Stockton.

May, E. (2000) *Strange Victory: Hitler's Conquest of France*. New York: Hill and Wang.

Paxton, R. (1992) "Darlan, Un Amiral entre Deux Blocs. Réflections sur une Biographie Récente," *Vingtième Siècle: Revue d'Histoire*, 36: 3–20.

Paxton, R. (1998) "Five Stages of Fascism," *Journal of Modern History*, 70 (1): 1–23.

Rémond, R. (1996) *Le "Fichier Juif." Rapport de la Commission*. Paris: Plon.

Sweets, J. (1988) "Hold that Pendulum! Redefining Fascism, Collaborationism and Resistance in France," *French Historical Studies*, 15 (4): 731–758.

Weber, E. (1994) *The Hollow Years: France in the 1930s*. New York: Norton.

Young, R. (1996) *France and the Origin of the Second World War*. New York: St. Martin's Press.

World War II: War in Asia

JOHN T. KUEHN

In 1937, Japan went to war in China, principally with the Nationalist government of Chiang Kai-shek. From that point on the shaky relationship between the Empire of Japan and the United States deteriorated. The United States, which saw itself as the protector of Chinese sovereignty, canceled trade treaties and imposed an ever-increasing regime of economic sanctions upon Japan as she continued this war and then began to expand southward into Indochina. By the summer of 1941, America had declared virtual financial and economic warfare on Japan and was Nationalist China's biggest material supporter in its war against Japan. When the United States cut off all of Japan's oil leases in an effort to stimulate negotiation about a Japanese withdrawal from China, the Japanese Supreme War council decided for war. Plans were quickly finalized for the Navy to strike a knock-out blow against Pearl Harbor using Vice Admiral Nagumo Chuichi's aircraft carriers of *Dai Ichi Kido Butai*. Other forces were programmed to overrun the resources of the so-called Southeast Asian Co-Prosperity Sphere (principally the British and Dutch East Indies).

The First Six Months

Before sunrise on December 8, the Japanese launched a series of coordinated attacks against British Malaysia. About an hour later, on the other side of the international dateline, the first wave of air groups arrived over Pearl Harbor, Hawaii. Several hours later, Japanese bombers from Formosa struck the Philippines. Never before in the history of warfare had any nation launched a synchronized attack on the land, air, and sea over such a broad geographic area over so short a period of time. The US Pacific Fleet was caught unaware on December 7, 1941. In addition to sinking or damaging all eight of the battleships present, the Japanese crippled the US Army Air Forces. Over 3,200 casualties resulted but the repair facilities and fuel depots surrounding Pearl Harbor were untouched.

The catastrophe in the Philippines was worse. Japanese aircraft flying from bases in Formosa found the Americans totally unprepared, despite the attack on Pearl Harbor hours earlier. Through a series of miscommunications, Japanese bombers and fighters found MacArthur's B-17 bombers on the ground. At one stroke the Japanese eliminated half of MacArthur's air force and the majority of his bombers. There were over 250 casualties, including 80 killed. With air superiority achieved, the Japanese returned on December 9 to pound Cavite naval yard. This attack damaged shore facilities, destroying the Asiatic Fleet's reserve of torpedoes, and sank a submarine and a minesweeper. Fortunately, Admiral Thomas Hart had already moved most of his ships to the south. The defense of the northern Philippines was now the responsibility of the combined US/Filipino Army. Meanwhile, Guam in the Marianas fell on December 10. Only at Wake Island, halfway to Hawaii, was there good news. The Japanese assault on December 11 was repulsed by Wake's navy and Marine defenders who sank several Japanese warships. A relief force under Rear Admiral F. Jack Fletcher was 425 miles away from Wake when the defenders were overwhelmed by a second Japanese assault on December 23. Meanwhile, Hong Kong surrendered to the Japanese on Christmas Day.

In the Philippines, events went from bad to worse. On December 22, 1941, the Japanese landed over 50,000 troops of General Homma Masaharu's Fourteenth Army at Lingayen Gulf on the main Philippine island of Luzon. With no air force or navy to speak of, MacArthur's plan for the defense of the Philippines now resembled the

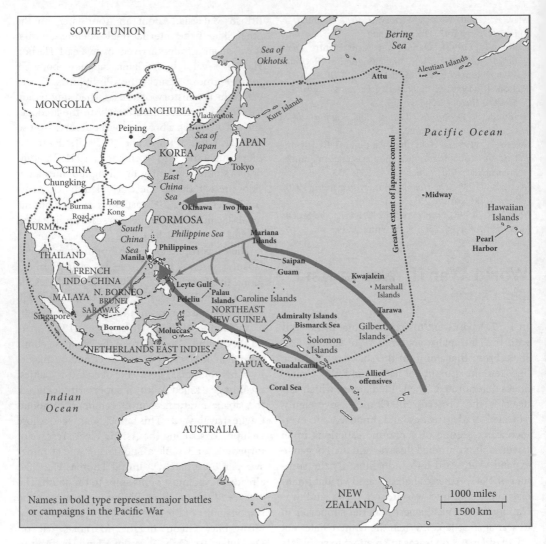

Map 21 World War II: War in Asia.

Alamo. MacArthur pulled back into a fortified line of defenses on Bataan. Here he would defend until relieved by the navy's Pacific Fleet. Any hope of this happening had disappeared at Pearl Harbor. MacArthur had little choice other than to hold out and tie down Japanese forces to prevent their use elsewhere. The fight settled into a siege, which the Japanese had not planned for. Roosevelt and General George C. Marshall, sensing that it might be bad for American morale to have MacArthur captured by the Japanese, ordered him to escape aboard PT boats with his family and staff. Upon his arrival in Australia he announced, "I shall return." In the meantime, the

horrors in Bataan continued. In April, 78,000 starving Americans and Filipinos in Bataan surrendered. Many of these prisoners suffered horribly during the infamous Bataan Death March. General Wainwright and 14,000 others held out until May on the small island of Corregidor.

While these events were taking place, the Allies established an American, British, Dutch, and Australian command under Field Marshal Sir Archibald Wavell to halt the Japanese advance to the south. Admiral Hart commanded Wavell's naval component. In addition to 29 submarines, Hart's force also included surface forces from all four nations, including several heavy and light cruisers as well as several squadrons of destroy-ers. US destroyers slipped in among Japanese transports at Balikpapan on the night of January 23–24, sinking four of them. They would have sunk more of them if not for defective torpedoes.

The event that doomed the East Indies was the fall of Singapore. General Yamashita Tomoyuki already had command of the air and sea after Japanese airmen sank the British capital ships *Prince of Wales* and *Repulse* a few days after Pearl Harbor. Yamashita then conducted a *Blitzkrieg*-style campaign against the British in Malaya. In the greatest Allied defeat of the Pacific War, Lieutenant General Sir Arthur Percival's forces were pushed out of the Malay Peninsula into Singapore, where he was forced to surrender over 130,000 soldiers and other personnel on February 15, 1942. Many of these men would die while building the infamous Thailand–Burma railroad for the Japanese. Wavell advised the Combined Chiefs of Staff (CCS) that further defense of the Indies was hopeless and turned over their defense to the Dutch. In late February, the Imperial Japanese Navy (IJN) smashed the remnants of Allied sea power at the Battle of the Java Sea.

The Dutch East Indies surrendered on March 9 and the Japanese now had nothing to impede their advance to the shores of Australia. Earlier in February, Nagumo's *Kido Butai* had conducted a punishing attack on Darwin, Australia. Moving south from their bases in the Marianas and Truk in the Carolines, the Japanese also captured the excellent harbor at Rabaul in the Bismarcks and began turning it into an impregnable fortress. Elsewhere they seized the Gilbert Islands, parts of the northern Solomons, and established them-selves along the northern shores of New Guinea.

Japan's efforts in the China–Burma–India (CBI) Theater were no less successful. The British colony of Burma had one objective – to protect India. To lose India was to lose the war. The Americans also wanted to defend Burma in order to protect the Burma Road to southern China through which American Lend-Lease aid flowed to the Nationalists. In early 1942, the Japanese began their offensive in Burma and captured Rangoon, the port terminus of Chiang's lifeline, in March. Roosevelt sent General Joseph Stillwell as his personal representative to Chiang's govern-ment and to coordinate with the British for com-bined operations against the Japanese. However,

this divided command structure and the inferior-ity of both the British and the Chinese troops resulted in catastrophe. Although Stillwell had been placed nominally in charge by Chiang, he found it very difficult to control his Chinese sub-ordinates. By May 1942, the British, Stillwell, and the Chinese had been run out of Burma. In Stillwell's words, "We got a hell of a beating."

Turning Points

Back at Pearl Harbor, Admiral Chester W. Nimitz arrived as Admiral Husband Kimmel's replace-ment. He retained Kimmel's staff and decided to conduct an active defense. With limited numbers of destroyers and oilers he made the decision to use task forces built around aircraft carriers because they were faster than the battleships. In Washington, DC, the American Joint Chiefs of Staff (JCS) under General Marshall implemented a divided command in the Pacific. MacArthur was put in charge of the Southwest Pacific Theater and Nimitz the Pacific (often called Central Pacific) Theater. The dividing line between the two theaters ran along the axis for Japanese offen-sive operations between New Guinea and the Solomons.

Nimitz initially conducted raids against the Japanese to give his inexperienced carrier aviators much-needed flying time. In April, the Americans launched Army medium bombers, commanded by Lieutenant Colonel "Jimmy" Doolittle, from the aircraft carrier *Hornet*. They bombed Tokyo on April 8. Although it caused little physical dam-age, the Japanese military leadership assigned hundreds of valuable Japanese aviators and air-craft to Japan for defense of the homeland. The Japanese Navy Staff proposed that the next step should be to sever Australia's sea lines of commu-nication (SLOC). Because of Doolittle's raid they now decided to approve Yamamoto's plan to bait the Pacific Fleet into a trap by seizing the west-ernmost island in the Hawaiian group – Midway. Also, they added the requirement to seize several islands in the Aleutians that they thought Doolittle's raiders had originated from. All this led to a watering down of the striking forces Yamamoto would have available for Midway.

Operations in the Southwest Pacific occurred first. Here the Japanese advanced to threaten

Australia's SLOC by seizing Tulagi in the southern Solomons and Port Moresby on the southeastern shore of New Guinea. In a series of
engagements during the first week of May the
American and Japanese navies clashed in the
Coral Sea. It was the first naval battle where neither side's ships saw each other. The Americans
lost the carrier *Lexington*, an oiler, and a destroyer
as well as suffering damage to the carrier
Yorktown. The Japanese lost the carrier *Shoho* and
suffered damage to the carrier *Shokaku*. The battle resulted in the cancellation of the invasion of
Port Moresby.

Coral Sea reduced the forces available for
Yamamoto's great battle. Two of the large carriers
used at Coral Sea were now unavailable for the
Midway operation. The Aleutian operation further diluted Yamamoto's available strength. On
the other side, Nimitz's codebreakers were reading Japanese naval signals and through subter-
fuge already knew that Midway was the target.
Unbeknownst to the IJN, Nimitz deployed his
carriers near Midway to ambush the Japanese.
The two forces were approximately equal in numbers of aircraft when the land-based army,
Marine, and navy aircraft at Midway are added.
Nimitz's task forces (TFs) were separated into two
groups – the *Yorktown* TF under Admiral Fletcher
(the overall commander), and a second carrier
force composed of *Enterprise* and *Hornet* under
Rear Admiral Raymond Spruance. On June 4, the
US Navy annihilated *Kido Butai*, sinking on one
day almost half of the Japanese carrier navy. On
the US side, the redoubtable *Yorktown* was critically damaged, abandoned, and placed under tow
back to Pearl. Two days later the Japanese submarine *I-168* sank *Yorktown* and her destroyer
escort.

Upon return to Japan the IJN declared that it
had won a great victory and withheld the extent
of its defeat from the Japanese army. As for the
forces attacking the Aleutians, they had accomplished their mission and captured the desolate
islands of Attu and Kiska. Yet even this victory
was pyrrhic, since they soon found that these
islands were virtually useless as air bases.
Yamamoto realized that his task had just become
infinitely harder. The opportunity now existed for
the United States to seize the initiative and launch
a strategic counterstroke. Midway and Coral
Sea had opened up new opportunities for two

commanders itching to go over to the offensive –
General MacArthur and Admiral Ernest King,
Nimitz's boss in Washington. King, alarmed by
the Japanese seizure of Rabaul, broached the idea
of a counteroffensive through the Solomon
Islands to capture it. Similarly, MacArthur, sensing the tide had turned, made a counterproposal
to use his command to seize Rabaul in a three-
week operation. The final outcome was a compromise that established the offensive pattern for
the war for the rest of 1942 and most of 1943.
Nimitz would execute the first phase by seizing
the Japanese bases at Tulagi and Guadalcanal in
the southern Solomon Islands. MacArthur was to
perform the second task, advancing along the
northern coast of New Guinea at the same time as
navy and Marine forces advanced in the
Solomons. The final phase, under MacArthur's
overall command, would involve the capture of
Rabaul.

The Japanese struck first, advancing over the
rugged Owen-Stanley mountains in New Guinea
to try to seize Port Moresby by the land route.
They advanced along the Kokoda Trail, believed
unable to support a major offensive. MacArthur
found himself on the defensive. A supporting
amphibious assault at Milne Bay on July 25 was
defeated by the Australians and a small contingent of US combat engineers. King, meanwhile,
exercising his command prerogative, launched
navy and Marine forces against Tulagi and
Guadalcanal on August 7, 1942. It was one of the
most important decisions of the Pacific War.
Guadalcanal was only invaded because the
Japanese were building an airfield there. It proved
to be a microcosm for the entire Pacific Theater –
a campaign of amphibious assaults and fierce
naval, air, and jungle battles. The Marines seized
Tulagi after a short, stiff fight. On Guadalcanal
they simply waded ashore as the Japanese construction workers ran off into the jungle. Upon
landing they found a pestilential, monsoon-swept
hell-hole. The airfield, with bonus Japanese bull-
dozers and earth rollers, was secured easily and
the Marines began to establish security perimeters, finish the airfield, and hunker down for the
Japanese counterattack.

The Eleventh (Navy) Air Fleet in Rabaul had
just the range to get its medium bombers to the
southern Solomons. But once there, they had little time to deliver their attacks and did so without

land-based fighter coverage. What was worse, Japanese carrier aviation was so reduced after the battles of Midway and Coral Sea that it could only provide temporary air coverage before it had to withdraw to refuel its few carriers in safer waters. The American carriers, as Admiral Fletcher had already pointed out, were under the same constraints and particularly vulnerable to Japanese submarines and land-based aircraft. The Japanese counterattacked immediately from air and sea, winning the lopsided night victory of Savo Island on August 8–9. However, the Japanese commander missed a golden opportunity after Savo Island to sink US transport and supply shipping, which slipped away and left the Marines to their own devices.

Ashore the Japanese made critical errors. Underestimating both the size and fighting prowess of the Marines, they landed the Ichiki Detachment (one battalion) in an attempt to quickly recapture the airstrip, now named Henderson Field. On August 21, these troops were wiped out at the Battle of the Ilu River. Additional Japanese reinforcements were turned back on August 24 thanks to the timely return of the US Navy. Over the course of the next six months there were six more major naval battles and at least nine more land battles, with air combat occurring daily. After a series of critical naval battles in November, the American army and Marine forces resumed their offensive to chase the Japanese off the island for good. By the time the campaign ended in early 1943, the IJN land-based aviation was as decimated as its carrier counterparts were. The Imperial Japanese Army (IJA) had had to withdraw from Guadalcanal. American losses were no less severe – however, the Americans could afford these losses and the Japanese could not.

The same attritional jungle battles were occurring in New Guinea. The Allied counteroffensive operated under the same harsh conditions that plagued their antagonists. By November, the Australians, with American support, had captured Kokoda. MacArthur now focused his efforts on the capture of the two key towns on the northern coast – Buna and Gona. While fierce fighting raged on Guadalcanal MacArthur's Aussies and Yanks met stiff opposition, especially at Buna. MacArthur, unhappy with progress, fired the commander of the Buna operation and told the new commander, Lieutenant General Bob Eichelberger, to "take Buna or don't come back alive" (Spector 1985: 216). Fortunately, the Australians captured Gona on December 9, 1942, and were able to assist the American effort and Buna fell in early January 1943. The Japanese garrison had virtually died to the last man.

Far to the north a deadly sideshow played itself out. Nimitz tried to cut off Japanese supply lines to the Japanese-occupied islands of Kiska and Attu with naval forces. In March 1943, a cruiser force under Rear Admiral Charles H. McMorris fought an indecisive engagement near the Komodorski Islands in the North Pacific with a superior force of Japanese warships under Vice Admiral Hosagaya. In early May 1943, the Americans landed on Attu. It was a bloody slog amid ice, snow, and fog for both sides. Another American division commander was relieved and the island was not secured for two weeks. The Japanese defenders had pulled into the interior and died fighting to the last man – a chilling preview of things to come.

Island Hopping

As the battles on Guadalcanal and New Guinea wound down, Allied leaders met in Casablanca to discuss the next steps in their global war. Through a very complicated series of negotiations the JCS/CCS agreed to underwrite offensives for both MacArthur and Nimitz – from this arrangement was born what has become known as the dual advance. Nimitz retained command of any navy forces not specifically assigned to MacArthur and so began to prepare for an operation based on the pre-war Orange Plan. Meanwhile, MacArthur retained overall strategic direction over the forces under his command as well as the nominally independent South Pacific forces of Admiral William Halsey. In this manner broad pressure would be applied against the Japanese defenses, preventing them from massing against any single offensive. The first phase of this dual advance became more generally known as "island hopping" because once Americans realized that they need not take every island, they began "hopping" around and over many of Japan's most formidable strongholds.

Fortunately, Halsey and MacArthur got along with each other. They came up with a new plan of mutually supporting offensives to take Rabaul that involved Halsey advancing up the Solomons while MacArthur advanced with American–Australian forces along the north shore of New Guinea. Eventually, the two offensives would converge on the island of New Britain where Rabaul was located.

MacArthur's air component (Fifth Air Force) was led by General George C. Kenney. Kenney's efforts, and those of the air-minded Halsey, would go a long way toward establishing permanent air dominance in MacArthur's theater. They learned that once an airfield or anchorage was seized, and a secure perimeter established, they could fight from a superior defensive posture against the ill-supplied Japanese ground forces. The Japanese, anticipating another round of US offensives, began moving divisions from other theaters to New Guinea. In early March 1943, Kenney's air forces, including B-25 medium bombers, located and annihilated a convoy carrying the Japanese 51st Division in the Bismarck Sea. Japanese General Headquarters overreacted to this battle by never attempting another major convoy again and routing most of their reinforcements through western New Guinea. This placed even more strain on the inadequate and lengthy Japanese supply lines.

That spring Admiral Yamamoto launched an air counteroffensive against Allied bases and shipping in an attempt to recapture the initiative. Using precious carrier pilots, he gained little as a result and lost about as many planes and pilots as he destroyed. Worse, Yamamoto lost his own life when US codebreakers detected his movement plans and ambushed the bombers transporting him and his staff with a squadron of P-38s. At one stroke the Japanese lost their most inspiring and farsighted naval commander.

That summer, MacArthur moved against the Trobriand Islands and along the coast of New Guinea to Nassau Bay. Almost simultaneously, Halsey moved against the Japanese airfield at Munda on New Georgia Island. MacArthur's attack relieved the pressure of a Japanese offensive against the Australian airfield at Wau, bypassing many of their defenses. Halsey's force, on the other hand, came under fierce attack by Japanese land, air, and naval forces. The ground battles

bogged down in the face of fierce resistance and another division commander was relieved. However, by the end of August the US Army had secured Munda. Throughout Halsey's operations a number of fierce naval surface battles occurred but the Japanese navy found itself faced by improving American surface ships which gave as good as they got. Halsey's next step was to bypass Kolombangara Island and land on lightly defended Vella Lavella further north, which had a better airfield anyway. Once this field was operational the threat from the air diminished rapidly. Fighters from Vella Lavella also provided escort for bombers flying raids against Rabaul.

MacArthur pushed on toward the Huon Peninsula that poked like a finger toward Rabaul from New Guinea. Using a secretly built airstrip, he first neutralized Japanese airpower in the area. MacArthur's forces then landed near the key villages of Lae and Salamaua, conducting the first operational airborne assault of the campaign in seizing a nearby airbase. By mid-September 1943, both objectives were in Allied hands. MacArthur, advancing his timetable, then preempted a Japanese move to beef up their garrison at Finschafen, New Guinea, by landing an Australian brigade first. After some very hard fighting the town was captured and all subsequent attempts to recapture it defeated.

Halsey needed to take the island of Bougainville as a precursor to MacArthur's operations against New Britain – he would not only distract the Japanese from MacArthur's upcoming thrust across the strait to Cape Gloucester, but fighters from the captured bases on Bougainville could escort both Halsey's and MacArthur's bombers in attacks against Rabaul. Nimitz also lent Halsey several of his precious aircraft carriers to contest the still potent Japanese air forces based at Rabaul and in the northern Solomons. The Japanese sent the bulk of their carrier-based aircraft from Truk to help contest these operations and defend Rabaul. The result was a punishing series of air and sea battles that erupted around Rabaul. These battles established American command of the sea and air around Bougainville and gave them an air umbrella over Rabaul. In late October, the Marines and New Zealanders conducted a series of diversionary attacks. The main landings in Empress Augusta Bay that November achieved surprise and went smoothly. The Americans learned they need not capture the entire island, just the airfields and enough defensive terrain.

With the Japanese fully distracted at Bougainville, MacArthur launched his assaults on western New Britain with the veteran First Marine Division landing unopposed the day after Christmas. Despite horrendous weather conditions, the Marines and army moved inland to secure their defensive perimeters and airfields. By February 1944, fighters were flying missions from airfields on New Britain. Allied aircraft punished Rabaul throughout these operations and by late February Imperial Japanese Headquarters decided to leave only ground forces to defend that bastion. By April 1944, Rabaul's airfields were no longer usable or defensible. The Allies, secure in their defensive positions, simply left the considerable Japanese ground forces to their own devices. Rabaul was no longer of any importance.

The offensive on the Central Pacific front got underway in late 1943. Situated on the flank of the advance were the Gilbert Islands, which the Japanese had seized at the beginning of the war. Nimitz and his staff felt it imperative to neutralize them prior to driving against the Marshall Islands where strong Japanese forces were based. The campaign opened with the seizure of heavily defended islands in the Tarawa atoll of the Gilberts, especially Betio, on November 20. It was a bloody opening to the campaign, with almost 3,000 casualties on Betio alone. Although Nimitz's Marines had sound amphibious doctrine, they had very little practical experience and were short of critical equipment like amphibious tractors (Amtracs) that could cross reefs at low tide. Tarawa was a slaughter that shocked the American public.

Nimitz and his planners used lessons learned at Tarawa against Kwajalein in the Marshall Islands for the next step of the advance. In late January 1944, the 4th Marine Division landed on the islands of Roi and Namur and the army's 7th Infantry Division landed on the main island of Kwajalein. Air support was provided principally by the new fast carrier task forces of Vice Admiral Raymond Spruance's Fifth Fleet. The Japanese navy, with no meaningful naval airpower, barely contested these operations. For the cost of about 800 American lives Spruance secured a major anchorage and operating base in the Central Pacific. Nimitz moved the timetable forward and

in a follow-on operation seized the important but lightly defended Eniwetok Atoll some 300 miles further west later in February. This time the air support came entirely from Spruance's fast carriers. In order to cover the Eniwetok landings, Spruance pushed Admiral Marc Mitscher's fast carriers west to attack the Japanese at Truk in the Carolines. The result was Pearl Harbor in reverse. Almost 200,000 tons of warship and merchant tonnage were sunk and 270 enemy aircraft destroyed. Truk, like Rabaul, had been neutralized and the Americans decided there was no need to capture it.

Meanwhile, problems continued in the "forgotten" CBI Theater. The Allies flew supplies for Chiang's forces "over the hump" of the Himalayas while at the same time they began construction on a new road from Ledo in British Assam to connect with portions of the Burma Road not taken by Japan into China. Most of 1943 was spent conducting raids, building roads, and in fruitless recriminations. Meanwhile, the Japanese surprised everyone by going on the offensive in the spring of 1944. Their goal was to cut the Ledo Road and drive the British from Assam. By now, Allied superiority in men, material, experience, and airpower had reached decisive levels. The British, now under General William Slim, defeated that Japanese at Aykab, Imphal, and Kohima. On the Japanese flank, Stillwell's forces were threatening Mitkyina by late May. The Japanese army literally fell apart as it retreated in defeat, many of its soldiers starving and resorting to cannibalism.

The Dual Advance Continues

By early 1944, Japan was on the horns of a strategic dilemma. Only in China and Burma, temporarily, were her military efforts successful. Meanwhile, her island empire, seized at little cost, was now being recaptured at great cost – to Japan. By mid-1943, the Americans had fixed the problems with their torpedoes and the Pacific Submarine Command under Vice Admiral Charles A. Lockwood was conducting history's first successful unrestricted submarine campaign. By early 1944, more than three million tons of Japanese shipping had been sunk. By the end of the war, US submarines sank over five million tons of enemy shipping. The Japanese were now without a merchant marine to supply their far-flung empire.

With the neutralization of Rabaul, MacArthur continued his audacious campaign, bypassing or outflanking Japanese strong points. MacArthur was driven by the knowledge that his theater had become secondary to Nimitz's. This was because the Marianas Islands, Nimitz's next objective, could provide bases for the new long-range B-29 to attack Japan. MacArthur hoped to invade the Philippines by early 1945, but Nimitz might get there first. In early 1944, MacArthur began his most celebrated campaign along the lengthy northern coast of New Guinea using limited air, sea, and land forces. In March, the Admiralty Islands fell and in late April MacArthur's forces seized Aitape airfield deep in the rear of the Japanese main army. The operations climaxed with Lieutenant General Robert Eichelberger's bold seizure of lightly defended Hollandia, with its airbases and anchorages. By late May, MacArthur had seized terrain on which to build heavy bomber bases that could reach the southern Philippines at Biak. While Spruance distracted the Japanese in the Central Pacific, MacArthur opportunistically seized the remainder of his objectives at the western end of New Guinea. MacArthur's seizure of the island of Morotai in September put his forces just 300 miles south of Mindanao in the Philippines.

While MacArthur conducted his "triphibious" *Blitzkrieg* up New Guinea, disaster visited the Japanese navy in the Philippine Sea. Spruance and the Fifth Fleet arrived with a juggernaut of their own to take the critical Marianas. The Japanese had been attempting to rebuild their carrier force to challenge Spruance. Operation A-GO, the defense of the Marianas, was to provide the ideal opportunity to turn the tables on the overconfident Americans. Over two days of aerial combat that became known as the Marianas Turkey Shoot, US carrier pilots and anti-aircraft gunners destroyed Japanese carrier aviation. Additionally, American submarines and aviators sank three more Japanese carriers. Ashore, the fighting was fierce, especially at Saipan where 30,000 Japanese inflicted 14,000 American casualties. Nonetheless, the disasters visited upon Japanese arms in the Marianas were so severe that the Tojo government resigned in disgrace.

The Japanese army and navy had no intention of quitting the fight. In fact, that summer in China the Japanese conducted a punishing series of offensives against the Nationalists – the Ichigo Offensive. Stillwell was removed and replaced by General Daniel Sultan in Burma and General Wedemeyer in China. The Japanese goal was to capture airbases in China from which the new B-29s of the Fourteenth Air Force had begun a strategic bombing campaign against Japan. Rapid movement of Chinese and American troops from Burma managed to save Chiang from complete collapse, but the airbases were lost. Japan simply did not have enough troops to complete the conquest. The Americans, however, simply moved the Fourteenth Air Force to the newly captured Marianas where they could continue the strategic bombardment of Japan from Saipan and Tinian.

Invasion of the Philippines

Throughout the spring and summer of 1944 the strategic councils were divided on which step to take next. Chief of Naval Operations Admiral Ernest King wanted to bypass the Philippines and strike closer to Japan by seizing Formosa as a stepping stone on the way to Japan. MacArthur was adamant in favor of an invasion of the Philippines, arguing it was the United States' sacred duty to keep his promise to return. Eventually, after a meeting with Nimitz and Roosevelt at Pearl Harbor, MacArthur prevailed. The decision was made to land in the central Philippines on the island of Leyte, with a follow-on invasion of the main island of Luzon. MacArthur made claims for a quick campaign that turned out to be grossly over-optimistic. However, the invasion of the Philippines might, itself, end the war, since their capture by the Americans would sever the Japanese home islands from her critical oil and other strategic resources in the Indies.

As a precursor to the invasion, Admiral Nimitz assigned the mission of seizing key islands in the Palaus and then the huge atoll and anchorage at Ulithi. In early September, Admiral Halsey sailed with 15 fast aircraft carriers and numerous escorts for a series of pre-invasion raids. Halsey found light defenses and he recommended to the JCS that the timetable for the Philippine invasion be moved up to October. He also recommended that several other invasions be canceled. Mindanao and Yap were canceled but Morotai and Peleliu went in mid-September. Peleliu turned out to be a charnel house and one of Nimitz's rare missteps during the war. The new Japanese strategy was simply to bleed the Americans and it worked, with a nearly one-to-one ratio of American to Japanese casualties during a two-month night-mare battle.

Halsey sortied from the newly seized base of Ulithi in early October to pound Formosa and the Ryukyus prior to the Philippine invasion. The Japanese mistakenly believed that an invasion of Formosa was underway. During a series of air battles the rookie Japanese pilots managed to damage two cruisers and shoot down some planes. However, they exaggerated their success so much that the leadership concluded that they had won a great victory. The American forces that sailed toward Leyte Gulf were the most powerful assemblage of ships and embarked men in history. Lieutenant General Walter Krueger commanded the Sixth Army (200,000 troops) embarked on the 738 ships of Vice Admiral Thomas Kinkaid's Seventh Fleet. Kinkaid was supported by Halsey's Third Fleet that included 17 aircraft carriers, six new battleships, and over 80 cruisers and destroyers. Only Kinkaid and Krueger were directly under MacArthur's command. Halsey, under Nimitz, had orders to destroy the Japanese fleet if it appeared. On October 20, Krueger's forces landed on Leyte.

The Japanese were stunned by the appearance of the US invasion fleet. The emperor personally canceled the plan to make the main fight in Luzon and ordered the army and the navy to concentrate on Leyte. The IJN's plan involved three forces that would converge on the US transports and amphibious ships in Leyte Gulf. The Southern and Center Forces were composed of Japan's still powerful surface fleet, while the Northern Force consisted of the pitiful remains of Japan's carriers and served as a decoy to lure Halsey to the north. On October 23, Halsey's carriers decimated the Japanese land-based air force, while submarines and aircraft slowly whittled down the strength of the main effort of Center Force under Admiral Kurita Takeo. The Center Force turned away after navy aircraft sank the super-battleship *Musashi*. On the night of October 24–25, PT boats, destroyers, cruisers, and the old battleships raised from Pearl Harbor destroyed the Southern Force. Meanwhile, Halsey detected the carriers and took the bait, leaving the San Bernadino Strait unguarded.

Kurita, meanwhile, pushed through the San Bernadino Strait undetected and collided on the morning of October 25 with Kinkaid's covering force of destroyers and escort carriers. Then the real "miracle" of the Pacific War occurred. The navy's "third string" commanded by Rear Admiral Clifton "Ziggy" Sprague aggressively attacked Kurita's potent force. Kurita, baffled by suicidal destroyer torpedo attacks and harassment by fighters and torpedo planes, came to believe he was actually up against Halsey. The Japanese admiral broke off the action and turned away within sight of Leyte Gulf. Sprague had lost three of his gallant escorts and one of his small carriers. Ironically, a small Kamikaze squadron also attacked Kinkaid's escort carriers and managed to sink as much as Kurita had. Meanwhile, Halsey savaged the decoy force, sinking several of the empty carriers, but had missed his chance to destroy Kurita.

The land fight bogged down. General Yamashita of Singapore fame moved more troops in to reinforce those already defending Leyte. Mother Nature seemed to aid the Japanese, too, with three typhoons, constant rain, and an earthquake making American operations more difficult, especially air support. The Japanese fought on, despite being cut off, and on December 15 MacArthur declared victory (combat would continue into April). General Krueger and the Sixth Army invaded Luzon on January 9, 1945, at the same location where the Japanese had landed three years earlier. Manila was destroyed in a fierce urban battle and Yamashita retired to the interior of the island. MacArthur spent the rest of the war liberating the Philippines. Yamashita held out until after the atomic bombs had been dropped.

Armageddon

With the effective destruction of the Japanese fleet and the fall of the Philippines imminent, America and her allies were now poised to begin the final destruction of Japan. The debates about how to do this varied, depending on which service you talked to. The navy thought a block-ade would starve the Japanese into surrender. The Army Air Force was just as convinced that the strategic bombing campaign would end the war. Finally, the army believed that an invasion of Japan would be necessary in order to bring about a Japanese capitulation. Roosevelt, and later Truman, believed the participation of the Soviet Union was also essential to end the war. The Japanese strategy was to bleed the Americans until public opinion in the United States forced an end to hostilities, leaving the emperor in place and with Japan-proper unoccupied. To this end the next great battles of the Pacific War reflect this grim strategy – Iwo Jima and Okinawa. The capture of these islands was considered abso-lutely essential. Iwo Jima, a sulfurous, volcanic rock some 600 miles south of Japan, had several airfields from which Japanese fighters could attack the B-29s flying strategic bombing mis-sions from the Marianas, as well as warn of impending raids. Okinawa, on the other hand, would serve as the principal staging base for the invasion of Japan.

Spruance's Fifth Fleet was given the task of cap-turing Iwo. The Marines landed on February 16, 1945. Despite an extensive air assault and a pow-erful naval bombardment, General Kuribayshi Tadamichi's 21,000 soldiers sold their lives dearly, burrowing into caves and then emerging from their subterranean sanctuaries to kill Marines. The Japanese died to the last man and inflicted over 28,000 casualties on the Americans in the bloodiest month in Marine Corps history.

Okinawa was in many ways simply Iwo Jima on a larger scale but with the new terror weapon of Kamikazes flying from Japan and Formosa added. General Simon B. Buckner, Jr had the Tenth Army with eventually over half a million men. During the course of the two-month campaign 21 ships were lost, 66 seriously damaged, and more than 10,000 sailors killed and wounded – the highest naval losses of the Pacific War after Guadalcanal. Ashore, the butcher bill was no less sobering, and a reflection of the horrors of total war. In addition to the annihilation of the 100,000-strong Japanese garrison, the civilian population lost at least 80,000 killed. American casualties numbered almost 70,000 killed, wounded, and missing, including General Buckner, who was killed during the last days of the campaign.

Okinawa was another strategic defeat for the Japanese, but the generals were not yet inclined to surrender, despite the fire bombings that had destroyed most of Japan's major cities. Surely another bloodbath would convince the Americans to back down from their harsh unconditional terms. American casualty estimates for the Kyushu operation and subsequent invasion of the Tokyo area on the island of Honshu amounted to 720,000 "dead and evacuated wounded" for the army and Army Air Force alone. Two other fac-tors came into play to end the war. As prepara-tions for the invasion of Japan proceeded apace, two atomic weapons produced by the secret Manhattan Project were shipped to a special B-29 unit located on Tinian. The other factor was the entry of the USSR into the contest.

On August 6, 1945, a B-29 piloted by Colonel Paul Tibbits dropped the first atomic bomb on the port city of Hiroshima, killing tens of thou-sands instantly, with the toll quickly climbing to 80,000 from residual blast and radiation deaths. On August 9, the Soviets invaded Manchuria. Over the next few weeks mechanized Soviet armies overran the Japanese puppet state there. Hours after the Soviets attacked, a second bomb obliterated Nagasaki and 35,000 more Japanese were incinerated. The Japanese army realized its strategy for defending Kyushu was hopeless if the Americans could vaporize their defenses. At the last moment, radical elements of the Japanese Guards Division in Tokyo attempted to prevent the emperor from broadcasting the surrender over the radio. Loyal troops suppressed this coup and on August 15 Hirohito asked his people to "endure the unendurable." On September 2, 1945, General MacArthur received the surrender of the Japanese dignitaries on behalf of the Allied Powers aboard the battleship Missouri in Tokyo Bay. The final bill in lives and property damage will never be known, but almost certainly the casualties directly due to the war exceeded 25 million (more than two-thirds civilians) if the start is moved up to 1937.

SEE ALSO: China, Invasion of (1931, 1937–1945).

Reference

Spector, R. H. (1985) *Eagle Against the Sun*. New York: Vintage.

Further Reading

Bergerud, E. M. (1996) *Fire in the Sky: The Air War in the South Pacific.* New York: Viking.

Carlson, E. (2011) *Joe Rochefort's War: The Odyssey of the Codebreaker Who Outwitted Yamamoto at Midway.* Annapolis. MD: Naval Institute Press.

Drea, E. J. (2009) *Japan's Imperial Army: Its Rise and Fall, 1853–1945.* Lawrence: University Press of Kansas.

Holwitt, J. I. (2009) *"Execute against Japan": The U.S. Decision to Conduct Unrestricted Submarine Warfare.* College Station: Texas A&M University Press.

Kuehn, J. T. and Giangreco, D. M. (2008) *Eyewitness Pacific Theater.* New York: Sterling Books.

Lundstrom, J. (2006) *Black Shoe Carrier Admiral.* Annapolis: Naval Institute Press.

Miller, E. S. (1991) *War Plan Orange.* Annapolis: Naval Institute Press.

Morison, S. E. (1963) *The Two-Ocean War: A Short History of the United States Navy in the Second World War.* Boston: Little, Brown.

Parshall, J. and Tully, A. (2005) *Shattered Sword: The Untold Story of the Battle of Midway.* Washington, DC: Potomac Books.

Prados, J. (1995) *Combined Fleet Decoded: The Secret History of American Intelligence and the Japanese Navy in World War II.* Annapolis, MD: Naval Institute Press.

Slim, Field Marshal Viscount W. (1956) *Defeat into Victory.* London: Cassell and Co. Ltd.

Y

Yugoslav Succession, Wars of (1990–1999)

JOHN E. ASHBROOK

The Wars of Yugoslav Succession were four major conflicts in Slovenia, Croatia, Bosnia-Hercegovina, and Serbia-Kosovo. Of these, the largest occurred in Croatia and Bosnia-Hercegovina in the early 1990s. The dissolution and wars resulted from a number of unresolved historical issues; the rise of opportunistic, nationalist politicians; a cumbersome federal government; and a long-term economic crisis.

The wars themselves stemmed in no small part from long-standing tensions between ethnic groups in Yugoslavia. Historically the three largest ethnicities – Muslims, Serbs, and Croats – lived together without much tension until modern nationalism seeped into the region in the nineteenth century. As new national boundaries emerged a struggle for power based on ethnic identity followed. Croats increasingly identified with the West through Roman Catholicism and the Serbs with Serbian Orthodoxy and the struggles against the Habsburgs and the Ottomans. The Muslims were latecomers to nation building, only fully developing an ethno-national identity in the twentieth century. Many Croats viewed the creation of the first Yugoslav state in 1918 as an exclusively Serbian entity, while some Serbs saw the Croats as internal traitors. The Muslims tended to be caught between the two sides, thus providing an impetus for the creation of a single Muslim ethnic identity. World War II unleashed a series of ethnic wars as all three nationalities perpetrated violence and ethnic cleansing on the "others." However, Tito's multi-ethnic Partisan movement joined members of all nations in the struggle against collaborators and their Italian and German patrons. Tito made a reputation for being an arbiter among the nations, and successfully recruited enough fighters to liberate Yugoslavia. As leader of the second Yugoslavia, Tito kept expressions of virulent nationalism suppressed while building Yugoslavia's reputation internationally. But Tito was less successful in establishing a widespread Yugoslav identity, as evident in his numerous governmental changes to balance the power between nations. Usually this entailed decentralizing federal power, while giving the republics and autonomous provinces more control of their internal affairs. During the 1960s, the country's economy, seemingly strong, reduced ethnic friction, but with the economic downturn in the 1970s and Tito's death in 1980, tensions reemerged without the leader's charm

Twentieth-Century War and Conflict: A Concise Encyclopedia, First Edition. Edited by Gordon Martel.
© 2015 John Wiley & Sons, Ltd. Published 2015 by John Wiley & Sons, Ltd.

or his ability to assuage them. A number of politicians and academics began to revive historical national grievances and to disparage the multinational experiment in communism for political and economic reasons, eventually throwing the country into the wars of dissolution.

Many scholars attribute the breakup to Serbian politician Slobodan Milošević. The opportunistic Milošević used the growing discontent with the Serbian republic's unique position as the only republic with two autonomous provinces and the plight of Serbian minorities outside Serbia to advance his career. He sought to recentralize the federation, leading to protests in Slovenia and Croatia, both of which demanded increased decentralization and multi-party elections.

The crises led to the collapse of the communist's monopoly on power as new parties won elections across the federation in 1990 and 1991. In Croatia the Croatian Democratic Alliance under Franjo Tuđman came to power, promising to resist recentralization and protect the republic's sovereignty. The victory worried the Serbian minority in the republic (12 percent of the population), especially the "revival" of Croatian symbols associated with the genocidal Ustaša regime of World War II, the ismissal of Serbs from government jobs, and changes to the constitution. Milošević used this agitation to goad them into rebellion. The Yugoslav People's Army (*Jugoslavenska Narodna Armija*, or JNA) supplied Serbs with weapons to resist secessionist drives in Croatia and Bosnia. Provocateurs and the few rabidly nationalist locals held meetings in the Krajina adopting symbols associated with the anti-Croatian Četnik movement of World War II.

In August 1990, Croatian Serbs voted to create an autonomous region, demanding to remain in a state with their fellow Serbs. To prevent government interference the rebels erected barriers on roads and railroads and expelled Croatian police. The government responded by flying special police teams to the scene, but JNA jets forced them to turn back. The JNA also tried to disarm the territorial defense forces of Slovenia and Croatia; however, the Slovenes responded quickly, managing to retain much of their equipment.

In a downward spiral of ethnic distrust and violence, Serbian paramilitaries targeted Croatian police and government officials in the Krajina. JNA colonel Ratko Mladić led the assault against

northern Dalmatian cities, shelling civilians and expelling Croats. Due to the violence, the United Nations (UN) imposed a weapons embargo on Yugoslavia. The embargo did not affect the JNA or its Serbian paramilitary clients, but it hampered their opponents' ability to defend themselves against attack and ethnic cleansing.

Slovenia and the 10-Day War

Both Slovenia and Croatia declared independence on June 25, 1991. Milošević knew that he could not justify keeping an almost ethnically homogeneous Slovenia in the crumbling federation. However, a show of force was needed. On June 26, the JNA mobilized to retake border posts. Slovenian security forces responded by surrounding JNA barracks and resisting the army.

After 10 days and several dozen deaths, the foreign-brokered Brioni Accord ended the war. The JNA withdrew, shifting its attention to Croatia and Bosnia.

The War in Croatia

In late July 1991, Krajina Serbs with JNA aid attacked targets in coastal Croatia. On September 11, they cut Dalmatia off from the rest of the country. Croatian forces halted this advance on coastal cities in mid-September, stabilizing the line until 1995. Further south the JNA and Montenegrin irregulars moved on Dubrovnik in October, destroying and ethnically cleansing much in their path. They cut off the city from its hinterland, shelling and sniping from the surrounding hillsides. Western Europe responded, condemning Serbian violence, demanding an end to the war, and imposing sanctions on Serbia.

In eastern Croatia, fighting on a large scale erupted in August 1991 around Vukovar. JNA troops and Serbian paramilitaries surrounded the city, besieging it for almost three months. The last of the Croatian defenders surrendered on November 18, and ended up in internment camps or were executed. Serbian forces then advanced on Osijek but could not break the Croatian defense around the city. The time bought at Vukovar saved Osijek from siege and destruction.

By the end of 1991, the Serbs held nearly a third of Croatia and their radical leadership proclaimed the Republic of Serbian Krajina (*Republika Srpska Krajina*, or RSK). With his territorial goals met and the increased internal and external pressures on his government, Milošević, much to the chagrin of the RSK, agreed to peace talks with Tuđman in December. This drove a lasting wedge between the RSK and Milošević, and ultimately led to the Serbian strongman's total abandonment of the entity in mid-1995.

In January 1992, the Vance Plan temporarily stopped most of the fighting. It established four UN Protected Areas in and near RSK territory with a UN Protection Force to keep the peace. It also meant to reverse the ethnic cleansing of the Krajina by encouraging the repatriation of displaced Croats, but the RSK continued expelling Croats with little UN interference. The JNA retreated into Bosnia, leaving resources and personnel for the RSK military.

Armed conflict in Croatia continued intermittently for the next three years. Two larger probing actions by the Croatian military occurred in 1993, leading to accusations of atrocities against Serbian civilians. The break allowed Tuđman to intervene in Bosnia-Hercegovina, justifying his actions by claiming that Bosnian Serbs supplied aid and comfort to the Krajina rebels.

In 1994, the Croatian government hired a US security firm to retrain its military. Until this point in time the United States had remained rather aloof from the situation. The Democrat candidate for president in the 1992 elections, Bill Clinton, campaigned against incumbent George Bush in part by promising to end the violence in the region. However, Clinton adopted a similar approach to Bush in his first year of office until Republicans in Congress pressured him into a more forceful approach, supposedly approving of the hire of Military Professional Resources, Inc. With the tacit approval of the United States and clandestine military support from foreign sources, the Croatian army (*Hrvatska Vojska*, or HV) transformed into a professional, highly qualified force. The war in Bosnia-Hercegovina and the international community's desire to end it permanently led to Croatia's final push against the Krajina in 1995.

The first of the two operations that ended the rebellion began on May 1, 1995, and concluded two days later. Operation Flash (*Bljesak*) targeted the western Slavonian pocket of the RSK. Resistance swiftly collapsed, showing the weakness of Krajina forces. Events in Bosnia allowed Tuđman to authorize the second action. In July, the Serbs overran the so-called UN safe zones in Srebrenica and Žepa. The Srebrenica massacre of over 7,000 men and boys galvanized western public opinion against the Serbs. Under pressure from various humanitarian agencies and politicians, the West, led by the Clinton administration, enlisted Croatian participation to end the violence by cobbling together an agreement between the Bosnian and Croatian governments, whereby the HV would end the rebellion, then turn south to engage Republika Srpska forces in Bosnia.

From August 4 to 8, Operation Storm's (*Oluja*) main thrust was aimed at liberating the Krajina capital, Knin, and linking with Bosnian forces. Storm, a spectacular success, cleared all resistance, precipitating an exodus of the Serbian population (estimated at between 150,000 and 200,000). Within days the rebellion collapsed, with only eastern Slavonia still under Serbian control. The international community brokered an agreement that returned it to Croatian jurisdiction in 1997. Thus the war in Croatia came to an end and the endgame in Bosnia began.

The War in Bosnia-Hercegovina

Unlike the other republics, there was no majority ethnic group in Bosnia-Hercegovina (BiH). In 1991, Bosnian Muslims (Bošnjaks) constituted 43 percent of the population, Serbs 31 percent, and Croats 17 percent. In general, most Bosnians were ethnically tolerant, especially in urban areas. However, three new political parties, each national in character, emerged and increasingly agitated against parties seeking to keep the country united. After the first elections the Serbian and Croatian parties radicalized, due in part to outside pressures from Serbia and Croatia. For Milošević and Tuđman, a functioning, multiethnic BiH was anathema to their nationalist projects. Both also desired an unstable Bosnia to focus internal discontent on an external crisis.

As in Croatia, the JNA distributed arms to Serbian defense units, ostensibly for protection against secessionist Croats, radical Muslims, and moderate Serbs. This sparked the Bošnjaks and Croats to seek weapons as well. As more arms flowed into the arsenals of paramilitaries, the Croats carved out an autonomous entity, Herceg Bosna, in regions with a substantial Croatian population in November 1991. The Serbs too established such an entity, Republika Srpska (RS), in January 1992.

The Bosnian government under Alija Izetbegović arranged a referendum on independence from Yugoslavia on February 29 and March 1, 1992. The Serbs boycotted it, but a majority of the electorate chose independence. Days later, Serbs blocked roads into RS, and ethnic cleansing escalated. Serbian paramilitaries and their JNA patrons took strategic and economically significant points across the country and surrounded Sarajevo. To hide his involvement, Milošević ordered the JNA to withdraw in May, but it left behind much of its equipment, Bosnian Serb soldiers and officers, and volunteers. Mladić took command of RS's military, which seized approximately 70 percent of the country, ethnically cleansing as it went and beginning a 44-month siege of Sarajevo. The violence prompted the UN to impose a number of sanctions and a weapons embargo.

It also prompted increased defense efforts from Croats and Muslims. Croatian volunteers swelled the ranks of the Croatian Defense Council, the military arm of Herceg Bosna, working reluctantly with the mostly Muslim Bosnian army (*Armija Republike Bosne i Hercegovine*, or ABiH). In March 1993, the nominal allies went to war against one another, much to the delight of the Serbs. Both sides worked with RS to procure weapons and ammunition. Further complicating the situation, a Bošnjak army in the Bihać region loyal to local strongman Fikret Abdić revolted against the Izetbegović government and openly colluded with RS and the Serbian Krajina against loyalist Muslims until August 1995.

Just before and during this confused war and three-sided ethnic cleansing, the international community attempted to stop the violence with a number of peace plans and the creation of UN-protected safe havens. The first, the Carrington-Cutileiro plan, called for ethnic power sharing and a decentralized federal government with a number of ethnically classified cantons. Croatian and Serbian leaders readily signed up to the agreement, but Izetbegović, after initially agreeing, reneged, claiming he would not support a plan that ethnically divided the country. UN special envoy Cyrus Vance and European Union representative Lord Owen brokered the second in January 1993. It divided the country into 10 autonomous territories to be protected and overseen by the UN. This time the Croats and Muslims agreed, but, because they had to return land, the Serbs rejected it in May. In August, the UN offered the Owen-Stoltenberg plan, which partitioned Bosnia along ethnic lines with the Serbs controlling 52 percent of its territory, the Croats 18 percent, and the Bošnjaks 30 percent. The Croats and Serbs accepted it, but Izetbegović did not.

The Croatian-Bošnjak war continued into 1994. By February, the West wanted a permanent solution to the Balkan instability and, under pressure from the United States, Tuđman and Izetbegović signed the Washington Agreement in March, establishing the Federation of Bosnia-Hercegovina, a joint government dividing the country into 10 cantons. The United States, Russia, France, Britain, and Germany formed the "Contact Group" and proposed yet another settlement to the war, but the Serbs refused to cooperate. In response, Milošević, wanting the West to lift the sanctions on Serbia, closed the border and imposed an embargo on RS, completely isolating it and exacerbating its economic problems.

The reconciled Croats and Bošnjaks began a series of operations with the Croatian army to cut off Knin from RS and to relieve the Muslims loyal to Izetbegović in the Bihać pocket in 1994. These maneuvers led to the successful joint operation against the forces of RS and the Krajina the following year.

By early summer 1995, RS planned attacks on the UN safe havens to remove the non-Serbian enclaves. Unfortunately for the Serbs, domestic pressure compelled President Bill Clinton to stop the war. When the Serbs attacked the safe havens and perpetrated ethnic cleansing, the West reacted. With the fall of Srebrenica and Žepa and the Serbian attacks on the Bihać pocket, the United States "green-lighted" the joint operation of the ABiH and HV against RS. In August, Croatian forces poured into BiH and, with the ABiH, liberated much of the western part of the country. This, combined with North Atlantic Treaty Organization (NATO) airstrikes against Serbian positions throughout the country, left RS broken and in disarray by September. Throughout September and October 1995, more sporadic operations took disputed territory and mopped up resistance in recaptured territories.

These defeats and the abandonment of RS by the Belgrade government led to the Dayton Accords of December 1995. Milošević and Tuđman represented the Bosnian Serbs and Bosnian Croats, while Izetbegović sat for the Federation. The accords ended the war, guaranteeing Bosnia's territorial integrity, but creating a government composed of two autonomous provinces with a UN high representative as a *de facto* executive power. The Federation controlled 51 percent and RS 49 percent of the country. It also shattered the nationalists' dream of a Greater Croatia and Greater Serbia, giving the West its desired regional "stability" until Milošević cracked down against Albanian separatists in Kosovo in 1998.

The Kosovo War

Tito kept ethnic tensions between Kosovar Serbs and Albanians, who made up nearly 90 percent of Kosovo's population, relatively quiet. They boiled over shortly after his death as Serbian nationalists brought up the question of the province's autonomy. This led to Milošević's meteoric rise to power. He purged the Kosovar Communist party and reduced the province's autonomy in 1989, sparking increased Albanian resistance. Ibrahim Rugova led a separatist movement employing non-violent means, while another, the Kosovo Liberation Army (KLA), used terrorism.

Rugova kept the region relatively calm during the wars in Croatia and Bosnia, but his ineffective policies led to the growth of the KLA. It began ethnically cleansing some rural areas by 1997. In response, Serbian security forces used brutal means to crush the uprising. Thousands of Albanians abandoned their homes, pouring into hastily erected refugee camps in neighboring Albania and Macedonia. The international community, sick of the violence and perceiving the Serbs as its root cause, condemned Belgrade's actions. In February and March 1999, NATO forced Serbian and Albanian leaders to a meeting at Rambouillet, France, to solve the crisis. However, Belgrade rejected the West's proposed solution, claiming it gave Kosovo too much autonomy. Because of this intransigence, NATO attacked Serbian targets across the country beginning on March 24. In reaction, Serbian forces stepped up attacks against Albanians, forcing hundreds of thousands more to flee. Operation Allied Force intended to stop the Serbs and coerce them to negotiate. Milošević, under pressure from both the bombing and domestic dissatisfaction, accepted NATO's terms on June 11. Serbian security forces evacuated, NATO troops entered, and Albanian refugees began to return, often purging the remaining non-Albanians as they came. Serbs either emigrated or moved into locales with significant Serbian populations for self-defense. In the long term, NATO forced Belgrade to reestablish Kosovo's autonomy, which led to the contentious declaration of Kosovo's independence in February 2008.

As a result of the wars of dissolution the ethnic map of the region permanently changed. Yugoslavia, once a single, multinational country with a significant level of ethnic toleration, fractured into six or seven independent states with much more homogeneous populations. The wars caused hundreds of millions of dollars of property damage, cost billions in revenue, displaced or killed hundreds of thousands of people, and resulted in the ethnic cleansing of large swaths of territory.

SEE ALSO: Ethnic Cleansing; Peacekeeping; War Crimes.

Further Reading

Ashbrook, J. and Bakich, S. (2010) "Storming to Partition: Croatia, the United States and Krajina in the Yugoslav War," *Small Wars and Insurgencies*: 21(4): 537–560.

Burg, S. and Shoup, P. (1999) *The War in Bosnia-Herzegovina: Ethnic Conflict and International Intervention*. Armonk, NY: M. E. Sharpe.

Finlan, A. (2004) *The Collapse of Yugoslavia, 1991–1999*. New York: Osprey.

Glenny, M. (1996) *The Fall of Yugoslavia*, 3rd ed. London: Penguin.

Gow, J. (2003) *The Serbian Project and Its Adversaries: A Strategy of War Crimes*. Montreal: McGill-Queen's University Press.

Magaš, B. and Žanić, I. (Eds.) (2001) *The War in Croatia and Bosnia-Herzegovina, 1991–1995*. London: Frank Cass.

Ramet, S. (2002) *Balkan Babel: The Disintegration of Yugoslavia from the Death of Tito to the Fall of Milošević*, 4th ed. Boulder, CO: Westview Press.

Silber, L. and Little, A. (1995) *Yugoslavia: The Death of a Nation*. London: Penguin.

Index

Twentieth-Century War and Conflict: A Concise Encyclopedia, First Edition. Edited by Gordon Martel.
© 2015 John Wiley & Sons, Ltd. Published 2015 by John Wiley & Sons, Ltd.